A
HISTORY
OF
FRENCH
CIVILIZATION

A
HISTORY
OF
FRENCH
CIVILIZATION

Georges Duby

Professor, Faculté des Lettres, Aix-en-Provence

AND

Robert Mandrou

Director of Studies, École Pratique des Hautes Études

Translated by JAMES BLAKELY ATKINSON

Random House   New York

Foreword

To PRESENT a history of French civilization in six hundred pages: what an impossible challenge! We are dealing with one of the most complex, if not the most refined, civilizations that ever existed; a civilization, moreover, dear to our hearts. Consequently, we must be explicit and point out that this history represents only a synthetic choice, systematizing, in an orderly fashion, a very rich history according to the most explanatory perspectives—and at the authors' pleasure. There are no exhaustive enumerations; no recapitulatory tables, complete and for all time. Furthermore, this book is not aimed at scholars; specialists in each period will learn nothing from it, and will note strange lacunae, according to their own viewpoint; most assuredly, it is useless to seek here a formal exposition of the thought of Thomas Aquinas, any more than a chronology of Impressionism. In fact, this short history of French civilization is directed to the advanced classes of French secondary schools and to students; to those abroad who are interested in French language and culture; and finally, to the public at large, or those among them who wish to have an overall view of French civilization. This book will have fulfilled its task if it arouses curiosity, if it inspires its readers to consult other, more scholarly and complete, books, and if it enables them better to grasp, oriented by ten centuries of history, the unique characteristics of that "person"—contemporary France.

GEORGES DUBY AND ROBERT MANDROU

Contents

Part I. The Middle Ages
BY GEORGES DUBY

Part II.   *Modern and Contemporary France*
BY ROBERT MANDROU

Illustrations

Part One

THE
MIDDLE
AGES

by

Georges Duby

I

The Year 1000

THE history of French civilization does not, obviously, begin at a precise moment. To determine the starting point of a book such as this, a choice must be made, and this choice must be somewhat arbitrary. Yet several reasons invite us to begin with the end of the tenth century. The first is that the age of the invasions has just ended. The last waves of marauders and conquerors broke over the regions of France before the middle of the century: the Danes, the pirates from North Africa or the Mediterranean islands, whom their contemporaries called the Saracens; the horsemen from the Steppes who carried their raids as far as Aquitaine and ended by settling in Hungary. There were still a few alarms in certain border areas; the shores of Provence, and especially the Rhône delta, were threatened for a very long time by Berber forays. But these were ordinary, short-lived passings-through; small localized raids.

We will pass over those great disturbances that had unsettled the deepest foundations of Europe's civilization and culture throughout the early Middle Ages, and omit those long, zigzag movements of migratory peoples who had destroyed much, but who, like catalysts, had occasioned changes. Since the end of the tenth century, the history of the West has proceeded without sudden ruptures from invasions. This marks a major stage. This is the threshold of a long period of material and spiritual progress.

Another consideration in choosing the end of the tenth century as our starting point, and one fundamental to the historian seeking the extremely scattered documents of these early periods, is that factual material becomes less misleading at this point. It is the end of the "Dark Ages." Actually, however, the illumination is merely relative; for a long time to come, light falls only on certain aspects of civilization, and not the most important nor even the most common aspects. The history of outstanding people (the rich and the learned) can be made out rather well; but the daily thread of existence, the modes of popular thought, and the reactions of the multitude are much less easily discerned. In any event, the texture of historical evidence becomes more tightly woven in the tenth century—one more reason for beginning there.

Finally, before the end of the tenth century, one can hardly be permitted to speak of a France, or of an actual French civilization. Indeed, up to this point, the territory of France consisted of poorly differentiated provinces merged into larger cultural units: Gaul, the Empire, Christendom. But from now on their personalities take shape: conditions of material life and patterns of thought and expression assume certain special features. These are, of course, faint and transitory indications, but they are truly the first fruits of a society unified by its civilization, one whose history it is henceforth legitimate to wish to follow.

In what geographic setting shall we pursue it? This is a new problem of delineation, and a new choice. For if one adopts the method—which seems a good one—of referring to the images that the word "France" could evoke in those tenth-century minds best equipped for thinking, one realizes that these images are very hazy. First of all, France is the small region of woods and fields, between Paris and Senlis, bounded by the Marne and the Oise. But in the language of the times, it is also the duchy and great military command north of the Loire, where a unit of provinces flanked by Normandy, Burgundy, and Lorraine has recently regrouped. Then, too, it is the realm, from the Scheldt to the borders of Catalonia, which marks the "frontier line of the four rivers" traced in 843 by the Treaty of Verdun, and now and then depending upon the Meuse, Saône, and Rhône. None of these various zones corresponds to the real extent of French civilization, which actually is formed gradually around multiple loci, and spread out in many directions. Moreover, these loci and directions did not remain static; we will have occasion to fix these crystallizing points over the course of this history, and to explore the orientation and limits of that expansion. And, since this inquiry into the past has as its essential goal a better understanding of the present, our concern here will be all the regions that form present-day France. This is a flexible setting. Let us place within it, as a prefatory setting, the chief aspects of civilization in the year 1000.

► **THE LAND, THE PEASANTS, AND THE LEADERS**

It is a completely peasant civilization and, for that reason, astonishingly rough. However, this rusticity has not always been so pervasive: there are vestiges of a different way of life, implanted formerly by the Roman conquerors for their own use and for that of the more advanced natives. Solidly built causeways, virtually undamaged, pass over farmland and thickets. These roads converge upon the former towns, more numerous and less dilapidated in the south, where skeletons of monuments, amphitheaters, public baths, and porticoes, constructed during the Imperial period and serving another mode of existence, are still standing. But these broad "paved roads," these routes laid out (according to legend) by Caesar, Brunhilde, or some local hero, are forsaken, broken up by difficult passages for want of maintenance, and eroded by floods or swamps. These towns are almost entirely empty. A few dozen vineyardists, graziers, and priests are gathered together within the narrow fortress walls built during the first Germanic migrations, feeling themselves very much in the open there; or else perhaps they spread out into the former urban areas in small groups, sticking close to some religious building, or some former ruin now used as a fortress or cattle shelter. This is what remains of Rome in the landscape: a dilapidated, useless stage set, overrun by fields or undergrowth. Because of the turmoil of the invasions and the gradually increasing torpor of commercial traffic, one after the other the rich abandoned their urban dwellings and retired to their country properties. There, in two or three generations, they forgot the culture and the customs of the towns. So all are peasants; a rustic nature, only thinly domesticated, completely dominates their existence.

Their miserable accoutrements do not protect them against cold or night. They live outside; the dwellings without fireplaces or windows are mere dens in which they entrench themselves only to sleep. The rhythm of life is wedded to the seasons. Winter is a long sleep; the days are short, for nothing is known about lighting. Men and animals grow sleepy rather than use up the inadequate food supply. In winter there is the huge Christmas blaze, sacrifices of hogs and bellyfuls of pig meat. Spring comes as a deliverance: the entire Middle Ages are illuminated by the lightheartedness of May, that brief respite in agricultural work, when begin, for the rich, the pleasures of military expeditions. Summer is feverish, a time of consuming work and fatigue. Because of its subservience to natural cycles, such an existence is brutal and one in which time, as duration of fluctuating value, is not measured.

These men are few in number, and their distribution in the space available to them is particularly uneven. Population density in the occupied territories seems to be as great as in the eighteenth century. (*Seems:* for the historian must move gropingly in this area bereft of almost all numerical evidence.) This density is too great for the level of agrarian techniques. But these settled places are extremely scattered. Separating these little islands are wildernesses—wide, uncultivated expanses surrounding and isolating each group of hamlets, here and there immense areas of forests or bogs devoid of permanent habitation. This state of affairs reveals one of the essential traits of the civilization of that time: isolation. There exists practically no adequate means of connecting the human groups; any contact is very difficult. These rustics are familiar with the wheel and, no doubt during this very period, adopt a harnessing process quite superior to that used in antiquity; but, because of a lack of draft animals and, especially, of a coherent system of way-stations, transportation beyond the limits of the territory is extraordinarily random. People move about on the rivers in little boats, or on foot accompanied by beasts of burden. In all these slow movements, distances are vast beyond measure; even the routes are useless in the absence of resting places. Also, travelers are rare; the society—split up into small, closed cells, regarding the passer-through, the "alien," as a suspect to be picked clean with impunity—has lost the habit of long-range communication.

Because of their dense groups, each isolated from the other, the peasants of the year 1000 are half-starved. The effects of chronic undernourishment are conspicuous in the skeletons exhumed from Merovingian cemeteries: the chafing of the teeth that indicates a grass-eating people, rickets, and an overwhelming preponderance of people who died young. Biological conditions have improved perhaps over those of the seventh century, yet the average age seems to be very low, due especially to the high incidence of infant mortality. There is never enough food for subsistence, and periodically the lack of food grows worse. For a year or two there will be a great famine; the chroniclers describe the graphic and horrible episodes of this catastrophe, complacently and rather excessively conjuring up people who eat dirt and sell human skin. If stomachs are empty, and children are stricken by disease before adolescence, in spite of the enormous extent of cultivatable and undeveloped land, it is because the equipment enabling men to extract their nourishment from the soil is very primitive and inadequate. There is little or no metal; iron is reserved for weapons. In the most comprehensive and advanced monastic farms, maintaining some hundred head of beef in their stables, one may find a scythe or two, a shovel, and an ax. Most of the tools are wooden—light swingplows, hoes with their points hardened by fire, unusable except in very loose ground and plowing even that imperfectly. This explains why the cultivated land is so limited, and why the peasants of those days are only half farmers, drawing a good portion of their meager means from unimproved nature.

The forest—nourishing indeed in its many aspects, where mighty virgin forests degenerate into brush, burned every ten or twenty years to wrest a harvest or two from the undeveloped land—fills the whole countryside. Many—hermits, shepherds, and woodsmen—live solely from it. But first and foremost, the forest provides everyone with that primordial material, wood, out of which castles, houses, fences, bowls, and all the daily implements are made. The forest furnishes all the many gathered products: honey, wax, berries (domestic fruit trees are still quite rare), and the plants buried or burned in the fields as fertilizer, as well as all the game. Finally, and this is its primary function, the forest provides pasture land for the livestock. Sometimes the oxen and horses are set free there; but especially wool- and cheese-yielding sheep and goats, and those black, half-savage pigs whose meat smoked or salted is eaten all year long, wander around there permanently.

The men work relentlessly to produce the rest of their provisions in the clearings that now and then punctuate this vast carpet of wilderness. Isolated settlement is the exception. Small enclosures called "messuages" are gathered together into little villages. These settlements comprise, as well as hovels for people, the stable animals, the harvests, the hemp fields, and the little area of fertile ground enriched by the household garbage and worked by hand daily, as well as the "curtilage," where garden produce is raised. Occasionally, huts are erected in the middle of these villages on a scale more comprehensive and numerous than that of the lord's manor. The *finage*** is around all this. Vine stocks are planted everywhere on the best-exposed plots of ground. In these areas, surrounded by permanent fences, the grapes have some chance of ripening, even in regions like the valley of the Oise and Normandy, where climatic conditions are rather unfavorable. Because wine-drinking has become a part of the practices of the rich, and the transport of this heavy commodity is quite difficult, people make every effort to produce the noble beverage within the region. The meadows of mowed crops stretch out in the moist areas, along the streams; these yield the winter food for the cattle, horses, and oxen raised, not for food, but for their labor. These animals are puny—they, too, are undernourished, and at the end of the winter they emerge astonishingly debilitated. The majority of the cleared land, however, is devoted to cereal grains, usually consumed as gruel, which forms the basis of human nourishment. Winter grains— wheat in warm terrains, rye and millet in backward regions—are grown; in climates where the summer heat does not settle in too quickly, people intermittently attempt to work in a grain crop, sowed in the Lenten season: barley and, much more rarely, oats. This agricultural system neces-

---

* *Finage*—in a medieval context, this word refers to the collection of lands cultivated by a village; in modern French it has come to mean the administrative area of a *commune*—preserving its local meaning.—Trans.

sitates a certain degree of nomadism, itinerant sowing on dubious patches
of burnt land at the edges of the wilderness, and the rotation of crops
on the plowed land, done according to an irregular rhythm. Because
the few cattle graze little, manure is rare, and the land is insufficiently
plowed under and poorly fertilized; hence, the system also entails long
fallow and sterile periods. The major part of the land is fallow, abandoned to grazing flocks roaming freely over the fields whose gates have
been knocked down during the period between harvest time and the first
sprouting of the grain. Yet in the sown areas, the yields are distressingly
small; in a normal year, the peasant scarcely harvests his sowings threefold. In addition, this cultivation must be stretched over great expanses
of land.

This primitive agriculture devours not only land but manpower. The
use of grain mills powered by running water and constructed by the
manor lords is just beginning to gain ground, and is a notable improvement. For the peasants, it saves all the time spent in crushing the grain
between rocks. Everyone, however, does not benefit; the poorest hesitate
to allow the manorial miller any portion of the flour of which they have
too little for their own allowance. Nevertheless, for want of equipment,
it is the vagaries of the land that lay claim to the heaviest toil. The peasants are divided into two social categories, depending on whether they
work their plot of ground with a team of oxen or dig it with a hoe. Farming with plows, or by hand: this deep schism in the rural world already
appears in the year 1000, and even today has not been entirely destroyed.

As a matter of fact, this unproductive land, so poorly repaying the
trouble people take with it, is unequally divided. Provided or not with
beasts of burden, many peasant families live independently by cultivating land that belongs freely to the family group and is passed on without
any regulations from one generation to the next. But well above the level
of these small freeholders, there exists a strong landed aristocracy, owning
almost all the uncultivated land and a good part of the cultivated areas.
These "rich," "nobles"—as contemporary documents designate them—
are, first of all, those who are considered to represent the sovereign in a
given region and who control large sections of royal land in recompense
for services they are reputed to have rendered. The "noble" class also
comprises religious institutions, dioceses, cathedral chapters, and monasteries; these, scattered everywhere, possess extensive property, endowed
by the donations of both rich and poor. Finally, the "noble" class includes a few large, more or less wealthy families, divided into multiple
branches, the origin of whose fortunes seems, from this vantage point,
obscure, but whose possessions—be they compact groups or dusty plots
of ground—nevertheless are distributed widely over entire provinces.

Owning the largest segment of the land, this aristocracy also owns a portion of rural society itself. For, like Roman Gaul, like primitive Germany, France in the year 1000 is a slaveholding region. Actually these slaves or—as the vernacular dialects designate them—"serfs" are in a minority among the peasants. Bought and sold like cattle, the serfs exist in a state of dependence almost as strict as that of the ancient slaves. They pass from generation to generation through the female line. They have no recourse to civil justice, are subject to arbitrary punishment, and must obey every order of their owners who, in turn, owe them nothing. Without delving into the origins of slavery itself, it is probable that the spread of Christian concepts caused the family rights of the serfs to be acknowledged. Nevertheless, what they own belongs first of all to the possessor of their person, and he is their first heir when they die. They are unable to marry without his permission, and one of them who wants to enter the Church is not admitted until after he has been officially freed.

There are slaves everywhere. Peasants of average means own one or two, but the greatest number of them are controlled by the rich. In small groups of twenty or thirty heads, a good portion of the human livestock lives in the owner's dwellings. Men and women who are fed in dining halls, dressed in goods handed out to them, deprived of wages or personal savings and their own family life, fulfill all the domestic tasks. They make tools and clothing for the entire group, and cultivate a portion of their owner's land—but a portion only. An explanation of this lies in the fact that, because they cost a great deal, eat, waste money, and give a minimum return for their work, it is in their owner's interest not to increase their number although they are far too few for the land. Also, the lord's "demesne," that portion of land set aside for his immediate profit, does not reward all the work put into it if it includes land which is not cultivatable. Only the best areas, the large *coutures*,* stretching out into the good sections of the *finages*, pay their way; the rest is given over in small lots to the tenants. Often the latter are free peasants whose ancestors, having only a small amount of allodial land, if any at all, agreed to work the land of other people. Sometimes, too, these tenants are serfs descended from domestic slaves whose owners once settled them on an independent farm, instructing them to provide their own food from their own plot of ground, but not to renounce the owner's service completely. Whether free men or serfs, they organize the development of their holdings freely, and if the land provides additional profits, these are at their disposal, succeeding at their death to their children. But, in exchange for the permanent grant that they enjoy, they must hand over to the manor lord rent and various fees, payable at fixed rates on occasions staggered throughout the year. Several pieces of money exist, though they

---

* *Couture* refers specifically to the large area of arable land which only the lord can farm.—Trans.

are rare; their presence proves that tenant farming is not a completely closed system and that the peasant normally sells a little at the markets. Or, though this is uncommon, they pay with some of the products of family industry—carved wood or pieces of cloth, required of the community during the preceding century. More often, they pay with fruits of the earth, portions of grain or wine, eggs, chickens, and now and then a sheep or a pig. In addition, the tenants must provide a certain number of workdays with their draft animals, if they own them. They come to lend the household servants a strong right arm for the heavy work: harvesting hay or grain, plowing, threshing, gathering grapes, and transporting the crops.

Such, then, are the landed manors. They rarely occupy an entire village; most of the time their holdings stretch over several districts, and their scattered lots are mingled with those of the small, freeholding peasants, or with the strips of neighboring lords, in various areas. Thanks to the work of a few dozen household serfs, the *corvées** of a few dozen tenants, and the fees everyone brings to the manor at Christmas, Easter, and St. Martin's Day, the rich—those few men controlling the largest amounts of land in a given area—can feed themselves well; themselves and their families, and, in addition, their guests and their transient friends, who are liberally received. The storerooms of the lord's messuage are always supplied with quarters of pork, with lard, peas, beans, and sacks of grain to see him through until the next harvest. The first privilege of the aristocracy is its right to escape the scarcity of food; thus the unequal distribution of land establishes small islands of gluttony in the common dearth of provisions. Small islands of idleness, too, are established for, above all else, the noble is the man who does nothing in the thick of so many rustics feverishly clawing up the earth; he is the man of leisure—because the old idea, deeming manual labor unworthy of the really free man and regarding the absence of productive activity as the most precious of distinctions, is indeed very much alive. In the long run, the manor lord's undertakings funnel the little money in circulation toward a few, and now and then put them in a position to buy those very rare commodities unobtainable from the patrimonial fields or the labor of servants.

As a matter of fact, commerce is not at a complete standstill in this rural universe, almost without roads or towns. It is even incorporated into the few vestiges of organization surviving in the waning of political institutions. In a given place, on a certain day of the week, a market is held in most villages. Here and there exist "ports"—that is, not unloading places but rather areas reserved for merchants to convene. Periodically, on fixed days, fairs authorized by the king are set up at a few

---

* The unpaid, forced labor services required by a lord of his subordinates.—Trans.

crossroads. Finally, there is the coining of money; but in fact only limited use is made of these pieces. There are abundant reserves of precious metals, used principally in making jewelry and objects of worked gold, extremely attractive to these primitive beings who delight in striking decoration and sparkling ornaments. Treasure is preserved not in monetary specie, but in the form of bracelets and cups, in the most protected nooks of the lord's house. The black coins, struck in a poor alloy of silver and lead, are small and so very thin that they are quickly worn out. The thickest of them is worth a *denier*, the twelfth part of a *sou*. Yet, because of their rarity, they have great purchasing power—an ox could be bought for some twenty *sous*. These simple means of exchange are used only when barter is impossible, yet the units producing them, scattered around the neighborhood of each of the main local markets, continue to produce them uninterruptedly. Be it a good or bad year, every peasant household garners a dozen or two of these *deniers*, through a few paltry sales of limited scope. But the manor lord takes in most of them.

In this fragmented world, a long-distance trade in luxury merchandise still survives, because of the circulation of local money on this intermittent basis, affecting only an imperceptible area on the fringes of the almost entirely self-sufficient rural cultivation. One can scarcely imagine the fundamental role dress played in the concerns and behavior of the people of these times; let us merely call to mind the warriors of Louis the German (the evidence comes from mid-ninth-century Germany, but is applicable to France in the year 1000), who had to be forbidden to appear on the battlefield dressed in silken and embroidered fabrics, for fear that they would fight among themselves over their tawdry finery and forget the enemy. Thus fabrics (material which, especially in its bright colors, was so unlike the rough woolen and hempen cloth made in domestic workshops—fabrics from which long, ostentatious tunics are made because the "nobles" dress differently from others, thereby demonstrating their superiority) and spices (those strangely flavored seeds used for hygiene and for the delectation of the tongue) are the two chief commodities that, being lightweight and very precious, travel immense distances despite all obstacles. In the main, they come from the Far East along multiple and diffuse routes: across northern Italy, or Moslem Spain; or else, following even longer routes, through the Baltic and the North Sea. But the trade in these commodities, used only by a few of the rich, is very defectively managed. More often than not they are gifts, rather than objects of commercial transactions, for offering gifts is a fundamental gesture. The nobles give them to their friends, especially the aristocracy whose prestige depends on such lavish generosity. Thus, pepper and red cloth make their way into the hands of the village *hobereau*.*

---

* Small, country gentlemen; provincial noblemen.—Trans.

There are also quite a few other purchases and sales, but made by professional merchants. Now and then, it is true, texts mention a few traders subsisting on their profession—such as the merchants from Verdun, in commercial relations with the Moslems in Spain—but this social type is a rarity. Most frequently, when someone wants to obtain exotic commodities, he instructs one of his servants to go and fetch them at great distances at one of those very rare main crossroads where it is known that these objects can occasionally be found.

So we see, in spite of the universal withdrawal to the land, a strongly hierarchical society. And in every forest clearing, in the midst of the peasantry, there emerges a noble family maintained by everybody's work. Surrounded by their household slaves, by their concubines covered with bracelets, gilded ornament, and multicolored apparel, demonstrating their wealth for all to see, these "powerful," "illustrious" men—as they are called—who ride fine horses cared for by others (another sign of their superiority), dominate these rustics from on high. Not all the peasantry are their serfs or tenants, but the village church belongs to them, and, in times of danger and hardship, it is their protection that is sought first. Their *de facto* power over the little group of human beings cut off from their fellows by distance and solitude is secure.

The organization of authoritative powers is adapted to this fragmented rural society, where the majority of the land belongs to a few. Most assuredly, all the efforts the Carolingian sovereigns made at the end of the eighth century to restore the monarchy are not lost. The prestige of the royal magistracy is still high. It is certain that in the heart of the most backward forest, the least of the peasants knows that a king exists, that he is chosen by the people, consecrated, anointed like a bishop with holy oil, invested by God Himself with the delegation of His own power, and instructed to maintain peace and justice over all the land in the kingdom. Actually, however, this prestige has no practical application. For, in a milieu where the movement of individuals is difficult, where education (as we shall see) is the privilege of a very limited élite, and where the use of writing and the awareness of abstract ideas both are lost, it is impossible to rule from a distance. And the lofty concepts people have of the king are not sufficient to subject men to him in actual fact. When he asserts himself, he is obeyed by everybody. But despite all his efforts to move about constantly—both to use up the products of his estates and to benefit on the spot from the fruitful hospitality of his subjects, as well as to show the power of the monarchy concretely in various locations— the realm is too vast, and he is unable to be everywhere at once. Since the election of 987, when the sovereign dignity was conferred on Hugh Capet, inheritor of the ancient dukes of France, the king is not really a leader except in his patrimonial estates around Paris and Orléans. And, in everyday life, the ruling power proceeding from royal authority (called the *ban*) * is divided. It is actually exercised by the count, a local leader, within a much more limited area, the *pays*. (In order to get some idea of the average dimensions of these divisions, it is worth noting that about ten exist between the Seine, Oise, and Somme.) Theoretically, the count is designated and invested by the king to represent him in a region; practically, he is independent of the king apart from a few intermittent demonstrations of allegiance. His inherited rights give him both his functions and his landed endowment. In several provinces, where a regrouping of authority took place—to the benefit of a dynasty of war leaders—during the invasions of the tenth century, the count acknowledges the superiority of a more powerful duke or count. Usually this is an extremely superficial protection, and does not prevent him from completely autonomous enjoyment of his prerogatives. These resemble almost exactly those of the sovereign: the right to gather an army of free men and lead them into battle; the right to preside at assemblies of justice, and to see that their sentences are carried out. The count exercises these rights personally, however, only over his landed aristocracy, the "rich" and the "noble." Minor officials assume control over free men of lesser wealth; justice is the concern of provosts; war-service is the domain of men-at-arms protecting the fortresses in the count's name and making an official round of control visits from time to time.

But the dissolution of power is pushed still further than this, because the count's authority is severely limited in practical affairs. It is limited, first of all, in space: in accordance with the privileges granted by the ancient kings, and since confirmed, the extensive estates of the large religious institutions are entirely free from the action of all custodians of the royal *ban*, and from the count and his subordinates. They form autonomous enclaves, the "privileged." Secondly, the count's authority is limited to a social group that consists only of the least poor among the free men; all the serfs are dependent only upon their owners; similarly, an increasing number of peasants find themselves, vis-à-vis the rich, in such a restricted economic dependence that their natural "liberty" has been forgotten. Finally, the count's authority is limited, ultimately, to a few extraordinary acts. All everyday activities go on beyond his reach. No one would dream, for example, that public power might levy direct taxes, or control family life; even justice and war are not entirely within his hands, since it is completely understood that a free man who has been the victim of an aggressor can avenge himself by use of arms (for the majority of conflicts are adjusted by friends, outside the arbitration of the

---

* *Ban* refers to the lord's power to rule and punish, as the king's representative in a given region; from this word proceeds the lord's *banal* privileges—his mill, for example, which the peasants must use, and *banalités*, the services the holder of the *ban* may exact.—Trans.

count's court). Also, under the guise of this official, political network, other sorts of relations flourish among men. These are private, but very effective and much more vital; they are more precisely adjusted to economic realities and to the natural multiplicity of social ties. The true power that governs men's daily behavior is organized into much less extensive patterns. One such pattern is the family relationship. Here the division of ancestral lands and their profits is settled, under the guidance of the family leaders; here, too, a threatened individual may find his first and best refuge. Another organizing group is that of neighbors living in the same hamlet, who are subject to certain collective restraints in farming the territory and who, in order that the common land may be parceled out, must decide on the harvest date, and the date when together they will begin building the temporary fences around cornfields and meadows. Another group is that of the landed manor lords, a community of work dominated by the economic power of the owner and by the permanent authority of the reeve—for the latter, being more close at hand, is often more burdensome. Again, there is the train of dependents, of "friends" coming from the middle aristocracy, that gathers around the very large landowners. And finally, there is the framework formed by the group of poor peasants who, in order to receive the aid of an earthly protector or to insure the good graces of the patron saint of a sanctuary, have entered into an hereditary dependence bordering on serfdom.

In short, extreme multiplicity is definitely the most characteristic feature of the material bases of French civilization in the year 1000. Only a few privileged people are able to escape, from time to time, these small, self-contained, rustic units in which too primitive techniques maintain an extremely low subsistence level. Only these few can, having a small surplus at their disposal, find means to travel, to meet, and to commission less ugly ornaments from local artisans, as well as to buy those brilliant and gaudy ornaments of superior craftsmanship, brought from far-distant countries by occasional peddlers. But this superiority is only superficial, for these village potentates have emerged hardly at all from the most barbaric rusticity. For centuries, throughout all France but especially in the north, the towns have ceased to be the centers of a worldly life, to which this landed aristocracy could now and then come and participate in certain more refined forms of culture. Culture has, for a long time, been the monopoly of a still more narrow élite, limited to a few dignitaries from the clergy and to monks from a few cloisters.

► **THE CLERGY AND LEARNED CULTURE**

The Church is firmly entrenched everywhere. The territory of France is now completely encompassed by the Christian framework, as a result

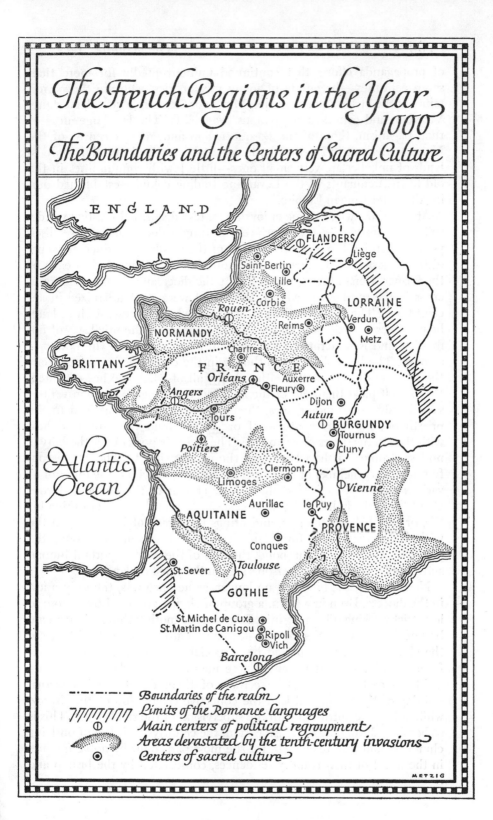

The French Regions in the Year 1000
The Boundaries and the Centers of Sacred Culture

ENGLAND

FLANDERS

Liège

Saint-Bertin

Lille

Corbie

Rouen

Reims

LORRAINE

Verdun

Metz

NORMANDY

Chartres

BRITTANY

FRANCE

Orléans

Auxerre

Fleury

Angers

Dijon

Tours

Autun

BURGUNDY

Tournus

Poitiers

Cluny

Atlantic Ocean

Clermont

Limoges

Vienne

Aurillac

le Puy

AQUITAINE

PROVENCE

Conques

St.Sever

Toulouse

GOTHIE

St.Michel de Cuxa

St.Martin de Canigou

Ripoll

Vich

Barcelona

Boundaries of the realm
Limits of the Romance languages
Main centers of political regroupment
Areas devastated by the tenth-century invasions
Centers of sacred culture

METZIG

of propaganda efforts that continued uninterruptedly for more than
seven centuries—the efforts of many missionaries, who are the patron
saints of the little village churches, Martin or Germain, Amand, Nectaire,
Valérien, and countless anonymous evangelists. The last large areas of
rural paganism, those of the Basque region and, more recently, of the
Norse settlement in Normandy, have just been wiped out. The only islands of unbelief are very small ones—little Jewish communities in the
old towns, remnants of the Levantine trading colonies established during the Later Roman Empire.

At this time, when Rome enjoys uncontested spiritual prestige yet despite the efforts of a few ninth-century popes does not exercise disciplinary guardianship over the Church of the Gauls, the principal agents
of the ecclesiastical body are the bishops. These are invested in each of
the former Roman towns, which is why the diocesan sees are more numerous in the southern provinces, those that were most urbanized in ancient times. The bishop is the pastor of the whole diocese. Rich in land,
he possesses a portion of the royal *ban* by means of the privileges of immunity, and is sometimes established in a town with all the power of
a count. The bishop's moral authority in the diocese is immense. He is
the respected leader of the entire clergy, all of whom he has educated.
He himself picks them out of the laity by conferring upon them various
sacred orders, first minor ones, then the major orders that lead to the
priesthood; the ritual gestures of ordination bind these men to him
with the strongest ties of patronage. The bishop's power over the laity is
no less strong: it is he who judges the gravest sins, he who is the confessor of every member of the upper aristocracy, he who is the initiator of
various charitable activities which draw crowds of the indigent devout
about the cathedral. He also, at times, causes miracles (either during his
life, or after), heals the sick, and brings the wrath of heaven upon the
wicked; he wields the formidable weapon of excommunication, the
power to sever the religious bond, the area of the most important human
activity, placing the guilty person's soul in the worst of dangers.

Nevertheless, the bishop is no longer, as he once was, the only priest
in the diocese. Even in a town, a group of clerics, governed by a more or
less strict working rule, is organized around the mother church. The members of this chapter—the canons—lead a partially communal existence in
the cloister and are supported by a special landed patrimony, distinct
from the bishop's endowment. These men are the prelate's immediate
assistants and share his tasks; certain of them direct the intellectual
training of the group and lead the collective celebration of the liturgy,
while others are entrusted with the supervision of the rural clergy. This is
so because, during the Frankish period, the countryside is full of outlying
churches—old private chapels, for the most part, built by noble families
in the midst of their country residences, consecrated by the bishop and

provided with a priest instructed to celebrate masses and distribute the usual sacraments there. This movement, tending to establish a center of sacramental life in each island of population, attains its end: by the close of the tenth century, one is able to trace the outlines of parishes within the solitary forest areas. Henceforth they form the essential framework of rural life. There, the total harvest is subjected to a deduction of a varying percentage—the tithe—for the sanctuary's benefit. With the exception of members of the manor lord's household, who attend the master's private chapel, every inhabitant brings his regular and fixed offering to the church where weekly liturgical services are held and where the principal rites which punctuate life are celebrated. The church is also a burial place for the dead and a center for distributing aid to the needy. In this way, in this society where country life is everything, primitive urban Christianity is finally ruralized. There is no longer a peasant who does not have a priest within reach; there abounds a superfluity of ministers of God, serving the faithful, nourished by huge landed riches. Their material situations are widely diverse for, within the clergy, social distances are as great as in the lay world. Bishops and canons are on the same level as the nobles who are their kinsmen; the priest in charge of a succursal chapel, provided with a special holding that he often farms himself, shares the way of life of the husbandman; and the freed son of a serf, whom a given manor lord installs as a household cleric in his chapel, is not materially—or perhaps even morally—in an appreciably higher position than is his brother, the stable boy.

The monks, who like the clergy entered God's militia by cutting their hair and laying down their secular arms, also form a part of the Church; but they have not been entrusted, as are the clergy, with the care of souls. Instead, they are withdrawn from the world, the better to prepare their salvation. A few, forerunners of a movement that is to permeate the entire eleventh century, are recluses—hermits who settle on the fringes of the clearings, living on alms and the gleanings from woodland areas. Most of the monks, however, practice collective isolation, and are gathered together in communities, almost exclusively communities of men because, in a world where women are in a very low position, religious life is a predominantly masculine affair. Ever since the beginning of the fifth century, when the earliest institutions spread the practices of the Egyptian cenobitic societies along the coast of Provence, Gaul gradually became dotted with monasteries. Toward the beginning of the tenth century, these monasteries are everywhere—just within the walls in the old towns, but especially in the country, in contact with agricultural work. Frequently they are very prosperous: popular piety has a special reverence for these sanctuaries of prayer; the rich gladly retire there in their old age, and place one of their sons there, at an early age, to pray for the family; many desire to be buried there—and all these attentions procure

substantial gifts of land for the community. From the Carolingian period on, all these monasteries were usually subject to the rules of Saint
Benedict. Hence, they are closed communities whose members are committed to permanent residence and placed under the authority of an abbot, their spiritual father, by the vows they have taken. They live in
chastity, but without excessive mortification of the flesh; they possess
nothing of their own, though the community itself may be rich. The
primitive obligation of manual labor has been greatly softened, and most
of the monks live like manor lords on the products of an area worked
by dependent peasants.

What is the spiritual influence of this large, omnipresent body? One
may judge it best by emphasizing the fundamental feature of this human
milieu formed during the Frankish period, a milieu which follows, in
part, from this very evangelization: the intimate coalescing of spiritual
and temporal elements, of the clergy with the faithful. The idea that the
leaders of the Carolingian church had tried to revive, that of a special
distinction of priestly functions, has been obliterated. In a society regulated in terms of land, where the Church, also become landlord, has
taken its place among the other landed powers, the dominion of the
bishop is indistinct from that of the count. The latter obtains analogous
profits and administers his holdings according to the same methods; and,
likewise, the holdings of the parish priest are indistinct from those of the
husbandman. No real barriers exist between these people. In daily life,
outside the ceremonies at which they officiate, what is there to distinguish the rural *curé* from the rustic, or the bishop—administrator of land,
head of a large group of dependents, willing leader in battle—from the
other "masters," all of whom hold, as he does, fragments of the royal authority? Even their clothing, food, and customs are the same. This in-
terpenetration is not without its advantages. It promotes direct contact
between the priest and his flock. It explains why the civilization of that
time, in its lowliest aspects and most primitive gestures, if not imbued
with ecclesiastical conceptions, at least is clothed in forms of an ecclesiastical origin. These are deep and lasting imprints on secular life; but,
even more, the spiritual suffers from being so closely mingled with the
material. Because the religious functions, always entailing the enjoyment of some landed income, are lucrative, and because there is little
feeling any more for their special dignity, it is the worldly powers who
dispose of them and distribute them—if in fact they do not arrogate the
right to exercise these functions themselves. The recruitment of church
personnel has, in general, been annexed by the secular. The parish
churches were built by the rich for their own use; their descendants regard them as personal property. They exploit them as one of the elements
—and the most profitable one—of their landed estates, like windmills or
village wine-presses, levying the various tithes and dues, offerings and

burial fees, accruing to the Church. In exchange for guaranteeing the celebration of worship, the rich designate the priest in charge of the suc- cursal chapels without any restraint whatsoever; in order to insure his devotion and to reduce maintenance costs, they take him from the lowli- est of their household staff. He is always a poor man who, lacking regu- lar touch with the upper clergy in the town, quickly forgets the little he has learned; because of his origins and the little plot of ground that in- sures his existence, he lives in total dependence on the lord of his church. In each tiny peasant clearing, religious functions are dominated by the village leaders.

Even at a high level of the ecclesiastical body, there is an intrusion of the upper aristocracy. The monasteries, too, are private establish- ments, integrated into the family's patrimony, and the monks do not choose their abbot without secular intervention. The patrons have their own puppets appointed and, without renouncing the world, are thus garbed in the abbatial dignity, reaping more of the monastery's riches for their own comfort. In the same way, every great family in a diocese re- serves for itself a place in the cathedral chapter; there it establishes one of its own members who in turn will hand his prebend down to some relative. As for the bishop whom the clergy and the people ought, in the- ory, to elect—he is chosen, according to a tradition asserted during the Frankish period, by royal authority; that is, by the king in a certain num- ber of towns, and in the rest, by the powerful few who have monopolized the attributes of monarchial power on a local scale. Thus, all the spiritual functions are carried out by nominees of the landed lords. These men have, to be sure, a certain solicitude (at least intermittently) for spiritual values, sometimes leading them to designate the people best qualified to perform their duty (the Church was not lacking, at the end of the tenth century, in men of high moral quality, even in the most exalted posi- tions); but they are not able to resist their own covetousness and, for that reason, often choose the most advantageous candidate, a younger son whose settlement is absolutely secure, a friend whose loyalty it is con- venient to have in one's pay—in fact, whoever offers the most tempting gift. And again, many accede to ecclesiastical dignities out of pure self- interest, without any vocation or special preparation, and the clergy is so entangled in the world that they do not deem it necessary to change their way of life or abandon their worldly customs. The outcome of all this is that a large segment of the Church is occupied by those whose be- havior and mental attitude are secular.

It is true that certain people sense the need for reform. Spreading out- ward from certain monasteries in Lorraine, closely connected with the bishops, and from Cluny, there is a movement that favors taking the ap- pointment of abbots and bishops out of the reach of unwarranted inter- vention by temporal powers. In 910, the founder of the Burgundian monastery at Cluny, concerned with insuring the integrity of religious life, had stipulated that the election of an abbot be effected without any exterior intervention, in conformity with the Benedictine rules. A fortunate innovation: the community became a model of spiritual strictness and, in the course of the tenth century, the patrons of other monasteries asked the Cluniac monks to come and reform theirs on the same principles. But this reaction, limited as it was to the monasteries, had scarcely any effect. On the whole, the Church remains under the patronage of the laity; hence, the moral state of ecclesiastical personnel is very unsteady. Brutes, boors, and libertines live side by side with pure and learned men, and often replace them. The texture of religious life, in warp and woof—both in and around the Church—is one of great diversity.

Moreover, this texture is rather difficult to characterize; the documents reveal scarcely anything but the most superficial practices, or else only those of the élite. One surmises that, at least for the better monks and clerics, the religious feeling in its highest form is nurtured much less by reading of the Gospel than by meditation on certain passages from the Old Testament—in particular, from the Book of Revelation. Thus the religion is not one of incarnation but of transcendence. Its vision is of a distant, powerful, terrible God punishing the living, a God who will return to judge the dead, dooming them to bliss or eternal suffering according to their merits. When? In certain elemental and popular strata the belief, intimately linked to primitive Christianity, in the imminent end of the world definitely survives; though we know today that the tenth century was unaware of that wave of collective terrors that the Romantics imagined, it is certain nonetheless that that idea of the senility of the world and the anxious expectation of the last judgment dominate even the upper echelons of the Church. It is these simple representations that feed the religiosity of the less enlightened clergy and all the laity. To save one's soul, to conciliate that terrifying divinity—this is the universal, primeval concern. The means to this end, undoubtedly, are much less those of attempting to conform one's life to the ill-known Evangelic ethical principles than of obtaining pardon for one's errors as soon as they are committed and insuring the assistance of efficacious intercessors—the saints. These countless, invisible, highly individualized powers, each attached in particular to such and such a church or holy location, are substituted by the collective conscience for the rustic divinities, the guardian spirits of the villages.

The support of the saints, who will defend one's soul at the heavenly tribunal, and God's pardon are purchased especially by alms "that wipe out sin as water puts out fire." Of all the religious acts, the principal one is the giving of land—on all occasions, but especially at one's death—in quantities meticulously proportioned to the offenses committed, and scrupulously divided among the sanctuaries considered to be the most conducive to salvation. This practice is so widespread that, in the rural areas, where trade is infrequent, pious donations, along with inheritance allotments, constitute the most active factor of economic mobility. Salvation is also earned by the performance of those multiple and exact rites that dry up natural piety: in this period, capable of only slight abstraction, it is gestures and concrete signs that count. Among these rites, those involving the veneration of relics are particularly well developed, for they answer the taste for the marvelous and the wonderful that invaded religious sensibility in the tenth century. These fragments, the concrete images of supernatural powers that have been in immediate or distant proximity to holy beings, are infused with a special efficacy for salvation. People want to touch them; they deal in them, and do not even hesitate to steal in order to have these relics for themselves. The practices encouraged by the Church thus are bound inextricably to superstitious and magical practices antedating the Christian veneer. The rural priests themselves must have had trouble distinguishing these magical practices from the official liturgy, for the councils in the latter part of the tenth century outlawed magic and divination, no doubt in vain. Such is Christianity, then: for all, a religion full not of joy and brotherly love but of guilt and prostrate fear; and for most, a collection of formulas and ritual attitudes built on a deeply rooted foundation of very primitive beliefs, involving homage to friendly spirits furnishing protection against demoniacal powers, worship of the dead whose survival is indisputable (only recently have people ceased to deposit in tombs the weapons and bowls of food for the use of the dead). Yet it is around this religious function, quite rudimentary in its most prevalent applications, that all the intellectual, literary, and artistic activities at that time are arranged.

All the activities, at least, that we know of. One can hardly doubt that a popular and lay culture existed as well; apart from a few minute, indirect, and almost indistinguishable traces, nothing remains of these expressions. They were extremely perishable: poetry, for example, was sung but not yet written down. Very exceptionally, something of this art has survived: some account of the Passion or song in honor of Saint Léger, "rustic cantilenas" or those liturgical derivatives that the faithful sang at Matins; or else decorations worked on short-lived materials like wood or terra cotta. We know nothing, either, about the education received by a rich man's son not headed for the Church, or anything about his tastes. On the other hand, the literary and artistic works devoted to the glory of God are invested with durable forms: parchment books, ivory plaques, masonry or incised stones.

In these higher aspects of culture, numerous survivals of Roman tradition are still ascertainable, although they are quite distorted. The intellectual apparatus and esthetic conceptions disseminated by Rome among the social élite had very greatly deteriorated in Gaul at the time of the Germanic migrations; and the decline of the towns and exodus of the upper classes to their rural estates brought an end to those schools that, until that time, had meted out unbiased instruction to the sons of the aristocracy. The invaders introduced an art completely different from that which the Gallo-Romans had cultivated—a nomadic art applied to objects of small dimensions, a blacksmith's and jeweler's art, a nonfigurative art in which animal themes, borrowed from the people of the Steppes, were integrated into a decorative geometrism. Nevertheless, this regression of classic culture, which continued into the seventh century and was especially pronounced in the north of Gaul, was not a complete one. The schools lived on, but were transformed into purely professional bodies, oriented exclusively toward the moulding of clerics and monks. For Christianity, a "religion of the book," is based on a certain number of texts that its ministers, at least, should be able to read and understand. In the Western countries these texts—central to which was the translation of the Bible that Saint Jerome made at the end of the fourth century—are written in classical Latin, and it is because of this essential scriptural element that the old schools were integrated into the Church. Founded as they were on the study of secular writers, these schools were first condemned as a stronghold of paganism. But gradually, as the language of the Scriptures ceased to be intelligible to a growing number of priests, because of both the corruption of the vernacular dialects and the progress of conversion beyond the limits of Latinity, the schools became one of the most indispensable organs of the Church. The forms of classical art, too, continued to stay alive. Stone buildings were still built in Gaul according to the Roman techniques whose secrets the masons passed on from one generation to the next; increasingly these were set aside for religious purposes. Figurative and humanist decoration, which had been repressed by the spread of barbarian art, progressively regained favor. One sees it in the damascene steel girdle plates decorated toward the end of the sixth century in the Parisian regions; and again, fixed in soft limestone, in the sides of sarcophagi, as in those of the funeral chapel at Jouarre; and, especially, in the illustrations for holy books. But the decisive remnant of what could still survive of antique culture, integrated into a Christian setting, was produced around 800 during the period of the "Carolingian Renaissance," that stubborn effort led by two generations of churchmen and heads of state to raise the intellectual level of the clergy and restore the ornamentation of the sanctuaries by borrowings from the vestiges of the Later Roman Empire that still existed, better preserved in Northern Italy and in English monasteries. Out of this recent renaissance directly proceeds the spiritual and artistic life of France at the beginning of the year 1000.

The basis of scholarly life is completely clerical; if it should happen that a young man from the upper aristocracy be admitted among the ecclesiastical pupils, without being particularly dedicated to the priesthood or monastic life, it is an exceptional case—during most of the Middle Ages the word "secular" is synonymous with "illiterate." Alcuin and the other scholars, with whose assistance Charlemagne revived learning, perfected a program, the continuation of that of Roman antiquity, for the schools established in the monasteries and cathedral chapters. This consisted of a group of disciplines called the "seven liberal arts" arranged in two cycles. The first, the *trivium*, is first and foremost an education in expression. "Grammar," the science of language (the Latin language, since no one knew Greek), stands at the threshold, communicated by the annotated reading of several profane poets—Vergil, Statius, Juvenal, Terence, Lucan—and especially by the concentrated study of the glosses of Donatus and Priscian. Next, "rhetoric," the art of literary composition—learned by reading Quintilian's *Institutio oratoria* and Cicero's *De oratore*, and by doing exercises in imitation of Cicero's orations against Catiline and Verres, or of the orations in Livy. And finally, "dialectic," the development of logical reasoning, based essentially on several treatises of philosophers or popularizers writing in Low Latin, such as Boethius and Porphyry, who transmit a very dim and distorted reflection of Aristotle and Plato. Following these comes the *quadrivium*, the goal of which is to give an encyclopedic knowledge of the world, though its branches are actually only slightly developed. "Geometry" and "arithmetic" meant simultaneously speculations on the mystical values of numbers (not without some relation to practices of magic, and thus answering a deep-rooted leaning of the medieval soul) in search of analogical correspondences and transpositions, and practical exercises where students become involved in the delicate handling of Roman figures. "Astronomy" is a simple and very primitive technique, applied either to "computation" (usually to calculate that pivotal date of the religious calendar, Easter) or to divination by means of the stars. "Music," finally, is an apprenticeship in the study of liturgical chant.

Such is the plan of the whole. But one must not imagine a progressive passage from one discipline to another. In these centers of learning, where students of all ages gather around a single teacher who, in the intervals between ritual exercises, reads and comments upon a text, everything becomes mingled—formal education, empirical recipes, spiritual meditation. Furthermore—perfectly consonant with the Carolingian tradition—the chief emphasis during this period is on the *trivium*, or the grammar cycle: that is to say, on the study of Latin. Although the system, again, is awkward in its methods, basically involving long ruminations on model texts that have been copied slavishly, it does make everyone who passes through the school bilingual. Indeed, because of the orientation of scholarly education, popular speech is definitively severed from the language of the intellectual, which is also that of the Church, of science, and of art. Far from being dead, this language is extremely lively, extremely flexible, capable of embracing every nuance of thought and expression—and it is the only written language. But the literature is extremely weak and of a totally academic nature: the library (whose resources were gathered in Carolingian times) and the workroom for writing and literary composition (the *scriptorium*) are annexes of the school. Its products are a few prayer-poems, and letters (for it is fitting that, during this period of physical isolation, cultivated men, scattered in the principal ecclesiastical posts and separated by very great distances, must resort to correspondence to exchange ideas with men of their own caliber). Only one genre flourished: history. In the most important religious establishments, regular annals are kept, more or less complete and open onto the world. The most skillful work of this period is the historical collection written by Richer between 991 and 995 in the school at Reims; it follows antique models, Sallust in particular, very closely.

As the schools are essentially religious in their intention, so is the art, in a sense that is consonant with the Carolingian Renaissance. Art contributes to the magnificence of the liturgical office—first, as a musical adornment. In this sphere, the end of the tenth century is a period when the technical innovations of the preceding hundred years take root and begin to grow: the first attempts at polyphony; notation by neumes,* although actually only in limited use, that first sketchy attempt at a graphic representation of the musical line, permitting the melody—until then committed to memory—to be fixed; and especially the trope, renewing Gregorian plainsong by arranging new, freely invented texts upon the modulations of the ritual chant, thus stimulating the religious lyric and making possible the advent of the earliest forms of liturgical plays— around 970, on Easter Morning, the monks at Fleury-sur-Loire acted out the discovery of Christ's resurrection, all the while chanting tropes.

The ornamentation of the sanctuary also renders homage to the glory of God. It is there that ancient traditions, revived at the end of the eighth century and during the ninth, are most alive: as formerly in Rome, this is an art of stone and of the human figure. Of stone, in order to build churches most of which are rectangular basilicas in the Roman style; but liturgical necessities, particularly the growth of relic-worship, have lately caused new attempts at transformation, the first fruits of a complete change in building techniques. These new techniques are particularly

---

* One of an early system of symbols developed from the Greek accents to indicate relative pitch, they date from *ca*. the eighth century. Neumes are dots and small strokes resembling shorthand symbols; written originally over the words to be sung (in order to give the singer a hint as to the rise and fall of the melody), they were later written between two horizontal lines which denoted a fixed pitch such as C or F. They were, thus, the first step leading to modern staff notation.—Trans.

relevant to two elements of the building: the entrance—that vestibule with side aisles and galleries for the use of pilgrims, which, extended, tends to become a kind of secondary church, topped by two towers and crowned by a belfry; and the chevet, where the crypt, surrounded by an ambulatory with radiating chapels, is arranged under the choir, around the main shrines. In the more massive of these constructions, new processes are tested: the pillar is substituted for the columns in a traditional basilica, vaults replace the framework. And, secondly, the representation of man takes a leading place in the ornamentation of the altar. The figure of Christ and those of the apostles and saints begin to appear— they are schematized, certainly, and mingle with the tracery and abstract elements of decoration, with the souvenirs of jewelers' techniques inherited from a nonfigurative, geometric, parti-colored esthetic formerly introduced into the Roman area by the Germanic infacers—but nevertheless these figures, in the center of the composition, are the major motifs. They can be seen styled in very low relief on the retables consisting of ivory panels or metal-covered wood; or, sometimes, erected in gold plate foreshadowing statuary art, as in those idols that southern France offers for the admiration of pilgrims, or those anthropomorphic shrines the most striking example of which is that of Sainte-Foy at Conques; or, finally, painted on the pages of holy books. Indeed, techniques of manuscript painting, the greatest of Carolingian arts, survived in the more active monasteries—at Saint-Bertin and Fleury, at Saint-Germain at Auxerre, and at Saint-Martial at Limoges. These images, enlarged, appear again in the form of wall frescoes.

The learned clerical culture, then, has its roots in Rome. But its basic outlines, its modes of expression and communication, were delineated definitively by the assistants of the great Carolingian sovereigns, within a special political construction. This intermediary stage accounts for some of its features, and first of all for its unity. Despite the distances separating the very rare centers of intellectual and cultural life, lost among the universal backwardness and scattered from one end of Gaul to the other, the tastes and modes of thought in this very small world of educated men are singularly homogeneous. As a matter of fact, all these areas were included in the empire built by Charlemagne; during the critical period lasting two or three generations, the true artisans of the Renaissance—abbots of the main monasteries, the great bishops of the first half of the ninth century, all enlisted in the few large, controlling families, all having received an identical education at the ruler's palace, were able to maintain close relations among themselves by periodic meetings of the upper echelons of the Church, by trips and written reports—all lived in a very narrow community of spirit. Thus, despite their subsequent isolation, the outlines of thought and of artistic creation stayed the same everywhere.

Thus a unity, but also a relative sterility, exists; in comparison with other regions of Western Christendom, the territory of France gives the picture of a people behind the times in the area of learned culture. Primarily, this is because the structures built by the Carolingians were too soon dislocated—and dislocated more than in the rest of the Empire, for the invasions were most pervasive there—and extended the decline of monarchial authority: schools and monastic workshops suffered more than other institutions by this reduction. The state of France is one of depression—as compared with both the other Germanic countries, staunch preservers of the Carolingian traditions, and the countries on the periphery of the Christian world, invigorated by their relations with other civilizations: the ports at the head of the Adriatic open Lombardy to Byzantium, where remnants of pagan teaching survive, and the best masters of masonry spread all over Europe; Islam, with her riches, refinement, and science, opens up Spain, as far as her Catalonian and Cantabrian borders.

Even within the regions of France, the geography of higher culture varies according to the intensity of the Carolingian imprint. This latter is much stronger in Neustria and Austrasia,* that is, in the truly Frankish regions north of the Loire. But in this zone, the original foundations were upset by the Norman invasions. Although devastated, the entire western area begins its slow recovery from the long depression. Revived by the increase of navigation on the North Sea and by a more active trade with England, a few centers spring up again: Corbie; Fleury, where the relics of St. Benedict, patriarch of the Western monks, are venerated; soon, Chartres. But the activity is still more intense in the eastern segment. To sheltered areas like Burgundy, which escaped the marauders, flocked all those who were able to flee the unsafe regions—including entire communities of monks, with their books and relics; and frontier areas such as Reims feel the beneficial influence of the large cultural centers along the Meuse and the upper Rhine Valley. On the other hand, the south of Gaul, including restive Aquitaine, was never very much subjected to Frankish domination, and thus was only superficially affected by the renaissance of art and erudition spread outward from the group around the Carolingian rulers. Other vital ferments, however, operate in this southern portion. Its heritage from the Roman past is much richer and better preserved, and less distorted by ecclesiastical intermediaries and the contamination of Germanic customs, than that of the area along the Seine. Between Poitiers, Toulouse, and Arles, Rome—the true Rome and not that single aspect of Latindom that received Christianity

---

* Clovis' son Lothair (Chlothar) at his death in 561, divided his land among his four sons. There followed a great feud resulting in three kingdoms: Austrasia, mainly Teutonic, whose capital was Metz; Neustria, mainly Gallo-Roman, whose capital was Soissons; and Burgundy. The three kingdoms were not unified until 613 under Lothair II.—Trans.

by assimilating to itself—is much more present, not only in the monuments but in the entire mental attitude as well. In short, this area is imbued with another force, one coming from Spain and reflecting the Mozarabic civilization.

Thus we begin to distinguish, in the northeast and in the south of France, two poles, two cultures of equal vitality but not of exactly the same hue. Already it would appear that the most fertile fruits are born of the interaction of these two cultural provinces—those sown in the soil of Carolingian tradition with seeds from the south, from that Latinity which, although the more authentic, is still penetrable by certain impulses from Islam. An example may be found in the career and personality of the most learned man of the period: Gerbert, who died as Pope Sylvester II, and who was remembered by subsequent generations as a magician with strange powers. He came from Aquitaine, and was educated in classical literature in the monastic cloister at Aurillac—at the edge of a corner of Auvergne where, sheltered from the invasions and oppressive dominations, the memories of Rome had remained much more deeply rooted. Later, from 967 to 970, he lived in Catalonia. On that frontier of the Arabized regions, where all sorts of commerce, of trading in spices and slaves, was conducted, where people traded artistic knowledge and techniques, and where the study of mathematics progressed much further than elsewhere, Gerbert grew familiar with the more refined techniques of computation and, in particular, with that calculating device known as the abacus. Between 972 and 982, as head of the episcopal school at Reims, he developed (as, simultaneously, did Abbon at Fleury-sur-Loire) scientific disciplines to parallel the *trivium*. He conducted the latter as a humanist, brought up on good authors, as both his correspondence and the literary competency of his pupil Richer prove. He introduced his pupils to astronomy—that foundation of the study of universal harmony—and taught the very fundaments of music, knowing how to make "different notes completely distinguishable by arranging them on a single-stringed instrument, dividing their consonances and harmonies into tones and halftones, ditones and dieses, and by methodically redistributing the tones into sounds." [1] *This was a systematic conquest of auditory subtleties, by their reduction to intelligible categories, and simultaneously a strict understanding of rhythm and tempo. Under Gerbert's stimulus, Reims became the most brilliant center of instruction in the kingdom of France. It became, too, the source of a great enrichment of learning, since Gerbert counted among his pupils (along with the future King Robert, son of Hugh Capet), Fulbert, who was to carry to Chartres, while directing its episcopal functions, the teachings of his master. There, applying his knowledge of mathematics, Fulbert was to adumbrate the structure of a whole new system of thought.

---

* Superscript numbers refer to the Notes section, which follows the text.

► REGIONAL DIVERSITIES

As Gerbert's activity and influence indicate, distance is not a drawback among intellectuals. Men, books, and ideas circulate from one center of studies to another, and local idiosyncrasies at the level of learned culture lessen because of this movement. This particular sphere, however, is an extremely limited one; considered in its entirety, the civilization of the year 1000 presents great contrasts. It must be remembered that France is immense—much vaster, relatively speaking, than the largest present-day empires because of the inadequate techniques of communication and the slight social fluidity. Among those small groups of peasants scattered in the midst of the wilderness, the customs and habits governing everyday life continue to develop autonomously in each closed unit; the dissolution of the Carolingian state and the parcelling out of royal power are, in point of fact, a normal adaptation of the political structures to the natural fragmentation of this human environment. Furthermore, certain regional incompatibilities are the heritage of the past. The various provinces of Gaul do not share the same history; we have just seen what differences these diverse vicissitudes introduced into the composition of their cultural heritage. Ever since the end of antiquity, the migration of peoples and the intrusions of marauders have affected these provinces unevenly; the varying intensity of exterior intervention has accentuated contrasts already perceptible in the pre-Roman substratum. France at this time is divided by frontiers, some of which are very precise while some, on the other hand, are wide, nebulous stretches—areas graduated from one slight difference to another. We shall close this chapter by giving some indication of their nature.

First, distinct and stable lines of division are formed by the linguistic barriers. On the periphery, these lines demarcate several areas where the Latin imprint was always superficial and, consequently, the language of Rome has now been supplanted by other tongues. There are the Germanic areas to the east of the Meuse and the Vosges, where invaders have obliterated almost entirely any trace of Rome—such as the northern part of the Flemish plain, formerly a graceless terrain and, moreover, inundated by the sea and virtually deserted, but now awakening to a commerce of river- and sea-going boats and already indicating perceptible signs of prosperity. Secondly, there are the Celtic areas in the western half of the Armorican peninsula. There, in the sixth century, the insular Bretons immigrated—with their special culture and their special, clan-oriented social structure, related to those of Ireland and Wales—and remained unsubjugated by Carolingian domination; throughout the Middle Ages, they remain several generations behind, out of the mainstream of French civilization. And finally, there is the small island of Basque dialect

south of Bordeaux, in a rather uninviting area—but Gascony, dominated by autonomous rulers, is on the way to becoming civilized after
long having formed an almost impenetrable obstacle of barbarity; it has
been Christianized only recently, and now serves as a more and more frequently used passageway into northeastern Spain. However, these areas of
linguistic particularity are limited, and exist in the backwaters of French
civilization which, taken in the aggregate, spoke Romance dialects;
those precise differentiations, established with the proliferation of vernacular literature and the formation of the literary languages of *langue d'oc*
and *langue d'oïl,** did not exist until the eleventh and twelfth centuries.
Undoubtedly some of the underlying divergences already have begun to
appear, as in the different manners in which the Latin roots are distorted
in the languages of north and south; but the transitions from one to the
other are imperceptible and each group of villages has its own phonetic
system. At this point, the differences felt by the people are of another
order: divisions of a political nature, some of which protract ethnic frontiers of more or less ancient standing.

The division by the Treaty of Verdun of 843 drew the eastern boundaries of the kingdom that is customarily called France. The boundaries
pass approximately along the Scheldt from its mouth on; reach the Meuse
through the Argonne, following the river's western banks for a good
distance; they are then determined, except for overlappings here and
there, by the course of the Saône, skirting the plains of Forez but including the Velay, and rejoining the small branch of the Rhône delta. A precise frontier: everyone, and in particular those professional scribes drafting charters, knows the district it encompasses and exactly where it lies;
yet it has absolutely no reality in everyday life. Having neither customs
stations nor garrisons, it is passed over without anyone being conscious
of, or caring about, it—it crosses manors, personal dependencies, and
finages without cutting them off. Beyond that, Lorraine, integrated into
the Germanic kingdom for a century, participates in the brilliant culture
of Otto the Great; it is permeated by an advanced ecclesiastical reform
movement, and, along the Moselle, by the prosperity of a major artery of
travel and commerce. Then, to the south of the Vosges, begins the
"Kingdom of Arles"—the combination of the two kingdoms of Burgundy and Provence—extending from Basel to Marseille; but its king, living in the area between Vienne and the upper Rhône, is totally power-
less. Combed by routes leading into Italy in the direction of the mountain passes, these southeastern regions are more Romanized and more

---

* The Romance dialects spoken south of the Loire River are referred to as the
langue d'oc, and those spoken north of the Loire as the *langue d'oïl.* The distinction
rests upon the former's word for "yes," *oc,* and the latter's word, *oïl (oui).* Provençal
was the professional, literary language developed by the troubadours living in the
southern part of medieval France.—Trans.

urban and have a strong manorial autonomy; in the southern regions, however, they suffered greatly under the brigandage of the Saracens, who were repulsed effectively only in the last few years. On the shores of the Mediterranean, commercial life is reduced to an insignificant coastal trade; the Bishop of Grenoble and the Count of Provence are kept busy restocking their devastated estates and distributing them, in large desolate pieces, to their faithful.

The kingdom itself is far from homogeneous. It is as if it scarcely owned those regions abandoned to the Scandinavian invaders—first, the banks of the lower Seine, then Bessin and Cotentin; this "Normandy," ruled by the Vikings' descendants, constitutes a special sovereignty whose political destinies are completely independent. Nevertheless, Norse settlement is limited to a few districts; the traces of destruction are quickly wiped out by the permanent settlement of the destroyers, and some of the major elements of the earlier civilization—Christianity, Latin and its popular derivatives, the manorial system—have reappeared there, enriched in more ways than one, and consolidated by foreign contributions. In the very heart of the territory to which, theoretically, the power of the *rex francorum* extends, three absolutely distinct zones appear—duchies that are sometimes, with a dogged reminiscence, called kingdoms and whose inhabitants are convinced that they form separate "peoples." These three large provinces were demarcated at the time of the Germanic migrations by the establishment of various groups of invaders; the Carolingian domination was unable to unify them. Of the three, Burgundy is the least individualized, a poor chip off the fifth-century region of the *Burgondes*, the majority of whose land lies beyond the borders of the kingdom. By contrast to this lack of individuation, the two other provinces are in strong opposition to one another. On the one hand, the true territory of France, around Paris, Orléans, and Tours—that of Clovis and his sons—continues the old Neustria; the ancestors of the new king had been dukes in the region. Then, the large area of Aquitaine, domain of the Visigoth invaders, which remained in strained resistance to the Frankish conquerors for a long time, is formed around two poles: Poitiers, the repository of Roman traditions and center of ducal power; and Toulouse, the head of the ancient Spanish frontier, on the edges of Carolingian military protection established opposite Islam on one side and the Western Pyrenees on the other. Between France and Aquitaine, from the lower Loire to Châlon-sur-Saône, runs the most deep-seated and vigorous border, separating rival political dominations much less than the more fundamental divergence in ways of life, opinions, and conceptions of the world. It is a border separating mutual incomprehension, reciprocal hostilities—listen to the Cluniac monk Raoul, who watched the procession bearing King Robert's new wife, passing by around the year 1000: "There then began to pour into France and

Burgundy men of the greatest vanity of spirit, coming from Auvergne and Aquitaine; men who were ridiculous in their customs and dress, immoderate in their military equipment and the saddlery of their horses, men who had their hair cropped to the middle of their skull, their beards trimmed in the style of clowns, their hose cut very immodestly—men totally incapable of remaining faithful to the sworn peace." [2]

Thus, diversity and division—this is the idea that once more asserts itself. The same backwardness, the same precariousness of the means of existence, are everywhere; and, in each of these rare and precarious sanctuaries preserving learned culture, one finds the same books, the same esthetic propensities. But between each little group of village clearings arranged around a crossroads, a cathedral, or a base of defensive operations, there is only very irregular contact; the barriers are erected, not only by the solitary space through which people hesitate to venture, but also by one people's mistrust of another. Such is France in the year 1000. But the period is not moving toward an even narrower regression: for several years, since the last attacks of brigandage were repulsed, conditions have begun to change. Already, the wilderness intermittently is pushed back by the more efficient tools of the peasants; already, travelers on the roads are more numerous, and among them there are peddlers of goods; already, there is a fermentation, harbinger of a coming release, rather than the terrified prostration of waiting for the end of the world. And gradually, a new unity of social relations, of customs and mental attitudes, the human framework of this advance, gets into working order. It is called feudalism.

II

Feudalism:
The Eleventh Century

ALTHOUGH the use of the term "feudalism" may be criticized on the ground that the fief is only one aspect of the newly arranged relations among men, and not the most important one, it is an accepted term; let us retain it while trying, at the same time, to make its content more explicit. The visible forms of social relations have been altered during the course of the eleventh century, and their mutation is an important one: henceforth, for many centuries, French civilization is to evolve within new frameworks which, even when they cease to form the skeleton of the society, continue permanently to influence patterns of thought. "Nobility," "chivalry," "honor," "homage"—these key words have reverberated for so long that even today they are not entirely mute. But this revolution was not in the least abrupt; for a long time, scarcely perceptible underground changes were preparing for it. The decades around the year 1020 produced the collective mind's grasp of these changes, their legal ratification and, simultaneously, the fixing and the final definition of social relations, until now conducted in the wake of instinctive reaction. These last represented the final, belated, adjustment to the milieu, the isolation of people in the clearings, the regressive economy, and that sinking into rural life characteristic of the tenth century.

"Feudal" society exhibits, actually, two fundamental features. First, power is divided into small, autonomous compartments; the abstract ideas that had once surrounded political relations are definitively obliterated. With the possible exception of a few clerics whose minds are better trained for thought, the ideas of sovereignty and public community no longer have any meaning; to command other men and to punish them is a personal attribute, sold and inherited like a piece of land, and those who are lucky enough to possess it, use it to their exclusive advantage without having to account to anyone for their acts. Further, if authority is to be recognized, it must appear concretely: no one obeys a lord whom he cannot see or whose voice he does not hear. Because the physical presence of the leader is indispensable, his power can be extended only over small groups of assembled men. The second feature of this society is the distinct dividing-line that now isolates the nobility from the bulk of mankind. This again is a simple solidification of awareness: the aristocracy, that class of well-born men provided with customary privileges, has existed for a long time; but from now on its rights and titles are openly acknowledged. Actually, the idea of the division of Christian society into "orders," rigidly delineated categories, is widely held by the end of the tenth century. These "orders" (classes) each have been entrusted by God with a particular mission and, by virtue of that call, each has the right to special treatment. Originally a concept of the learned, formulated long ago in educated Church circles, it was applied first to priests and monks to separate them from the laity; now, it subdivides the laity into two groups. On the one hand, there is the minority of the lords, the rich, the leisure class; in order to merit the material advantages Providence has accorded them, they are obliged to turn their entire attention to the art of war, and to the armed defense of the other social categories. On the other hand, there is the "order" (class) of laborers, the mass of little people—the poor, the rustics—who, according to divine plan, have the responsibility of supporting with their labor those specialists in prayer and combat, in exchange for the spiritual and temporal protection these latter provide them.

► CASTLES AND POWER

To a great extent, the new social structure is organized in terms of the military edifice—the castle. This is, in the eleventh century, an extremely simple building: a squat rectangular tower with two floors. The lower floor is a storehouse for provisions; the upper, whose door is accessible to the ground by means of a light, removable ladder, serves as the place for temporary habitation or withdrawal from which, when it is necessary, its defense is directed. Except in the Mediterranean regions, where good beams are scarce, the walls are made of wood, the material most accessible and most easily worked. The inconvenience is that it is inflammable: thus, no heat can be brought into the castle; the kitchen must be set up outside and some distance away; and, most importantly, fire becomes the assailants' most effective weapon, from which the defenders protect themselves by putting freshly skinned animal hides at the most vulnerable points of the exterior walls. The mounting of the guard is a delicate task; the greatest lords, those who have the means, attempt to construct stone towers on the order of the donjon erected at the end of the tenth century at Langeais by the Count of Anjou, or that at Montbazon in the Touraine. But this substitution of stone for wood is rarely undertaken because of the expense of hiring quarriers and professional masons; stone strongholds are not really in general use before the second half of the twelfth century. We see, then, that during the formation of feudalism the castle, like all human dwellings of that time, is primitive and weak. Its permanence and the better part of its strength come from its situation. The tower is perched on a site which at once is elevated and difficult of access; if no escarpment is provided by nature, an artificial mound, the *motte,* is built and surrounded by a deep moat. Finally, some distance away, an embankment capped by a palisade girdles the center of defense. This embankment serves as the first line, and is capable of halting an aggressor; it protects a large enclosure where the neighboring population can find refuge during an alarum. Thus the castle or the *ferté** is the very image of collective security, the symbol and seat of power for the military command through all the surrounding villages.

These strongholds are not very numerous. Not all the nobles of the eleventh century are chatelains—far from it. Actually, the number of strongholds varies according to the locality: a greater number along the major passages, or on the outskirts where regional dominions are contested; fewer, on the other hand, in heavily wooded terrains. The concentration of castles during this period seems comparable to that of the present-day French county seats—on the average, there is a stronghold for every twenty or thirty local settlements of peasants. Furthermore, the majority of these entrenchments are, at this time, already old buildings. When, first, the partitioning of the empire into rival kingdoms, and then the deeper and deeper penetrations of the Scandinavian, Hungarian, and Saracen raids, demanded that the martial regime of the frontier areas be extended to the whole territory, these fortresses were almost all constructed in Carolingian times under sovereign control, be it of the king or the count. Here and there, of course, a few adventurers aided by disorder and insecurity were able to build strongholds on their

---

* *Ferté:* a fort or stronghold; the word still survives in place-names such as La Ferté-Saint-Aubain, south of Orléans.—Trans.

own initiative rather than on the authority of the king. But this was an extremely risky undertaking: one had to elude the vigilance of the leaders of the people and overcome the peasants' resistance; "illegitimate" castles seem to have been the exception. Most strongholds, therefore, were the king's buildings, held by his representatives. They remained so for some time. For this reason, when in the tenth century the last ties uniting the holders of the royal *ban* at different levels were broken, when all power became private and personal, it was the castle—repository of the final memories of the idea of sovereignty, yet now the hereditary possession of its guardian—around which the new conceptions of authority were formed.

In the eleventh century it sometimes happens that one lone leader is still in personal command of several castles, residing in each from time to time and leaving them, between visits, in the hands of devoted and subservient guardians; such a network of defensive points constitutes the skeleton of a kind of principality, like those held by the counts of Anjou and Flanders. But more often, each castle is the seat of an isolated rule, free of all exterior control. This is true especially in the southern part of France, but even in the north it is common: in the heart of the little region where the king has not lost all his power, between his towns of Paris and Orléans, there exist chatelains like the lords of Montlhéry or Puiset who, independent in fact, are sole possessors of their towers and of the attendant power over the neighboring terrain. And, even in the regions where the count has retained several castles under his control, his power derives not from his title, but, locally, from his function as chatelain of each of his forts. This is perhaps the fundamental characteristic of feudalism: the division of ruling power over various military bases of operation.

This small earthen and wooden fortress is, everywhere, the property of the richest man of the region—the one who holds the greatest part of the large surrounding forests and vast stretches of cleared land. But, more than wealth, it is his position in the fortress that places him so high above all the other large landholders who are his neighbors. Living there surrounded by his armed servants, the *sergents*,* the chatelain is indeed master, in the highest sense of the word—only he, the count, and the bishop are called "lord" or "sir" in the official records. His power is of the same sort as the king's, whence, in fact, it originates: it is his duty and right to maintain peace and justice in his region. He has also the task of defense against outside enemies. In case of an emergency, the chatelain sounds the alert and, uttering what is called *"le cri de château,"* summons his warriors who, from then on, are subject to a strict discipline.

---

* *Sergent* refers to men whose rank was below that of the knights. They served the lord in his household, or else went into the field as a knight's attendant, but less heavily armed than he.—Trans.

And it is his function, primary in this period when everyone lives in terror of sudden marauders (who gave the tenth century such glamour in their ancestors' eyes), to let the people huddle in the stronghold and, sustained by the neighboring population, free themselves gradually from all control. It is his job also to maintain justice within the group. Like the old kings, the chatelain is a peacemaker who quells all conflicts: he punishes the most serious crimes—premeditated murder, adultery—that rupture the peace and contaminate the community; he convenes legal assemblies about his person and executes their decisions; and, to forestall conflicts, he enacts regulations and compels obedience to them. This authority, although it has the air of royal prerogative, is now the lord's personal possession; he has inherited it, and does with it what he pleases. Aided by his men, he exploits it as he exploits his estates, his mills, or his churches. For him, the *ban* is a source of profit, an opportunity to impose fines on, and extort "gifts" from, those he protects. There is no recourse against his authority; consequently, he is tempted to exact still more. Nonetheless, this encroaching power does know one limit: "custom"—the sum of former practices recorded in the collective memory. This is a fluid law, because it is unwritten, ascertainable by questioning the oldest members of the village; yet it compels everyone's recognition as intangible legislation. Indeed, it is by the very word *coutumes** that the chatelain's prerogatives are designated.

Originating in the wooden tower and its enclosure, this tribute-exacting power radiates outward across a territory called either simply the *ban,* or the "district" (because the lord has the right to use his power within it) or else the *"sauvement"* because it is under his protection. It is a limited territory—a man can always walk from the castle to the most distant populated areas, and back, in one day. Its borders are, at first, vague and shifting; but little by little, defined by the opposing claims of neighboring chatelains, they become explicit and stable.

Thus were formed the *châtellenies,*† those political divisions fundamental to the entire Middle Ages. Today, traces of them linger reminiscently about the French countryside: the borders of the present-day *cantons,* assigned at the time of the Revolution, often adopt the same contours as the small dominions formed around each castle in the eleventh century. At that time, everyone who lived in the *châtellenie,* every *manant* (the word means, strictly, "one who lives"), were subject to the lord's power. But this power did not fall with equal weight on all and, in the early eleventh century, we see a new social classification come into being with respect to the lord and the castle.

---

* *coutumes:* taxes and services due to a lord having a *ban.*—Trans.
† The use in this translation of the word "chatelain" (and *châtellenie* for the region under his jurisdiction) is to emphasize the distinction between a manor lord who owns a fief or estate (*seigneur, seigneurie*) and the lord who is governor or owner of a castle.—Trans.

The first change is that slavery no longer exists. In tenth-century society, the clearest legal distinction (one inherited from the Roman and
Germanic past) is that which contrasts the free man—simply and forth-
rightly a member of the popular community—with the slave, who is deprived of all legal qualification. Actually this social representation, preserved by language and by many habits of thought, did not correspond to
real conditions. Within the lower classes, the free man and the slave
were brought close together by many causes: first, the pervasive Christian philosophy, which conferred a new dignity upon these non-free people who, baptized participants in the parish community, could no longer
be considered mere *things*; second, the spread of personal dependencies,
which placed more and more theoretically free peasants in a state of strict
submission that extended to their descendants and attached them to
their owner as rigidly as might any ties of slavery; and, finally, the obliter-
ation of even the idea of a public community, governed by special institutions, from which certain persons could be excluded. In practice, after
the year 1000, medieval France no longer experiences slavery in the old
sense that put a man in the position of a domestic animal. (The only
exception is the extreme southern borders, which are influenced by Islam; there, a slave trade, of non-Christians supplied by piracy, continued
throughout all the Middle Ages.) Obviously, there remains for a long
time the extremely depressed social condition of domestic servants,
shared with a great number of others who are practically without rights,
without family, and without personal will. Certain mental habits and
verbal survivals of slavery also remain; but ultimately the language itself
adjusts. In the provinces most faithful to Roman traditions, where the
keenest sense of legal Latin has survived, people soon ceased to use the
word *servus* in charters, since it seemed to imply too great a subjection,
conjuring up a degraded existence that no longer had any reality. And
if, in many popular dialects, the term "serf" remained in common use,
it now designated a condition which had no real connection with that of
the slave—a condition more accurately described by calling one person
the "man" of another. In this manner, the concept of personal dependence replaces the older one of slavery. The concept expands, gathers
strength, and grows into one of the major axes of social classification.
And it is accompanied by a completely new idea of human relations, in
particular the notion that the ties between man and man are those of
mutually exchanged services—that the lowliest dependent has the right
to expect help from the protector he serves.

As for the line dividing society into two major classes, it has been
moved to a higher level of the social structure and is drawn according to a
new criterion: the distinction is now established with respect to military
capability. The bearing of arms was, in fact, one of the privileges of freedom in ancient times—which caused a great many poor, careless people,

who had no real desire to abandon their little plots of land in the summer months, to join royal expeditions and to accept a personal dependence in exchange for exemption from servitude. And to bear arms was also, in all probability, the most conspicuous indication of a man's free state. In the ideas of Germanic origin that had fashioned the political behavior of the early Middle Ages, the "freeman" was first and foremost a warrior—and, because military service was their prime public duty, free men nowhere felt themselves more a part of the social community than in the army, gathered on the edge of the battlefield. By virtue of developments accelerated by the tenth-century invasions, fighting methods have been transformed: in the midst of the soldiers, the small group of horsemen, more heavily armed, already placed in a better position and relieved of the fatigue of long marches, had gradually taken the leading position in battle. Foot soldiers, reduced to a minor and soon negligible role, had ceased to be called up regularly; ultimately, they were entirely exempt from service and no longer participated in expeditions except in the case of serious local alerts. Therefore, at the beginning of the eleventh century, the full brunt, but also the full prestige, of military duty are the privilege of the mounted fighting-men: they alone are true soldiers. Documents written in Latin begin to give them the title *miles* to distinguish them from the others. Popular dialects are more explicit: *miles* is the translation of "horsemen," or in northern France, "knight" [*chevalier*]. In this way, as long as the idea persists that fighting is the special activity of free men, total freedom is confined to a small military élite.

It is an élite of people of means: to be a horseman, one must be rich. Fighting men during the early Middle Ages were obliged to equip themselves without any assistance from the commanding authority. Lacking the means, most of them appear to have been fitted with the most primitive equipment, and one of the Carolingian capitularies* had to state explicitly that it did not suffice to bring along a club. In a time when livestock were poorly fed and, indeed, sadly lacking, a horse—by which we mean a fighting horse, capable of carrying an armed man and his military accoutrements—was a very rare item of equipment, one whose maintenance presupposed his owner's superabundance of provisions; hence, available only to possessors of considerable capital. Furthermore, leisure was an especial necessity, as well as sufficient means to have one's estates cultivated by others and to entrust the maintenance of one's house to numerous tenants and domestics—for these men had to be trained in the difficult techniques of mounted warfare, had to spend time garrisoned in fortresses, and had to join the expeditions regularly undertaken in spring and summer—just when the land required the most constant care.

---

* The name given to a collection of legislative acts drawn up by the Carolingian kings and divided into chapters (*capitula*).—Trans.

Consequently, in the eleventh century, military duty becomes the pre-rogative of those who, by virtue of a patron's "blessing" but more often by inheritance, control a large estate, rich in land, one of those fine manors, furnished with abundant personnel, yielding sufficient food and funds to improve one's equipment. Thus the line of division, incised more deeply every day, places the "peasants" and *vilains* (men who, born in a hamlet, never leave it)* below the "warrior order"; it is the dis-tinction that, even in antiquity, separated the small group of lazy, well-fed *hobereaux* from the laborers. In most of the French provinces, the militia or "knights" tend to become identical with the landed aristoc-racy—the rich, the lords, the nobles.

The knights, who erect their residences on the chatelain's land, are placed under the stronghold owner's authority. This is so clearly recog-nized that people call them *milites castri*, the "knights of the castle," be-cause the fort is their assembly point, the chief area of the military activ-ity that distinguishes them from the bulk of mankind. But the authority of the leader is exercised over them in a special way, for they are soldiers like him; he treats them as associates. It is usually the case that they are his "men," so it is a question of an honorable dependence, a free and personal attachment producing that spirit of mutual camaraderie uniting the fighting groups—not a blind subordination. They are exempted from the usual constraints: no *coutumes* for them, nor any of the exploitation out of which the lord's *ban* materializes. In this way is formed the idea that lasts so long and has such extensive consequences: that the military vocation produces a special immunity, that a certain exemption is due to anyone who risks his life and gives his blood.

By contrast, the entire burden of the lords' power rests on those who are unarmed, on the *vilains*. For them, the entry into personal depend-ence, the state of "belonging" to another man, means obedience to all his orders, the retreat into a strict and, most important, an hereditary, subjection from which it is impossible henceforth to break away. These are the people whom the lord exploits, through the medium of his provosts, his foresters, and those auxiliaries who, though of low birth, pull themselves up upon their invested powers and, exceeding their rights, quickly make their fortune. These last are the real and immediate con-trollers of the *manants* whom they often tyrannize. It happens sometimes, in cases of great emergency, that the rustics are called into combat—or rather, into preparations for the real combat of the knights. At such times, they are despised cannon-fodder, armed only with ridiculous farm imple-ments. Normally, their co-operation in the common defense takes forms that are deemed degrading: delivery of provisions for the castle garrison and in particular hay and oats for the maintenance of the horses; or even

* *Vilains* come from *villanus* and means *villa* dweller; *vilain* refers to someone who lives in a village—by extension, a peasant.—Trans.

corvées, theoretically devoted to the periodic repair of the fortifications, but often diverted into farm labor for the chatelain. Over them prevails the manor lord's justice, all the more strict and ready in that it is so profitable: fines in *deniers* whose total amount is customarily determined by a barbaric and undifferentiated code (seven *sous* for any kind of blow, sixty if blood flows, whether or not the wound be serious) cause the few peasant savings to pass into the lord's coffers and his agent's purse. If the guilty person is unable to pay he is imprisoned; this is not a punishment, but a means for accelerating the adjustment of the monetary penalties. In the case of serious crimes, the perpetrators are at the mercy of the chatelain: he can confiscate all their property, inflict corporal punishments such as mutilation of the guilty hand, or even death—for the gallows is another symbol of lofty power. Finally, as a price for the protection accorded them, the peasants whom the lord shelters owe him material "aids." They offer him lodging when he needs it—and if the chatelain himself rarely comes to his *manants'* huts to eat the family gruel, his knights, men, and hunting dogs take advantage of this gratuitous allowance—a periodic and dreaded drain on family food reserves, although most of the time, in fact, it is limited by custom. On the other hand, the leader's right to take from the *vilain's* house whatever he needs, whenever he needs it—called the *taille**—is exercised arbitrarily.

Thus a heavier lordship, that of the controller of the *ban,* weighs on the eleventh-century peasantry. For the tenants carry this burden in addition to the services they owe the owners of the land they farm and, for parish members, it augments the tithes and other fees given to the altar of the sanctuary. It is this coercion that leads the rural population, in order better to defend itself, to gather within the framework of the parish, where different hamlets join forces in a closer community, the guardian of the *coutumes.* This collectivity of the village, that other unit basic to the French countryside, germ of the present-day *commune,* the organ of resistance to the lords' demands, acquires form and texture around the church, the place of refuge. The establishment of the manor, through the net of exactions that spares the fortunes of the nobility but transfers into the lord's hands a good part of the peasants' small profits, is another means of accentuating the differences in position within the economic hierarchy. It raises the lord of a castle even higher over the others and, more important, it isolates more than ever the small knightly élite from the mass of backward people.

► **THE KNIGHTS**

Since we always glimpse him through exterior evidence, we know almost nothing about the peasant of this period—unless it be the way in which

---

* The *taille* is a direct tax levied by a lord on the wealth of those under his control; later, it is often levied on the land held from him.—Trans.

he is exploited by his masters. On the other hand, the knights appear
in full illumination. They are a closed group: everything converged then
to make knightly rank and its privileges a condition handed down from
father to son, and to make that limited élite of rich people and warriors
an inherited society. The first cause of this was the extreme shrinking of
the economy, which made appreciable variations in individual fortunes
impossible, except in very rare instances, and maintained, from one generation to the next, an equal distance among the various family inheritances. Secondly, the exactions of the chatelain placed a new obstacle in
the way of the peasants' chances of enriching themselves. Third, the
strength of blood ties and the intimate solidarity of kinship prohibited
the very thought that, at the father's death, the son, even though impoverished, might lose the high rank he had shared during his father's lifetime. Fourth, the multiplicity of family alliances set up an extremely effective barrier to all surreptitious social advancement, in that milieu
where lasting changes of position were rare and where everyone knew his
neighbor's genealogy and situation. Fifth, class consciousness was formed
early and aroused scorn for all those who were not members of the class
by birth. And finally, there was the vigilance of those who held the coercive power and who were directly concerned that few newcomers share
the privileges and exemptions of the *coutumes*. In contrast to England,
for example, or the countries of the Empire, knighthood in France is, beginning in the eleventh century, a nobility in the strictest sense of the
term—a normally hereditary condition.

One becomes a knight by means of a ceremony of initiation, a very
expressive ritual called dubbing. Upon emerging from childhood—that
is, at about fourteen—the young noble is admitted into the company of
the warriors. An older member of the group, ordinarily his father or uncle, solemnly hands him the shoulder-belt and sword, symbols of his vocation, then gives him a blow across the face, the *paumée*, doubtless a
dim reminiscence of an ancient test of strength and self-mastery. Then
the new knight proves his physical ability by performing a series of exercises in knightly combat before the assembly gathered for the occasion:

> Then did he don a beautiful cuirass;
> A helmet green he laced about his head.
> At his left side Guillaume then hung his sword
> And strapped around his arm a mighty shield.
> His good horse was the noblest in the world.
>
> *Chanson de Guillaume*, lines 1075-1079

In this basic pattern, the ceremony is entirely secular and military. Set
phrases for the consecration of the sword are known as far back as the
tenth century, but the process by which Christian rites came to be mingled in the dubbing—as already they were mingled in other principal
events of life—was a very slow one, difficult to trace.

Thus, the superiority of the knight is publicly exhibited by these acts, applied to all warriors' sons not destined for the priesthood or for monastic life. Yet knightly existence is intimately intertwined with that of the peasants. The only member of his rank among his brothers in the parish, the knight spends the best part of his time on the land that gives him his living. His place of residence, flanked by stables and storehouses, differs only in its slightly ampler dimensions from the huts inhabited by the rustics. He has many servants, and a few rare villagers are his "men." He judges the cases that may arise in connection with the twenty or thirty holdings operated for his profit. Often the church belongs to him, in which case the bulk of the tithes finds its way into his barn. His rights, the harvests of his land, and his tenants' provisions furnish for him a great amount of food, but little money: his authority and wealth stop short at this point. Those knights who own a castle are slightly less drawn into the agricultural life, and collect *deniers* in greater abundance. Like all the others, however, they lead a singularly crude life; like all the others they are practically defenseless against darkness, disease, and cold—for the use of chimneys, coming in with stone construction, becomes widespread only very slowly in the twelfth century. Undoubtedly the most highly placed men of the period had a nervous constitution appreciably different from ours, which made them more resistant to physical pain although less capable of curbing their emotional and imaginative impulses. Their helplessness before nature explains the rash of superstitions as a continual commerce with supernatural forces. This helplessness also leads to a gregarious life; the only lived-in room of the castle is always full of people: there, the lord eats the dishes his head servant brings him from the distant kitchen, and rubs elbows with all of his people. And at night, the whole company sleeps on the floor, huddled about the lord's bed. Man in the eleventh century is never alone, but is always in the midst of a flock of others; solitude seems one of the most difficult and most admirable exercises of the ascetic life of the period.

Close as he is to the peasant, by virtue of his vulnerability to natural dangers, the knight differs from him in one fundamental connection: he does not work. Manual labor is, in fact, an obligation unworthy of a well-born man, and only he who is fed by other people's work is held to be truly noble. The ideal is to do nothing yet, at the same time, not to be unduly attached to one's wealth: once the nobility is aware of itself, one of its necessary virtues is what chivalric literature will later extol under the name of "liberality" [*largesse*]—a disinterestedness or, more accurately, a propensity toward wastefulness. More than by his titles or by legal criteria, the knight differs from the husbandman in that not only is he unproductive, but also that he uses, spends, and destroys more than anyone else. And beyond this, his is an existence entirely oriented toward strife.

Strife, first of all, against wild animals: for the king, as for the lowest of the *hobereaux*, the hunt is the most everyday of pleasures. We know the enormous areas occupied by uncultivated space in the countryside at that time. This virgin land belongs to the rich, who open a portion of it on which the peasants' cattle graze, but who also reserve a large part of it for hunting ground—which then appropriately was called the "forest." They hunt the larger animals with spears and with packs of hounds whose maintenance the chatelain imposes on his dependents. These expeditions, primitive and dangerous, are, in themselves, good training for war from which they differ only slightly in weapons and tactics; in addition, they furnish a valuable supplement to the food supply. The hunt, rather than stock farming, was the chief supplier of meat in those days. The noble is a carnivorous being (another of his distinctive characteristics) and *la vénerie* (the art of the chase), that sum of formulas and rules by which the body disciplines itself in intimate contact with savage nature, is for centuries one of the essential elements of the noble's mental equipment. Nonetheless, combat, the thing that truly defines knightly existence, lies at the heart of the knight's activity.

First and most essential, there are his tools for fighting. The horse is the warrior's indispensable implement and the most conspicuous sign of his social superiority, but all the knight's special trappings are very expensive: his armor alone would buy a good piece of farm land; we see again why this life is reserved for the very rich. These two elements—horse and armor—do not exist independently and, during the course of the eleventh century, they gradually become an increasingly harmonious and efficient combination. In the year 1000, equipment was still very simple. For a military engagement one needed a short lance, used like a javelin and thrown by the knight at his adversary from a distance. This method can still be seen on the Bayeux "Tapestry," embroidered about 1080, which narrates the battles of William the Conqueror, Duke of Normandy. For hand-to-hand fighting, there is the very long, very heavy sword. This is the knight's principal weapon: in the epic accounts he gives it a proper name, as he does his horse. It is fashioned with extraordinary ability, according to techniques inherited from the ironsmiths of the early Middle Ages. Then, for protection, he needs a metal helmet; a cuirass—a leather shirt reinforced in places with thicker plates arranged like scales; and he needs a round or triangular shield or buckler, also made of leather. All of this equipment is relatively light and permits great freedom of movement. The spread of iron smelting, a major event of this period but one about which we know little, was a sign of progress first manifested in the improvement of defensive weapons. A metal plate, the nasal, protecting the front part of the face, was joined to the helmet; the hauberk, a long cape, made of iron links or rings, which followed the shape of the body from the head to just below the knees, was substituted for the cuirass. This new equipment made the warrior virtually invulnerable to hurled weapons, like javelins or arrows shot from a small bow; reducing the role of attacks at a distance, it emphasized the decisiveness of hand-to-hand combat. It also made the knight more unwieldy, harder to carry, and less free in his movements. Because of this, the horse had to be adapted to a new function. Formerly, horses were used principally to approach the enemy, for surprise attacks, and for skirmishes and pursuits; but they were abandoned during sword fighting, which was done on foot. But two elements made it possible for the knights gradually to use horses in the center of battle: first, the use of the stirrup and the large saddle, which gave the warrior more balance and made him, to a greater degree, one with his mount; and second, the improvement of the horse itself, which became more sturdy and capable, with no loss of agility, of carrying the fighter dressed in his new armor. Thus, the military engagement became, in the final years of the eleventh century, a cavalry attack, a joust. Henceforth the lance was the pre-eminent offensive weapon. Carrying it at his side, the knight, dashing at a gallop, used it to unseat his adversary who, fallen to the ground, entangled in his coat of mail, was at his mercy—his *miséricorde*—for a few moments. *Miséricorde* is even the name given the short dagger which, when inserted by the knight between the plates of the cuirass, then enabled him to finish off his enemy:

> When Roland hears him (God, he has such pain)
> He spurs his horse on, lets him have full rein
> And strikes the count as fiercely as he can. . . .
> *Chanson de Roland*, lines 1196-1198

This is a major transformation. It makes even wider the distance between the mounted warrior and the foot-soldier, whose role has become contemptible. It changed, too, the mental habits of the warriors: adequately protected from blows dealt from a distance, they were compelled to fight at close hand, which permitted a dialogue, a bargaining, between the opponent, thrown from the horse, and his vanquisher. Thus, a portion of the murderous quality of warfare vanished: the practice of ransom, required under oath of the enemy whom one had foregone killing, made its way into the usage of warfare, appreciably modifying its conduct. Finally, battle formations took on a new aspect. During the early years of the twelfth century, they became a succession of alternating charges, with each group of knights leaving to meet their opponents, then returning at a gallop to take cover and regroup behind a screen of foot-soldiers armed with pikes. This new combat arrangement necessitated certain preparations, in particular the choice of a flat and unconfined terrain which lent itself to the knights' maneuvers; consequently, there had to be a kind of preliminary understanding between the opposing groups. Because of this there came into being the function, so startling to us, of war heralds—emissaries charged with fixing in advance the day and place for the encounter. In this way, through the improvement of equipment, war became an art, a skilled sport. To be sure, it is not without its risks: the appeal of ransom is not powerful enough to curb entirely the brutality of these men, accustomed as they are to fighting wild animals, and incapable of checking their anger. The battlefields described in the *chansons de geste* are strewn with severed heads and scattered brains. Nonetheless, this sport is governed by rules that it is convenient to respect. One of the basic elements of knightly ethics was to play the game fairly, and one of the noble's duties is that of placing a ban on all treacherous "devices" that might pervert its outcome.

Yet war is a transitory pleasure. There remain the winter months, a dead season for military expeditions. There are also moments of peace, perhaps more frequent and longer-lasting than is generally supposed. But, during these intervals, the knight does not settle back entirely into village life. In the first place, he must be quartered for periods of time in neighboring castles; during an instruction period (called a *stage*) lasting a month or two, he lives at his chatelain's expense, away from his own lands, in company with a few other warriors also taking their turns at "guard duty." Moreover, he is sustained by those substitutes for real combat—the tournaments. These reached their greatest period of popularity in the twelfth century, a century that saw the flourishing of those occasions of large assemblies arranged long in advance which, accompanied by much publicity, attracted participants from great distances away. The practice of organizing meetings where knights can train at their favorite sport originated, however, much earlier. These competitions are as brutal as battles; like battles, the tournaments set two groups of knights against one another on a large field; they enjoy themselves thoroughly, attempting to take prisoners and win ransoms, but sometimes miscalculating their blows so as to kill their adversary.

> Each one gives a great deal of help to his companions, striking hard and taking prisoners, defending themselves and backing up one another. . . . They separated at the hour of Nones but they did not depart, for there were still things to do. Some looked for saddles and equipment. Still others asked those who had been to the battle what they knew of their relatives and friends who had taken them. And those who were captives on parole asked their friends for their ransom or a bond.
>
> *Vie de Guillaume le Maréchal*, lines 2981-2996.

So does the anonymous author of the narrative of Guillaume le Maréchal reconstruct, with especial skill, the atmosphere of a tournament (which, taking place at the beginning of the thirteenth century, is a rather late one). After the engagement, the hero of this narrative, "his head bent to the anvil," labored to have his dented helmet straightened by the ironsmith. But these games of war were too similar to their models. The powers whose interests lay in maintaining the public peace—the Church and those sovereigns who were conscious of their conciliatory mission—condemned the tournaments and, for the same reasons, condemned private skirmishes. Thus "real" combat comes to constitute the culminating point of noble life, and military efficiency conditions the entire behavior and mental structure of the nobility, who shut up in monasteries all those sons unfit for war, and place above all other virtues physical excellence, bravery, prowess, valiance, true "valor."

Respect for the sworn word, and loyalty toward those to whom one is bound by oath, constitute another major support of the knight's ethics. This warrior class is free from every constraint on the part of those powers that reaped the remains of public authority; knowing none of the punishments inflicted by the chatelain on the peasants, they are actually the feudal class, in the strictest sense of the term: that class in which political relations are ordered by means of an ethical understanding established between one man and another, in the terms of vassalage and the fief.

The practice of "commendation," that is, of personal devotion to a protector, was old among both the aristocracy and the lower classes. Flocks of retainers formed spontaneously around the greatest men, and, as early as the ninth century, the Carolingian rulers had tried to codify these unofficial practices—which they themselves used to tighten their hold on the kingdom—in order to obtain fuller submission from their provincial representatives and to attach the more influential manor lords more directly to themselves. These practices were most deeply rooted in the area between the Loire and the Rhine; gradually they spread to the southern regions, assuming more strength with the collapse of royal power. And, at the same time, this personal bond took on a special form in the "order" of the knights, as these men became more and more differentiated from the peasants. At the beginning of the eleventh century, when the chatelain, speaking of his domestic serf or of his knight serving his *stage* in the fortress, ordinarily calls both of them "my man" (although there does exist a specific term, "vassal," for designating a noble retainer), the service he expects of each of them, their position with respect to himself, and the feeling he has for them, are of a sharply different nature. This difference is already noticeable in the vocabulary: the lord is the "master" to the peasant, but only the *senior* for the knight; the latter thus acknowledges in him, not the coercive powers, but only his moral superiority, analogous to that of the oldest member of the family.

The rites that bind the vassal to his lord express this character even more distinctly. The ceremony is enacted in two phases. First there is the "homage": bareheaded, unarmed, and kneeling, the man who is about to place himself in vassalage puts his two hands, in a gesture of submission and of total self-surrender, between those of the man who, by this gesture, becomes his lord. Thus from the outset, the subordination of the vassal—who from that moment ceases to be his own master—is manifested, as he hands himself over completely into the power of another. But he does not long remain in this attitude of humility: the lord immediately makes him rise, and kisses him upon the mouth. In this way the ritual clearly indicates that the two men are henceforth to exist upon the same level, and that the bond they have just entered is one of friendship, not of subjection. Next the vassal, standing, swears to be loyal "in good faith, with no evil devices, as a man ought to be with his lord." This is the second act, that of faith or fealty. A religious gesture, this oath is doubtless a more recent addition, another sign of the gradual permeation of social relations by Christian practices. But it also affirms the fact that a vassal's obligations proceed from a personal and free commitment, not from external coercions.

This commitment is lasting: what has been given by the presentation of the hands and by the sworn word cannot be taken back again. Lord and vassal are bound together for their entire life. Yet a vassal's submission, unlike that of a peasant, is not transferable to his descendants, but is a strictly individual act. Furthermore, it is agreed that this bond can legitimately be broken—by another ritual ceremony, the *défi*, which is the reverse of the homage: different, but equally expressive, gestures— such as the staff that is broken and thrown onto the ground—signify the rupture which takes place when one of the two men neglects his obligations. For the bond of vassalage does oblige those who enter it to fulfill certain duties. Let us examine their scope and their nature. At such time —when law is preserved only by the collective memory and is very fluid, and when sensibilities are especially attuned to external formalism—no precise and fixed codification exists of the duties called forth by homage. Yet by the beginning of the eleventh century men were forced to obtain a clearer awareness of them. Let us examine the reply given about 1020 by Bishop Fulbert of Chartres to an inquiry of the Duke of Aquitaine. Fulbert's mind was trained in the loftiest intellectual culture; he was accustomed to judicial considerations and quite conversant with the mentality and the reactions of the manorial world, in which he participated by virtue of his family origins and even his functions; his statement furnishes the best evidence of the way the duties of vassalage were then interpreted. He first defines with great precision what seem to him the basic obligations of fealty, and what expressly it is advisable to fulfill in order not to be guilty of what was called *félonie*: to do nothing that might be prejudicial to a lord with respect to his person, his property, or his "honor." A vassal's bond, then, establishes permanently, and most importantly, a pledge, a guarantee of security between the two men.

However, this negative attitude is not sufficient: ". . . For it is not enough to refrain from doing wrong," says the bishop from Chartres, "one must also do what is good." But actually these positive requirements are presented in much vaguer terms, using only two words—which are, however, the governing words of the feudal world: "aid" and "counsel." It is a universal conviction that the retainer must indeed "aid" his lord, that is, lend him, when he is in difficulty, a strong hand in a variety of ways: by helping him, when he is old and sick, in the administration of his property; by testifying for him in legal proceedings; and, later, in the twelfth century when money is of more importance, by giving him *deniers*—to pay his ransom, to dower his daughter, to equip his son for newly entered knighthood. But it is quite obvious that in this milieu, organized entirely in terms of combat, the pre-eminent aid is military. It is by means of his weapons that the vassal ordinarily comes to the rescue of his "friend," and vassalage consists primarily of harnessing the warriors' camaraderie. The duty of counsel answers to another need. We have noted the gregariousness of life in these times: it is inconceivable that a powerful man would live alone or, in particular, that he would make an important decision without seeking the opinion, the "counsel," of his men. As often as he is summoned, the vassal must proceed to the side of the man who has received his homage, that the latter may be surrounded by his *cour*, those whose friendship he deems indispensable. These periodic visits which last for a few days, during which those in fealty live in close touch with their leader, have another result as well: they renew the attachment that, without repeated contact, would tend to become lax at a time when distance deprives the leader of his authority.

All of these duties are reciprocal. Fulbert of Chartres is very precise on this point: "In all things, the lord must render the like to his vassal"; he must do nothing against his interests, and must support him with weapons, advice, and even, if necessary, with *deniers*. Still, it is true that the obligation is much more exacting for the retainer. Only for him is the obligation one of "service"—that word used not long ago with reference to slavery. But this service is spontaneous in fact, and the more active the attachment between the two men, the more extensive it is. This affection frequently dates from childhood; customarily, a vassal's son spends several years of his youth in the lord's household, learning to handle weapons and control the hounds in the company of the boy whose "man" he will later become. The precise terms of this service are sometimes, after mutual discussion, specified by the oath of fealty. But nonetheless, as Fulbert expressly indicates, the "service" is rewarded: if the vassal must give aid and counsel, it is "to be worthy of his fief." The protector's "beneficence" is in proportion to the service of the dependent.

More important than anything else is the generosity of the lord; it is his liberality that earns him the friendship of those who are in fealty to him. They expect from him a good table, a supply of weapons, horses, and money, and particularly those objects of finery so highly valued in that world. In the minds of the primitive, commended warrior, the vassal was indeed totally dependent on his leader, living with him like a real servant; even in the eleventh century, there were many castles in which two or three warriors stayed all their lives, vassals to their lord, but completely integrated into his family. "The land you claim I cannot give you," replied Guillaume Longue Épée, Duke of Normandy, to the men who begged him for it, "but I shall gladly give you all the furnishings, bracelets, cross-belts, helmets, greaves, horses, and axes, and all the beautiful swords, magnificently decorated with gold, that I own; you will always enjoy my friendship, and the glory of service in my household." [1] Still, we see from this that what the men preferred was the gift of an estate, the thing of greatest value in that period, which alone could spare them the embarrassment of being permanently commended. As a matter of fact, at the beginning of the eleventh century it was usual for the lord to grant a good piece of land to his "man," once the latter entered his vassalage. This was called the *chasement*, or, more commonly, the fief. Varying in size, the fief can comprise a church, a share of the tithe, the right to command and exploit some family of peasants, perhaps a mill or a single field. Over all this, the lord remains the eminent master; but, by the ritual act of investiture, he hands over the entire holding to the vassal, who "holds" it, so long as he fulfills the obligations of homage—that is to say, so long as he is not *félon*—until his death. The profits from this property are the payment for his fealty.

Introduced by chance into the heart of the vassalage relationship, the feudal holding became the main element, as was inevitable in this time when the only things that really mattered were those that could be seen and touched; as early as the second half of the eleventh century, it was considered that homage had been rendered "because of the fief." The phrase "feudal system" well expresses the new primacy of the landed relation: men were now bound to one another in terms of tangible property. Human relations were appreciably affected by this. In a sense, it resulted in a certain strengthening of the manor lord's authority; because of the holding and of everything related to it, the vassal was subject henceforth to the laws of the lord who, on the other hand, now had the means to punish every departure from the vassal's sworn word: the threat of confiscation of the fief, on the counsel of his other vassals. At the same time, vassalage ceased to be an individual bond, uniting two men until death in a chosen friendship. For how could one take back, from the inheritors of an integrated vassalage, the fief that had been intermingled with the family lands for a whole lifetime? The lord was obliged to let them keep

the holding and, because of it, usually admitted them into his vassalage
—even, against his better judgment, when their services seemed to him
dubious or inadequate. Next, since it was recognized that the vassal
could leave the fief to his survivors, people began to think that he could
also sell it or give it away. Naturally, the lord's consent had to be obtained, sometimes purchased with a gift, and every new owner had to
pay homage in advance; nonetheless, this mobility of the fief made fealty
much less durable, and, particularly, much less deeply felt. The lord saw
inheritors and buyers of vassalages come into his service, men whom he
had not selected, who were obliged to serve him, not through the free
impulse of their will but in order to obtain the income from the land;
often, it soon became apparent, the fief passed to widows, girls, and weak
men who were incapable of giving him even military aid. A still more
serious consequence was the fact that the same man, as a result of
changes in his lands, had a good chance of holding several fiefs, under
the jurisdiction of different lords, obliging him to render more than one
homage. Which of these multiple lords should he serve; for which
should he bear arms when one was fighting the other? This resulted in a
curious dispersal of the personal devotion that, in the original conception of vassalage, ought to have been complete; when one was divided
in this manner among contradictory obligations, one ended up by being
reduced to discreet abstentions. But in spite of these attenuations, the
sense of vassalage remained one of the principal axes of the knight's mentality, pervading every ethical conception of the period, from the nobles
on down. Among these fighting men, left to their impulses and covetousness, did this flexible aggregate of prohibitions and obligations, guiding all their political behavior, maintain a modicum of discipline?

The network of fiefs and fealties was, in the eleventh century, without any real coherence. It was in no way arranged in a pyramid that
would, ascending in successive stages, have converged the fealty of all the
knights in France in the person of the king. This extremely complex network, complicated at every level by the multiplicity of homages, and
constantly upset by the effects of inheritances and sales, was parceled out
in a multitude of small, almost isolated dependencies grouped around
each local power. Thus there was discontinuity; but the rigor of organization varied from province to province. Throughout southern France,
feudal institutions, belatedly superimposed upon other structures, were
always less stable than elsewhere; particularly in this region, many fiefs
existed independently of all service throughout the Middle Ages. Furthermore, to a great extent, the effectiveness of the vassal's attachment
depended simultaneously on the actual proximity between the lord and
his man, and on the distance that separated them within the social hierarchy. The simple knight from the village, a quasi-peasant, was absolutely
subjected to the chatelain by his homage; all the more restrictively, since

the vassal lived nearer the stronghold. Amidst the little group of warriors and hunters forming a unified "house," a *mesnie,* around the lord, we see instances of real mutual aid: friendship confirmed by communal life and family alliances, and also obedience to the decisions of a leader capable of suppressing any quarrels; a leader whose authority, whenever it led those men assembled under his banner into combat, was never questioned. It was this way for centuries. But when the same ritual gesture joined two lords of equal power, who had little contact with one another—the homage, for example, that linked the Count of Flanders to the King—it became no more than a simple and imperfect security pact, implying no true subordination. Finally, even at its most strict, the feudal relation was not enough to control all the behavior of the vassal; for the knight was under the lord's jurisdiction only when he broke his fealty, and even then only by virtue of his fief (a portion that often was of little importance to his fortune, which consisted particularly of allodial land, of good, free land). The vassal could commit the worst misdeeds; if they were not directly prejudicial to the lord's interest, the latter had no right to intervene. Had he done so, he would not have been supported by the indispensable counsel of his other men. Thus, checked only by homage, the knight was actually free in most of his acts, and enjoyed a landed independence. For proof of this, one need only consider the effects of legal practices then in use among the nobles.

What if a crime has been committed, in one of those transports of rage that so quickly took hold of these rough creatures? What if a man actually suffered "injury"—that is, an act derogating his rights—from another knight? The first reaction of the victim and of his friends is not to lodge a complaint—what jurisdiction would be effective?—but to make, on the spot, his own law. Private revenge, exercise of which is limited among the peasantry by the diligent interventions of a chatelain's repressive laws, is most fully developed in the world of the nobles. It occasions most of the armed conflicts, to such an extent that the word *guerre,* originating as a particular designation of these revengeful enterprises, came to be applied generally to every military confrontation. Every violent act of this sort has extended repercussions; for it is not just two individuals pitched one against the other, but two groups: each adversary calls on the "aid" of his relatives, his vassals, his lord, and all of his friends. He aims his retaliations not against the aggressor alone, but against all of his men as well. Thus cruelties answer cruelties, each hanging upon the one before; the chronicles have handed down the memory of hatreds that, prolonged and extended, have decimated the entire nobility of a province. But there comes a moment when most of those involved want to end the quarrel. Certain among the friends have some connections in both camps, and these serve as intermediaries; gradually, the principal antagonists agree to make peace. The ill feelings must still be soothed; an

arbitration is necessary, and this involves accounting for the damages suffered on both sides, estimating the sum of the settlement that will redeem the spilled blood and the loss of materials. Arbitration is rarely entrusted to the established powers, to the counts and lords who are
eager to serve as judges when there are peasants to be fined, but who
are hardly tempted to play the delicate and unprofitable role of this sort
of conciliator. Most often a special assembly, whose seats are allotted,
half and half, to supporters of both adversaries, is called together. No in-
quest is conducted to measure the respective wrongs; people's confidence
in invisible forces is sufficient for them to wait for God's indication of
whose cause is just—hence, the practice of the ordeal. The old ordeals,
which made guilt manifest itself by the way in which the powers of water or fire behaved toward the accused, are too tainted with paganism,
and have fallen into desuetude in French territory. The most common
test, and the one best adapted to the military temper, is the duel: single
combat decides between the litigants, who are replaced, when unable to
fight themselves, by "champions." Under the influence of the Church,
people rely also on oaths, required of both the adversaries and their
friends. The divine wrath upon the perjurer is indeed so dreaded that no
one would dare knowingly pledge his word if he were not certain of being in the right. Instructed by means of these methods, the adjudicators
render a sentence that is rarely impartial but, apportioning the object
of the litigation, endeavors to satisfy one party or the other. But this decision must be accepted, and peace is not concluded finally until after
other parleys and oaths, with the indispensable rites of mutual pardon.

These arbitration proceedings in the knightly world are singularly in-
efficient: they are slow and they are imperfect—and fail to rectify all the
wrongs; they are costly, for gifts must be distributed to the intermediaries,
adjudicators, champions, and witnesses. It is better not to resort to them.
For this reason an aggregate of practices, intended to forestall dissension,
enters the aristocratic customs of the eleventh century. When a knight
concludes a settlement, he is required first to pledge his soul with an
oath; furthermore, for a surer guarantee, he must surround himself
with a group of men responsible for his acts, by asking his next of kin,
who also swear their word as to his integrity, to become his "pledges."
They are morally concerned that the agreement be maintained, and are
obliged, if it is broken, to put themselves in the hands of the opposing
party as hostages, and remain at his disposal until peace is restored. This
system of precautions appeals to the two forces that constitute the most
powerful means of moral compulsion for the knights: the cohesion of
the group, encompassing and binding the individual; and respect for the
oath, that religious act and "sacrament" delivered while touching a sacred
object, a relic or the Gospel, while begging for the help of God Himself.
It would be unimaginable to break this oath without risking the gravest

spiritual injury. In these two forces is contained the entire value of the bond of vassalage; but they may also be seen parallel with the feudal organization and, to a large extent, they correct its imperfections.

Nowhere is group cohesiveness so powerful as in the natural community joined—perhaps more closely in the eleventh century than ever before or since—by blood lines. Indeed, this is the time when, among the nobles, the individual ancestor's surname begins to be borne by all his descendants, and becomes the rallying symbol of the family or, more precisely, the *lignage* (lineage). Just as the insecurity that resulted from the diminution of regional powers, goading each man into seeking the support of those close to him, caused the vassalage dependencies to proliferate, so undoubtedly did it cause the gathering together of kinsmen. And family solidarity is also tightened by the economic arrangement which makes the ancestral land the basis of all wealth. Twenty or thirty people, sometimes more—married sons, their children, and even their grandchildren (for people are considered to be fully mature at fourteen; they marry young, and there is little age difference between generations)— live side by side around the same fire and the same cooking pot, sometimes in one room which serves as a nocturnal retreat. Together they administer, under the direction of the eldest, the inheritance left in their joint possession. Such, then, is the noble family. Their interdependence is tyrannical; no one has any savings at his disposal that would allow him to lead his life as he pleases. Many of the characteristics of the knightly mentality may be explained by the constraints of this joint family possession: the taste for far-off adventure, the roaming in search of pillage and profit, the bad blood that sets the sons against the father who is too slow to die while the former dream of leading, in turn, the group of relatives, and seek refuge with rival lords. On the other hand, the joint possession is the most powerful factor of cohesion; it inures people to discipline. The inheritance of the fief and of the title of knight were the inevitable results of the practices of exploiting communities; and joint possession also makes the family the most reliable of the associations for mutual defense. The first recourse, in times of danger or combat, is the kinsman; he is called upon, too, to help one avenge oneself, to prove one's right, or to save one's soul by means of alms or propitiatory rites. The personality of these clans is much stronger than that of the individual; and fundamentally, vassalage is only a surrogate for kinship; homage, a means of artifically establishing a kinlike bond between two men. It is quite rare for a knight to act alone, rather than while surrounded by men of his own blood. He takes shelter behind them, but also he must submit to their opinions and suppress his individual impulses in order to follow the will of the group. Because of this, such a structure, in which the family has such power, acts effectively against the excessive turbulence of the age.

Another kind of group, one based solely upon the oath, is the association for peace. A void had been left when the collapse of the Carolingian state caused the disappearance of those institutions that had insured order in the Frankish society, and the Church now wished to asssume the mission that the kings were no longer in a position to fulfill: that of making the peace of God rule over the earth. The movement was launched in the final years of the tenth century in Aquitaine—the region of the greatest disintegration of state powers—and in councils that gathered the regional nobility about the bishops. It spread quickly, and found its way into the control of the Church leaders in the most unified principalities north of the Loire; then, in 1095, the papacy took over its direction and again enlarged its scope. Its aim was to restrict, within precise limits, the instances of recourse to violence—but to restrict only the limits; it was never a question of prohibiting violence, nor of the disarming of a social group, of an "order," organized in the same terms as combat, nor of challenging the legitimacy of the right of revenge. In the first place, certain things had special protection and were safeguarded by the "peace" of God Himself. These included certain places (the churches and their surroundings), periods of time (the days of the week consecrated to prayer or penitence, liturgical feasts, and Lent) and certain social categories (the clerics and all those who had no means of defense: merchants and peasants).* The associations also served for the codification of private war, which must not be exercised beyond the group of knights which, even so restrained, still runs afoul of truces and sanctuaries. The sanctions of this code are primarily spiritual—anathema and excommunication. And, in fact, these sanctions are effective, if not in checking the fightingman's aggressive excesses and compelling him, in the joy of battle and destruction, to respect the prohibitions, then at least in causing him to regret his mistakes and make amends for them quickly. Over and above all these things, the peace is conceived of as a true pact; at the call of the bishops, the knights present at the council, one after another, swear on relics to respect the agreement; to withdraw, jointly and severally, their friendship from the instigators of trouble, and to chase after them.

This venture in collective discipline, quite active until well into the middle of the twelfth century, dependent as it was upon concern for salvation and respect of the oath, certainly was not completely successful in curbing the violence of the knights. The feudal period remains a savage era, during which the season of war is ablaze with outbreaks of fires in

---

* The French word *paix* has been translated literally in this paragraph. However there are two simultaneous movements, the Peace of God and the Truce of God. The Truce of God is more limited both in extent and efficacy, and it attempts to ameliorate the harshness of warfare by prohibiting it on specific days and during specific seasons.—Trans.

the harvests and in peasant huts; during which murder, rape, and maiming are perpetrated—even in the most venerated sanctuaries—at the very feet of those altars that attest to the terrifying power of God the avenger, even in the bosom of the most closely knit families, even in the bosom of the families or vassal groups. But the search for peace was sustained and paralleled by other attempts, led by the clergy, to Christianize military customs; these attempts, by means of the blessing of weapons and the introduction of liturgical practices into the dubbing ritual, paved the way for the gradual conversion of the knight's morals, the imperceptible orientation of knightly prowess toward the service of Christ. Combined with the multiple oaths—of vassalage, surety, or individual peace—that every man in the nobility is called upon to utter; associated with the natural bonds of kinship that, in a milieu stabilized by exclusively landed wealth, in which migrations are rare, unite all the neighbors; this conversion enmeshes the knight in a network of obligations and interdependencies that, more often than not, prevent him from doing much harm. Therefore, there is discipline, but no coercion. These men, with their horses and weapons, are most distinctively characterized, not by their idleness or their wastefulness, but rather by their manner of obedience which, given freely, is a matter solely of loyalty and of honor.

► THE FORTUNES OF CULTURE

In the secular world, the knights are the only class to attain self-expression. Their sons fill all the upper echelons of the Church. It is, therefore, their customs and their reactions that give eleventh-century civilization its special tonality, even in the world of the spirit.

Feudal manners penetrate into those ecclesiastical circles which serve as the custodians of learned culture. The estates of the Church have, by means of the development of immunity privileges, become independent manors whose *manants*, the men in the service of the holy patron, are judged, punished, and ordered about on behalf of the clerics or monks. Each bishop and abbot has his knights and vassals, who render him homage, receive landed fiefs—frequently even parish churches—and, when they have just completed their obligations of aid and counsel, introduce their warlike unruliness into the cloisters. But this contamination goes even deeper: it is by means of the same gestures of investiture that the secular lords, patrons of the bishoprics and monasteries, hand over the crosier, the distinguishing mark of the episcopal function, to the dignitary whose election they have brought about. Now in the secular rites of feudalism, since the fief is intimately linked to the vassalage, investiture tends to become inseparable from homage; gradually, the idea gains acceptance that the spiritual mission is itself a fief, and that he who fills it is a vassal and owes service for it. This is a dangerous introduction of sacred matters into the aggregation of temporal powers. Furthermore, a number of bishops, abbots, and canons—all of them descended from noble families and scarcely detached from family bonds—are driven by their functions to lead the life of worldly lords. Like the latter, they live in a tower, surrounded by fighting men, household knights, or vassals in their instruction *stage*; they must organize expeditions against those who fail to recognize the rights of their church, or those who kill their serfs or pillage their stables. Whether or not they want to be, most of them are caught up by that atmosphere of bodily and mental primitiveness that was theirs from childhood. A prelate of those days liked war and hunting, to say nothing of that sexual freedom which, in that feudal world where one's lawful wife rarely was one's sole companion and where the passing guest found easy ladies at his disposal in every castle, was almost never curbed.

But indeed, the movement of reaction whose goal was the disengagement of the Church from temporal corruption gains ground daily. The eleventh century, in particular, witnesses the rapid success of the Cluniac reform. In southern and central France, in Provence, then in Lorraine, the Benedictine communities, one after the other, are won over to the strict observance of the rule by those astonishing men, the abbots of the Burgundian monastery. And, that the purification may last, the reformers take care to bind to themselves, with the strictest of ties, the religious houses they have just reformed. Henceforth, all these houses have the same abbot, one from Cluny; by the end of the century there are several hundred such houses in France, and together they form a congregation, a special *ordo* in the heart of the monastic family—the first of the religious "orders." The feudal world has no influence on their way of life; the Cluniac priories are small islands of purity and moral strictness.

Yet, even in this organization whose unity comes from its very independence of temporal powers, there are certain areas in which the monks' style of life is permeated to some extent by knightly attitudes. Thus, the manner in which those at Cluny deviated from the original instructions of St. Benedict's rule—as when they reduced the part played by manual labor in daily activity to an insignificant role—closely parallels the noble's notion of the unworthiness of hard work. This is a perfect instance of the adaptation of monastic life to the lord's regime and to the secular society's recent affirmation of class differences: the monks, as idle as the knights, surrounded by servants who relieve them of lowly tasks, have their maintenance assured them by the provisions and *corvées* of their dependent peasants; and the care that people take to vary their menus in the dining halls, to mix spices into the wine that is served them, to renovate various items of their wardrobe before they wear out, and to maintain a princely stable for dignitaries, indicates both an aristocratic conception of the religious profession and the conviction that

God's servant ought to eat better bread, wear more lavish clothes, and travel in company different from the workingman's.

But this infiltration of the nobility's ways of life, thought, and behavior into the ecclesiastical structure is not limited to the surface. In the mutual osmosis of the temporal and the spiritual, the profound penetration of knightly conceptions into the heart of the religious profession corresponds to the gradual Christianization of the military ethic, homage, and dubbing. In the beginning of the eleventh century occurs the moment when the old attitude of prayer—the gesture of outstretched arms which may be seen in the old *orante**—is replaced by a kneeling posture, with head bared and hands joined; the same posture, that is, as the vassal's. Now in a world where gesture is the pre-eminent sign, this change is more than a mere repercussion: the "faithful" man (the confusion is already inherent in this word that is also one of the synonyms for "vassal") is aware of incurring a sort of commendation, a pact which generates consequent services, but mutual ones. And particularly, a quasi-military conception of spiritual life gains acceptance. The Christian is a fighting man; he wins his salvation by fighting, in his Lord's service and with His aid, against the powers of the Adversary. The feeling of this conflict of soul and body, this psychomachia, is present in every mind. The first graphic representations of the "Enemy," appearing toward the middle of the eleventh century in the illuminated Apocalyptic books in Aquitaine, give evidence of this battle as well as of the detailed precision with which, during the same period, the Cluniac chronicler Raoul [Glaber] describes the devil, an habitué of monastic dormitories. The religious life becomes a joust in which the qualities of strength and will have great value: at this time, to be saintly is to be ascetic, and to be a hero is to be master of one's body. For the religious man, as for the knight, valor is more necessary than book learning.

Also, the beginning of the eleventh century marks a certain regression of the educational aspect of intellectual activity. This is very distinct in secular life, where the practice of having written agreements, drawn up by professional copyists (more lastingly maintained in the southern provinces) rapidly disappears. Writing becomes, in secular life, an object of distrust; only the gesture and the word matter. But this regression is perceptible, as well, in the most cultivated circles of the Church. It is true, of course, that schools patterned after the one at Chartres created by Bishop Fulbert, schools in which methods of teaching and of thought once perfected by Gerbert d'Aurillac are patiently improved, during this period can see their enlightenment extend to the most developed region of northern France. But hostility to studies dominates the most vital part of the Church, the Cluniac world. In the be-

---

* A statue in early Christian art, generally of a woman standing with her arms outstretched as if in prayer.—Trans.

ginning of the eleventh century, the great abbot Odilon condemns the reading of Latin classics; by so doing, he is faithful to the purest Benedictine tradition, following the line set down by Benedict of Aniane* who, in the better days of the Carolingian Renaissance but in reaction to it, banished literary humanism from the monasteries. For Odilon, the aim of the monastic life is not the deepening of faith by intellectual pursuits, but the celebration of God's glory by collective prayer.

For this reason, Cluny is the most magnificent liturgical construction of Western Christianity, a construction both musical and plastic. Sacred chants proliferate about the mass and orisons that are spread over the hours of the day, and the choral function absorbs all the monks' activity and invades their lives. In addition, nothing is spared in decorating the sanctuary, building an appropriate monument which, by the magnificence of its architecture and ornament, is itself a prayer and an homage to divine majesty. Thus, Cluny stimulates the efforts of musicians, builders, and carvers; in this lies its contribution to the progress of civilization. At the same time, however, insofar as it expresses and realizes a certain religious ideal, Cluny reveals its harmony with certain of the knights' behavioral tendencies: this may be seen in the preference for collective rites, the attraction to fasting, the quality of wastefulness. There is an obvious similarity between the finery of the military life and the gilded objects Saint Odilon ordered to decorate the principal altar of the church he had just built: for this decoration he used, in fact, silver ingots offered by several knights out of their share of the spoils from a victory over Saracen pirates. This similarity is no less evident between the hagiographic literature and sung poems, like the *Vie de Saint Alexis* (composed in the Norman regions around 1040), in which suffering and the spirit of sacrifice are extolled in the vernacular, and those as yet untranscribed warsongs and genealogical narratives that so pleased the military gatherings, sometimes copied down by certain clerics on the order of their lord (as happened with Doon de Saint-Quentin, a servant of the dukes of Normandy, around 1020). We shall see that, in the last three decades of the eleventh century, all the creative activities, in which converge the aspirations of the two élites—the orders of those who pray and those who fight —are about to undergo a prodigious development; a development that is the product of economic progress, and the fruit of the peasant's toil.

---

* This is not St. Benedict of Nursia, the founder of the Benedictine order, but an early ninth-century reformer of the order's rules.—Trans.

III

*The Century
of Great Progress*

1070-1180

Suddenly, midway through the eleventh century, we begin to see signs
of a newly awakened vitality—signs which increase sooner in some areas,
later in others, because the territory of France is so diverse and does not
evolve at the same rate. For example, the history of the interior of Brittany or of the Gévaudan is at least a hundred years behind the pace set
by those areas on the banks of the lower Seine, or the road junctions in
the Lauraguais, or the passes in Burgundy. A period of accelerated progress begins at this time, the most rapid phase of which occurs between
1080 and 1120; its rate of speed is comparable in every respect to that period beginning about 1750, with whose trends we are still moving. Of this
progress, contemporary intellectuals were fully aware, as they ceased to
live like so many previous generations, whose eyes were fixed on an exemplary, but departed, Golden Age, anxiously watching for signs presaging the end of the world. On the contrary: they were confident that they
saw further and more clearly than their predecessors, and they were
confident in themselves. The tone of the twelfth century is one of universal fermentation, of a rather chaotic, but burgeoning and creative,

daring. This century begins, to my mind, in about 1070 and comes to an end around 1180; its admirable landmarks are the abbey of the Trinity, in Caen, at its beginning, and the choir of Notre-Dame in Paris at its end. It is a century whose early years schooled the author of the written version of *La Chanson de Roland*; a century that closed with the death of Chrétien de Troyes and the birth of Francis of Assisi. The great twelfth century, the century of Abélard and St. Bernard of Clairvaux, is the most productive of the Middle Ages; and this productivity may be seen by its vast enrichment of the still-imperfect framework of feudal society.

▶ THE PROGRESS OF AGRICULTURAL TECHNIQUES

The twelfth-century expansion was sustained by a long-term, auspicious economic tendency that took shape in the West before the year 1000, as early as the end of the last invasions, and continued in an unbroken course from then on. By 1050, one begins to see its beneficent effects: a rapid increase in wealth and, even before this, prosperity in the peasant world of the fields. Indeed, the eleventh and twelfth centuries witness the most intense period within a movement of renovation of agrarian techniques. This movement is widespread; but it is impossible to follow all the details and permutations of its progress, because of the total absence of any remnants of tools, the lack of precision in illustrated documents, sketches, or sculptures, all of which are distorted by artistic techniques, and the great silence of the written evidence, which failed to record the scarcely perceptible modifications in the most common gestures of everyday life. However, this seems to have been the only great total renewal of peasant practices to affect the French countryside from the Neolithic period until the "agricultural revolution" of modern times. We find ourselves, here, concerned with one of those essential spheres of civilization in which historical research knocks against insurmountable factual difficulties, and hypotheses must be built upon a few, very rarely conclusive indications; but as far as one can judge it, this technical progress in no way was determined by recent inventions or (with a few exceptions) by processes hitherto unknown in the West; instead, it came about through the general diffusion of methods that had been applied until then only on a few model farmlands such as the estates of the large Carolingian monasteries between the Loire and the Rhine, and in other very limited and scattered sectors of the rural world.

The improvement of peasant equipment and of rural techniques by the dissemination and, even more important, the combination of many individually perfected details: surely this is the deep mainspring of progress in all civilizations. And it is true that, in the middle of the twelfth century, the *vilain's* tools are undeniably more complex and efficient than those his ancestors used in 1000. First of all, the mills, which already were turning on a good number of streams, became even more numerous. The lowliest of the manor lords harnessed the village streams with canal reaches and locks, while dams and landing stages were set up on the large rivers to accommodate paddlewheels; sometimes dozens of these constructions were concentrated in the same place, as at the Bazacle de Toulouse. Thus, flour mills are now available to every peasant family; in certain areas peasants are forced to use them by the manorial *ban,* but in any case the practice of abandoning the hand-operated pounding and crushing devices takes hold everywhere. The result of this abandonment is a considerable liberation of manpower, as well as a revolution in diet, since bread is substituted for cereal gruels and millet gives way to bread-making grains. Already, in certain areas, axles set in motion by the movement of water are joined to other machines, driving pedals to full cloth or to break hemp. The way is open for other improvements, and the moment is already being ushered in when the drop hammer will be used in forging metal. In the towns and the most developed areas, the thirteenth century witnesses (through the initiative of the merchants and contractors) that period of all the industrial and mechanical skills that are to introduce into the rural districts many new tasks that will, for centuries to come, associate the contributions of the working classes to the tilling of the ancestral soil. Men also harnessed the power of the winds: the first windmills date from the closing years of the twelfth century, in Normandy.

At the same time, tools are improved. Iron is no longer as rare in the rural areas around 1150; as it becomes available, weapons more efficient for the conquest of nature come into general use, among them large clearing axes and, especially, plows with moldboards. This last is a heavy and awkward instrument, drawn by four, six, or eight oxen (people now know how to shoe oxen, and how better to harness them: with a yoke in front); but it has, at least, the great advantage of being able to penetrate the densest and heaviest soil, to turn it over thoroughly and, hence, to restore its fertility. These plows are expensive instruments indeed, first used only on the manor lord's land, but later, present in the villages where people share their use; finally, they are to be found in every region with deep soil. Along with iron there appears, in all the villages, the blacksmith, "smith," or "forger"; he is the domestic servant of a lord, but his services are available to the peasant community as well. We first hear of him (by chance) in Anjou around 1080, then in the area near Mâcon around 1140; not until modern times—and even now, he has not been entirely replaced by the mechanic—does he cease to be, in these villages, the only specialized worker.

Finally, by virtue of improvements in the planning of crop rotation, there is a better balance within the agricultural system. A regular three-year cycle produces, on the same land, the successive sowing of winter grains—wheat or rye—followed by a sowing of cereals—oats or barley—in spring, and then by a fallow period. By means of stages that, unfortunately, are barely traceable, this three-field system replaces the primitive practices of itinerant cultivation of patches of burnt land, or ill-regulated rotation. This progression is an extremely slow one: its origin probably dates from the very early Middle Ages, and it is not completed before the close of the thirteenth century. It spreads outward along each terrain, from the central areas to the most disordered borderlands, from the large manorial *coutures* to the little plots of ground belonging to the poor, hidden out among the frontiers of the waste lands. It started, in French territories, among the plains of the river basins around Paris and the Lorraine, and continued as far south as climatic conditions permitted—as long as the hot weather, disastrous to March wheat, did not come too early in spring and impose another cycle, that of the Roman two-field system. The new system, leaving the land fallow only every third year, gives rise to an increased cereal production. It also develops the cultivation of oats and, doubtless, thereby improves the breed of horses. If feudal civilization is essentially equine, this characteristic is not without connection with the agrarian structure; for there is the peasant's horse as well as that of the warrior, and the gradual substitution, in the northeast, of the swifter horse for the ox in the plowing of farmland serves as one more sign of the complete renovation in processes for working the fields.

This renovation is, of course, imperfect. Limited to a certain part of France, it is at first truly widespread only in the northern part of the Kingdom, and this unequal dissemination of improved techniques is one reason for the relative deterioration of civilization in the Midi. For natural reasons, such as the quality of its soil and of its climate, this area remained a region of light swingplows and fallow land twice a year; in spite of the planting of several new crops in its Mediterranean borderlands after the Crusades, the Midi was from then on agriculturally inferior by comparison with the rejuvenated north. Because the new equipment is expensive, the renovation is limited—even in the provinces where it is the most advanced, even on the better farms, even in the best regions. In the twelfth-century village, the poorest villagers, working the most unpromising districts, do not cease to employ swingplows, wooden hoes whose points are hardened in fire, and grain mortars; there is still agrarian nomadism on barren land, little patches of which are plowed, now and then, to yield a dubious harvest. For a long time to come, farming will remain unsystematic, and will tolerate the coexistence of diverse practices; it is not before the end of the Middle Ages that we witness those coherent terrains organized into the regularly rotated crop fields that presuppose a strict village community subject to collective restraints. An incomplete renovation, then—one that does not solve the problem of fertilizer or that of the periodic reconstitution of the soil. There are few cattle, little fodder, little manure, and long fallow periods. And the yields are still very small: on the estates of the Cluny monastery —and these are at the apex of agrarian progress—people harvest, in the mid-twelfth century, six times their sowing on the best lands, and only twice their sowing on the worst. Nonetheless, this is a fundamental revolution, one that overthrows every way of life; for, because of it, the peasant now is able to extract more food from a smaller area of cultivation, and to do so with less expenditure of time and trouble.

The first result of the increase in agricultural yields is that the rural family now can be certain of a more abundant and, particularly, of a less irregular supply of food. Less vulnerable to disease, the family becomes more stable and larger; children grow up, and the generative force is no longer canceled out by infant mortality. Yet, despite this enlargement of the family group, cultivation of land can be confined to a smaller area because of the increased intensiveness of agriculture. As a matter of fact, between the beginning of the eleventh and the middle of the twelfth centuries, the large messuages of the early Middle Ages are broken up, and are divided into *métairies,** "quarters," and "heritages" of limited scope. The resultant demographic expansion brings about the first fundamental change: the former territories are much more densely populated around 1150.

Therefore, more manpower is available to the village. And at the same time the manor lord, in turn, has become less demanding, since his resources in kind also have increased—and much more than those of the rustics. As the owner of mills he has built, he deducts from the lands his advance "fee"—a part of the grain harvest; as holder of the parish tithe, he receives a proportional tax on the same harvest. Thus he is the first to profit, and he does so with no pains other than a careful supervision of the increased yields of the peasants' land; he simply watches his storehouses fill up by themselves. Less concerned with supplementing profits than with avoiding worries, he consequently reduces the cultivated areas on his own estates. Not to the point of becoming a pure landed proprietor, however; until the end of the Middle Ages, the lords' residences, even those of the king and the more powerful barons, all retain an agricultural annex, a household of herdsmen and plowmen, and, within their dependencies, vineyards, meadows, and patches of plowed land. But, now that his estate is less extensive and, furthermore, well-equipped

---

* A *métayer* is a small farmer who receives his supplies and equipment from a landowner, in return for which the former pays his rent in kind. This is known as the *métayage* system, and the land in question is called a *métairie*. It is analogous to the American sharecropping system.—Trans.

with modern tools, the lord requires much less labor; a team of dependents suffices to develop it, and only now and then do these need reinforcement by supplementary manpower—no more than on several of the busier days of the year. Thus the numerous *corvées* that, before the year 1000, had so closely associated the tenants with cultivation of the manorial land—disappear. What use was it to retain the representatives of each dependent family who, according to the old custom, came three days a week to the lord's house and put themselves at his disposition? No one knew what work to assign to them, and they had to be fed for doing nothing; better, then, to send them back home. Or sometimes the lords may ask of them, in exchange for their welcome release, a few compensations: several of those pieces of silver that the tenants now have more opportunity to earn, and the lord, in turn, has more opportunity to spend. Now that they are almost exclusively committed to payment in kind—and, more and more, payment in *deniers* rather than in labor—the tenants' holdings are changed into autonomous farms.

It follows that the social climate of the villages is considerably changed. No more is the large estate that narrow working community which almost daily united the impoverished tenants from surrounding holdings in collective labor on the lord's *coutures*; and, because of this, the human bonds connecting villager and knight are markedly distorted. As opposed to his grandfathers (who spent most of their time in the ranks of the lord's laborers, compelled to cultivate—and badly— someone else's land) and to his grandmothers (who gathered together in the manorial workroom to spin and weave), the twelfth-century *vilain* feels that he pushes the plow, sows, and harvests for himself. Once he is done with the rare days of hay harvesting, hauling, or plowing that are still demanded of him—moreover, far from doing them himself, he entrusts them to the least vigorous man in his household—his only obligation is the periodic donation of some meat, grain, and wine to the manorial seat. Certainly the dues are greater than they once were, but they are also less burdensome, since the family land is capable of producing more. In any case, the peasant manages his property in complete independence. His situation as a tenant is hardly different from that of his neighbors whose lands are allodial, that is, are not dependent on a landed manor—for the heaviest charges, the taxes, the *coutumes*, and the *taille* levied by the chatelain as defender of the peace, weigh equally on everyone in the village. The clearest social distinction in the rural world now is that which is established between the servants and the cultivators of land, be the latter freeholders or not. Servants are quite numerous at this time: at all levels of the economic scale, the first use people can find for their affluence is to cause the poorest possible person to enter their household, to pledge him to unconditional service in exchange for his complete maintenance. These poor devils have no scrap of individual freedom, own nothing of their own; they are real chattels, the property of their masters "from the soles of the feet to the roots of the hair," punished with no curb on their owner's authority. Among the cultivators of land, on the other hand, the rift that separates the husbandman provided with a team of oxen from "those who turn the land with a hoe, by the strength of their own hands," deepens somewhat, because of the improvement of agricultural implements; for the latter group, however, the exactions of the owner's *ban* have been lightened.

Another consequence of the improvement in rural techniques is that the cultivated areas have been extended: this is the great clearing movement that is, perhaps, the most important event in the history of medieval France. The improvement of tools furnished much more efficient means for felling trees, removing stumps, and, especially, for plowing the denser soils that had previously been ignored, not because of their lack of richness, but because they had heretofore been impossible to cultivate. Furthermore, the newly perfected agricultural system freed labor that could be used outside the limits of the area formerly plowed by peasants—freed labor both directly, by increasing the output of human work, and indirectly, by decreasing the work teams needed on the manors. And, finally, because it permitted more production of food, this extension of the cultivated land area stimulated the population growth in already populated districts, as well as inviting expansion to new ones.

The earliest evidence of this onslaught against waste land appears about the middle of the tenth century and proliferates after 1050; it is then that the period of intense effort, which was to continue for a century and a half, began. The struggle against trees, waste lands, and marshlands assumed many forms. The most common, although the least apparent, is the gradual enlargement of the village clearing. The peasants, having at their disposal both more time and better tools, extended the fields bit by bit, on the outskirts of old fields and in the scrub areas, already thinned out by temporary burning, which led into the forests of full-grown trees. New areas, previously used for pasture or itinerant farming, in this manner are integrated into the territory, retaining from their primitive state only special names: *bussière, artigue, novelle.* The tall trees and marshlands are next to be tackled. After having been drained, the freshly cleared ground, at first divided into mown meadows, produces wheat and vineyards in its rotation, and the frontier of conquest over nature is pushed a little farther forward. In this way, woods and pastures are forced back to the periphery of the parish territory, and sometimes reduced to a few small islands on the outskirts of the districts—often, even, reduced excessively, so that the farms lack that indispensable complement that waste lands provide within the agricultural system. Sometimes the lords co-operated in this extension of the outlying lands, imposing group discipline for the most difficult work, such as the drainage arrangements. But more often, this form of clearing is an individual, often even clandestine effort, eating away at the manor lord's land without the knowledge of his foresters.

The creation of new *finages* in the heart of the "deserts" was altogether a different matter. There, manorial initiative is the rule. Abbots and chatelains, who keep the large woodland spaces within their estates, understand what profit they would derive by populating and farming them; they gladly welcome the pioneers who arrive in the virgin lands from overpopulated villages. These "hosts" become very numerous throughout the forests of France in the beginning of the twelfth century. Sometimes they attract clearers of land by issuing settlement charters, promising favored treatment to newcomers—a minimal rent for land, no *corvées*, exemption from arbitrary *tailles*, reduced military service, and improved legal proceedings. They guide them to the well-wooded sections most amenable to settlement, organize them into communities, sometimes provide them with their initial equipment and renounce their own hunting rights. They assign each household its share of the land, and soon start a church for the spiritual needs of the population. In this way a unified village comes into being—often called Villeneuve, Neuville, or Lessart. Frequently, these towns are strung out along forest riding roads, where good land has been leveled and where agriculture has prevailed: the houses sit side by side and, behind them in long strips, the fields stretch out, gradually extended at the expense of the woods. These new terrains, carving up the uncultivated land, tend ultimately to meet. Conducted at the outset within the framework of the village, the clearing process frequently extends, during the course of the twelfth century, to isolated farm areas. Is this because of newly improved tools? Has the fear of solitude been conquered? Or rather, is it another manifestation of the breaking of manorial bonds? Throughout entire regions, in any case, it gives birth to a new form of working the land: houses are scattered, each surrounded by a small, individual clearing; the lots are enclosed by small belts of trees or shrubs that protect the tiny islands of cultivation from forests, moors, or animals (domesticated or otherwise). The countryside is completely different now: broken into pieces, cut up into "plains" and "fields," instead of the earlier wooded districts.

Thus we see, between 1000 and the end of the twelfth century, the French countryside receives a new face, and receives it through enormous human effort: countless hatchet strokes, hoes wielded by generations of pioneers, create all those drainage ditches, light all those brush fires, and plant all those new vineyards. One of the first alterations is that the distribution of people over the land becomes much less fluid, assumes a sort of rigidity; at the terrains' borders, now much more distinct, the contours of wooded areas and of the spaces thrown open to the free grazing of flocks are clearly fixed. The clusters of villages are definitively differentiated from the former manorial center. Ultimately, contrasts assert themselves among the various rural landscapes: in northern France, there are open fields where nothing obstructs the vision; wooded belts which, in the areas remaining unfriendly for a longer time to the settler, intimately mingle farmland and forests; little groups of irregular fields that alternate, in the southern regions, with moors. But the pioneers also have provided, by virtue of their toil in these virgin and very rich lands, a considerable addition to the food supply, and the means for the population increase. Although innumerable indications vouch for this increase, in the absence of all numerical evidence it is impossible to evaluate it even approximately. Nevertheless we can imagine, by comparison with England for which some statistical data do exist, that the number of men in France was at least trebled over the course of two centuries. Hence there are more consumers, but also more producers, causing the expansion to continue, and, for a long time, the creation of new wealth to remain slightly ahead of the population advance. In short, the peopling of the empty spaces, and the drying-up of the marshlands that blocked the large river valleys, reduced the distance between human groups, and permitted more frequent contact, facilitating communication within that large, inert, partitioned body, punctuated with immense solitary areas, that France still was in the year 1000. The great progress of the twelfth century—that major accident in the development of French civilization—is certainly the result of agricultural success.

► VOYAGES, COMMERCE, AND MONEY

In reality, there was no immediate, radical transformation in the way of life. And even for the mass of peasants—about whom we know little, actually, since written documents are made for the rich, and scarcely describe the lives of these dark, hairy men who hardly speak the French language—it can be said that there was no change. With the exception of one thing, and an essential one: these people no longer go hungry. From one year to another, the production of basic food supplies still varies considerably, according to variations in the climate; nevertheless, from about 1050 on, there are no more of those appalling famines that periodically ravaged the early Middle Ages, and for generations, the French countryside enjoys the basic good fortune of security against hunger.

In the world of the secular or ecclesiastical lords, on the other hand, the conduct of everyday life underwent modifications that were clearer and more immediate. These rich people had always eaten as much as they wanted, but previously they had been supported very close to the land. At this time, they break away from it. In the first place, the abundance of manorial profits gives rise in each noble household to the enlargement of that basic social group then called the *cour*, the group of commended men and obligees with which every wellborn man must be surrounded. The servants, becoming more numerous, tend also to become specialists; several "department heads" grow up among them. And ranking guests, especially, arrive in greater numbers; for it is much easier in the twelfth century to move about and to visit one's friends; material progress, too, permits more mobility. At this time, travel is the only means of escaping the quicksand of rural life, the burdensome claustrophobia of family life; it is a means of extending one's experience and one's knowledge: the only means of being oneself. Therefore, despite the dangers, the weariness, the slowness of the routes, travel furnishes an exciting and necessary diversion. The period is one of other travelers, too, solitary or in company: scholars in search of new books or other learning; monks who, despite their obligations to the cloister (and the great indignation of reformers), are alert to any pretext for breathing the open air of the roads; and, above all, pilgrims. Because of the new ease in traveling, trips to famous sanctuaries definitely have become the most popular pious practice at the end of the eleventh century, and, reputedly, the most efficacious in blotting out sins and acquiring the favor of the saints. Rich and poor alike, heedless of distances, counting on the monasteries' hospitality and waysiders' charity along their route, set off on complicated itineraries, lasting months and years. Their endless wanderings, calculated to omit no relic, tend most often toward one of the three high places of Christendom: Rome, St. James of Compostela, or Jerusalem. This proliferation of travelers is an essential aspect of the great twelfth-century expansion—the aspect which, above all the others, impressed the contemporary mind.

Just as the roads were coming to life, so too did trade awaken. In the well-being brought about by agricultural progress, knights and peasants now have less difficulty in satisfying their deep-seated taste for finery and ornament—all those strange objects so unlike the usual domestic, the rustic; and this difference is, of course, what gives them value. Therefore, there is, and will be for a long time to come, a trade in important luxury articles. It is only the commodities of high value, spices and magnificent cloths, that come from great distances. But the customer is less restricted, his tastes are more varied and his means more ample; consequently, the movement of trade is more active. Meanwhile, most of Western Europe gradually abandons its isolation and stagnation by means of three factors: first, by the gradual integration into Latin Christendom of the Scandinavian maritime communities and the half-savage Slavic clans on the great northern plain; second, by the livelier commercial relations with Islam, from the Spanish marches and the southern part of the Italian peninsula, as well as with Byzantium from the base of the Adriatic; third, and most decisively, by the military recapturing from the Mos-

lems of the islands in the Tyrrhenian Sea and of Sicily—this reconquest
results in trade being rendered less risky between the two Mediterranean basins for the Christians. An as yet embryonic system of merchant
traffic is established across the territories of France; it has three poles.
The first is organized around maritime Flanders, the Oise valley and the
lower Seine; simultaneously it is a center for the manufacture of that fine
wool and brightly colored cloth whose noble buyers are more and more
numerous; and the way-station for exporting, to the British Isles or the
banks of the North Sea and the Baltic, the goods which gather there
from sea and river coastal traffic: the salt from the Atlantic coast, the
wine from the Seine and the Loire. The second pole is Catalonia, gateway to Infidel Spain, where Christian traders exchange weapons and
slaves for the valuable products of Mozarabic artisans. And the final
point of attraction is Italy, whose sailors, recently coming only from Venice and Amalfi, but now from Pisa and Genoa as well, bring in commodities from the east. These three sources are connected, across the French
countryside, by inland water routes and endlessly branching passages,
over which more and more goods travel.

And in fact, between about 1030 and 1075, a new social type appears
and spreads: the man who does not work the land, yet who is neither a
lord nor a beggar nor even (except occasionally) a bandit, but who earns
his living all the same—the professional merchant. He is always a traveling adventurer, for at this time the merchant does not wait for customers
in a shop; he visits them, unpacks his wares for them in the castles, where
the lord's purchases are counseled by his surrounding vassals; or else, he
unpacks them at the doorsteps of churches that fall along a pilgrim route,
urging the nobles who come, attracted by high feast days, to buy. And
this certainly is a great innovation: formerly, the rich sent their servants
far afield to bring back exotic objects; the laying-in of supplies was always a dubious undertaking, decided upon far in advance. Now, on the
contrary, the itinerant merchant anticipates and stimulates the lord's desires. And, in order to acquire the tempting objects, the lord draws
upon the reserves of precious metal or of rough and unproductive jewels,
which he did not know what to do with a short time ago. Thus, by the establishment of new relations between purchaser and supplier, the wealth
of the churches and manorial chambers is partially liberated during the
course of the eleventh century. Precious metals—of which the West was
not totally devoid, but which had been immobilized by the paralysis of
commercial movement during the early Middle Ages—began to be put
into circulation again. Hence, currency is more plentiful in the twelfth
century. New pieces have been struck, using the silver from cups, bracelets, and altar ornaments. And *deniers* are not the only means of exchange: sacks of pepper and gold dust are also used. Above all, currency
now circulates much more quickly. And, since they are more common,

the pieces of money have less value: in the closing years of the eleventh century there begins a rise in the price of provisions, one that it is impossible to evaluate, but which continues regularly. Men then begin to realize that the pieces coming out of these numerous and increasingly active mints—one of which was needed, in moments of extreme economic recession, near each fairly well frequented market—were not all of equal value. The idea of the circulation of money is new; it is accompanied by new trades: that of changer, weigher, financier, coin-clipper,* and, finally, money-lender.

The twelfth-century merchant, then, is a vagabond; he takes with him all the commodities he owns, carrying them on his back or, more often, in saddlepacks on beasts of burden. Sometimes he carries them great distances, as did those Italian protégés of the pope who, as early as the reign of Philip I, had to submit to royal tax demands in the regions around Paris. Begrimed from his trip he is, like the pilgrim, a "dusty one" (as they were called from the Anglo-Norman regions to the area around Mâcon), an "alien," an unknown. Consequently, he is an object of scorn as well as of scandal: this because he gets rich without any visible effort, because he carries away people's money, because—contrary to the precepts of charity—he resells to his brothers what they need, and does so at a profit, which cannot put him in the good graces of God. He is, finally, the object of covetousness: his double bags are full of extraordinary objects, of more *deniers* than anyone in the country has ever seen at one time. Since 1000, nonetheless, these passers-through, these travelers, merchants, have gradually made a place for themselves. The roads have been put in some sort of order; most of the present-day foundations of French bridges date from the eleventh century, when their upkeep was considered a charitable deed—one analogous to the building of houses of God erected, during the same period, along all the main itineraries—comforting places of refuge for travelers who are received, refreshed, and cared for by confraternities of charitable men. These places are also for the purpose of security. Because their lives are not without danger, merchants ordinarily travel in groups, in disciplined and armed caravans. These caravans bring together, at the beginning of the summer months, all the merchants from the same town who are planning to use the same route, and they embark on a commercial campaign curiously similar to a military expedition. But the organization of this group is not always sufficient protection against the dangers of a still highly disunified world—a world in which each local strong-man controls all the rights over any intruder who, since he is not a resident in the

---

* An "occupation" in which men would shave or clip the edges of slightly overweight coins. Reducing the coin to standard weight, these men could either accumulate enough shavings to be made into new coins or sell the clippings. The milled edges on today's silver coins were first devised as a way to end this practice.—Trans.

territory, does not live under the lord's *ban*. Around 1075, for example, the merchants from Langres, who made their way each summer to the monastery of Cluny, which then was a large center of consumption, were grouped together in a traveling and defensive partnership; nonetheless, a local chatelain could not overcome the temptation to relieve them of their cargo. The regulations of the peace of God, of course, specially promised that the merchants be spared; but the caravans' security really was assured only by a new institution, the "conduct." When entering a chatelain's territory, the travelers entered, equally, into his protection; in exchange for his taking care of them, they paid a special tax, the "toll," as insurance against theft. Ultimately it became necessary to insure a peace for the fairs, those great commercial gatherings that were so indispensable, given the condition of communication, for they permitted traders from an entire region to come into periodic contact with merchants from other places; there they renewed their stock by offering their own wares to these foreigners in exchange for commodities of more distant origin. These numerous fairs, held on fixed occasions, and lasting several days, had grown up since the early Middle Ages. Originating under the stimulus of powerful and far-seeing lords like the counts of Champagne or Flanders, or the abbots of Saint-Denis (men who knew how to obtain effective protection, and obtain it effortlessly, for the merchants), several of these fairs became the most active centers of commercial revival at the beginning of the twelfth century.

Furthermore, the progress in traveling and in exchange was accompanied by progress in urban life. At the junctures of the great main roads, at the doorways of sanctuaries containing relics, at the terminal points of river navigation, at the foot of mountain passes, at the head of bridges, at the usual pedestrian stops throughout the plains—in all these places, there had to be fixed points where merchants and pilgrims on the move could find rest. These points needed to be equipped with auxiliary personnel: unloaders and boatmen, suppliers of immediately consumable meals—this last, indispensable to all those travelers not carrying food supplies along with them. It was necessary also to have more prolonged stopovers for the merchants to use during winter, a dead season in their selling campaigns. As a matter of fact, all the twelfth-century merchants roaming the roads are actually attached to one town or another; "aliens," "dusty ones" though they be for those who see them pass, they are still the dependents of some lord, who controls the built-up area where they live in the interval between commercial expeditions, and to whom they appeal whenever they have a bone to pick with the toll-collectors. Thus, by the passage of travelers in the summer and the residence of professional merchants during the winter, the essential function of the towns is restored. A burst of urbanization, earlier and more continuous along the great axes of trade, takes hold of France from the middle of the eleventh century on; it gives rise to land developments, and to the construction of new parish units. New districts within the towns, called *bourgs*, are formed in the vicinity of old Roman towns, several influential castles, or famous monasteries, ones most often visited by pilgrims. These *bourgs* consist of lines of flimsy huts, clustered around a large market square and along roads opening out into the countryside. They are completely rustic areas, simple and built-up outgrowths of squalor, wretched and fragile by comparison to the old part of the town, where people go to seek refuge and to barricade themselves in emergencies. Still, the new *bourg* is the prosperous center of the new traveling and mercantile activity.

In truth, twelfth-century towns still are very small: a few hundred inhabitants—at most four or five thousand for exceptionally lively towns. Since they are stopovers for travelers who do not obtain their own food from the land, they are centers of large agricultural consumption. Thus, in the environs of each *bourg* and way-station, a certain trade in provisions flourishes. Furthermore, many merchants now buy in greater quantity those products that come from the land—wine, wool, plants for dye-stuffs—stimulating livelier production of these commodities. A little of the peasant's work is thus of a commercial sort and, by degrees, even in the center of those wooded spaces being opened by the work of the land-clearers, each of the peasants becomes accustomed to a more frequent usage of *deniers* and to a greater mobility of wealth.

Also, the great twelfth-century system of landed cultivation becomes a much more flexible organism. The spread of a money economy within society was partially responsible for the former payments in work or harvest crops being replaced by fees in *deniers*; this in turn caused a conspicuous relaxation of the bonds between tenant and landlord. Furthermore, we see the development of a wage-earning class, as well as a set of completely new relations among the rich who, because they have regular cash resources at their disposal, prefer to hire salaried servants for specific jobs; the jobs are, thus, performed better, and the poorest of the villagers are happy to earn, by work done on a temporary basis, those pieces of silver now found in use everywhere. As for the manorial class, whose lives are centered in the castle, they too adapt themselves to a livelier circulation of money. The lord of the *ban* increases the levies of *tailles*, the "collection in *deniers*," as soon as he senses that his *manants* have accumulated some savings; on the other hand, a number of personal obligations are paid in periodic installments, and this, too, relaxes men's commitments to one another.

But the most obvious effect of the economic changes was the formation of a new social group, whose differences from the rural world were sufficient to designate it, in the closing years of the eleventh century, by a new term: the "bourgeois," or people of the *bourg*. Actually, the *bourg* at this time is not really separate from the rural milieu. It is not yet surrounded by a wall; fields and vineyards fill the areas that have not been built up, and these plots are subject, by virtue of the old peasant agricultural holdings, to dues in *corvées* (plowing or harvesting hay) or in wheat. The population comes primarily from peasant stock—recently arrived from nearby villages, whence they are drawn by the advantages of the traveling professions—one side of whose lives is concerned with rural activities. They all—even the few strangers who settled there, obtaining a holding of land, and the community of Jews who live apart on their own street in each town—keep animals in their houses, dress their vines, and harvest their grain. Like the village *manants*, each is subjected to the *ban* of the town's lord, who judges them and extorts *tailles* from them. They are not distinguishable from the rustics: their own way of life, their food, their clothing, their mentality, are equally crude.

But their professional functions differentiate them from the *vilains*. Almost all the heads of bourgeois families practice a trade, a *métier* (the word, a contemporary one, designates specialized economic activity, distinct from "ordinary" work, that is, the working of the land). At first this trade is a mere sideline, but gradually it begins to steal the march on their peasant tasks, occasionally becoming so engrossing and profitable that, to devote themselves to it entirely, the most enterprising permit their plot of ground to lie fallow, despite the threats of the landlord. Many run inns, or bake bread for the passers-by; many are butchers— that is, not only do they raise cattle but they also supply meat, tan leather, and sell salt. In every medieval town, the butchers are the most numerous, the first organized, and often the most affluent. A few bourgeois are *merciers*, that is, dealers in all kinds of exotic commodities, who offer their wares to the rich. All these ventures, cut off as they are from the agricultural world, allow a direct profit in *deniers*; this fact is responsible for the other characteristic of the bourgeois: the distinctive nature of his wealth. It consists of transferable assets, precious metals in bullion or scraps of coin from various mintings, to which peasant hands are still unaccustomed. It is a much more private fortune, one that can be buried in some hiding place and thus, unlike a peasant's livestock, ham, or grain reserve, escape the lord's exactions. It is also a more personal fortune and, unlike ancestral lands, is not the common property of the family group. This group is, in the towns, a much looser organism; here, a man is more independent of his brothers and of his sons, and this tendency toward individualism is strengthened by the merchant's partially itinerant life. Most important, the bourgeois fortune is a much less stable one. The *bourg* is the only place in which, by means of his activity, a man has the opportunity to make money quickly. Hence, ideas of profit, advantage, and thrift are introduced into some people's minds—ideas strange to country people, be they peasants or lords. And these ideas do not arise without producing some bad conscience: quite often the newly rich man, fearing punishment for so many sins against charity, bequeaths the greatest part of his wealth to the Church. Thus, the churches of his town profit indirectly from the new prosperity; from the middle of the twelfth century on, they command financial means far beyond those of the rural religious communities, whose wealth is solely in land. Thus, in the cities, fortunes are unmade as quickly as they are made; it is not until after 1150 that some of these townspeople begin to invest a fraction of their individual profits in less unstable assets: they build those stone houses, signs of their affluence, some of which still stand today in southern France.

Another major difference is that the people of the new *bourgs* are freer and better protected, because their wealth is in *deniers*, from the lord's arbitrary exactions. Very clearly, as early as the mid-eleventh century in Flanders, Saint-Omer, and Valenciennes, merchants in the same town entered partnership to organize caravans and to form a united front against customers and outside suppliers. Often these mutual aid associations—which, gathering about a patron saint and expressing themselves in group prayers and processions, had a religious aspect—encompassed the total population of the *bourg*, drawing it into a tight interdependence based on a collective oath. This "amity" is a true compact, designed to maintain order among the population and to insure a stronger security in these places open to the world, filled with strangers and unknowns, and stocked with easily stolen wealth: "All those who belong to the town's amity have pledged, by their word and oath, that each will aid the other, that they will be brothers in service and courtesy . . . if someone is in great extremity, because of a fire in his house, capture, or the obligation to ransom himself, each one will give a *denier* toward the assistance of his impoverished *ami*. . . ." [1] These regulations of the charter of Aire-sur-la-Lys show clearly that they concern a fraternity whose solidarity is that which unites the family group.

This gathering for mutual profit, "commune" in the terms of the day, led naturally to a further consequence: the head of the *bourg*, whether bishop, abbot, or count, was asked to abolish certain manorial demands which, although tolerable to a rural area before urbanization, were particularly restrictive upon businessmen. These included arbitrary and unforeseeable taxes, too heavy tolls that alienated passers-through, primitive judicial procedures poorly adapted to merchant activity, and military requisitions that broke off trade during the season devoted to fairs and commercial travels. Occasionally, the commune even claimed the right to manage some of the interests of the group—particularly in southern France, where it included the resident knights, who took over its control.

The communes, then, existed to claim the bourgeois rights. From the light shed by imprecise documentation, we gather that they appeared for the first time at Le Mans in 1070; then in the Oise Valley, in Flanders, and in the area around Toulouse, always proliferating along the main trade arteries. (There is rivalry among urban communities, each wanting to obtain equal advantages: if the bourgeois in Tournus on the Saône acted so violently against their lord in 1170, it was because they had the distressing feeling that they were the laughingstock of every stranger passing through—for they still paid a certain tax, though a very slight one, that had been abolished everywhere else.) The negotiations were almost always peaceful, for the bourgeois had quantities of that silver so tempting to the lord. A generous gift of *deniers*, agreement to taxes that were both regular and productive—and the lord granted "exemptions" which, without ever cutting him out, limited the exercise of his power in certain areas and, especially, abolished its arbitrary character. Yet in some towns—when the lords were ecclesiastics, less free to dispose of the *ban*, since they felt themselves to be only its administrators, the real lord being the patron saint of the church—there was some resistance to this bargaining. And, too, this sort of lord was less pressed for money, for the religious communities benefited from bourgeois alms and participated in commerce themselves. This resistance led to conflicts and often to violence, as in Laon where, in 1116, the bishop was murdered by the enraged bourgeois. These insurrections met with varying success, but for a while they tainted the communes' actions, in certain ecclesiastical circles, with scandal: "Commune—a new name, a detestable name if it is a name at all. For all those who are subjected to a personal tax, liquidate the *coutumes* of servitude by means of a single annual payment, and are liable to a fixed fine if they commit a misdemeanor, since the other fees of the lords, normally resting upon the serfs, are spared them." [2]

Yet the movement is irresistible. In the middle of the twelfth century, in several towns north of the Loire, justice is administered by the mayor and the municipal magistrates [*échevins*], representatives of the bourgeois community; in the south, the *consulats* are small, autonomous, aristocratic associations; and in all the *bourgs* of any importance throughout the French provinces, people breathe a greater freedom inside the walls that the bourgeois are beginning to build, here and there, financed by raising subscriptions. This is the beginning of that political differentiation between town and country which will be so lasting in Old France. And yet, as early as this period, several village communities also have obtained "exemptions," which have been recorded in a charter and are very similar to those of the towns. This time the initiative comes from the lord, who wants to attract immigrants to his lands; nonetheless, it is still a direct effect of economic progress.

But if most of the social ties have become more flexible, the standard of living for the majority has not noticeably improved. Pious practice, and the belief in the redemptive efficacy of alms, dictate that a good part of the peasants' and bourgeois' newly created wealth be offered to God and the saints—that is, to the clerics and monks who serve them. Furthermore, embracing the same rhythm of agricultural and commercial progress, manorial finances have improved. All the *deniers* coming into the peasants' hands have gladly been transferred into those of their lords, in exchange for the discontinuation of *corvées*, and a reduction in the amount of wheat or wine with which they must furnish him. At the same time, to offset the new freedom granted by the town's lord, the bourgeois cheerfully agree to his tapping their cash reserves more fully, and more frequently.

Thus, in the twelfth century, the peasants are better fed, better armed against disease, and more capable of raising their children into adolescence. Their tools are more sophisticated; sometimes they go into town to buy a little salt, some shoes, some iron to be made by the smith into plowshares and axes. But their lodgings are still primitive—unfurnished, except for a few bowls and a tripod for the fire; they dress in wild animal skins, in cloth made of the wool from their own sheep or from the hemp growing behind the stable; they have not yet acquired the habit of spending money. But then, we must add, neither have the bourgeois. However rich they may be in precious metals, they still live in the style of peasants. In a word, all of the new profits are for the two élites—that of prayer and that of warfare. The entire monetary flow terminates in the hands of the knights and the men of the high church; for them only does it produce an improvement in living conditions, and a rise in culture.

▶ THE SERVICE AND THE KNOWLEDGE OF GOD

During the first half of the twelfth century—in the days of St. Bernard, Peter the Venerable, and the Abbot Suger—the Church of France manifests singular changes. It has become richer, more erudite, and, at the same time, more independent: as a result of the long program directed by the papacy from the mid-eleventh century on, which the historians call the Gregorian Reform, the Church has much greater freedom from feudal life. For the entire manorial world, from the kings down to the last *hobereau*, this liberation was not an easy one; for it was these people who had had authority, to a greater or lesser degree, over the religious media. This struggle, although less bitter and dramatic in France than in other countries of the Empire, was stubborn and coercive enough. Its propaganda radiated out of the very heart of the feudal system, spread by countless men, half of them of the Church and half of the world (the very symbiosis it was trying to disrupt). It was directed from the top by amazingly active personalities: Hugh of Die, the papal legate and archbishop of Lyon; and Urban II, a former Cluniac monk, whose official

tour through central France in 1095 dates the decisive phase of the reform.

At this time, the chatelains and village knights give up their interests in
all the rural churches. Whether they do this for the salvation of their souls
(and do it with the many reservations and the sidesteppings of heirs who
are poor losers of their ancestral wealth) or through fear of the excommunication by which they feel threatened, they donate these lands to
God, most frequently to a monastery. To be sure, they often retain the
tithes, rendered so profitable by technical progress; they keep the right of
review over the designation of the succursal priest. But the "altar" is no
longer in their hands, nor can they appropriate burial fees or the seasonal
offerings of the faithful; spiritual activity has ceased to be a manorial exploitation. As a consequence of this release, the parish organization becomes stricter. The extension of cultivated clearings, the repossession of
uncultivated border regions, have enabled the boundaries of the parish to
be more sharply defined. The new leaders of the Church carefully see to
it that all the religious activity of the people within the parish is enclosed
within these borders: the people cannot go elsewhere to hear mass, to receive the sacraments, nor, especially, to be buried or donate alms. It is
within this framework—gathering together, in regions of scattered population, all the remote areas—that we have seen the village community
take definite shape around pious fraternities and associations that supervise church maintenance and distribute its charity. But the transfer of the
rural churches into the patrimony of the religious community has not appreciably improved the quality of ecclesiastical personnel. The monks, as
a matter of fact, do not themselves even minister to the succursal chapels
in their parishes; rather, they entrust these chapels to the care of serfs'
sons, as did the lords. And the village *curé* stays a poor man; inevitably
he is married, and burdened with children; uneducated, poorly supervised, and half-starved, he is tempted consequently to exploit his flock by
taking advantage of the magical prestige surrounding his function. He
does not preach; doubtless, the liturgical life of the faithful is limited to
periodic meetings around the sanctuary, group chants whose meaning is
barely understood, exorcisms, pat phrases. And this deficiency in the
rural clergy, which was to outlast by far the Middle Ages, poses the problem of Christianity's actual pervasiveness within the peasants' world.
Who was Christ for a twelfth-century husbandman? What reflection of
Gospel teachings could this sort of man perceive? How was his spiritual
universe organized, where were interdicts located for him? Unfortunately,
it is impossible even to conjecture.

But it was in the upper echelons of the Church that the reform was
most unequivocally successful. In all the monasteries of twelfth-century
France, the monks live according to the rule, and freely elect their abbot.
As a result of the social and religious evolution, these monks are recruited

almost exclusively from sons of knights, and in increasing numbers have access to the priesthood. Concomitant with this, a lower category of religious man is designated: the "lay brother," a man of peasant stock, who is restricted to material tasks. In the cathedral chapters (where, too, the prebends are reserved for nobles; the sons of the newly-rich bourgeois do not begin to enter before the end of the century) canonical regulations are better observed, and people have reverted to a certain austerity. Ultimately, all the bishops are designated by the canons, and the king and high nobles use more discretion in the recommendation of their candidates. Much more frequently than before, however, these candidates are worthy of their function; they are the best educated, the most energetic, of all contenders, and even—sometimes—are those whose morals are the purest. At any rate, it is increasingly rare that one finds incompetents or ruffians among the dignitaries of the monastery or the members of the upper clergy. Almost all of them now have a loftier and clearer conception of their mission; in particular, they feel the necessity for serving God better by adorning the sanctuary, encouraging scholarly activity and intellectual research—all this with the resources of their church, resources that are much more abundant, not only because of the increase in the lords' revenue, but also because these revenues no longer are shared with secular patrons or misappropriated by poor management. In this way, the reform produced the simultaneous appearance of the first system of original thought, and the first—the only—great sacred art in French civilization.

One of the first uses to which the new wealth was put was the fuller realization of that Cluniac ideal: liturgical magnificence. St. Hugh, Abbot of Cluny until 1109, proclaimed openly that precious metals should not accumulate in their treasury but, rather, should be used for the adornment of the House of God. Hence, artistic progress grew out of those French provinces most under the influence of Cluny—that is, the provinces of the Midi. These regions—around Poitiers, Toulouse, Clermont, Autun, Lyon, Vienne, Arles—were also the most retentive repositories and faithful guardians of the antique civilization, places where Roman monuments survived in the greatest number and in the least deteriorated state. Entire generations passed before these monuments without seeing them; but around the year 1000, people had begun to admire them, to look upon them as sources of inspiration. Such, then, is the new art: the techniques of Rome are assimilated by Cluny, which is to say, by a Christianity directed toward the ostentatious celebration, both musical and plastic, of the glory of God. This art begins the attempt to find itself in several isolated experiments during the end of the tenth century; at the outset of the twelfth it is flourishing south of the Loire and on the edge of Burgundy, with brilliant success.

The Church is the sole object of this art. The main artistic act, that around which all others are ordered, is building—building with beautiful, well-matched stones, according to the Roman models, that vessel capable of containing and developing the intoned chant of the liturgy. Thus, the artistic renaissance is manifested most obviously in the opening of new quarries. Because it is an art centered on building, it is a costly one—for Romanesque churches spring forth neither from the earth by the spontaneous and voluntary efforts of the faithful, nor by the work of the men of God themselves, nor by the unpaid *corvées* of peasant tenants. Rather, the churches are the work of craftsmen—quarriers, stonecutters, transporters (the finest material is not always that which is nearest at hand), and masons—all of whom demand a salary; these, organized into itinerant companies, certainly formed the first unified group of specialized workmen. It must be understood that the materialization of the long, preparatory researches, the blossoming forth of Romanesque architecture, the flowering of white churches so moving to the men of that time—all occur at the exact moment when the movement of economic expansion was sufficiently launched; when money was finding its way everywhere, when silver was leaving the treasuries and going into circulation; when there was a rebirth of towns, a new creation of tools, and an increased number of merchants. It must also be understood that although the completion of those enormous and magnificent works of art, the large sanctuaries, could be very rapid when the undertaking was backed by abundant and regularly augmented financial resources (as at Cluny where the immense basilica, the third, was begun in 1088 and almost finished by 1118), it could also drag on indefinitely, with long interruptions, despite the collection rounds and the publicity that surrounded new relics or new miracles. Because of the long spreading out in time of the construction, elements of the buildings are often disparate, finished according to different esthetics or techniques from those chosen by the original creator.

For the Romanesque builders of southern France, the problem is to build churches entirely of stone—not only the walls, but the ceiling as well. This is done, not merely for increased security or protection against fires (which actually had destroyed many sanctuaries) but also out of adherence to a new conception of architectural beauty. Indeed, the vault is the main element of a special esthetic, whose essential aim is the creation of an enclosed interior space around the altar, cut off from the world—a space whose atmosphere is of a different quality: a receptacle and a coffer for the resonance of sacred music. The problem was that to the naves of the ancient basilica, with their rhythmic processions of pillars and arcades, had to be adapted one of those vaults—barrel or groined—that had already been used by the Carolingian builders in the new parts of the church, in the crypts, and the *clochers-porches*. But the present state of architectural technique required, for reasons of balance, that the walls be thick and not too tall, with only a few openings. These churches, then, were relatively dark, but this half-light—which bestowed all their import upon the sanctuary fire and the lighting so necessary to the liturgy and the contemporary religious manifestations—is precisely one of the principal components of that sacred space consecrated to collective prayer. The churches are squat: the builders are concerned less with width and height than with balance of proportions. Harmony, balance, rhythm, rational organization of both space and time (for we cannot separate the research of the builders from that of the musicians)—these, made possible by a greater familiarity with arithmetic, are responsible for the beauty of the Romanesque buildings, whose silhouettes and interior proportions are identical with those of the last buildings left by classical antiquity.

The churches of the twelfth century are, nonetheless, very different from one another; in this world where, despite progress in transportation, real distances remain enormous, research is conducted in isolation, in a creative fever that ends in the development of new solutions. Furthermore, architects, as we use the word today, do not yet exist: it is the leader of the religious community, he who has decided to rebuild the sanctuary, who alone conceives the project. In conceiving it, he calls upon his memory of the buildings he has seen on trips, sometimes sending for measurements to be taken at the site of whatever building he has chosen as a model; he calls upon empirical knowledge as well—and here we see the part played in the artistic renewal by the reforms, whose recruitment of new personnel purified the upper echelons of the Church and disseminated mathematical knowledge within the religious schools. Because plans are often conceived from memory, a certain relation exists among buildings in the same region; for it is the forms of the closest churches, those seen most often, that take hold of the builders' minds. Nevertheless, the affinities are not exclusively provincial. The effects of proximity are counteracted by other influences: spiritual ties that join two distant monasteries, prompting their leaders, who are accustomed to visiting each other despite the distance, to adopt the same style as a token of brotherhood. And, on the other hand, an antagonism may exist between neighboring prelates: for this reason, at the beginning of the twelfth century, the bishop of Autun chooses, for his cathedral's new dependent churches, an architectural model different from that which the nearby Cluny, which he could not endure, proposed. What diversity, what richness, in the naves of Cahors, Périgueux, and Angoulême, each capped with a series of domes—a solution that passed through Solignac and Poitiers, and went as far as Fontevrault; in daring contrast, Saint-Philibert, Tournus, employs a refined harmony of pink and white stone, the high cylindrical masonwork pillars supporting a succession of juxtaposed transverse barrel vaults. At the same time, there is an enormous development of pilgrim basilicas arranged, with many coupled naves and radiating chapels around the ambulatories, to facilitate the movement of crowds—these may be seen today in Saint-Sernin, Toulouse, and in Sainte-Foy, Conques; they once existed as well in Saint-Martial, Limoges, and Saint-Martin, Tours. And then again, we see the strange motley of Notre-Dame, Puy; the churches in the region around Brionne, all the more luminous because of their high windows opening into the principal nave above the side aisles, with their groin vaults that served as a pattern for Vézelay; the Autun cathedral's strict fidelity to the fluted pilasters of its Roman models; and the porches of the very simple churches of Provence, with their Corinthian capitals supporting triangular pediments.

But these new sanctuaries are ornamented, too—and in the ornamentation lies, undoubtedly, the principal esthetic innovation of southern France. These ornaments previously would have been confined to a prescribed area around the altar—hence the illuminated pages of Gospel books, wood-and-ivory reliefs on the covers of sacred volumes, and stone engravings decorating the altar table—but now the ornament is incorporated into the building itself, transposed in terms of architectural particulars. During the eleventh century, the work of the artists who, in the writing and illuminating workrooms of the monasteries in Burgundy and Aquitaine, drew from the great Mozarabic or Italo-Byzantine illustrations the inspiration for embellishing their Books of Revelation; the work of those at Limoges who, in touch with the earliest enamelers, decorated their Prayer Books in a touching and agitated style, with magnificent reds, blues, golds; the work of the carvers from Pyrenean quarries, chipping away at the sides of sarcophagi—all this gradually is transferred to the construction yards. So it is, at first, that the great monumental painting developed. In the twelfth century, frescoes—palely harmonious in Poitou and the Loire Valley, lively and contrasted in the small churches of the Roussillon and the Puy cathedral, stretching out on a dark background in the Cluniac priory of Berzé-la-Ville—decorate all the apses and walls with few openings. Sometimes, according to a new trend, they even cover the vaults, which at Saint-Savin-sur-Gartempe are specially arranged to receive the painted decoration; thus, long rhythmical series of figures dwell in the half-light of the sacred area. This is a narrative, figurative style of painting, which offers—passionately at Vic, meditatively but fervently at Brinay, feverishly and vigorously at Tavant—the same imagery of the manuscripts, but offers it to a much larger public than could be found in the very rare users of books. Still, the Romanesque creations in this sphere are only the flourishing of a very old, traditional idea promoted by the entire civilization's progress, encouraged by conciliar meetings, supported by public opinion: a church was not complete as long as it was not decorated.

Completely new and revolutionary, on the other hand, is the appearance of a sculpture that is no longer abstract, geometric, reduced to tracery and, at most, to floral stylization; the new sculpture is lifelike and representational. This innovation is not attributable to the mere rediscovery of a lost technique; it marks a profound change in taste, also originating in the southern provinces. Indeed, it was the "former mode and ancient custom, in all the regions of Auvergne, Rouergue, and Toulouse, as in all the contiguous regions, that each man erect a statue to his saint, in gold, silver, or some other metal, according to his means; a statue in which the head, or the most conspicuous part of the body, was reproduced with veneration." [3]

But this sense of volume, this need for the plastic representation of sacred figures, had been progressively spreading south of the Loire since the year 1000; it was eventually applied to the decoration of the building as well. Thus, relief sculpture gradually invaded the walls of the church, beginning with the early, awkward lintels in Roussillon's mountain chapels, and continuing through the complex and almost theatrical arrangement of the façades in the region around Angoulême. It is true nonetheless that, in the early twelfth century, sculpture is still almost invariably a minor art, the servant of architecture, rarely calling attention to itself. Caught in the wall, scarcely emerging from it, sculpture, like the frescoes, is covered with colors; often it appears as the mere introduction of some relief into a part of the painted decoration, at a few limited parts of the building. Again faithful to Roman tradition, the men in charge of the building in those days handed over to the sculptors only those areas which, in the ancient temples, had been decorated with reliefs: on the one hand, the capitals, where figures and monsters at first worked their way among the acanthus volutes, ultimately replacing leafy designs completely; on the other, the façade—a much larger area, sometimes completely utilized in a decorative profusion, as in Notre-Dame-la-Grande, Poitiers. But more frequently sculpture is confined to the vicinity of the doors—unassuming figures of the virtues or of virgins, moulded to the curves of the archings of Saintonge and Poitou churches; complex scenes inscribed in the semicircle of the tympanum. There, if nowhere else, when Burgundian and Toulousian monks of the Cluniac order decided to offer divine figures for the contemplation of the faithful at the threshold of the sanctuary, they opened the way to one of the most perfect triumphs of Christian art. Thus we see, at Saint-Sernin, Toulouse, the fleshy and rounded forms of the stylobates, very earthy and very close to the Roman models; in the Last Judgment at Saint-Foy, Conques, the devils gesticulating like clowns, the good-natured faces of the elect, are presented to the great crowds of pilgrims in a manner that is too popular, too peasant-like, too much compromised by popular edification. But the art of relief realizes the most perfect representation of the religious sentiment of the clerics in several sublime works: at Moissac the inaccessible God of apocalyptic vision appears, surrounded by aged musicians; on the tympanum of Autun, the artist plays with human forms with the most daring freedom, but knows how to express in the faces of his figures, with their plantlike sinuosities, all the piety, somewhat tinged with terror, of those days; finally, at Vézelay, the most beautiful figure of God the Omnipotent the Christian world knew how to conceive, is surrounded by the whole Church, manifested in the blaze of the Pentecost.

Such, then, is the French art called Romanesque. It is above all else a monastic art, a liturgical art, an art of men trained to calculation by the mathematical games of the *quadrivium*. It is an art of divine transcendence, nurtured on the Psalms and the Prophetic Books, completely steeped in the apocalyptic fantasies that the early Middle Ages bequeathed to Western Christianity. It is an art of composers of sacred chants, who conceived the universe in harmonic forms: St. Hugh wanted to see represented, in a series of marvelous capitals around the main altar of Cluny, the tones of this music, a music related to the intellectual activities and spiritual aspirations of mankind as well as to the cosmic rhythms of the seasons. This art flowers most beautifully around 1100; after the first third of the twelfth century it begins to decline, as when, at Charlieu and at Saint-Julien-de-Jonzy, the Burgundian sculptor's ability is lost in pure virtuosity and bizarre fantasy. The exception is Provence where, forty years later, this art produces a strange blossoming in the Saint-Gilles portal—that meeting point of many artistic currents where man-eating lions, from the protohistoric art of the Rhône Valley, combine with Roman friezes, the whole treated in the style of the Lombard stonecutters. In this tenacious remnant, situated in the most Roman of the French regions, there appears once more the close link among Romanesque art, the plastic expression of southern France, and Mediterranean esthetic traditions transmitted by Rome.

North of the Loire, in the regions where the Carolingian imprint had been deepest, the beginning of the twelfth century saw appreciably different tastes. There, people knew how to decorate books marvelously: the most beautiful illuminated manuscripts of the time come from the monastic *scriptoria* of Flanders and Artois, where influences from Winchester coincide with those of the workrooms along the Meuse. But people there are not accustomed to monumental, figurative sculpture. At the beginning of the eleventh century, the head of the episcopal school at Angers, having returned from a trip into Aquitaine, was scandalized by the "idols" and images of saints, rendered overly concrete by the techniques of relief. He saw there the "continuation of the rites of formerly worshiped gods, or rather demons. To me, completely ignorant as I am," he said, "it seemed quite perverse, and contrary to Christian religion,

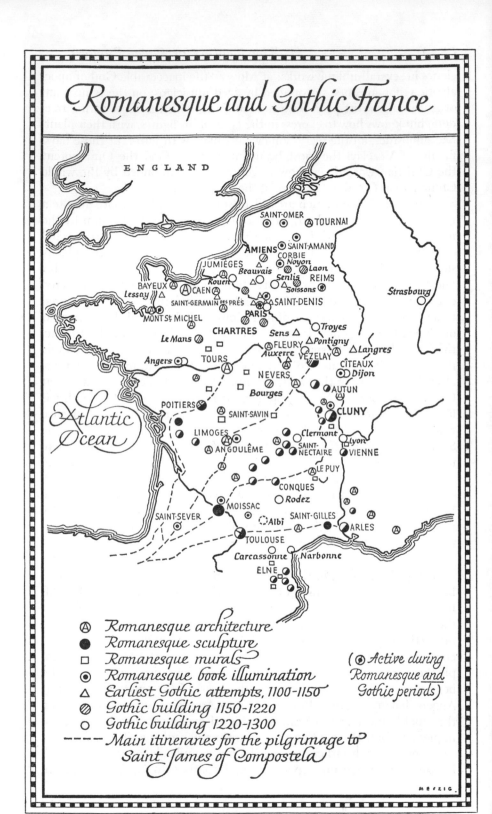

Romanesque and Gothic France

ENGLAND

SAINT-OMER · TOURNAI
AMIENS · SAINT-AMAND
CORBIE
Noyon
JUMIÈGES · Beauvais · Laon
BAYEUX · Rouen · Senlis · REIMS
Lessay · CAEN · Soissons
SAINT-GERMAIN DES PRÉS · SAINT-DENIS
MONT St MICHEL · PARIS
Le Mans · CHARTRES · Sens · Troyes
Angers · TOURS · FLEURY · Pontigny · Langres
Auxerre · VÉZELAY
NEVERS · CÎTEAUX · Dijon
Bourges · AUTUN
POITIERS · CLUNY
SAINT-SAVIN
LIMOGES · Clermont · Lyon
ANGOULÊME · SAINT- · VIENNE
NECTAIRE
LE PUY
CONQUES
Rodez
MOISSAC
SAINT-SEVER · SAINT-GILLES
Albi · ARLES
TOULOUSE
Carcassonne · Narbonne
ELNE

Strasbourg

Atlantic Ocean

Ⓐ Romanesque architecture
● Romanesque sculpture
☐ Romanesque murals
◉ Romanesque book illumination
△ Earliest Gothic attempts, 1100-1150
◍ Gothic building 1150-1220
○ Gothic building 1220-1300
---- Main itineraries for the pilgrimage to
Saint James of Compostela

(◉ Active during
Romanesque and
Gothic periods)

MERZIG

when I saw for the first time that statue of St. Géraud, set on an altar . . . modeled exactly after the form of the human face, so much so that, to most of the peasants who contemplated it, it seemed to look at them with a penetrating eye, and answer their prayers with more benevolence through the reflection of its gaze." [4] In a word, the prelates north of the Loire did not yet demand, in the building of churches, that perfect harmony, that quality of interior atmosphere accomplished by stone vaults; faithful to the imperial traditions revived not long ago by Charlemagne and his sons, they loved vast proportions, large and unmysterious light, the vertical thrust of steeples, elevated walls. And they were satisfied with wooden timber-work to cover the high, luminous naves.

Nevertheless, in the regions which had long been reduced to a state of cultural deficiency, after the still poorly repaired devastation of the Scandinavian invasions, artistic pursuits had also been passionately conducted since the middle of the eleventh century, accelerated by a more rapid economic progress and by earlier reforms of ecclesiastical organization. These pursuits occurred first of all in Normandy, the principal province, and the most prosperous and active one. Between 1060 and 1100, abbeys or cathedrals were erected between the Cotentin Peninsula and the Seine, at Caen, Jumièges, Bernay, and Bayeux—buildings with high, bare façades, extended by towers toward the sky, whose interior elevation was organized around superimposed tiers, arcades, galleries, and tall windows. As yet, no vaults: but, in the early years of the twelfth century, a new means of roofing, the ogival transept—broad arcs, carrying the stone vault's thrusts into the corner pillars, thus permitting it to project on higher and airier walls—was applied as an afterthought to those vast buildings. This had already been used in some areas of Romanesque France, but essentially for decorative intent without the builders, who did not have the same structural problems to solve, being too much interested in exploiting its possibilities. From the Norman regions, between 1120 and 1140, the use of the still-crude ogival arch spread into the little churches around Beauvais, Paris, and in Picardy; then into buildings of greater scale, on the borders of Romanesque Burgundy, at Sens, Charité-sur-Loire, and at the cathedral of Langres. But it was in an exemplary building, among the group directed by the Abbot Suger at the Abbey of Saint-Denis between 1132 and 1144, that this architectural formula became the principal expression of a new esthetic.

Saint-Denis-en-France had become the "master abbey" by the beginning of the twelfth century. Celebrated in the *chansons de geste*, it was a venerable monastery, upon which the Merovingians had already been showering their alms. It was enriched by famous relics of the Passion, and was the most royal of all the monastic establishments: since the seventh century, it had received the bodies of dead sovereigns, and preserved, along with the insignias of royalty, the banner of the royal host, the oriflamme. Its claims to being "master abbey" rested as well on several new and simultaneous factors: its material prosperity, due to the success of the Lendit fair which had been revived by the expansion of shipping trade on the Seine and the Oise; its religious regularity, restored by the reform of 1127; its increased and learned circulation of saints' lives; and, especially, because of the personality of its abbot, Suger, friend of Louis VI and Louis VII, regent of the kingdom in 1147 when the King departed for the Holy Land—Suger who, among all the great ecclesiastical figures with such various callings in the first half of the twelfth century, represents the administrator, the perfect manager of the temporal wealth of God and his saints. In his trips beyond the Loire, Suger had acquired the taste for beautiful buildings. He wanted to give his church a sanctuary worthy of its fame, and in his conception of this new building he shared the Cluniac predilection for liturgical pomp: his primary aim, in his words, was "to celebrate the sacred mysteries in a truly divine manner." But he also brought to the project two conceptions that were responsible for the originality of his work. First, he held the appeal of light to be the perfect link between man and God, the vehicle of grace and prayer, the means for transcending the appearances of the senses and arriving at the realities of the spirit. He expresses this in a meditation on the reflections of precious stones, in which, "transposing the material into the immaterial," he sees himself "living as if truly in some strange region of the universe that does not entirely exist, either on the mud of the earth or in the purity of the sky;" and again, in two lines he wanted to inscribe on the threshold of the new church, "The unilluminated spirit raises itself to truth by traversing the material; through light it is reborn from its previous submersion"; and, repeated on the doors, his desire to see his work "illuminate men's spirits, and, lighting their way truly, lead them to the true Light, to which Christ is the real door." This mystical conception of light is not his personal one; it derived from the Neoplatonism then being taught in the schools of Chartres. In any case, this idea, until then the subject only of meditations or of lyrical representations, became the basis of a new art of building, with the help of Suger. No longer was it oriented toward the creation of an interior half-light filled with vigil fires, but instead, toward the total illumination of the house of God—toward Gothic art, the poetry of light. Suger's other new intention, distinguishing him from the Romanesque designers, was his eagerness to demonstrate, by means of the symbolic image, the agreement between the Old and New Testaments. For, through a decisive change that occurred in the most progressive milieux of northern France at the beginning of the twelfth century, a Biblical and apocalyptic inspiration, a contemplation of divine transcendence, flows into the Gospels, into the sense of the humanity of God, and through this, into the conception of man and of his natural environment. In this way, a new iconography took shape at Saint-Denis: painters and sculptors were urged, for the first time, to represent the human element of the Christian mysteries, instead of monsters, or divine, terrifying, glorious effigies.

Unable to abandon the ancient basilica said to have been built by Christ himself, Suger began by affixing a new entrance to it. This solid, architectonic mass, whose upward-aspiring appearance resembles that of the large Norman façades, is the first of the Gothic façades, by virtue of certain major innovations: the complete integration of the two towers into the building, the large rose-window opening on the upper chapel, and the arrangement of the porch. The narrative tympanums of the Burgundian and Toulousian churches combine there with the arches of the Poitou region, supported by statue-columns of kings and queens—one of Suger's inspired inventions; sculptors, probably invited from the great workrooms of the south, have represented here the story of the entire creation, placing the Virgin among the apostles of the Last Judgment, as well as Suger himself in an offertory attitude: these two figures introduce the very image of maternity and succorable human weakness into this depiction of the power and justice of God. That the new building be pervaded with light, that "the whole church be resplendent with a marvelous, uninterrupted light, radiating from windows of maximum luminosity," Suger built the choir, taking advantage there of the ogival transept. There are no more partitions betwen the radiating chapels; instead there are slender, stone columns and large bays enriched with those ornaments previously considered subordinate—stained-glass windows.

Suger did not have the time to join the porch to the choir; nonetheless, his work marks the beginning of the new art. For Saint-Denis was at the intersection of the great routes of this region along the Seine, this area now surpassing the former wealth of the Romanesque provinces; the wealth of its rejuvenated countryside, the activity of its navigable rivers, brought amazing progress. The undertakings of Suger also offered to the bishops of the region, now well supplied with *deniers* by the commercial Christendom of their fully developed towns, ready-to-use teams of masons, stonecarvers and glassmakers, to say nothing of an unsurpassable model. Thus, the abbey of Saint-Denis is the leader of the whole line of cathedrals in the royal domain: Noyon, where work began in 1145; Senlis, whose bishop began its reconstruction in 1153 aided by Louis VII; Laon, whose construction yards opened in 1155, and, finally, Notre-Dame, Paris, whose choir went up in 1163, and whose nave in 1180—the same year work on the new church in Soissons got under way. As the work progressed, construction techniques improved. The flying buttress, a monumental innovation permitting the complete breakaway from Romanesque constructions, was used on the nave of Notre-Dame in Paris, which consequently can stretch to the then unheard-of height of 105 feet. Thus, the Gothic style of architecture takes its definitive shape, through the assertion of the vertical, the fluting of the walls, and the larger and larger admittances of the unreal, stained-glass light.

At the same time, after Saint-Denis, the character of the new decorative style is defined as well. In this, Chartres—where, after 1145, the workshops of sculptors trained by Suger went to make new decorations for the portal—takes the lead, through the marvelous success of its statue-columns. These mark the first movement toward a radically different conception of the face: the lowered eyebrows and puckered lids that give the Romanesque eye a Gothic glance; the mouth that becomes more and more alive, all the human personality gradually revealed in the graphic symbols of Romanesque imagery. And, especially, the contribution of Chartres lies in the illustration of a new theme, the Nativity, the most directly available expression of divine incarnation, where Christ appears in the vulnerable form of a child, and where for the first time the Virgin is the central figure. The whole of this is immediately copied at Le Mans, Saint-Loup-de-Naud, Bourges, and Étampes; its influence can be seen even in the Romanesque figures on the porch of Saint-Trophime in Arles. But only in the last years of the twelfth century does the most striking characteristic of the new sculpture—its religious tenderness— appear. We see it at Laon, where the Christ of the Last Judgment extends his hands, revealing the marks of his suffering, and at Senlis, where the whole portal is devoted to the glory of the Virgin: she appears triumphantly on one of the tympanums, being crowned by Jesus, and is placed on the same level as he.

Thus, between 1120 and 1180, the Ile-de-France recovers from its lag and assimilates the artistic discoveries of the southern regions—and, in assimilating them, creates its own artistic style. And this birth of Gothic art is accompanied by an astonishing flowering of polyphonic music, this too having been transplanted from Saint-Martial, Limoges, to the banks of the Seine. It was for the new naves of Notre-Dame, Paris, that Pérotin the Great composed *conducti* and *organa** for four voices, which are among the most beautiful works of medieval music. It is a sacred art, but it is also one which, by uniting the development of religious feeling with the progress in intellectual equipment, frees itself from the terrifying and the imaginary—an art in which God becomes a friend, draws close to man through the intercession of the mediating

---

* Perotinus Magnus was the director of music at Notre-Dame from about 1183 to 1236. A *conductus* uses a metrical poem for a text, to which is attached a fixed song with a freely invented melody (the plainsong melody is no longer used); the long, sustained notes become organized rhythmically, with words no longer attached to every part. An *organum* is the voice part accompanying a fixed song (*cantus firmus*) in parallel fourths, fifths, or octaves, improvising a melody with uniform rhythm.— Trans.

Virgin, and takes his place in the center of a reconciled nature. It is the art of an urbanized Christianity, and this localization answers the new economic conditions; the rural monasteries that had been, since the seventh century, the liveliest centers of learned culture, are henceforth eclipsed by the cathedrals of the old towns and the collegiate churches of the *bourgs*. The Ile-de-France and the towns assume the leadership, not only in art and music, but, as will be seen, in the rebirth of studies as well.

At the beginning of the twelfth century, the monkish distrust of intellectual activity is asserted: reading the secular works of Roman antiquity becomes a sinful pleasure. One does not draw near to God by reflection, but by purely affective steps: by letting the soul ascend on the modulations of sacred music, by destroying the carnal portion of the human self through asceticism. There are no more studies in the monasteries, but in the worldly Church, the directors are of an opposite opinion: a cleric's mission is to learn, his piety must be fed on knowledge. So, opposite the cloisters, there emerge the schools. Traditionally, these are cathedral annexes, set up by one of the canons, the *écolâtre** —the only teacher—disseminating his knowledge among his brother monks, young and old, and to the rare stranger to the community: visiting clerics in search of new learning, or, very rarely, sons of the greatest manorial families. More often than not, the schools are very colorless, devoted strictly to professional, liturgical, and choral education; but sometimes, when their leader is talented and when they have a few good books in their collections, they are brilliant. In any case, the effectiveness of the capitulary schools of the eleventh century was subject to many modes of variation. But after 1080, certain of them, all north of the Loire, began to flourish: first Tournai, then, for several years, Laon; more permanently, Angers, Tours, and Orléans (which specialized in reading, and commenting on, poetry). Chartres, whose old school was reactivated by the Bishop Yves, continued its bent toward the Platonically inspired study of numbers and philosophy, and experienced its greatest success up to about 1150; and, finally, Paris began to advance with the twelfth century.

These centers of study attract a larger and larger number of students. And this movement of scholarly concentration is the result of economic changes: it is in fact the diffusion of money that enables students, as well as other men, to move about more easily, to detach themselves from the soil that nurtured them, to leave the production communities of monasteries and chapters and establish themselves in new surroundings —in the towns. In the twelfth century, money became a prerequisite of

---

* Director of a cathedral school—Trans.

school life, as we see from those letters written by students in Angers or Orléans, asking their families for *deniers*. And, at this point, the very structure of the teaching apparatus is modified. One *écolâtre* is no longer enough for each group of students; he secures additional teachers by that delegation of the power to instruct known as the *licence*, freely conferred by the ecclesiastical authorities, and resting only on an examination of ability. The scholarly center or *studium* thus becomes much more complex: it has many teachers, enlarged and diversified programs, and longer-lasting studies (for students pass from one to another professor, each of whom has his own specialty). The common meeting in the cathedral cloister is replaced by small study groups, each a unified section resolutely gathered around a teacher with whom they choose to study for several years; they are real work communities—living communities as well, for the teacher often boards there—where firm friendships are established, and where the professor feels supported and sustained by his followers who stimulate him, drawing him into the search for new things. These schools are particularly active instruments of intellectual achievement, and yet they function in very primitive material circumstances, conducted as often as possible outside, along streets, under church porches, or in some rented shop in a new house of the *bourg*. There the students squat with their slates, doing exercises in the morning, taking notes on the teacher's reading and commentary, and, in the evening, ending the day with prayer and collective meditation. The increased concentration of students in several privileged centers, the appearance of teacher-specialists whose profession earns them a living, and the differentiation into groups of scholarly work—all these clearly encouraged the enrichment of learning and the improvement of intellectual techniques.

There was, first of all, more intimate contact with classical Latin culture. Without abuse of the word "Renaissance," it is nonetheless clear that a period of intense and ardent reference to ancient Roman models of writing and thought can be located around 1130: that is to say, between the Carolingian Renaissance—which restored in all its purity the Latin of Cicero, Vergil, and St. Jerome, making of it a scholarly language entirely distinct from popular speech—and the Renaissance of the Italian humanists in the fourteenth century, or the French and Rhenish humanists in the sixteenth. There is perfect competency in Latin prose and poetry, handled according to the methods particularly inculcated in the schools along the Loire and around Orléans; this is exemplified in the astonishing adaptation of style to thought existing equally in the *Policraticus* by John of Salisbury (born in England but, like so many other Englishmen, educated at Chartres and Paris) and the abundant flowering of lyric poems, religious poems scanned according to Gregorian sequences, playful love poems composed by erudite prelates living along the Loire (Marbode of Angers, for example, the Abbot of Bourgueil, or the Bishop of Mans) and the laughing or drinking songs of the Goliards. There is a virtuosity of form apparent even in the style of a stubborn opponent of the schools like St. Bernard, a virtuosity often bordering on the precious, as in those overly subtle poetic constructions which the Abbot of Cluny, Peter the Venerable, enjoyed putting together for his own amusement, in the little literary groups he used to organize in the middle of the woods, at some distance from the monastery. This is a century of orators, and of fiery rhymers—indeed, of rhymer-musicians, for this poetic drive is supported constantly by the development of a music about which we know little, but which is perhaps the most important creation of medieval civilization. It is also a century of humanists; to the best of the twelfth-century clerics, the Romans were the masters of thought; Cicero, Suetonius, and Seneca opened these students' perspectives onto a completely new moral universe, and communicated to them a new sense of personal worth and endeavor, a sense of that affective relation called *amicitia*. This imbued even the purest of the Christian mystics in such a way that reminiscences of Ovid's *Art of Love* can be found in *On the Nature of Love*, the work of a Cistercian, Guillaume de Saint-Thierry. The rapid refinement of feeling at the beginning of the twelfth century derives in large measure from the greater familiarity with the classics—whence derives also the new attention paid to the traces of Roman art and its decorative elements, as well as the new plastic sense that liberates the statue from the relief surface that formerly had held it. And the aspiration toward a more incarnate religion, manifested in early Gothic sculpture, is certainly a function of the Church's leaders having been permeated with humanism.

The enrichment, however, is not merely literary. It affects the entire organization of ideas: indeed, the birth of a broad movement, ultimately transforming the structure of the European spirit, can be located in the cultural world of France at the beginning of the twelfth century. Until then, the principal approach to learning was intuitive; in the perceptible world, and in that microcosm that man seemed, each person saw images of God—obscure images, however, whose deeper meaning could be discovered only through the arduous and slow deciphering of many signs. Consequently, in order to attain to higher knowledge, the knowledge of God, it was necessary to interpret symbols, to seek correspondences and apprehend harmonies, for which reason music and the study of numbers were fundamental disciplines. This is the cause, also, of the intense passion, continuing throughout the entire Middle Ages, for analogy and the anagogic commentary of texts. But books were only one indication, among many others, of this attitude; more than study of logic, the most productive practice was still contemplation—silent and ascetic meditation.

But another conception of knowledge began to form in the new scholarly circles: no longer sensing or divining, but understanding by rational deduction—*intelligere,* that is, defining, classifying, observing. In this way the higher modes of understanding gradually were brought to perfection. This transformation is confined at first to the small world of the Schoolmen; but it is destined to expand, during the following generations, to increasingly larger circles. Dialectic—the art of reasoning—figured among the knowledge (or, rather, the intellectual techniques) taught in the first cycle of the liberal arts. This furnished a very limited sort of training, since, at best, it was confined to the passive reading of popularized philosophical manuals, handed down from very late Latinity, which communicated only a very dim reflection of the great systems of Greek thought. Nonetheless, as early as the beginning of the eleventh century, the first forward steps were taken at Chartres where the fruits of simple scholarly exercise were pursued further than in other centers of learning: an example of this is the discussion involving the problem of universals, the reality of general ideas, enumerated in detail in one of these elementary manuals. With respect to this scholarly question, the professional thinkers of northern France soon were divided into two groups: the "nominalists," who denied the reality of concepts and, opposing them, the "realists." This gratuitous mental gymnastic was primarily of value in bringing about a better appreciation of reason, "the honor of mankind," "which is in itself the very image of God," as was proudly explained by Béranger, the *écolâtre* of Tours, the first who dared, shortly before 1050, to apply reasoning to the shadowy areas of Christian dogma. Then followed the first reaction, the first scandals; the first Council meetings, examining the arguments of these reasoners, and the first condemnations. But the movement was launched. In the closing years of the eleventh century, many men in the Church already regarded dialectic as a discipline essential to the education of a cleric, furnishing the surest means of apprehending divine truth. Henceforth, faith can no longer be blind: it must be probed deeply, and illuminated by the intelligence. This is expressed, now with everyone's approbation, by St. Anselm—that Lombard who directed the monastic school of Bec in Normandy, who died in 1109 as Archbishop of Canterbury, and who, because he knew enough not to let his intellectual pursuits deviate from the orthodox, legitimized the recourse to reason in resolving problems of faith.

This promotion of reason into the forefront of the faculties of the soul makes possible the twelfth century's great achievement. Contemporaneous with the formation of the large centers of learning, this conquest was promoted first by the discovery of new texts for study, by the sudden enrichment of intellectual material. Until that time, Western thought was fed solely on the very poor heritage left it by a moribund Rome, a Rome that cared little for logic or rational exactitude; and the professors of

Christian studies, primarily concerned with methods of procedure and with grammar, made little effort to increase this paltry equipment. As a result of the material prosperity, greater ease of movement, and military expansion beginning in 1100, unknown fragments of Greek science and philosophy found their way to the schools along the Loire and Seine—in particular, to the professors at Chartres, through Byzantine and Arab intermediaries coming from Sicily and, even more, from Spain. The Englishman Adelhard of Bath, a product of Chartres, in this way brought back different documents, one by Euclid, from his trips to the East between 1115 and 1140. At Pisa and Palermo, and especially at recaptured Toledo, teams of translators gradually brought Ptolemy, the *Phaedo*, Hippocrates, and Galen to light. And they revealed through their work the fascinating thought of Aristotle: with intense emotion, the Schoolmen discovered the entire *Organon*, the *Logic*, and some fragments from the *Nicomachean Ethics*, in the course of two generations—works that comprise, in a word, the whole method of thought people were looking for, a method of thought supplied alone, reduced to a bare intellectual mechanism, and detached from a *Weltanschauung* which, too greatly opposed to the Christian universe, would have hindered its acceptance.

This was a decisive acquisition. But, to make it truly fruitful, the main centers of study had to improve their working methods between 1100 and 1180. Until then, the basic scholarly exercise had been the "lesson," the reading of an "author"—an "authority." The reading was explicated, but still stayed respectfully close to the text. Now, gradually, magisterial commentary, "glosses," with which professors surrounded Latin poems (at Orléans) or exemplary texts of dialectic (at Chartres and Paris), became more widely used. The teacher drafted these glosses and gave them to his followers to transcribe; they became autonomous texts, original and truly creative work, and were the objects, in turn, of new commentaries. Furthermore, when, in the course of the annotated reading, special difficulties of interpretation emerged, people got into the habit by the beginning of the twelfth century of formulating the problem clearly, of asking what they called the "question"—and it was to solve precisely these well-defined difficulties that the methods of logical reasoning, newly perfected with the aid of Aristotle's treatises, were applied. Such an attitude toward the text—a text which the tenth- or eleventh-century *écolâtre*, paralyzed with respect, would not have dared to question—is a singularly active and productive improvement.

This freedom asserted itself in the reading of even the most respected authorities—the *divina pagina*, Scripture, the Church Fathers—reading which, after 1100, was beginning to become the business of specialized teachers, the object of a new cycle of studies, and the goal and highest triumph of the liberal arts. Out of a primary concern for clarity, Anselm of Laon and Peter Lombard, who directed a school in Paris, worked hard at putting dogma into order by reducing it to "sentences," a succession of simple and clear statements. Actually, the statements were too clear— they accentuated the contradictions, the "questions" that it was important to resolve. Then appeared their too brilliant follower, Abélard; dissatisfied with his teachers and passionately fond of his profession, he later became one of the most winning professors of the Parisian schools which, in part, were initiated by him and which, specializing in dialectic, soon eclipsed those at Chartres. His students urged him to push ahead: "They called for human and philosophic reason, and they required understandable explanations rather than assertions; they said that it is useless to talk if you do not make your remarks intelligible, that only what has been understood can be believed . . ." (here, twenty years after the death of St. Anselm, we can see the progress of the logical spirit, the need and the demand for rational clarity) ". . . and that it is ridiculous to teach others what neither you nor those whom you teach understand. . . ." Abélard was, primarily, a logician. By means of a more subtle argumentation he began by resolving the poorly posed problems of universals, then established the rational method of "theology" (the very word comes into use at this time, designating the new science of sacred texts) in his *Sic et Non, circa* 1135, in which he gathered all of the contradictions of the "sentences." Let us remember that he did this with no spirit of negation; it would be the worst of misunderstandings to place Pierre Abélard on the fringe of the Church for, as he wrote Héloïse in one of the wonderful letters which are—in their sincerity, psychological depth, and evidence of the best humanist education—one of the finest products of the era's ecclesiastical culture: "I do not want to be a follower of Aristotle if that separates me from Christ . . . and, to banish your anxious concern and all the anguish in your heart, know that I have established my conscience on the cornerstone where Christ has built His Church. . . ."

We know that Abélard's condemnation by the Council of 1140 broke his heart. Yet for him, for the Parisian teacher, religion is no longer either a mere collection of efficacious formulas against the hostilities of supernatural power or an outpouring of sentiment. It is the basis of a system of logical thought—that is, of Scholasticism—which is more than the mental attitude of the Schoolmen: it is the first philosophy of the West.

After 1150, this passion for the intelligible, this fervor for the syllogism, rages among the Parisian students, whose numbers increase as their outlooks become more diversified. Like the taste for choral polyphony, for harmony, for vertical and linear architecture, for large monumental sculpture and illuminated manuscripts, it is the privilege of the upper Church reformed in its practices, freed from the thumb of secular powers —yet remaining nicely situated at the crossroads of trade, nicely provided with good land which, now better developed, is very rich. But, because of its reform, its wealth, and in particular because of the amazing cultural progress that it has achieved in a very few years from this wealth, this small group of prelates, canons, Cluniac monks, teachers and their followers—several thousand men, at most, in all of France—were much more separated from the humbler clergy and all the faithful to whom the lofty musical, dialectical, and architectural manifestations of sacred culture, including even the highly erudite symbolic ornamentation of the churches, were inaccessible. Now, among the populace, and in certain areas of the Church itself, the renewal of these things awakens religious aspirations that arc no longer so in keeping with the superficial activity of the Cluniac monasteries and cathedral chapters. Uneasiness and tension grow out of this and, to begin with, a dissatisfaction that is actually heresy. This is another sign and another product, very early manifested, of progress.

These currents of soul-searching run along two very different levels. Certain of them disturb humble social planes, very distant from learned culture: the first people persecuted as heretics were peasants, who lived in Champagne around the year 1000, and some bourgeois who lived in Arras in 1225. These heresies accept only the authority of the Gospel, and manifest themselves simultaneously in attacks against Church directors whose morals are deemed unworthy of their mission and in a need for moral rigor, a feeling that salvation is attained, not by mere ritual gestures, but by asceticism. Consequently, there arises the desire for a religion truly lived through the imitation of Christ. To these aspirations, which seem to be very widespread, but usually arc unformulated and come to light only intermittently, when acts of persecution attempt to repress them, corresponds a parallel tendency at a much higher level—this time in the very heart of the Church. Among the clerics and monks participating in the Gregorian movement, many think that the reform ought not to aim solely at extricating the ecclesiastical functions from the control of the laity, but ought instead to be a true conversion of the entire Church, a complete rupture with temporal power, with the material; a return to the spiritual state of primitive Christianity, to what was then called the "apostolic life"—for, since Carolingian times, the Church has combined unbecomingly with the secular town. This conception, too, is nourished by meditation on the Gospels; it aspires to renunciation, to a liberation of the soul by victory over the flesh, and consequently, it is more and more vigorously opposed to both the liturgical magnificence of Cluniac Christianity and the intellectual and rational Christianity of the *écolâtres*.

Those who share this conception likewise depart from the framework of the established Church. They are recluses, who go and live in the middle of the woods in order to embody to perfection their ideal of rupture with the temporal; or they are wandering preachers who proclaim the

Gospel at crossroads, for preaching is an essential act in the apostolic life. With these sermons, they answer the spiritual aspiration of the humble. The end of the eleventh century is the era when great masses of simple people are unsettled by religious orators. There are crowds led insanely toward Jerusalem by Peter the Hermit—crowds of women, too, like those Robert of Arbrissel assembles and inflames in Anjou where wives and daughters of knights and princes mingle with former concubines of the priests who, won over by the reform, are pledged to celibacy, and with repentant prostitutes, according to the example of Mary Magdalene, whose relics people then begin to venerate, and whose life is told everywhere.

Nonetheless, within the Church, the main result of this desire for religious purification is the establishment of new religious communities. Many of these hermits and leaders of crowds end up by grouping several followers around them and withdrawing from the world. Thus, clerics join together in canonical communities, but subject to a very rigid rule inspired by St. Augustine, group around the former professor, William of Champeaux, at Saint-Victor in Paris, and around Saint-Norbert in Prémontré. Monks follow the example of Étienne de Muret, gathering at Grandmont in the Limousin as early as 1074, each living in an individual hut in contemplation and total poverty, nourished by alms collected for them by servants. And monks are the associates that St. Bruno, former *écolâtre* of Reims, established in 1084 in the mountain retreat of Chartreuse—ascetics and anchorites who break the silence and isolation of their cell only a few hours a week. Each one of those prayer and austerity groups, in turn, forms new cells, and these offshoots constitute new congregations whose spirit is opposed to that of the Benedictine group at Cluny.

So rapid a spread indicates how deep was the need for a new style of religious life; it is also one indication among many of the great population growth between 1075 and 1120. Of all these new associations, Cîteaux had the greatest success. It too was formed by a hermit, Robert de Molesme, who set himself up in 1078 in the heart of the swampy and still uncleared forest in the Saône Valley; it too was born out of an avowed opposition to the Cluniac monasticism. But its foundation was Benedictine, and it was destined to restore the literal purity of the Benedictine rule. Cîteaux owed its fecundity to the personality of St. Bernard, who made his profession there in 1112, along with about thirty knights' sons who were his relatives and friends; his arrival revived that small, worn-out group, enabling it immediately to spread and establish affiliated monasteries. Bernard himself became the abbot of one of them, Clairvaux; he became, in particular, the heart of the congregation. A man of rugged will, he was always taking trips, despite the fact that his health was impaired by asceticism; he was a talented preacher, a stubborn opponent of the teachers of Scholasticism, an organizer of crusades, and a mentor to popes. Bernard truly directed the conscience of all Christianity between 1130 and 1150, and directed it strictly. In the Cistercian rule are balanced all the different tendencies in the current of spiritual renewal and of return to the apostolic life. One tendency is solitude: the Cistercian monasteries are established in the "desert" at a good distance from the villages—although, out of fidelity to St. Benedict, a communal life is led there. And there is poverty, total renunciation: a *livre* of black bread a day, a few unseasoned vegetables, watered wine, a sack of straw to sleep on, a tattered and rent tunic of coarse wool, and a disdain for bodily cleanliness, which was considered superfluous homage rendered to the flesh. And the churches are bare (we know the impulsive criticisms Bernard formulated with respect to Cluniac art, whose luxury and imagery distracted man from his search for God), devoid of all figurative decoration, their windows of plain, grayish glass, their engaging beauty deriving, as at Fontenay and Thoronet, solely from purity of line, harmony of proportion, quality of stone. But, though unadorned, these churches have sound material possessions, guaranteed by carefully preserved charters, which constitute the indispensable support of the communal life.

Another characteristic of this life, perhaps the greatest Cistercian innovation, is the re-establishment of manual labor; in accord with popular evangelism, this rejects both the liturgical sloth of Cluny and the contemplative vacuity of Grandmont. There is also the condemnation of the manorial form of life; "because they did not read, either in the rule or in the life of Saint Benedict, that this master had had altars of churches, oblations or sepulchers, tithes from other men, ovens, mills, villages, peasants—they rejected all these things." [5] Consequently they made a strict rule of developing their land with their own hands. Still, they did not reject entirely the aristocratic idea of the religious profession; indeed, there exist at Cîteaux, as in all the new communities, two categories of brothers—the superior class recruited from the clergy and from knightly families, the other formed of peasants' sons who are assigned to the heavy, material tasks.

"The work in the barns is done by lay brothers and by paid workers. . . ." [6] They cleared much less land than has been supposed; instead, they specialized in raising animals, producing wool, leather, cheese, and meat—all the commodities in more and more urgent demand throughout the expanding towns of the mid-twelfth century. The Cistercian estates very quickly became allied with the trade circuits; situated in the best economic position, having abundantly zealous and unfettered manpower, they soon experienced excessive prosperity. The monks in no way renounced their asceticism, but they were not known to emerge from their retreats except for trading. Soon after St. Bernard's death, criticism was active against the religious men who were too eager to defend their legal rights, too prompt to purchase their plots of land from peasants handicapped after a poor harvest or from impoverished knights—above all, too much isolated from the world and too indifferent to the spiritual needs of the poor.

But all these attempts to adjust monastic life to the spirit of the Gospel were, in fact, evasions. Christianity could not take entirely to the desert. Abandoned by the best men, left to pastors who were either too ignorant or too learned, too rich or too "impure," those who stayed in the world remained dissatisfied. And especially the people who were in areas most open to innovation, already emerging from the passivity of the country-side, in the new *bourgs* and in knightly society—these continued to listen to the wandering preachers, who were still as numerous, con-demned by the hierarchy but avowing their devotion to Christ, and were convinced that they were more "perfect" than the clerics who con-demned them. Because of this, they went on preaching the Gospel, preaching detachment from wealth and reform of morals; they grouped around them small, fervent sects, who were on the fringes of orthodoxy, scattered through all the provinces of France. Around 1140 or 1150, a somewhat different religious attitude crept into this agitation; diffuse at first, it became more firmly established between the Massif Central and the Pyrenees, and there, after 1167, it organized into a real church, rival-ing orthodoxy with its own hierarchy, its own councils. No one knew at first what to call its believers; they came to be called "Cathars"—a Greek name, for the movement was linked, through northern Italy, with the Byzantine Balkans—the "pure." This movement, too, involved aspira-tion toward the purification of the soul. In its most rigorous form (but, in this strictest form, it was undoubtedly accessible to very few, and very rarely formulated with clarity), Catharism was a religion completely alien to Christianity. As dogma, it appears to be a very simple dualism: the universe, and man himself, consist of two principles, the one spiritual and the other material. One must support the side of the Good and help it triumph; therefore, one must break with matter, must be poor, pure, and detached—thus, one attains to perfection and thence to salvation. Otherwise, the soul is reincarnated by means of a series of transmigra-tions, until it arrives at perfect purity, and is liberated. But to the masses this doctrine, cloaked as it was by a vocabulary and aggregate of symbols borrowed from Christianity (the figure of Christ, as well as the Gospels, had its place there), appeared to be plainer Christianity, divested of every obscure rite and professed by men who, in striking contrast to the official clergy, truly practiced the evangelic virtues. Consequently, it had extraordinary success in the southern part of Aquitaine. Already, even before the heretical movement had coalesced, the round of orthodox propaganda directed against it in 1145 by St. Bernard had completely failed. In 1177, the Count of Toulouse issued the alarm: the churches were empty. At Albi, the bishop was alone with his chapter; not a man was spiritually obedient to him. Everyone had found a living and truly apostolic religion, completely outside the Church.

Beyond the Cistercian cloisters, beyond the Albigensian and definitely rebellious Midi, others were eagerly seeking the evangelic way of life, hoping to be able to lead it without breaking with the clergy. This was true particularly in the towns, where the ecclesiastical force was insufficient and where the majority of men, too quickly grown rich, were more sensitive to the problems of poverty and of salvation. Such was the case of the merchant Peter Waldo of Lyon who, deciding to translate the Gospel into his own language, sold all his goods in 1176, distributed his money among the poor, and set about preaching penitence, gathering around him those who were willing to be "poor," in spirit and in fact. He worked unceasingly to remain within the bosom of the Church, but —ultimately intractable because of the persuasion that he was inspired by God—he was condemned and entered into heresy; and his followers, called the "Waldenses," were readily confused with the Cathars. All this unrest—the thousands who, faced with the first exercises of rational theology, seek solitary forests and propose a religion of pure love and moral application; people in business who are attentive to the prescriptions of the Gospel; hermits nourished on alms; the new popularity of the many inspired orators, dressed in sacks, always on the move—all the religious disturbance in this period of great progress is the result of a refinement of religious feeling among the laity. In some localities, the non-clerical world, in its highest levels, actually is beginning to extricate itself from the peasant state of semi-sorcery—for the Cathar followers and the preachers' audiences are knights, or the richest of the bourgeois; those in search of poverty are, needless to say, not the poorest, but those with the most wealth. Gradually these people become aware that the salvation whose images they see on the tympanums of the new churches cannot be attained by rites, but by a form of life. This is a singularly more sophisticated conception, but it is merely one aspect of a total transformation of thought; for, at this point, all the sensibilities, all the intellectual faculties among the élite of the lay "order," are undergoing a process of growth.

► THE APPEARANCE OF A SECULAR CULTURE

At the same time that the increased production and expanded wealth benefit the monasteries and the cathedral clergy, they benefit the knights as well. Their fathers have ample supplies of food: enough to feed their dogs and horses, to maintain a large staff of servants, and to entertain their friends; their essential social superiority lies in this certain abundance of food. But beyond this, from the end of the eleventh century onward, they have money. For, as we have seen, the circulating *deniers* end up in their hands. The peasant spends hardly anything, nor does he save the few pieces earned by selling part of his harvest in town or on the roads; for him, they have no tangible value, and are worth far less than his daily meal; so he barters or gives them to the lord of his land in exchange for the latter's abolishing the *corvées* or the demands for provisions in kind. If any remain, they go to the chatelain, whose *sergents* levy the *taille*, the price of public safety. As for the man of the *bourg*, doubtless he manages to hold on for a little longer to those profits allowed him by his craft or trade; but what he does not offer as charity to the Church goes, in large quantities, to the toll collectors who stop him on the roads, the attendants at fairs, or the lord of the town who sells exemptions at a high price. So that, for the knights, the new economic conditions mean money—scraps, and sometimes a larger ingot, of silver; less often, a pinch of gold, to be stored away in a corner along with festival finery.

Actually, this is not equally true for everyone. The supply of precious metal is much more abundant for those who, having a castle, possess the power to command and to levy *coutumes*, those who ensure peace over a large area of land, and, particularly, those who rule an active town—one with a well-attended fair, and with a good Jewish community that from time to time can be extorted. Nonetheless, this inequality of cash revenue is less important in practice than would be supposed, for the first duty of a lord is to gather around his wealth the greatest possible number of his peers. The more *deniers* he earns—and he does not save them, either, since the virtue of liberality is still exalted in noble spheres, increasing in proportion to the means for spending—the more numerous and brilliant is his court. And in the social framework of this court are located the deepest advances of lay culture in the twelfth century. Courtly outings unite hunters and warriors after the winter's torpor, catching them up in revelry and physical exploits. But these hunters and warriors gradually become habituated to diversions other than those of arms, and women become, for them, more than the girl from whom one takes one's pleasure, or the legal wife who runs one's household.

The first use of the extra *deniers* was, obviously, to improve arms, and the first sign of progress in the knight's world was the perfection of military tools, saddles, and cuirasses. (See pp. 43-44). But the new resources also permitted more frequent trips, excursions away from the castle or village. The purpose of these trips was sometimes religious (the nobles are a definite majority among the pilgrims) but, just as often, it was military. The arrangement of the institutions promoting peace, and the reinforcement of repressive authority appearing after the mid-eleventh century in certain principalities of advanced political evolution, like Normandy, made the carrying out of wars more difficult; and the period of the large tournaments has not yet arrived. For all those superfluous sons—curbed by parental power and, in many cases, remaining unmarried in order not to increase the family community beyond measure—who dream of leaving the confining family solidarity, often seething with unbearable hostilities, this is their means of doing so. A few have already left; they tell how they made their fortunes outside of the realm.

In the eleventh century a good many knights were flung into distant adventure because of the profuse birth rate, the removal of many impediments to traffic, and by the superiority of military techniques which guarantees their success over less well-armed opponents. Particularly spectacular was the expedition in 1066 of William, Duke of Normandy, when, in his conquest of the kingdom of England, he led troops of adventurers who had come from all over, attracted from Flanders to Brittany by the lure of booty and of feats of valor. But we should remember all the Norman knights who, one after the other, uncle attracting nephew, had been leaving for southern Italy since the beginning of the eleventh century. At first they were mercenaries in the service of Greek cities or Lombard lords; then, conquerors and founders of kingdoms, wrenching Sicily away from Islam. And we should recall as well all the knights from Burgundy and Champagne who, habitual travelers on the road to St. James of Compostela, joined with the Christians to hurl back the Infidels from Spain, pushed southward the borders of Castile and built the kingdom of Portugal.

In Sicily and in Spain, their adversary was the adversary of Christ as well, and it was in these successful struggles against the Saracens that there developed the totally new idea of a holy war. It was a combination of pilgrimage and combat, assuring the participants of pleasure in arms and, at the same time, salutary indulgences; martyrs' palms for the dead warriors and, for the others, the fruits of victory. In this manner, the pilgrimage to Jerusalem—though the Arabs' tolerant attitude had not altered—gradually assumed the form of an armed expedition, led by small groups and surrounded by knights. This happens even before the pilgrimage becomes, through papal initiative in 1095, the Crusade—the pious work to which warriors from every French province were to devote their enthusiasm for a century, convinced that, by delivering the Holy Places under the sign of the Cross, they were the instruments of what Guibert de Nogent called God's deed. In this new attention paid to the way of Jesus, we find further evidence of that rediscovery of the Gospel then being accomplished by Christendom. In the thirty years after the great departure of 1097, before the first withdrawals from Islam had aroused the great relief expedition of the Second Crusade, everything indicates that at least half the knights of France departed in little groups for adventures in the Levant or the Pyrenees. These were mere excursions lasting several months or at most a few years—and though many died on the way (were killed in combat, drowned in the wretched ships of the period, or, particularly, were victims of the sharp change of biological milieu) very few left with the intention of remaining in the conquered lands; nonetheless these temporary migrations toward the Spanish confines or the Holy Land exercised a profound influence upon the evolution of knightly civilization.

First of all, these migrations caused an appreciable change in military mores. By diverting the aggressiveness of the warmaking specialists to external matters, against the Infidels, the armed pilgrimages contributed to insuring the peace of God. The Church people were aware of this; at Clermont in Auvergne in 1095, when Pope Urban was launching the Crusade, he sanctioned with his authority the instructions of the peace councils; all disagreements among Christian warriors, united in a common struggle, had to cease. As a matter of fact, the departure of the most turbulent men immediately reduced tensions within families and among rival manors. Furthermore, the conception, clerical in origin, of the *miles Christi*, the knight who devotes his activity to the service of God, agreeing to participate only in just combat against unbelievers and evildoers, spreads within the perspectives of the Crusades. The first signs of the gradual ritualization of chivalry appear simultaneously with the first expeditions of the holy war. The role of the priest extends into the dubbing ceremony; whereas formerly he blessed the sword, now he assumes the moral preparation of the future knight. In this way, certain Christian virtues tend to be incorporated into the military and feudal ethic, which was based on bravery and loyalty. The valiant knight, the man of true wisdom and integrity, the *prud'homme*, rights wrongs and defends the oppressed; extolled as a "new militia" by St. Bernard, the "order" of the knights gradually acquires the characteristics of a religious brotherhood. Soon there exist many indications of this ideal: the monk-soldier confraternities, for example, founded in conquered Jerusalem at the beginning of the twelfth century, for the protection of pilgrims but, more important, for the permanent defense of the Holy Places; houses of these confraternities soon spread throughout all France, fed by the charity of all those who were not able personally to participate in the overseas journey. Dedicated to effective warfare, well-fed, careful of their weapons, exempt from excessive liturgical obligations—yet living in austerity and in a certain humility (they must not recount their feats of valor), renouncing hunting and luxury (no pads or ornaments on military equipment)—the Templars and Hospitalers are the exemplary types for the new generation of knights.

Crossing the Pyrenees, embarking at Genoa, at Venice, and, soon, at Marseille—setting out with a few neighbors, a few cousins, closely grouped under the banner of a local chatelain who has pledged his land to borrow gold and silver—this was the discovery of a new world. The Christian reconquests of Islam (those of Sicily and the Spanish regions much more than that of the Holy Land) were of enormous importance for learned culture, bestowing upon the hitherto inward-turning West the Mozarabic artistic processes, and Byzantine and Islamic book learning. In particular, it revealed—at Saragossa, Constantinople, and Antioch—a much less crude way of living. During their stay in the Mediterranean countries, these rough men were dazzled by the decoration, the scent and flavor of fruits and spices, the glitter of jewels, the gaudy clothes which contrasted joyfully with the grays and dull browns of the woolen or hempen clothes woven for them by servants on their estates. To be sure, people had some notion of these eastern splendors as early as the year 1000; a few had been on pilgrimages; but for almost everyone, this was only a dream, kept alive by the memory of a few amazing objects seen among the Church's "treasure": a collection of relics and ornaments. Once they returned home, the Crusaders brought back much livelier impressions, and often they even brought back customs which became transferred to those who had stayed home. There was a greater aversion to domestic frugality, an active taste for more abundant commodities whose acquisition was facilitated by the revitalized traffic in money. There was, most noticeably, a refinement in dress. Clothing is the essential luxury of this period, the great object of expenditure, and one of the principal centers of interest in the life of society, if one judges by the role that descriptions of finery occupy in twelfth-century chivalric literature. Around 1100, the style changes: men's as well as women's clothing becomes much longer. The tunic reaches to the feet and is covered by a long-sleeved *bliaut* (smock), with a trailing coat "sweeping the dust" like that which Duke Robert of Normandy (d.1106) was apparently in the habit of wearing in Sicily, and with a "surcoat" which later becomes good form to wear over the hauberk. This fullness of dress, in contrast with the very close-fitting apparel of the *vilain*, denotes two things: the tendency toward a less restless, more sequestered life, one less exclusively oriented toward physical efficiency; and greater affluence. This is all the more true since the fabrics are no longer made at home. Silk goods are still quite rare, imported from Asia Minor for the upper aristocracy, but a great range of tinted and patterned cloth, made by specialists, finds an increasingly wider and more demanding clientele within the knightly class. The refined taste of the nobles, and their augmented resources, therefore encouraged the growth of the first industrial centers—producers of quality fabrics in Flanders, Artois, and Picardy—between 1075 and 1180, and also stimulated several skilled professions: by the middle of the twelfth century, the Limoges enamellers did not work for religious establishments alone, but for princes.

At the same time, the knight's mental universe was enriched. To those things which had occupied their thoughts almost exclusively—extremely primitive religious beliefs, fighting and hunting formulas, feudal and family rules of behavior—came to be added other acquisitions. Several echoes of the intellectual training received in the schools could be heard in noble society after the twelfth century. There was no aristocratic family that did not number among its members a canon, a man who had studied, who had perhaps read some book; in any case, he was used to writing, accustomed to a certain precision of reasoning. Yet he remained in close touch with his own family, visited them often, chose among his nephews the one who would succeed him and prepared him for this succession. These intra-family contacts alone meant that the enrichment of the ecclesiastical culture had extensive repercussions in chivalric society. Beyond this, in the warrior milieu, people began to think that a school education was not a burden to the future knight, that there might be some benefit in having their sons educated, even those not intended for the Church; thus, Abélard's father, who had received such instruction in his youth, wanted his sons to profit by it. New attention was paid to intellectual values, and a greater number of young nobles entered monastic or secular establishments of learning as free pupils: at age five, St. Bernard, without being particularly headed for a religious life, had been placed in a canon's school at Châtillon-sur-Seine. This new orientation also brought about an increase in family tutors, sometimes students who interrupted their studies for several years and entered a castle household to earn a little money, or clerics who specialized exclusively in this new profession of educator.

In increasing numbers, men devoted to the service of God receive a school education, then find the opportunity to capitalize on their intellectual abilities and forge a career outside of the Church; and because of this opportunity (among other reasons) scholars flock to the centers of ecclesiastical studies. In the service of a manor lord, they perform all the tasks that involve writing, and make themselves useful in every situation requiring a little reasoning. They are paid to draw up charters, but also, more and more frequently, to provide intellectual entertainments for a castle society which, growing less untutored, is beginning to develop taste. In this gradual permeation of the chivalric mentality by learned ways of thought and expression, the courts of the greatest lords played a major role. These courts were the crossroads of social life, the centers of attraction for the knights of an entire province, the places where a whole group of clerics, well educated in the schools, were permanently maintained. Among these courts, that of the Capetian king still cuts a sorry figure. Most brilliant are the ones in southern France, at Poitiers around the Duke of Aquitaine, at Narbonne, at Nîmes, at Saint-Gilles on the Rhône around the Count of Toulouse; and, north of the Loire, around the Duke of Normandy and the Count of Anjou (Normandy and Anjou soon unite with Aquitaine under the single rule of the Plantagenets); later, in the second half of the twelfth century, around the Count of Champagne and the Count of Flanders.

It was in these permanent gatherings, whose members continually were renewed, that new styles of dress were initiated, and cloth and spice merchants found their best and most regular clientele; here too, people acquired a taste for games of intelligence, like chess (whose governing piece, we note, is feminine), and, at the lord's command, monks or clerics composed Latin chronicles and even works intended to entertain, such as the love poems after Ovid that Baudri of Bourgeuil or Hildebert of Lavardin dedicated to the Norman princesses. Here, too, the poetic works recited before a knightly audience were, for the first time at the end of the eleventh century, deemed worthy of being written down. These works most often were written by professional churchmen, intellectual servants attached to one of the manor houses, or even by wandering scholars, exploiting their talent hither and yon; their interpretation was left to the *jongleurs*, those specialists in recitation, who supplied pleasure which varied greatly in quality. Certain works were created, in the most advanced noble societies of Aquitaine, by the knights themselves, amateurs who found a new pleasure in this interplay of words and music, and found in it, as well, a still newer aspect—a motive for glory and for personal success. They were composed in Romance languages; not, actually, those ordinary tongues that changed from canton to canton, but in semi-artificial, erudite languages common to this milieu that was so pervaded with littérateurs; languages which could be understood, however, by all the knights who formed the itinerant interpreters' audience. This is an important fact, presupposing as it does an effort of transposition, an educating, intellectual gymnastic on the part of the listeners. Thus, a new factor of social differentiation is added: the knight is a man able to understand and speak a language his stableboy cannot share: the dialect of the courts, the dialect of wit.

There are two principal creative centers, two literary languages; hence, because the mental habits of the public differ, two sources of inspiration. Between Normandy, the Loire Valley, and the Ile-de-France, we see the appearance of epic poems, written down for the first time at the very close of the eleventh century, whose forms and themes slowly had been worked out and transmitted orally: the *chansons de geste*. Perhaps the first to be put in writing was that masterpiece composed by a scholar of genius who knew his Vergil and Lucan: the *Chanson de Roland*. It was an immediate, immense success. These poems—long successions of assonanced lines, scanned aloud to a primitive musical accompaniment —are constructed to please specialists in military technique, and those feudal men whose moral life is in large measure organized around vassalic devotion—men who took up the cross, or who dreamed of doing so.

Their heroes spring from the Carolingian era, for this is the period of the first Christian expansion at the expense of Islam (of which all who followed the paths of St. James of Compostela have seen the traces), and the period that gave birth to the feudal aristocracy, to which each princely or chatelain family returns to locate its principal ancestors, the roots of its genealogy. These heroes are divided by desire for personal glory, greed, duties toward relatives, and vassalic obligation. They meet one another in battles whose phases are minutely and tirelessly described. Most of them are, in short, models of an heroic Christianity engaged in holy wars in the service of God; their enemies, the Saracens, are also the enemies of Christ, of the Crusaders, of the pilgrims to Spain; and those jousts, those gallops, those conflicts between sworn word and immoderate impulse are set among the pine, the olive tree, the Alyscamps at Arles, the Pyrenean ports, Orange, and Constantinople.

At the same time, between Poitiers and Limoges, the first written evidence of a literature in *langue d'oc* comes to light. Its tone is quite different: there are short songs whose secular texts are set to more complex melodies, derived from those liturgical, intoned psalms of whose creation Saint-Martial, Limoges, was one of the most prolific centers. Their dominant theme is love, and their first known author is one of the greatest lords—William IX, Duke of Aquitaine. Their distinctiveness results from the special stamp assumed by chivalric civilization south of the Loire. The feudal and vassalic institutions there do not mold the main framework of the noble society, which itself is less occupied with military activity; rather, in this region where the traditions of urban life were not so sharply interrupted during the early Middle Ages, society is more civil, accustomed to human confrontations other than court sittings or the formation of combat groups. The area south of the Loire is in closer touch with southern countries, with Mozarabic and Moslem Spain, from which may have come the inspiration for their secular songs. Scholarly life is much less developed; the clerics, educated by a culture both Latin and Christian, are less numerous, and religion is more deeply imbued with the Cluniac spirit and strongly oriented toward music and ornament. And, finally, it is unquestionably this region which first experienced that all-important social transformation: the promotion of women in the chivalric world.

Until that time, the noble woman, sharing the mores of the warriors —a hunting enthusiast, appreciated for her physical abilities and bodily strength, often beating her maidservants to death—was relegated to a very inferior position. Being unable to bear arms, she was considered as a minor and excluded from the feudal setting; completely dependent during her youth upon her father, she then passed into her husband's dependence through an arrangement concluded over her head by the males of the two families: when she was widowed, the dependence was transferred to her sons or to the lord of the fief who imposed a husband of his own choice upon her. From a spiritual point of view, her position was no better, since most Churchmen saw in women the source of evil and the seed of weakness. She could not have her own religious life; again, a man—her husband or father—had the responsibility for it before God. All this changed in the closing years of the eleventh century. In religion, attention decidedly shifted to feminine figures, those of saints like Mary Magdalene, for whose relics people were just beginning to compete, and, above all, of the Virgin, increasingly present as the indispensable intermediary, always present alongside of Jesus. Even piety ceased to be a purely masculine attitude. Many of the wandering preachers addressed themselves to women; convents were founded for them. The most famous of these is Fontevrault, the head of the order, where all the noblewomen at the beginning of the twelfth century dreamed of ending their days, located exactly between Angers and Poitiers in the region where scholars are copying Latin love poetry and where the earliest secular love poems originated. At the same time, the rights of women were asserted. Repudiation, an habitual act for the eleventh-century husband who had tired of his wife (he needed merely to compensate the family, or to find a man willing to pick up the forsaken woman), passed into the control of ecclesiastical courts; wisely, the Church (unless the lord was too formidable) defended these women abandoned in spite of themselves. Gradually, people granted that a woman was able to administer a manor during her husband's absence; increased traveling and the long separations of the Crusades established this new custom. Soon, she could do homage for a fief. To be sure, the warriors' wives were always treated roughly, chastised like servants; in the indiscriminate mingling of the hall they rubbed elbows with their husbands' concubines and bastard sons. Yet their place in chivalric life was less restricted. Respect for the woman (the noble woman, of course; the attitude toward the *vilaine* was entirely different) became one of the imperatives of the gallant knight's ethos. And, in particular, between battles and forays, in the courts—in those rooms of narrower dimension, those alcoves for conversation that began to be arranged off the large hall in the most modern castles, and used for intimate meetings—contact with women took its place among the amenities of the noble life. In the most advanced circles at the end of the eleventh century, there are knights who seek to please them. As early as the *Chanson de Roland*, it is said (in lines 957-958) in passing of the Saracen Margaris of Seville:

> the ladies fell in love with his beauty
> not one of them seeing him, can but beam.

But this concern for the opinion of women is simultaneously made much more lively by the fashionable society of Poitou, of the Limousin, and of Languedoc.

There, between 1100 and 1140, a new conception of the relations between men and women was formulated. This already emerges on several occasions in William of Aquitaine's work, throughout which he is particularly given to the celebration—for the coarse laughter of an essentially masculine audience—of physical pleasure. This conception was taken up and refined by the troubadours, to become what is called courtly love. Doubtless it owes something to the *amicitia* which the humanists discovered in Cicero, and owes more, perhaps, to the love dialectic of Arab Andalusia; in certain respects, too, it is a transposition of religious piety and vassalic devotion—its use of a whole vocabulary of service, homage, and valor, borrowed from feudal terminology, is very significant. Yet it is still an original conception. This love is located outside of Christian marriage (the chosen woman is generally the wife of another); it is definitely not a bodiless love but retains, contrary to popular belief, physical union as its precise aim. But—and here is the change, the sign of a refinement of sensibility—it adapts itself to the interval between physical desire and its satisfaction, and strives to fill it with pleasures of sentiment.

The increasingly frequent exchanges across the Loire, the expansion of travel, effected a transplantation of all the ideas that Provençal lyrics had been expressing for several years to the chivalric courts of northern France toward the middle of the twelfth century. This transfer was hastened by fortuitous political circumstances: in 1137, Louis VII had married Eleanor, daughter and heiress of the Duke of Aquitaine; for fifteen years the queen and her entourage tried to introduce into the Ile-de-France something of the spirit of the court at Poitiers. But the fashionable southern customs were too far removed from the Capetian austerity, and Eleanor's divorce itself is proof of the distance that still separated the pattern of life and thought of the *langue d'oïl* regions from those around Poitiers. On the other hand, the union of Aquitaine, Anjou, and Normandy under Henry Plantagenet and his sons, and the personal influence exercised by Eleanor's daughters (one married the Count of Blois, the other the Count of Champagne) were much more effective. To be sure, the popularity of the epic did not diminish north of the Loire; purely military poems continued to flourish, organizing themselves (like the Westerns of today's cinema) in cycles around popular characters. But the vector of good taste in the most-frequented fashionable gatherings was directed elsewhere. While the humanists rediscovered Ovid, the professional littérateurs worked hard at treatises on love and courtly good manners; treatises prepared the way for the principal book of the new style, which influenced generations of writers—the treatise (in Latin) *The Art of Courtly Love*. Andreas, Marie de Champagne's chaplain, dedicated it to that great woman in 1184; in it, according to the Scholastic method, he gave form—not without some pedantry—to the doctrine of courtly love.

At the same time a new literary genre was rapidly developing: the romance. Differing from the *chansons de geste* in its form—it is a poetry freed from song, with shorter lines rhymed in couplets—the romance was intended to be read aloud, but in a much more intimate circle (which proves the development, in upper secular society, not only of the practice of reading but also of the faculty for attention). It differed primarily, though, in spirit: it was escape literature, outside of the real or the rational—a succession of marvelous amorous or martial adventures, linked by the method of a voyage in the dream world or a "quest." These narratives were at first constructed upon skeletons borrowed from ancient literature, an indication of how immense was the influence of clerics and scholars on the moulding of secular culture. In the *Roman de Thèbes*, rhymed about 1150, then in the story of Aeneas, then in the *Roman de Troie*, we can see the new genre gradually disengaging itself from the epic, abandoning the great theme of the confrontation of Christian and pagan warriors, developing scenes describing life at court, and analyzing increasingly subtle love plots. There appeared in 1170 the "matter of Brittany," all the make-believe elements and all the symbols of Celtic fable, introduced into Normandy and Aquitaine from Cornwall and Wales, transplanted and amplified by the Plantagenet entourage —who, to augment their prestige, doubtless wanted to set this new poetic universe against the "matter of France," that is, against the songs of Carolingian inspiration exalting "sweet France," St. Denis, and hence the power of their rival Capetians. Legends of Tristan, of the Grail, of the exemplar of courtesy, King Arthur, and his Knights of the Round Table—all these were embellished by Marie de France, the first woman whose writings were preserved; by Gautier d'Arras, son of a chatelain and the first of the northern-French noble poets; and finally, the greatest of all, Chrétien de Troyes, a cleric steeped in classical culture, and servant to the Counts of Champagne and of Flanders. His last work, *Perceval*, written between 1174 and 1180, delineates a new change of direction in the romance, this time toward a sense of mysticism: there is a sublimation of courtly love, a glorification of chastity and purity, those virtues of a new, overtly religious, "chivalry."

Such is the course pursued by the mental habits of the manor lords, in their development during this century of great progress. It is plain that only the best of the literary men, and only a few men of fashion, in the most educated chivalric circles of Normandy, Champagne, or Poitou, truly participated in this rapid refinement of sensibility, this annexation of new values that relegated the primitive militarism to the periphery of consciousness. For the great mass of knights, when they were aware of it at all, courtly love was then but a poorly understood attitude. These men were still, and would be for a long time to come, hardened old soldiers, uneducated and incapable of suppressing their appetites, having only elementary religious reflexes—in the least civilized provinces, they were sometimes formidably savage pillagers, dressed in foxskins; murderers of monks, robbers of merchants, abductors of women. In this vast country, where the means of communication were still so primitive, the chronological lag in the development of manners and sensibilities within the same social group was enormous. But for most of the members of the warrior class, at least, this was a period of decisive change.

Ultimately, the history of literature—like that of sacred art, thought, or education—brings out another tendency, of which one more indication is the development around 1150 of a new literary language, based on the dialect of the Ile-de-France, which very quickly won out over the others. This is a gradual concentration toward the France of the Seine, the region where the fruits of these diverse and widespread experiments were still being assimilated in 1100. Thus, at Chartres, in the commercial towns of Champagne, and in Paris, toward the middle of the twelfth century, a synthesis is being prepared, and at the same time a political regrouping begins to take shape around the royal province.

IV

The Capetian Synthesis

1180-1270

WITHIN the French Middle Ages, the thirteenth century is the period of great and general prosperity—primarily, of course, a rural prosperity, for this land is still fundamentaly agricultural, and its people still very close to the soil that nurtures them. Although agricultural techniques are no longer being perfected, all the possibilities are being drawn from former improvements, and although the distribution of still-virgin lands is in the process of slowing down (except in the southwest), production continues to increase and the villages are rich. The three-field system is more widely diffused, and the breeds of domestic animals are improved. Particularly, there is a continuation of the population growth, the most active factor in the forward movement: at the end of the thirteenth century, the population of rural France is denser than it ever has been, denser than it ever will be again before the great eighteenth-century spurt. But storerooms and storehouses are full, and the memory of famine has been erased.

But what is new, from 1180 on, is the uninterrupted progress of transportation and commerce. The towns are flourishing. Indeed, in those urban centers revived during the preceding generations, this is the period of great development in trade and of prosperity among merchants. Despite the fact that, on the whole, French civilization remains profoundly imbued with rural nature and oriented toward the peasant, it begins, in several of its most advanced manifestations, to assume certain new characteristics, which come from the towns.

▶ **URBAN PROSPERITY**

From the mid-twelfth century on, France benefits fully from the strides of European commerce, whose way was paved a hundred years earlier by the offensives against Islam—the opening of the Strait of Messina through the reconquest of Sicily; the development of naval activity in the Italian maritime towns; the construction of large fleets, intended to transport the Crusaders to the Holy Land, but also receivers of cargoes of goods. This commerce was next promoted by the gradual integration of the northern countries into the trading economy. By degrees, England emerged from a state of rustic savagery, and the banks of the Baltic were colonized by German peasants and merchants. Thus France—the France of Burgundy, of Champagne, of Paris, and especially of Artois— has become the central crossroads of an immense commercial network which interacts at Bruges (center of trade with the Nordic regions), at Genoa, Pisa, Venice, and the cities of the Po Valley, all of which are way-stations in the trade of eastern commodities. The outposts of this network are connecting links with other merchant worlds—Novgorod, Alexandria, the cities of the caravan traffic in Syria and at the base of the Black Sea.

There would be no way to account for the commercial prosperity, were it not for the constantly increasing demand for luxury products— those objects not made domestically whose use has now become habitual. Numerous new needs are established in social milieus whose boundaries, through the affluence originating in the more productive rural areas, are constantly being pushed back. In houses—no longer, except for the most miserable, dens made out of branches—there are now fireplaces; discomfort begins to diminish. People become better accustomed to arming themselves against the night, using lights hitherto reserved exclusively for the sanctuary—and this victory over darkness, combined with a new notion of time developed by the musicians, necessarily leads to the replacement of the old system, in which the hours' length varied according to the season, by a time in which hours are of fixed duration independent of the seasonal change in nightfall. The first furnishings appear: chests with iron-reinforced hinges and locks; tapestries for blocking out drafts as much as for decoration; bedding whose items are carefully enumerated in wills. During the thirteenth century, pans and metal vessels are added—even in certain of the more affluent peasant households—to the old wooden and terra-cotta utensils. Certain refinements in food preparation come to ameliorate the simple gluttony of the previous age: at the chatelains' tables—but also at certain knightly houses and in the towns, at the banquets held on fixed dates which assemble the members of the countless guilds, brotherhoods, and associations of all kinds—people drink more and more wine even in regions where grapes grow badly, and become more particular about quality. The consumption of meat—or, during the long periods of fasting, fish—increases, as does that of spices. These latter are simultaneously cures and condiments, with multiple uses during this period when wine, for example, is scarcely ever drunk unless it is augmented with exotic flavors. But clothing is still the principal luxury. "You ought to dress well," said Louis IX in the presence of Joinville, "because your wives will love you better for it, and your dependents think more highly of you." It is by distributing fine woolen cloth that, in the spring, the king and aristocracy reward their household officers and their servants. "Bright scarlets, deep scarlets, madder violets, sea-green, brownish black"—all fabrics are, for the rich, of bright colors; for this is a glittering and parti-colored century, and the crowds at large festivals, royal coronations, and occasions of state have the vividness, the variety of hue, of stained-glass windows. Tunics and outer coats are cut from these heavy woolens, often lined with furs; and the ladies, "most tightly laced," begin to wear clothes different from those of the men—smocks ("a woman is comelier and daintier in a smock than in a tunic"), and at the end of the century, bold-colored coats and surcoats. Most important, wardrobes become larger. Normally, a knight's wife has three outfits: one for great occasions, another for Sundays, and a third for everyday wear. A 1279 statute, under the reign of Philip the Bold, limited the number of gowns a man could purchase each year; five fur-lined gowns for the aristocrats, from two to four for gentlemen; a bourgeois whose capital was a thousand *livres* could buy one for himself, and two for his wife.

To satisfy these increasingly numerous and exacting buyers, the large production centers develop. The means of transportation are improved —not the roads, maintained by no one but the users, but the equipment: on this route or that, one finds teams of specialized carriers, who possess beasts of burden or river boats. Way-stations are set up, shipping techniques improve. All this encourages concentration and specialization. In the river regions, on the Seine and lower Loire, around La Rochelle and Bordeaux, wine production is clearly oriented toward exportation. Some centers of craft manufacture appear, two of which, by the end of the century, far surpass all the others: Paris for her skilled professions, and Artois and Flanders for their beautiful fabrics. The production of the heaviest and best woolens, dyed in the most popular colors, is gradually concentrated around Arras, Douai, Ypres, and then Ghent. Despite this concentration in a few towns, the preparation of the fabric is broken up there into a large number of small family workshops, whose owners—

weavers, fullers, dyers, shearers—each fulfill only one of the multiple phases of the work. The equipment is primitive, and technical innovations are generally forbidden by the urban authorities. But the large assemblies of manufacturers, whose entire effort tends, under close control of the merchants, toward the improvement of quality, gives rise to an active commercial movement: a flow of raw materials; more and more wool coming from England; alum imported from Asia Minor; dyestuffs, most of which are drawn from neighboring countrysides (such as madder and, especially, woad or pastel, source of all the gradations of blue and green, of which Amiens merchants were the most important retailers) but some of which, like indigo, are brought by Italian traders from the farthest Orient.

The constant progress of commerce entails an improvement in currency. The great merchants preferred, to the black irregular money with its ever-changing value, circulated near every old market by the lesser lords (but circulating no farther than the neighboring districts), the pieces of standard quality and weight which were struck in a few of the better managed workshops. The thirteenth century is extricating itself gradually from the monetary diversity that had settled in during the time when trade was so greatly constricted. People become used to figuring the amounts by reference to the more broadly regional currency like that minted at Vienne (the *viennois*), in the Saône and Rhône Valleys, and—rapidly gaining over all the provinces of the realm—the king's currency, minted at Tours (the *tournois*) and at Paris (the *parisis*). Imitating those coins introduced by Italian merchants, there are struck in 1266 some pieces of money of higher value—the *gros*, worth twelve of the former *deniers*. Finally, gold currency, abandoned since Merovingian times with the disappearance of the last traces of antiquity's commercial activity, is revived and issued by Louis IX, at the same time that Italian gold pieces are circulating increasingly throughout the kingdom. And the slow rise in agricultural prices, a fortunate stimulus to production, continues during the entire century, accompanying this constant acceleration of monetary circulation.

But, since this circulation does not answer all needs, the use of credit becomes more widespread. For the most part, this is consumer credit, practiced in very primitive forms and ordinarily backed by land, which is the only true wealth. This credit takes the form of money lent at a high interest rate, longer-range loans pledged with urban or rural resources, purchases or sales of *rentes* in perpetuity, based on fields, houses, and various forms of revenue. The creditors are Jews, merchants, small-town clerics; but in the most active urban centers, professional financiers gradually are established: strangers, men from the south called first "Cahorsains" and then (the word has stuck) "Lombards"—for, in actual fact, most of them come from beyond the Alps. Hated by their debtors (who feel they are being unjustly squeezed dry) and, in fact, by everyone, since they are known to be rich and to live apart in groups defensively ranged along the same street, these aliens are in need of the lord's protection, and the latter makes them pay very dearly for it. After the middle of the century, we can see credit movements at the princely courts and in the large business centers. These involve much larger sums. Sometimes the lenders are local financiers, as is the case in Arras, but more often they are representatives of Italian companies, coming from Siena, Lucca, or Piacenza. But even in the most advanced (and very limited) sectors of financial activity, the methods for handling funds are uncommonly primitive; accounting methods, too, are insufficient to permit transfer from one account to another, and the bill of exchange is unknown. In order to move cash from one place to another, yet avoid the transfer of specie, the most efficient means is still the use of Templar houses, scattered everywhere and organized to collect the Crusade subsidies and forward them to the Holy Land; the king makes use of them, and so do many others, so that the popular distrust of moneyed men is attached to the Templars as well. The only noteworthy progress in handling the circulation of wealth occurs in the improvement of an institution linked to the most elementary forms of itinerant commerce: the fair. Here again we find a concentration has taken place, in the form of the organization of cycles of fairs, occurring successively during the summer months in the same region, and constituting a sort of permanent meeting place for every merchant. Such are the fairs founded by the counts of Flanders at Ypres, Lille, Metz, Bruges, and Thourout, which contribute a great deal to the polarization of the quality woolen industry in that region; and in particular, such are the fairs in Champagne.

Ancient in origin, but revived in the twelfth century by counts able to attract foreign traders by means of meaningful guarantees, these large gatherings are the chief commercial crossroads in thirteenth-century Western Europe. They are divided into six stages, spaced out from spring through the beginning of winter; because of them, an immense concentration of tents and temporary shelters appears for several weeks in the vicinity of four small, important towns: Troyes, Provins, Lagny, and Bar-sur-Aube. There, all the merchants from the length of the basin around Paris, from Flanders, from the Rhineland, meet their Italian counterparts. (In 1278 at Lagny, twenty-three *consuls* represented businessmen from Genoa, Venice, Piacenza, Milan, Bologna, Lucca, Asti, Siena, Florence, and Rome.) Each fair is enacted according to a definite rhythm: eight days of "entry," during which the merchants set up their booths, unpack their goods, visit one another, and establish their prices; next comes the period of sales—first woolens, then "cordovans," that is, all leather goods, then those items whose value is determined by weighing them on scales, generally called items "of weight" (*avoir du poids*):

"spices" and the dyeing or perfuming materials from the Levant and Italy. After this period, whose length varies from fair to fair, the transactions terminate, and the money-changers "lower their tables"; there begins the period of "issues," when accounts are closed, and settlements in kind effected, while merchandise is stowed away and transport caravans formed.

Thus the fairs in Champagne fulfilled a double function. The first is commercial: until about 1260, before the Italians started going into the Netherlands to negotiate their business directly, they established the principal juncture between the two main currents of European commerce—the transalpine importers of "spices" and the brokers who disposed of woolens from Artois and Flanders. The following statistic will give some idea of these transactions: in 1280, at the fairs in Provins alone, 55,000 pieces of woolen cloth were traded, half of which were of Flemish origin. The second function of the fairs is financial—and this function, continuing as it did beyond 1300, is even more important and durable. Since the greatest commercial matters of the Western world were negotiated here, the Champagne fairs happened to be designated as the place where debts were to fall due; particularly, since the settlement of all operations was postponed until the "issues" of each gathering, a vast system of paying off debts was established among the merchants during the entire fair. This system enabled them to buy and sell for much higher stakes than the value of the money actually in circulation; in this way the fairs corrected the dearth of precious metals from which the European economy suffered. At any rate, the fairs appeared in the middle of French prosperity, and their geographic position clearly indicates the economic preponderance of northern France over the Midi, which—in spite of the activity of Marseille adventurers, the establishing of Aigues-Mortes, the fairs at Pézenas, the gradual revival of Lyon as a commercial center, and the much more active strides of Toulouse and Bordeaux—remains more somnolent. These fairs are the center of this prosperity; or they seem so if one regards them as including their natural extensions: the very large city of Paris, for example, is a permanent fair—an uninterrupted market connected with the gatherings in Champagne by close bonds and a complete network of riverways—its economic role is already making inroads into that of the fairs, and continues to expand.

Throughout the twelfth century, the towns continue to grow; during the reign of Louis IX, they contain a much greater proportion of the population. Certainly Paris, with its population of at least eighty thousand, perhaps even a hundred fifty thousand, is a giant, not only in France but in the entire Christian world as well. Yet even local crossroads like Toulouse, or industrial centers like Arras, bring together thirty or forty thousand people, and each of the small straggling villages that surround the bishoprics and large monasteries has several thousand. Furthermore, urban society no longer is a mere excrescence of the rural areas, imperfectly liberated from them; it has assumed a personality. Of course, the built-up areas of the bourgeois are still totally steeped in peasant activities, containing much undeveloped land, gardens, even fields and pastures; the streets are as muddy, as littered with cattle, poultry, and manure, as those of the village, and the dates of harvests and vintaging are very important on the urban calendar. All the townspeople cultivate property outside the city walls—vineyard plots especially, since every medieval town is wreathed by vinestocks. Nevertheless, there is one fundamental difference: the town is now strictly enclosed, surrounded by a wall whose guarded gates are closed at nightfall. Therefore, it is clearly distinct from the countryside—the "flat-country"— which is open and vulnerable. The town, then, becomes a private world, a world whose houses, tending to grow taller and more solid, follow a different arrangement, and whose people dress and eat in a different fashion—a world whose days proceed according to another rhythm.

While urban population has increased due to the constant immigration from the country and to the diversification of economic functions, the social structure has lost its uniformity. Following the example of the merchants, who had banded together ever since the beginning of the commercial revival to form seasonal caravans, these retailers and craftsmen who specialize in manufacture or distribution of the same product have formed their own communities—the guilds. These associations are predominantly religious, united around a patron saint to pray for their dead members and give charity to those living in need of it. Closed groups, monopolizing a given activity, they are governed by regulations enacted and administered by the town authority, which takes care to avoid competition and to protect the consumers by fixed prices and quality control. Not counting servants, troublemakers, beggars, and vagrants, all of whom are closely surveyed and subject to a special set of rules, every man in the town—all those who exercise their franchises and who bear the title of bourgeois—thus can be included in these professional associations.

Enrollment in a guild, then, would be an equalizing social factor. There are no large enterprises but, rather, small workshops combined with showrooms, grouped according to profession along the same street. For the most part, these are wide open to the light of the day, for people would not know how to work by candlelight; the work is done in full view of everyone, with inadequate tools. The master and his one or two journeymen, an apprentice or two (more often than not his sons) live together with the young children and servants, eat out of the same pot, in an atmosphere quite similar to that of the rural family group. For the urban working group is a family represented by its leader within the guild, but satisfying individually the needs of each of its members; within it, antagonisms of economic origin are unknown. Still, there exist "big" or "little" guilds, a hierarchy among professional activities that particularly manifests itself, whenever there are large collective ceremonies, in orders of precedence in the processions. People do not get rich as quickly in one profession as in another, and the standard of living varies. These differences appear much more distinctly in those towns that respond to the most active commercial currents, and those that produce objects for export to distant lands. Thus at Arras, Douai, and Lille, the woolen workers are organized into guilds like everyone else; but the foremen of the small workshops are entirely dependent upon the large contractors who supply them with raw materials, undertake to dispose of their products, often give them credit, and sometimes own their equipment—and who patronize and defraud them. These foremen are actually wage-earners; since their activity is part of a vast trade cycle, they are at the mercy of the slightest obstacle to commercial trade, and are open to unemployment, in other words, to poverty. Because of this, they are harder on their assistants, some of whom are hired by the week and live in even greater insecurity. All this produces a tense atmosphere, a distinct conflict between an aggressive proletariat and a commercial aristocracy; there are struggles among guilds to obtain autonomous administration of their own interests. And there are strikes, the first of which appear at Douai, in 1245. Actually, these areas are exceptional. But outside of these advanced sectors, in every thirteenth-century town, several rich families, clearly distinguishable from the "ordinary" people, begin to put down roots.

They are distinguishable by the nature of their wealth; these well-to-do bourgeois are, as they say in Lyon, *terriers*; a large part of their wealth is invested in land. They live in the towns, in extremely beautiful, well-furnished *hôtels**built, like castles and churches, of stone. They own many houses, merchant stalls, and shops, which they rent out. In the country, they are manor lords, and the best part of their fortune consists of fertile lands, worked by tenants who supply their household with food, hence they themselves never lift a finger. These rich men keep an eye on the shop of the small merchant, the dealer in spices or cloth, the money-changer from whom their father earned his money. But these are men of leisure, and they monopolize the municipal offices. In turn they are *échevins* in the north and *consuls* in the south. It is they who make the rules governing both commerce and the town working classes,

---

* In an urban context, *hôtel* refers to a town-house or mansion; in subsequent centuries, possessing an *hôtel* becomes increasingly a sign of social superiority. In an administrative context (*see* p. 128), *hôtel* first refers to an urban location where Louis IX and his successors concentrated their bureaucracy. Hence, *hôtel de ville* today means the city, or town, hall.—Trans.

but they make them in their own best interests: because they sell wine and wheat, they keep these prices high, while keeping down the prices of those commodities they must buy for resale elsewhere. They make the finances of the urban community their personal concern, falsify tax bases to their advantage, and lend public funds at interest. They are a well-established oligarchy, remaining open to newcomers as long as business goes well, and hardly even threatened by the first signs of lower-class unrest at the close of the century. They form a new, fundamentally practical, cultural élite, one acquired by management of a commercial enterprise, hewn realism and from direct worldly and material experience; yet they do sometimes surrender to intellectual and artistic pleasures. Indeed, the richest of the bourgeois devoted a portion of their wealth to the decoration of their churches. The guilds paid for some of the stained-glass windows in the new sanctuaries; the entire decorative profusion of the cathedral at Amiens was supplied by the woad producers' prosperity, and, in the smaller towns, the rich constantly financed the creations of sacred art. Thus, a Mâcon bourgeois, and not one of the richest, who died sometime before 1250, offered to the mother church of the city holy vessels of gold and silver, paid with his own *deniers* for the addition of an ogival transept at the entrance to the choir on an old Romanesque arch, and finally established a private chapel for his family. Becoming habituated to wealth and feeling the lure of the noble life, the bourgeois élite adopts certain customs and tastes heretofore peculiar to knights, and so creates a new clientele for the artists as well as a new audience for writers. At the beginning of the thirteenth century, Arras, a large town of cloth merchants and financiers, thus became a very great literary center, harboring more than one hundred eighty poets—professional or amateur—who throughout the century gathered around an old, half religious, half-literary association known as the Puy, which became a sort of academy. There they used every genre, and tried every poetic form.

Yet the results of the commercial development make themselves felt beyond the walls of the towns, extending to the end of the cart paths which lead to the new villages, and to the isolated huts on the borders of the newly cleared land. Indeed, agricultural products sell better and better, in greater quantities and at higher prices; they are provisions for the overpopulated towns, where people are now too much occupied with their private work to feed themselves exclusively from the cultivated plots, large and small, maintained by the bourgeois. Agriculture furnishes, as well, commodities that are the object of a much wider trade: flocks of cattle from Normandy or the Morvan make their way to Parisian butcher-shops; dyeing materials are exported to England; wine is drunk as far away as the base of the Baltic. We do not know how, and by what means, the farmer enters into the stream of commerce, yet more and more signs indicate clearly the attention he is now paying to trade. In the charters of the freedoms granted here and there to village communities, the peasants force the lord to acknowledge their rights to control weights and measures themselves, and compel him to create a weekly market and seasonal fairs.

Not everyone is so skillful or fortunate in managing lands or dealing with buyers; the trading economy, as it penetrates deeper into the peasantry, emphasizes social inequalities. The opposition is still between the husbandman and the day laborer. Yet, among the day laborers, there are some for whom poverty is more immediate; who, to confront a given calamity, must borrow, and sell *rentes* on their land, the interest on which is henceforth to be paid off in *deniers*. This becomes an oppressive burden on the family, depriving it of any hope of recovery, driving it to obtain new loans, to accept, in exchange for help, a tighter subjection of family property (which, instead of remaining allodial, becomes a holding), or even a personal subjection. In certain provinces, a new serfdom is restored in this way, at the lowest level of the hierarchy of wealth —a serfdom of the glebe and of the poor into which one falls through poverty, although one buys oneself out again as soon as one is rich enough. This form of servitude is to last, in some areas, until the Revolution. On the other hand, among the husbandmen, there are some who work their way up. There are fortunate family alliances, a keener eagerness for work, greater craftiness in concealing one's cache of *deniers* from the lord's agents who are responsible for levying the *taille*. The usual path for the enrichment of the country person, however, is in the fulfillment of a minor office on the manor. In the village, the big men are primarily the provost, the forester, and all the lord's agents, who in this office are able to avoid taxes and keep as their own remuneration a portion of the taxes they collect. They keep, too, the profits from the justice they render in the name of their lords. It is they who are, in short, the real owners of the *manants*, exploiting them as they please, and accepting or requiring gifts. Furthermore, they are often instructed by their lords to sell off the surplus rents in the form of grain and wine accumulating in the tithe-collectors' barns and get them into the markets. They lease out the better portion of the lords' old manor on profitable terms; they divert whatever still remains of the village *corvées* to their own advantage; they are the first to benefit from the new commercial channels. These newly-rich peasants live like idle lords: tenants work their land; they have acquired the cash income levied on the patrimony of the poorest. They gladly marry the dowerless daughter of a knight and push some of their sons into study, preparing them for fine, ecclesiastical careers. With their savings, they purchase noble land. Some become judges, some become lords of fiefs who settle down in the manor houses of now ruined *hobereaux*. The theme of the newly-rich *vilain* who, stinking and boorish, nonetheless occupies the place of a gentleman, is current in thirteenth-century chivalric literature, indicating the indignation of the well-born at the rise—through money—of the vulgarian.

For the effect of money is a challenge to the knight's superiority and even to the whole idea of nobility. Money upsets the distribution of landed wealth, whose stability, not long before, gave the various social categories the appearance of immutable castes; money makes of the spice merchant or the no-account peasant the lord's creditor, his son-in-law, and, sometimes, his successor. Indeed, for most of the nobles, the new times are a period of constraint and financial difficulty. Accustomed from childhood to disdain profit, very rarely are the lords mindful of increasing the yield of their inheritances. Thus, in France the lord who is attentive to agricultural improvements, who is careful about fencing in his territory to withdraw it from the common land, about improving his livestock and planting new vines, is not (as is the case in England) the knight, but rather the fat bourgeois on the newly acquired manor which he will exploit like a business. No treatises on good management exist among the books intended for a noble public. The nobles do not know, or want to know, how to utilize favorable conditions. Desiring above all else to obtain a stable revenue and to free themselves from all supervisory concerns, and not even dreaming of the profits they could derive by selling their wheat, wine, or woad themselves, they farm out to bailiffs those fields cultivated by their great-grandfathers' servants. Furthermore, they relieve their tenants of providing marketable commodities in exchange for their paying fees in *deniers*.

These fees are fixed; they drop in value as a result of the continued rise in prices. Hence, while the noble's revenues become reduced, his need for money continues to increase. Everything, now, requires money: marrying off one's daughter, since the custom of the cash dowry began to gain acceptance; buying one's salvation, for now, at one's death, endowments (in good *deniers*), masses, one's saint's day, and offerings of income based on the inheritance which saddles the heirs' budget forever, a burden whose weight increases generation by generation—all these are substituted for the former alms of land donations. Much more money is necessary than before to maintain one's position—for, at the same time that finery and dress become more expensive, there is continual improvement in military equipment. In backward regions, primitive arms are discarded and no one can get along without a hauberk—which by the early thirteenth century has become, in the most advanced areas, a delicately worked garment extended by gloves and hose of mail, and very expensive. As for the helmet, it is now a closed box, fashioned much more complexly to surround the entire head; this element produces, in consequence, not only the abandonment of the beard and adoption of a much shorter haircut, but—since one's enemy is not recognizable by his looks—the necessity of indicating one's identity by distinctive marks and painted symbols: whence the origin of the coat of arms, and all the heraldic techniques that form a major ingredient of a noble's education after 1300. Furthermore, the knight's dwelling changes; it becomes an abbreviated replica of the castle, a *maison-forte*, or stronghold, with moat and towers. All this is unquestionably done, not out of concern for security (on the contrary, this is a relatively peaceful period), but because men at arms are more independent of the chatelain; because, too, they are bent on the external indication of their rank, the separation of themselves from the rustics of the villages, who are no longer so remote from them in terms of wealth. The whole business is expensive: where can money be found to replace a horse, killed in battle or at a tournament, or to finance the formal dubbing of one's son, and, when the occasion arises, give a lavish party for a whole crowd of friends? One borrows—an old custom. But whereas, in the preceding century, one could obtain the several pieces necessary through one's cousin or lord, now, for these larger sums, one must approach less conciliatory lenders who intend to derive a guaranteed profit from their loan. Hardly anyone worries, any more, about the Church's condemnation of lending money at interest. Thence follows debt; pledging part of one's land, the income from which henceforth accrues to the creditor; the impossibility, of course, of repayment; new financial difficulties; one has to sell, at a bad price—and even this relief is short-lived for, once more, one finds oneself needing more *deniers* than the manor can supply. In this way the patrimony dwindles, passing in dribs and drabs, then in larger portions, into the hands of those who profit by the whole thing: the newly-rich. Also, in spite of their casualness, the nobles have begun to realize that their position is no longer so certain as it was, that entry into their caste is being forced by the bourgeois, the manorial agents, descendants of their ancestors' slaves, and increasingly numerous hired mercenaries who, although they too are professional soldiers, are nonetheless of mean birth. That is why, after the beginning of the thirteenth century, the aristocracy organizes its defense against the intruders—though they are impoverished, they have the solidarity of their privileges, their type of life, and their common ideas. There is a more precise assertion of the notion that nobility is not a function of wealth nor of a military profession, that the expensive dubbing ceremony can be put off until long after a young man's coming of age, without his ceasing to be considered a noble. New noble titles appear—squire (*écuyer* in northern France and *damoiseau* in the Midi)— which show just that inherent superiority of a man of good ancestry who, because he could not arm himself, was not able to call himself a knight. The idea of *gentilesse*, that social distinction based solely on birth, transmitted from father to son by blood, becomes more clearly conceived.

This distinction is thought to entitle men to special honors and external considerations that disguise the actual overthrow of the formerly dominant family bonds—a conception not yet faded from men's minds, the legacy of a feudal society which, because of the increased mobility of wealth and the very prosperity of trade, disintegrated during the course of the thirteenth century.

Thus the old, rural élite finds itself considerably humbled. The activity of the grain, wine, and cattle brokers, the effect of all the debts that bound both impecunious peasants and *hobereaux* fallen on hard times to the bourgeois financiers, the grafting of newly-rich merchants onto the village manors—all these contributed to causing the small, rural areas to become dependent on the neighboring towns. Every straggling village becomes a real capital, the main center of all social relations. Proof of this lies in the fact that the nearby chatelains and knights now want to have a residence, an *hôtel* where they come to spend their most pleasant days.

The attraction of urban life is a very important innovation. It results, first of all, in profound changes in the division of power. In the thirteenth century the stronghold of political power is no longer the rural castle but the town—itself a stronghold, with its ramparts, moats, and gates. It is the seat of a special authority, a bailiwick or provostry, extending over the surrounding villages; a place where *tailles* are the most profitable, where sources of cash income are the most abundant. Cultural leaders no longer are located in the wandering courts, which unite only warriors and domestic clerics; they settle in the largest towns, where their public is much larger, both in size and scope.

► ROYAL FRANCE

Since the last quarter of the twelfth century, the constant development of commerce as well as the growth of towns has encouraged political concentration. From now on, it is the Treasury, rather than friends, land, or retainers, which secures power. Philip Augustus certainly sensed this: in the "testament" he drafted in 1190 before departing for the Holy Land, his first concern was with his reserve of wealth. The Treasury alone enables war to be waged effectively. The palisades of stakes behind which the eleventh-century chatelain defied his enemies are no longer worthy of being called defensive. Because of the contact with Byzantium, the art of siege has made rapid strides since the Crusades; a real stronghold, one furnishing the means for holding a region, must therefore be of good stone, with round towers, a reinforced base, and such accoutrements as arrow-slits and machicolations. But to modernize an old castle takes enormous amounts of money. Still more money is necessary to build and maintain siege apparatus—stone-hurlers, mangonels, and catapults—whose projectiles demolish the walls of the old forts. Furthermore, the best and most effective warriors—those who know their profession, who once they are in open country do not desert on the pretext that their period of feudal service is terminated, who do not exact ransoms but instead destroy, and who are able to scale walls and handle the crossbow, that complicated and terrible weapon that no hauberk can withstand—these men are mercenaries, foreigners coming from poor regions, "Brabançons" or "Basques" banded together in groups called *routes*. But it takes money to pay them. By distributing *fiefs de bourse*, that is, fiefs formed by annual cash revenues, the Treasury also enables new retainers to be annexed, and annexed more closely together since all infractions can be met with immediate sanctions. Thanks to the Treasury, one can purchase, from nobles in need of money, their homage for land hitherto allodial. Thanks to the Treasury, finally, one can rule from a distance—something that had been impossible for centuries—through the use of agents who, instead of being rewarded by a gift of land, are paid by salary, so that they are reliable and more easily replaced. Money confers real power. It assures, among the countless lords who divided the power of command and punishment into little fragments, absolute superiority for a few lords, those dukes and, occasionally, counts who are heirs to the former regional magistracies, and who extend their authority over the great commercial channels, fairs, and towns. For these are the men who are able to exploit the bourgeois and the Lombards; they alone can obtain limitless and advantageous credit from the richest businessmen, since the latter find their best and steadiest clients among these lords. In this way the progress in commerce and monetary circulation contributes to the gradual restoration of vast and organized principalities. At first these grow up in the areas best situated along heavily traveled trade routes—Normandy, Flanders, Champagne, and Anjou; then, after the middle of the twelfth century, in the area around Paris, that is, in the royal region.

The royalty had not been completely suppressed by feudal pressure. The king of France retains three secure assets. First, his title: the unrivaled privilege of having been anointed, impregnated with divine power (hence the belief, popular in the eleventh century, in the sovereign's magic power to cure scrofula by touching those afflicted), of having a sacred quality like that of Charlemagne, that great emperor whose figure fills the new literature and haunts the chivalric imagination—of being, therefore, like him, the recognized protector of all Christians within the confines of the realm, that immense territory requiring more than a month to cross. Secondly, the king of France towers over the infinitely tangled network of vassalic relations; unentangled by that maze, he renders homage to none. Only he among all the nobles does not kneel, with bared head and clasped hands, before anyone—save God, his only lord. On the contrary: the loftiest barons and dukes, the most powerful counts, are loyal to him, as their ancestors were to Charlemagne; it is within the king's entourage that the notion (at first quite false, but one to which reality had to be adjusted) came into being of the feudal system in the shape of a pyramid, with the king at its apex, which connected him by successive stages with every knight in France, down to the very lowest. And thirdly, the king is the head of a large family manor —his domain.

Chance, this time, lasting over two centuries since the election of Hugh Capet, has made the royal magistracy hereditary, because each sovereign was lucky enough to have had a son, and has had the astuteness to have him elected and crowned during his own lifetime; by this hereditary transmission, the personal patrimony of the first Capetian, the old principality of the dukes of France (Paris, Orléans, and a few dependencies along the Aisne and the Somme) was attached to the sovereign dignity and became the king's strongest support. Gradually, this introduced into the minds of the kings a love for the ancestral land and a feeling that it must not leave the family but, on the contrary, must be enlarged as much as possible. Not that the Capetians ever dreamed of extending this domain far enough to make it coincide with the borders of the realm —how could they have imagined their one family being able to administer and use to fullest advantage that enormous space, only a small part of which they had even seen? This would have been to foresee an unthinkable circumstance: the suppression of the feudal structure. Yet, ever since the reign of Philip I, the Capetians wanted to have secure possession, amid their vassals' manors, of a principality large enough that, once the servants of God had been given their alms and the youngest sons had been well established on those appanages that let them hold the rank of princes, there would be enough land and resources left over for the heir of the title to maintain his family well and live on a scale worthy of his royal dignity. This conception is very moderate; it broadened imperceptibly, as opportunities opened up, as the needs of the court grew, and as the very idea of royalty became more grandiose. Therefore, the domain expanded, and with it the king's powers—a gradual expansion, induced by chance and by alterations in the economic, social, and political environments more than by the king's personal initiative. That fat campaigner on horseback, Louis VI (the first of the "good" kings in the traditional and ridiculous gallery of the kings of France), certainly more obtuse than his father, Philip I, had even been, had demolished—with head lowered, torch in hand, and in company with a small band of comrades—the strongholds in the very heart of the Capetian region which had set up multiple, independent enclaves.

But the real departure occurred in the next generation, in the time of

Louis VII, a misunderstood king who should be assigned to his true, and important, place in history. His was the period of the first excursions outside of the Ile-de-France, and even outside the kingdom itself: an Aquitaine marriage, pilgrimages to St. James of Compostela and Canterbury, a visit to the Carthusian monastery in the Alps, and particularly a crusade that put the king into fruitful contact with a great many nobles who had never seen him at close hand. His was not only the period of the first confrontations with the Plantagenets, the great princes in the West, but also the setting up of the first outposts for a wider extension of the domain, creeping into the southeast toward the regions along the Saône and Rhône, into the provinces that lacked political backbone, where the king appears in the role of administrator of justice, defender of churches and merchants, and the terror of pillaging chatelains. In addition to receiving the homage of the main strongholds, the king also obtains the right to participate in certain ecclesiastical manors, and the wherewithal to establish permanent representatives there. Here we have the roots for a new domain which, spreading step by step in small, imperceptible stages, soon encompasses the entire area, gnawing away at feudal powers until they are weakened and then driven out. The decisive turning point occurs during the reign of Philip Augustus, when the conditions for political action are altered at a stroke, and when money permits undertakings to be conducted on a much larger scale. There are twenty years of exhausting expeditions, interminable sieges, setbacks, retreats, desperate flights during which baggage and records are lost, perseverance—and finally Bouvines—and the Plantagenet power is completely destroyed. Artois, the region of the great wool-weaving towns; Normandy, an area richer by far than all the old Capetian inheritance; Anjou and Poitou—all are reunited with the domain whose extent is more than tripled and, consequently, whose structure is changed. To administer it, new instruments, new officials—the "bailiffs"—have to be created. And though these men are far from Paris, where the realm's political center is established and the king's justice effected, they are charged with organizing the vassals into bands for military expeditions and with gathering *deniers* to be sent to the Temple's treasury.

With the death of Philip, Louis VIII approaches another area, the region around Toulouse and Carcassonne; there he regains control of the struggle conducted for several years by the barons of the Ile-de-France, against a nobility contaminated by the Catharistic heresy. Contracting a fever in those Mediterranean regions, he dies very shortly, but unwittingly prepares a new advance of the royal domain—the area of "Languedoc," as it is called—so far-off, so different in its dialect and customs, that it has led an almost autonomous existence for centuries. After a female regent—the first, and another indication of the new position women are granted in the feudal world—there comes a saint: Louis IX.

His methods of governing are still singularly primitive: "Many a time it came to pass that during the summer months he would go and sit down in the Forest of Vincennes after mass, lean against a chestnut tree, and have us sit around him; all those who had business with him came to speak to him without troubling themselves about a bailiff, or any other official." [1] Council sessions are held on the ground, on the floor, or on the lawn of the royal orchard, or on some staircase; no distance exists between the king and his subjects, nor does any intermediary save for some clerics and knights in the *hôtel* and the household who specialize in receiving petitions, preparing lawsuits, and auditing accounts. But the reign of Louis IX is particularly memorable for the settlement of the old quarrel with the king of England; for the concern with just and charitable government; for the investigators sent in circuits through the domain to curb the power abuses of the king's men; for the statutes enacted by the sovereign, applicable to the whole kingdom, which, though their intention is entirely a moralistic one (for the king, acting as God's representative, resumes the peaceful work once carried on by the Church, punishes blasphemers, and obstructs private wars), nonetheless open the way for the idea of the king's law. St. Louis—foremost sovereign of the West, arbiter in every conflict, martyr on a crusade for Christ, considered a saint long before his death—causes veneration for royal dignity to make its way at a single stroke into even the dullest of peasant minds. When he dies in 1270, the administrative mechanism still needs to be improved, and formulas of sovereignty still must be discovered in Roman law—but France is truly a kingdom.

Such, then, is the path blazed by several kingly figures, for, until Louis IX, authority is exclusively personal and the king's person is everything; once he goes away, ages or sickens, cannot ride horseback and joust, or cannot himself pass the sentences made by his councilors, the stimulus for expansion relaxes. But in the principalities that have not come to be merged with the king's domain—in the "county" of Flanders, in the duchy of Burgundy, in Brittany, in Guyenne (which remains the king of England's), and outside the realm, in Savoy and in Provence—the power of the duke or count becomes stronger, at the same rate and by similar means: the extension of personal lordship, the creation of a body of tractable officials, the utilization of feudal rights for the benefit of the lord, and the establishment of a higher degree of security. At the end of the thirteenth century, political feudalism is dead, the former castles merge into the knights' strongholds, and all are controlled by a higher power. The network of homage converges toward the supreme authority; the impoverished, needy nobility has been domesticated.

The first effect of the establishment of these extensive principalities is the formation of a new social group, one containing the auxiliaries of power. On the payroll of the king and the great lords, divided into specialized sections in their *hôtel* or gathered into small teams in the main towns of local districts, are men of service, already numerous at the end of the century. They are drawn from all milieux: from those clerics who received a scholarly education; from those still rarer men who went to Italy, in particular Bologna, to learn about Roman law; from the upper bourgeoisie who are accustomed to handling finances; and, finally, from the lower knightly classes and noble families feeling the pinch of financial difficulties, for whom both the wages paid by king or duke and the authority delegated by them are means of escaping the impoverishment, the humiliation, the deposition, almost, that they feel in the face of the rising classes. These men are placed in diverse situations: they are employed as copyists for those documents that play an increasingly important role in social relations, as humble bookkeepers, legal clerks, notaries who have the authority to register contracts and who become, in the *bourgs* and soon in the rural districts as well, indispensable intermediaries called upon whenever someone wants to contract a loan, engage a servant, draw up a will, or order a work of art. There are also guardians of castles, bailiffs, and *grands administrateurs*—these last are always nobles, if not by birth, then dubbed as knights by their lords—for they are *d'épée* and hold managerial positions in the lords' names. Yet both great and small officials are brought together by common thought and behavior. They owe everything they have to the prince, and their fortune is bound closely to his; they are his most ardent defenders, eager to extend his privileges and to increase his benefits. It is in this manner that the officers of the king of France, more than the king himself, extend his domain through their initiative, astuteness, opportunism; through these men, totally imbued with the notion of royal superiority, the idea spreads gradually among the most ready minds. Furthermore, along with the ecclesiastics, they constitute a second group of literate men, for whom a book is not merely a decorative object preserved like a jewel in one's treasury and displayed on ceremonial occasions, but is rather a tool, an instrument of knowledge. But theirs is a special culture—essentially, a legal one. Some of them, known as "legists," particularly numerous in southern France, learned scholarly law, Roman or Canon law, either in the schools of Italy and Montpellier, or in newer centers like those in Orléans or Paris where legal texts are commented upon through the use of the Scholastic method with its glosses and questions. Most of them, not speaking Latin, are educated by experience. To these men falls the enormous job of taking the tangled mass of usages—those supreme rules of society known as "customs," which differ from district to district and are preserved in men's memories, full of lacunas and contradictions—setting them down in writing, and making them a part of the rational intelligence; whence arise after 1240 the *coutumiers* of Normandy and Anjou. Around the mid-thirteenth century, casebooks such as Pierre de Fontaines' *Conseils* and works like the *Livre de Justice et de Plaid* (drawn up at Orléans around 1260), in which the principles of scholarly law are popularized, are written for these experts. Finally there is another victory for the vernacular: translations, like that of Justinian's *Code* and *Institutes*, are introduced for the first time in the middle of the century. But these jurists and administrators also become interested in other types of literature. They form a new public for chronicles, encyclopedias, and the collections of curios that flourish around 1250; some sample chivalric romances and the poems of courtly love. The most famous of these agents of power, Philippe de Rémi, from Picardy, Lord of Beaumanoir, and bailiff of Vermandois for the king of France, not only drafted the "customs" of the Beauvaisis, thereby establishing his historical importance, but also wrote two love romances and many songs between 1276 and 1285. Thus, new centers of learning augment the cultivated circles of the schools, the upper echelons of the Church, and the large manorial courts. But these centers are directed toward quite different goals. They are much closer to reality and action; more particularly, they are much less tightly closed, much more widely disseminated, and have direct contact with much humbler classes of society.

On the other hand, the reconstitution of the privileged social categories is accompanied by a reinforcement of security. Not only is the era of Louis IX the time of a prosperity, nostalgic memories of which are handed down from generation to generation for a long period, but it is one of peace as well. These two things are allied. Forced into the least accessible districts, military brigandage diminishes; the disturbances of the knights are curbed; private wars are thwarted—according to royal regulations, the injured party must wait forty days before retaliating against the one who wronged him, the delay allowing anger to cool, and intermediary friends to re-establish harmony. The use of arms is also controlled through "assurances" by which any threatened man may put himself under the direct protection of the king or duke. In a word, society is becoming civilized. At the same time, it becomes looser: family interdependence, losing its utility, begins to be an encumbrance. Bonds begin to slacken, and, because there is less joint possession, each brother becomes more independent of the others. The narrow petty-manorial confines, which until recently enclosed small isolated worlds within the chatelain's *ban* and guardianship, are very rapidly being dissolved. To be sure, private jurisdictions, far from moribund, are still quite viable; but royal power is set over them. One can appeal the sentence passed by a *hobereau* to the neighboring bailiff, who never misses an occasion to come between *manants* and their lords. In practice, the lord carries out less and less frequently those basic functions of protection which, in the eleventh and twelfth centuries, had justified his exactions and his *taille*. The advent of mercenaries, and the omnipresent royal or ducal sergeants (the best police force possible), again call into question the lords' social function, as well as that of the nobles whose invulnerability vanished with their economic superiority.

As the old interdependence relaxes, there is a commingling of social groups and, concurrently, a reduction of particularisms. The regions controlled by the chatelain are re-absorbed into broader political groups on the scale of the new social relations; the drafting of regional "customs" and the institution of appellate jurisdiction cause narrowly local practices to disappear. The Albigensian Crusade establishes Parisian customs in Languedoc, conquered by knights from the Ile-de-France; common practices, similar ways of behavior, are spread abroad gradually by the *grands administrateurs,* all of whom are trained alike in the prince's entourage, have no attachment to the particular region, and are shifted about too often to put down any roots. In this manner, by means of those in the king's pay, the Parisian courtly speech and the administrative language spread to the regions around Angoulême and Lyon where the Capetian influence begins to spread into the lands of the Empire at the end of the century. It should be pointed out that this tendency toward unity is equally apparent in the body of the Church of France where, in each diocese, the bonds between bishop and clergy become closer. Since the early years of the thirteenth century, two highly disciplined and singularly effective spiritual militias have been finding their way into every town: the mendicant orders of the Dominicans and the Franciscans. These two orders, wholeheartedly committed to this world (as opposed to the old Benedictine communities), finally realize within the Church the ideals of poverty and the apostolic way—which for a long time troubled souls have been able to find only in heresy—and compensate for the deficiencies in the secular clergy by spreading a sound and consistent doctrine. Confronted with heresy, these orders superimpose upon the ordinary means of jurisdiction the instruments for a spiritual policing which successfully rectify heterodox currents and cause the dissident sects that flourished in the twelfth century to disappear, collecting the faithful into an at least apparent unity of belief. The thirteenth century is truly the century of regroupment. After the burgeoning diversity of feudalism, a synthesis is realized in the heart of the Capetian region and is imposed as far as the borders of the kingdom—indeed, well beyond them.

► THE SYNTHESIS OF THE ILE-DE-FRANCE

The lines of force, whether economic or political, in the thirteenth century converge toward the center of the basin around Paris. In this period southern France, the cradle of Romanesque civilization, recedes into the background. Its farmlands have been less thoroughly renovated; the most traveled trade routes, now, are no longer those to Spain, but to Italy, and so do not pass through Aquitaine. With the destruction of the Plantagenet "empire," Anjou and Poitou have turned to face the north and Paris; there still remains little Guyenne, open to England and the sea, but increasingly turning its back upon the continent; and if Provence, comprising the activity of Marseille, the lower Rhône, and the Durance, is more prosperous and active than ever, the old region known as Gothie, around Toulouse and Carcassonne, center of the Catharistic heresy, was beaten down by the Albigensian Crusade and by the Inquisition which struck the élite in particular. New ruling classes have been grafted on here, and there is an atmosphere of distrust; for a while, the decline of this area is all too evident. This decay accentuates the predominance of the Ile-de-France and, primarily, Paris, the royal city—the only large town in the Western world. Less diverse than recently, French civilization in at least several of its aspects begins to acquire a Parisian tone as early as the thirteenth century.

In the eleventh century, Paris was still a little city among many others, well situated on a river axis, but no more. It was far from surpassing the other Capetian city, the one on the Loire: Orléans—which, like Paris, was a trade center, but which, with its famous schools, was more of a cultural center than Paris. The kings did not dwell any longer in Paris than they did in the other towns where they had palaces, but divided their residence among all of them. Parisian ascendancy dates from the twelfth century, for three related reasons: the development of Seine commerce, connected with the rise of the Champagne fairs; the success of the professors, drawing crowds of students; and, finally, the king's choice of it for his favorite resort—for a variety of motives, but perhaps primarily because that town is the best situated with respect to hunting grounds. Henceforth, Paris continues to grow; after the thirteenth century, it becomes an enormous center with five or six times the population of the largest French towns.

The function of Paris is threefold. It is a capital—Europe's first capital to fix the center of a state—an economic center, and an intellectual crossroads. As a town, too, its function is treble; on one of the islands in the Seine, is the *cité*, the old redoubt in which urban life was developed during the early Middle Ages. The *cité* is surrounded by a very old wall, many sections of which are still standing; at the eastern point, the new cathedral of Notre-Dame (whose two façade towers were finished around 1230) rises above the chapter houses and the charitable establishments; at the other end, enclosed within a wall, stands the king's palace, combining gardens, orchards, various buildings and oratories, among which is Sainte-Chapelle, built by Louis IX. This is not the only royal residence (the king also lives on the right bank in the fortress of the Louvre, at Vincennes, and in other castles in the immediate environs), but it serves as the nexus of royal administration, the *hôtel*, that is, of the numerous household of clerics, knights, and valets. Formerly, the *île de la cité* was the commercial center, along such streets as the Draperie and Juiverie; and the cloister of Notre-Dame, the center of scholarly life. But in the second half of the twelfth century, these activities are transferred to the two banks of the Seine: the Jews, expelled by Philip Augustus in 1180, once grouped around the principal route of the Frankish centers, thus came to be settled on the right bank—in the new merchant quarter, the "town."

Protected since 1190 by a high defensive wall (beyond which it soon extended), and better bordered on the northeast by the marshland of the still undeveloped Marais, the quarter known as the "town" is organized around two streets, paved by order of Philip Augustus. One leads to the Cluniac priory of Saint-Martin des Champs; close by, around Saint-Jacques de la Boucherie, are clustered the stalls of the meat guilds. On the other, the Saint-Denis road, between the Innocents and Sainte-Opportune, the Champeaux market is held, where peasants from the surrounding area offer their wares every Saturday. This market opens onto the Grand Pont, a six-arched bridge blocked at one end by the Châtelet, where most of the royal provost's sergeants have their headquarters and which is the most secure part of Paris—consequently, almost all of the moneychangers' shops are to be found there. But the most active crossroads is the Grève, the steep riverbank where, upstream from the bridge under which they cannot readily pass, the "water merchants' " boats unload grain, wood, and especially wine from the upper Seine, and items from the fairs in Champagne; at the same time, salt and fish from Rouen are unloaded at the Châtelet. Near the Châtelet, too, are the streets of the Lombards. Farther on there is the Temple, a group of strongholds where the king's money is kept. This is a teeming quarter, alive simultaneously with industry and trade. Indeed, Paris is a large craft center, but one whose products are infinitely more diverse than those of the woolen-weaving towns in Artois and Flanders. It is, in particular, a center for the art objects and luxury articles made in a multitude of workshops and not destined for local consumption. In his *Livre des Métiers*, Étienne Boileau, provost of Paris during the days of Louis IX, lists some hundred and fifty professional associations, comprising almost five thousand masters—and even so, he is interested only in the most important ones. Paris is also a major commercial way station. This commerce is both local and foreign. The former is maintained simply by the presence of an enormous mass of people, and is dominated by the butchers who are very rich men whose numerous aides have dangerous weapons at their command. The latter is supplied by the community of water merchants whose "board of directors," with the merchant provost as chairman, is considered by the king as spokesman for the Parisian bourgeois—who have not yet received an enfranchising charter.

On the other side of the river, the atmosphere is different. Between the abbey of Saint-Germain-des-Prés on the one hand, whose broad expanse of vineyards and meadows isolates the little peasant *bourg* that formed around it, and the abbey of Saint-Victor on the other, ascending through the gardens along the Rue Saint-Jacques (the road to Orléans), along the slopes of Sainte-Geneviève, lies the area of the old Roman town, a number of whose buildings are still standing, still in use—this is the quarter of the schools. It begins at the Petit Pont, whose shops were occupied by professors in the twelfth century, includes the Petit Châtelet, residence of the king's provost, and extends around Saint-Séverin and Saint-Julien le Pauvre, along the axis of the Rue de Garlande as far as the Place Maubert, where the food guilds are bunched together. This quarter has grown larger with the increased fame of the Parisian schools, which, since about 1160, have become the leading schools in Christendom for the study of dialectic and sacred learning. These studies now constitute a *studium generale*, a vast center for inquiry with many teachers, the seminary of the entire upper clergy, the seedbed for bishops and Church administrators, a place where many popes studied—a place whose connections extend throughout France, and into England, Italy, Germany, and the Scandinavian countries.

The students, coming from all over the world, differ widely in customs and ways of life. Sometimes they are rich, but more often starving. They pass the nights under church porticoes, earn a few *deniers* by working as servants or tutors for their richer friends, or as copyists or cantors; often they are obliged to interrupt their studies, abandoning theology for law or medicine so they may carve out a career more rapidly.

This influx of students posed serious accommodation problems after the end of the twelfth century. As it expanded, the student center shifted from the outskirts of Notre-Dame toward Sainte-Geneviève. In order to serve the students, an entire secular population, whose interests were closely linked with their needs, gathered there—landlords, makers of parchment, ink, and books. In order to alleviate student poverty, relief associations were created, modeled after the hospices offered along the roads to the pilgrims; after 1180, the income from charity let them offer to each of eighteen poor students a bed in the city's Hôtel-Dieu and a scholarship of twelve *deniers*. Soon other *collèges* were founded by private charity, among which was the one Robert de Sorbon, a friend of Louis IX, intended for students of theology, while each of the large religious orders gave their attention to organizing a welcome center for their members near the Parisian *studium*. Ultimately, in order to insure for themselves the discipline of their studies, and to defend their interests against those of the town bourgeois, the king's men, and the episcopal authority, the students and teachers gathered into a community quite similar to the associations for peace, the "charities" and the professional associations of the towns—having periodic banquets, religious services, and funerals—and formed an organization, known after 1208 as the University. Upheld by the papacy against the royal provost and the bishop's chancellor, this association—with the help of brawls and strikes —gradually gained official recognition between the years 1192 and 1231, and obtained certain privileges, in particular, legal immunity.

As the University body grows larger, it also becomes more diversified. Four special mutual aid groups are formed: the "nations" of France, Picardy, Normandy, and England, among which the students and teachers are divided according to their birthplace and the vernacular dialect they speak in the interval between classes and studies. At the same time, teaching is divided into four educational branches or departments called "faculties" first in 1219. To begin with, there is the "arts faculty," a preparatory "faculty" gathering together by far the greatest number of students, as well as the youngest. One enters it at about age twelve or thirteen and takes the *baccalauréat* examinations at nineteen. Then, after two years of additional studies, the *licence* is granted. There is an initiation ceremony analogous to that which admits one to the guilds, involving a "masterpiece" (the inaugural lecture), the taking of an oath, and the treating of one's colleagues to a banquet. In this manner, one becomes a "master," qualified to open a school. The three other "faculties" are very highly specialized. Law and Medicine are actually only slightly developed; theology, on the other hand, considered the queen of the studies, is taken up by the best masters of arts when they become mature, and is the study that makes available the highest ecclesiastical careers.

Such, then, is the triple aspect of Paris; of Paris which, although it is not the only creative center—in the thirteenth century, other towns, particularly Troyes and Arras, play an essential role in formulating the new culture—is still situated very much at the forefront, and is the initiator of new fashions. Thus, for example, the carvers who sculpted the ornaments of Notre-Dame were a good twenty years ahead of those who worked in Amiens, Reims, or Strasbourg, both in the themes they chose and the manner in which they treated them. Two facts confer this mastery upon Paris. First, Paris is the possessor of a receptive atmosphere, much more concentrated and more highly developed than any other—an atmosphere not determined by the court, if one understands by that word (as was understood in the twelfth or fifteenth centuries) that group of lords surrounding the king; the Paris court is very modest in scale, austere and somewhat rustic—culture in Paris then is not that of the worldly. Rather, the atmosphere is determined by the numerous company of royal servants, knights, and clerics, the richest bourgeois, and the people connected with the University. This milieu differs completely from that of courtly society; it is rationalistic, and oriented toward reality. Secondly, the artistic and intellectual currents, until recently directed by forces that were essentially religious—connections between monasteries, personal relations among the prelates—now follow the major commercial paths whose great juncture is at Paris.

Another great thirteenth-century innovation is the shop: there, one's money can buy books or art objects which can be taken away or resold— another aspect of the permeation of the monetary economy. In the eleventh and twelfth centuries, books were written in monastic workrooms for the enrichment of the monastery's library; sometimes offered as presents, more often than not they remained in the community, belonging to all, as did the sanctuary and the altar decorations. Like the latter, they had been put together very slowly with careful attention to formal perfection and—since this work was considered a means of spiritual elevation—with piety. For the new world of students and administrators, the book is a totally different thing, an instrument which, first of all, must be useful. Hence, bookcraft underwent a great change during the course of the twelfth century: now, it is a business, with paid copyists, often impoverished students; the work is done with an eye to speed; it utilizes an abbreviated, cursive handwriting and dismisses all superfluous decoration. They are craftsmen oriented toward sales; the first bookstores begin to appear, a fundamental revolution in cultural history. At the same time, we note that some artists no longer work in teams when they build and decorate churches or work in a lord's household; rather, they own shops, offering buyers their output of illuminations or enamels and ivory worked into little statues or relief plaques—small, transportable objects. Customers are still very few, and the artist usually works only when commissioned. Yet, with the advent of bookbuying and bookselling, small illuminated chests, portable altarpieces, Madonna-and-Child groups that are faithful copies of monumental works—all these, transported in merchants' packs as far as the lower Baltic and Sicily, spread new tastes, intellectual attainments, and forms. This diffusion greatly promoted the primacy of Parisian culture.

In the thirteenth century, the resources of this culture are formed by the ecclesiastical tradition, particularly vital in the Capetian entourage which, through a deep sense of royal responsibility and a sense of fidelity to the memory of the Carolingian period, remains much more under clerical influence than other manorial courts of France. Hence, it is characterized by the religious art of Saint-Denis and of Chartres; by liturgical polyphony, and by the dialectical search for God. But this tradition has been deflected by three new contributions. First, there is the sense of the world's diversity and richness, a sense that is very much alive among those men—the new cultural participants—whom either business, administration, or education has led into a lucid observation of reality, men who are in daily contact with foreigners, with Lombard financiers, students from England or Cologne. Secondly, there is the discovery of a system of thought completely foreign to the Christian intellectual universe, that of Aristotle—not Aristotle the logician, whom people knew well, and from whom they had extracted the Scholastic method, but the "new Aristotle," the moralist and metaphysician. The *Ethics*, the *Metaphysics*, the *Natural Philosophy*, and the *Politics*, accompanied by the commentaries of Arab or Jewish thinkers from the Moslem world, like Avicenna and Averroës, are translated in Sicily, in Spain, even in Paris. These translations result in the bewildering entry into the schools of an attractive and stimulating rational construction, a construction that acts as a solvent for that thought hitherto grafted onto an unproblematic faith. It is, in particular, the revelation of a philosophic system ordered around man and nature, one no longer enchanted by supernatural mysteries.

The third innovation is the introduction of the Franciscan sensibility. Answering the needs of the urban masses, growing both in number and in sophistication, who were begging in vain for spiritual nourishment from an inadequate, routine-bound, and ritualistic secular clergy, the followers of St. Francis spread rapidly through French towns during the first half of the thirteenth century; as early as 1219, there were Minorites in the Parisian Schools. Their influence was considerable, despite the resistance of the parish priests, hostile to these intruders, contending with them for their flocks. This influence was exercised by moral preaching, by the spread of sacramental practices, and by exhorting men to imitate the life of Christ. Their effect on the spirituality of Louis IX, for example, was of prime importance. As a consequence, there was a complete renovation of Christianity, an enrichment of the life of the affections, not limited to a few groups of esthetes. To be sure, these innovations found their way only gradually into the minds of the people, and civilization did not really show signs of the Franciscan influence before the fourteenth century. Nevertheless, this gradual permeation must be counted among the principal elements of the synthesis of the Ile-de-France.

Finally, the most striking characteristic of the Parisian apex of thirteenth-century culture appears to be a sense of equilibrium, a maturity of intellectual faculties which from now on are capable of disciplining, without emaciating them, the vital pressures that had tumultuously opened out in the preceding century. In this prosperous world, freed from famine and war, such an equilibrium reigns between reason and feeling, between nature and divinity. This harmony of extremes is indicated, primarily, through what one might call a growth in wisdom of the feudal and courtly tradition which, released from the irrational and returned to reality, is re-integrated into logic at the same time that it assigns to itself a more precise place within the framework of Christian life.

In the thirteenth century, the vogue for chivalric literature is still as great as ever. There is a widespread public on all sides for the literature of sport and love, of fantasy; for epic poems, romances, and Provençal lyrics —for one would be mistaken to believe that the Albigensian Crusade reduced the number of love poems written in *langue d'oc*. This is the era of chatelain-poets, while patronage, formerly indulged in only by the richest lords, now tends to spread far and wide: the greater facility of communication promotes the dissemination of small literary centers. But this taste becomes provincial, and in the avant-garde centers—that is, those of the basin around Paris, and Paris itself—we discern a new and complex modulation. On the one hand there is deeper inquiry into, and description of, all the ramifications of courtly love, through the learned process of allegory, combining all the resources of literary culture with all the logical steps of Scholasticism: the *Roman de la Rose*, by Guillaume de Lorris from around Orléans, is a genuine *summa* of courtliness (this university word is well suited to that dialectical construct, enlivened by an astonishing oratorical felicity); the totality of love literature culminates in it, but it does so by clarifying itself and clothing itself in balance and grace. In a completely different sense, however, there is a return to the concrete. This tendency appears early in the century in some romances, in particular those of Jean Renart who asserts, in the beginning of *L'Escoufle*, his preference for truth and reason; and in *Guillaume de Dole*, he proves his mettle as observer: as ironic as the unknown author of the charming *Aucassin et Nicolette*, he is at great pains to analyze character, and is interested in both bourgeois and peasants. But this tendency toward the concrete is brilliantly expressed in the success of the chronicles—real stories told by witnesses in plain, vernacular prose.

Consequently, there results a complete change in the chivalric mentality. Impulsive violence, preference for fables, and a limited and formalistic religiosity give way to a sense of duty and action, to lucid self-mastery. A new type of model man appears: the man of experience and integrity, the *prud'homme*—". . . so great and good a thing, one need only say the word, it fills the mouth. . . ." Louis IX, who was an expert, placed the *prud'homme* above the "Beghard," the devout man seeking his salvation outside this world. The former is bent on following the example of Christ, but is reasonable, easy-going, and fun-loving; still as enthusiastic about horses and jousts as ever, but knowing how to control his animal instincts. The best example of this complete change is St. Louis himself, as he is presented, ingenuously and without excessive stylization, by the old Joinville. Louis is a rather exceptional man, to be sure, but a more meaningful representative of the ideal of an era and a class than any literary character, or the statue of St. Theodore at Chartres, or that of Saul at Reims. The king "loved God with all his heart, and followed his example . . . and risked his life several times for the love he bore his people"; "understanding that one should not spend all one's time in trifling matters nor in the querulous demands of this world"; the king "began to study and read Holy Scripture, for he had a glossed Bible and original manuscripts from St. Augustine and other saints, as well as other books of Holy Scripture, which he read, and had read aloud to him many times at dinner and at bedtime." [2] The king, in the same posture as St. Francis, washes the feet of the poor on Holy Thursday, feeds lepers with his own hands, and mortifies his own flesh; becoming involved with the idea of a crusade (though this notion was falling into disrepute), he animates it anew with his personal zeal and he makes the holy trip twice, the second time in defiance of his associates, and ends by dying a martyr's death. This, then, is a mysticism, echoing that of the prose *Lancelot*'s hero; but what is new is that this is a mysticism tempered with reality. St. Louis respected priests, yet was always opposed to their infringements; he refused to support the pope in his struggle against the emperor, and valued freedom more than devotion. Health, balance between the virtues of the Gospel (considered the model for living) and those of chivalry, both tempered with good sense: such is the new form of the aristocratic ideal.

This same growth of wisdom, disciplining the passion of the previous age, and this same equilibrium, are expressed in the art of the Ile-de-France—in the Classic Gothic, whose characteristics come to light in the early years of the thirteenth century on the façade of Notre-Dame in Paris. These characteristics materialize once more in Paris around 1250, in the Sainte-Chapelle of the Palace, and again at Chartres, Amiens, and Reims. There, too, the tendency is toward unity, and the architectural formula worked out in these places is asserted subsequently, for more than three centuries, in most of the countries of the West. By improving the design of the ogival arch and by substituting flying buttresses for abutments, the builders could become even more independent of weight and mass. First of all, the new style is one of thrust and liberation from matter: vaults and spires are raised as high as possible, sometimes, as at Beauvais (where the vault of the choir had unwisely been raised to 157 feet and the spire to 492), to the point of collapse. There is also a general tendency toward elongation, an accentuation of upward soaring, effected inside the church by the gradual discontinuation of capitals, of friezes, of anything that might interrupt the free thrust of the pillars; outside the church, it is done by adding triangular window canopies, pinnacles, sharp angles, and pointed spires shooting into the sky. An art of upward thrust, then, and also one of light: the building is usually confined to a skeleton of pillars and arches; the windows become taller and broader, and, for the first time at Chartres, they take up the whole bay. In order to open the structure even more, the intermediary gallery, borrowed from Norman churches by the architects of Notre-Dame, is replaced

by a light, blind arcade, which is mere decoration. The upper chapel of
Sainte-Chapelle is nothing more than a dazzling stained-glass window,
while on the southern façade of the Notre-Dame transept Jean de Chelles
opens up the first of those immense and radiant rose-windows which
soon fill all that can still remain of the unoccupied space. Yet in this research for the ethereal and the immaterial, achieved through ascension
and illumination, we see the continuation of a balance at its most robust and healthy, the continuation of that sense of order that gives such
harmony to the proportions of Chartres, that bestows its supreme balance on the façade of Notre-Dame—that mathematical severity in the disposition of lines and angles, which, like the great polyphonies, is a victory of reason.

Decorative art, too, tends toward the unreal, insofar as it is dominated
by the stained-glass window, the principal means of expression now that
the wall has disappeared. At the beginning of the thirteenth century,
the Chartres glassmakers and those working in Paris after 1245—both on
the Sainte-Chapelle and on the rose-window of Notre-Dame's transept
—produce the lyrical masterpieces of the period. A lyricism of pure, dazzling color, this is infinitely more stirring than the brown or green
earth-tones in the Romanesque frescoes, and more luminous than
those masterpieces of precious stones that conveyed to Suger the most
subtle of enjoyments. The pure interaction of their reds and intense
blues in the separated partitions of the windows causes their icono-
graphic pretext to be forgotten. The stained-glass window also dominates
all the graphic arts, giving its special accent to the miniatures—with their
stiff, dark circles of stilted people, their schematized landscapes, their
golden backgrounds where vivid colors sing—of which Paris, along with
Winchester, is then the great European center. But it is in sculpture that
this equilibrium—combining mystical love, preference for reality, and
good sense in the balance so basic to Parisian culture—stands out most
admirably. The carvers are in close touch, on the one hand, with Franciscan preachers, like them considering the Gospel to be the sole point of
reference, and they remake Christianity into a religion of incarnation.
On the other hand, their contact with the scholars of the schools restores
nature to its place in the intelligible universe. A victory, then, over
the irrational: no more monsters, no more distortions. No longer are
purely decorative elements borrowed either from fanciful bestiaries or
from unreal compositions of abstract forms. Rather, we see the plants of
the Ile-de-France—detailed reminders of pastoral nature, the seed and
fundamental source of this still-peasant equilibrium: ivy, vine, and let-
tuce leaves, closely observed, sprout up at every point where their presence does not interfere with the upward thrust of the architecture. The
victory of humanism bursts forth in the great art of statuary. Marian
themes are developed and expanded by those taken from the life of Jesus,

by the glorification of Christian heroes, apostles, and saints who move forward out of the walls and columns to stand on the porches in the same proportions and attitudes of life. These are men, now become accessible, brotherly, living, free from the ecstasy that enthralled the figures on the Romanesque transepts and bas-reliefs. Thus, the face of the *beau Dieu*, on a pier at Amiens—among all the images of Christ, one of the most perfect representations of a religion uniting man and the supernatural—where divine majesty and knowledge are joined with human tenderness. In the same way, a sweetness radiates from the scenes of Christ's childhood sculpted on the portal of the Notre-Dame cloister: kindness, sweetness, but not suffering. A felicitous incarnation: that of man's reconciliation of nature and divinity. In plastic art, the thirteenth century is one of the rare periods of the smile—a smile still awkward, childish, ready to laugh, but one freed from the obsession with unknown forces, from holy fear. When it achieves perfect expression of the human balance, Classic Gothic rejoins Greek sculpture—sometimes, as in the Visitation group at Reims, in an unsettling fashion.

The attitude that can be seen in the new directions of courtly literature, the new features of sculptured faces—the acclaiming of natural beauty, the attempt to harmonize extremes in the light of understanding—can also be seen, even more pronouncedly, in the world which is still narrow yet much more open than it had been upon other social milieux—those of the professional scholars and philosophers. Since the days of Abélard, the instruments of logical knowledge have continually been improving in the Parisian Schools. Virtuosity in handling the syllogism assumes still more agility with a new exercise, the *disputatio* or debate, which publicly discusses the contradictions of authors. At the beginning of the thirteenth century, this method tends to take precedence over all other learned activities, and is for students what the tournament is for the knights—a friendly battle, the means for simultaneously training oneself, breaking oneself in, and making the most of oneself. The knowledge thus acquired is systematically put in its place: in the abstracts of their magisterial teaching that the great professors draw up, the *summae*—condensed manuals that permit the students to go further and transcend the reading of texts. Finally, and most important, new translations of Aristotle and his commentators provide not only a framework of rational thought but also the wherewithal to fill it with unsuspected intellectual wealth. Reading these unknown texts had greatly contributed to the success of the *studium* in Paris, in the closing years of the twelfth century. Urged on by their students, teachers—especially those in the arts faculty, whose students were younger and more rash—took more and more risks, intoxicated by the discovery of a logical system in which everything was arranged to human scale, and without mystery. Some teachers ventured so far from the traditional framework of Christian thought that they

seemed dangerous: in 1210, a council condemned two Parisian professors
—Amauri de Bène and David de Dinant. The readings from [Aristotle's] *Natural Philosophy* and its glosses were henceforth forbidden; for
several years people restricted themselves, as they had formerly, to reading logic only. It soon became apparent to the directors of the University,
and to the pope who once studied there, that these barriers could not remain standing for long, that it would undoubtedly be less dangerous to
confront the new doctrine and try to reconcile it with that of the Church.
The forgers of this reconciliation were scholars from the Mendicant orders, who now had monasteries on Sainte-Geneviève, and who provided
every guarantee of orthodoxy since they were closely subject to pontifical
power. Faced with Aristotelianism, the Franciscans placed themselves in
a permanent current of Christian thought, for which St. Augustine had
shown the way in the early Middle Ages, and which was expanded in the
twelfth century in the school of Saint-Victor and the Cistercian monasteries. This current of thought was opposed to the advances of rational
theology, and the Franciscans declared in favor of the affections, and of
mysticism. But it was a moderate, reasonable, tempered mysticism, open
to creative thought, in total conformity with the spirit of St. Francis; a
mysticism capable, through the illumination of grace, of linking Nature
—whose beauty and power Greek philosophy had lately revealed—to
the Divine. The Dominicans, on the other hand, took the body of natural
philosophy in hand and, by a dazzling gymnastic of the intellect, gradually beat down the countless contradictions that set Aristotelianism in
rational opposition to Christian dogma. Although the groundwork for
this was laid by Albertus Magnus, and continued to a great extent in the
monasteries along the Rue Saint-Jacques, it was the work of the Italian,
Thomas Aquinas—with his *summae*, attesting in all their vigor and boldness to the dominant tendency of cultivated men in the century of St.
Louis: the relentless effort to reduce everything to unity, to reconcile
everything into a common whole.

In point of fact, the Thomist venture surpassed all bounds. It risked
falling from some very perilous heights, higher and more delicate than
cathedral spires, and inaccessible to most. It did not prevent the boldest
intellectuals from coming under the spell of Aristotelian thought, from
considering the reconciliation of dogma and philosophy impossible and,
through studying Averroës, from gaining increased doctrinal independence. Among the philosophers and theologians in the schools around
1270, there is an efflorescence of life, a frenzy of discovery, passion, and
opposition. They are at the threshold of a moral crisis which is to call
their intellectual values into doubt.

More characteristic of this phase in the evolving culture, and also more
causative, is the state of mind that spreads, from the little circles of Parisian students clustered around teachers, to other cultivated areas in Paris

and in the large towns of northern France. This is sometimes called the "bourgeois spirit"—wrongly so, for, although it is indeed peculiar to townspeople and does not affect the rural nobility (or, even less, the amorphous mass of peasants), it is still common to many social groups: to the rich merchants to the extent (a limited one except perhaps in Paris and other highly oligarchical towns, like Arras) that they are interested in things other than their profession and the salvation of their souls; but also to clerics, canons, *curés* of urban parishes, university men, former students who have become doctors, notaries, bookkeepers, knights in the royal household, petty town-dwelling nobles, artists, illuminators, carvers. All of these social groups have much stronger intellectual powers than they used to; lucidity and perspicacity, as well as curiosity about the universe, are what most clearly distinguish their mental attitude from that of their twelfth-century ancestors. The thirteenth century is the time of the great encyclopedias, where everything everyone knows about the world is collected and begins to be organized; the period of the *Mirrors*, the *Treasuries*, the *Lapidaries*, and the *Bestiaries*—collections of strange things which, though imparted naïvely, nonetheless open minds to the diversity of creation, and make them discover that reality is as astonishing as fantasy, that it can gradually be inventoried and brought under the light of intelligence. These people have a positive world view, a will not to be duped. Their belief is absolutely intact, a calm, natural piety is integrated into their daily behavior, and increasingly they address God through familiar intercessors such as the omnipresent Virgin and saints. Theirs is a religion without anxiety. But they have attained a major advance in the face of the world: a sense of irony. All excess is irreverently criticized: courtly conventions, the devotion to women which, subordinating man, disrupts the order of things; the braggart nobility caught up with priorities no longer justified by moral or material superiority; excesses in religious practice, such as the deplorable discrepancy between the ecclesiastics' mission and the way in which they conduct their lives. There is a sense of equilibrium, a sense of what is possible, an alliance between a healthy and profound faith and a very open severity toward the priesthood—appearing now because the priests are not the only ones who can express themselves, and indicating a better awareness of religious values, a greater exigency, and a participation of the laity in spiritual life. These men know how to make fun of themselves. A whole literature, in which relaxation gives birth to laughter, develops for them: satirical plays such as those the great musician and producer Adam de la Halle puts on; amusing tales in which newly-rich peasants, women, braggarts, and especially monks and priests, appear in grotesque postures; parodies and fables in which animals point out the failings of human society. An intelligence that is overly rational and sometimes slightly pedantic—but one of vitality, grace, robust beauty, and ingenuousness—everything that the Parisian Rutebeuf expresses in his poems: this is the tone of the thirteenth century.

By means of merchants, of former students at the University who now have become bishops or provincial *écolâtres*, of court gentlemen sent from Paris on temporary missions or to fulfill some office, the tastes, ways of feeling and of self-expression formed in the heart of the Capetian region from 1180 on spread rapidly through the entire kingdom. This impregnation is basically attributable to the towns, on which the king's hand fell heavily because of their bad job of handling finances. All France north of the Loire (excepting part of the "county" of Flanders, north of Lille, and that of Douai with its Germanic dialect, withdrawing more and more from the realm) and all of Burgundy as far as the outskirts of Lyon are now entirely under the influence of the Ile-de-France. Further to the south, in the regions of Aquitaine—so profoundly alien, even in the mid-twelfth century, to the civilization of the "Franks"—the infiltration begins. Parisian Scholasticism establishes a center of diffusion at Toulouse, where a *studium generale* is founded in 1229, to augment with doctrinal weapons the fight against the Cathar heresy; *francien*, the official language of the court and that spoken in the Ile-de-France, slowly wins out over *occitan*, extending the audience of Parisian and Picard authors into the Midi; prelates in the second half of the thirteenth century adopt the style of "France" for their churches—Clermont, Limoges, Rodez, and Narbonne are inspired by Amiens, and Saint-Nazaire de Carcassonne by the Sainte-Chapelle; thus the Gothic style, of which the Cistercians had already introduced several elements, progressively forces the Romanesque tradition into retreat.

Finally, along the commercial routes and the great European political axes, the spread of Parisian culture far exceeds the borders of that realm which Louis IX had made the most marvelous in Christendom. In the Empire whose frontiers, in Forez, Velay, Gévaudan, and soon, Lyon, are slowly receding before the Capetian advance, the regions of the Hainault and the Barrois, the "county" of Burgundy, and Dauphiny are completely oriented toward the kingdom—by virtue of the language and all that it conveys, by virtue of the great course of commerce, and of the pervasiveness of artistic styles. At the same time, the French influence begins to seep into Provence, ruled by a brother of Louis IX. If England, closely associated with France at the end of the eleventh century and throughout the twelfth, now begins to draw away from the continent and to forge its own civilization, then, on the other hand, the secular and religious aristocracy of the Germanic regions, emerging from Carolingian rusticity, now adopt French manners. Troubadour rhythms and themes from the romances written in Champagne have been taken up by the *minnesänger* in the closing years of the twelfth century. In the valley of the Rhine, Main, and Lahn rivers, the new cathedrals have the same silhouette as those in Laon or Soissons. French building techniques appear from Scandinavia to the region of the middle Danube. The sculpture of Reims finds a faithful echo in Bamberg, an extension in Strasbourg. Similarly, since the majority of the French Crusaders were knights from the north, the Christian colonies established in the Near East—in Syria, Cyprus, and Morea—are "Frankish" in their language, the style of their castles and churches, and in the sort of life led by their lords. In Castile, at Burgos, León, and Toledo, the architecture and ornamentation of the new religious buildings again are French. The same is true in Italy: although faithful to the Roman tradition and remaining somewhat aloof to Gothic influence, she is imbued by lesser works of art—those ivory statuettes, for example, that may have been one of Giotto's sources of inspiration—and by literature: the literary dialects of France are those of fashionable entertainment, and the Florentine Brunetto Latini is not the only one to choose the French language for his vernacular works. From one end of Christendom to the other, everyone not entirely engulfed by the rural life—great merchants in touch with the Champagne fairs, Church dignitaries, courtiers, knights wandering from tournament to tournament—all have picked up some trace of the synthesis of the Ile-de-France. The thirteenth century is, without a doubt, the moment when European civilization is, at its farthest reaches, most intensely French.

V

The End of
the Middle Ages

The Fourteenth &
Fifteenth Centuries

A PERIOD of astonishing progress. The regions of France are settled; the
landscapes are molded, while an agricultural system achieves its final
form and subsequently remains almost unchanged until the eighteenth
century; new commercial circuits are established, reawakening the towns;
Christianity ceases to be merely a collection of propitiatory rites and becomes, for most men, a moral framework; logical instruments and sensibility become, for a few élite groups, enormously richer. Such is the first
era in the development of French civilization. Its roots are immersed in
Carolingian times and, beyond that, go back through the dark depths of
barbarism to rejoin Roman antiquity. Yet this era does not extend over
all that great chronological stretch habitually referred to by historians as
the Middle Ages. There is another "Middle Ages," both in Western history and in that of France—better known, more immediate, than the
other: the one revived by the Romantics, appreciably different from the
first. The point of transition from one to the other occurs immediately
after the death of Louis IX, in the 1270s. Three major alterations take
place at that time: a change in the attitude toward knowledge, a new

conception of political power, and a complete about-face of economic conditions.

The first of these changes affects only a very limited sphere, that of the intellectuals; but since it is they who hand down ways of thinking and feeling to later generations, this change, confined at first to the schools, involves the whole future. At the University of Paris, the Dominicans had tried to reconcile the new Aristotle with Christian dogma. This indicated their trust in Greek philosophy; they encouraged those numerous teachers and students in the arts faculty to study it for its own sake, its own value, without concerning themselves about integrating it into the mental perspectives ordered with respect to Christianity. Actually, around 1260, a group of dialecticians formed around Siger of Brabant—men inspired exclusively by Aristotle and by Averroës, who was the former's most daring and simultaneously his least religious commentator; they constructed, for enthusiastic followers, a purely logical world system so fundamentally at odds with Christian perspectives that it shocked many. Such temerity persuaded everyone who had long feared the seeping of dialectic into religious behavior to react. They did so brutally: the Parisian Averroists were condemned formally in 1270 and again in 1277; the second condemnation extended to the doctrine of Thomas Aquinas.

Thus, any reconciliation of Aristotle and Scripture was deemed impossible—and useless, dangerously useless—as were the attempts of generations of clerics, since the time of St. Anselm and the first murmurs of Scholasticism, to render intelligible the mysteries of dogma, and to effect a union of faith and reason. This constitutes the great rupture. The new position of the intellectuals, of which Duns Scotus, the prime example in the early years of fourteenth-century Paris, is the Franciscan. This position rejoins that other Christian speculative tendency which, prior to the triumph of Aristotle, relied upon mystical illumination: one can attain to God, not through the intellect, but through the will propelled by love. This position separates, once and for all, the religious attitude from the progress of reason.

Indeed, from now on it seems to everyone that logic cannot be applied to revealed truth, that all rational theology is without interest. Henceforth, faith is a matter of pure feeling, and the religious life becomes purely affective. Moreover, it is at this very time, after fifty or so years of gradual penetration—thwarted by the laity, and also, perhaps, by the coolness of many of the faithful who saw in the Mendicants the "pope's men"—that the Franciscan influence truly asserts itself in the religious behavior of the urban masses. (Let us take note that this influence is limited to the towns, a fact that accentuates the growing opposition between the urban and the rural civilization.) Scattered in all the centers, living in the streets, in constant contact with the laity, the gray friars are the artisans of a total renewal of religious practices; they act by example, by preaching, by auricular confession—of which they were the propagators. The Christianity they preach does not reason with itself—it lives, behind a suffering Jesus; to obtain perfect delight it calls upon the efficacy, not of the intellectual faculties, but of humility, charity, and a childlike spirit. Thus, the new scholarly concerns indicate a close correspondence with the new forms of popular piety: both lead to mysticism.

On the other hand, however, in the views introduced by Duns Scotus, human reason can be applied to everything but revelation, that is, everything located on a human scale, within the scope of human intellect —and, furthermore, human reason can do so with complete impunity, since faith is not concerned. The ideas of Duns Scotus are taken up and extended by William of Ockham, the most influential of the Parisian teachers, whose teaching, during the entire second quarter of the fourteenth century, decisively changed intellectual history—despite the condemnations that he, too, suffered. Thus, at the same time all dogmatic constraints are released, philosophy—banished almost totally from theological investigation—is liberated and is oriented toward the facts of experience. A singularly immense range of *practical* application unfurls in front of philosophy: the study of man and the world. Actually (and here again, we see a distinct correspondence between the attitude in the Universities and the real curiosity that the laity attuned to culture have manifested since the middle of the thirteenth century), logical methods are beginning to be applied to the understanding of natural phenomena in fourteenth-century France. The teachers Jean Buridan and Nicolas Oresme venture to observe the physical world by using the experimental method, although this method is still tentative and unasserted. Subsequently, there is distinct progress in the exact sciences—mathematics and optics. Through these, the sense of numerical precision, hitherto so strange to the most educated minds, begins to penetrate these minds and brings with it an increasingly sharper awareness of space and time. This latter is apparent in the appearance of the first attempts at perspective, occurring in mid-fourteenth-century miniatures, and in the rhythmic subtlety of *Ars Nova* musicians; it is reinforced by the installation of the first public clocks at Paris and Caen.

In another connection, rational analysis is brought to bear on political and social relations. The speculations on power were based less on the *Defensor Pacis*—that attack upon papal theocracy written by Marsilius of Padua, rector of the University of Paris in 1312, and by John of Jandun, regent of the Collège de Navarre, which, though prohibited, continued to be read and commented upon in the schools—than on Aristotle, in particular the *Politics*, translated into the vernacular by Nicolas Oresme between 1370 and 1377. The university men in the entourage of Charles V worked out a theory of "good policy," that is, of good government: the king, God's minister on earth, must imitate "his Royal Highness Saint Louis," practicing all the Christian virtues and governing for the "common weal"; to attain this end, the king must receive assistance from a council, a good, select, efficient council, comprised of a limited number of intelligent, *reasonable* men who will see to it that he limits himself to the resources of his domain, and that he is not too extreme against the wicked. If a monarchy does not succeed in thus tempering itself with reason, it becomes a tyranny. And, at the beginning of the fifteenth century, at the height of the struggle between the Armagnac and the Burgundian factions, and after the assassination of Louis d'Orléans, another university man—Jean Petit—publicly demonstrates with the aid of syllogisms, before the whole court, the necessity of tyrannicide.

But the application of rational reflection to the understanding of the world is not the only explanation for this quickened political conscientiousness. In actual fact, the nature and application of power have been altered radically since the last quarter of the thirteenth century. From Louis VII to Louis IX, the growth of royal authority was accomplished within the framework of feudalism; what the Capetians had done was a simple development of their authority as lord. This is "feudal monarchy" —the king administered his justice surrounded by a council of his vassals; he had them behind him in warfare; he requested their "aid" in *deniers* when he had to meet an expense that the resources of his personal estates could not cover. The idea of a sovereign power, superior to any feudal one, did not occur clearly to anyone—for, in everyone's eyes, the direct, personal, and patriarchal power of the king was exercised in the familiar form of an "amity" originating in homage and linking the retainer to the owner of his fief. But, after 1270, royalty assumed a completely different aspect; first of all, by the enlarging of its apparatus for administration. In the days of Louis IX, the "king's men" were already numerous, and during the closing years of the thirteenth century the number increased enormously. About a dozen court clerks, law officers, sergeants-at-arms, and police sergeants were connected with each bailiff's and seneschal's court, each royal fortress; hundreds of auxiliary men of all ranks, of the clergy or laity, were at the heart of the government where the personnel of the *hôtel*, charged with the maintenance of the royal house, was now completely separated from that of the "court," whose sergeants themselves were differentiated, into the Parlement with its "chambers," Chancery, and Chambre des Comptes.

Compared to that of a modern government, this is still a primitive administration, one that is improvised, flexible, totally domestic in its spirit and its way of life. Its leaders live on familiar terms with the king; its agents move willingly from one job to another, as they are needed. But this administration soon acquires regularity and order; in a world habituated to the direct exercise of power, to hand-to-hand and verbal contact between a leader and his men, it takes on an air of gigantism, of a heavy machine capable of running itself, whatever may be the personality of the king. But in that lies the great innovation: the grandson of Louis IX, Philip the Fair, is the first French king of whom we do not know whether he is responsible for all the acts of his reign; personal action, for him, may have begun to be eclipsed by that of his principal advisors. After Philip, sovereigns can lose their prestige; no longer need they personally lead their armies into war, but rather they entrust this to their captains, directing things from a distant study; even a king's madness does not prevent justice from being done, war from being conducted, and taxes from being levied—all in his name. At the outset of the fourteenth century, power ceases to be confined strictly to the royal person.

Furthermore, this complex organism, managed collectively by so plentiful a number of officers who, scattered everywhere, are fervent propagators of royal claims, extends its action much further than did the "feudal" monarchy. The king of France no longer conceives his sole mission as the creation of a reign of peace and justice within the territory entrusted to him by God, no longer thinks of himself as leading his people on a crusade for their common salvation. He stands at the frontiers of the kingdom—from which are separated, in spirit if not officially, the Catalonian and Flemish regions—and sees, beyond these frontiers, in Lyon and then in Dauphiny, his interests and (from his point of view) those of his subjects thwarted by the work of foreign lords.

The period of great armed conflicts begins in Europe with the fourteenth century. In feudal France, warfare—formerly a seasonal plundering expedition against a neighboring people—had become local, even familial, banditry; individual revenge and sporadic agitation by little bands, filling the intervals between the peace of God, on the outskirts of manors—short forays regulated by the customs of "honor." The only large-scale expeditions organized against distant objectives were the Crusades. But henceforth, war was to be a matter of conspicuously more bitter confrontations, on the scale of the large political entities that gradually became disengaged from the feudal structure. Most of the time, the pretexts are still quarrels over fiefs and vassalage, or family differences; but these conflicts are inflamed by economic interests and the slow germination in the heart of the collective consciousness, not of national feeling but of xenophobia—that is, of an aggressiveness toward foreigners—at its liveliest around the frontier regions, which now have acquired more real meaning as borders of states. In this lies a profound change in European living conditions, the causes and forms of which would merit close study.

In order to conduct these wars which, because they were of greater duration, necessitated a more sustained effort, the modes of action furnished to the French king by feudal customs are inadequate. How can effective operations be undertaken, when the host of vassals is slowly gathered by their bailiff, then unhurriedly dispatched to the point of concentration? These men, often equipped with decaying saddlery, are concerned with enjoying themselves at the lord's or king's expense, in the company of their rediscovered friends; lacking any notion of discipline, they leave the army on the eve of a battle, at the height of a siege, absolutely determined to return home once the forty days' service they owe for their fief has been completed. Ever since the twelfth century, kings have been employing mercenary armies, specialists in modern weapons and conscientious workers. During the reign of Philip the Fair, the entire army is paid a sum which varies according to the fighters' excellence and armaments. Vassals also become mercenaries, thus permitting unlimited service to be exacted from them; they can be equipped appropriately (that is, inspected in "musters") and can be grouped into well-led companies. This system is efficient but expensive. At a time when the maintenance of the king's house, court, and government agents normally necessitates only limited recourse to money, to mobilize an army for two or three months is enough to triple or quadruple cash expenses and to empty the treasury at one fell swoop, even though the army be a scanty one, never comprising more than two or three thousand knights. A slightly drawn-out siege results in several years of financial difficulties.

Thus, adapting the army to the new warfare necessitated the sudden augmentation of royal finances. Now, the idea that the king—like every lord—ought to be content with the resources of his own domain and the aid of his vassals, and that the *coutumes* are restricted to very precise occasions, is a deep-seated one. Has the king the right to ask for more, to levy taxes? This is one of the questions that particularly engrossed the minds of political theorists during the reign of Charles V; and, if the author of the *Songe du Verger* holds the opinion that the sovereign, being responsible for the common good, can claim subsidies in his own right for the general welfare, the contrary opinion is held by Nicolas Oresme, who makes the "extraordinary" levies depend on the express consent of the governed. In point of fact, despite this reluctance, the king's men do raise the money they lack—as they can, by the use of all sorts of expediencies. There are loans, but also various taxes. The king's financial system begins to weigh on the kingdom and, beyond that, to connect both feudal intermediaries and his subjects' wealth to that of the sovereign.

Ultimately, another conception of royal authority is formulated in the final quarter of the thirteenth century, among the monarchy's assistants who are desperately seeking the resources for a larger-scale policy. A policy propagated especially by the officers from new estates in Languedoc—the "legists," educated in Roman law at the universities of Bologna and Montpellier—the doctrine of sovereignty they worked out is completely opposed to the notion that grew out of the feudal manor. The king of France is, for them, "emperor in his kingdom"—which means, primarily, that he is independent of all other power, save that of God. He is independent of the Emperor (but since the death of Frederick Barbarossa, the Empire is nothing in the West); independent, too, of the pope. It is at this point that the kingdom breaks loose, and violently: we know how bitter was the conflict waged by Philip the Fair against Boniface VIII; we know that the papal ascendancy made the French Church begin to think about forming a united body more closely attached to the king than to the Holy See. Also, to speak of the king's *imperium* is to assert baldly that he possesses an unopposable sovereign authority over all his subjects—a revival of the *lèse-majesté* idea, a definitive disengagement of royal power from its feudal trappings. But it thereby became necessary to establish types of communication between monarch and subject other than those that once followed from link to link in the chain of homage. Hence, the first meetings of the "estates." These were, in effect, mere adaptations of the feudal "counsel": the king summoned, in addition to the barons and prelates, representatives of other "orders"—the bourgeois from the prosperous towns and from the University. These assemblies were without any regularity: the king decided to convene them whenever a particular difficulty arose, when he felt the need of unity on the part of the kingdom's principal members, for a decision he wanted to make. The large gathering that took place in Paris in 1302 is the first to make its impression upon contemporaries for, at the height of the struggle over papal decisions, it was concerned with preparing public opinion for the possible excommunication of the king and with trying to find out how far people's resistance would extend. Subsequent meetings were held more for the purpose of advising people of financial difficulties and plans for taxation. These "estates" were diversely constituted: the assemblies settling the dynastic problems when Philip the Fair's sons died were composed exclusively of nobles and Church dignitaries, whereas, whenever money was concerned, bourgeois delegates were dominant. Never were the estates "general" in this kingdom that was still so vast and so varied; Languedoc still had its own private ones, and in the regions of *langue d'oïl*, they were often convened province by province. There was no regular representation—only those came who were summoned by the king's men—nor any discussion: one listened to the royal will. Nevertheless, during the first half of the fourteenth century, a dialogue between king and subject began to be established through these means. With warfare and increased financial exigencies, the estates were convened more and more frequently. Bargaining began on the fringes of the plenary assemblies; the king's men had to promise certain reforms as payment for aids. Confronted with a less personal, less sovereign royal power, one that gradually was forging its instruments of government, the grievances of the people became apparent, and the idea was born of a possible control, conforming to the theories of the political philosophers: in this sphere, again, the close of the Middle Ages possesses a markedly different color.

Characteristics of the economy differentiate it even more. In fact, the decades surrounding the year 1300 produce a complete reversal of the combination of favorable trade circumstances. The full expansion movement, which had progressed steadily, distributing prosperity throughout France for three centuries, slowed down around 1270, and then stopped. This is the beginning of a long period of stagnation, slump, and recession; of a falling-off in production and trade that compels a bitter struggle against thousands of connected difficulties, clouding over daily life. Can we say that this entails a decline in everything? Must we, like Huizinga and so many historians after him, speak of the fourteenth and fifteenth centuries in terms of twilight and decline? Must we consider everyone in this period to be neurotic, incapable of producing balanced creations, lost in a dream-world, divided between excessive mysticism and a frenzied search for wild pleasure? There is a trace of Romanticism in this pessimistic view. The historian ought to be on his guard, for three reasons: first, because his documentary material, which is beginning to become overabundant, forces him increasingly to choose, to scrutinize it, for it is now the exceptional features which make an impression, threatening to obscure the normal, the everyday balance of life. Secondly, because, by dint of being on the lookout for novelties, eager to apprehend them when they appear, the historian forgets all the things which, coming from the prosperous era of the Middle Ages, penetrate and reinforce a period of adversity: the savings, the reserves, and that enormous torrent of reassuring customs. Thirdly, because the world, still so vigorously rooted in the soil, so close to nature, so hardened and fundamentally primitive in its ways of life and its reflexes, is less vulnerable, less affected by the ups and downs of fortune than we—from the viewpoint of our frail and complicated civilization—might believe. Just as the methods, the inquisitiveness, the ways of reasoning and of considering the world continue among intellectuals, scarcely and imperceptibly deflected by the new philosophical options; just as the feudal and manorial system remains as the basic framework of political relations, despite the advances of royal sovereignty; just as the *banalités* are infinitely more important in men's eyes than the meetings of the "estates," or recourse to royal justice: just as, in this period of intense crisis, the overwhelming majority of Frenchmen—peasants anxious to harvest only what can be eaten before the next summer, provincial *hobereaux*, ignorant of all luxury, busying themselves with hunting and family meetings, modest townspeople, suburban vine-growers, and small craftsmen with only a few customers—felt, we are sure, merely very much subdued, aware of little more than the effects of those fluctuations in the circulation of money, those interruptions of commercial routes that, in the rare developed sectors of economic activity, more markedly modified the living scale for a few. This is certainly a period of hard times—but a period in which sufficient vitality is conserved to maintain and renew cultural traditions; to initiate, at the height of the fiftccnth century, the revival that brought about the appearance of the first seething signs of the Renaissance.

► HARD TIMES

Although they are most heart-rending when they come from the poorest classes, then just beginning to express themselves, lamentations echo through all social strata during the fourteenth century. At first these cries are intermittent, isolated; gradually, from around 1330 on, they become louder; and finally, between 1420 and 1430, they merge into a universal moan. There is a weariness in the face of material difficulties; and in the face of a menacing death, an apprehension and anxiety expressed in the literary works—the turgidly rhetorical occasional poems, the more precise manner of intimate writings—journals, memoirs and, more tragically, the testaments and inventories where the hardness of the time appears in no uncertain terms. Among these perils, which are not clearly separable, there arise three obsessive calamities: famine, war, and pestilence.

To the contemporaries of Du Guesclin and Joan of Arc, the good days —the golden age, the days of his royal highness St. Louis—were, above all, the era when everyone had enough to eat. This was, to be sure, a delusion: the twelfth and thirteenth centuries had known bad years, summers that were too rainy, winters that were too severe, times between harvests when people had to mix less edible foodstuffs in with the good grain, and to tighten the belt as well, in order to stave off hunger. Nonetheless, in comparison with the feudal era, the end of the Middle Ages is a period of dietary insecurity; the shortages are more frequent and more serious, and there are famines to which men have grown unaccustomed during the course of two or more centuries. At the heart of all the difficulties of the period, then, we see the dearth of provisions. Where does it come from?

Before the fourteenth century, before the development of princely financial systems, and also before the establishment of a new sense of statistical precision, no one ever bothered to take a census of a town's or province's inhabitants. The earliest document preserved in the French Archives bearing any resemblance to our modern census dates from 1328; this is the "condition of the fires in the jurisdiction of bailiffs and seneschals"—who, in the royal domain, add up, parish by parish, the "fires," that is, the taxable units—a very delicate matter to interpret. All the evidence leads us to believe, however, that since the beginning of the eleventh century population had been increasing at a rapid rate. But this advance was constantly accompanied and stimulated by a no less lively growth of agricultural production, due to gradual technical improvement and to the continuous extension of arable land, the reclaiming of ponds, fallow terrain, and large forests. Now, after the end of the thirteenth century, it would certainly appear that the crops no longer are increasing. By now, the best processes of cultivation have spread everywhere they can reach. There are no new improvements, there is no more clearing of land—because, on the one hand, it is no longer possible to reduce the forest and pasture area any further without altering the agricultural system; and, on the other, the burst of acquisitiveness caused men to clear land so unfertile that, after a few mediocre harvests, it was exhausted. Far from man's being able to extend the fields any farther, it was necessary to return them to less barren soil. This resulted in a standstill, if not a recession, in production. Since the upward rise of population was to continue for some time to come, the equilibrium was therefore broken. France—with, almost certainly, fewer than fifteen million inhabitants—was an overpopulated country at the beginning of the fourteenth century, one in which many were unable to find enough to eat. The shortage becomes chronic, then the irregularity of agricultural prices, following upon the first wheat crisis, spreads between 1315 and 1317, and becomes permanently established. The difference that henceforth holds sway between the value of provisions and that of other merchant products, seems to have perceptibly changed the mentality of the peasant producers. The main concern, now, is survival from one year to the next, as it was before the great agricultural advance. What good to extract from the land more than is necessary to feed and clothe one's household? People return to the same old habits of an almost closed economy; they slam their doors upon those "thieves" who wish to sell their products for them—that is (from the peasant viewpoint), to grow fat at their expense—and upon peddlers, since one is no longer accustomed to spending much money. They revive their ancestors' primitive ways, which prosperity had allowed them to abandon; and within a very short time, three or four generations, have returned to animal life, bent upon food alone. This revival of the peasantry, which had been beginning to open up to the trade economy, was the first element

in the economic malaise—a malaise fostered and aggravated by a second
unbalancing factor: war.

The thirteenth century had not yet ended when the long period of
large-scale conflict began. In effect, the campaigns led by Philip the Fair
in Guyenne and Flanders were the prelude to a war, officially declared
in 1337, against the king of England: the Hundred Years' War. The expression is inexact: the armed struggle, continuing until 1453, actually
continued for more than a century; but it has the merit of pointing out
conveniently the permanence of the hostilities—perhaps the most important characteristic of the era. Henceforth, everyday life had to make
room for war; men were born who were never to know, despite the testimony of their grandfathers, what peace was. What sort of war was it?

It was a war that was not waged in exactly the same way as in the
days of Philip Augustus or of Louis IX. Taking into consideration all the
elements of habit that remain in a warrior's acts and equipment—how
many poor *hobereaux* must have rejoined the king's army with the
weapons and cuirasses forged by their grandfathers during the period of
rural prosperity—and the strength of those old customs which impose a
certain attitude toward the enemy, there were still many changes in the
fourteenth century.

The main innovation doubtless results from the greater efficacy of pro-
jectile weapons: the crossbow, complicated and fragile, but precise,
whose special feature, the bolt or "quarrel," has a frightening power to
puncture; the long-bow, which shoots far and hard, and which can be
drawn with extraordinary rapidity; to say nothing of the artillery and ex-
plosive weapons, whose building was made possible by advances in
metalworking, but which, as they are still not too easy to handle, are
used primarily in sieges to replace the old catapults—they are particularly
effective in pitched battles because of the noise they make, terrifying
both men and horses. This improvement in long-range, offensive weapons renders absurd the use of leather shields and the old shirts of mail
for protection. The first consequence is that armor has to adapt itself:
iron plates are affixed to the hauberk at its most vulnerable points, first
placed side by side, then organized in a sufficiently resistant shell which,
becoming increasingly improved through the introduction of hinges,
becomes increasingly heavy as well. In the fifteenth century, a more
modern type of armor weighs 130 to 175 pounds; thus, a warrior is unable to arm himself, let alone support himself—he is also unable to
make the most ordinary gestures, is obliged to walk straight ahead and to
strike only at things directly in front of him. He is unable to lift himself up if he falls to the ground, and, if the ground is muddy, he is
bogged down in it. Furthermore, the possibilities of cavalry are appreciably diminished; first of all, because no horse can carry such heavy riders
either very far or very fast; secondly, because the horse, having no cuirass,

is rapidly put out of combat by the arrows of the archers or crossbowmen. Hence, the increasing importance of fighting on the ground. French knights adapt themselves, slowly and awkwardly and by suffering stinging defeats, to the new tactics introduced by the English—fighting in armor, but on foot, using a short arm like the mace or sword. The ancestral superiority of the man equipped with a horse diminishes as the role of the infantryman grows: archers and *coutiliers* who lunge with daggers for the interstices of the armored shell, either attacking when an armed man has fallen to the ground or surprising him from the rear since he is unable to turn around. By degrees, the man clothed in armor, the jousting horseman—once the only warrior worthy of the name—is integrated into a combat group that surrounds him, consisting of two archers, now mounted so as to be more mobile (very often these are nobles too poor to carry plate armor), a *coutilier* (again, in the fifteenth century, this duty is sometimes performed by gentlemen), and the valet and page, who are responsible for taking care of the weapons and for guarding the horses during battle. This team is called the "lance," the attendants of men-at-arms.

Such changes also involve modifications in the warrior mentality. Difficult to eradicate as were the moral rules formed in the old jousts now that killing is done from a distance and the foot soldier is deadly, combat gradually loses all semblance of a duel, an *affaire d'honneur* carried out honestly without "evil devices." The French soldiers came into contact with mercenary specialists who treated war as a profession, desired only to be effective, and cared little (unless they had arrived at the acme of an exceptional career) for courtesy and chivalric deeds—men who very often come from the wildest provinces, the least polished social groups. Through this contact with the mercenaries and through their gradually being contaminated with xenophobic attitudes, the French knights—faced with an enemy speaking a foreign language, and with that enemy's very behavior (for the English, accustomed to merciless fighting against Scotland and Wales, had the most brutal habits imaginable)—acquired the habit of opportunistic guile and, perhaps, less respect for human life. At any rate, they engage in military operations with an entirely new way of doing things. Pitched battles, arranged in advance, are increasingly rare. The main action consists of rapid, surprise forays, pursuits, ambushes, and badgering skirmishes by small and very mobile bands—and consists, above all, of sieges, which become the major episodes of battles, as can readily be seen in the chronicles as well as in the illuminations of history books. Since defense techniques are far ahead of offensive ones, the sieges are interminable; castles and towns are virtually impregnable, and blockades are rarely total. There are lengthy sieges of fortified places, and this produces something new: the season for warmaking is extended into winter. During these long sieges, the beseiger settles himself in, erecting his own fortresses and temporary lodgings opposite those of the enemy. Yet these periods are, for the besieged, times of austerity and affliction, even after expendable mouths have been dispensed with—and for the others, times of idleness and boredom, of growing impatience; they fall ill when the hard times last and, finally, massacre the defenders when they have held out too long. Nevertheless, these sieges concentrate the armies on one point for a long time, thus leaving the rest of the country in peace: such is the new warfare.

This new warfare, infinitely less destructive than the modern variety, presents on the whole few physical dangers for the combatants: despite the fresh outbreak of aggressiveness and the growing inurement to murder and suffering, essentially war is still (more than ever, perhaps) a race for ransom, a great money-game, in which one risks all his fortune in the hope of winning someone else's—the poor, having no wherewithal to ransom themselves, are unhesitatingly massacred—a game in which, before the battle, one conspires with several others to capture the big prey alive and so to share the profits. One does not kill the conquered if one knows they are well provided for—that would ruin everything; it is quite by accident that, in the fluster of an unexpected victory, frightened by a false alert, Henry V of England had most of his prisoners killed when night fell at Agincourt: a disastrous waste, long deplored. Normally, all battles stop once the enemy abandons the terrain. There is no pursuit; the conquerors, sure of their prisoners, would not risk losing them for anything. Therefore, no battle is decisive. Unless there is a mishap, then, the noble combatant preserves his life, but he risks long years of captivity; for generally, the ransom is very high (honor demands that one overbid in the dealings that follow defeat), too high a sum for the family to raise easily, even with the help of the feudal *coutume* that obliges the vassals and retainers to render "aid" in those exceptional cases when the lord is taken prisoner. The periods of captivity are more or less arduous, but they take the knight out of his natural milieu for a protracted period, easing the habitual family and vassal ties. They are equally tedious and expensive for the "masters" obliged to maintain the prisoner. Often they get rid of him by ceding their "rebate" rights to other captors, and ultimately this practice gives rise, at a time when cash is rare, to an enormous movement of silver and gold currency, diverting this money from its normal circuit. These ill-regulated transfers throw the nobility's wealth into disequilibrium.

For those who do not wage it, war is not so disastrous, either, as one might think; indeed, the total strength of the armies is extremely weak. Setting out to conquer France, and stretching to their limits all the military and financial resources of his kingdom to succeed in this undertaking, Henry V of England landed in 1417 with fewer than eleven thousand men. In 1429, the defenders of Orléans numbered about a thousand, and it was Joan of Arc's arrival with reinforcements, amounting to two hundred men-at-arms, that reversed the situation. As few troops as these, therefore, cannot destroy very much. Either they are always on the move—in which case all the noncombatant has to do is to be attentive, provide for some hiding place for his valuables, and sit patiently for a few days in the woods or swamps with his animals—or else the army sets itself up for a siege, in which case the pillaging is limited to a very small area. In short, war is never sustained because no one has the means to wage it for long. People do get used to fighting during the winter, but not without some reluctance; for most of the warriors action is limited, as formerly, to a session of several weeks during the summer months of the year. Consequently, hostilities are always interrupted by agreements, truces, and "abstentions from war" determined for a longer or shorter period, but a period during which the ravages can be repaired.

Though it never affects more than a few districts, interrupted by countless respites, and is, all things considered, not very deadly, the new war is disastrous nevertheless, much more so than the feudal conflicts of old. First, it is more profoundly and deliberately destructive. The English raids during the earlier period of the Hundred Years' War were expeditions of systematic pillaging, with long wagon trains taking the booty back to the ships. Then, after the French sustained amazing defeats in great pitched battles at Crécy and Poitiers, they answered these incursions with a new tactic: lay waste to the region beforehand, take the heart out of the enemy by destroying, before his very eyes, what he was preparing to take. Above all, war is now a matter for professionals, and here lies the principal misfortune. The kings of France and of England, and later the princes, are no longer content with their vassals' paid services. At the point of undertaking a campaign, they negotiate with captains, combat contractors, adventurers from many parts (England, Germany, Brittany, Franche-Comté, the Basque region, Spain, and the Lorraine), most of the time noblemen: these men put their "company," their mercenaries (*routes*) at the ruler's disposal—once they take their cut. These groups are strongly united under the authority of a leader who is the better obeyed since he is brave and can both supply and defend his men. Such a band has fifteen to thirty armed men, rarely more; there are nobles too, but poor or bastard ones, sometimes even former peasants. They are accompanied by auxiliary forces, servants, blacksmiths, and always a cleric to keep the accounts and to give communion. These mercenaries wage war and wage it well. But when their employer can no longer pay them, or whenever the truces put them out of work, all the companies do not break up. The majority, formed of combatants now uprooted from their normal surroundings and unable to take up their

former life, continue to pillage for their own provisions—and more ruth-
lessly than before, because they are in no one's pay. They get their food
from the land and move on when it is exhausted; they cut off the roads,
intercept merchant caravans, and impose, in exchange for relative security, regular tribute upon both peasant and urban communities. Not only
prolonging and deepening the hardships of war, but also making violence an everyday occurrence, rendering the truces more distressing than
the active phases of battle, since during the latter the soldiers are at least
busy fighting and, in a few cases, dying, these companies are the real
plague. There is a fresh outbreak of disorder after every general peace:
after the Peace of Brétigny in 1360, *grandes compagnies* overrun the
untouched provinces in Burgundy and the Rhône Valley. People do not
know what to do about these men who threaten the pope in Avignon,
and refuse to leave on a Crusade. Finally, Du Guesclin succeeds in drag-
ging them off to Castile. After Arras in 1435, we hear of the *écorcheurs*,*
the "shearers" [*retondeurs*] "who recut what the first pillagers had failed
to snatch up and take." These men are brigands—the word is contemporary, and the French word *brigand* comes from a piece of military
equipment—but their leaders are not banned from society (it is from
them, we must recall, that Joan of Arc recruited her associates). These
leaders continue to negotiate with kings, pride themselves on their courtesy, are finicky about valor; sometimes they make good marriages, purchase manors (if they have been prudent), and often die in the most
edifying piety. War is, in short, a disaster because, even waged with such
mediocre means, with such little power, and without prolonged effort, it
is nonetheless extremely expensive, consuming money and ruining kings'
finances.

It was primarily the need to pay the soldiers and to meet the expenses
incurred by war (such as the enormous ransom for King John, taken
prisoner at Poitiers in 1356) that brought about the regular tapping of pri
vate savings for the needs of the prince: the establishment of taxes in
France. These were established gradually, were judged by many to be
scandalous; there was interminable discussion with the "estates" of the
realm, there were opposition and stubborn revolts. Thus the salt tax
(*gabelle*), the aids collected in the towns on the sale of the principal consumer goods, and the *taille* levied in the rural communities by "fires," diverted a great portion of the money in circulation to unproductive expenditures. Still, this sort of taxation was inadequate: the king's men
were forced to other expedients, like that of "stirring money," that is,
changing the face value of coins. These were delicate manipulations in
a bimetallic system where the flow of gold and silver was extremely variable; upsetting prices and thereby restraining trade, they were con-

---

* Literally, "flayers," gangs of armed marauders who laid waste to large areas of
France during the reigns of Charles VI and Charles VII.—Trans.

demned as fraudulent, even by members of the king's entourage: Nicolas Oresme, for the edification of Charles V, brought forth a theory of money stability based on the Aristotelian notion of the common good. Both the financial system and the unforeseeable fluctuations in value also led to recession, to money hoarding, aggravations of the economic uneasiness caused by the insufficient agricultural production. A good part of the gloom that hangs over the final centuries of the Middle Ages is attributable even more to the monetary consequences of the wars than to the devastation they wrought.

There is a third scourge, even more deadly, since no one knows whence comes its power nor how to find protection from it: disease. Ineffective medical prescriptions and poor hygiene—for although people possessed a few habits of cleanliness, their diet was irregular and unbalanced, their homes badly ventilated, their lives beset by swarms of parasites—opened the door to epidemics. Yet, in the twelfth and thirteenth centuries, the epidemics' development had not reached catastrophic proportions, doubtless because the human organism was accustomed to attacks of disease, occurring in unvarying forms; it gradually became immune to them. This biological equilibrium was disrupted in the fourteenth century, first because the populace, having become too numerous and consequently ill-fed, went into a chronic state of physical deficiency aggravated still more by the war's abuses—forced evacuations or else congested huddling behind the walls of a besieged town. More particularly, a new disease is suddenly introduced into Europe: the plague, in its bubonic and pulmonary forms. The "Black Death," as it was called, came from the commercial ports of the Levant, conveyed by the commercial ships; it penetrated into France early in 1348, through Marseille and the ports of Languedoc. Through Avignon, that great crossroads, it spread in all directions. Precautions were taken—withdrawal from towns, military cordons at ports, flights to rural sanctuaries, large fires fed by aromatic herbs that people thought useful for disinfecting the air, the group penances, and the processions of flagellants seeking, first in Flanders, then in Picardy and Champagne, to appease heaven through public mortification of the flesh, the massacres of Jews, blamed for the calamity when the people stopped laying this responsibility at the door of the Mendicant orders, the research under the king's aegis into cures undertaken by the teachers of the medical faculty at the University of Paris. But notwithstanding all these precautions, the disease gained ground everywhere, and reached its apex in the summer of 1348. It was a terrible slaughter. Froissart thought, as did his contemporaries, that a third of mankind disappeared during that time—an estimate that seems too high for the rural regions, but actually not high enough for the towns. The parish records for the little market town of Givry in Burgundy indicate that half the population died in that year (680 died during August, September, and October, at a time when the normal monthly average was five, and the total population perhaps twelve to fifteen hundred); and the mortality rate was terrible in denser groups like monasteries, cathedral chapters, and fighting units. In Marseille, every Franciscan died; at Montpellier, seven Dominicans out of one hundred thirty survived. This extraordinarily brutal shock changed living conditions for a long time. One can imagine the repercussions: the terror, augmented by the swiftness of the disease which attacked the strongest men first; the sudden lack of priests, and consequently the confusion in men's souls; a clergy bled white by the annihilation of its best members; the labor shortage, and the sudden rise in wages; the halting of wars throughout Europe for six or seven years; the huge turnover in inheritance rights; and the sort of vital madness seizing the survivors. Having periods of abatement, then returning for another offensive phase (as in 1361, 1373, 1380, and so on), during which people were again unable to bury their dead, the plague established itself to stay.

It was in about the middle of the century, when the effects of these three major calamities began to converge, that the hardship of the times became evident and increasingly conspicuous. Destruction of the rural areas was of an uneven sort: far-reaching only in those provinces where the hostilities lasted—Normandy, Ile-de-France, the outskirts of Guyenne, and Provence; more often than not, the destruction was temporary, and was doggedly patched up in the intervals between the military crossings and deaths. Yet the landscape was changed: devastation and abandonment of inhabited areas, setbacks in the vineyards, increased wastelands and forest areas which sometimes remained permanent as in Puisaye or the Dombes. For the population decrease was immense and widespread: it is estimated that Normandy, inhabited by a million and a half people at the close of the thirteenth century, could not have numbered more than a half-million a hundred and fifty years later. Sometimes this depopulation was total and permanent, stretching over wide areas: in 1417, the last three inhabitants of a Saintonge parish departed it to take refuge in Bordeaux; the village of Magny-les-Hameaux, near Paris, remained completely deserted from 1431 until 1455, when "three poor Normands" came there to settle. Nevertheless, those peasants who were not dead or evacuated actually found themselves in a better position with respect to their masters, for they were far less numerous. As a matter of fact, when the knights and their stewards called the workers to arms after each alert and supervised the restoration of the land to cultivation, the repair of the hovels, the planting of new vineyards, and the reconstruction of the manors, were to the peasants' advantage.

It is in this manner that, as the fourteenth century emerges, the majority of those whose ancestors were chained in hereditary serfdom—

Aquitainian *questaux*, the Burgundian *hommes couchants et levants*—
attained their freedom. They do so by running far from their homes, taking possession of the unoccupied land in the depopulated regions, and
by coming to amicable terms with the owner of their person—for he too
is racked by problems. After the middle of the fifteenth century, serfdom in France survives only sporadically. On the other hand, the rent for
the land is reduced, by the very depreciation of money, but also by agreement with the lord: during the truces, when it was necessary to find
new takers for the deserted holdings, the villagers all solidly refused to
accept them without a reduction in quitrents (*cens*),* often, the *métayage* system, extremely widespread during thirteenth-century rural prosperity, was replaced by a reasonable rent, paid in money. Gathered
into family communities, probably more closely knit than before these
difficult times, almost all the farmers are working larger, more concentrated, and more productive farms by the end of the Hunded Years' War.
Yet, since their ways are cruder than in earlier times, they undoubtedly
live more miserably than their ancestors. In 1465 (during a time, that
is, when many wounds were already healed), the Englishman John For-
tescue, traveling through France, was astonished to see peasants dressed
in flimsy tatters, drinking plain water, eating apples and rye bread,
never eating meat except in the forms of lard, tripe, and the heads of animals slaughtered for bourgeois and nobles. An obviously sparse population, a lower standard of living, a perceptible recession in cultivatable
lands, a pronounced tendency, within farming communities, to reduce
the number of exchanges with the outside world: such is the new appearance of rural France after the middle of the fourteenth century.

Within the urban centers, something of the countryside is present:
cattle, fermentation vats, gardens, plowed-up plots of ground between
houses—more numerous, perhaps, because the buildings are sparser and
the obsession with hunger is more pressing. Despite all this, the breach
between the towns and the rural world is more overt than it was before.
Always enclosed, straitly surrounded by ramparts, for the outlying areas
were destroyed in the face of the enemy (English or mercenary), the
cities are less exposed to the ravages of war. If they are captured, they
are more at the mercy of pillagers and rapists; but their walls are strong
and, except when they are betrayed or surprised, it takes more patience
than the captains usually have to bring them to their knees. The towns
are refuges, islands of security, into which the most unfortunate, the uprooted, and the derelicts of rural society, try to wedge themselves—but
these attempts are rarely successful; the bourgeois close their doors to
outsiders, for the latter are new mouths to be fed during famines,
and probably carriers of plague germs to boot. Yet actually, the towns

---

* An annual sum paid by a peasant to his lord either in kind or specie; it was based
on the proportion of land held by a peasant.—Trans.

escape neither calamity nor anxiety: they are struck violently by the
death rate, they worry more about provisions, and, above all, they are affected in their most basic function by the slackening of commercial activity.

From the end of the thirteenth century onward, the geography of
Western business is appreciably changed. The large woolen industry of
Flanders and Artois enters into a period of decline for a variety of reasons, doubtless the most important being the change in style: heavy wool
cloth falls into disrepute, and those who care about elegance prefer silk
goods, lighter woolens, or linens lined with fur. Business stagnates at
Douai, and the town rapidly declines. Arras does not fail completely, because a new industry, that of smooth-faced tapestries which become indispensable ornaments in princely households, is established there during the course of the fourteenth century. But, generally speaking, the
preparation of cloth is now scattered over a great number of urban centers, often even more greatly diffuse, into rural areas where the work
avoids the very strict control of the guilds and, especially, where salaries
are much lower—are, indeed, a token, off-season contribution to the
needy peasants. Widely scattered outside of France, the textile industry henceforth is much less concentrated even in France, with a few
more active areas in Normandy, Champagne, and the southern regions
of Languedoc. Another major center of the old economic system also
slackens: the fairs in Champagne. The main European trade ceased to be
organized around them as early as 1270; they preserved their financial
function for some time, until about 1310, and finally they lost it very
rapidly.

Actually, from the fourteenth century on, the trade economy of the
West acquires more complexity. It is no longer so simply gathered about
the Flanders-Italy axis which, passing through France, had made it so astonishingly prosperous until now. This fact derives from political partitioning, from the gradual isolation of kingdoms whose rulers, seeking
to drain pieces of gold into their coffers by every means at their command, try blunderingly to direct foreign trade and thereby throw it into
disharmony which, after the return of bimetallism, affects the monetary
system. Then, too, there is the establishment of new trade itineraries: the
advances in naval technique make possible direct connections between
the Italian ports, England, and the North Sea; there are also improvements in the Alpine trails, enabling Italian merchants to reach the Netherlands through Switzerland, the Bavarian plateau, and the Rhône Valley. France, once the commercial crossroads of Christendom, now finds
herself somewhat in the background; the large economic centers and the
major areas of prosperity, where business practices are being revived, are
no longer in France but in Italy, along the North Sea, and on the Ibe-
rian peninsula.

The paralysis of commercial activity in France is partially the result of the shifting of the major trade circuits. Yet much more than war itself —which never absolutely obstructed commercial movement, since the small sectors of hostilities could be skirted—the most basic causes of this paralysis are, first of all, the shortage of cash, closely linked with the economic disorders, and still more the decrease in purchasing power, brought about by the wasteful expenditures for warmaking, the recession in agricultural production, and the minimal yield of the manors. This stagnation is not really universal; a few centers of great commercial prosperity continue to exist. They are the political capitals, those privileged points where, sucked out by the new fiscal measures, all the taxed gold converges and flows into the hands of the princes, and of their households, servants, and guests; for, levying it under the pretext of warfare, they consume it all in luxury and entertainments. There are still powerful little centers of feudal principalities such as Orthez, the capital of the Béarn. The two major centers are Avignon and Paris. Avignon is the city of the pope and of his cardinals' houses; it shares in the activity of Italy by virtue of Marseille and the Durance, and all Christendom supplies it with precious metal—before the Schism. Paris continues to grow; at the beginning of the fifteenth century its population is two hundred thousand and perhaps more. Because of the presence of the Royal Court, it replaces the fairs of Champagne as the principal locality for commerce and money between the Alps and the Netherlands. In the few towns in which Italian companies are represented, business is better than ever. A group of important merchants supplying the prince prosper there; they are integrated closely into his finances, the management of which they actually have been given control in exchange for lending him money. These islands of prosperity, however, are altogether exceptional amid the general lassitude.

All the other towns are in decline. Ruins, entire areas of devastated houses, attest to their impoverishment. Tax registers indicate, on the one hand, a falling-off of population (forty thousand in Toulouse at the beginning of the fourteenth century; only twenty thousand a hundred years later), and, on the other, the dissolution of the large fortunes. The craftsmen and retailers have a much more difficult life: their customers have dwindled because of the peasants' few purchases and the nobles' financial difficulties, so they seek a remedy for their difficulties by strengthening professional restrictions. After the beginning of the fourteenth century, the guilds become more rigid, enclosing themselves in a network of fussy regulations, and refusing to admit newcomers. Thus, in 1319, the Arras municipal magistrates decide that from then on they will not accept into the fishmonger guild

> any more colleagues than there are now, unless they are the grown-up children of colleagues, born of an honest marriage, and no one

else . . . to avoid the trouble and inconvenience that was in the city, which burdened the common profit . . . because of the large number of colleagues that existed in the said guild, growing every day, and thus raising the price of goods. . . .[1]

But this blind reaction that congealed manufacturing processes and paralyzed venturesome initiative by protecting the weakest and most routine industries increased the stagnation even more. There followed a very unequivocal depression. If we compare the activity, mentality, and the way of life of the provincial French merchant with those of his Italian contemporary, he seems singularly behind the times. His customers are few, because the majority of men fill their basic needs by farming a little plot of ground, thus bypassing the merchant in this period of withdrawal. He is unable to specialize, but sells everything, for his role varies according to the fluctuations in the local agricultural production: in the years of plenty, he supplies those few commodities the estate cannot produce itself—oil, salt, dried fish for fast-days, and, especially, fabrics; in the lean years, he becomes primarily a purveyor of grain. He can often be seen along the roads transporting his own merchandise. Having very few helpers, using archaic methods of bookkeeping (the use of Arabic numerals is not introduced until after 1430 and even then they catch on slowly), he leads a life of extreme simplicity, with few books except some devotional ones in the vernacular, no works of art except a few crude religious objects; his only luxuries are display fabrics which hang from his walls, and a suit of unusually rich fabric. And as soon as he has accumulated a little money, the merchant buys some land, which is the best investment possible, assuring that primary asset: secure provisions. The merchant's ideal is to become a landed manor lord as soon as he can, and to lead a noble, idle, rural life. Not even the slightest prefiguration of the capitalist spirit is discernible in his attitude toward his wealth.

A stagnation of techniques, then, and a setback in both production and trade; the lively upward mobility of social classes in the thirteenth century has now reached almost a standstill. In the decades subsequent to the reversal of this tendency, until about 1380, as the result of the first shocks of monetary changes, wars, and plagues, a few spasms trouble the social body. There is confusion in the years from 1349 to 1351, directly after the passing of the Black Death, when the government tries, with meager means, to restore order in the setting of prices and in the labor market. There follow peasant revolts—the Jacquerie of the Ile-de-France in 1357, and the Tuchins of Languedoc in 1381—reflex actions of uncontrolled rage in the face of an excessive poverty, insurrections of a few who, having in their fury slaughtered the king's men and the lords, fall into a panic, do not know what to do; they killed at random and, so that they would not be the only guilty ones, forced others to follow them. These revolts are leaderless, programless, hopeless movements, and finally are trampled down by men-at-arms. There are also bourgeois uprisings against taxation, at Rouen and Paris in 1380, when people become aware that the fiscal machine is continuing to function despite the deathbed promises of Charles V, who considered the levying of taxes to be a mistaken action. But after these sudden and issueless convulsions, the economic depression manifests itself in the social structure only through a general depreciation.

In the towns, save in Paris, the large fortunes are destroyed; and if the group of vagrants cast out from the bourgeois community, mendicants enrolled on church registers for relief allowances—if that group of the most wretched, the dregs of misery and war, has grown much larger, still the distance between the "fat" and the "lean" has diminished appreciably, and the tension between them runs much less high than it did at the close of the thirteenth century. There is even depression among the nobility. The village *hobereaux* have suffered from the devastation of the countryside much more than the peasants have; the landed manors, patiently reconstructed after each calamity, nevertheless yield less and less; the sum of tithes and rents has diminished, and the quitrents have lost their value. Less power, fewer resources, yet as great or greater need for money. Now, in wartime, with the exception of some leaders and mercenaries descended from very poor stock, profits and losses balance each other in an interplay in which, as Froissart says, "one side would win and the other lose, in such a way that some ventures turn out as battles." Intermittently the knightly families are subjected to sudden blows: a ransom, taking years to pay, that definitively ruins the whole family; an unusually murderous battle, like Agincourt or Verneuil; exile for the gentlemen who, anxious not to betray their fealty to the king, their natural lord, prefer to leave the "Anglicized" provinces.

A number of family lines died out, therefore, or saw their manors pass into the hands of religious communities, enriched by pious donations and bequests—for lavish alms-giving was by no means checked during the hard times—or into the hands of fortunate adventurers, or those of an occasional bourgeois looking for a good investment. But on the whole, the fourteenth and fifteenth centuries were for most people a period of continued decline, not into mediocrity—the nobility remained liberal and prodigal, with its love of finery and wastefulness—but into financial difficulties, worries capable of solution only in terms of large dowries, pillaging, or pensions distributed by princes.

Out of this general depression, however, a few individuals emerge with some wealth—and the fortunes of these few men who fill their pockets with gold seem even more dazzling and scandalous considered against this background of poverty. Happy amid the hard times are the few war contractors, such as the leader who joined the fighting in Brittany during the mid-fourteenth century, a man

> . . . called Croquart, who had been in his youth a poor boy, a some-
> time page to the Lord d'Ercle in Holland [who] bore himself very
> well. It happened that, at an engagement where they were, his mas-
> ter was killed; but for his vassalage, his comrades elected him leader
> in place of his master, and he stayed there. Then, in a short while,
> he won so much, acquired and profited from ransoms and from the
> capture of towns and castles, that he became so rich it was rumored
> he had a fortune of sixty thousand *écus*; not counting his horses,
> numbering about twenty or thirty in his stables, fine chargers and
> pairs of cobs. And withal, he was reputed to be the best expert with
> a sword in the region . . . And the king of France promised him
> that if he wanted to become French, the king would make him a
> knight and marry him off handsomely and richly, and would give
> him two thousand *livres* in revenue every year, but he was in no wise
> willing.[2]

Fifty years later, Perrinet Gressart was such a man, doubtless the son of some humble royal finance agent—first a mercenary, later a leader who captured the fortress of Charité-sur-Loire and kept it as his own, making it the heart of a strong principality, investing his profits in landed manors, litigating for a long time in defense of his estates; a man who gave himself the title of "noble"—for as Jouvencel said, "arms ennoble the man, whoever he may be"—and who died rich and universally respected. But the real, abundant, secure wealth is destined for the princely families. Whatever the misfortunes and the dangers, the best means of making a lasting profit is to have some of that money that is so universally lacking— to have it by sharing in power, by being connected directly with a fiscal circuit, by having one's hand in those coffers that are constantly being filled with salt-taxes, aids, or *maltôtes*.* This is true at any level: on a small scale, in the local capitals—for example Hugues Jossart, Bachelor of Laws, who first became bursar for the Archbishop of Lyon, then lieutenant for the royal bailiff, finally the king's counselor in his native town, acquiring several nobles' lands and being himself ennobled in 1398 by Charles VI. More brilliant fortunes are made around the king—as was the case with Arnaud de Corbie, counselor and then president of the Parisian Parlement, then chancellor, trebling his large regular salary by extra pay, receiving on every hand gifts and lucrative sinecures. In short, one makes a fortune by scandalous means— like those of the nobles in the princely houses, who parade through court in a whirlpool of insane lavishness.

.   .   .

---

* Sales taxes levied for the king's needs.—Trans.

These men with empty stomachs and empty purses, so jealous of those very rare individuals living too easily from the poverty of others, have another cause for worry: the feeling of no longer being led by their natural guides. First, in the matter of religious authority: for a long time, people in France had been mocking an overly Italianate pope, one too much concerned with temporal power and financial profits and, apparently, too much bound up with the Sienese and Florentine banking interests. Early in the fourteenth century, the retreats of Boniface VIII before King Philip had destroyed the peoples' habits of respect in one fell swoop by puncturing Rome's inflated claims. Then, to please the king, the papal court moved to Avignon, settled down there, and invested so much money in buildings that its stay seemed permanent. The papal residence was not strictly inside the kingdom, but was at its door, within the French territory. Surrounded by cardinals, the majority of whom were from Aquitaine, who feared Italy, its assassins, and its miasmas, the Holy See thus appeared in everyone's eyes as an obedient satellite. It shocked many people throughout Europe. Yet to the royal government the "Babylonian Captivity" was of such great moral and material benefit that when, in 1378, it appeared that it was about to end and that the pope was to return to Rome for good, Charles V could not accept it, and had no scruples about throwing the elections into chaos, thereby causing a schism. This brutal shock had enormous consequences. Two popes, and then three, confronted one another, each excommunicating his opponent and all his opponent's supporters. Before their stubbornness and their ill will in seeking an understanding, the Conciliar propositions gradually developed in the University of Paris, motivated by the idea that papal power, like that of kings, ought, when it becomes tyrannical, to be controlled by an assembly of the faithful, represented by the wisest among them. Yet actually, the challenge to papal authority was articulated clearly only within a few exclusive intellectual and powerful circles; for most believers, catching only distant echoes of the divisions (and these echoes were distorted by their being embedded in zones of cruder and cruder comprehension) there was always one pope, the true one. Nevertheless, lasting changes were brought about. The Church of France gradually acquired the habit of constituting an independent body, forming ranks behind the king, a habit that began with its adherence to the acts of Philip the Fair and lasted until the movement of "subtraction of obedience," launched at the end of the fourteenth century to force the competing popes to compromise. Furthermore—and this is a still more radical change—the doubts raised with respect to pontifical dignity, the antagonisms among the great prelates, encouraged a tendency that was already powerful: the faithful were pushed into living their religious life outside the framework of the hierarchy, seeking, in an attitude of individual and intimate piety, a direct contact with God. This was a popular mysticism, more or less developed, exacerbated during plagues by superstitious anxieties, and spread far and wide in the Midi by the itinerant preaching of the Spirituals, those Franciscan dissidents so fiercely antagonistic to the Avignon pope.

But there was something else, much more tangible, clearly apparent not only to a few initiates within the power structure but also—at least during certain critical periods—to all the members of the feudal system and the entire population of the good towns; the source of material unrest affecting almost everyone: the decline of royal authority. At the beginning of the fourteenth century, an entirely new question was posed, one that remained quite engrossing for more than a century: that of the legitimacy of the man who calls himself king. This was a question of blood and of succession, for the hereditary character of the royal dignity was never doubted. By pure accident, all the kings after Hugh Capet had sons to succeed them. But the three sons of Philip the Fair left only daughters when they died. Upon the death of the last, the barons and bishops elected a cousin, Philip of Valois, the closest male descendant of Louis IX who was also "of the realm." This choice was arbitrary, for there were other pretenders with reliable claims: Edward III, King of England, and Charles the Bad, King of Navarre. It was the occasion for all those who were dissatisfied with the "found" king to rebel, to transfer their homage, to break their allegiance and to form hostile parties. The dynastic change, apart from the fact that it put inexperienced and irresponsible sovereigns on the throne—men who were perfect types of chivalric insouciance, having the wasteful habits of the nobility—also established a dangerous breach of loyalty. Philip VI, John the Good, and even, at the outset of his reign, the sickly and suspicious Charles V, were surrounded with factions, were never certain of their vassals, and lived in fear of poison or sorcery—those insidious means of destruction that were beginning to seep into France from Italy. At the beginning of the fifteenth century, a new crisis erupted. It was not that anyone had ever believed in the hereditary claims insisted upon by Henry V, King of England, to justify his expedition of conquest; but there was the presumption of bastardy, based on disconcerting evidence, which hung over the Dauphin, and which was dispelled only after the coronation at Reims—the most decisive result of the venture of Joan of Arc. All these doubts, reinforced by the sovereign's military defeats and interpreted as signs of divine condemnation of the ursurper—this uncertainty insinuated itself deep in the minds of the people ("dirt, dirt, filth of a king; our only king is God; do you think they got honestly what they have? They tax me, and tax me again"—said Guillaume le Juponnier of Orléans, publicly, in 1385—"a poor man with a wife and four children to care for. . . ."),[3] and put the royalty in a state of least resistance against two hostile forces.

No longer is feudalism one of these forces; it is now harmless. Instead, there are the "estates" whose role has grown larger with the financial difficulties springing out of the war. They are a vehicle of expression and action, if not for all the ruling classes, at least for the townspeople, and more precisely the Parisian bourgeoisie. The Parisians alone, actually, have considerable power, born of the university men's political thinking and supported by the humbler people who, weary of taxation, are better aware than anyone else of the wastefulness of the Court. On two occasions—under Étienne Marcel's leadership, in the hard years between 1355 and 1358, surrounding the Poitiers disaster when King John was captured, and again in 1413, at the height of the rivalry between princely factions, in the tumult and riot led by the butchers—did the Parisians attempt to establish a limited monarchy, in which the levying and allocation of taxes would have been tightly controlled by the estates. These attempts were fruitless, and took on a degree of seriousness only when a prince tried to derive some benefit from them—thus Charles the Bad in the fourteenth century and, in the fifteenth, John the Fearless, Duke of Burgundy, who knew how to speak in public, and did so in a big-town setting where the harangue was then the most effective means of stirring up peoples' minds. The truly hostile force undermining royal power came, indeed, from the princes. Large-scale feudalism was dead, except for such principalities as had become, in reality, foreign like Brittany, Flanders, Guyenne, and, on the periphery of the realm, the manors in the Pyrenees. There remained the threat of the king's next of kin, possible pretenders to the crown, unpunishable by ordinary means. They derived part of their power from their appanage, that portion of the royal domain usually given to younger sons to help them maintain their station—a portion which the prodigal Valois had unduly augmented. Their power came, too, from the exceedingly great authority additionally entrusted to them, and particularly from their privilege of direct access to the king, allowing them to profit from his affection, or at least from that good will a king could not refuse one of his family line, and to obtain all sorts of personal favors, unfair promotions, undeserved pardons. This power expanded dangerously when the king was weak, immature, or sick, for then the prince could direct the kingdom's resources and personnel in order to effect his own policies. Some princes dreamed of nothing but good living—like that soft egoist, John of Berry, brother of Charles V and a marvel of wastefulness; others—like the Angevins, rulers of Provence who were enchanted by the kingdom of Naples—carried out distant adventures. But, for several reasons, the most dangerous prince at the beginning of the fifteenth century was certainly the Duke of Burgundy, ruler of the Netherlands. His power was on the brink of eclipsing even that of the king; his possessions formed an actual state, only half-incorporated into the kingdom, and a national sentiment germinated there whose nature was antagonistic to the spirit then prevalent in the royal provinces.

This uneasiness, induced by the weakening of traditional frames of reference, was never more serious than during the period between 1410 and 1435. The mad king, the princes, and the nobles were all divided into two opposing cliques, Armagnacs and Burgundians, by murders unpunishable by royal justice since their perpetrators were too highly placed; by an English invasion; by a dauphin disavowed by his family; by a schism; by a council set against the pope—the anxiety infected the humblest social strata, extending even to the outermost edge of the realm, to Domremy, where it stirred the heart of an untutored little peasant girl. This is the period, too, when the depths of misery are reached: war refugees are everywhere, death is rampant—

> . . . and, to comfort the poor, they revived those children of the Hellish Adversary, to wit, taxes, both *quatrièmes* and *maltôtes*; and those trusted to administer them were lazy folk who, having no wherewithal, taxed everything so hard that goods ceased to come to Paris, as much because of the money as because of the taxes . . . Everything was then so expensive that people in Paris complained at great length . . . And on the dunghills of Paris, in 1429, you could have found ten, twenty, or thirty children, boys and girls alike, dying there of hunger and cold, and no heart could be so hard as to hear their cries at night—"Ah! I die of hunger"—without pitying them; but the poor administrators were not able to help them, for they had no bread, nor wheat, nor fuel.[4]

▶ THE LEGACY OF THE GOTHIC PERIOD

Those were, to be sure, years of exceptional misery. To picture the whole fourteenth century in such somber tones would be to emphasize only the weaknesses and the afflictions that chroniclers, memoirists, and preachers complacently describe—and to forget all the quotidian matters that remain healthy, balanced, and inveterate. Certainly, the contemporaries of Philip VI and Charles V lost the comfortable security that had rendered so replete "the century of St. Louis." Certainly, in all social milieus, culture is in visible decline, repressed by the difficulties of material life and the brutalities of wartime, and customs have become unquestionably crude, with that inurement to physical pain that makes the early fifteenth-century atrocities seem less surprising. And yet this period is less sterile and more consonant with the tradition of the classic Middle Ages than it is usually said to be or than it seems at first sight. Protected at least from famine and the ravages of war, if not from plague, many isolated areas of ease continue to exist—around prosperous captains and in urban religious communities well provided with alms and revenue, to say nothing of the courts at Avignon and Paris. And the great art forms, the currents of ideas, that had flourished in the preceding century continue to develop without any perceptible decline. They do so, however, with less fullness; there exists a noticeable contraction and, above all, a tendency to withdraw gradually from everyday reality. At the same time, a new, exquisite culture is formulated in a very few privileged locations, but it is reserved for a very limited élite and completely cut off from the world.

Two books—the key books of the period, to my mind—help us grasp to perfection the continuance of the tradition. The first of these, one which even presents itself as the culmination of all courtly literature, was written between 1265 and 1290, that is, at the beginning of those difficult times, yet it enjoyed the liveliest possible vogue throughout the fourteenth century: Jean de Meun's continuation of the *Roman de la Rose*. The other is the *Chroniques* of Jean Froissart, in which the whole of the epoch's good society complacently recognized itself. The two books are, actually, completely different in tone, and each corresponds to one of the two poles of "Gothic" culture: in Jean de Meun, scholastic irony; in Froissart, the chivalric ideal.

In the second part of the *Roman de la Rose*, the fourteenth century found all the knowledge accumulated by the University in the thirteenth century, now presented within everyone's understanding, in particular the understanding of those men at Court who had never gone to school but were anxious for knowledge. For two-thirds of the eighteen thousand lines Jean de Meun added to the springlike sequences of Guillaume de Lorris, translated the *auctores*, the Latin classics, and especially Ovid —but also the great Aristotelian thinkers of the Schools: Abélard, Alain de Lille, Guillaume de Saint-Amour. It is a *summa*, an encyclopedia in which one painlessly can acquire that culture it is advantageous to display, and from which one can satisfy the curiosity the preceding generation had awakened. It is also something more: the most striking expression of one of the aspects of the medieval mind, of that critical and rational faculty which was one of the thirteenth century's triumphs. There are three principal allegories—for, like all the authors of his time, Jean de Meun presents abstract ideas only as personifications: Venus, who is the invitation to love—but to a love undeviant, uncomplicated, unrepressed—the straightforward love, that is, of the *fabliaux*; and, especially, Reason and Nature, who really manage the show. In the name of these latter principles, taken from Aristotle, social conventions and customs are called into doubt. All courtly manners are criticized vehemently, and women are restored to the low position that they occupy in fact, in this society which, particularly in the realms of study and of war, has remained very masculine. The conception of power and of the social hierarchy is in line with the speculations of the political theorists, as in the picture of a king governing for the common good; simultaneously, the *Roman* sets the true nobility, that of heart and soul, in contradistinction to the aristocracy of birth, which is but empty pride:

> If someone, contradicting me,
> Prides himself on ancestry,
> And claims the gentleman (for thus
> Is he called by the populace),
> Because of blood and parentage,
> Holds a place of privilege
> Above the man who tills the earth
> I say no one is thoroughbred
> Who is not by the virtues led.

Roman de la Rose, 18607-18615

Furthermore, the mysticism of the Mendicant friars has been hacked to bits in the person of False Seeming, while an intellectual and balanced Christianity, an activist piety unseparated from the world, is extolled. All enlightened people used this manual of ready wisdom and comforting irony, and during the years 1401 and 1402—at a time when its asperity, far from being blunted, became more evident, when people were more sensitive to the liberating possibilities of social criticism, and when a good number of the old values began to waver—the work of Jean de Meun was the center of an impassioned debate among literary people. Champions of courtliness, like Christine de Pisan, and defenders of a sentimental and respectful attitude to religion, like Gerson, stood in opposition to the "humanists" of the young group that was laying the foundations for a new structure.

The brilliant reportage of Froissart was no less highly valued. Here, against the backdrop of the Hundred Years' War, we see the dream, the masque, the finery, the well-regulated ballet of chivalry and courtly life; the escape through "great adventures," in which the attitudes and "quests" of Lancelot and the Knights of the Round Table are transposed —conserving, however, a good part of their gratuitousness—into real life. There is the glorification of prowess, that is, acts through which "expertise in arms," military bravery, physical courage, and the art of handling both lance and horse are expressed, but expressed with honor, loyalty, and respect for forms: "so commendable and noble a virtue that one must not take too brief notice of it, for it is the very matter and light of the gentleman; and as the log cannot burn without fire, so without prowess the gentleman cannot attain honor and glory." [5] It is a virtue that even the least scrupulous captain practices at times, and always respects at least from afar, even when he spends his life lying in wait for ransoms and pillage; for it is the virtue that ennobles him, makes him a true gentleman. Largess, or liberality, is on the same level; for the *preux*, the man of prowess, lives a life of festivals, of the joyous consumption of wealth, in the company of ladies who are his partners in the complicated games of amorous courtliness. Thus we see the vigor that remains in the customs gradually initiated into the feudal courts two centuries earlier —more vigor than ever, perhaps, for it is at this very point, when the struggle against the English unveils an aspect of warfare in utter opposition to them, that noble society reaches its highest point of saturation with the chivalric romances.

Actually, despite the movements upsetting the hierarchy of social position, despite the spread of other methods of governing and judging men, the fourteenth century is still wholly encompassed by vassalage. In the immediate entourage of the princes, people may possibly attach less value to an enfeoffed man's devotion, to respect for the sworn word, and to the duties of aid and counsel. These latter features preserve their fundamental value for the large majority of nobles, who are gathered into the closely knit network of homage. Perhaps this era is actually more feudal, in its intimate structure, than the eleventh century, when fiefs were certainly less numerous and a vassal's obligations less strictly codified. There is no doubt that, in its spirit and gestures, if not in its motivating forces and crucial acts, this is a more chivalric era. The fourteenth century is the period of emblems, of the development of heraldry; the period of knights errant defending noble ladies against brigands and mercenaries who lurk along the roads; the heyday of tournaments, which are beginning to become spectacles. In 1351, in a Brittany torn by Franco-English rivalries, thirty knightly champions from each of two parties confronted one another, according to the rules of courtliness yet giving no quarter, in a battle that was not forgotten—confronted one another "for love of their lady friends," but also so "that people would talk of it, in the rooms, the palaces, and other places throughout the world, in times to come"; and still more, to submit to the general conflict for the judgment of God, in conformity with the old belief. The first meeting of the Ordre de l'Étoile, the first order of secular chivalry, created in France by King John, was held in the following year. Doubtless its intention was to surround the king more closely with particularly trusted friends; but the religious aspect of this confraternity—in which survived the ideal of the old knight-monk brotherhoods, though adapted to the courtly style—extolled the moral philosophy and behavior of the paladins in Arthurian legends. The extraordinary vigor of the idea of a crusade attests to the period's fidelity to the old frames of reference; no one, in noble circles, detected the anachronism. Holy wars are led against those pagans surviving in the Baltic countries; thousands of

French knights meet once again for thrilling hunts, with human quarries; the trip to Jerusalem becomes an obsession (for which Philip de Mézières is the touching propagator) dominating all noble hearts. In 1391, Louis de Bourbon, brother-in-law of Charles V, is sole leader of an expedition, with his friends and vassals, against Tunis, an expedition in the style of St. Louis, his patron saint; while others, like those dragged along by John, the future Duke of Burgundy, or the Maréchal de Boucicault, go and confront the Turks in the Balkans.

Another legacy from the days of Louis IX is preserved with piety: the décor, the esthetic backdrop. The intellectual perfection of the High Gothic triumphs during the fourteenth century, of which Reims, Amiens, and the Sainte-Chapelle are model buildings, the very image of beauty. Several changes in artistic currents can readily be distinguished but they are, in the end, secondary. There is a change in scale, a tendency toward less ambitious undertakings, deriving from the difficulties of the times but also from the fact that the large buildings have just been entirely renovated, and the only things remaining to be done are completing and attaching the accessories: spires, window canopies, pinnacles, porches, and rood screens. There are very few spacious buildings, except in the Languedoc region of the Midi which, having been cured of the burdensome Albigensian malaise, erected its two masterpieces: the Church of the Preaching Friars at Toulouse and the Cathedral at Albi. Instead, there are numerous outbuildings of very limited dimensions. During this period chapels are added, bay by bay, all along the side aisles and ambulatories of the large churches; or merely tombstones, in flat-bottomed funeral niches joined to the walls; or "raised" tombs, built like isolated monuments. Most of these are ordered by the rich, whose opulence is founded on the common poverty; who, in their wills, spend lavishly, emptying their financial reserves in one blow, burdening their heirs for all time with extremely heavy arrears, in order to enjoy plentiful and personal orisons after death. For, in the fourteenth century, with political upheaval and the faster movement of wealth loosening social ties, and with the penchant for mysticism freeing piety from its priestly framework, devotion too tends to become individual and self-oriented. Artists work more and more for patrons and for lay people. This is a major change, and its effects already can be distinguished, even in the works executed for ecclesiastical communities. Art attempts to please. Certainly all the works are religiously inspired, and it is still true that only things of God seem to merit lasting ornament; but now room has been made for a sentiment of the beautiful, and for esthetic pleasure. What is it that insinuates itself into the supreme forms of the Classic Gothic? It is grace. A new sense of the beauty of the human body is expressed in the miniatures and bas-reliefs which, at the very end of the thirteenth century, illustrate the Creation in nudes executed in amaz-

ingly pure line, and, more tenderly, in the figures of the resurrected in
the Cathedral at Bourges. In statues, this new sense of beauty leads to a
breaking of the vertical, by means of a hip-shot attitude as if at the beginning of a dance; for this is a style of dances, smiles, springtime, of
delicacy of both angels and young people, a style which, though it slips
sometimes into slight affectation, has achieved pliancy. This is true even
of the stained-glass windows, where brilliant yellows prevail over blues
and reds, in which the forms begin to escape from the lead circles that
girdle them, to develop an independent suppleness. Indeed, this is an
art of increased freedom, increased liberation from liturgical and scriptural restraints; it is, too, more attentive to reality, to likeness, and to
visible appearances, to the very degree that it avoids religious symbolism.

But the culture of the fourteenth century is not entirely an inheritance
from the central Middle Ages. In spite of material difficulties, it has
gone on enriching itself. In particular, some very valuable contributions
have come to it from Italy, the *trecento* Italy at the height of its commercial prosperity and its intellectual and artistic excitement. These
come through Avignon, where the papal Curia maintains its ties with
Rome, attracting financiers, artists, and writers from beyond the Alps—
and, perhaps even more, through the very active merchant and banking
colony of Lombards established in Paris. Indeed, it is primarily at Paris,
around the Court—around those Valois, who so loved beautiful things,
and who, breaking with Capetian austerity, introduced the style of the
grand gesture, lavishly spending on buildings, books, and precious stones
the money levied to finance the Crusade, or the war against England—
there is formed a totality of tastes and worldly customs—a subtle, fragile
greenhouse flower, enclosed in a protected setting—an extremely refined
and elegant totality, one which, from Paris and the appanage capitals,
proliferated throughout all upper European society.

The élite is much more limited, more essentially aristocratic, than
that of the twelfth-century feudal courts had ever been—more intimate,
furthermore, and closed. It is also further separated from nature: no
longer is this culture set into orchards or lawns, as in the days of Louis
IX, but into houses—not, by now, mere dens where people take cover
against the dark or cold or when danger threatens, but places fitted out
for a sheltered life: country châteaux whose exterior shell is still that of a
fortress—with towers, moats, and drawbridges—but, behind this defensive screen, the residential buildings are pleasingly arranged on courts
whose wide, decorated bays give a sense of openness. In the towns, especially, the *hôtels* have a less military appearance; see, for example, those
built in the new quarter of Paris, on the right bank, south of Saint-
Antoine, some of which form the new royal residence, Saint-Paul. Scattered among gardens and menageries, built by Charles V and enlarged

and decorated by Charles VI, this residence is better adapted to the style of the day than the Palace on the Cité, or Vincennes, or the Louvre. It is a building of modest dimensions, but allows a great deal more comfort. Those large, cold rooms that remain serve only for balls or large audiences. Daily life takes place in small rooms, connected by spiral staircases, furnished with tables and backed chairs, and hung with tapestries, of which John the Good had more than two hundred fifty prepared —tapestries made at Arras and especially at Paris. These rooms are heated by fireplaces and, at night, are better lit than before: to the amazement of Froissart, the Count of Foix, Gaston Phœbus, had twelve torches to light his supper every evening. The day is spent in passing from one room to another, "near a good, glowing fire, in well-covered rooms." Thus, for Charles V, after a morning divided among mass, a recital of the hours, the affairs of council, and an hour's nap, there was

> a period with his intimates, during which he would frolic about doing pleasant things, looking at jewels, or other riches . . . then he went to Vespers, after which, in summer, the Queen sometimes came to him with his children. Sometimes people gave him there strange gifts from different countries: guns, military equipment, and various other things, or merchants came bringing velvet, golden cloth, and all sorts of beautiful, strange things or jewels, that he showed to the experts he had in his household. In winter, he especially kept himself busy, often by hearing reading from various beautiful stories from Holy Scripture or the *Faits des Romains* or *Moralités des Philosophes*, or other knowledge, until the hour came for supper, to which he sat down rather early and at which he ate lightly; after supper, the barons and knights gave a merry play, then he retired and went to bed.[6]

Protected in this milieu against natural forces, people do their best not to think of the plague—besides, it strikes down few of the well-fed and well-tended—and readily manage to forget the mercenaries, the high cost of living, and the burning villages; they take pleasure in the new, the "strange," the subtle, and the piquant. The princes, who still hunt, joust, and fight but differ from their late ancestors in not becoming torpid when night falls or winter arrives, must have entertainment to fill the hours, the seasons, when open-air games are impossible. Now more than ever, for all the indoor assemblies, torchlight balls, readings-aloud, and musical recitals, dress is a pleasure; made up in lighter, more elegant and elaborate fabric, no longer cut at home by female servants but rather by professional "dressmakers" and "linen-drapers"; and men's clothing, doublets and breeches, is now completely differentiated from women's, if not by its colors and the delicacy of fabric, at least by its shape. Women's clothing, with lower necklines, corresponds more and more to the silhouette of the body; one feels, seeing the artificial means for making the figure slim and emphasizing the bosom, the arbitrary modeling, the bondage to style and to the feminine profile, that living habits are getting farther away from nature, that the courts during this period experienced an advance into eroticism, a refinement and early intellectual conquest of physical life—in essence only the culmination of the subtleties late courtliness had embroidered around erotic sentiment.

To this public are offered artistic and literary creations which, being very mannered and slightly fragile, also bear the stamp of the excessive pursuit of the elegant, the novel, the hitherto unknown. But far from indicating a backward step, a decline, or even the insipidity of the preceding age's culture, these creations march boldly forward to announce an esthetic change. Thus, for example, in the *Ars Nova*, do musicians exhibit their desire for modernity—as in the great Guillaume de Machaut's *Messe de Notre-Dame*, doubtless the first mass written to be sung in parts, and in numerous other, secular melodies, all of which free vocalization once and for all from the old Gregorian matrix, break up the rhythm, and toy with syncopation. Simultaneously the musicians of this period of death and impoverishment—one of the greatest eras of song—renew the whole lyric tradition, elaborating poetic forms that are to flourish for three centuries: the virelay, the rondeau, and the ballade. There is also a deeper and farther-reaching renewal: that of book illumination, that art of the private collector so highly esteemed by the "experts" of Charles V's entourage, each of whom vied for the possession of the most beautiful library. Paris, more than ever, is the capital of these new arts. Artists come there from all over, to work for the whole of Europe, and styles are born in the Parisian workshops; in the fourteenth century, it is there, perhaps even more than in Florence and Siena, that the first steps toward the pictorial revolution of the West are taken. One becomes aware, during the few exhibitions for which illuminated manuscripts are taken out of their repositories, that the Italian cities are less open to the outside world, less receptive to all the tendencies and pursuits that were in the air, than is Paris. After the death of Louis IX, book illuminators begin gradually to free themselves from Gothic symbolism. They begin by making their design more flexible, thus introducing movement, transposing onto parchment the dance-motions of the new sculpture. Gradually they gain an extraordinary calligraphic dexterity, filling the margins with a profusion of flowers and animals so that the text is placed in the middle of floral and sylvan life, of that life of nature they knew better and better how to observe— and in this we see the influences of both Aristotelian naturalism and of the Franciscan tenderness face to face with Creation.

But the main triumph, the one that changed everything, is that of the third dimension. Jean Pucelle was the first who sought to represent space and atmosphere, around the holy figures in the breviaries and books of hours he illustrated about 1325; he may have been tempted to do so by the new attitudes of the people in the schools, who were becoming more experienced in geometry and optics, and were also gradually discovering the rational notions of scale and distance. Or perhaps he caught an echo of the inquiries carried out along the same line as his own by the Italian fresco painters. At any rate, the processes he used to give the illusion of depth, although they are still awkward, ushered in a new way of perceiving. A few years after his death, the golden backgrounds surrounding painted figures with unreality, then the gaudy squares borrowed from the makers of stained-glass windows, gave way to landscapes and interiors. It is at this point that painting ceases to be a symbol, and becomes an interpretation of the real world.

This advance of the musicians, poets, and painters at court culminates around 1400 at an apex of exceptional inventiveness in the entourage of Charles VI and his brother, Louis d'Orléans, and their uncles, the appanage dukes of Berry, Anjou, and Burgundy. Throughout this period— when all of enlightened European Christendom was awaiting the Paris University men's resolution of the Schism; when teachers like Pierre d'Ailly and Jean Gerson were seeking to give a more balanced and regular, less incoherent, form to the currents of mysticism coming from the Netherlands and along the Rhine, to that devotion which, too, was "modern"; when the Dutchman Claus Sluter, in the service of Philip of Burgundy, suddenly brought into the Carthusian monastery at Dijon a world of forms which, in their fiery and dense, thick and brutal, vulgar and harsh vigor, were violently opposed to the traditionally elegant and graceful images of French art—a new humanism was flourishing in Paris: quite different from that of the twelfth century, and much freer of religious considerations. Admirers of Latin literature were then, by and large, scholars and university men, like Gerson and Pierre d'Ailly, Nicolas de Clamanges and Gontier Col, but not all were. Jean de Montreuil, secretary to Charles VI, for example, was infatuated with Vergil and Terence—he had studied "arts" at the University, though he did not graduate and did not have a job with the Church; and Christine de Pisan, an Italian woman, derived an income from her writings.

The influence of Italy on the contemporary mental attitude, as a matter of fact, was distinct; Jean de Montreuil corresponded with Collucio Salutati, the pundit of humanism; Boccaccio's *De Claris mulieribus, De Casibus virorum illustrium,* and *Decameron* were translated by Laurent de Premierfait, and the *De remediis utriusque fortunae* by Petrarch, who had come on a mission to Paris in 1361. What is important, however, is the avid curiosity for fine Latin style and for all of Roman antiquity. As early as 1350, John the Good had had the walls of his castle at Vaudreuil painted with scenes from the life of Caesar. The end of the fourteenth century was a great period for translations which enormously enriched the vernacular and began to endow it with the syntactical rigor necessary for reasoning, formerly the prerogative of Latin, to say nothing of giving it a much more extensive vocabulary, far better adapted to describing the impulses of the soul and calculated to refine the psychological sense of those who had not studied at the University. In the *Collection of Memorable Deeds and Sayings* by Valerius Maximus, translated by Simon de Hesdin, and in the version of Livy's *Annals of the Roman Republic* executed by Petrarch's friend Bersuire, Rome at last emerged liberated from the distorting plots of old romances; the Romans were no longer *preux*, but heroes.

For princes lavishly spending the gold extorted by the fiscal machine (despite temporary interruptions by the English assaults) from a people now accustomed to taxation, the Parisian workshops simultaneously were producing magnificent works of art. Thus the most beautiful collection of tapestries we know—the Apocalypse series, ordered by the Duke of Anjou—was created between 1375 and 1379 by Nicolas Bataille, from the designs of Jean Bandol. Pictorial creation was especially intense. There was already some panel painting, the most beautiful of which is by Jean Bellechose, but in essence this was miniature-work, transposed among jewels and chasing onto the gold of precious curios. Yet there was also some portraiture, likenesses of princes who desired to see their own features immortalized, perhaps because of the recent concern for individual glory that was fostered by humanism. Illuminated books were in profusion: the French artists were joined by more and more Italians from Lombardy and, especially, more artists from the north, such as Beauneveu de Valenciennes and the three Limbourg brothers. In the illustrations made for these books, the richest of which were painted for the Duke of Berry, all the elegance and subtlety of daily life are magnificently displayed; there are landscapes in which reality undergoes an extraordinary poetic transformation, processions come from a legendary, sumptuous, and gaudy East, which again exaggerate the extravagances of the court's style. At the same time, isolated and poignant among this series of festivals, surged the pathetic cry of the master of the *Heures de Rohan*, like an echo of the misery and death which, on all sides, surrounds the enjoyments of the rich.

And indeed, this renaissance—coming as early as the Florentine one, yet encompassing all the richness of the Gothic, Courtly, and Scholastic civilization—was cut off abruptly. Its first blossoms appeared during the reign of a mad king, amid balls and masques; when it was still delicate, a bit feverish but ready to swell with life, political uprisings struck directly at Paris, which was its center. Then, in 1413, the Saint-Paul gardens were overrun by riot; next the Armagnac mercenaries ravaged the Lombard banks, forcing the financiers to flee and ruining one of the most essential ingredients of Parisian prosperity. Five years later, Jean de Montreuil and Gontier Col were killed by bands of the opposing faction. Henceforth, for years to come a besieged town, Paris was bound to the Burgundians, isolated from the world, deserted by the king's court and the princes' houses. Paris was sterile. But at that very moment, in France as a whole, we see indications of a recovery.

▶ THE DÉTENTE

In 1435, the King of Bourges* is reconciled with his Burgundian cousin at Arras. In 1444, truces stop the war against the English, for a while, and in the following year royal enactments set up "companies" of permanent, regularly paid men-at-arms who, billeted by the populace, consequently can be counted on not to fall on the region and recklessly prey upon it between battles. In 1453, the army and artillery of Charles VII expel the last English troops from the realm. In certain sectors of the economy, a few signs of recovery reveal themselves.

Its earliest movements come to light here and there around 1440, among, for example, the merchants of Toulouse. But this is still timid, uncertain, and halting; a few short-lived and personal successes on the part of bold individuals—often foreign adventurers, like those Genoese who then established themselves at Marseille, or businessmen having semi-official status at court, whose ventures are stimulated by their private and profitable service to a prince. The fortune of Jacques Coeur, which so astounded his contemporaries, shows simultaneously the characteristics and the limitations of this early recovery: his father was one of the suppliers to the Duke of Berry, and possessed only a modest fortune, since the prince's court was resident only intermittently in Bourges. It was Jacques Coeur's good luck that one of the governments of France—assembled around the Dauphin Charles, who before long became King of Bourges—was, at the risk of civil strife, transferred into the town. The Dauphin had with him a large and permanent train of dependents, and Jacques Coeur, like his relatives, busied himself in supplying them with luxury goods. With this aim in mind, he traveled in 1432 into Egypt, Syria, and Cyprus—but did so as a petty merchant, having no capital, shipping goods on other people's boats. Like the traders of the early Middle Ages, he was obliged to transport his merchandise amid perils (on his return voyage, for example, he was captured in Corsica by pirates, and ransomed). Yet in this way he achieved proximity to all the instruments of the financial system. In the improvised accommodations

---

* Charles VII, so called because, in Paris, the Burgundians had backed the infant Henry VI of England and the regency of the Duke of Bedford as the ruling faction of France, while Joan of Arc's Dauphin remained in Bourges, proclaiming himself king, until he was crowned in Reims in 1429.—Trans.

of the royal court, this virtually domestic trader, since he was accustomed to handling precious metals, was entrusted with minting money. At first he was condemned, though not harshly, for imprudent speculation; but he held on tenaciously to his financial functions, which he rightly considered to be the safest mainstay for his concerns. All his activity, therefore, was intimately linked with the royal house; and his prosperity, from the Peace of Arras on, coincides essentially with that of Charles VII. The latter expected his zealous servant to supply him with the most beautiful finery, the best spices, but with the least possible drain on his monetary reserves. Thus Jacques Coeur's mission was twofold: to increase the king's liquid assets and to furnish luxury goods. The first entailed the finding of precious metals; and, like so many other fifteenth-century men thirsting for gold and silver, Jacques Coeur sought them in the bowels of the earth; he acquired an interest in the mines around Lyon, and also played with currency fluctuation and exchanged silver against gold with the Berbers. Secondly, he sought luxury goods at their source, in the Mediterranean Levant—but to save money, had to avoid passing through any Italian intermediaries; hence, he formed a fleet based in Montpellier, then in Marseille, and managed it with a small team of devoted "agents" integrated into his household. Successful because he was quite close to the king, he, like his ancestors, invested most of his profit in land. He became very rich—too rich: he is envied, he is destroyed, by 1453 he is ruined. What a beautiful example for moralists, and for those whose sermons evoke the reversals of the wheel of fortune! Yet his case, by virtue of its very isolation and, still more, by virtue of its archaic methods, gives proof of the deep torpor still gripping the areas of French business.

Actually, the great upheaval occurs some twenty-five years later, around 1475, after the final cessation of hostilities. The following are certain effects of the peace: the strain is removed from the king's treasury, money stops fluctuating and, in particular, the countryside's reconstruction no longer is canceled out by a new wave of destruction every ten years. A quarter of a century suffices to repair every part of this essentially landed economy. There are a few good harvests, enough to eat, means for nourishing children and fortifying them against the onslaught of disease; too, the villages are more populated, consequently, there is a larger labor force, and the outlying areas of the farming terrains are recovered from lying fallow. The peasant ease of the days of Louis IX is recovered. But it is not surpassed, for farming and breeding processes have not been improved. Manure is as rarely used as ever, the yields are as low; for quite a few generations to come there is the same discrepancy in production from one year to the next, the same lack of reserves, and the same fear of want. After so much misery, destruction, and famine, some surplus, at least, exists from time to time. As a result, there is an increasingly ample flow of trade, money circulating, and a general feeling of relaxation.

Nevertheless, the basic cause of the new prosperity, more than the end of the wars, is a shifting in the combination of favorable trade circumstances. With the rest of Europe, France is again swept along by a movement which picks up speed, in the closing years of the fifteenth century, and turns into a long period of expansion. The period of great merchant ease returns, to medium-size towns as well as to the very large ones, where (a sure sign) Italian businessmen once again settle. Traffic becomes more active, and also more rapid on roads that are better planned and well equipped with way stations, as well as on larger and more stable boats. It is then that the new orientation in the flow of wealth becomes noticeable. First, there is the opening of the Atlantic region, and the horizon becomes, within a few years, enormously expanded on this side: shortly before 1480, sugar arrives from Madeira, through Marseille and more especially Rouen; in 1483, sailors from Honfleur call on the Cape Verde Islands; twenty years later, the first navigators, natives of Normandy, sight Brazil. Paris has remained the great city for all the professions and trades, but she now has competitors, for there are other points of convergence: Orléans, Troyes, Limoges, Rouen—a traveler in 1500 believes the latter town to be more heavily populated than Nuremberg, and its population has, in fact, trebled. Another basic center comes into being: Lyon, the way station for everything coming from Italy, the town whose fairs, initiated at the beginning of the century, have for a long time been outpacing those at Chalon-sur-Saône and, more recently, those in Geneva—the latter is a consequence of royal action: in 1462, the king forbade French merchants to frequent the Geneva rendezvous. Indeed, royal authority, measuring its wealth by the amount of money circulating within the realm, now takes care to control trade, and aspires to direct it. To avoid purchases from foreign suppliers, the government thus encourages the manufacture of precious fabrics, woolens from Rouen and Montivilliers, and silk recently manufactured in Tours and Lyon. But at the end of the fifteenth century, French merchants, unlike those of Italy or the Netherlands, are a very sober lot, mindful only of dressing well, acquiring a good piece of land with which to establish their families, and contributing, for the salvation of their souls, to the adornment of their churches—they are little concerned with culture, but they do fear God. They amass gold and silver, but far less than one would think, for cash is rare. To be sure, upon this revived activity, in which "everyone, except the nobles (and I do not exclude all of them), takes part in trade," the first lasting fortunes are built and the first dynasties of new men are founded. But, as before, the striking success belongs only to those who combine the exercise of political office with that of managing business. And if, as the sixteenth century draws near, everyone is plowing and working, in a France where no trace of the afflictions of Joan of Arc's time any longer appears—a France where, as Claude Seyssel says of Louis XII's glory, "possession, revenue, and riches increase with the people"—the real profits are still for the king, his friends, and those who serve him.

This is a period of departure—but departure into a transformed world; for, during the hard times, many features of medieval civilization were definitively obliterated. First of all, the primacy of Paris is over, for a while. This relative eclipse resulted from the same quartering of France, sundered from 1415 until 1435 by the Armagnacs, the Burgundians, and the English. During and after this period, the royal town is situated in the middle of a wide belt of active warfare, laying diagonal hold of the kingdom between the Somme and the Loire, from Picardy to Lyon. This is a major area of insecurity, cutting off all normal relations: thus, political connections, commerce, and intellectual life had to be organized from a provincial standpoint around local centers. This separation was encouraged also by the gradual strengthening of the appanages: each *fleur-de-lys* prince and each of the great aristocrats whose principalities had never belonged to the royal domain, wanted to have his private administration, a court distinct from that of the king, and his own capital. And when, during the last quarter of the fifteenth century, these little "states," like Anjou, Provence, and Brittany, were reunited one after the other with the crown, each of the princely towns—with its noble *hôtels, pieds-à-terre* for its neighboring country gentlemen, art workshops, and cultural traditions—preserved its function and its provincial splendor. But Paris, since it was no longer a royal town, suffered a great deal more. In 1418, it had declared itself with the Burgundians. Now, monarchial loyalty went out to the Dauphin Charles, a refugee beyond the Loire in the territory of his uncle, the Duke of Berry; it was around him that the resistance to the English was organized, supported by the ever-developing xenophobia. Charles VII, as King of Bourges, lived partly in Orléans and partly in Chinon, and set up the central services of royal administration at Poitiers. With peace restored and Paris won over to his side, he frequented the Loire Valley, and the Court stayed there from then on. Consequently Paris, though by the end of the century it is to regain all its activities and become far and away the most heavily populated town in Europe, is nevertheless no longer the only axis of French civilization. This civilization often flowers more exquisitely elsewhere, in the royal residences around Tours or Orléans, at Dijon, Beaune, Aix, or Moulins—and in the astonishingly ascendant Lyon, gateway to Italy and center of large-scale business negotiations and new industries.

This is but a temporary lapse; on the other hand, that of one of the principal mainstays of medieval culture—the University of Paris—was definitive. Here again, it is a question for the most part of the same decentralization originating in the political lacerations of the realm. Furthermore, the multiplication of other universities was encouraged by the freer movement of thought: scholars were less interested in congregating all together at one point, now that they could correspond more readily, visit one another, and exchange books. Due to this relaxation, therefore, universities sprang up throughout fifteenth-century Europe; from that time on they proliferated, not only in Germany, Italy, and Spain, but in every French province as well. The princes' interest in controlling the education of their clergy and officials led to the foundation of new teaching centers at Poitiers, Aix, Bordeaux, Dôle, then in Besançon, Grenoble, Cahors, and Valence—not to mention Toulouse, and the very old medical school at Montpellier. Paris suffered from this competition. But even more, it suffered from the loss of its old franchises, its legal privileges, its reserves of ecclesiastical benefices for its graduates—all of which the kings and popes had conspired to withdraw—and from poverty, for the war and the monetary depreciation had rendered worthless most of those *rentes* that supported the *collèges*. Its boarders were less numerous and insufficiently maintained, and a greater number of starving students, like the companions of François Villon, studied perfunctorily and lived by their wits. Finally, the University suffered from the political discord, the internal troubles, and the English occupations which brought about the promotion of second-rate men and a consequent laxity of discipline. Thus it was that the great machine of thought began to rust. Respected by all at the beginning of the century, consulted by people everywhere, it had exercised a real political authority; but, at first terrified by the riots that Caboche* led, then very tightly muzzled, it very quickly lost all its influence in this sphere. The only thing left to it was its specialty theology. Yet the best theologians had long since been diverted toward mystical experience; Gerson, for example, once in contact with the Brothers of the Common Life, had formulated a doctrine concerning the love of God which he disseminated by means of little treatises, written first in Latin and then in the vernacular; he dreamed of a reform in studies which would be nurtured by the inner life. This invigorating mysticism was momentarily spread in the Collège de Navarre, through the teachings of Nicolas de Clamanges, the last of the great Parisian professors. But when he died in 1437, the "Terminists" † concerned themselves exclusively with formal logic and

---

* Caboche, a Parisian butcher during the reign of Charles VI, was the leader of a faction that agitated for, and received, administrative and legal reforms in 1413.—Trans.

† The University of Paris had two rival factions, the Thomists or Scotists (the "Ancients") and the "Terminists" or Occamites (the "Moderns"). By the close of the fifteenth century, they had combined forces against the inroads of humanism.—Trans.

word-juggling; and the teachers at the Collège de Sorbonne, embedded in routine, preferred out of sheer laziness Peter Lombard's very convenient, three-hundred-year-old *Sentences,* instead of direct Biblical commentary. Thus the great Scholastic venture—which had given thought a rational framework and had prepared the West for the scientific and technical conquest of the natural world—ended in pedantry, in the vain refinement of the syllogism, the ruminations of a language too abstract, too technical and inexact, and ridiculed by all great minds.

Another basic support of the earlier civilization which did not regain its strength during the general recovery was the manorial framework. Certainly the notions of honor and fidelity, and the entire interplay of show and response that had gathered around feudalism and chivalry, still were conspicuous during the reigns of Louis XI and Charles VIII. On the other hand, the very soul of the medieval system was dead forever—that human intimacy between protector and protected, between the patron who insures peace and pacifies strife, and his dependents who support, serve, and "aid" him, in return for the security they enjoy. In the rebuilt countrysides, the ties between the landowner and the farmer are taken up again, but—established by means of long-term supports and *métayage* contracts—their nature is purely economic and void of any sentimental content. Often represented by managers who are the only ones to be in touch with the peasants, these great owners—gentlemen, bourgeois, clergy—are now, in truth, pure landed proprietors. There is an almost complete divorce between the village and the noble's house which, with its dovecotes and hunting privileges, is situated on the outskirts of things. On the other hand, the old *banal* rights, such as legal powers of justice, tolls, *maréchaussée,** and *blaierie,** have for the most part survived the war, but no longer have they any meaning, since no longer are they justified by the defense functions formerly assumed by their holders. When the *écorcheurs* roamed over the countryside, "carving up the throats" of the peasants to learn where their savings were hidden, or when the arrival of the English, the Burgundians, or the king's soldiers, was announced, the lords of the manors were, more often than not, absent—either enlisted, captured, or run away. During the troubled times, many a manor changed owners, and the natural lord— he who was connected to the villagers by ancestry and by centuries of mutual aid—was replaced by newcomers: foreigners, mercenaries, traitors rewarded by the conquering faction; men with money who, more than anything else, were anxious to extract the maximum profit from their new rights. These transfers were responsible for ruining loyalty and for undermining that mutual confidence which, in feudal times, had insured, despite the provosts' abusive exactions, a solidarity between

---

* *Maréchaussée* refers to the allowances of oats required by a lord for his horses; *blaierie* governs the lord's rights with respect to wheat grown by his tenants.

chatelain and *manant*. At the close of the fifteenth century, making allowances, of course, for the more long-lived remnants, those provinces
least disturbed by war, the communities of rural France are no longer
supported and guided by manorial power. They no longer have any true
intermediaries, any spokesmen against the king's men—tax collectors or
troops to be billeted—who appear from time to time. For, in this collapse of the old local frameworks, royal power alone can make itself felt;
after some temporary setbacks, it is regenerated in battle.

To his subjects, the king is still the object of that veneration attached
to those impregnated with the essence of divinity. He is the healer, the
guide, the son of St. Louis, from whom moral authority is expected—
hence, the confusion about Charles VII, the first to flaunt the existence
of his mistress. "In the final week of April [1448]," wrote the student
known as the "Bourgeois de Paris" in his *Journal*, "there arrived in Paris
a young lady, said to be loved publicly by the king of France who, without faith or law, breaks his word given to the good queen, his wife . . .
Alas, what a pity to see the leader of the kingdom giving such a bad
example to his people." Yet he remains, beyond all else, the sovereign. It
was he who drove the English away, and he who gave the people real
protection. In the long struggle, he won the right to levy the taxes that
make those the chatelains still exact seem excessive; and his power to
impose them is so firmly established that he no longer consults the
"estates," except in a few provinces. He has forged an army well supplied
with artillery, entirely under his control, which grants him decisive superiority over anyone in the realm who might aspire to political power.
In the closing decades of the fifteenth century—by virtue of a series of
fortunate circumstances as much as by his willful tenacity—he effected
what no other sovereign had ever hoped for before the Hundred Years'
War: the abolition both of the appanages and of the feudal states. After
the destruction of the Burgundian state, which was partly in the realm
and partly in the Empire, which Charles the Bold had dreamed of setting
up as an entirely independent sovereignty, the king's domain is, in the
people's mind, identical with the realm, apart from a few isolated spots
still remaining autonomous—regions that are scarcely important any
more, like the Bourbonnais principality, the feudal areas in the Pyrenees,
Albert, and Foix. To be sure, there remain some dependencies, groups of
armed men, private castles, and powerful habits of insubordination, and
for a long time to come these will make themselves known through
rebellions and outbursts of impatience running from end to end of the
kingdom—and frequently these will be stirred up by the one person who
is now a threat to the king: his brother, or else his sons. But henceforth
these rebellions are merely short-lived, unimportant clashes, *guerres
folles*. No longer is France the sum of her manors: now the realm belongs, truly, to the king.

. . .

But the fifteenth century should not, because it saw the disintegration of two of the principal mainstays of medieval civilization—Scholasticism and the manorial system—be considered a falling-off period in the development of French civilization. Quite the contrary; in the sphere of the mind, it is a period of youth, renewal, and great productivity. Nevertheless, progress is situated on another level. In particular, the twelfth and thirteenth centuries had blazed paths toward a rational understanding of man and nature; the fifteenth marks a major stage in the development of sensibility. This advance coincides with the permeation of certain cultural forms—those that appeal to feeling and hence are most immediately accessible to people not specially educated in reason—of much deeper social strata, a permeation extending (but only in the cities) into the subsoil of the populace. This is wrought by new means: first of all, by the sermon, the most popular and sought-after entertainment of the period. A famous preacher, be he a Preaching Friar or a Franciscan, is expected for weeks in advance in all the towns; he is preceded by his reputation for being inspired, people have heard he heals the sick, some have seen him walk on water. In one of the new churches built by the Mendicant orders—a vast preaching hall oriented more around the pulpit than the altar—or else in an open-air square, he will hold the attention of an entire populace of hundreds of thousands of listeners (men on one side, women on the other) for hours. Without rhetorical artifice, in language that is daring and intentionally coarse—the language of the most humble—he speaks not about theology, but about practical morality: How do you earn salvation? He manipulates his public, tells funny stories when their attention wanders, makes them quake with fear by conjuring up the sufferings of Christ, the punishment of the damned, the unpredictability of death. Violently he attacks the miserly, the rich, even the princes and high clergy, thus urging a freer religious life, one less respectful of the clergy, and sowing the seeds of the reform spirit. But he also teaches the less gifted how to think, and enriches their sensibility. The more skillful of these holy speakers sometimes instigate real moral revolutions during their tours: thus the Parisians, returning from one preacher's sermons, were

> so disposed to devotion that in less than three or four days they lit more than a hundred fires, in which they burned backgammon boards, playing cards, taws, billiard balls and cues, anything that could lead to anger or cursing in gambling games; on the same day and the next, the women burned all their hair-dressing paraphernalia, like hairpieces, pieces of leather or whalebone they put in their hair to stiffen it or pull it up in front; the young girls abandoned their pointed headdresses, pigtails, and a huge pile of powderpuffs. . . .[7]

But the most effective work is done day by day, by those men who, in the intervals between these oratorical spectacles, preach and hear confession: the friars from the local convents.

Along with the sermon, and very close to it in basic method and effect, there is the theater. The fifteenth century passionately loved the productions, pantomimes, and *tableaux vivants* the preachers staged to increase the impact of their words; and the living scenery that was strewn through the streets for marriages, funerals, and entries of princes, constituted, in effect, theatrical performances. For example, when the king of England entered Paris in 1420,

> the whole of the wide Rue Saint-Denis, from the second gate to Notre-Dame, was nobly behung and bedecked; most of the prominent people were dressed in red; a very moving passion play, modeled on the one painted around the choir of Notre-Dame, was set up in front of the Palais on the Rue de la Calandre.[8]

These plays were sheer entertainment—there were farces, moralities, and satires, but in particular there were the religious dramas, the mystery plays, which were much more highly thought of and which caused infinitely more lasting repercussions. These plays constitute, along with the sermons, the principal communal diversions of the fifteenth century. During this period, these mystery plays, staged by pious confraternities who made a specialty of them, were illustrations of the Passion of Christ. These interminable works—the best of them, composed by Arnoul Gréban, director of the choir school at Notre-Dame, Paris, ran to more than thirty-four thousand lines— were played over the course of several days. Their success was enormous—because in them one could see the central problem of all Christianity, that is, salvation, set forth in a readily understandable allegory in the prologue; because, between the scenes which recounted the Gospels, entertaining episodes were inserted—like the entrance of the devils or secular dialogue or stories taken from unauthentic legends like that involving the Sinner Mary Magdalene; and because, especially, they were fascinating spectacles, with their hundreds of characters and supernumeraries, their disguises and scenery, the subtlety of a staging already served by a set of perfected contrivances. These visual and musical impressions, sustained by the droning of the text, were powerful contributions to the education of the popular soul.

By comparison with the profound influence exerted by the sermon and the theater, the role of printing seems very limited. Introduced to Paris in 1470 by teachers at the Sorbonne, three years later taking root in Lyon, then spread hither and thither by patrons who could afford the very high price of installation, the new technique—used almost exclusively in the making of devotional books—did not appreciably modify reading conditions before the end of the fifteenth century. But to counterbalance this, there was the process of wood engraving, which had been much longer in use and was now much more widely disseminated. It too contributed to the refinement of sensibility, by distributing pictures over a broad area, either singly or combined with others in little pamphlets. These, again, were devotional pictures, fixing and prolonging the affective impression of the drama and preachings.

Thus, all these combined effects bring about a sudden flowering of religious feeling. People are sometimes inclined to consider the fifteenth century to be less Christian than that of St. Louis. This is an illusion: on the contrary, it is much more religious, and more deeply so. But what is expressed now is another kind of Christianity, for we are at the moment when the religion of the priests really becomes popular, begins to be truly felt and lived by the entire (at least urban) society. As is true with all popularization, this transfer of religious conceptions from a small group of intellectuals to a particularly sensitive and emotional mass entails a change in tonality—all the more so because the hold on the mass consciousness is maintained by rather free means, since the faithful are no longer so closely hemmed in by the clergy. For the Church of France, too, suffered from the hard times. Its most active communities were struck by the black plague, then ruined by the war, so that, as Jean Molinet says, all that remained of the greatest monasteries were

> Storerooms wheatless, poor-plates coinless,
> Prelates shameful, brothers muddied,
> Empty ovens, cellars wineless,
> Ruined cells and cloisters bloodied. . . .

After the end of the troubles, then, the situation of the lower clergy was more deplorable than ever: revenues cornered by non-resident curates, poorly educated priests in charge of succursal chapels, mocked by their flock, and, above all, poverty—a clergy, thin, stricken and consequently greedy, particularly bent on selling sacraments and indulgences at the best price.

Accordingly, religion is more intimate, personal, and familiar. In a universe where the line between natural and supernatural is blurred, the saint fulfills the functions of exorciser of evil, intermediary, and protector —functions taken on by the priest only imperfectly. There are individual patron saints, those whose names people bear, though it is scarcely before the end of the thirteenth century that it becomes the general custom to give young children the names not of ancestors but of venerated saints who thus become associated with the family. Then there are the collective patron saints of professional organizations, of the "charities," those groups for good works, prayer, and burial, then multiplying prodigiously in both urban and rural districts; or else, patron saints of military brotherhoods, those of archers, crossbowmen, which form a framework for the urban infantry, of which they are the real captains. And there are even guardian saints, objects of widespread worship: those who protect against sudden death, like St. Christopher and St. Barbara; who are in charge of this or that disease, like St. Roch and St. Anthony; saints with whom it is wise to be on good terms. Every one of them is present in the most quotidian acts; they live all the more intensely among these people because their faces are depicted on stained-glass windows, retables, and banners; and because they have been seen to act and speak, armed with all their traditional attributes, in processions or theatrical performances. But, dominating this gaudy and reassuring crowd of patron saints, extending her cloak over everyone like a shield against earthly perils and the wrath of God alike, is the interceding Virgin, the object of a devotion that now experiences an enormous development, with the appearance of the rosary and many confraternities of all sorts devoted exclusively to her service. Indeed, it is during the fifteenth century, among those crowds surrendering themselves to religious consciousness, that the gradual development of medieval Christianity—of which Mary has become the central figure—reaches its climax. Next to her, Christ almost never appears in any form other than that of the infant Jesus, whom she supports and suckles; or else, dead, spread over her knees in the touching group of the Pietà. Around these two principal representations—Virgin and Child, Virgin of Sorrows—devotional life is organized and the new orientation of piety is asserted, an orientation propounded for two centuries by the Franciscans, one directed toward tenderness and, particularly, toward drama.

It is a religion of pathos. During this period, the practice of making the Stations of the Cross spreads, the confraternities stage the Passion time after time; Philip de Mézières has recently founded an Order of the Passion, and Isabella of Bavaria has a meditation on the Stations written for her use. The sermons of the Franciscans describe the torture instruments and the wounds of Christ, one by one, with alarming precision; the image of the crucifix—with outstretched arms, and rigid body whose weight pulls upon the hands—assumes the look of the gallows; painters, sculptors, wood engravers distribute far and wide the picture of the Man of Sorrows, crowned with thorns, awaiting His suffering; and, in the imagination of the devout, the body of Christ becomes a fountain of youth, sprinkling sinners with the blood of redemption. These are the times when participation in the Passion has become the principal act of piety. One prepares, then, for death, for the "good death" that now has become the converging point for all religious concern. Indeed, it is an obsession: history as written by the Romantics took pleasure in turning up every one of its manifestation: bodies in a state of decay, opened stomachs, had been represented on tombs since the very end of the fourteenth century; and the very image of Death, who is personified armed with his spear, appears in many Books of Hours, or even in the old story of the Three Dead and the Three Living, which the Duke of Berry ordered carved in stone in 1400. It appears still more impressively in the Dance of Death, first depicted around 1425 in the Parisian cemetery of the Innocents, then copied everywhere, and finally popularized by means of printed illustrations. But we must truly understand why this theme is significant. It is symptomatic neither of psychical disturbance nor of the collapse of a world tortured by hardships and tormented by war. Actually, in books like the *Ars moriendi,* a treatise on how to die well, which spread by the processes of wood-engraving and printing, was enormously successful in France after 1480, the thought of death is a stimulus—either to take better advantage of the pleasures of life (and the theme of physical decay becoming an incentive for immediate enjoyment is carried by a whole body of literature into the sixteenth century) or else, not to let oneself be caught napping, but to defend oneself better against sin. This more popular and common religion is henceforth based less on the love for or intellectual contemplation of God, than on the idea of sin, on the fear of a hell made even more dreadful by the proliferation of a whole new set of imagery. This is one of the great fifteenth-century innovations. All the religious sensibility of the poor and ignorant, which until now had its outlet in practices and beliefs that fell outside of the forms of worship, are stimulated by the propagandization of the Mendicant Friars, and seep into Christianity, giving it a new outlook for centuries to come. But at the same time, roused by this eruption of irrational feeling, many other beliefs begin to be prevalent. Demons are no less real, no less active, than saints: the Devil is everywhere—people feel him, see him, and prosecute his adepts before lay or inquisitional tribunals, condemning them over a wide area of France either individually or en masse—as in Arras in 1459 and 1465, or Lyon in 1480. Visionaries, mystics, and miracle workers fill all of the fifteenth century; this in turn opens onto the great period of witchcraft. And this inquisitive era which, seeking to understand, is nonetheless weary of Aristotle and rejects the fossilized logic of the schools, finds the cause of phenomena in the actions of invisible beings, in the influence of stars, or in relationships that have nothing to do with reason. Doctors are also astrologers, and even the most intellectual are engrossed in magic and occultism. Hence, the powerful forces of popular feeling converge with the manifestations of high culture; for the latter, too, is undergoing a thorough renovation.

The war's hardships had been too limited, both in time and in space, to dam up the deep-rooted currents of princely culture, or even to change their course. In encircled and "anglicized" Paris, the workshops of the illuminators, ivory sculptors, and tombstone makers are disbanded, or have slowed down to a snail's pace. But the writers and artists have gathered elsewhere, regrouping themselves around princes well supplied with gold, and have an eye out for their own glory. The fifteenth century is the period of highborn patrons, and it is worthy of note that the era's greatest poet, Charles d'Orléans, was a prince. (The greatest poet with the exception of François Villon who was student, pimp, burglar, murderer; who stands, as he should, alone, and who was the only one to be able to introduce the perturbing song of his own misery into the extremely rigid structure of the new lyric forms.) Also, one of the greatest painters of the time was a prince: René d'Anjou, recently supposed to be the artist of those amazing miniatures, studies in esoteric lighting (sunrise over meadows, dim bedchambers at night) that decorate the most beautiful copy of his mediocre romance, *Le Livre du cœur d'amour épris*. The liveliest centers of art are around the aristocratic lords, at Tours, Bourges, and Orléans where the kings live; at Angers and Aix; and at Moulins, which toward the end of the century becomes, under the Duke of Bourbon, one of the most brilliant capitals. The court of the Dukes of Burgundy, clearly superior in luxury, is actually set somewhat apart; it is provincial, indurate, and lags behind the times to the extent that the chivalric spirit rigidifies there, unrenewed. This spirit becomes the dominant theme of a vast and tightly regulated ostentation whose formality subsequently passes to Austria and Spain, then appears again in France during the reign of Louis XIV. The Burgundian courtliness, love-casuistry, and allegory become ossified in the vain and numbing virtuosity of the Grands Rhétoriqueurs. Since the days of Sluter, and since its center was transferred to Flanders, the court of the Burgundian dukes has become increasingly foreign; its great creations—the tombs in Dijon with their cortege of mourners, the great paintings of Van Eyck and Rogier van der Weyden, the music of Ockeghem—all these are no longer French, but come from Flanders, Hainault, and Brabant. But, on the other hand, in the *fleur de lys* courts along the Loire and Rhône, there surges around 1440 a creative force which, although certainly influenced by the Italian, is not Latin, but sinks its most nourishing roots deep into Gothic civilization—a fact which too often makes people forget that this force is, already, truly of the Renaissance.

A renaissance, first of all, of architectural ornament. After the long domination in the Ile-de-France of the High Gothic, there is a complete change in method, around 1420, causing the sudden appearance of an entirely different art: Flamboyant Gothic, an art of extremely pronounced angles, assertive moldings, sharp breaks in lines and curves, all reacting insistently against the slimness, the soft accents, that had sapped fourteenth-century cathedral architecture. It is as natural an art as the old one, but is swollen with a new vitality that causes the transepts of the arches to spring forth from the very shaft of the columns; and it is a highly skillful art, simplifying construction and reducing it to its essential means. Most especially, it is a freer art, combining brackets of curves and counter-curves in decorative exuberance, making all the lines writhe as if they were on fire, causing leaves to break out in curl-clusters, garlands, and bouquets, around the mullions of windows, on the main floors of *hôtels*, and on the rood-screens and tombs of votive churches, masking the base structure of the building under an independent sculptural surface. Stimulated by all the attempts at rebuilding, a new departure spreads from Paris and Normandy to Brou and as far as Auch. Taken up in its liveliest form by the sixteenth century, Flamboyant Gothic actually forms the solid support over which Italian ornamentation lies like a superficial veneer; yet this style was to remain in France, until the seventeenth century, as the skeleton of every building.

And, at the same time, great painting is born. Art lovers now definitely prefer painting on wooden panels to illuminations in books. The advantage of the former is that it can be displayed in the small, intimate rooms where people like to live, or on the altars of private chapels; at the same time, it preserves all the vividness and precious richness of the miniature. Once again, the greatest creators are in the service of princes; hence the existence of three provinces of French painting, corresponding to the three regions where princes usually live—apart from Burgundy, where the style of painting is Flemish. First, there is the Loire Valley, where Charles VII and Louis XI liked to live. There, the style of the decorators who illustrated books for the Duke of Anjou or Jean de Berry was enriched by the contributions of the masters who emigrated from Paris after the English occupation. This style saw its supreme flowering in the art of Fouquet, who had returned from a trip to Italy, bringing not only an ornamental repertory inspired by the antique, but also a sense of space and of volume. His calm figures, arranged outside of time, are not without correspondence to those then being painted by Piero della Francesca; but Fouquet's are bathed in a different light, that of the Loire country, less precisely defined, slightly softened—and a light in which the humid atmosphere lends softness to flesh tones, in which exotic pinks and yellows glisten. The second region of painting is in Provence, where the painters' efforts were stimulated, first by the orders of the cardinals living in Avignon after the Curia's return to Rome, then by those of René d'Anjou, when he brought his court to Aix. In Provence, the vision of the Sienese decorators, who in the preceding century had embellished the pontifical dwellings, was combined with Flemish influences. Toward the middle of the century, a very powerful style asserted itself, one that owed its strong architectonic quality to a sense of balanced composition and to an analysis of the unequivocal light which, around Avignon, simplifies all forms, and throws into relief the limestone hills of the Comtat Vernaissin. Thirdly, and somewhat later, the Duke of Bourbon had the greatest image-makers of his time working at Moulins; among those who

designed the stained-glass windows of the collegiate church and decorated the ducal castle, one of them also did wooden panel paintings of
purity, simplicity, and sweetness: portraits of the princesses, Nativity
scenes, and triumphs of the Virgin. In those large workshops which set
the tone for a whole body of minor work, perspective and form appear in
some areas, then, in the long run, prevail. This vigorous art, one that
is much more muscular than that of the court of Charles VI, certainly
owes a great deal to the Flemish and Italian sculptural discoveries; yet it
has completely assimilated them, and asserts its originality in grace, harmony, and circumspection—the qualities of the Gothic canon of beauty.
And it is certainly this period, around 1450, in Tours and Avignon—
much more important for all French painting than the Italianizing interlude at Fontainebleau—from which the Renaissance must truly be
dated.

This renaissance, lastly, is one of the intellect. It occurs much later
than the artistic renaissance, is much more limited and more dependent
on Italy. Yet, in the midst of the decaying university life, the intellectual renaissance is the last sign of vitality in the waning Middle Ages.
After 1470, Guillaume Fichet, a member of the Société de Sorbonne, had
brought the first infusion of humanism into the University of Paris. Fichet
came from Savoy, and had been nourished on Petrarch and the Latin
classics during his studies in Avignon; also, in Milan he had recently
come into direct contact with Italian intellectuals. The presses, for whose
installation he was responsible, printed Valla's *Elegantiae*, which is, in
short, the basic text of the new philology. Next, around Robert Gaguin,
dean of the law faculty, a small society of admirers of ancient letters was
formed, consisting of some Italian professors, some Greek refugees who
were spreading Platonist doctrines. These were men of the court or the
university, who lived piously and were attracted by monastic life and
ascetic mysticism; yet they were anxious to rediscover the purity of clas
sical Latin—as distinguished from the jargon of the Scholastics—and
re-establish a truly soul-nourishing philosophy, again in contradistinction
to those in the arts faculty, who redigested empty logic. To do so, they
were lured by Platonism. It was a very small group, but Jacques Lefèvre
d'Étaples was a member. At that time he was dreaming of a monastic reform, according to the tradition of St. Bernard, and sought the answers
to his anxieties in the Cabala. At the same time, on his return from Italy,
he published a paraphrase of Aristotle and a treatise on natural magic.

According to the history textbooks, the Middle Ages ends there. Yet
does it really? And when? A vain question, when one considers the closing years of the century, a period not of falling-off, but of bursting forth,
a period which finds, in its meditation upon death, a recrudescence of
fervor and creative energy. Agricultural techniques have stagnated; ar-
chaism and routine reign in small-town shops. But, in the West, a new

world is already opening up for the sailors from Normandy and Saintonge. The honeyed tones of courtly rhetoric and the absurd verbiage of
those at the Sorbonne are inconsequential, compared with the flourishing of religious sentiment, compared with all the nascent forms germi-
nating out of the Gothic tradition, compared with this current of
thought and of new curiosity which, although now scarcely beginning to
form, swells rapidly; a current from which the young Rabelais is soon to
quench his thirst.

Part Two

MODERN

AND

CONTEMPORARY
FRANCE

by

Robert Mandrou

Introduction

WHAT have these fifteenth-century Frenchmen in common with our contemporaries of the mid-twentieth century? Less than half a millennium in the history of this people, scarcely less than the preceding period: those Middle Ages, already so rich. And yet it is as if an abyss separated the men of 1480 from French civilization today. Then, they burned to discover worlds both new and ancient; they were fervent Christians to their dying day; they were entirely open to the joy of being alive in those generations liberated from the great cataclysms of an interminable war. Simultaneously, they were so rough, so very withdrawn into their little birthplace—the narrow social framework of parish and province. Compared with the France of today, what is the fifteenth century, that time of rich contrasts and of exceptional lives, that flowering of the Middle Ages that presaged a new era? The apex and heart of the greatest technical revolution man has ever lived through, the France of today is in the forefront, carrying out her great role there through all the efforts of her scientists, artists, technicians, intellectuals; simultaneously, she allows many reminiscences of a former France to survive in her rural areas and sleepy little provincial towns. At the rate at which the scientific ascendancy rushes headlong into everyday living, the rate at which movies and television and speed of transportation are transforming ways of both thought and life, the prodigious and sometimes frightening twentieth century would deserve, if we dared, to have half, if not more, of this study devoted to it. Is not the man of the 1880s, astonished by the railroad, that prime marvel of yesterday, a closer relative to an associate of Louis XII than to ourselves who, overrun and served by mechanical objects, live in direct and permanent contact with new worlds which, having finally come about after three centuries of distant connections, are now upsetting the old Europe? Undoubtedly, this earlier part of the twentieth century alone contains more promises, more innovations already made, which bear on an entire civilization, than the four hundred years that precede it.*

This incredible twentieth century is not, it is true, the product of an abrupt change or an historical leap, despite the importance of a few dates. The first industrial revolution governs the two subsequent ones; the Paris of today has concluded the polarization of French civilization because the entire nineteenth century prepared the way for the gigantic growth of that capital, harbinger of the "French desert"; and yesterday's revolutions continue to inspire and orient both political thought and that passion for the *respublica* which dominates opinion and which has the power of multiple traditions and inventive boldness. Therefore, let us make our distinctions according to a more classic—too classic—division of two movements: preceding the "contemporary" France, which evolved from the social and political revolution and then the economic and social transformations—before 1789, or else 1781, if we need a date—there are the three hundred years of "modern" France, during which the still provincial civilization of the Old Regime flourishes; three hundred years that come to maturity in the eighteenth century—with its *fêtes galantes*, its Encyclopedia, its Europe of the Enlightenment—when France taught all Europe both its language and its arts.

Besides, does not fifteenth-century France, too, possess political and social frameworks, economic structures that will last until the Revolution? By then, the dominant elements have been fixed: and, if one had the space, one would need only follow the fate for the three centuries of a small provincial capital—Arras, Dijon, or Moulins—in order to understand these elements. Each of these towns wins its own success in difficult human endeavor; they grow, spread out over the lowlands; they conduct trade; they exchange books and ideas with Paris and with their neighbors. But their inner life still reflects the great conflicts and powerful exchanges that have nourished France for so long: jolts and assimilations of the manorial society, inherited from the Middle Ages and from the ascendant bourgeois society, whose power grows as trade and law enlarge its future; the successes and reverses of monarchial society, firm in principle, weak in daily practice—leaning on the bourgeoisie for support, fearing its former ally the nobility, making use of the clergy, and at the same time controlling their action over the people. During the era of Louis XV and the *philosophes*, France—still poorly centralized, vulnerable in its badly guarded frontiers to the other European countries,

---

* One is tempted to make the two parts of this study as disproportionate as those of their subject, and to reserve as much room for the last fifty years as for the four centuries preceding; we still lack—to cede for a moment—dozens of sound studies about the artistic and social role of movies and radio, about the psychological and physiological transformations attributable to mechanization.

open to Dürer's Renaissance Germany, or Siglo-de-Oro Spain, sensitive
to all regionalism, poorly unified despite all the indications of patriotism betokened by the deadly wars—France, then, still displays many of
the features that the overly rich fifteenth century carried, at least in seed,
within it.

Modern France, contemporary France. The two are hinged by the eighteenth century, by the night of August fourth or twenty-sixth, 1789; the
old, classic, academic divisions have some worth.

MODERN FRANCE

The Sixteenth to the
Eighteenth Centuries

VI

The Rural Milieu and Mentality: End of the Fifteenth Century to the Beginning of the Eighteenth Century

For more than two centuries, from the end of the fifteenth century—when the scars of the Hundred Years' War and the crises then experienced by Western Europe were forgotten—to the beginning of the eighteenth, around 1730 or 1740, rural France did not suffer any deep or violent alteration. In the country—but only there—France remained, as it were, unchanged.

The economic and social structures of France (and, one might say, of all Europe, all the countries of the Old Regime) are determined in such a way that it is legitimate momentarily to separate, at least in spirit, town from country; for, no matter how indispensable to each other, how closely connected, the two are, the former develops very quickly and the latter remains, for a long time, just as it had been. The nutritive base of France, her agricultural foundations, have varied only slightly for centuries on end; where the basic lines were established between plowed land and forests around 1500, they still remain, or very nearly so, in 1700. All the villages, then, are pegged out in the beginning of the sixteenth century—and we find them there even today. The same bases, then; can one also say the same constraints? The same narrow, unextended lives?

During those first two centuries of modern France, the rural heritage of the Middle Ages remains, weighing upon the country as an almost unshakable burden; we see its survival in the social organization, the village community that is more or less organized, administered or, at least, dominated by the lord, the *curé*, and the royal agent. This system is perpetuated in the economic organization: the peasants unquestionably feed the nearby towns and in their small way promote large-scale trade, at least through the intermediary of those landed proprietors—nobles, bishops, and also the bourgeois who, from the thirteenth through the fifteenth centuries, were acquiring land—who are all large sellers of agricultural products. Yet, on the whole, the prevailing economic system is still of narrow scope, resting on limited resources. The village lives an introverted life; to be sure, it is open to the external world existing beyound its heaths and forests, thanks to the *curé* who reads the royal enactments every Sunday, thanks to the soldiers, that dreaded lot all too often seen, and even to that other affliction, the tramps. But this is much and little at the same time.

With the exception of the outskirts of large, innovating, demanding towns—for example, those plains that are the granary of Paris, in Brie, Picardy, and the Beauce—and with the exception, too, of such villages as are frequently passed through along rivers and roads, the rural world leads a life apart, removed, by the great distances of the period, from that of the towns, whose adventures, riches, joys, and ordeals are more varied and changeable. This does not mean that rural living is peaceful. Its risks, misfortunes, latent insecurities, traditions, or rare pleasures are, as we are told incessantly by the scanty literature treating of rural life, almost immutable. This is so despite the variety in ways of living brought about by geographical contrasts, climate, and soil—from the broad cereal-producing plains of the Beauce to the pugnacious flocks being moved about in the Pyrenees or in Haute-Provence; despite that variety fostered by the rare agricultural operations of the day, such as woad in the valley around Toulouse, vineyards along the Rhône; despite everything that history has incorporated in some areas, into everyday life, of features hitherto unknown (thus, in western France, which had to be rebuilt after the Hundred Years' War, the peasant was allowed a relative freedom, while in eastern regions, like Burgundy, Lorraine, or Franche-Comté, a more severe regime prevailed, continuing the long-persistent blemish of serfdom). But his deceptive diversity is not really much, after all, during these times when the primary concern is to be assured of sustenance, fundamental to the needs of the community; when the basis of all food, of all life, is bread. Coming before all regional diversities is a general design whose major features we must describe in more detail.

▶ MATERIAL INSECURITY

The basis of this precariousness, or at best this mediocrity (as in the fertile soils and climate of Poitou and Aquitaine) is the "natural economy," that is to say, the economy of sufficiency. Settled on the plot of ground of which he feels himself master, devoted to those communal practices that constitute rural interdependence, yet at the same time weighed down by all sorts of burdens, the small peasant has only one ambition: to produce what he needs—wheat, first of all, then barley or oats and also a little wine, even in the northern regions.* Depend on no one but yourself, and a few close neighbors—like weavers or cartwrights—who soon return services you render them; this rule of life remained applicable until the middle of the nineteenth century, a golden rule observed even today in those regions of small, family farming that remain in the Massif Central and parts of Aquitaine—a rule that returned to favor even as recently as between 1940 and 1944. And the juxtaposition of these two periods is not accidental: the idea of providing everything for oneself has great (indeed, excessively great) prestige, in times when life is difficult and everyone fears that one day or other he will lack the basic necessities, originating in constant want, famine, and "high prices," it is an idea incorporated into the economic conditions that are a heritage of the past.

Georges Lefebvre has said it quite well: "The typical rural Frenchman is the peasant who farms for himself and, at best, for the nearest town."[1] He was speaking of the eighteenth-century peasant; it is even truer of that peasant's ancestors in the preceding centuries. The French peasant is a small-scale farmer† on the land of his parish, owning a half-dozen

---

* Just before the Revolution, *intendants* were still reporting on all the important vineyards in Brittany, the present-day Nord, the Perche, and the Caux regions, *i.e.*, quite far beyond the alleged northern boundary of the wine-growing region.

† From the point of view of rural farming, the only noteworthy exception is doubtless that of the farmer on the plains surrounding Paris; as a tenant farmer, he gathers many scattered fields around him, or farms a large property whose holder lives in town. However, this type of farmer is still rare—and besides he himself sells a part of the harvest; he is treated with respect in villages either in the Ile-de-France or the Beauce.

sparse plots in different exposures, often in very different types of soil. Thus he cultivates his part of each field, those large, age-old segments of crop rotations, so different in their simplicity from the rotations of today —the three-field system in the north, the two-field in the south. They are aware of no method of improving arable land other than letting it stand fallow, sometimes for an extended period. This small farmer can thus make twenty-five to forty acres (as we would measure them today) "produce"; also, along with his neighbors, he makes use of the very extensive communal property: heaths, forests, swampy pasture-land, and so on; with these he feeds his family, supports and clothes himself with the wool from his lambs and the hemp from his hempfields along a stream. He repairs his implements with the wood from his forest, which is regularly distributed, and covers his house with the straw from his harvest. Whether or not he owns his land, he brings in very few goods from the outside; "capitalist" ownership has progressed over the course of the modern centuries, but only in the vicinity of towns, for it is a fact of great urban importance, as much as, if not more than, rural. And it is at this point that we come across the rich peasants: men who farm with a plow, who own several horses or oxen. For, to farm a hundred and twenty-five or a hundred and fifty acres, you need more than one beast of burden.

Many a day-laborer of that time did not have even the two or three heads of cattle necessary for the hardest work. Rather, they rented out their services to a neighbor who was better off and, in exchange, borrowed the latter's team of oxen, and sometimes his swingplow. This predominance of small farming, so many examples of which remain today, is not an unalterable thing; we need not trace it back to Neolithic times but can content ourselves with noting that the Middle Ages, with its manorial regime and the destructiveness of its invasions and wars (see above, pp. 161-62) encouraged it. Let us note, also, that it was tenacious; for, during these same sixteenth and seventeenth centuries, it was severely abused by neighboring England and by Germany beyond the Elbe, to the advantage of both the large estates and the large farms. In any case, rural France never experienced any movement of enclosure comparable to England's, even during the century of the Physiocrats; this was so for many reasons, the chief being the glamor and attractiveness of French urban life, to which French nobles were more sensitive than were their English counterparts, those great "enclosers."

The stability of small farms, especially the cereal-producing ones, would in itself suffice to explain the mediocrity of the peasants' condition, during a time when the granaries were well-stocked and everyone ate as much as three *livres* of bread a day.* Actually, this stability is

---

* Bread, the basic foodstuff even in the cities, is the food richest in calories, as Europeans have known for centuries.[2]

linked closely to the collective life, almost no traces of which survive today (except in the fields divided into small plots, existing especially in Lorraine). Each peasant's land is integrated into a common territory, where crops are the same year in and year out: hence, the peasant does not dispose as he sees fit of his own plots of earth—as he might dispose of dead- or live-wood, or the ferns and huckleberries of the forest—but does so only with the permission of the rest of the village or parish. The paucity of the estates necessitates mutual aid, and all work is done jointly, during weeks of communal living, when all the participants help each other month after month*: harvesting grain crops with sickles (the standard practice until the nineteenth century); plowing with those swingplows that are so hard to handle, yet so small; cutting down great quantities of wood from the forests; and also gathering grapes. Thus the parish community has its own profound reality—which partially explains why new techniques and new crops have been so slowly adopted until recently in French rural districts: corn and the bean, brought back from America during the sixteenth century, did not win over southern France for many decades; and also later, the same was true of tobacco and, a better-known example, potatoes. It is the same story for agricultural implements and techniques: the swingplow, used in tilling the soil, remained the same or almost the same, from antiquity down to the eighteenth century; still used today in the mountainous districts of the Massif Central, Velay, and Combrailles, it is easy to identify through its kinship with the old instruments. A still better example: Roger Thabault, in his great book from which we shall quote later on, tells how the all-metal wheel-plow came slowly and discreetly into ordinary use, in the middle of the nineteenth century, in his village of Mazières-en-Gâtine.[3] But the Mazières innovator is then the master of his field; his neighbors come, perhaps jeeringly, to watch him try out his tool—they cannot prevent him from doing so; then, two or three years later, seeing his field entirely rid of ferns and broom grasses, they doubtless make up their minds. On the other hand, in the sixteenth and seventeenth centuries, such an innovation is unlikely from the very first. The peasant described by La Bruyère farms like his neighbor and his father; he cannot farm any other way, and he does not try to. Is there, in these difficult times, one single peasant who is free in his actions? Documents do not tell us of any, unless it be one in some village of the Haute-Saône Valley in 1636, or in the Bourbonnais in 1662—the final survivor of an atrocious famine.

---

* Rural individualism, so strong today, is a recent fact; the only peasant individualists of the past are the vine-growers of Aquitaine and Burgundy, already producing well-known wines and uninterested in collective structures; they come and go from their vinepatch to Dijon or Bordeaux where they sell their wines and buy their hogsheads and bread. To be sure, they are wedded to the land, but the commercial life they lead makes them actually townspeople.

Actually, the agricultural techniques and habits have been used from time immemorial; despite certain innovations, the contributions brought by the Arabs to the Mediterranean regions during the Middle Ages (see above, p. 103) are practices easily listed and described: winter and spring cereals occupy the best land; kitchen gardens and fruit trees are planted near the village or near isolated houses; the peasant always farms according to the same routine and with the same wooden implements because iron is expensive (not rare, but difficult to shape); since few coppers pass through his hands during the course of a year, he buys as little as possible: an ax, a pruning hook, a sickle, a spade, a point for his swingplow. So, the majority of his implements are wooden: harrows, yokes, flails, wheelbarrows, and wagons, often with rimless wheels. On the other hand, what poor yields, from this repeated use of a common forest! The swingplow, turning and scratching up four inches of soil, does not pull up the weeds; and how slow is the harvesting of cereal crops with a sickle—and what an expense of energy!* Fertilizing the soil, which they know to be necessary, is still not certain, first of all because there is not enough livestock; everywhere land is left fallow and this restores it, but very slowly. Weeds are not yet used to vary crop rotations, and not until the eighteenth century does such a practice become widespread. In many mountainous regions, the soil is left fallow for years, until it is gradually overrun by broom grasses, ferns, and low coppices which presage and precede forests: all this is cut, one fine day, then burned, and this process enriches the soil—for a few seasons. This method of burning the land is a system that has not entirely disappeared by the nineteenth century.[4]

Fertilizing the farm does not make up for this method of resting land. Cattle are scanty and thin, for the peasant can provide them with an allowance consisting only of rank weeds from the lowlands, straw from the harvested fields, and the few grasses from the underbrush. There are few meadows of mown corn crops and no plentiful fodder. Cattle-breeding is a mere complement to the raising of cereal products, even in the mountainous regions where the use of high pasture land enables people to have larger flocks. Thus, the livestock does not provide for an abundant supply of manure. Few meadows mean little wheat. In the vicinity of towns, where wagons and, soon, post-horse way stations necessitate large stables, the big farms that supply the towns with fodder and horses are better provided for: there are always exceptions—slight exceptions.

Finally, these small peasants are unable to improve their crops by the purchase of selected seeds which are adapted, as they are today, to soils

---

* We know the classic comparison of productivity in our day: two and a half acres harvested in an hour by fifty men with sickles, twenty-five with scythes, ten with a mechanical reaper.

and climates. For both seed culture—a very modern technique born of a science then nonexistent—and money are lacking. Peasants always use their own grain, from one year to the next, and are happy to obtain yields in the ratio of six or even four to one.

In every tradition, the greatest part is that of mental habit: man is caught up in a network of acquired customs, accepted from childhood through the authority of the family, and maintained without effort. It is not that this life, withdrawn into village or ancestral neighborhood, with peasants and artisans forming a body, seems to them to be perfect; they are all too well aware of its deficiencies, being themselves victims, and daily victims, of its precariousness. They lack too many things, even assuming heaven and earth are kind to them—and their chief lack is money.

In this life resting on its own support, the small peasant has no resources: this explains the numerous small craft professions, for they are capable of bringing in a little extra revenue. They grow up around commercial towns—even at some distance from them—and are based on the use of leisure time forced upon the peasants by the winter. We must recall that the sixteenth-century peasant sells hardly any of his products. Not that he produces just the amount he needs to live on—the grain harvests, especially during the good years, are more generous—but the agents of both lords and bishops take a healthy cut of his output. The grain that has been cut but not yet taken in passes through the hands of the tithe-owner on the field, and he removes (depending on the region) one sheaf in six, in seven, in fifteen, or in twenty. Then this grain must be ground—in the *banal* mill—and baked—in the *banal* oven. Each time, a payment is made in kind. The same thing is true of the manorial wine-press, and of the hemp when it must be fulled. We readily grant that these little village functionaries, representing a lord who is either absent or scorns such chores, are often more exacting and unkind than he himself would be. Added to this, it is true, within the framework of the same manorial order, are the cash payments whose real value was considerably reduced by inflation in the Middle Ages, and particularly in the sixteenth century. But in many provinces, the *champart** remained a payment in kind; therefore, it was a very heavy one. Besides this, the accounts were calculated and recalculated (amounting to multiple taxation);[5] when the peasant paid his tithe, when he discharged various manorial fees and then arranged for his *banalités,* and finally when he stored his seed away—this alone could consume more than a quarter of his harvest, while the tithe and *banalité* together could constitute twenty-five or thirty per cent of the same harvest. Only what remained in his granary could be used to feed his family. And if the price of wheat increases in urban markets, where the tithe-owners or wheat-

---

* A tax levied on the sheaves of grain collected by the lord.—Trans.

marketers and hucksters entrusted with disposing of the manorial reserves sell them, it is not the peasant who profits. These facts, then, help
to explain two things: that, in fact, the peasant profits but little in the
urban monetary economy, selling at the annual local fair only a few capons, some butter, perhaps a calf; and, that he devotes the little bit of
money he receives to discharging his royal taxes, such as the *taille* and
the salt tax. As Vauban asserts,[6] while he does not always go so far as to
neglect his land in order to pay less (a very understandable reaction, we
must add, and one taking the longer view), still, he is convinced that
these overwhelming charges are the great, the chief, cause of his distress;
and so convinced is he of this that often he is ready to take up arms—
gun, pitchfork, or flail—to protect himself against the "collectors."
The greatest disturbances of the sixteenth and seventeenth centuries,
the revolts of the *croquants*,* were directed against royal agents, the
collectors of cash, that is, of fiscal tax surcharges. The first and most burdensome of these (these violent movements should not mislead us) are
the tithe and the *banalités*—taxes in kind.

Under these conditions, how difficult is material life in rural France!
That peasant who, through the tithe-owner and the lords' *intendants*,
feeds the towns, he whose products are thus even able to enter international circuits of commerce—wheat from Provence to the Mediterranean,
from Aquitaine to Spain—feeds himself with great difficulty. A bad harvest, a heavy April frost, a storm over his fields in July, and his harvest is,
if not destroyed, at least reduced†; a heavy frost is especially dreaded.
Chronicles of the times abound in descriptions of terrible winters, the
kind France does not have any more: the Seine and Loire completely
frozen over, so that people can cross on the ice without any danger; and,
along the Mediterranean, ice floes. Reduced or insufficient grain harvests
mean, first of all, that fees are heavier, since they represent a percentage, and also because the tithe-owners and nobles' *intendants* become
all the more exacting when the receipts are low and when, therefore, the
total income is decreased. Above all, a reduced grain harvest means
that, several months later, the next harvest is jeopardized; having discharged his debts, the peasant has whatever remains in his storehouses
to live on, once the seeding is done—for this represents a fixed amount,
not a percentage: for a harvest of a hundred or a hundred-fifty sacks, he
will always need twenty-five bags of seeds. If his storehouse is empty,

---

* The name given to the peasants who revolted under Henry IV and Louis XIII.—
Trans.
† Need one go into this damage? In an economy as fragile as this one, a fifty per
cent loss (which could be the result of a frost, or even of a bad storm) is a catastrophe for which village solidarity cannot compensate. Then the peasant borrows
some wheat from the *aisez* or rich. Disaster! [7]

he has to eat plants and roots, for better or for worse, in order to hold out until July. And how is he to hold out, if he cannot even survive the winter? In this way, shortage and famine run rampant over the countryside before they affect the towns—the opposite of what France experienced in the years 1940-44, when the towns suffered much more than the country.

Shortage, high prices, famine: contemporaries are careful to distinguish very significant gradations among these.* Shortage is dire poverty; bread is made from ferns or bran, but it is a situation that is not fatal, except perhaps to a few old people. Famine is much worse: villages destroyed, even towns and provinces laid waste, and, says a seventeenth-century doctor, "horrible things that make your hair stand on end." † Sometimes localized in a corner of one province, since storing and circulating grain throughout the realm was not well organized, famines are often spread by the speculation of the collectors, who hoard their grain, gamble and win on a price rise over a period of months, in those very towns being assailed by the peasants who, fleeing their thatched cottages, come to town to beg for their bread. Thus, during a series of bleak years, 1630-32, 1636-38, and again in 1709, there are great catastrophes based on poverty, cold, and chronic hunger. A final ingredient completes the picture: during, or after, the famines, the epidemics found the ground already prepared for them in these peoples' undernourished bodies. Hence the fear of bubonic plague carriers [*bubbons*]—strangers, beggars, or the ordinary passer-by crossing a village—the man no one knows, whose tramp's or vagrant's pack perhaps harbors those dangerous, unknown animals who carry the plague, that dreaded and always lethal disease that is, in these crises, at its strongest.[10] Villages that one day are heavily populated are deserted six months later—further explanation is unnecessary. And, on a nationwide scale, fifteen or sixteen million people would, after such ordeals, be reduced to thirteen or fourteen million; would return to seventeen or twenty million, or more, after twenty or so fairly good years had passed. These figures are approximate, but the observation of details explains it rather well: a given village, in a normal year, records fifteen deaths—then in 1709, fifty-five; in 1710, thirty.

Yet what expansive pleasure, rejoicing, good meals, and cheerful sing-

---

* Evidence concerning the frequency of want and the horror of famines is abundant; reflective works like the *Dixme royale*, emphasizing the chronic distress of Vézelay: "The common people . . . rarely drink wine, eat meat three times a year, and have only a little bit of salt. . . . We should not be surprised if such people have so little strength. To this we should add that what they suffer at the hands of nudity contributes a great deal to it: three-fourths of them are dressed only in half-rotten or torn cloth, and wooden shoes in both winter and summer . . . weak and unhealthy people." [8]
† "A child who had already eaten one of his hands. . . ." [9]

ing and dancing, when the grain harvest is finished, a harvest large enough to let them garner a fine store of wheat, barley, or oats. These copious rural feasts, a few traces of which remain today, have the fullest significance of a victory over death, a future gained for the next several months. And again, what fervor of rustic faith when, during an extremely long dry spell, preventing the grain from growing taller, on an already too hot June morning the whole parish, and the *curé*, with the beadle in front, depart in a procession to the Church, carrying across the fields, with a thousand precautions, the statue of St. Médard,* the good saint who makes it rain—carrying him amidst a hum of prayers, going so far as to dip him into the last spring still containing water, in order to make it quite clear to him what it is that they expect. And yet, supposing everything succeeds—a good harvest, a fine tillage, a fairly mild winter, a fairly clear summer—they still incur some risks. For example, in the mere passing through of some soldiers. Strictly speaking, the peasant in this "modern" France finds little help around him; the social framework of the period is, for him, oppressive, without any consideration for the feelings either of *vilains* or *croquants*. Richelieu compares them to mules who are accustomed to burdens—and who deteriorate more from a long rest than from work.

► **SOCIAL INSECURITY**

A bad play on words, this subtitle, for the modern reader. And yet what better way to call attention to the breaking of the social equilibrium, characterizing the situation of this "modern" French peasantry, unbalanced and unstable despite its dependence on the land? Numerous day laborers in the country do not even have a garden; they rent out their services in various locations, depending upon the season, and travel a great deal. As vagrants they are dangerous, because they might easily become soldiers or—almost the same thing—brigands. Circumstances are limited among these masses of peasants—deprived of all social backing, excluded from all privileged communities, yet situated in the immediate vicinity of towns, within sight of their ramparts; limited, too, for those who stake out their claims along rivers on the still very rare main roads. Even their contemporaries realize how tragic their isolation is.

Nevertheless, social frameworks do exist: there is the chatelain lord, the landowner (in some areas, still, the owner of men as a result of certain monastic communities) who—the fees that people pay him are a sure indication of this—is the recognized protector of the village. If he has recently been replaced by one of those newly rich fourteenth- or fifteenth-century bourgeois who like to put their money into land, the

---

* The French equivalent of St. Swithin, whose "day" is July 15.—Trans.

fees are still gathered, and the protection consequently must continue to exist in the shadow of the castle, the dovecote, and the other exterior indications of the dependence. Then the chatelain's neighbor, the *curé*, who is the spiritual protector as the *hobereau* is the temporal one, insures everyone of the last religious rites in his terrestrial life and of his passage to the life beyond. But if the priest and chatelains are still there, if the *curé* can still assemble all his parishioners each Sunday in church and the castle dweller can (but less often) bid his peasants to broach a half-hogshead of wine in the castle courtyard when a son is born or when a daughter marries—nonetheless, the daily social reality is no longer that of the early Middle Ages (see above, pp. 13-14).

"The poor people," as Vauban calls them, are oppressed, more than protected, by the lord. The great tragedy of rural France, unsolved until 1789, is the maintenance of the lord's rights and of the standard fees; those fees that in former times assured the noble's defense of the local territory, but that are now reduced to ponderous indications of his social, almost racial, superiority (his "blue blood"). And we must evaluate this fairly: we must regard as exceptions those lords who desecrate the order, those of the "haultes Sévennes," the Gévaudan, and the Cantal mentioned by Fléchier, who become marauders, laying waste to their own countryside, looting their own neighbors, ransoming travelers: nor, for that matter, did the Grands Jours in the Auvergne rid the mountains of the Massif Central of them. Nonetheless, let us steadfastly believe that in Champagne or Sologne the noble was content with receiving his income, doing justice, sitting in the first row of the church on Sunday, watching over "his" peasants to make sure that they do no poaching, picking quarrels with the royal agents who come onto his lands; this is already quite a bit. It has been said often enough that the little village *hobereau* lives as crudely, ignorantly, and miserably as his peasants; to be sure, he does not read Homer in the original, or even Ronsard.* Perhaps even his twelfth- or thirteenth-century ancestors, before the great medieval growth of towns, were less boorish than he (see above, pp. 103-104). But he remains the "master," all the more attached to his rights in proportion to the reduction by incessant and subtle inflation of his style of living, and his too quickly threadbare clothes fail to distinguish him from the common people. We shall see that these feelings become stronger with the great price "revolution" of the sixteenth century, which continues into the eighteenth: such feelings are basic. For social connections are very much a matter of tradition and, especially, of mental habit: the sixteenth-century *hobereau*, no longer dreaming, as did his ancestors, of crusades to Jerusalem or Constantinople, lives day in, day out near his dovecote, passing over his moats—whenever these still exist.

---

* Said François d'Estut, Seigneur of Chassy: "The f—— people don't even know how to read." [11]

And this is likewise true, one may perhaps say more so, for the bourgeois from Lyon—he who discreetly purchased a "noble ground" in Forez, ten leagues from the town in which he had made his fortune in silk, spices, or gold, and who came there to settle, proudly, into his new title. From this type, someone just arrived to nobility, the peasant can expect nothing more. This man is undoubtedly rich, more so than the *hobereau* of old stock, but, along with a few good friends from town, he is still using his wealth for speculation in grain—from Feurs or Lyon. What makes him noble is not a vocation as redresser of wrongs or as philanthropist.

The lords' protection of former days has long since disappeared. What remain, then, are the burdens and inflictions, which are more frequent than the good times, and all sorts of obligations. *Corvées* are still required, for example, and against this and other practices, the monarchy has not acted very strongly; and although it has whittled down feudal fees and cut into them considerably, it has done so to the particular advantage of those in the towns. Hence, to the peasantry the royal hand appears, above all, as that of the salt-tax collectors, and collectors of the other royal duties. No longer is the lord the "natural protector." * Yet, on the other hand, the peasant still expects much from his *curé*, on a completely different level: that of a world beyond, the existence of which he does not doubt for a moment, and which, he even believes, is constantly present, mixed with this lower world: natural and supernatural commingled.

Despite their important social and political role (that of more or less intelligent readers of, commentators on, royal enactments), despite the volume of their relief work (many poorhouses and charitable institutions still exist in sixteenth-century towns), nonetheless the lower clergy of the rural areas cannot provide adequate protection for the peasants. The rural *curé* is not a rich man; rather, he lives as penuriously as his flock. The tithes he receives are passed on to his bishops, who in most dioceses have them collected by lay people; he receives an annual fixed viaticum (becoming in the sixteenth century an annual emolument), and has nothing to expect from his faithful expect a few good meals at the château. Also, the *curé* never leaves his village, and sees his bishop only once a year, for confirmations.† He never received the spiritual education that his station might prescribe, but was given, instead, a slipshod training, more often than not by his predecessor—who, choosing the

---

* This is a fine expression, if one thinks that such an ancestral protection created, in the long run, a "nature." But M. Mousnier is of the opinion that the lord always protects; he takes his argument from the fact that the peasant revolts of the seventeenth century were directed primarily against royal agents. This is true; but his conclusion is debatable.[12]

† At this time, the pastoral tour of duty takes place: the state of the roads or else bad weather are often good reason for not making it.

most alert among his large flock of little peasants, taught him the rudiments of the catechism. Provided, then, with a few words of Latin, only those parts of the Gospels which are necessary to the saying of the Mass, ignorant of the Church Fathers and even of the Old Testament, the good *curé* lives amid a moral poverty comparable to that of his peasants. This is doubtless a distant effect of the exacting Gallican movement which, from the time of Charles VII to that of Francis I, caused the nomination of bishops to be put in the hands of the king. More often than not, the *curé* in his rural parish is a poor, dirty, unkempt chap, cut off from any official support, living in the middle of a village on which he willingly lavishes a few more or less orthodox rudiments of Christianity—and ultimately shares the feelings, the intense emotions, the same revolts,* of his faithful, much more than he governs them.

Finally, the insecurity is measurable in terms of relations with the outside world. The social life of the village is only as closed as the economy. The peasants whom La Bruyère and Vauban alone observed and described did not restrict themselves to collective work, evenings spent with one another, Sunday mass. They did know a few other classes of their distant contemporaries: those nuisances the king's agents, collectors of the *taille* and of the salt tax; and sometimes, nearby or in the distance, they catch a fleeting glimpse of a princely or royal journey, passing by on the roads with a long procession of carriages and bedizened horsemen. Again, sometimes a few city dwellers pass through; these people love the country, of course, but, having it always at their back door, rarely feel the need of it, and merely leave Lyon for Saint-Rambert, Paris for Saint-Cloud or Montmartre. (Madame de Sévigné, who loved Les Rochers,† was an eccentric, in that she traveled widely and did so for pleasure.) None of these people are too dangerous, except for the fiscal agents who are empowered to evict one, with all one's belongings, when they are not paid. The most dreaded visitors are soldiers and brigands.

French archives (the B series of *départemental* Archives, for example) spew forth complaints and horrible tales about the detested soldiers, who leave so many bad memories in their wake. The soldiers arrive, to be billeted or not; on duty, in the field or not; friends or enemies, it is no longer important: their behavior is always the same. One need not be surprised at this: they are all mercenaries, their talent is for sale, and they care little for the cause they serve, provided it pays them. And, too often, their pillaging can be excused because their pay is in arrears; war is expensive, for kings, for princes, even for Charles V. Therefore, except for rare instances which are always mentioned with hyperbolic admira-

---

* Porchnev quotes priests in Angoulême leading their parishioners in a riot against the salt-tax collectors in 1636.[13]
† The Sévigné château in Brittany.—Trans.

tion, the soldiers lay waste to villages, pillaging and ravaging ". . . furniture, linens, clothing, beds, plowing equipment . . . sheep, calves, and other smaller livestock . . . shooting at hens, manhandling several people and beating them up, and, with drawn swords in their hands, chasing after young girls. . . ." * What devastation, when troops fall upon a defenseless village in this manner! These fine soldiers, who love to live dangerously (or who, sometimes, have been condemned to such a life, according to the contemporary legal formula, ". . . compulsory service of the king, for ten or twenty years . . ."), have no thought whatever for the peasants. And the latter, in the long run, are perhaps more defenseless against the soldiers than were their ancestors of the early Middle Ages against invasions.

Standing crops, storehouses, livestock, heavy armor, women—all these are threatened, as well, by brigands, the subject of endless village discussions on long winter nights. "Brigand" is a generic term; it can, and does, include soldiers, especially those of exotic origins (Spanish, German, and, particularly by the end of the seventeenth century, English). The brigands are of various types: lazy nobles, deserters from the army, highwaymen, and unpunished pillagers who cannot be flushed out of the high mountains in their eagles' nests above the valleys—Crussol on the Rhône, Nonette on the Allier, and many other locations. They organize bands for pillaging those regions, such as the Gévaudan, which are almost completely unprotected by royal troops. Led by some ablebodied rogue, they turn to attacking the villages when their best prey—merchants laden with gold and valuables, whom they surprise on the roads or on dangerous rivers—is scarce, which happens particularly in winter when trade is slow. Braudel[15] has demonstrated the ubiquity of modern banditry and of this social type, the brigand—someone who is on the fringes of society, who is dreaded, but not always detested. For numerous legends revolve about him: the justice-loving bandit; the bandit who punishes salt-tax collectors and pillages lords; the avenging bandit, who uses evil means for good ends. Not detested, then, until the day when, aided by hunger or by an unrewarding hunt, he is forced to serve his needs from the village which is, always, defenseless.

In the end, to whom can the peasant turn? The royal provost and, for even better reasons, the bailiff live far away, in town. And even if the town is only a league distant, this is still too far. For the league must be traveled on a dirt road, impassable in winter, when it is covered with mud, its ruts frozen over with frost. For the peasant, going into town—to Saint-Michel or Saint-Martin—is an expedition, undertaken once or twice a year, and usually in a group. But to go for immediate defense, urgent protection? Never. And then, more generally, the town,

---

* Let us curtail these picturesque descriptions.[14]

which is farther away than actual distance can indicate—lying at the
end of a road, beyond the rather unsafe forest into which even the bailiff
does not enter without an armed escort—does not particularly welcome the peasant. Once danger—unknown soldiers or threatening
bands—is spotted from high on the ramparts, the gates of the town are
closed. Whenever want grips the countryside and whenever, in April or
May, the poor peasant leaves his thatched cottage where there is no grain,
and comes into town to beg, he is greeted coolly.* At the least warning,
whenever epidemic is spreading or the town granaries, too, are empty,
the *échevins* or *consuls* push the whole mass of beggars outside the
gates; for the "vagabonds" are not part of the city; the town is not
called upon to insure the protection of the countryfolk. Despite the re-
semblances between them, despite the rustic ways of the largest towns,
despite the continual osmosis that establishes a reciprocal traffic, the occupations of the town and its manner of life are too foreign to the rural
world. The countryside, which twenty years without large-scale famine,
that is, without demographic reduction, have sufficed to overpopulate,
does not live with the town in perfect symbiosis. The flat regions stop at
the ramparts, at the constantly guarded gates from which comings and
goings are surveyed all day long; the peasants are of another world. The
rural parish, with its collective tragedies in times of war and misery, with
its economic crises unbearable enough to rout the population from
their thatched cottages, is a small, almost closed, world, one that does
not fully participate in the expanding economic life, the complex social
organizations, or the brilliant, even sumptuous, artistic and intellectual
life, of the towns. We always talk about French "civilization"; yet the
plural is more accurate—yesterday as today.

► **BELIEFS AND OPINIONS**

Nor need we contrast one rural mentality with the changing colors of
urban civilization—the Florentine Lyon and Flemish Lille, and then
Besançon, which leans toward Spain. It is beyond any question that regional variations exist. Just as the sworn enemy varied according to
the area—in Picardy it was the English, in Burgundy the Spanish or Germans—so too did the mental habits of the peasantry undoubtedly
exhibit regional features, destined to be preserved until the nineteenth
century, that time of large-scale destruction. These features were largely
unrecognized, one would suspect, like everything conveyed by an
oral civilization. On the other hand, it is possible to reconstruct, on the
near side of these unique regional characteristics, some dominant attitudes of feeling from which to evoke a mental atmosphere, a level of

---

* "In the year 1631, the great poverty and abundance of poor people who died in
the moats around the present town of Puy . . ." [16]

civilization. There is a fear, then, born of and maintained by the widespread insecurity; a simple faith of Catholic stamp, but rich in pagan
souvenirs; a political belief, a faith in the monarchy—uneven in the
Ile-de-France or Champagne—which, as far south as the most forsaken
depths of the Limousin, bears witness to the royal presence. Doubtless,
this picture is incomplete.

Fear and panic predominate, and explain many aspects of village
life. The fears, because they are daily, are more intense than those
of the twentieth century, though the latter has a heavy share. There is a
firm belief, one that directs all thought, that the threat of doom hangs
constantly over the lives of men and beasts, over the harvests. A shooting star in the heavens, the gallop of a horse snorting in a field, the disordered words of an idiot or those of a neighbor dallying in the tavern
after mass—everything gives a form to this fear. Forest brigands, Englishmen, bubonic plague carriers—the frolic work of imaginations
crazed by chronic malnutrition. One has only to notice that these panics
multiply on the eve of the harvest, when the slightest cry is suspect and
the visitor or "stranger" roaming along the roads is a menace: the grain
crop will be burned, the fine harvest lost the night before it is cut; and,
to avoid these misfortunes, people quickly take up pitchforks and flails.
A healthy number of the seventeenth-century popular movements can
be explained in this way;[17] with the help of the alarm bell, this sort of
agricultural panic can move about, engulfing one village and then another, and soon entire provinces—as in Provence in 1630. There is a sort
of rhythm in rural life, as the great period of relaxation follows an untroubled harvest, gathered without any losses (though losses are fairly
frequent). But this context of fear, with the violence of its emotions,
in which tomorrow's life is at stake, explains both the great exuberant
joys and those impulses of anger, of unthinking hatred, against collectors, *sergens*, enemies, or mere strangers—"all those inveterate animosi-
ties and hates that are perpetuated in peasant families." [18]

In this atmosphere, then, everything is the object of fear; and, more
important, everything is possible.[19] Earth, sky, and water, the world inhabited by our sixteenth-century peasants is not the one we know. It is a
world in which there is no distinction between natural and supernatural,
reason and unreason—a world, in fact, in which such a distinction has
no meaning. It is "normal," for example, to accuse a shepherd, licensed
by a large Brie farmer, of having caused the deaths within six months of
three hundred and ninety-five head of cattle, sheep, horses, and cows—a
rude and rather simple act of revenge, effected by casting a spell over
them: a natural act, one within anyone's capability; one has only to
know the tested formula. It is equally "normal" to hold "processions for
good weather, which the land greatly needs." Religious faith, then, acquires a peculiar tonality: it is not a question, here, of separating the
wheat from the chaff (something quite orthodox) nor of depriving one-

self of the intercession of some holy protector (something going far beyond orthodoxy).* Need we point out, then, that all the purges undertaken by the Council of Trent in the mid-sixteenth century were without effect in the countryside, and remained so for a long time to come!

Most assuredly this countryside is Christian. "From birth to death," according to the phrase of Lucien Febvre, the *curé* is there near his flock, from the baptismal font to extreme unction. The annual Paschal communion is the principal religious act, along with the Sunday mass, of course.† Easter communion is so scrupulously observed that, in the eighteenth century, the monarchy's *intendants*, always in love with statistics, used this communion to count the number of people in the parish. No, it is not in the village that ungodliness is to be sought. To be sure, it will happen that people joke about the priests' celibacy, interrupting the *curé* in the middle of a sermon on the joys of marriage to tell him, amidst much laughter, that he is speaking of something he knows nothing about. But this is no more than occasional disorder, happening now and again; it is not anticlericalism, nor blasphemy. The freethinkers of the sixteenth and especially the seventeenth centuries will have to be sought in the towns.

Nevertheless, the rural faith does present original characteristics remote from all Christian orthodoxy; the worship of saints readily commingles with superstitious practices, so termed after the beginning of the seventeenth century. Moreover, belief in the unmitigated power of sorcerers, sorceresses, neighbors endowed with the evil eye who are in the habit of riding broomsticks and rambling through clearings at night —all occupy an enormous place. The devil is at least as often present as the benevolent God. In 1679, a learned *abbé* writes a *Traité des superstitions*, a great work by an experienced theologian who would no more venture a formal denial of sorcery than he would one of miracles or of the intercessions of those multiple patron saints of vineyards, bees, or pigs. With various references to the Church Fathers (more than to his contemporaries, which is a great shame), he studies the superstitions current in the country (and, for that matter, in the towns); he examines the prayers, which he deems ridiculous. One reads:

> Little white Pate'-Noster made by God,
> named by God,
> placed by God in Paradise:

---

* There is a host of patron saints; dozens, on the order of St. Médard, who starts or halts rain; St. Séverin, who protects the grape crop; St. Nicolas, who is responsible for harvest fires; and St. Dominic, who is invoked against hail, etc. These come from the region around Paris.
† In some localities, archive documents report the absence of mass; *curés* in those days did not have an Abbé Boulard to prompt them to make statistics. It is difficult to interpret these often succinct texts, or to draw conclusions from them.

At night when I go to bed
I find three angels by my bed,
one at the foot, two at the head.
Among them is the Virgin Mary,
she says, Lie down and do not worry.
For the good God is my father
  the good Virgin is my mother
  the three Virgins are my sisters
  the three Apostles are my brothers.

The little shirt where God was born
wraps me round and keeps me warm.
  Cross of Saint Margaret
  upon my breast is writ.

Madame cries out to God along
fields she walks over. Meets Saint John,
  Sir Saint John, where are you from?
From the *Ave Salus* I come.
  Have you not then seen Our Lord?
Yes I have and there is he
  there upon the cross and tree
   his hands nailed up,
    his feet hung down,
little white thorn hat is his crown.

Who says this three times morn and even
In the end will go to Heaven.[20]

He examines also the marvelous medical practices, and the prescriptions*
which never ceased to circulate until the nineteenth—indeed, even the
twentieth—century, and which those great seekers after oral tradition,
the folklorists, have collected with varying success over the past fifty
years. This old foundation of belief provides both form and explanation for sorcery. An easy transition, if it be true that, to make the girl
next door amorous, one need only sprinkle her door with toad ashes.
The sorceress who returns from the Witches' Sabbath, her bag laden with
enough evil spells to kill off an entire village—animals, people, plants—
must necessarily be endowed with tenfold power, in this domain where
the relations of cause and effect take on some astonishing aspects. Furthermore, the belief in witchcraft seems universal. The persecutions
(stretching approximately between the fourteenth and seventeenth cen-

---

* Let us quote, among countless ones, one example: Fasten a nail taken from a crucifix onto an epileptic's arm, and he will be cured.

turies) did not fail to strengthen the extraordinary extent of this belief.

What a source of horrible and continually renewed evil spells was the devil's daily intervention into men's lives! Even in the towns, few minds —few regions, even—resisted his charm. People thought in those days that evil was greater in the north than in the Midi: "It is well known that there are more sorcerers in the northern districts, where people's minds are simpler and more gullible than in the southern regions, where they are more refined." [21] Despite this rather silly geographic determinism, this is a delicate question: the spread of sorcerers in Franche-Comté, Lorraine, and Flanders was more easily possible, perhaps, and encouraged by the local legal proceedings in regions whose law was that of custom. But what fear! Someone in Lyon wrote in 1660:

> All you need is one scoundrel who needs a piece of your field, to whom you would not want to have sold one stone of your inheritance, who hopes to have it by the sale of your property—one base churl, calling attention to a word you chanced to let slip, could bring about the beginning of your total ruin.[22]

The maleficent supernatural is always present to the mind; when, for example, a cow shows signs of weakness, one remembers that a short time ago the woman who lives next door passed by the stable, scratching the nape of her neck. Might one conclude that religious practices form, particularly in hard times, a defense against that invading Devil who finds so many willing helpers in the villages? This chancy conclusion does admit of partial truth.

This world of the spirit is, in certain respects, terrifying. Where, then, can brightness and peace be found?

First of all, in the energy with which these peasants are able to face all the evils overwhelming them. Want and famine, the lords' exactions and the bandits' raids, soldiers' misdeeds and supernatural disasters— they endure everything. After the war, the villages are burned out and the population decimated, as in Burgundy during the Thirty Years' War; but the survivors return to work, rebuild those houses that have been the most lightly affected, and go back to plowing the fields. The energy of these peasants, faced with the metamorphoses of a life that is always uncertain, is limitless, and every village is rapidly rebuilt after even the worst disasters. Even the widows, always so numerous in the country (much more so than today, and serving as the very symbol of this chronic insecurity) go back to work, return to their ravaged houses, and resume their place in the community. Given twenty or thirty years without war, epidemic, or poor harvests, the peasants restore their population and their activities, as if by the miracle of an ever-renewed will, and to the astonishment of even their own contemporaries.

Secondly, there are the great feast days, heralded long in advance;
there are both those of the Christian calendar—Christmas, Easter, All
Saints' Day—and those Christianized feasts that disguise the ancient, ill-
forgotten customs—like Saint John of the Solstice, when "passing
through fire cures prickly heat." Then to some extent, but less so since
they are ornamented with the darkest possible tales (and herein lies
their attraction), there are the family evenings spent around the fire,
those long winter evenings where, under the sometimes burdensome authority of the father, the traditions and songs about a simultaneously
monstrous and gilded legendary figure (of which we have only fragments)[23] are handed down and kept alive.

Finally there is undoubtedly a political confidence, although this is
uneven and varies according to the region. The king, a protector of the
peasants, is still too remote from the peasants and the poor by the end
of the eighteenth century. Yet this faith in royal benevolence is always
alive, and is based on a religious belief whose extraordinary acceptance
has a deep political meaning: the faith in the French kings' supernatural
and miracle-working power.[24] A potent master, he is deceived by his sergeants and by the hated collectors; he is, too, the distant suzerain of
those so often unbearable local *hobereaux*. Although no one would
dare to leave the Bourbonnais or Poitou to seek out the king in Paris
and ask for a favor—such a long and difficult trip to claim just restoration for a theft or even a crime—they would go see him if he were to
visit their provinces. And it is not rare that people do go and see him,
on the great feast days when, in the galleries of the Louvre, at Amboise
or Fontainebleau, he touches and heals the sick. Foreigners from Spain,
Italy, Franche-Comté, and the Rhineland mingle with Frenchmen as
they come to have their foreheads touched, that they may be cured of
their suppurating wounds, ugly to see and unpleasant to smell—that
disease of the undernourished called scrofula or the "king's evil" in the
sixteenth century, and which doctors now call adenitis. Thus the faith in
religion, in miracle-working, forms the basis of political faith; for, in the
popular mind, the king is placed among the ranks of those numerous
saints whose relics, distributed throughout old France, cause so many
miracles. The king of France shares his powers over scrofula with St.
Marcoul de Corbeny—to whom, moreover, he pays a visit on the day
after his coronation at Reims.* Let us put to one side, for a moment,

* The King of France's legendary privilege of healing scrofula on his coronation day
involves two saints: St. Remigius (St. Remi) and St. Marcoul de Corbeny. St. Remigius (d. 530), known as the "Apostle of the Franks," was the Bishop of Reims. He
was the saint who converted his friend Clovis to Christianity—for the ceremony, a
dove is said to have brought St. Remigius a vial of oil from Heaven. Remigius conferred upon St. Marcoul, who in turn gave to Clovis and succeeding kings, the right
to cure the "king's evil." The remains of St. Marcoul (d. 552), Abbot of Nanteuil,
are at Corbeny near Reims; hence, the royal pilgrimage at coronation time.—Trans.

the *de facto* religious authority of the king, his acquired right to direct the Church of France, and the strange reticence on the part of seventeenth-century theorists of royal authority, from Savaron to Bossuet, who rarely mention this tangible indication of the sacred character of royalty; still, how nourishing it must have been to the staunch, popular faith, a faith that has survived much longer than the silences of Bossuet, and has even found expression in family record books, those intimate diaries of yesteryear: "Here shall I praise our Lord for having had the grace to grant us a so Catholic and benign king [this text is written in 1600], so fortunate in all he undertakes, who has conquered all his enemies, who stands so well in the grace of God that he heals sicknesses." *

► NEW ELEMENTS

This mental and material universe of the French peasantry does not remain entirely without modification during the course of two centuries or more; but, for some time to come, the fundamental structures remain solid and stable. Within this whole, changes come about through small, imperceptible steps: if only one could map the progress of the bean in garden plots and fields throughout the sixteenth century, or chart the attempts to split up the communal lands—this is the ambition of nobles concerned with "agronomy," or the powerful desire of day laborers who have no land. The large structures that remain are not without intermittent cracks, especially around the towns which everywhere are agitating forces for renovation. From Amiens to Arras to Calais, the peasant is not at all the same as he is in the Haute-Auvergne, ten mountainous leagues from Aurillac, a town of five thousand. Yet, because our documents so rarely discuss those "humbler classes," we are forced to refer to the general developments revealed by the towns, and to the testimony of other contemporaries. For example, the refrain of material insecurity, whose permanence is established by voice after echoing voice. A family record-book for 1596 reads: "If you had seen the poor peasants, eating chick-peas out of the fields, cutting the heads of wheat to eat; a remarkably pathetic sight, the gathering of the wheat, somehow not dying of hunger, having it cooked in the oven—and it is this way everywhere in the region." To which a traveler at Blois in 1660 replies: "Want is so great here that peasants lacking bread fall upon decaying carcasses . . . malignant fevers are beginning to kindle . . ."; and in 1694 around Mâcon: "The *curé* of Bissy la Maconnaise claims that the population of that province is utterly reduced to grass, weeds, and ferns, that people are forced to eat without salt, because of their poverty." Such re-

---

* The "sicknesses" referred to in the quotation are probably scrofula.—Trans.[25]

ports continue through 1709, that terrible year at the gateway to such a critical century. Despite the progress of large-scale proprietorship—which does not always follow large-scale farming—there is the same stability on the social level until the Great Fear and the night of August fourth, thus even beyond the innovations of the eighteenth century.

There remains the vast area of peasant opinions and beliefs, an area so difficult to explore. It is impossible to grasp and pinpoint here those alterations that perhaps were undergone during the course of two hundred years of evenings before the fire, by the old wives' tales and the fertile fantasies of children, the hagiographic legends and the fairy tales, the stories of chivalry and of the Devil. Good old Perrault gave us some tales—a small part of that children's and grownups' chronicle, written in the middle of the seventeenth century—but not too much about that immense oral tradition, which is hinted at (for the seventeenth and especially eighteenth centuries) by the Bibliothèque Bleue of Troyes.* It is impossible even to grasp the totality of the village customs, how the habit of *charivari*, the mock-serenade of newly married people, is continued despite so many bailiffs' and provosts' enactments attempting to forbid this brutal practice.

What one can get a sense of—and certainly it is no trifle—is the strengthening of religious faith, a sort of purification, which comes about in several ways. First, although this did not spread for a long time, there is the appearance of the Protestant minister. Educated on the spiritual level by several years' study at Geneva, experienced in disputation, aware of all the "Roman weaknesses," this man with a staunch faith carries with him, everywhere he goes, his method, his direct reading of the Gospels, and that presence of mind which makes him so formidable to the lower, Catholic clergy who are in no way trained in theological controversy. But this minister is only a passer-through, for Geneva cannot educate the thousands of them that would be necessary to "spread the Gospel" through the countryside, to wrest it from the Catholic "militia" that fills all the parishes. The none-too-numerous ministers go wherever they are summoned by urgent calls—to the towns, that is, that are to be gained step by step. One could push one's thesis a little further, and state that rural Protestantism became widespread only in the second half of the seventeenth century when persecutions—before 1685 as after —made life impossible for urban Protestants. Yet what rapid changes— first, wherever the Protestant minister passes, later, wherever he settles. Everyone suddenly must know how to read, must have a Bible in his possession; thus people open their minds to logic, one of the great resources of the Calvinist spirit. There is a rapid decrease in superstition,

---

* This is a collection of folklore and popular medieval romances of chivalry bound in blue covers established in the seventeenth century at Troyes by Dudot. The venture was continued until the mid-nineteenth century.—Trans.

the mind opens out onto exterior life, onto relations with the outside world both French and foreign (for the books and the ministers come from abroad): for example, the Cévennes shortly before the revolt of the Camisards.*

At the same time, the Catholic Church came close to disciplinary reforms that might have enabled it to rectify, or reinforce, the superstitious faith of the rural districts. The Council of Trent, so sensitive to Protestant criticism, decided to create diocesan seminaries: a reform only slowly set in motion for want of a professional staff which the religious orders and even the Society of Jesus could not supply en masse. Even in the seventeenth century, St. Vincent de Paul and Abbé Olier, fully aware of the necessity of supplying future priests with a sound theological education rather than the former empirical casualness, founded important, although short-lived establishments (see Chapter IX). Again, in some areas, a bishop like Fénelon at Cambrai, at odds with the court, could become concerned about his young parish priests and establish a house near the bishop's palace and improve the spiritual level of an entire diocese for a period of a few years. But such action was brief and not at all along the lines of what the Council of Trent had, perhaps idealistically, hoped for.

If, at the end of the seventeenth century, the lower clergy awakens and assumes a consciousness worthy of its rule, if they read their breviaries with intense emotion and have not yet read *Candide* or the *Profession de foi du vicaire savoyard*, this moral consciousness is probably attributable not to the seminaries but rather to the Formulary Affair of 1661-65. Louis XIV, in the ardor of his battle with the "Jansenist heresy," enjoined all the clergy to sign a formulary which expressly forbade "the five propositions extracted from the book of Cornelius Jansenius"—and said nothing more. Whence comes an extremely understandable reaction of curiosity concerning this Jansenius, of whom no *curé* in the remote regions of Rouergue or Brittany had ever heard; and then, more important, another reaction—that of reflection upon the importance of a simple *curé* in the framework of the ecclesiastical life, if the king and bishop demand his signature at the bottom of this small text so portentous in its peremptory form. For many rural *curés*—absorbed in the petty parochial tasks which were especially burdensome since, to improve their normal standards of living, many of them farm the land too—this administrative formality of signature could be the beginning of reflections whose ramifications are undreamed of: ramifications which even, perhaps, lead us to the contentious, philosophizing, political *curés* of the eighteenth century. At any rate, priestly activity begins to become more

---

* Even today the attentive observer successively visiting, for example, in the Haute-Loire at Cambon-sur-Lignon, then in the Ardèche at Saint-Agrève, several kilometers from one another, can see the contrast.[26]

deliberate and productive; the closing years of the century of Louis XIV, then, are a moment of progress for rural Catholicism.

Finally, one question. We have seen that the town and the country form two different worlds whose contact is formal and, with the exception of the riverside dwellers on the ramparts, none too frequent: annual fairs, traditional feast days, and the visits of princes, sovereigns, and bishops attract the people from the surrounding countryside. Or else the contacts are tragic, as in times of famine and plague. But the sixteenth century, and a good part of the seventeenth, formed a period of astonishing urban expansion—not just in Paris, which was already beginning to accumulate the administrative, commercial, and "industrial" functions of a capital, but also in Lyon, that great city of the triumphant sixteenth century, and Atlantic ports like La Rochelle and Le Havre—towns that build, that fill themselves with people, that maintain themselves. In all probability the labor comes from the more immediate countryside; so too provisions, but from farther away, through the medium of the landholders. But how do these rural provenders benefit from the urban progress? By ideas, new activities, a new backdrop for living? Ten or twenty leagues from Lyon, or from Bayonne—that town at the frontier of Spain, overflowing with financial activity—what do we see? We are accustomed to our encroaching suburbs, stringing out along the roads of the most insignificant "county seat"; to a network of multiple connections established between town and country by today's railroads and highways; thus, we are tempted to believe that the country receives something from the town. We are tempted, that is, by gross anachronism. For, having passed beyond the *focés*, the moats of the city, a different world begins. Paris is, without a doubt, an exception, for the *ville jolie* of Marot is already, for the period, enormous; it needs the Seine, Marne, and Oise to feed itself, and is connected with already distant rural areas, connected to them more closely than Limoges or Le Puy could ever be to their own "flat land." But one must wait until the eighteenth, even the nineteenth, century for the still-forming town to give life to the surrounding countryside. However attractive, diverse, rich the Renaissance town may be, its walls enclose all the ostentation, grandeur, and risks of a tiny minority. During the sixteenth century, when the population growth was strong and when rural crises were less frequent than in the seventeenth, the population of France oscillated between thirteen and sixteen million: the lives of ten to fifteen million of these have been described in this chapter. All the rest, from Ronsard to Racine, Calvin to Bossuet, Leonardo da Vinci to Fontenelle—all these are the achievements of a very small minority, rich in glory; a minority which is, ordinarily, the only thing we see.

VII

❊

Urban Progress During the Sixteenth Century

*1500-1640/60**

❊ ❊

We have said that the town and the country exist in opposition—or better, in contradistinction—to one another. Yet, at the point at which we try to encompass the French towns in one glance, their first characteristic, an obtrusive one that it is important to take into account, is their rural aspect. Even inside the ramparts, there are gardens and fields; this feature is well known. Actually, the inhabitants of the towns remain peasants, false city dwellers, even when they are fulfilling the very Parisian functions of President in the Chambre des Comptes or in Parlement; in their moderation at table, their pastimes, beliefs, and customs, they are still fresh-air men, sunburned, accustomed to wind, to sun, to horseback riding and outdoor living.

The sixteenth-century town, unlike that of 1900 or even 1860, is not equipped with the comfort that signals a different way of seeing and

---

* The dates, for one of which we offer an alternative, are approximate; they are for guidance only, and have no other meaning. It would be impossible for them to have the precision of, say, a birth date in the twentieth century. Why, however, 1640-60 rather than 1610? *See* below, pp. 252 ff., "The Economic Advances. . . ."

understanding the world. Life is rugged there, to a point scarcely imaginable, and the urban splendor is only relative. Undoubtedly, the heavy gates open not only onto little dirt paths, but also onto paved roads as well as riverways whose horizons surpass, and cannot be compared to, the line of forest or broom-grass marking the boundary of the village terrain. One is bound to point out the glory of these still frequently traveled waterways, from the royal routes like the Seine and Loire, to the Allier and Isère; they triumph over the unsafe roads, which are very slow and difficult despite the accelerated pace of postal way stations. Thus the modern town, still only slightly developed, is a center for exchange, an aperture onto the vast world, at this time when the world is growing larger, asserting itself, and offering, as the century progresses, markets, interests, new products, in increasing quantity. In 1500 Lyon, along Rue Mercière, a bourgeois awaits news of pepper coming from Lisbon or Venice, and is prepared to order and pledge his fortune on a rapid delivery. His drawers contain bills of exchange, letters of credit, signed Fugger, Augsburg; Martin Kléberg, Lyon; F. Spinola, Genoa. And in 1557, when the king of France and Philip II go bankrupt almost simultaneously, he experiences moments of extreme anxiety. His whole outlook is one completely foreign to, say, his tenant farmer in Francheville, who brings him two capons, a goose, and several cheeses each Michaelmas, and who often borrows a few *sous* from him to buy salt.

Thus, in every town, two types of trade are juxtaposed: first, the small trade from the nearby flat country, the goods that pass through noble and episcopal storehouses, through a host of trivial, personal relations, ultimately to feed the town; secondly, the large-scale exchange of silver and gold money, spices, ivory, fabrics, and weapons, which determine the warp and weft of international commerce—and, added to the banking activities (bills of exchange, contracts), the high points of economic progress, determine its continuity as well. Whether it occupies the first place in France (as did Lyon in the sixteenth century) or is a mere way station (be it a town, a bridge, or a crossroad—Moulins on the Allier, Montereau on the Seine), the center is inhabited by people who are still daredevils, lovers of great adventure: trips, loans, risky investments. There are the merchants and, in their shadow, the carters and craftsmen of countless urban professions, working for the merchants, and with them—a whole world, in short, that has no rural equivalent.

The town, then, is a commercial center; it is also a small administrative capital, the seat of the diocese. There, in the shadow of the recently completed cathedral, everyone mills about all the shops protected by the buttresses, gossips and argues with the clerics—canons from the chapter house, *curés* from urban parishes, bishop-appointed ecclesiastical judges, students and their teachers from the diocesan schools and those medieval universities whose fame is limitless (Medicine at Montpellier, Law at Orléans), and all the petty professions living off the Church: makers of tapers, candelabra, rosaries; Bible-printers; and, shall we add, discreet dealers in relics. Whether it be the seat of a balliage, a presidial, or mere provostry, the town is still a gathering place for royal agents and bourgeois, for newly-rich men basking in royal service who remain zealous until, in the seventeenth century, they are rebuffed. These are surrounded, too, by a group of people knowledgeable in law, eager pedants (for the study of Law loves commas), attorneys, other men of the law, writers—who argue in court, write, present reports and petitions, and excellently foster the pettifogging minds of merchants tempted by usury and underhanded pacts. These people form a second urban world. Although they travel less than the men of commerce, they travel far in their minds; they read a great deal, keep themselves and others informed, and argue incessantly.

All this is distant enough from the village and the monotonous cycle of works and days; then, the sixteenth century gives an extraordinary impetus to urban work—through the book and printing, so quickly becoming a part of men's habits, and through the new treasures from America. An insouciant cobbler in Romorantin could ignore Gutenberg and Christopher Columbus, and let the year 1492 slip by without marking it on his calendar. But fifty years later! The enormous vitality of this long sixteenth century which owes so much to America, is manifested in hundreds, thousands of ways; even to the progress of a growing population—insofar as precision can be obtained from learnedly extrapolated calculations and estimates—in a gradual but constant fashion, abetted by a respite from famine, an acceleration of trade, and the prosperity of those towns already glutted with wealth, hence more surely so with men. Herein is the vitality of the sixteenth century.

► CITYFOLK, COUNTRYFOLK

When the Frenchman of the Renaissance settled in the town, he did so of necessity, for his work: he did not come to live better than he could elsewhere, or to enjoy commodities unobtainable beyond the town walls. As a matter of fact, "the town does not hold on to men." * It is an overgrown village, not unaware of the most daily of peasant concerns. For example, shortly before the harvests, does not the provost of a very small town (then, as now, Bourbon Lancy) decree in 1665: "All

---

* The turn of phrase is that of Febvre. This work [1] [see Notes] is a quick and distinguished picture of daily town life during the Renaissance. It need hardly be said that we owe him a great debt.

those having dogs will affix and attach heavy logs to their collars, so that they will be prevented from going into the vineyards; failing to accomplish this, it is herewith permitted that the dogs be killed." The same in 1648: "Orders for those who keep dogs and swine . . ."[2] We are not concerned here with a village in Burgundy or a château in Bordeaux, but rather with an ordinary town maintaining rural activities like any other place, maintaining them, so to speak, between the houses. There are gardens, little walled-in yards of greenery that are part of every home-owner's property—meadows, pastures, little patches of oats for feeding horses and chickens; finally there are vineyards, enabling the well-off bourgeois to emulate the medieval bishop or nobleman, to "drink his own wine"—always a French ambition. Thus, it is not just the dogs who wander around in the streets, but also the hens, goats, and pigs. All the accoutrements of rural life are present: many families have an oven and a storehouse where they accumulate the reserves gathered in autumn for the entire year; sometimes, at a bend in the street, there is a pile of manure. Even Paris, *ma grand'ville* in the days of Henry IV and Boileau, scarcely avoids all this—there are bad odors coming up from the overheated walls in summer, and streets like cesspools, accumulating refuse which, thrown up by the wheels of carriages, spatters the walls. By these very accumulations, by the density of the urban centers, the large towns do not have a very appetizing aspect: already in the sixteenth century, and more so in the seventeenth, some people move away when they can, leaving the dense areas of Paris around Sainte-Chapelle and Notre-Dame, to go and take refuge in the hills. Olivier d'Ormesson, while visiting Issy, comments with obvious admiration: "One of the splendors of France is seeing the private pleasure-houses in the vicinity of Paris. . . ." Moreover: ". . . so ornate are they . . ."[3] but the important thing is that they are *pleasure*-houses. Paris was not a pleasant place in which to live.

Let us look a little more closely at the life in the towns. The urban house is certainly more solid, better protected against wind and rain, than a house in the country; after the sixteenth century, it often has windowpanes, is made of stone and is well roofed. There are none of the "little wooden and thatched cottages that they (the peasants) make with small tree branches, almost like baskets or panniers covered with a little lime or grain cockles."[4] It is a better refuge than the one large rural room where men and cattle sleep together; but it is still a precarious refuge. The city dweller dreads the cold and wind, against which he is badly protected, for good, efficient heating is very difficult. Only a few square feet of the large rooms can be heated by the large fireplace with an immense hood going up to the ceiling;[5] and yet, even this does not always exist in the country: "A number of peasants have no fireplaces in their houses and they build their fires in the corner of a room; the smoke disappears from some window or door of the house, or a hole left high up in a board." [6] This fireplace is the only resource; the arrangement of the houses is still an obstacle for the rooms are laid out in rows without the corridors and symmetries that might facilitate adjustment to the climate. The sixteenth-century city dweller is still a fresh-air fellow; one might even say a sportsman, but this would be misleading, since it is not a game, a conscious simplification of one's life, but a necessity. The king himself is always hunting, or conducting battle or combat out of doors; and the merchants or their transport agents are always on the roads—in summertime more than winter, to be sure, yet they are always ready and willing to travel; and the covered stalls of the day open onto the street, have no expensive windows nor even, sometimes, any shutters. Houses, even those of princes, are cold and cheerless. There are huge hangings, Bergamot tapestries, gilded leather from Spain, curtains at the windows, rugs on the floor—all attempts at gaining protection against the cold and the icy dampness of the house as are those large beds, curtained on all sides, and those nightcaps and nightgowns. All these arrangements for interior protection are not easy for us to visualize, accustomed as we are to taking off hat and coat when we return home. People in the sixteenth century would almost do the opposite.

But this city dweller, this manager of money, or else of non-monetary wealth—is he, perhaps, better fed than the peasant? Is he, consequently, better protected from the inside, by his nutritious calories, against the cold and bad weather? Has he more resistance, more strength? To a certain extent, but we must not exaggerate. Bread is better, for example, only in good years: the little rolls from Gonesse,* so much lamented by the *parlementaires* of the Fronde, are an upper-bourgeois delicacy; the journeyman and small craftsman, like the countryfolk, eat bread made from mixed flours, wheat and rye, along with the warm gruel that appears almost every day on modest menus. For the rich—bourgeois, nobles, clergy—there is meat, and for everyone there is fowl or game. Wines are more commonly drunk; and, on such occasions as feast days, the entrance of a prince, or some confraternity celebration, there is the good red beef which does not appear on each table every day. Apart from this—for, according to the beliefs of the period, there are inferior meats—the great luxury of the sixteenth century remains the medieval spices, pepper, cinnamon, ginger, which, even when the supply of them is abundant, are very much in favor, well into the seventeenth century when coffee, sugar, and cocoa make their appearance. Also, along with the spices and to help wash them down, there are wines—the good ones and the less good, all certainly inferior to our *grand crus* of today;

---

* Gonesse is a little town just outside Paris. In the sixteenth and seventeenth centuries, its bakers used to send their very highly esteemed bread and rolls into Paris daily.—Trans.

they keep hardly a year. They are used also as cordials, and to compensate for the scarcer alcohol: at the end of the century, Henry IV revives a Parisian noblewoman, who fainted while presenting a petition to him, by having a glass of wine brought. Is luxury of the table widespread? Moderation does not seem extraordinary; contemporaries present it without excessive praise (or, for that matter, blame): "He was very moderate, eating little meat, and of the most ordinary sort, at dinner, and contenting himself with a little soup with two eggs in the evening." [7] Nevertheless, the basis of nutrition is bread; in the town just as in the country, it is bread that insures the life of the entire population. Once want prevails in the flat regions, once the peasants begin to pour into the towns, everyone keeps an eye on his storeroom of provisions and tries to assure his own future. And when famine makes inroads, in turn, upon the towns, the authorities quickly become worried: Paris is restocked by the king, directly, for fear of revolts: "It is made known that His Majesty, for the relief of his people, has caused a quantity of wheat to arrive in his good city of Paris, the distribution of which will be made next Saturday and on subsequent days to the citizens of Paris, from the galleries of the Louvre . . ." *

Is the city-dwelling Frenchman, then, in the glorious days of the Renaissance, sheltered behind his ramparts and protected by his granaries? Still only imperfectly. Famine can reach him, for his granaries are not inexhaustible. When brigands pillage the countryside, soldiers can certainly be quartered in the towns, but only with the agreement of the municipal authorities who negotiate over questions of their total strength, the length of their stay, and indemnities; and it is the authorities who distribute the troops and officers. Billeting soldiers is a serious matter, certainly not a chance to profiteer. For the brigands, who were not so policed, it is another story: pickpockets at fairs, stone-broke students, bold counterfeiters, low-born pimps—the towns certainly have their underworld, which in turn is not unrelated to the rogues on the main roads. These troublemakers manage to disrupt the urban nights; they are masters of the streets, which have almost no lighting and little police supervision; they take pleasure in "insulting or desecrating, roaming about the streets, giving false alarms, throwing stones against windows, battering in tavernkeepers' doors . . . and other noisy nuisances." [8] Then, too, city dwellers fall prey, less to famines than to the subsequent epidemics, which sometimes even get a head start, arriving before the hunger and spreading like brushfires through those unkempt alleys, into the houses huddled together around the cathedral. These are horrible pestilences, incurable in spite of all the types of medication†

---

* In 1649, the king had wheat brought from Hamburg and Danzig.
† Lotions of vinegar with rosemary and lavendar added, and many others.

that are hawked and extorted from the pillagers of plague-stricken houses—men who risk their lives for the theft—and in spite of all the precautions that are taken: fairs postponed, departures forbidden for weeks on end, boats quarantined upon entering ports. After one little treatise on the measure to be taken against plagues has enumerated all the prescriptions for disinfectants, perfumes to be burned and to bathe in, it frankly confesses on the last page: "The greatest cure of all is to flee, very far away, and to return much later." And Montaigne, who is no more cowardly than the next man, knew this fact well. Famine brings the peasants to the gates of the town; epidemics scatter townspeople throughout the countryside for many months; courts suspend their sessions and shops stay closed, until the atmosphere becomes healthier.

Let us pursue similarities even slightly further. Our modern townspeople owe to this crude life of the sixteenth-century townspeople— only slightly less crude than that of the "savage" peasants—the feeling that all their nerve-ends are exposed: hot-tempered dispositions, easily excited. There is unbridled laughter on high feast-days or on *Joyeuses Entrées,* when the *échevins* have mulled wine and brioches served on the square; and, equally, there are tears and rioting fury against the heretics at the end of the century, against the fiscal agents as well, and even especially, because their exactions are always dreaded and their financial constraints are regarded as iniquitous. "On the fifteenth of June, 1594, there was great dissension and emotion among women over in the court of the king, about a hundred fifty women having taken the king to judgment saying they had no wish to pay the *tailles* imposed upon them, having the wherewithal neither to pay, nor to feed their poor children." [9] Both men and women were violently emotional about their hard life, which seemed—as if in merciless battle—always to be lived in danger.

In any case, what could the rural people find to envy in this town that is already large but not yet anonymous? The extremely relative material security is doubtless paid for by enormous risks, travels, transactions of which the peasant knows little and considers with more fear than envy, a fear still persisting today wherever the "capitalist" spirit has not captivated the countryfolk; yet therein are lodged the charms and the originality peculiar to urban life.

▶ **URBAN ASSOCIATIONS: GUILDS AND SOCIAL GROUPS**

Born and developed as they were outside and against the feudal system, the urban associations still did not escape the rule of imitation. A carefully established and constantly controlled hierarchy dominated urban relations, particularly during this period in which the financial and merchant bourgeoisie broke away from the *robins**—that new nobility that wanted to be foremost in the city, as was the other nobility in the village and elsewhere. Hence, there is a regime of protocol, an urban order. If, even today in French towns, the bourgeois who is well provided for, with secure *rentes* (if he can still find any!), finds it important to distinguish himself from the common people—and there are multiple indications that this is indeed the case: beautiful neighborhoods, worldly vanities in abundance, luxurious automobiles—still, our modern bourgeois no longer has the opportunities he would have had in the sixteenth or seventeenth century of making manifest his taste for the social hierarchy. For thcn, communal living presented numerous ceremonies during which the entire population of a town could be found, carefully classed, lined up, at least for several hours, in an order whose priorities were now and again disputed but which remained, nonetheless, obligatory. The entry of a prince or queen, the reception of a bishop (and, good year or bad, there are at least a dozen of these large processions in a town)—these are the great moments when everyone is carefully established in his precise place: captains of young nobles authorized to proceed on horseback, outside the town, preceding the great personage who is to be received; nobles and those who "live nobly"; clergymen; the municipal corps—*échevins, consuls,* court judges, and guards—each group nicely placed in front of the city gates or the cathedral or in the main square; then the professional men, also very carefully classed, from wool merchants, small-wares dealers and goldsmiths, down to water-carriers, who bring up the rear or are put at the most distant end of the square. We will ignore the clashes between nobles and bourgeois, and among the *robins,* for whom the rows of ermine have as much meaning as do the stars and bars for our military men of today—running battles, accompanied by insults, by blows with the flat of the sword. It is more important to see how much this hierarchy, accepted by everyone as the order of the city, is the object of real admiration. Beautiful processions, nicely arranged by a diligent clergy; grand entries, followed by evening celebrations; fireworks; dances; distributions of food; and, in particular, drinking bouts—these always appear prominently in family record-books, as sights to be relished and commented upon at length. Even around Easter, when processions occur every other day, they are always worth mentioning. This is already a show, and not the only one, of which the peasant is not even aware.

Of these urban masses, crowding in good order before an episcopal or royal coach, let us forget about the noble families who are not too numerous in the sixteenth-century towns. The seventeenth is the century

---

* *Robin* refers pejoratively to anyone having to do with the legal profession—"unworthy men of the robe."—Trans.

of urbanization, when society life develops and, particularly, when Louis XIV sets the fashion by imposing a new style upon the life of the nobility. But in the sixteenth century, the patrimonial châteaux are still often occupied by their owners; to be more precise, nobles love to travel from château to château, even from château to town, but it is not yet pleasant to live shut up in the latter; hunting, real and simulated battle, are more attractive.

For those of the townspeople who do not "live nobly," there are two possible occupations: merchandise or the law. "Merchandise" is to be taken in its broad sense, to include the financier or banker who deals in money, and also the small artisan whose stall opens onto a narrow street, who sells his cloth and commodities directly; the law, too, is to be taken broadly: judges and clerks, doctors and lawyers, students and notaries, something like what we now call "the professions." Economically speaking, it is the merchandising professions that gain the upper hand, even in those towns of the Midi, like Aix and Montpellier, which have longstanding legal traditions. Yet the *haute bourgeoisie*—the dominant class, which in part patterns its ways of life on the old nobility (*noblesse d'épée*) which rules and administers the town, receives the king's agents, and consents to those loans without which, as early as the sixteenth century, the monarchy would be unable to live—consists simultaneously of those judges, presidents, councilmen to the Parlement (in seventeen towns) and the presidial, and of the large-scale merchants and "tourists." The concerns of these last go beyond the limits of the monarchy, so that, by the end of the sixteenth century, men from Saint-Malo are trading with Spain, men from Marseille are trading with Genoa, Venice, Barcelona, the Levantine ports, the markets of the Barbary Coast. The rich, sixteenth-century bourgeois turns toward commerce—big financial dealing, commerce in spices and especially in cloth—and his fortune is completed with the help, direct or indirect, of America and Asia. But in the seventeenth century the pendulum swings in the other direction, toward the *robin*. He purchases offices and urges his sons into them, and officialdom triumphs over commerce, for its attractions are stronger. All this almost certainly corresponds to a double economic movement: first, expansion, when prices rise and business expands, continuing through the sixteenth century and gradually tapering off between 1620 and 1650; then, stagnation, the seventeenth-century withdrawal into itself. Yet, the psychological movement cannot be exactly superimposed upon the economic one: already, in the closing years of the Middle Ages, office-holding had many attractions, and these were handled by royalty in such a way as to create for itself a docile, loyal, zealous personnel, a very fortunate replacement for those troublesome and awkward feudal servants, both petty and elevated. In the seventeenth century, there is the same policy, and it is increasingly successful. In 1604, when Henry IV institutes the *paulette*, that annual privilege enabling office holders to determine to whom their functions would be handed down, thus adding an hereditary feature to the system, he imparted an air of nobility to every *robin*. Obviously it is not the same to be heir to the office of First President of the Parlement of Grenoble, as to be heir to land or ancestral property in La Tour du Pin. But making office-holding hereditary gave a new attraction to those already highly valued, honor-laden sinecures. The fact that it did not promote respect for royal authority is another matter.

Sens, Chalon, Rouen; small provincial center or large seaport: every town has two aspects. On the one hand, it is a local market, where the surrounding area's agricultural offerings accumulate, passing through the hands of tithe-owners, wheat-marketers, and hucksters; to secure the food supplies of a townful of people is (as the eighteenth century will demonstrate) no small factor in urban life. On the other hand, every town is a way station, a halting place on the high roads of international commerce which crisscross France, for she is a privileged European isthmus, between the Mediterranean and the Atlantic, the North Sea and Central Europe. This is an international world, dominated by large trading centers—yesterday the Hanseatic towns, Bruges, and Venice; tomorrow, Lisbon, Seville, and Antwerp—and a world actuated by an uneven monetary circulation, still under the impetus of the large fairs that force merchants, money-changers, and goldsmiths to travel, to Besançon, then to Piacenza, Lyon, then Antwerp (which, by the end of the century, established a permanent fair, by virtue of its bourse). Ports and seaways serve as its arteries, transporting, at great risk but with less expense,* everything that is lifeblood to these traders who are certainly more numerous at Lyon than at Grenoble, at Toulouse than at Carcassonne, at Roanne than at Clermont-Ferrand. There exist degrees, steps, between this large-scale commerce whose base is the Mediterranean, Atlantic, and Baltic, and the little trade, say, from Choisy to Paris; between the two there are the rivers, even the second-rate ones. And these are crossed by merchants, whose ambitions and roles are more modest, of whom the chronicles have not recorded very much †—small retailers with minimal expenses, minimal risks, minimal profits. On the other hand, the real merchant, who serves as an example of the triumphant sixteenth century, is a man of long trips, great adventures; a man who places his luck in a galley on the Mediterranean, a galleon or ship in the Atlantic, and whose whole fortune hangs in the balance for

---

* For, says a little treatise called the *Prest gratuit* in 1679: "the costs of land transportation, when added up, are more than fifty times that of ocean transportation."
† "Pierre Bertrand and Georgette Auclerc, his wife, living in Notre-Dame du Puy in the Auvergne, having a small business in Auvergne cheeses which they were going to sell in Nevers, and from Nevers, crockery which they were going to sell in the Auvergne . . ." [10]

Sixteenth Century French Imports

Atlantic Ocean

North Sea

SCANDINAVIA
gold, silver, metals, sulphur, saltpeter, furs

COPENHAGEN

LÜBECK   STETTIN

HAMBURG

AMSTERDAM

ENGLAND
tin, lead, copper, leather, tallow, cloth

LONDON

LOW COUNTRIES

GERMANY
gold, silver, copper, metals, wax, jewels

ANTWERP
serge from Arras and Lille, satins from Bruges, tapestries, linen, batiste, spices, jewels, sugar

BRUGES

FRANKFURT

STUTTGART

AUGSBURG

DIEPPE
ROUEN

LE HAVRE

PARIS

St MALO
NANTES

ORLEANS

ANGERS

NEVERS

LA ROCHELLE

ROANNE

LYON

VENICE

ITALY
silk cloth, armor, spices, drugs, saffron, porcelains, Venetian crystal, Milanese fustian

GENOA

BAYONNE

ARLES

MARSEILLE

metals for minting copper, saffron.

TOULOUSE

SPAIN

BARCELONA

THE LEVANT

NAPLES

PORTUGAL

MEDINA DEL CAMPO

MADRID

LISBON
spices, drugs, gems, perfumes

SEVILLE

Mediterranean Sea

MOROCCO
sugar, wax, almonds, dates, leather

SALÉ

SAFI

Products from
Morocco-Spain-Portugal
Italy and the Levant
England
Northern Trade

METZIG

months—for distances and voyages by sea are that long and that changeable, even over an almost identical course. *Almost* identical: depending
upon the conditions under which sailors take their bearings and follow
their course, as well as upon fear of squalls and of pirates. And what
anxious periods of waiting in port, what alarming news, at Rouen and
Marseille, Lyon and Paris, when the delays continue beyond the
bounds of probability, not to mention the speculation, the insurance,
and all the gambling, protection, and risks surrounding even the most
modest operations! What an adventure, even, to hazard an ordinary trip
by land, from Orléans to Étampes, Étampes to Paris, or to risk the possi-
bility of a small load of pepper on the sandy bottom of the Loire from
Nantes to Sully! Among all these merchants, the foremost undoubtedly
are the large handlers of silver and copper who, during the early decades
of the century, underwrite the partners of the large expeditions to the
Indies; who lend money to kings and princes, and who have agents in
Venice, Lisbon, Seville, Medina de Campo, and Lyon. In the regions
around Lyon and Antwerp, these men are the new capitalists, of whom
Ehrenburg gives a penetrating study in his classic work.[11] All the same,
this is a cosmopolitan world, one in which foreigners—Germans; Italians
from Venice, Florence and especially, at the end of the century, Genoa
—are very numerous. In the largest "merchandising" triumphs, the
French are not very much in evidence, a fact noted before with reference to the medieval period (see above, pp. 165-66), which cannot be
easily explained—some people have thought it attributable to the
Church's condemnation of usury, but this practice prevailed everywhere: in Italy, in Germany, even among the Lutherans; and would
Protestantism have freed merchants from their scruples, glorifying the
completely earthly success of large-scale trade? A mere sign, and not a
sure key to the problem. No, other elements must be set forth, to explain the pre-eminence of Seville, Augsburg, and Antwerp over Rouen,
Lyon, or Marseille, such as the burden of public finances which, always
running at a deficit, gouged great holes in private fortunes, which always grant loans;* or the loans on the *"aisez,"* all kinds of forced loans,
recovering the silver in silver-plate; but this, too, is insufficient as a reason, for Spanish bankruptcies are worth quite as much. There remains
the fact that large merchant families in Lyon and Rouen do not escape
the temptations of the period: the legal profession and, especially in the
sixteenth century but in the seventeenth as well, the buying of land,
which constitutes a very safe asset and is the best means of becoming
noble. And, although its profits are more modest than those of large-
scale trade, they "fall" regularly—and without any risks.

---

* The king of France reigns over fools, no one dares refuse him allegiance. His revenues . . . *"Essere tanta quanta ne vuole il re"*—["to be as much as the king
wants . . ."—Trans.][12]

At the forefront of the commercial bourgeoisie, then, are the leaders of the world economy; their transport agents, warehouse managers, prince's agents, either those having power of attorney or simply supervisors, are numerous in some places, rarer in others; they swarm all over Lyon, for example, but are infrequent in Bruges, which no longer enjoys the good days of Jacques Coeur's time. Then come the small businessmen, whose risks are hardly greater than those of our present-day grocers and other small retailers—the "feeding corps," bakers, and butchers. Next come the artisan-craftsmen, subdivided into rigidly defined guilds each of which has its own proficiency, its own detailed regulations. Amid the flux of sixteenth-century business, these have become less respected, and have undergone a diversified profusion (according to region, where local products attain a certain repute): "tanners, bootmakers, glovers, and pelisse-makers" among the leather workers; linen from Brittany, linen and wool from Flanders (see map p. 239). This multiplicity of closely related professions is a prime indicator of the radical decay of the guilds, which are undermined by the free professions, by the stability of the masters' dynasties, and, even, by demand. Nor has this diffusion fostered technical progress; for, in these trades, the tools vary, particularly in the minute details of methods and tricks of the trade; and the chief handicap is that the only energy comes from water-power or manual strength which consume a large amount of manpower. Thus, the "humbler classes, living by the work of their hands" are distributed throughout a number of small workshops of three, five, or ten journeymen, even in the new professions like printing. Again in this we see the great inelasticity of production: fabrics, tapestries, weapons, furnishings, houses, carriages—all are still expensive items because they are completely hand-made, and are time-consuming operations. But then there are also art objects; assuming that the client allows the craftsman enough time to perfect the work, artist and artisan are one and the same. In this way, the name of a town or a region is made very quickly, according to the demand for the product and the ability of the craftsmen: the Angoulême paper-makers supply the most beautiful paper in France; the Thiers cutlers' products sell very well in Paris.

The craftsmen in their workrooms—simultaneously businessmen and manufacturers who work linen, hemp, or wool supplied by the nearby countryside, iron that all the French forests can then supply, from the Langres plateau to the Canigou, the Limoges region to the Jura—are not industrialists in the modern sense of the word. Modest weavers' workshops, fullers in the mountainous regions, humbler "mines" and forges in the forests, all are small enterprises, yielding and producing little. In sixteenth-century France there is hardly a town of twenty thousand or more whose activities, exclusively industrial or metallurgical, can call forth a larger specialization. Saint-Étienne is an exception, astonishing

and horrifying contemporaries with its noise and its ravenous activity—
but this is a weak exception. The following description expresses it rather
well:

> At two leagues from Saint-Rambert sur Loire, the port for this manu-
> facturing town, there is the town of Saint-Étienne de Furen, which
> one would take rather for a hell inhabited by devils than for a place
> of human habitation, were it not for the large cross erected on one
> of the town's gates. . . . There are three mountains near this town,
> constantly burning and throwing flames like Vesuvius in Italy; they
> also yield coal and iron mines which the inhabitants, the best work-
> men in France, use to forge all kinds of weapons and iron products.
> The town is such that, approaching it, one hears only the sound of
> hammers on anvils, making more noise than thunder. One sees only
> dirty-faced men, more frightening than goblins, with no white on
> them except for their teeth and eyes. . . .[13]

Financiers and merchants, Lyon bankers dealing with Antwerp and
Genoa, woad dealers in Toulouse, Tourangeais silk transporters, shipowners from La Rochelle trading with Lisbon and Bayonne, craftsmen,
masters selling beautiful pieces of silverplate, furniture clumsily carved
with large designs of St. George crushing the dragon, small journeymen
already motivated by feelings of animosity against their (small) employers: all this multiple and diverse world of the sixteenth century is about
to experience the greatest economic venture the European world has
known since Trajan and the gold of the Dacians. Yet opposite it, or
rather, let us say beside it—for there is no watertight bulkhead between
one group and another (no more than there is, at least until the days of
Colbert, between noble and bourgeois)—beside the merchants, then,
there are the men of law, so indispensable to city life, judging, arguing,
drawing up contracts and insurance. In spite of all their abuses and
dilatoriness, disparaged by subsequent generations, they are men of
great service, much more than those who effect the summary manorial
justice in the country. They are men of another stamp, too: sedentary
like all scholars and men of much intellectual activity, speaking Latin—
and, more and more after the 1539 enactment imposing it on all writs,
French.* They are adept at unraveling an abstruse set of laws, which are
complicated (without apparent reason) by diverse traditions of Roman
law, feudal custom, canon law, and the king's pleasure. Among the
citizenry, it is these men who are of the royal service, attached to the
monarchy by vocation and by a complex feeling of admiring hostility to
the old nobility, against whom their offices have been created and are

---

* With the Édict de Villers-Cotterets, Francis I ordered all subsequent official judicial
acts and pronouncements to be made in French, not Latin.—Trans.

consolidated. In the forefront of all the *robins* are the judges and councilors of the Grandes Chambres, Courts, and Parlements; pridefully decked out in the titles and privileges of office, they are usually very well pleased with themselves, and with their complacently flaunted role as defenders of the monarchy. Very quickly, well before the establishment of the *paulette*, they develop caste—or at least class—feelings, distinguishing themselves from the lower classes and, in particular, from the "merchandisers." Did not Olivier d'Ormesson say, in the middle of the seventeenth century, regarding one of his friends in the Paris Parlement: "He is marrying below his station, and is acquiring only money"? [14]

As early as the sixteenth century, and especially in the seventeenth, the security of the higher offices, which put them in the foremost place in these provincial small-town societies, renders devotion to the king rather suspect. There are many good reasons for these men to feel independent: the purchase of their offices at a high price, the honor of serving the king, their place at the head of their small towns, their power to dictate over a host of humbler people, and, ultimately, the security added by the *paulette*. The rest is accomplished by the civil wars at the close of the century, and by the revolts during the Regency. The *robins* very quickly become unruly officials who think nothing of betraying the king by disobedience, using their privilege of *remontrance*, trouble-making, and the refusal to register or to apply his laws. Strange servants of a monarchy which, after the time of Francis I, was called absolute, yet which was particularly defenseless confronted with such doings. The magistrates and *robins*, who guard jealously their authority and prerogatives and who are experienced in administrative life, frequently form the municipal officialdom of the towns; they do not fear to run counter to royal power when circumstances, poverty, or financial oppression lend them support.* Imagine today courts refusing to render justice, revenue officials collecting taxes as suits their pleasure—the comparison is a shaky one, but the officials' brazenness was along these lines.

Organized in this manner, the "modern" town presents us with a social diversity, a burgeoning complexity, a richness of relations between individuals and groups—all in very vivid contrast to the poverty and simplicity of the village. Especially at this time no town, not even Paris, wants or is able to section off its districts; consequently, nobles and bourgeois, rich and poor, masters and journeymen meet and cross paths a hundred times a day. And the course of business, the necessities of social life, create intellectual needs—reading, reckoning, writing; or merely holding discussions, over a piece of cloth in front of a judge; or over a good, fresh jug of wine or cider in the rear of an ill-famed tavern

---

* In 1666, a calm year, Poitiers refused to subscribe to Colbert's East India Company: "It is ruined by taxes, by the soldiers passing through the town, and by the billeting of sixteen hundred of His Majesty's guards, imposed on it in 1665."

nestled at the foot of a cathedral—not just once a week, on Sundays, but every day, they participate in an interrelated life, with multiple holidays, both civil and religious, feasts of public and of personal patron saints, a life embroiled in students' disputes, as well as in their practical jokes and their misadventures with women of easy virtue. This life is, then, more "civilized" than the one lived on the other side of the ramparts, despite certain similarities—a fact of which contemporaries are well aware.*

▶ INTELLECTUAL ADVANCES DURING THE SIXTEENTH CENTURY: THE BOOK

The town is, beyond a doubt, the center of artistic and intellectual life (before the advent of the book, these two are inseparable) from the Middle Ages on (see especially above, pp. 118-119). Urban accoutrements in this field are impressive: sculpture workshops annexed to every cathedral, episcopal schools and universities, even, under pressure from the bourgeois, parish schools, where merchants' sons are taught their ABCs; there is an entire little world of masters of arts, learned professors, clerical students and monks, who teach and are taught. A little world, nonetheless: a few hundred in the most famous towns like Montpellier and Paris; a few dozen elsewhere. Gutenberg's discovery, so quickly perfected and spread throughout Europe, was the equivalent of a revolution and was to transform modern intellectual life for three centuries, finding an equal only in the revolution of today's communication industries.

If we are to try to evaluate this transformation, we must try first to reconstruct the mentality of the scanty urban masses who, despite their increasingly well-established intellectual frameworks—active and well-managed urban parishes, schools, and universities with important social ramifications—are none too easily distinguishable from those rural mentalities we have already discussed. Despite these intellectual frameworks, despite the "technical" needs of the commercial and business life, and, one might say, despite the book itself, which at first codified and disseminated all the beliefs and opinions accepted, inherited, and sustained by centuries of oral tradition, and, at the same time, made available the philosophical and artistic works of the Ancients. Lucien Febvre, in his *Problème de l'Incroyance*,† has admirably demonstrated now the mentality of the sixteenth- and seventeenth-century intellectuals is usually not too orderly, and is still rich in approximations, imprecisions, and

---

* How, we are asked in 1664, can the seventeenth-century pastoral romances present us with such attractive shepherds? "Several people thought that there was something incredible about making Shepherds and Shepherdesses talk and behave as if they were the most polished courtiers, whereas ordinarily rustic people are vulgar and stupid." [15]

† and in the articles already cited in note 19, p. 220.

contradictions, gradually passing into the rhythm of personal reflections, the logical requirements of each individual, with a slowness consonant with each mind, much more than in a universal progression toward the Enlightenment. All one can say is that the sense of the rational occurs more frequently in the cities than in the country. Febvre quotes M. de Monconys,[16] a learned seventeenth-century traveler valuing good and reliable knowledge, who puts no stock in an abbess showing him a permanent miracle in her convent; yet, several hours or days later, under a set of similar circumstances, he is quick to accept the reality of a demonic spell or practice. And he is not any more a fool than Jean Bodin, the learned author of the *Six livres de la République* and a great economist who engages with his contemporaries in polemics about rising prices, when he publishes, in addition, a *Démonomanie des Sorciers*, a learned catalogue of the thousand-and-one tricks of the Evil One. Nor again is he alone: for every witchcraft trial, every burning at the stake of those difficult days, was staged and arranged by scholarly jurists, learned experts of a superabundant jurisprudence, who were also scrupulous about cataloguing the Sabbath crimes that could be made out of a simple theft. This credulity (as we might call it, though the word is anachronistic) was similar to that extant in the country, though it was perhaps less in the towns. Thus, the unconscious confusion of rational and irrational, natural and supernatural, is still widespread; a heritage from long centuries of familiarity with those saints' lives, assimilated by a rather undiscriminating piety to the authentic Gospel accounts. The *Journal* of L'Estoile, for example, tells us a charming story—for these accounts, so like tall tales to us, do have their own zest; but let us remember that for Pierre de l'Estoile, who does not for a moment hesitate or let his pen falter, it is no "tale":

> On December 20, 1593, it happened that a Neapolitan, desperately in love with a bootmaker's wife, sent to her requesting three drops of her milk (for she was nursing) for an eye disease that he claimed to have; he sent her three *écus*, which she very readily took with her husband's permission. He, having a goat, advised her to take milk from it and send three drops to the Neapolitan, letting him think that it was her own. The Neapolitan, overjoyed, thought to complete his *mystère* (which was to make the bootmaker's wife so in love with him, that she would run after him and seek for him wherever he went); he put charms into the three drops of milk that had been sent him, which made the goat so much in love that it began to jump around and become maddened, finally escaping from its master's house and, finding this Spaniard in the Neapolitan guard corps, forthwith jumped on his neck, and kissed him, and gave him thousands of caresses.[17]

One may, at least, assume that the intellectual and professional equipment of a townsman of this time is less deficient. Merchants handle *livres, sous,* and *deniers* daily; money-changers and goldsmiths have to weigh things, to determine the value of the foreign money flowing into the border towns and even into the center of France; they are large-scale traders who know the exchange rate, who must come to grips with a currency which is constantly being reminted and clipped. All these men know how to read and count, at least, and are not, like the villagers, the slaves of oral tradition. This is all true. But let us be sensible: granted they no longer try, as do their rural compatriots, to count entrances and exits by notches made on a wooden slat, as the peasants count the number of sacks of wheat carried to the mill; but they are still far removed from our use of "mental arithmetic," a schoolboy exercise learned very young and sticking with us. Neither lengths of time, nor matters of business, are easily measured in figures; and, in order to represent numerical figures, one has to be able to write fast. In 1665, M. d'Ormesson is present at a gallstone operation undergone by his father; the stone is crushed between the ends of the forceps, and the surgeon is forced to use a spoon to remove the particles. How long did all that last? "More than the length of two Misereres." [18] Making up one's accounts involves the slow writing of everything, and then the working out of one's calculations; in family record books as in many other documents the processes speak for themselves: the addition for 50 plus 45, and 150 plus 30 plus 4, must be set down; subtraction is a puzzling task in which, most of the time, the carried-over numbers are overlooked. One would like to think that the great accountants of the period, like Martin Kléberg of Lyon, the statesmen, and the great financiers like Cardinal de Tournon, knew how to manage things a little better. But the errors, the common difficulties, are all too significant, at a time when the book—not really widespread until the sixteenth century since there is a definite lag between the technical discovery and its practical application on a scale large enough to constitute a fact of civilization—already furnishes arithmetical models and tables applicable to daily use.

But, above and beyond all the mental and intellectual realities, let us take full cognizance of the fact that the townspeople, even before the spread of books, find some degree of intellectual framework and sustenance in two institutions unknown in the villages: the urban parishes, so alive and active; and the schools and universities which, originally reserved for clerics, are eventually open to the laity as well.

The urban parishes, like the rural ones, furnish a skeletal structure upon which the spiritual life of the townspeople can mold itself. True— but the urban structure is unquestionably a better support, in the sense that the urban *curés* and *vicaires* have a much more powerful spiritual "presence" than does the poor, rural *curé*. This presence amounts to attentive supervision, sometimes augmented by sanctions, to which, even in mild instances, the people are responsive: ". . . for which reason he refused the role of godfather, offered him by the Sieur Morice, ensign in the cavalry company of the Sieur of Saint-Jamain; for the *vicaire* had said that he was not able to do this, not having taken the Easter Sacrament." [19] He has even greater reason to watch over those suspected of heresy: "Françoise Blondin, suspected of Protestantism, because she had not heard mass for two months. . . ." [20] As we shall also see, the erudite skeptics, as described by René Pintard, never miss Mass, in order to avoid all suspicion.[21] There is discipline, then, in this control, in these holy days of obligation that are so numerous—soon too numerous, in Colbert's opinion. The parish is still the center of the inner life; through its sculpture and its stained-glass windows, the Church furnishes, as we know well, a commentary upon religious life. Nevertheless, from the very fact that people are accustomed to it, the Church is less effective than the shrines upon which miracles are perpetuated, and, especially, less effective than the preaching—so vivid even in this century of the book—and the singing of that extraordinarily rich repertory of hymns, carefully cultivated in order that worship be celebrated, and celebrated by the faithful themselves, in the most beautiful manner possible.

There are magnificent shrines, more carefully guarded than all the silver-plated service for worship, and shrines on which the most skillful craftsmen have worked for years. Each parish has a few, containing authentic remains, unique in all Christendom—thorns, bits of linen, shrouds, pieces of wood from the Cross, drops of blood, tears—piously accumulated treasures, objects of renewed veneration, always glorified, despite the horrible trafficking in such objects which has been going on for a long time * Intermittently, they bring about wonderful miracles, over which the entire village rejoices at great length.

Then there are the preachers, mendicant types specially trained to deal with the urban public, secular priests traveling from one parish to the other, bringing the good word to a public greedy to hear it, a public willing to run and hear a sermon undoubtedly more pleasant than those inevitably monotonous Sunday services. At the height of the seventeenth century, the most literate Parisians, those who have a library and friends, two good reasons for self-sufficiency, throw everything to the winds in order to hear a Jesuit father's sermon, or that of a Capuchin of great renown (the latter ordinarily being the preferable one). A de-

---

* Listen to a small craftsman from Puy boast of the relics in his cathedral: "In the first place, the said town is honored to have in its cathedral of Notre-Dame the most beautiful relics and holy objects in the world, namely: Our Saviour's holy foreskin, that is from his very own body, and there is none other, in any other part of the world."

manding public, certainly, and an exclusive one; in the small provincial towns, where the humbler classes do not always speak French, preaching does not have as much importance.* Theological discussions, discussions of the great and grave problems of this time, these centuries when Western Christianity is irreparably tearing itself apart—with these the preachers supply our *robins,* who are admirers of fine words and who are habituated to long disputes over texts to be interpreted. Undoubtedly, they supply, in addition, a less dainty diet.† In an activity as important as this one, not everything can be of top quality. And finally, the townsman finds, in his church and cathedral, that other pleasure of the ear (but then, as Lucien Febvre has competently demonstrated, the sixteenth century is more oriented toward the auditory than the visual): the hymns, lovingly cultivated by the bishops (their "choirs"). There are the rhythmic masses, always in the unalterable order of six ritual parts: Kyrie, Gloria, Credo, Sanctus, Benedictus, and Agnus Dei; particularly, there are the motets, the texts of which are taken from the Proper of the Office, and are lyric poems, upon which the composers embellish melodic designs adapted to each voice. These simple compositions, delighting their hearers, found their sixteenth-century masters in Palestrina and Tomás Luis de Victoria among others.

Thus the urban parish furnishes a living and stable framework of intellectual life for the townspeople—who are so very privileged by comparison with the parish life on the other side of the ramparts. Privileged indeed, despite the imperfections of the system: the urban residences of bishops and *curés,* who are appointed by the king of France himself, are not always provided with the best men (again, a direct consequence of the Concordat of Bologna, signed in 1516): the Bishop of Lodève, appointed by Henry IV when he was only four years old, is a well-known example. And sixty years later, Fléchier, participating in the *Grands Jours* in Auvergne at Clermont, discovers a bishop of Auvergne who does not inspire him with great respect: "M. the President Montorcier was speaking to him one day, in theological terms, about the priesthood in his region; he constantly turned to a priest and asked him if these propositions were Catholic!" [24] However, even from this point of view, the seventeenth century was one of progress in disciplinary reform, in the efforts at recruitment, and especially, in great religious polemic.

Curés and *vicaires,* canons and bishops, and those many monks— popular Capuchins, Benedictines, Jesuits, Dominicans—all are constantly present in the life of the towns. Listened to and, at the same

---

* Brunot quotes an informative text by the bishop of Apt (1709): "These sermons scarcely ever bear fruit, for most of the preachers that are sent do not know how to speak the local patois, and the peasants and craftsmen do not understand them when they speak in French." [22]

† "The preachers, often more sedulous about humoring their audience than about correcting its faults, never miss an opportunity to second popular opinions." [23]

time, observed with that strain of malice, that old background of too-
facile jokes, dating back to the *fabliaux*, concerning priests and nuns
(from which La Fontaine fashioned the cleverest tales ever written)—
they were always in the forefront of everyone's thoughts, thanks to the
flourishing life of the parishes, and also to those other ecclesiastical institutions, the episcopal schools and the universities. This is a world in
motion during the days of Rabelais, Montaigne, Descartes, those great
"reformers," who gave voice to their contemporaries' innumerable complaints,* and of those reforms drafted on so many occasions: bold efforts of Francis I or the Jesuits, and later the Oratorians and Jansenists.
But the schools, with the students' hullabaloo, the staunchly maintained
traditions, by giving the *robins'* and merchants' children the necessary
knowledge in the arts, still assure their part in the urban intellectual life.
There are the disputations, the trials before the assembled faculties—
what we now call the dissertation defense—which draw a large audience
to listen gravely to a treatise at the Faculté de Médicine in Paris. In
1648, "Is Woman an Imperfect Work of Nature?"; in 1668, "Is the Application of the Gall of a Fish, as a Cure for Blindness, Natural?" [*La
cure de Tobie*]—bizarre subjects in our eyes, but the fruits of a scientific
state whose basis is formed by Aristotle's writings. The schools and
collèges still furnish the town with drama—those learned performances
to which parents and friends of the young actors as well as the merely
inquisitive flock in order to see the story of Daniel, or of St. Alexis, those
dramas taken either from the Bible or from the *Legenda Aurea*. Thus
these scholarly establishments, perhaps stifled by Scholasticism, nonetheless determine the tone of the intellectual life, governing its rhythms
with their semesters and vacations, their festivals and debates.

Let us note once again how much prestige, during all this, the spoken
word has retained, even when the book has invaded everything; the
churches are never large enough and the most popular preachers speak
in the open air. Sermons, fine effects, are as much sought after as, today,
people run to the latest art exhibit, and snobbism is, of course, one of
the motives in either case.† The revolution brought about by the book

---

* Despite many fine programs, progress (outside of that attributable to the advent
of the book) is minimal in the pedagogical sphere. At the end of the seventeenth century, J. Rou still complains: (I, 4) "That barbarous method of teaching a child by
rote, by rules he does not understand . . . the horrible *singula riter nominativo* of my
first declensions, its *Indicativo modo*, *Tempore præsenti* are now so many spec-
ters . . ."

† A seventeenth-century Parisian like Olivier d'Ormesson is not afraid to go hear several sermons, one after another, during a single afternoon, and he does not do so for
snobbish reasons: "Sunday, December 6, 1643, I was at the home of the Chancellor
of the Seal. After dinner, went to Saint Paul's for the sermon of Father Joseph
Morlaye, who performed wonders . . . from there, to the Annonciade . . . I heard
the sermon of a Jesuit from The Hague." [25]

is not a revolution in habits, in the rhythm of social life, so defined; its action in this sphere was slower, and books more often than not gain ground only at the point where one's profession, technical necessity, or the need for knowledge prepare the way. It is certain that the book causes an enlargement of the intellectual world, but this enlargement is difficult to gauge precisely. For the clerics themselves, it certainly produced an extraordinary transformation, only with difficulty imaginable to us in the twentieth century, no matter what our profession, who read, at the lowest possible estimate, seven to nine pounds of paper (posters, newspapers, income-tax forms, etc.) per year. In one century, let us say from 1450 to 1550, how can the clerics and their friends pass from those very rare, expensive, precious manuscripts, sometimes difficult to decipher, always difficult to handle, and, even more, to preserve—to books, the estimable book that is solid, well-bound, all of whose copies are put at everyone's disposal? What we know most about is the overwhelming triumph of the book. There are the inventions perfected in the fifteenth century: from the 1420 *Biblia Pauperum*,* to the fine inks and lead type of Gutenberg, the workshops proliferate everywhere. In 1470, despite the protestations of the professional scriveners, who, in the shadow of the early Sorbonne, earn a good part of their living unhurriedly copying the reliable old texts and courses, the first printers' shops are set up in Paris, at the Sorbonne itself. In 1500, the town of Lyon alone has fifty shops, and a new profession is already being organized there—one which consumes large amounts of capital for its machines and its increasingly necessary paper. This new profession is singularly free and bold, printing everything that has fallen into its hands: school books; Church books, the Gospels and Church Fathers first of all, enabling everyone to read Luke and Matthew at one sitting without having to wait for the reading and commentary at church on Sundays; then the manuscripts from Latin and Greek antiquity, gradually being turned up by the oldest monasteries—the good republican Cicero, the philosophers Plato and Seneca, the histories of Thucydides, and that *summa* of ancient biography, Plutarch's *Lives of Famous Men*, translated by Amyot, the huge success of the sixteenth century; somewhat later, but without any relaxation of that curiosity, that passion for publishing things, appear those treatises that are sometimes reflections on, sometimes reworkings of, ancient thought, mingled with contemporary observations, like the *République* of Bodin, the learned studies on marvels by Ambroise Paré, and the treatises on magic and alchemy, written in excellent Latin. Then there are all those satires at whose infinite numbers

---

* A Vulgate Bible appearing in numerous editions with a Latin text and many woodblock illustrations, of both the scenes described in the text and analogues in other parts of the Bible—particularly Old Testament ones for New Testament events. *See* the edition by Paul Kristeller, Berlin: Cassirer, 1906.—Trans.

we can only guess, relating an unusual event in a few pages, and commenting upon it in a dozen or so lines. How many copies printed? For what audience? We do not know; very often, we know no more than the name of the author.* After the sixteenth century, one could almost speak of a real mania for printed matter.

At the end of the fifteenth century, the greatest luxuries of the big-city bourgeois were having panes put in their windows, purchasing heavy, round-topped cupboards of carved wood, and, in particular, beautiful tapestries. From now on, they add another passion to these, as we know by the inventories taken after someone's death, a passion we know to be headed for a fine future: beautiful books, bound in calf, with gold stamping; quarto or octavo relating saints' lives, the exploits of Cyrus the Great, the marvels of the New World. Nicely lined up along the walls, within reach of both hands and eyes: the passion of a Montaigne, and of how many others! Is it too bold, then, to assert that the Renaissance and Reformation are entirely the daughters of the printing press, which propagated itself through the European world; that Luther would not have been any more dangerous (or would have been only a little more so) than Jan Huss, if the ninety-five theses of Wittenberg had not been spread through all Germany in a few weeks, and soon through all Europe? We shall not play the childish game of remaking history; but such an hypothesis is valid when the transformation reaches as great an extent as this.

However, it is a double movement. On the one hand, culture and the intellectual life are enlarged, finding their best support in this instrument of diffusion, going beyond the confines of the clerics and schools, to appeal to all of the upper urban society, won over with enthusiasm (the fervor of the humanists, for example, like Robert Estienne in the sixteenth century and Cramoisy in the seventeenth, who were simultaneously great scholars and printers); the intellectual life gains in scope and achieves a partial separation from the artistic life. But, on the other hand, the discussion and invention, the thirst for knowledge and understanding, emerge from the monasteries and schools, passing into the *salons*, the jurists' conversations (which, in turn, enlarge their scope even further); hence, the cultural life of those groups stimulated by books separates itself from that of the ordinary little people—craftsmen, peasants—who have neither the leisure nor the means to read, and who consequently are left behind. Every parishioner of Notre-Dame, Chartres,

---

* An example which gives us a good idea of the spirit of the times, the importance of the written word: "An admirable and prodigious discourse concerning a lynx who entered the city of Vienne, Saturday, March 5, 1616. And after having been pursued for a long time, it took refuge in the large Church of Saint-Maurice." [26] "A miraculous, very admirable, prodigious, and true discourse concerning a person of false religion from La Coste Saint André in Dauphiny, who, for having blasphemed against the Blessed Sacrament, was horribly eaten by rats." [27]

passing before the royal portal, knows its meaning by "reading" the sculpture. But Ronsard and Du Bellay do not write for everybody; and even when René Descartes furnishes a French translation of his *Discours de la Méthode*, obviously thought out and written in Latin, he does not and can not hope to have it read by his shoemaker or by the peasants of La Haye* in the Touraine. We shall gradually see this rapid and rough sketch take on gradations with the passing of time, which changes everything. A schema such as this does not work out, for example, the major questions of popular literature or of *préciosité*; yet it has its value.

► THE ECONOMIC ADVANCES DURING THE SIXTEENTH CENTURY: THE TREASURES FROM AMERICA

It took a century for contemporaries to grasp all the implications of the revolution brought by the book into the intellectual and spiritual life. The often quoted exclamation of Campanella dates from 1620, at a time when books had already invaded everything, private accounts and artistic schools: "Our century has more history contained in its hundred years than the whole world has, in the four thousand previous ones; more books have been published in the last century than in the five thousand years that went before." On the other hand, it is after 1550 or 1560 that the "perspicacious observers" mentioned by Braudel[28] realized the enormous economic revolution through which they were living. Next, Jean Bodin announces, in a justly famous passage:

> Spain, which survives only because of France, being constrained, as she is, by inevitable forces to obtain her wheat, linens, woolens, woad, *rodon*, paper, books, even her woodwork, from us, and all her handmade products, goes out and looks all over the world for the gold and silver with which to pay us." †

This is a readily acknowledged fact and one which, with the end of the century, becomes a commonplace, one of those ready-made ideas of which businessmen and statesmen took some time to rid themselves: Spain, the Indies of European nations.

Thus, during the long sixteenth century, the hunger for gold and silver—which overwhelmed medieval merchants and was still rife at the end of the fifteenth century, despite the overflowing activity of the German and Scandinavian mines—gave way to an unprecedented abun-

---

* Descartes was born in a small town about thirty miles south of Tours now known as La Haye-Descartes.—Trans.
† Concerning *rodon*, I can only concur with M. Hauser's note in his "Commentaire," p. 86—"Nous n'avons pu identifier cette marchandise." Moore's translation suggests "tanner's sumach."—Trans.[29]

dance of monetary specie. This abundance is, beyond a doubt, relative, for the continuous wars, the acceleration of trade, constantly demanded more. Yet during this long century, Spain received gold and silver by the ton; there were galleons laden with entire cargoes of metals, carefully shipped from the Antilles to Spain—some hundred and eighty tons of gold and seventeen thousand tons of silver between 1500 and 1640. What a waterfall into the monetary stream of Europe! In the early years of the century there was a river of gold, followed by an inundation of silver between 1550 and 1610, followed in turn by the enormous circulation, in the seventeenth century, of nickel-and-copper alloys, of silver, and of copper—that little coin of daily urban trade. And these quantities of metal, brutally thrown into circulation, explain the contemporaries' admiration, and the meaning the word "Peru" retained for a long time: reference to an inexhaustible source of wealth!

Why do this gold, this silver, those "doubloons" and "reals" from Spain, pass into France? Because, soon after the conquest, Spain—placed at the head of immense realms from Mexico to Paraguay—is unable to exploit them by herself. She lacks wood, sails, and cordage for her large Atlantic fleet, as well as flour, meat, and fruits for the crews; she is unable to supply the arms, textiles, and tools for which the Conquistadores are crying out. Like every other European country at that time, Spain does not have at its disposal a sufficiently elastic agriculture and industry to swell with pride at the demands made upon it, or to supply such powerful needs. She is, then, obliged to appeal to her neighbors —to the French (for wheat, linen, and furnishings), and to the Italians: Genoese, Florentines, and Venetians. Then as time passes, aided by smuggling, and by licit trade—from Marseille, Bordeaux, or Saint-Malo, as well as Antwerp and Genoa—and by the diminishing population of Spain, whose strength was being drained into those immense, unexplored continents: the Spanish economy was less and less able to supply itself with weapons, fabric, and grain, for which her greedy neighbors ask a steeper and steeper price in Seville. Great days for the Mediterranean and the Atlantic, which are crisscrossed in every direction; great days for the fortunes of Bordeaux merchants, Toulousian suppliers of wheat and woad, woolen and linen sellers from Rouen and Saint-Malo. We ought to add, to round off this account of the invasion of Spanish money from the south and west, a mention of the tactics of the great politicians, Charles V and Philip II, who sent their precious convoys through France, or along her borders from Milan to Besançon and to Antwerp, later bribing the League. France's monetary enrichment, then, comes out of this bleeding of Spain, which is a gaping wound of money. And it continues: at the beginning of the seventeenth century, the rural districts of Aragon are deserted, and people from the Cantal in the Auvergne head toward the Ebro for their grain harvests.

This new enrichment does not, of course, distribute its benefits equally, either among all the regions of France or among all the social classes. First, it involves a brutal rise in prices, all the more violent because French artisan production was not as elastic as Spain's. It is possible that in some localities the demand was able to promote some technical research (weavers of Lyon and Rouen, for example, inaugurate new professions).* The only means by which the price rise is held in check—and, of necessity, not a negligible one, though it falls short—is the hoarding done by families and by ecclesiastical groups, who absorb ciborium pieces, jewelry, and table services, via the self-seeking mediation of money-changers and goldsmiths. All the rest feed the commercial speculation and the trade in money, whose speed of circulation increases with the demand, and whose modalities of investment multiply with the need—exploding all barriers, even including the Church's ban on usury, which fell to the inflation movement—too high a bidder, too strong a temptation, and in certain respects a temptation comparable to the one France experienced after the Liberation. Private fortunes, as well as public finances, suffered miscellaneous fates: unusual successes and deep crises, even, on occasion, bankruptcy.[30] In terms of this movement, France, with her large trade with Spain, the Mediterranean, and the Atlantic, carried on along the Aquitaine border and as far as Saint-Malo and Rouen, did not experience the "money troubles, Mediterranean troubles" that destroyed the Italian cities—Florence in particular—at the end of the century.[31] But she is somewhat jolted by watching the progress of her large ports—even Marseille and especially La Rochelle, Saint-Malo, Rouen, and Le Havre; and her large financial centers, especially Lyon—as well as the sight of the medieval social balance threatened by this economic movement which slows down between 1610 and 1630, then gives way to a recession spreading over the second half of the seventeenth century.

In this urban fever, in which fortunes are made and unmade with unheard-of rapidity, in which bankers maintain a rhythm of loans and advances dizzying to the contemporary observer, and in which large-scale commerce, war, and princely ambition mingle their demands, thereby maddening money-changers and heads of finance in the Chambre des Monnaies alike[32]—who, in this febrile economy, are the beneficiaries? Who the victims? At first sight, every class is a victim; journeymen and craftsmen are crushed by the rise in prices; bankers dwell constantly on the edge of a precipice, and sometimes fall into the abyss below; "industrialists" are unable to impose their own prices, or to supply

---

* Actually, it is legitimate to speak of technical stagnation; there is not much advance either in the vital equipment of each profession, nor in its own techniques. And the investigations of Leonardo da Vinci, which come before this great movement, are mere diagrams, untranslated into immediate industrial use.

the demand. Yet distinctions can be made. There are at least two groups that indubitably are victims. First, there are those who are pushed to one side, who, though they should have profited from the price rise (even in agriculture) do not sell their wheat—small grain-growing peasants whose "business" is limited to one or two sales a year at fairs, and whose meager profit is quickly absorbed by the voracity of royal finances—more exacting than ever in these times of long wars—not to mention the voracity of the lords. Apart from the husbandmen in the Beauce, the woad-growers around Toulouse, the vineyardists from Bordeaux, there are, with few exceptions, no gains for the peasants. The only consolation is that, because they buy so little, there are also few losses. The second group is the mass of the urban populace. These are more severely affected: journeymen, garret-craftsmen, and small craftsmen, suffer with each rise in prices, whether it be wheat, drink, or meat, commodities whose prices dance a frenzied sarabande. Yet these people do not earn much more than they did, for their wages increase slowly, very slowly;* as a matter of fact, in terms of actual recompense, they decrease terribly. Times, then, are hard indeed for the small wage earner in the towns; the nervousness of the masses at the end of the century, the League's troops, the image-toppling groups from the Flemish regions—all these and more cannot be understood without this economic context and the serious poverty it signifies. The gold and silver brought back by Spain from the ends of the world hardly ever refill these modest purses. And, in this period of urban overpopulation, in which manpower is abundant and the journeyman can make scarcely any demands, his dissatisfaction—which, because of the virtual nonexistence of class consciousness, is not directed toward social demands—breaks out at every turn.

On the other hand, there are some people who do benefit. Those who were most sure to profit from the price rise were, beyond a doubt, the land proprietors whose storehouses received impressive harvests as a result of their privileges in kind; and, after 1530 or 1540, they were able to sell these harvests, which they had so easily garnered and delivered, to the urban merchants at a much higher price. These were clear, easy, riskless gains, always attractive to those merchants and bankers having the wherewithal for a secure investment. In opposition to the more substantial dangers (and profits), then, of the large-scale business, there is also that resource within arm's reach: the acquisition of good land, a few leagues away from the town. Thus, the estates around Paris and Lyon are not mere promises of ennoblement—that constantly sought-after satisfaction of vanity—they are also investments, yielding much and risking little, for in the sixteenth century land values, too, are on the way up. But, as everyone knows, those nobles who were contemporaries of Henry III

---

* Braudel quotes precise figures: given an index of 100 for the period between 1550 and 1559, wages move up to 107.4 in the period from 1610 to 1619.[33]

and Louis XIII complained bitterly that they were the victims, and not the beneficiaries, of the merchants' success. For several reasons, their incontestable but nominal gains seemed, to them, to carry little weight: they were "eaten up" by the ascending cost of the products they purchased—tapestries, golden and silken cloth, woolens, paintings, furnishings, and so forth, whose prices increased no less than did that of grain, especially since the nobles had become very large, indeed insatiable, consumers of those products which, in those days, passed for luxury items. Hence they have the impression—already present during the great commercial centuries of the Middle Ages (see above, pp. 166-167) but becoming, in this century of gold, silver, and luxury, a throbbing ache—of being shockingly outdone by those town-dwelling *roturiers** and *manants* who are their purveyors, and who do not themselves scorn luxurious tapestries and magnificent paintings.† These proprietors forget their gains, in the face of such large expenses and constantly increasing needs; daily comparison between the modest ease of the château and the ostentation of the cities is inevitable. Such then are the landed proprietors, nobles and clergy alike—the ungrateful beneficiaries of the economic revolution.

Despite all the blows of fate, despite the ships that are lost, run aground, or seized by privateers, despite the bankruptcies of lavish kings and the commercial rivalries with Italians and Flemings, there are still those who profit from this economic boom. Merchants trading on a large scale, small manufacturers, famous craftsmen, handlers of gold—money, good and bad, passes back and forth through their hands. It is this passing of money, not its sterile accumulation, which makes fortunes. Merchandise crowds the back rooms of shops whose floors are littered with packing cases and baskets, recently arrived and inventoried, then immediately sent out again. The fortune of the sixteenth century is that of those people in Lyon, La Rochelle, and Brittany who gather treasuries of silver table-services, buy up good noble land, and lend money to the king —who, ruined by his wars and his castles, is always scraping the bottom. These men live on a grand scale; their *hôtels* are built in the new residential districts of the large commercial towns, far from their stores and warehouses; they furnish and decorate these houses, the direct result of their success, with their own portraits. Moreover, they are not unaware

---

* A *roturier* is a person of common birth who has recently joined the ranks of the newly-rich; in the eighteenth century, they are a part of the Third Estate's upper stratum.—Trans.
† After the beginning of the sixteenth century, Erasmus emphasized this point in a line that became as well known as the medieval explanation, "When Adam delved and Eve span, who then was the gentleman"; in one of the *Colloquies,* called "The Horseless Knight, or False Nobility," he says, "Indeed what is more unbearable? A vulgar merchant bursts with wealth, while a knight has nothing to give to courtesans, nothing with which to gamble!"

that they are snapping their fingers in the face of the old *noblesse de sang* and, while they enjoy doing so, they are always seeking to insinuate themselves discreetly into its ranks. This perceptible rivalry, which the Capetian monarchy had known how to manipulate marvelously (*see p. 128*), is exacerbated by the economic strides of the sixteenth century.*

In this climate of social division, but also of flowing and continually renewed wealth, in this atmosphere of conquest where gold, silver, and alloys flow from the south, west, and north, there flourishes a chatelain and urban civilization which prides itself on its rejuvenation, even to the point of insolence: from Lefèvre d'Étaples to Saint-Cyran, from Leonardo to Philippe de Champaigne, from Pierre Lescot to Louis Le Vau.

---

* This is particularly true of the "hybrid" class known as the *noblesse de robe* which, bourgeois in origin and prompt to repudiate it, also aspires to intermingle with the *noblesse de sang*. From these contradictions, a materialist philosopher said recently, modern thought would have emerged. Like all a priori constructions, it is an extreme thesis—but an interesting one.

VIII

From
Innovators to Fanatics

Aspects of the
Sixteenth Century

THE century is filled with glory, filled to overflowing. Already its merits are considerable: it has extended Europe into America and Asia, across seas and oceans; it has added new worlds to the old Mediterranean; it has founded an art of living in society upon the book—that new means of communication which has replaced and extended the spoken word by the written one. To these achievements it adds many others: new religions which quarter the Catholic Church, forcing her back into her cradle, the Mediterranean domain, which becomes her strongest support; a rebirth of all of antiquity, diffused through the century's arts, philosophy, and science, which built a new universe—a universe in which men of every time since have seemed to recognize themselves and their lives: thus the eighteenth-century humanists like Montesquieu and D'Alembert, who venerate their glorious predecessors; twentieth-century artists and writers like Paul Valéry, seeking the secret of all artistic and scientific thought in Leonardo da Vinci; and scientists themselves of the nineteen-hundreds, rightly or wrongly discovering a precursor in Rabelais. Surely, this is too rich a century.

We seek to understand it more fully, not to diminish it, when we distinguish within that colossus stretched along the great dates of Western or French history (1492, 1598, 1610), not one homogeneous sixteenth century, but several successive movements in an extremely diverse collective drama, one whose various actors bear scarce resemblance to one another: contrast Calvin and Montaigne, for example, or Marguerite de Navarre and Marguerite de Valois. That great sixteenth century firmly planted in the heart of France, along the supremely peaceful scenery of the Loire, which authored the most sensational and infinitely expansive dramatic turn of events ever recorded in French history: the Renaissance and Reformation—that century contains, perhaps, a little stage setting, a healthy dose of well-meaning deception. Instead of this dramatic "great turning point," * this irremediable about-face or sundering, too well accredited in our time, when distinguished men of letters proclaim the tragic end of civilizations—instead, let us see a series of passages and transitions, which respect the past and would not think of nullifying it. It is thus that the atmosphere of those days changes, without overly sudden stoppages (we are tempted to say, as might the Scholastics: *natura non fecit saltus*,† a kind of historical nature). The air breathed by Francis I, Lefèvre, Briçonnet and their contemporaries is not that of the rough years of the 1560s, when burnings at the stake proliferate, when the Antichrist, dreaded and detested, is everywhere a menace, when passions explode for thirty years throughout all of France and the adjacent Netherlands. It seems as though an abyss separated the men who heard the alarum of St. Bartholomew's and those of the years 1500 to 1515 or 1520, years containing the glorious homecomings from Italy, the trips to Fontainebleau, and the witty dissertations of Erasmus upon reforms necessary for the Roman Church. The three or four generations (four, let us say, for life is short then; but we shall not attach too much importance to this confusing idea) which overlap the sixteenth century on the calendar experience a different France. The later years become more difficult and severe; in a word, more fanatic: D'Aubigné follows Ronsard, Montluc comes after Lefèvre d'Étaples. Yet the transitions from one to the other are clear.

To define these successive climates, of course, does not explain everything; nonetheless, it is quite certain that no man, however full of genius he may be, is completely detachable from his time, from his beliefs, and the means at his disposal—and this is particularly true in those

---

* The expression is borrowed from the most recent historian of the drama of modern history, conjured up in all its horror, for the author is full of fondness for the Middle Ages.[1]

† "Nature makes no leaps (in her operations)"—a phrase generally attributed to Jacques Tissot, *Discours véritable de la vie*, and later used by Leibniz in his *New Essays* (IV, 16). In either case what is being stated is an established maxim from physics.—Trans.

spheres of creation, like music and painting, that are dominated by an exacting technique. But even he who needs only a pen and a piece of paper; he who desires, like all founders of religions, to become a prophet, to speak, to appeal, to mankind for an eternity—does not Calvin, in the *Institutes of the Christian Religion*, know his contemporaries extremely well? What risks he runs, what false interpretations he brings down upon himself, when he is careful to confront the partisans of Averroës with his definition of Predestination! The atmosphere of a time, while it is unable to explain prefiguring genius, locates and encloses it. Lucien Febvre has supplied a masterly demonstration of this point, as he studies Rabelais, dissecting him and putting him back together again, snatching him away from the anticlerical interpretation of Abel Lefranc.[2] This does not mean that a flash of genius is impossible. But such a flash attains its true coloration when it is placed, and accurately placed, against the dark or light background of the sky across which, for a moment, it zigzags.

Let us look at our men of the sixteenth century. In the years between 1520 and 1530, they are still astonished and delighted with the new or very recent discoveries, delighted to learn that the human universe extends beyond the area along the Mediterranean and oriented toward it, and even more astonished at the idea that this round earth is, perhaps, only a point in space: but very few attempt to take in this last idea, and pending the advent of better telescopes, of ardent mathematicians from Kepler to Newton, say neither yes nor no. Anything, after all, is possible. They pay attention to new things, but still are not absolutely new creatures themselves, carrying the debts to a recent past—to the Italian Quattrocento, which gave life to the French Renaissance and preceded it by a century, just as the French has, in many respects, about the same advance over the Renaissance in England. Finally, these new men are overwhelmed, too, by the weighty heritage they bear from Antiquity, which delights and enchants them—but deprives them of leisure, of the desire to seek elsewhere and to see other things. What is truly new among the contemporaries of Charles VIII, Louis XII, and Francis I is their happiness, their thirst to live, discover and know—yes, but also to read and build, in a fervor that is frightened by nothing, that shrinks from almost nothing—their *curiosity*: a stronger word than it is today, meaning what the Germans call *Lust*. *Lustig* men, those men of 1520, rich in money, easy profits, leisure, hopes; men who are curious about books, regions, worlds unknown, or little known (for the medieval clerics were not unaware of antiquity). Here, then, are the men of the early sixteenth century, completely happy to know that these treasures, for which their fathers neither knew the taste nor suspected the existence, are within their reach. They are truly indefatigable: Amyot, a humanist knowing three ancient languages, Latin, Greek, and Hebrew, reads and re-reads the most difficult manuscripts, translates all of Plutarch into the good French of his day; the self-taught Leonardo, who masters all the science of his time—Aristotle naturally, the *summa* of medieval science, but also the rediscovered scholars of antiquity, Pliny, Varro, and many others—and who dreamed, in drawings still admired today for their precision and intuition, of new machines. Scholars in the encyclopedic and enumerative fashion of those times; impassioned artists—that extraordinary early sixteenth century flowers with boldness and life; but it is short-lived. After 1560 they are replaced by the *tristes hommes*, the sad generation, turning away from riches and joys, toward death. Other men, in another key: somber, with avenging hands. The sixteenth century illustrates, better than any other, that primary truth: men in modern times live their lives most intensely, surpass themselves, in two interpenetrating domains which, nourishing each other, are not of the same stamp: Art, which dominates in the early years, until about 1530 or 1540; and Religion, which between 1570 and 1590 becomes a deadly weapon.

► **THE ITALIAN SCHOOL**

"Italy, land of the arts . . . mother of the arts," true. It is from Italy that noble gentlemen and kings of France, following those merchants who had known the roads for quite some time, learned how to give to France her new aspects, from Chambord to Fontainebleau and the Louvre, faces that fifty years ago so shocked the good old Courajod, that passionate defender of Gothic art, that obdurately artistic Gallican, to whom that love of Italy which ended in the rediscovery of antiquity was entirely foreign.

And yet, this artistic outburst, which almost coincides with the ostentatious reign of Francis I, is not a surprise; rather, it is a culmination, a vigorous advance produced at a time when, on the other side of the Alps, artistic life attains a fullness which is its zenith. Charles VIII returns from Italy loaded down with booty; Francis I comes back with one of the greatest geniuses of Leo X's century in his entourage; both kings have discovered, with boundless admiration, the height of the Italian Renaissance, a height quickly followed by decline which—if one believes what Montaigne, traveling there around 1580, says of it in his *Journal*—is best not evoked. Between 1500 and 1520, the Italy of Leonardo, Michelangelo, and Raphael (for Fra Angelico, Filippo Lippi, and Giotto have passed into the background) offers to the French knights an already saturated image of a country where artistic display has been a daily matter for more than a century, where the rich arts of stone and color constitute the only luxury that the merchant Italy of the end of the Middle Ages, the triumphant director of world commerce, had wanted to permit herself. Herein lies the explanation for the ecstasy of Charles VIII, bemused with admiration,* as well as the cupidity with which his companions and those of Francis I, from Milan to Naples, threw themselves on everything they could buy or carry off: jewels, paintings, statues, and particularly artists, for months and years. The French and the Italians: the masters receiving (and putting up with) the Barbarians, as they used to enjoy saying—together they lived this life of wars, of occupied and evacuated towns, of constantly resurging clashes in an Italy where every prince is a little Machiavel. Yet amid these conflicts, the artistic enthusiasm of the French warriors, who have been shrewdly misled into this wasps' nest, is the salvation of the large expeditions led by Charles VIII and Francis I.

The groundwork for this enthusiasm was laid a long time ago. If it is true that sixteenth-century Italy accomplishes its own return to antiquity, getting caught up in veneration for the ruins of the Coliseum, for the last column still standing in the Forum, doggedly deciphering the riches of Trajan's Column—then it is also true that the French, certainly since the days of the Avignon Captivity, and at least since the time of the Angevin expeditions to Naples, find this Italian renewal more than suspect: did not Giotto associate with the French artists brought into Italy by those ambitious princes whose cumbersome heritage Louis XII and his successors had only to gather up? All those noble lords, those knights *sans peur et sans reproche*, who leave their king behind to go and conquer these southern principalities (no doubt completely happy with the windfall, the long rides, the great swordfights—for centuries the French nobility has not been able to do without them, and scarcely can abstain today)—all the great names and the small of France depart, too, to explore those opulent towns, those palaces, those humming workshops, whose reputation has spread quickly throughout France from Villeneuve-lès-Avignon and Lyon to Orléans, Angers, and Paris. In France, Italian styles had preceded the conquerors of Fornovo; their return caused a veritable tidal wave, submerging all other traditions.

So it is that the companions of Charles VIII and Francis I, loyal vassals led into the conquest by their suzerains, are not satisfied with pillaging. They have discovered the Italy of the Medici and those towns that still overflowed with wantonly "wasted" riches, in the countless craftsmen's workshops flourishing in the shadow of princely palaces, alongside of

---

* Bemused: a somewhat ungainly word, yet a rather accurate translation of the style of the king and his companions who, like many of their contemporaries, hardly ever described anything without using the words "beautiful" or "rich." Thus, in the *Lettre du roi à Pierre de Bourbon*, March 28, 1495: "Furthermore, you would not believe the *beautiful* gardens I saw in that town. For, on my word, it seemed all that lacked was an Adam and Eve in order to make a terrestrial paradise out of it, it was so *beautiful* and full of all sorts of good and *beautiful* things . . . and in addition, I found in this country thousands of painters, to whom I shall send you in order to have the most *beautiful* possible ceilings made. . . ."

their open-handed patrons. These workshops are astonishing: full of experts working together, talking profusely for hours on end, relating their good luck while they mix their earth-tones, conversing about rival workshops, about the great masters,* those who have to turn away the apprentices clustered around their school. These are mobile workshops, if we may use the term, since all the masters, great and small, follow princes and bankers, and are not reluctant to heed the summons of the most generous popes; accepting all orders, they divide up the work on the large projects—and Michelangelo is thought to be an eccentric because he wants to handle by himself what others would have done in a team. In these towns, already glutted with artistic work, littered with artists, where the Italian bourgeois and some of the nobility argue about art with an esthetic sense refined by centuries of lavish patronage—in this environment the French have only to choose. They admire both the works and the men; for an "adventurer" like Benvenuto Cellini, who has somewhat boastingly and truculently related his life to us, can but compel admiration, both by the extent of his talents (though the art of the specialist has not yet acquired the prestige it subsequently gains), and by the verve with which he narrates, just as he undertakes, without any care for the future, trips, jobs, and pleasures. The French dream of returning home to reproduce those marvels,

> those very singular things . . . houses with sweet little windows, tall, long, wide, full galleries, pleasant gardens—little courtyards, alleys, gates, hills, little rivers for enjoying yourself and frolicking, where there are old statues in alabaster, white marble, and also porphyry.[3]

The Renaissance—misused word—lies there: in the trip down to the Mediterranean and Naples, taken by those knights weary of their old, ruinous castles, in the trip down to the new world, abounding in extraordinary riches which ask nothing better than to be allowed to escape to France or Germany.† Thus, the noble companions of Charles VIII and Francis I follow the merchants who, for a long time, have been shipping new wares to Lyon, Besançon, and Paris from Italy; these men succeed their Angevin predecessors of the previous century. Italy overflows with riches; France is greedy. When the expeditions draw to a close, when Charles VIII returns to the side of Queen Anne, followed by an endless procession of wagons laden with all that Naples could offer —statues and manuscripts, jewels and holy images—he also brings back

---

* The teaching is oral, and scarcely resembles the way the arts are currently taught; for then, the spoken word is highly esteemed, and the "sciences" of nature are taught simultaneously with the art of painting canvas or sculpting marble. This kind of teaching helps us to understand the universal Leonardo.
† The question of why Italy is so generous with her wealth exceeds the confines of this book; let us put it aside.

painters, engravers, sculptors, even musicians and carpenters, none of whom hesitate for a moment to follow those glorious princes who promise houses, pensions, and commissions in a country which is said to be as beautiful as Italy and where there is so much to be done. Projects run rampant: Charles VIII and Francis I have large ones, and the nobles, small. Cardinal Briçonnet says somewhere that, in Naples, Charles VIII cannot bear to think about Amboise which, before his departure, was his favorite château, and that he is going to build something else; his successor, too, never tires of commissioning châteaux or prospects reminiscent of Italian splendors to be built along the Loire or Seine. These large-scale operations are entrusted to Italians who are honored at the French court and made much of by both the ladies and the nobles—who, in turn, give them more commissions. Italian workshops set the fashion in France, while the king is under the spell of Andrea del Sarto, Rosso de' Rossi, Cellini, and Leonardo—masters who are accompanied by numerous followers, as Il Rosso is surrounded by Miniali, Luca Penni, Domenico de Barbiere—all those who constitute what is pompously called the School of Fontainebleau.

Despite the prestige of the "Mona Lisa" and the wonders of Fontainebleau, what is foremost in this mania for Italy that seized the French aristocracy is the passion for construction, the era's fever of gold running through the fingers, more plentifully than ever before—a fever shared by the Fuggers and the Welsers in Augsburg, those other Italianate princes outside of Italy. For the France of Francis I, the châteaux of the Loire are the passion of the century. Upon the traditional and calm décor of a monarchy recently threatened from the north by the Burgundians and forced to retreat, Francis I and his men grafted this majestic series of large buildings devoted to royal amusements.* They are bold compositions which mingle the old art—with its moats and terrepleins, its wide, round towers, and a whole décor reminiscent of the fortified castle—and Italian art, enamored of symmetry of windows and of the arrangement of doors, and particularly framed decoration in an old style, involving a transposition of antique orders onto the modern building, thus decorating it and giving it that Italian aspect without which nothing would be beautiful for a Briçonnet or a Francis I. Likewise, the interior ornamentation is executed according to the Italian taste, with marble and sculpture from Genoa and Carrara. Foremen, whom people are beginning to call architects, are brought up on texts by Vitruvius and given learned advice by Alberti and Serlio, the great theoreticians of the new architecture; all these designers repeat one another by sketching very "ancient" designs and formulas, which are the secret of perfect success.

---

* If a model is necessary—though each work has its own features and history—let us choose Chambord, begun in 1524.

Its façade must have ornamentation and majesty, and be divided like the human face; the door below and in the center, as is a man's mouth, through which all nourishment passes into the body. The windows correspond to the eyes, one on one side and one on the other; and this is also true of the decoration—the arcades, columns, and pilasters. . . . The first entrance hall is magnificent and corresponds precisely to the human throat, and it is to be wide and open so that files of knights or pedestrians who will frequently pass through there will not cause accidents when they enter in a crowd, for festivals or for other celebrations . . . The courtyard corresponds to the human body, it will be a perfect square or, like the whole body, a rectangle . . .[4]

Let us cut short this rather forced anthropomorphism—which is, however, quite characteristic of the period—and look at the concern for festivals, mentioned above in connection with the entrance hall. The large sixteenth-century châteaux, from Amboise to Saint-Germain, are adapted to that setting for noble life which the kings so greatly enjoy: it is an open-air life, with continuous games in which the court excels, because it is the king's will. The Loire Valley was not merely the last entrenchment of the French kings in the bad days of the past; it was also the setting for the great royal hunts: Chenonceaux and Blois, as well as the large forests of Saint-Germain and Fontainebleau. What kings and princes found in these châteaux—these transient dwellings, one might say, if the words were not offensive—is a joyful resting-place during those trips in which they range over the entire Loire Valley from Orléans to Saumur, from one hunt to the next. Their life consists of long rides, of clashes and tournaments before ladies who also ride horseback, and who participate in the excursions and picnics in the forest, and who sleep out of doors if they do not reach the nearest château by nightfall.*

These large châteaux set among the water and woods of the valley, with their pilasters and their cornices, are also—this should not be overlooked—layover spots and ostentatious hunting lodges, capable of gracefully and effortlessly housing and entertaining, in their long suites of rooms, some hundred-odd people newly arrived from a long outing in the woods, from a picnic whose informality was never intimate. To see Chambord or Blois is to see a long company of knights and ladies, re-

---

* Febvre notes somewhere how sunburned the favorites of the gallant Francis I were. They were constantly on hills and in valleys, in boats or on horseback, taking the sun and rain at the beck and call of the indefatigable sovereign. We are still far from the time when feminine beauty is of a white, indoor kind—a century away from it, as a matter of fact, for Madame de Maintenon notes in 1650 that to go to observe turkeys: "They crammed a mask on our noses, because they feared we would become sunburned." [5] Here the feminine face reflects the ideal of the fashionable world.

turning to the foot of the terraces or the long staircases, with the game they have killed: roe-deer and hinds that have either been thrown to the dogs or roasted in the tall fireplaces.

Furthermore, only the royal entourage can allow itself the ostentation of these large buildings, and their ornamentation. The noble lords, returning from Italy drunk with sun and admiration, and anxious to destroy their old fortified castles without a moment's delay, quickly saw the cost of doing so and realized that such luxury is not within everyone's reach. Moreover, the more ambitious again fall in with one another around the king, who spends money without thinking about it, gives it away as long as there is any in his purse, and attracts all the valuable artists and their followers—those Frenchmen who are beginning to set the fashion. Between the years 1530 and 1540, young Frenchmen by the hundreds—having been seized by the atmosphere of Fontainebleau where the ornamentation of the château, its stucco and old motifs, profusion of unicorns, Bacchuses, and Adonises, serves as a model for everyone—depart in droves for Italy, to round off their work at Florence, Carrara, or Rome. There are many more of them in the 1580s, for it is commonly held that antiquity and nature* can be learned only there.

But thanks to the king's munificence, thanks to the best product of the lord's *rentes* (that is, we should remember, thanks to Spanish gold and silver), and thanks to the proliferation of artists (although this proliferation certainly does not reach the heights that it did in Italy)—châteaux and large residences, rectilinear and symmetrical even to their false windows, gradually increase in the north and in the Midi. From 1550 to 1580, all secular architecture begins to be in the Italian style, adopting its window architraves, its pediments, and its colonnades. In one of those ill-tempered outbursts that came so easily to him, Montaigne said:

> I can hardly contain myself when I hear our architects puffing up with those large words like pilaster, architrave, cornice, Corinthian and Doric style, and other similar words in their jargon; nor can I prevent my imagination from seizing upon the palace of Apollidon at once; and in fact, I find that they are the worthless parts of my kitchen door.[6]

We shall not try to have the last word: this is the moment when princely architecture, that luxury of the "great king Francis," passes into the realm of bourgeois architecture. Somewhat later, colonnades, Doric and Corinthian pediments, meet again in the towns, especially after a

---

* "Attain to the true imitation of nature, for the more one does so the more what one does will be beautiful."[7] In this we see the complete definition of the painting and sculpture of Fontainebleau and the Louvre.

pause at the end of the century, in the great awakening of the years 1600 to 1650.

Returning from Italy, the companions of the king of France—be they the glorious conquerors of 1515 or the sorry defeated army of 1525, be they nobles or not—no longer desired to see anything but palaces, decorations, gardens, in the Italian manner; they dragged behind them, from Naples and Florence, display pieces, foremen, valuable manuscripts* that are responsible for the advance of humanism at that very moment when the work multiplies on the French châteaux. A double movement, then, occurs simultaneously, one aspect of which astonishes the contemporaries who gaze at the work on the Louvre or Jean Goujon's Grecian nymphs in the heart of Paris, while the other leads, less gloriously, to the monopoly of a small number of initiates, who celebrate, in their own way, the return of an antiquity of superabundant and inexhaustible riches.†

► **HUMANIST DARING**

Indeed, during this first part of the sixteenth century, the enthusiasm and fervor for discovery and creation are not the sole property of the artists whose studios France sees springing up on all sides. They are also —at least until 1540—the achievement of those men who spend their lives closeted with manuscripts and old texts, the discoverers of an ever richer antiquity from Rome to Athens. Fearless discoverers (these pre-Christian and post-Christian texts are not without some danger), they are fortunately protected by Queen Marguerite de Navarre and by Francis I himself. In 1530, the latter founds the Collège de France for his humanist friends. Again, humanism is not born with this century; its origins were in Italy. But, until 1534-36 and the fears of the Reformation, it is a glorious age for the admirers of Erasmus, and for the friends of Lefèvre d'Étaples and Guillaume Budé,‡ prince of the humanists.

Prince, not founder. Humanism's parallel with the artistic movement is complete in that genealogy is of little consequence. Thus, in Paris, Lyon, Meaux, and a dozen other cities, there is the same proliferation of re-

---

* We also know and only too well, that Frenchmen brought the "Neapolitan disease" back from Italy. The devastation this produced, though difficult to measure, was undoubtedly very great, as early as the mid-sixteenth century. It was a dread disease, and only so great a lover of laughter as Rabelais can dare to joke about it, presenting his *Gargantua* to: "You most illustrious boozers and precious syphilitic friends. . . ."

† Let us emphasize only the main lines: it stands to reason that confronted with the Italo-Antique invasion, realistic Gothic art does not disappear in France overnight. Even after 1530, when it had taken refuge in tombstone sculpture, recumbent or kneeling figures, it still has a few beautiful results.

‡ It is not just chance that the group proposing to defend "Les Belles-Lettres" and to promote studies in them today, is called the Association Guillaume Budé.

search into an antique world (which the medieval cleric had kept to himself), opening out upon man, the center of the universe. Let us attempt no further definition of this dangerous "ism" which is now to be found everywhere, since we hear on the one hand of the humanism of Dante, on the other of that of the twelfth century. Is not the important thing to recognize the common spirit which prompts Budé to translate, annotate, edit, and similarly prompts Dolet, Sébastien Gryphe, and Robert Estienne? When, between 1520 and 1530, men are all translating and editing; when they protest against the university routine, tied as it is to its *trivium* and *quadrivium*; when they correspond with Erasmus; and when Budé persuades the king to send to Italy, and even to Constantinople, in search of manuscripts—then "humanism" can certainly be defined, however loosely,* as the study and the heightened discovery of man.

What are the attitudes of these erudite scholars of the French Renaissance? First of all a feeling, a spiritual impulse, one not surprising on their part but one which demands careful examination; the strong conviction of the superiority of the intellectual life and spiritual pursuits. Undoubtedly, this assumes the notion of a hierarchy of human activities, and perhaps a touch of vanity as well, on the part of these scholars reading and re-reading their Xenophon or Thucydides, comparing manuscripts, nimbly wielding Greek, Latin, and French. In a sense, the intellectuals have transposed the social hierarchy into their own realm.† To them, the epitome of noble activity is the exercise of the mind, intellectual creation or simple reflection, to which they are proud to devote their lives—with a hint of disdain for manual work. Painters and sculptors writing polemics on the virtues of their respective arts adopt, during this period, the same view: "They (the painters) say that the real difficulties lie in the mind, and not in the body, that the things which by their nature require study and more knowledge are infinitely more noble than the things which bring into play only physical strength." [8] This is a widespread idea from Erasmus to Budé and Dolet, although there are a few dissenters here and there: the good friar Jean de Rabelais, an industrious monk who worked with his hands even during Holy Service; and later, Ronsard: "I hate idle hands" [9]—and who, moreover, calls upon his hands to take up the lute and not a rope or carpenter's plane.

Thus, these men have a streak of pride in their great task, that of

---

* It is not a bad thing to mention one detail, even in a text as cursory as this: the word "humanism" does not exist before the nineteenth century; the supplement to the *Littré* mentions it only cautiously by referring to a text in the *Revue Critique* in 1874.

† They are undoubtedly not responsible for the hierarchy of professions and human endeavor; yet they give it renewed strength, and, until the nineteenth and twentieth century, it is a viable idea transposed even in the newest professions.

investing the mind with a new life; and an unabashed delight in the riches revealed, in the course of these discoveries, by an antique world long buried deep in the monasteries. Yet, they do not, strictly speaking, repudiate the Middle Ages, the Gothic period so markedly scorned in the following century.

Architects and sculptors admire Vitruvius and ruins. The humanists, too, accumulate objects of admiration—the history of Thucydides, and the marvelous "everlasting possession" which served as its purpose, justifies all their toil; the vigor of the Roman soul, that ancient *virtus* of which Cicero, Cato, and numerous others, boasted; finally, to cut the list short, the wealth of knowledge about the world which Pliny discloses in his *Natural History*. Yet one must mention Amyot's monumental *Plutarch* too,* and Robert Estienne's annotated translations of Xenophon and the "divine" Plato, published in Lyon after 1507.

Among specialists in this extremely prolific period, we hear again and again the term "Neoplatonism," necessitated by the importance universally accorded to the author of *The Republic* and *Gorgias*—an antidote to the Aristotle of the schools and the Scholastic Aristotle.† Indeed, there is a double pleasure: that of discovering, understanding, amassing, but also that of sharing one's discoveries by publishing and offering to one's friends a Polybius or a Tacitus. The humanist entourage of Charles V, the champions of Petrarch, could not have known the sense of triumph we can so readily appreciate when we scan the long list of publications and re-publications that these scholarly professors of the Collège de France, those vigorous publishers like Gryphe and Estienne, constantly offer to their friends. They offer them, as well, to that wider public of *robins*, bishops, and monks who gather in various localities, at Meaux, at Fontenay-le-Comte, and especially around Champier at Lyon, to read, compare, discuss. This fervor of humanism is not the achievement of a handful of scholars; it reaches a wider audience, acquainted with Budé, Briçonnet, and that great teacher, Erasmus. It comprises, in fact, a long lineage, from which the second generation is recruited in the 1540s;

---

* Here is an example of this tranquil admiration in a letter by Amyot, in 1559, a long time after Homer, Plato, Herodotus, Polybius, Caesar, Sallust, or Titus Livy: "There is so much pleasure, instruction, and profit in a book, no matter in what style it may be written, provided it is comprehensible, it cannot help being well received by everyone of good judgment, although it is, in short, an abridged collection of everything that is the most memorable and most worthy thing said or done by the greatest kings, captains, and wisest men of the two most noble, virtuous, and powerful nations that ever existed in the world."

† So many Greek names may lead to a misconception; for the Romans were also taken up, and as abundantly commented upon and translated as the Greeks; doubtless because connections with Greece were not as easy, despite the good relations between Francis I and the Sultan. The world of the monastery on Mount Athos, the Acropolis, and the Piraeus were not as familiar to the humanists as were Italy and her ruins, which had been visited and admired by men from Charles VIII to Du Bellay.

those who matured and chose both their style and task amid the menace of prosecutions and of the stake. This is the generation of Scève and Louise Labé, Ronsard (born in 1524) and the Pléiade, and of the good Montaigne who "muses, records, and dictates" with "all his books arranged about him on five rows of shelves," rifling the work of his predecessors. It is the generation which publishes countless elegiac stanzas —but also *La Deffence et Illustration de la Langue Francayse* in 1549, and *Essais* in 1580.

Already a new spirit begins to emerge. But to define that of Budé, Postel, Dolet, and Lefèvre—men who are *sçavans*, complicated, difficult to grasp—what should be put in the foreground? Should we emphasize what Budé, defining his craft, calls philology, the restoration of antique texts, a compilation which is actually discovery (for most of these manuscripts have been buried in monastery libraries and are unknown)? Philology is, strictly speaking, textual criticism. A laborious proceeding, indeed: one surrounds oneself with three or four manuscripts that present variations, interpolations, omissions attributable to the copyist's carelessness or to the poor quality of paper or parchment. Among all these variant readings, one finds the best (not always the most frequently occurring), establishes the most reliable text, and then—child's play after the text has thus been determined—proceeds to translate it. What noble work, then, for Budé to tackle Thucydides, that author who exacts a rare understanding of his language and syntax, as well as a sound knowledge of Greek history and civilization! Textual criticism entails, too, its own justification, in the form of commentaries and explications (hence, Dolet's publication of *Commentaries on Cicero*), and this work of the first humanists corresponds to an intellectual attitude: it is the spirit of criticism, in the best sense of the word—what the *honnêtes gens* of the next century call *l'esprit de finesse*.

The philological method itself gives one some idea of the craving which prompted the compilation, shaping, and enthusiastic publication of all these ancient works: each one discloses a fresh, previously unknown aspect of ancient civilization. There is, for example, the discovery in Seneca, Epictetus, and Marcus Aurelius of a complete philosophy of the art of war, and especially a military morality. To be sure, the generation of Erasmus and Budé did not have the time to comment on everything, but their successors try to, and in the same spirit. Toward the end of the century, the famous Leyden humanist Justus Lipsius publishes a *De re militia libri quinque*, a Stoic military treatise echoed in 1608 by Jean de Billon's *Principes de l'art militaire*.* Thus, the inspiration of humanism is transmitted into all areas, with that encyclopedic curiosity which, at the beginning of this period, animated the author of

---

* Another example: Guillaume Budé published in 1514 a treatise on currency, *De asse*, which led him to deal with the entire material civilization of the Romans.

The Praise of Folly in 1511—the man whom all lovers of antiquity, from 'Spain and Italy to the North Sea, acknowledge as their master: Erasmus.

A period of tireless discovery, a sort of reconstruction of the world, of ancient thought, and of the most diversified ways of life. The most significant possessor of this endless curiosity is Rabelais himself, the Rabelais of *Gargantua* (1534) and *Pantagruel* (1532)—those kindly giants towering several feet above the common run of "completely doltish" mankind—and of Thélème, where "there was no one . . . who could not read, write, sing, play musical instruments, speak five or ten languages, and compare both verse and prose in all of them"; the Rabelais of encyclopedic knowledge and inexhaustible laughter.

But the publisher of Rabelais had some trouble in 1543. *Gargantua* dates from 1534, when there is talk of Protestantism (*i.e.*, Lutheranism, until Calvin in 1536). The humanists antedate the reformers by a few years; not only are they contemporaries, but Calvin also had been the admiring pupil of Budé until the latter refused him and his "innovations." And, to many facile explicators, the humanists—those pagans whose only subject-matter is man—are the harbingers, if not the treacherous antecedents, of the Reformation.

Budé and Lefèvre d'Étaples, the commentator on the Epistles of St. Paul (1512) and translator of the Bible into French (1530), are not of that ilk. Undoubtedly they are capable of criticizing, and sharply, the weaknesses everyone recognized in the Church of Rome: its traffic in indulgences, probably, and a good many other evils which their friend Erasmus, as well, did not refrain from castigating. They are capable, too, of laughing at the little failings of monastic life—laughing as innocently as did the *conteurs* of an earlier age. But beyond that? Guillaume Budé makes room in his Christian faith for ancient culture. Following the example of the early Church, which assimilated pagan tradition and assented to the continued study of pre-Christian authors in its schools, Budé feels that the ancient world cannot help but be a good introduction. Writing his *De transitu hellenismi in Christianismum* in 1535—knowing well at the time the nature of Calvin's temptation when he "disappeared" the year before—he states his conviction that love of belles-lettres contributes to a better understanding of Christian truths. Perhaps there is some slight touch of mysticism in this Greek scholar, but nonetheless Lefèvre and Erasmus share his basic attitude: Lefèvre refuses to go over to the other side, and Erasmus even writes polemics against Luther (*De libero arbitrio*). These admirers of Plato and his doctrine of the soul's immortality, these believers in a God that is neither Zeus nor any lesser Olympian deity, are content to read—in a good text—the Gospels of the Old Testament. They are far from repudiating the Church and the tradition of the early Church Fathers. Calvin cannot pardon them for this, reviles them, and regards them as fools, as Nicodemites. He has spent some time in their schools (even at Geneva, he is capable of throwing their solecisms back at them), but, desiring to carry things further than they are willing to, he pretends to think that they dissimulate out of fear, and that they recoil before the steps to be taken and perhaps the risks to be run.

Another hypothesis maintains that pagan humanism leads to something still worse: atheism—that tremendous word which is all but anachronistic in this century, so steeped in religion.[10] Rabelais, an unbeliever? Or Budé, captivated though he be by the wiles of the ancient world? The danger is not a real one. After all, amassing as they were the entire heritage of the ancients, both before and after Christ, it is natural that the humanists should have "stumbled" on dangerous writings, texts of that quarrelsome period in the early Christian centuries, when Christianity was attacked simultaneously by the Jews and by the supporters of the Hellenistic culture surviving in Alexandria and Byzantium. Thus, we have the polemics of Origen and Celsus—Origen's awkward refutation of the Hellenist Celsus (*Contra Celsum*)—and, similarly, several centuries later, St. Cyril's attack on the emperor Julian the Apostate (*Adversus Julianum imperatorem*). When our scholarly Latinists discover in the words of these weighty refuters the arguments of the Adversary which, going to the heart of the problem, deny the divinity of Christ, they avert their eyes and pass over these impious propositions as foolish ideas. Only one man among them took these writings literally. He dared to revive them, without, however, accepting responsibility for them since (prudently) his work appeared anonymously. Yet he dared: the *Cymbalum Mundi*, published in 1537, is the work of a humanist who presents the Incarnation in terms devoid of mystery, denying the divine nature of Christ. Neither Dolet—worried on several occasions by his questionable writings, suspect not because of their unbelief but for their seeming Protestantism—nor Rabelais went as far as he. Bonaventure des Périers is without a doubt a precursor, almost unique in his time; almost —because in the last years of the century a second-generation humanist, Jean Bodin, circulated but did not publish a work in the same vein: the *Heptaplomeres*, not published until much later. But these humanists of the 1530s obviously are not "free-thinkers" in Pascal's sense.

Those are a few of the complications, and only the most important ones. Let us merely note in passing all the epigrams and scholarly poems of that little world which revolves about the greater names, and which, year in, year out, turns out imitations of Horace, Ovid, and Petronius, in fine distiches and iambs. Its members are quick to quarrel, quick to reconcile. They use surnames and latinized names without rhyme or reason. They compare themselves constantly to Homer and Vergil. Scaliger, Doletus, Vulteïs, Macrinus:* competent versifiers, discoursing on every-

---

* Giulio Cesare Scaligero—an Italian doctor, scholar, and humanist, his *Poetics* is his most famous book; Étienne Dolet—humanist and printer, burned at the stake

thing—or nothing—with that same curiosity which animates the greatest scholars. The great ones are those who write in French—Marot and Rabelais; who compare science and magic (disclosed by Pliny and Varro) with the teachings of the universities and the *collèges*. And it must be remembered that neither Erasmus nor Rabelais has much tenderness for the universities, while the *collèges*—annexes of the Arts Faculty—are hardly a success either, if one is to believe Ronsard and especially Montaigne.*

Thus the humanists nurture belles-lettres, but nurture the sciences as well—for everyone, not merely Rabelais, regards these two as one. The distinction we make today was not current then, and their desire for knowledge did not recoil before the sciences, which were originally collections, accumulations or observations, and descriptions, on the order of Pliny's histories. None of these men—scientists or humanists—are scientists in the modern sense, not even Leonardo da Vinci, who seeks and invents machines of every description: flying machines, "covered cars" behind which the infantry need only march unobstructed, trenches for draining the deepest moats, and means for pulling down high defensive walls. They do not compare hypotheses and experiments, progressing from law to law. Rather, they are primarily compilers, admiring marvels and monsters, accumulating the truths given by the Church (and jealously guarded by the Sorbonne) along with every innovation. The "Copernican Revolution" is no real revolution in minds that are quick to believe everything, and it is Galileo who, somewhat later, pays the price.† Humanistic science is science feeling its way, looking in all directions, utilizing no precise method, posing no precise problems. It is just beginning to use truly scientific tools—that is, numbers and experimentation. Even so, mathematics is still regarded as a system of harmonious, musical, Pythagorean laws which have extraordinary virtue in all fields—hidden virtue, applicable to human things as well. For, in mathematics as well, the distinction between natural sciences and humanistic ones has no meaning. When Bodin deals with the equilibrium of governments within the Republic, he speaks like a mathematician:

---

for his unorthodox opinions; Jean Visagier, often called Voulté and Jean Salomon, nicknamed Maigret—the latter two were also French humanists and scholars.—Trans.
* Famous quotations: Rabelais claims that they "corrupt all the flower of youth," I, 15; Montaigne says of the *collèges*, I, 26, in "On the Education of Children," "They are truly a jail of captive young people. People make them dissolute by punishing them for it in advance. Enter just when they are beginning their lessons: you will hear nothing but cries, both from agonized children and from teachers mad with anger."
† Copernicus' great work, *De revolutionibus orbium cœlestium* dates from 1543: the belief in a heliocentric universe is condemned in the person of Galileo, who publishes his *Dialogo . . . sopra i due massimi sistemi del mondo* in 1632. (This is the famous "Dialogue on the Two Chief World Systems".—Trans.)

One must follow harmonic justice and couple these four points together, to know law, equity, enforcement of law, and the magistrate's duty . . . for just as in the four numbers 4, 6, 8, 12, the same ratio exists from 4 to 6 as from 8 to 12, by the same rule we can determine the relation between enforcement of law and the magistrate's duty. . . .[11]

At the end of the century, Cardan and Viète are still seekers of numerical virtues—and this leads them to Algebra.

It is still experimentation which reveals the works of antiquity. Ambroise Paré, and even Vesalius (who publishes his *De corporis humani fabrica* in 1543) are still steeped in Galen and Hippocrates, both of whom could be read in translation after 1526. They know, too, of Theophrastus, whose *History of Plants* had been published even before that. Vesalius somewhat mixes up those long listings of observations and therapies, and adds great doses of observation which are his own. These conflicts are, as it were, dogmatic; and out of them comes a vague naturalism, difficult to define in our modern terminology imbued with scientific precision. Ready-made ideas, horror of the vacuum, ideas outside nature, the intercession of the spirit world, charms, *virtus dormitiva* —all these ideas are mixed inextricably together. Thus, too, in Ambroise Paré with his animals, monsters, and marvels.*

As a matter of fact, at the end of numerous compilations, numerous studies, in which the Italian universities (especially Padua) had the greatest part of rationalist daring because of their frequent handling of Lucretius and Lucian, at the end of these diligent readings of ancient philosophers and scholars, it is only by bits and pieces, fleeting impulses quickly forgotten, that these scholars came to state the problem of determinism, key to all research. In a short-lived moment without any scientific descendant, Étienne Dolet gave forth his famous expression, without believing it worthy of a better fate than any other: "The order and succession of causes, whose sequence from cause to cause engenders all things." This is the period of science's first halting words.

Without a doubt, their minds are better equipped in the area of theology. Despite distance and the swiftly alerted defiance of the authorities, Lutheranism is very successful in France from 1530 on. There is the incredibly bold Affaire des Placards at Amboise in 1534, and Calvin's *Institutes of the Christian Religion* in 1536. Immediately thereafter,

---

* Worlds where everything is possible, worlds of the why not—dragons, dogs with chicken heads, fish whose bodies are made up of a bunch of grapes, in the *Discours de la momie et de la licorne*. A mentality returning again today among people who, unable to follow the scientific movement, merely record new resourcefulness, often clumsily popularized by local newspapers; irradiated wheat made as fat as a fist? Supermen like Rostand's supertoads? Why not?

prosecutions and burnings at the stake occur—those of Servet at Geneva and of Dolet. The humanistic impetus is not killed, but prudence becomes the rule of the day. How many publications are frustrated, like the *Traité de l'opinion* which Dolet had considered? Greece is still honored, and Du Bellay goes to Rome, publishes the *Antiquitez*, daydreams among the ruins and in the Roman countryside. But insipid elegy can be, in its own way, a means of withdrawal. Ronsard publishes his first collection of *Amours* in 1552, and from 1560 to 1570 he is the official poet and idle charmer of a court that does not want to believe in the calamities awaiting it. Finally, beautiful years, centered about Marguerite de Berry, who does not have the daring of that other Marguerite— Briçonnet's and Lefèvre's. The light verse inspired by Horace and Anacreon, by Cassandra and Helen, will soon be silenced, as will the delicate chansons, courtly love lyrics, love songs, and cantos evoking the great battles of the past—the glory of Marignano by Jannequin, the worthy successor of Josquin des Prés. The St. Bartholomew's Day Massacre in 1572, that slaughter which signaled the beginning of merciless struggle, put an end to it all. Montaigne, withdrawn in his château, found it a good time to leave his troubled country, and from 1580 to 1581 he traveled through Germany and Italy. He had published his *Essais*, in which the eternal question *que sais-je?* is balanced (or, perhaps, screened) by the "Apology for Raymond Sebond," a long eulogy of an undistinguished theological treatise whose virtue lay in its guaranteed orthodoxy. And even Ronsard, at the same time he was producing countless eclogues, ballets, and *entrées*, put the *Misères du Temps* into verse. From 1572 to D'Aubigné's *Les Tragiques*—that outcry of ruthless warfare—there is silence, although not, obviously, total silence. This age of wars is a time of contrasts more violent than usual: Ronsard is fawned upon, set to music, praised everywhere, admired by the court of Charles IX, even after St. Bartholomew's, and he does not really become silent, although aged and isolated by the deaths of his friends, until after 1574. But in the reign of Henry III, in addition to the notorious pleasures of the court, a few episodic pleasures remain, their existence depending on individual cities or the fortunes of war. There are the academies of minor poets, lovers of reading and storytelling; Antoine de Baïf's "Academy of Music" in Paris, which sets to music Psalms and light verse, and warmly hails welcome talents like that of Jacques Mauduit. These activities are oases in the middle of a desert, and witnesses, *rari nantes*, of past grandeur.

This brings us to a final, but important, point. What light does this fluctuating and diverse humanism shed on the France of Francis I and Henry II? We can see hundreds of these works—editions of ancient texts, translations, commentaries—lined up on the shelves of our great libraries. We can even measure their success, count their republications (especially since their printings are small, one or two hundred copies at best)—Rabelais, Lefèvre, Erasmus, Amyot, Plutarch. We can still see these enthusiastic scholars, who by no means concealed their whereabouts, traveling and discussing across France and across Europe—from Lyon to Paris, Meaux to the Loire Valley*—often imprudently, like Servet when he took refuge in Geneva. We see them, sometimes we can just guess at their presence, undertaking long discussions and scholarly debates at their learned gatherings, for example those of Sébastien Gryphe, the great Lyonnais publisher. We see these loquacious commentators on new works, constantly amenable to the most flattering comparisons, as Jean Bodin's *Six Livres de la République* with the *Republic* of Plato. Eventually their polemics grapple even with the difficult problem of currency, as in the case of Malestroit, Bodin, and La Tourette around 1568. What, in short, do they amount to? Several hundred Lyonnais and Parisians, several dozen lawyers and clerics, Latinist scholars from the better *collèges* taking pleasure in recounting the most minor news item in Latin, and dreaming of some great work. In that period, when the universities had recently opened their doors to laymen not destined for the priesthood; when the *collèges*, distant forebears of secondary education—that intermediate path between the thinking avant-garde and the bulk of the people—are still very scarce in the shadow of the universities; in that time when the ideal of the dominating class, a pugnacious nobility applauding Henry II until his last breath, rests on sword thrusts and large hunts rather than on scholarly studies (despite Ronsard and Du Bellay)—in that time, the great humanist impetus and its intellectual ideal remain the privilege of a few thousand Frenchmen who think and speak in Latin, live an intellectual adventure whose outcome they cannot, and often will not, measure. They are precipitated into a discovery whose applications have not yet been exhausted without thought of the immense multitudes who do not, cannot, follow them. It is not yet the time when spoken Latin becomes an objectionable piece of snobbery, an affectation distinguishing the speaker from the *vulgum pecus*.† Eventually, they are unknown to the rest of the

---

* One would not set up a geography of sixteenth-century French humanism like a solidly factual collection of maps of the châteaux. Birthplaces do not mean very much, and the places where they resided are badly known. We can readily discern several large centers: Lyon, Paris, the Loire Valley—with the court and the châteaux; then Nérac, because of Marguerite de Navarre. But the entire Massif Central and Brittany would not be included, nor would the Lorraine which certainly seems void of any humanist influence.

† This occurs in the following century, when accusations are frequently heard against little writers who speak Latin so they will not be understood. Sorel, in *La Bibliothèque française*, speaks his mind about an author of a treatise addressed to Guez de Balzac in the following manner: "They did not avoid the opportunity to reproach him for having written this work in Latin in order to deprive interested people of

population, which does not read and which has no source of culture other than oral tradition and the stone images placed before their eyes. These scholarly humanists were unable to attain the effectiveness of the other great actors in the century, the Reformers. But, in Calvin's instance and in that of the other leaders of Geneva, Basel, and Strasbourg, the conflict is in another sphere; it is a conflict encompassing the total man, involving his own salvation—not the death of Socrates, however beautiful.

► **RELIGIOUS DARING: CALVIN TO LOYOLA**

The Reformation in France: some feel that it has already begun in the Paris of 1530 when, at the Sorbonne, the good and gentle Lefèvre d'Étaples lovingly comments on St. Paul; and in this same city—or at its gates, in Montmartre—in the very same year, a strange person comes to make his retreat, a person who dreams of reconquest: Ignatius Loyola, soon to be the founder of the Society of Jesus. Actually Lefèvre, who favors the monastic reforms of the 1520s, is not an "evangelist"; at most, he is a thorough reader of the Gospels, and is charmed by the narratives which set the living Jesus, the Jesus of Golgotha, before his eyes. But he goes no further, and does not consent to derive, from an imprudent phrase of St. Paul, that "justification by faith alone" which Luther had been extolling for years.

Before Calvin, therefore, France had to deal primarily with Lutheranism. When, as a very young man (he was born in 1509), Calvin studies with Budé, preparing and then publishing his commentary on Seneca's *De Clementia* in 1532, like any other good humanist who has chosen his field and supplements the common knowledge in this fashion—during this time the new doctrines are already widespread, even among the entourage of the prince of learning, where someone called Farel is making ready to desert belles-lettres for a battle having other implications.*

After 1517 when Luther launched his Ninety-five Wittenberg Theses throughout Germany, when he experienced his extraordinary adventure —excommunication, pursuit, refuge at Wartburg—his ideas were making their way into France: through the free city of Strasbourg, a town as wide open to currents of thought as to those of trade, a place of wel-

---

any knowledge of it; people who mainly were women and a few courtesans who understood no other language but French." On the other hand it is true, and much more frequent, that there is a concern for making everyone understand; Descartes himself translates his *Discours de la Méthode*.

* Farel left Paris and spent most of the rest of his life in Switzerland working for Protestantism. He entered Geneva in 1533 and "conquered" it by 1535 when he held a public debate on the issues involved in the Reform Movement, and the people of the city declared in favor of him. He immediately brought Calvin there; the latter stayed in Geneva until his death in 1564 except for a brief period of "exile" from 1538-1541.—Trans.

come and contact between two worlds, where protestations against Rome created an endless competition; and even through Alsace, going up the Rhine and the Ill to Mulhouse and Basel, then proceeding through Burgundy, and from there simultaneously to both Paris and Lyon.* This pathetic appeal of the Augustinian monk, to a faith returned to its sources, purified of all the redundancies with which centuries of tradition had encumbered it, certainly moved more than one heart, even among the entourage of Francis I. It fails to win over Briçonnet or Marguerite de Navarre to the German prophet, for they lean to a more orthodox interpretation of the most dubious texts; yet around these people many others, less prudent or less scrupulous, adhere enthusiastically to him—perhaps as early as 1520. But the truly dramatic turn in events, the moment when the king had his counselors take cognizance—worried and frightened cognizance—of how thoroughly Lutheranism has impregnated France, occurs in 1534: the Affaire des Placards involves posters which spread a few Lutheran "truths" even into the château where the king is residing. Despite some misgivings on the part of Francis I—diplomatic misgivings, or other kinds, due to his foreign policy against Charles V—suppression follows, and, until 1598, suppression and then open struggle scarcely cease for a moment.

In 1534, however, John Calvin—that young man with the dark stare—enters into the fray. He leaves the dangers of France for Strasbourg, then Basel, and is already drafting his *Institutes*, whose Latin version appeared in Basel in 1536, followed by numerous French editions from 1541 on. At twenty-seven this humanist, who doubled as a jurist, who knew the best teachers of his day, in Orléans and Paris, takes arms against the Church of Rome. He rallies to his side the persecuted French Protestants who have been bewildered by the king's attitude which, until 1534, had seemed almost favorable, and is unafraid to defy his king to whom the *Institutes* are dedicated. Calvin says that he still hopes for the king's understanding, and appeals simultaneously to his heart and to his intelligence; he vows his companions' obedience, but in the final *envoi*, foresees the worst, with a serenity which indicates fairly well how many illusions he harbored with respect to Francis I: "But if, on the one hand, the vilifications of the malevolent so possess your ears that the accused have no place in which to defend themselves; and on the other hand, if you fail to restore order and the hot-headed furies continue to practice their cruelties with imprisonments, whips, tortures, maimings, and burnings; we, like sheep consigned to the slaughterhouse, will certainly be reduced to the farthest extremity, so much so moreover that we shall

---

* But not through the Lorraine, or at least not the southern part: Metz, even more than Nancy, is a town without either a great intellectual life or a great religious one —there are no more Protestants there than humanists. But Alsace was enough to insure the transmission of ideas, along with that other way station of Flanders-Picardy.

possess our souls in patience; and we shall await the mighty hand of the Lord, which will unquestionably show itself when the time is ripe, and will appear so armed as to deliver the poor from their affliction and to punish the scornful who so brazenly make merry at this hour. May the Lord, King of kings, grant that your throne be established in righteousness, and your Kingdom in equity."

This John Calvin covers the ground traveled twenty years earlier by Luther, yet he is not satisfied with following in the footsteps of the Augustinian monk, even though he too foretells the downfall of the Church of the Antichrist. Calvin goes off in a different direction, in a manner one might call more crude, more logical, and more mystical; he uses another interpretation of the Gospels to found not Lutheran churches, but a Church, a Calvinist one. He establishes himself in Geneva in 1541, and reveals himself to be an admirable organizer of the new Rome, which Luther was never able to do. He is a new prophet, with an amazing polemical talent—we have already alluded to his *Excuse à Messieurs les Nicodémites*,* which rallies around him the hesitant French Protestants, straws in the wind, blowing from Zwingli to Bucer, Farel, and Castalion. The Calvin of Geneva, of the *Institutes*, founds a new Christian religion.

Undoubtedly his point of departure is the same as Luther's: a return to Scripture as the sole source of faith against tradition and against all the "farrago" the Church Fathers have heaped upon the pages of Matthew, Mark, Luke, and John. These interpretations and commentaries have no more value than one's reflection in a looking glass; the ideal is still the primitive Church, if not Palestine itself, "at the never-to-be-forgotten hour of the Apostles." Similarly, there is to be a return to a religion whose center is Jesus—and God the Father; but it will have no place, not even the smallest one, for the manifold saints who proliferated in the Middle Ages, no place either, or almost none, for the Virgin, that ill-used Mother, whose worship—so lively since the days of St. Bernard —is in Calvin's eyes a kind of idolatry. Finally, there is to be a return to Saints Paul and Augustine, especially to Paul, whose Epistles supply a healthy part of the Calvinist arsenal. All this implies the same disdain for Rome, for her abuses, her traffic in indulgences, her practices—Rome, home of the Antichrist. But Calvin takes it up with a more rigorous attitude than that of his German predecessor; hence, he comes to rather different conclusions about doctrine and practices.

Calvin accepts justification not by, or according to, works, but justification only by faith. But he stops short there and goes straight on to predestination, all the while imposing the same "morality" on the faithful

---

* See p. 268n. with reference to Budé. The title alone is a beautiful touch: Nicodemus was the high-ranking Pharisee who went to visit Jesus at night: the most timid of the timid. The full title is: *Excuse à Messieurs les Nicodémites, sur la complainte qu'ils font de sa trop grand'rigueur.*

as that of the Catholics; this morality, based on the gratuity of the moral act, is far from Luther's too famous *pecca fortiter sed crede fortius*. And, for Calvin, predestination is the basis of God's freedom, His omnipotence, and His divine grace. There are none of those misgivings, that foreknowledge mixed with predestination, which for Luther further confuse things that are already not simple. Similarly, Calvin rejects transubstantiation, as well as the real presence in the communion—another compromise in Luther, another bit of clarity in the Frenchman, who reduces the bread and wine to visible symbols—symbols of a promise which has actually been made, and which Calvin does not question. Hence, Calvinist thought is not so much a reworking of Lutheranism as it is a meditation, passionately lucid, even to the remote boundaries of mysticism.

Thus, Calvin offers the Protestants as coherent as possible an image of the Word, as he reads it in the Gospels. To be sure, his basis, like Luther's, is the Christian's personal encounter with his God; the Church has no goal other than the facilitation of this encounter, this act of love. But for Calvin one may say that the divergence separating him from Catholic thought is greater, the rupture more total. Calvin extends his will, so full of logical energy, as far as it will go, into every realm, and breaks with Luther once more in the *Institutes* on the subject of the relations between Church and State. Refusing to replace the Pope's authority with that of the Prince, as was done in Germany, Calvin separates the Church from secular authority, be it exercised by magistrates or princes; he allows co-operation between them, in order to enforce Christian precepts—precisely as he did in Geneva—but maintains two distinct powers. This is a bold conception whose political implications are obvious, although they are not immediately felt, so closely associated are the town councils, during the first experiment at Geneva, with the decision of the Consistory. No less important, however, are the definitions given in the *Institutes* concerning the duties of Christian citizens, those "lesser authorities" to whom Calvin gives a special place in the ecclesiastical administration entrusted to those assemblies of ministers and elders which are just like little democratic communities—even to the risks presented by the "confused animal" in the Consistories. The care with which, in his *Institutes*, Calvin defines himself with respect to philosophy, men of letters—so often Nicodemites—and the state, reveal even more of this orderly man, to whom such carefulness is more than petty detail.*

---

* He even concerns himself with music, to which, like everyone in those days, he attaches a great deal of importance. In Geneva he prescribes the singing of hymns—in unison, not in parts—Psalm recitatives or purified popular songs. This is the church music that played so large a part in the Calvinist triumph in the most diverse milieux.

Confronted with so many prophets of Protestantism, founders of churches which, although they lack stability, blaze with divine love, at Strasbourg, that city of Protestant experimentation, at Wittenberg and Zurich—the man from Geneva makes of this second-rate town inhabited by merchants who, until his arrival, are greedy for wealth and pleasures, his capital and his frame of reference. After Farel, who with Théodore de Bèze and many others, aroused it as early as 1538, Calvin makes it an austere town, allowing no images or statues; it remained the Calvinist capital, directed by the Consistory and the Councils with an iron hand that punished the slightest deviation and quelled all rebellion; in it Calvin remains until his death in 1564. And, in the heart of this city so quickly won over to that exigent religion, there are the Academy and the University, where Calvin educates the ministers who are to spread the good word through all French-speaking countries, and even several others—those ministers who are held in awe because of their missionary spirit and their intellectual strength. The Academy, both seminary and theological faculty, indeed holds on to the young men who flock there from the Swiss cantons, from all over France and the Rhine Valley, for years on end. Based on a sound humanist education, followed by an extensive study of theology, necessarily involving the study of Catholicism as well as the new faith, this Academy turns out disciples of the new Rome. These men are zealots, learned polemicists, who win over to their side the nobles and bourgeois of the towns where they go and preach. They besiege France—even Paris—from within, reconquering the entire Parisian basin from the Lutherans and stretching the length of the Rhine Valley, spreading far and wide the little pamphlets of the *Ordonnances Ecclésiastiques*, the vade mecum of good Calvinists. Now, between 1530 and 1540, even before the Academy, not organized until 1559, is able to supply these legions of missionaries that Geneva sends as far away as Poland and Scotland, Calvinist writings have won over to his cause not only the many little, inspired preachers, but also a whole segment of the nobility and the commercial bourgeoisie living in the France of Henry II. This latter continued, throughout his entire reign, to prepare for the inevitable repression—even to the point of making peace with Philip II in 1559, for the purpose, as people usually say, of devoting himself entirely to it.*

While, during the decade between 1560 and 1570, Frenchmen gradually are becoming accustomed to civil war, Calvinism is winning over all of France: a success which is relative only in that there are no towns or regions of which one can say with certainty that they were conquered entirely by the new faith before the wars. There are increasingly numerous towns having reform groups, some even with churches, town meet-

---

* The Peace of Cateau-Cambrésis—virtually ending *foreign* French wars for the remainder of the sixteenth century.—Trans.

ings, and skeletal consistories—from Lyon to Montpellier, from Pau to
Abbeville and Amiens, passing through the towns along the Loire, and
Paris. But on the other hand, the countryside constitutes a great mass,
unresponsive and largely unaffected, except in the environs of the
towns; a passive mass, not hostile, because the Genevans are not numerous enough to preach the Gospel to all those in the country. And,
prompted by persecutions that gradually increase after 1547, the Protestants are getting out of towns and kingdoms that are too dangerous,
taking refuge in Geneva—which to the great displeasure of the natives
becomes invaded by Frenchmen—or in the towns of Alsace, part of the
Empire, or in Swiss cantons. As Febvre describes them, they are the first
people to be "uprooted for their faith" and their mobility is one of the
most powerful means for the spreading of the Calvinist doctrine. In this
second half of the sixteenth century, they are already creating that European solidarity of Protestantism which, after St. Bartholomew's Day, asserts itself, extending from the Netherlands, lately revolted against
Philip II, to Germany. It confronts that other, traditional solidarity of
Catholic countries, sustained (perhaps partly because of the Inquisition
and of the zeal of Philip II) by the two Mediterranean peninsulas—
Italy and Spain.

Yet at the point where the Calvinist nobles no longer fear to use their
weapons in defense of their right to affirm Calvin's God, at the point
where, despite the appeals for leniency coming from Catholics like Anne
du Bourg and Protestants like Sébastien Castalion,* both parties prepare to come to blows—at this point the Catholic Church has all its
forces reassembled, and has the militia for reconquest: the Society of
Jesus.

This immoderate effort, both to regain lost ground (a term all too
well taken over from military strategy) and to restore to western Europe
that Catholic unity upon which the medieval centuries had lived, also
shows the capacity of "this century which wills to believe" † for religious
boldness. Side by side with those kings for whom religious unity is a
political axiom (as it is for princes as well: Germany, at the time of the
Religious Peace of Augsburg, does not think any differently), the Catholics of the years between 1530-1550 are living through something like a

---

* *De hæreticis, an sint persequendi* (1554). In 1559, Anne de Bourg, a member of
the Parisian Parlement, protests against the persecution of "those who call, from
among the flames, upon the name of Jesus Christ."
† The expression is from Febvre: with this extremely fortunate expression he charac-
terizes, with a stroke of the pen, the entire religious spirit of the sixteenth century;
for the preceding medieval centuries, so fervent in their piety, did not *will* to believe
at all; faith was taken for granted, without the intense emotion that Luther, Calvin,
and Loyola must bring to it. The difference is that between simple belief and the
desire to believe, the latter being noteworthy for the multiplication of new institutions: the Sacred Heart and the Immaculate Conception are two such impulses of
faith.

moral crisis, which for some is full of fervor, for others (still numerous in 1560) full of hope for reconciliation and settlement. For Ignatius Loyola, who in 1526 wrote the *Spiritual Exercises,* a method of strengthening an attacked faith, this crisis is mystical: in a Paris which between 1530 and 1534 is overrun by the satirical lampoons of the Lutherans, he conceives the idea of that society dedicated to collective reconquest. He has it approved in Rome, and immediately heads for the two besieged areas, Germany and France. A former soldier, he founds an army which strikingly resembles the Calvinist troops in Geneva. First, the dozen or so years of classical education, and then theology, give these soldiers of Rome the same intellectual soundness that they give the Calvinists. Discipline and obedience to Rome do the rest, and in particular that missionary spirit that soon will be unfurled not only throughout Europe, but through the new worlds as well, from Paraguay to Japan. In a Catholic world already encumbered with monastic orders which remain lively and active, this is an extraordinary triumph.

The first achievement of the Society of Jesus is the leadership of the Council of Trent which lasted, with a few pauses along the way, from 1542 to 1563. Many bishops came there, still hoping for the impossible doctrinal conciliation; it was there that the Society brought about the total reaffirmation of the traditional doctrinal positions—those dealing with the central problem of justification by faith, as well as on all the other points, we might say the details, such as the worship of saints. This reaffirmation is made with extreme caution, reproducing the contested texts and commenting upon them word by word,* thus scrupulously anathematizing Protestant writings line by line. Finally, the Council gives a great deal of space in its decrees to disciplinary reform of the clergy. Introduction of this reform into France after 1563 creates problems: it undermines the royal privileges acknowledged in Bologna in 1516.

However, from the 1560s on, the Society's greatest triumph is reconquest. Even in the heart of the civil wars the Jesuits, who are skillful confessors (too skillful, people will soon exclaim), circumspect spiritual advisors, adapt themselves to the exigencies of the faithful. Taking care not to entrust the *Spiritual Exercises* to run-of-the-mill penitents, they rapidly acquire a reputation in the towns, a reputation which attracts to

---

* The Decree on justification reads in part: ". . . whereas the Apostle says that man is *justified by faith and freely:* (Rom. 3:24, 28) these words must be understood in that sense which the perpetual consent of the Church has held and expressed, namely, that we are said to be *justified by faith* because faith is the beginning of salvation, the basis and root of all justification . . . *justified freely* because nothing preceding justification, neither faith nor works, merits the very grace of justification. . . ." [12] And an example from a Canon: if anyone says that from the time of Adam on, man's free will is lost and extinct, that it is only a name, or rather a name without reality, or else a fiction introduced by the devil . . . as he is against the Church so be he anathematized.

them both the exceptional and the lukewarm. They also are the founders of new *collèges* near their houses, and thus can offer to the townspeople, who have been living for years in a humanist atmosphere, a new form of education. This is codified in 1584, in the Society's *Ratio Studiorum:* as always, Latin is taught, and a place is made therein for pre-Christian antiquity, duly purged of all dangerous writings (Lucretius, and even certain pages of Cicero), an antiquity which, on the contrary, is made to approach Christianity, thus enjoying the prestige of humanism. But the Jesuit *collèges* also teach the fine ways of urban life—dancing, music, deportment, manners—worldly lessons that certainly did much for the reputation of the famous Collège de Clermont at Paris, as well as for several of the others. From that point, as early as before 1570, there are amazing results,* even more in Germany, indeed, than in France. The Society of Jesus seems omnipresent. With several thousand men, it has emissaries everywhere, and by the end of the century its *collèges* are all over France—despite the handicaps, the dangers of war, with which the Society finds itself involved. The Jesuits rapidly come to symbolize the Party of Rome, as opposed to the old Gallicans, whose insularity was strengthened by the very excesses of foreign interventions. But at this point we enter upon another period, for the proponents of the Counter-Reformation as well as for the Protestants.

► **THE AGE OF FANATICS**

For almost forty years, from 1560 to 1598, the French lived through civil war, the war of brother against brother, mingled with English and Spanish interventions. Although it undoubtedly did not make of France that cadaverous body in which the skillful management of public opinion, on the part of good King Henry's entourage, would have us believe, the better to glorify the recovery during the early years of peace, from 1598 to 1610—still, it was a relentless war, when fanatic violence prevailed over the spirit of proportion, over that desire for peace which ordinarily actuates Frenchmen. It was a bitter experience: religious passion was backed up by resentment and political opportunism; and royal authority —which for centuries had consolidated France's unity, strengthened her interior peace, and reinforced her boundaries—was severely shaken and, to a certain extent, this crisis of authority governs the seventeenth century and the future of the monarchy.

Between the reigns of Francis II and Henry IV there are eight religious wars, with intermittent respites during which the antagonists catch their breath, seek new forces and allies; these are marked by long parleys, in

---

* But this is not yet the Society's most glorious period; after their reinstatement in 1603, a magnificent era begins, during which the Jesuits—royal confessors, masters of towns, great baptizers—momentarily seem to be the omnipotent directors of the Church. *See* Chapter IX.

Protestant expansion until 1560 and the large Roman Catholic Collèges around 1640

ENGLAND

ANTWERP
HONDSCHOOTE
IEPER
ARMENTIÈRES
BOULOGNE · TOURNAI
LILLE · BAVAY
ABBEVILLE
CHARLEVILLE
MAINZ
EU
DIEPPE · AMIENS SAINT-QUENTIN
YVETOT BEAUVAIS NOYON
BAYEUX ROUEN · CLERMONT-de-l'Ois REIMS
St-LÔ CAEN LISIEUX · PONTOISE · SENLIS EPERNAY VERDUN · METZ
EVREUX JUILLY · CHÂTEAU-CHÂLONS PONT-à-MOUSSON
St-MALO PARIS MEAUX THIERRY BAR-LE-DUC NANCY
ALENÇON VITRY STRASBOURG
RENNES VITRÉ PITHIVIERS TROYES VASSY
LE MANS ORLÉANS MONTARGIS MULHOUSE
LAVAL VENDÔME VESOUL BASEL
ANGERS LA FLÈCHE BLOIS DIJON MONTBÉLIARD
TOURS VIERZON SANCERRE BESANÇON
SAUMUR BEAUNE DÔLE BERN
NANTES CHINON BOURGES NEVERS NEUCHÂTEL
POITIERS SAINT-AMAND AUTUN POLIGNY LAUSANNE
FONTENAY SAINT-MAXIENT LA CHÂTRE MOULINS GENEVA
NIORT
LA ROCHELLE EFFIAT ROANNE
SAINTES LIMOGES RIOM BILLOM LYON CHAMBÉRY
COGNAC
PÉRIGUEUX MONTBRISON VIENNE
BORDEAUX SARLAT GRENOBLE
TOURNON
PRIVAS VALENCE
BERGERAC VALS
CAHORS RODEZ AUBENAS EMBRUN
NÉRAC AGEN JOYEUSE CARPENTRAS SISTERON
CONDOM MONTAUBAN NÎMES AVIGNON
TOULOUSE MONTPELLIER BEAUCAIRE
PÉZENAS AIX
CARCASSONNE TOULON
LIMOUX

Atlantic Ocean

● Pre-1536 centers of Protestantism
◉ Protestant strides from 1536 to 1560 } I
◐ Collèges sponsored by the Oratorians } II
⊕ Collèges sponsored by the Jesuits
○ indicates towns of I and II
xxxx Boundary about 1560

METZIG

which the moderate factions of the two parties tried to establish, if not a basic conciliation allowing a real peace, at least a *modus vivendi*. Before St. Bartholomew's Day, even Catherine de' Medici strove to do so, not without some hesitation; she distinguished between those heretics who erred only in their faith, who could be brought back to the fold by the "path of leniency," and those who were in a state of "manifest sedition," for whom "severity" was in order.[13] This compromise was promptly condemned by the intense emotions of both groups involved in the war: thus Amboise, Beaulieu, and Saint-Germain, places where truces were made and discussions held, echo the large battles of Arques and Ivry, as well as the ravaged towns of Issoire, Montbrison, and Privas, which were captured and then taken back again. The merciless war gradually increases the number of *politiques*, French patriots who repulsed the excesses of both parties and disavowed the action of the Leaguers as well as those of the bloodier Huguenots. Among those patriots, in the terrible years between 1584 and 1594, is the very talented author of the *Satyre Ménippée*.*

How was this war maintained for so long, what excesses did the Protestants and Catholics commit? The war went through many metamorphoses both of appearance and of meaning, during those forty years—from the mutual exchange of blows at the beginning, to the Parisian and Spanish insurrection under Henry IV. The year 1572 was a carnage; after 1584, with the death of the Duke of Anjou, last heir of the Valois, it became a patriotic war. There are, however, a few dominating characteristics: first, the intense religious emotion that knows no tolerance, that second-rate virtue rejected with scorn by anyone who knows in his heart that he holds the truth. Secondly, there are the prudent *politiques* who, in the wilderness, preach an unthinkable coexistence, and seem to be cowards or, at the very least, men of little faith. In a time when the all-too-famous phrase "Who is not with me, is against me," is on everyone's lips, the truth torn between two powerful parties quickens both sides' eagerness for battle.

Religious truth is commingled with politics: the Catholics defend, certainly, the kingdom's political unity, but they want also to protect the close union between the Catholic Church and the monarchy repre-

---

* The high point of this satire's vehemence occurs in its denunciations of the Spanish king's underhanded maneuvers in France—the speech by the Sieur d'Aubray: "His doubloons and his men came only after they had long been sticking out their tongues at us, and only when we could do no more, no matter how much earlier he had been able to help us; he is fattening us up to sell us, as butchers do with their hogs; yet out of fear too that we will die too soon, for he is anxious to preserve us for the greatest possible ruin, he prolongs our languishing lives, which he gives us in small doses as a jailer feeds criminals in order to make them last until their executions. What has become of all those millions of doubloons he brags of having spent to save our State? We see none of them in the hands of the people; most of them are in the hands of our enemies—in your hands, Sirs, princes, governors, captains, preachers, you who keep them tightly locked in your coffers."

sented by Reims—with its symbol-laden ostentation—by the release of
ring-doves, and the visit to Saint-Marcoul de Corbeny the day after the
ceremony. However, the Protestants could not hope to win all of France:
those of them who cannot bring a personal faith to the royal miracles
hoped, at the very most, to impose a Protestant king on a France that
remained Catholic, at the time when that relapsed heretic, Henry of
Navarre, finds himself the only heir to the crown and still a Protestant—
would they, in this manner, make all of France into a new Geneva?
For them, religious unity is a goal which is, at least, more remote: yet
this unity, this great idea of the times, does not explain everything.

Thanks to other intense emotions, the war is continued, renewed, re-
kindled. For twenty years, Protestants and Catholics are led by the
nobles, the dukes, the great names of France—the Guise, Rohan, and
many others, even Montluc and that terrible Baron des Adrets; in the
struggle for or against the king they find their unique opportunity, which
for half a century had been missing, of hacking the enemy in two, of
leading the rough camp life, of following in hot pursuits and laying
ambushes. All this is within the old tradition of feudal unrest, which,
under the heavy hands of the preceding kings, Francis I and Henry II,
had tended to pass into the condition of old and pious memories.

Not that men like Coligny, the Guise, Sully, and Mayenne were
hurled into the fray without having any religious convictions; not that
they did not sell out, some to German princes or Elizabeth I of England,
others to Philip II of Spain. In the complex psychology of these great
swashbucklers, who joyfully abandon mock battles, tournaments, and
other fantasies for real warfare, religious passions are of prime importance. But feudal atavisms and the justifiable fear of the extension of
royal powers have their place too. On the battlefields and in the war
councils, the nobility rediscovers the military and political role of which
a far-seeing monarchy had, for a long time, been gradually and skillfully
depriving them. And the good towns followed in the wake of this fervent
nobility: jurists won over by Calvin's fiery logic; merchants and financiers, attracted by the re-establishment of terrestrial success which Calvinism seems to grant to the more fortunate of that century; *bons bourgeois* and humbler people, concerned with their eternal salvation, and
swept along by the long-famous energy and fervor of the Leaguers'
sermons.* The towns supplied the money, weapons, and fortresses, and

---

* An energy rather well divided, in this time when everything is put into the bad
verse, anagrams, and puns that we find collected in L'Estoile's *Journal*. The Duke of
Mayenne is treated by his opponents thus:

Duke of Monks

You traitor and black-magician, base Lorraine parricide,
Cheater stuffed with ambition, bastard without title,
You paternosterizing, hypocritical rebel,
Damned atheist: God, faith, and law you have denied. . . .

the foot soldiers, and kept alive a war that the nobles could not have maintained by themselves; the clerics fanaticized the towns, but the men of power led them into paths which were not always merely religious.

Let us turn from this strife, which ends in 1598 when the Edict of Nantes brings about a Catholic victory, and look only at the weakening of royal authority. From the facts, it is rather clear that the reign of Henry III was not so bad as the Leaguers said it was, and that it was fairly easy for Henry IV to re-establish order, after his conversion in 1594. Yet in those years of peacemaking, the greatest harm has already been done: the monarchic ideal has been severely injured by the "millions and millions" of satiric lampoons and subversive theories which were born in the heat of wartime and spread throughout the cities. In this fact lies one of the keys to the relentlessness with which, in the following century, the successors of Henry IV had to go about restoring and consolidating royal authority. The Protestants were the first to contest this authority—immediately after St. Bartholomew's Day, that unspeakable treason, that royal perjury perpetrated by Catherine de' Medici and Charles IX. Within several months, some extremely serious treatises, which set forth how and why a monarchial power ceases to be legitimate, spread throughout France. There were the lectures of Théodore de Bèze at the Calvinist Academy, the *Droit des magistrats sur leurs sujets*, which emphasizes the duties as well as the rights; the learned treatise by a legal expert, Hotman, called *Franco-Gallia* (1574); somewhat later, in 1579, *Vindiciæ contra tyrannos*. Not to mention the numerous pamphlets against the "misbehavior of Catherine de' Medici" (*Tocsin des Massacreurs, Réveil matin des Français, Vie de sainte Catherine*). Henceforth, the Protestants, for whom obedience to the prince was previously an unquestioned part of their doctrine, acknowledge that the subjects of a perjured king are absolved of obedience to him. Hotman and the new theoreticians bring up a contract theory, which is a democratic basis of the social order. Most of the Protestant nobility were killed in Paris on August 25, 1572; thus, this theory is emphasized in the hands of those jurists brought up on history and Roman law, those ministers long inured by their consistory life to an egalitarian society. The French Protestant will never return to the monarchical devotion of the Catholics.

There is a reversal of roles, a return of violent emotion. After 1584, when according to the "Salic" law, Henry III has no legitimate heir save Henry of Navarre, when the Leaguers' monks let loose against Henry III, in the whole kingdom and even in Paris, the time comes for the most exalted among them to speak of tyrants and tyranny, and particularly to set forth the idea of the legitimacy of tyrannicide: regicide is a duty for subjects of a king who becomes illegitimate that day he stops protecting the good Frenchmen of the League, the day he ceases to be king of the

Catholics. To be sure, in these vituperations* of what the *Satyre Ménip-pée* aptly calls the "Jesuit cudgels," and of the other Capuchins let loose against the two Henrys, it is not a matter of a social-contract theory, but simply of striking out once more against that person to whom the Church gives a sacred character, against that king who is the Lord's Anointed. Furthermore, contemporaries who have seen Henry III and Henry IV assassinated have no delusions about the matter. In 1589, after the death of Henry III, that "monstrous and prodigious assassination" by the monk Jacques Clément, the following extremely lucid lampoon circulates through Paris:

> Now, with his belly pierced by an envenomed dagger,
> Falls the *anointed* king, by a monk's deceit and hand.
> Fear, Bourbon! And all of you, pursued by so many shades,
> Fear! And for you too, Sixtus, the same doom awaits! Why Not!
> Now at last *are revealed the holy secrets of kingdoms;*
> *We learn that the Gods are nothing at all, those who*
> *Were said to be Gods even by God Himself.*†

The war is over in 1598. The Spanish withdraw to their own lands, in Flanders and Spain; Philip II renounces at Vervins the ambitions he cherished for putting his daughter on the French throne; the Protestants are admitted into the kingdom by the Edict of Nantes, a true peace treaty, signed by the king and those companions-at-arms who had become his opponents. It is, beyond a doubt, a Catholic victory, one that was established as early as 1593-1594, when Henry IV decided to be instructed in Catholicism, and abjured, for the second and last time, his Protestant faith. But the victory is difficult and incomplete: in his preamble to the Edict, the king does not conceal the fact that this provisional situation seriously interferes with the unity of the kingdom, and that he will await a more auspicious moment, one conducive to his restoration. At the point when the Protestants gained their right to live in the kingdom, at the point when the king recognized this right, the old ideal, which had been reduced to myth, is dangerously reaffirmed as a precept for the future. The victory is difficult in another sense: the

---

* There is violence of words, violence of calls to arms, violence of curses hurled against the kings. Here is what L'Estoile relates on June 6, 1593: "Today the Franciscan friar Fenardent, who was preaching at Saint Jean's, having spewed forth millions of abuses against the king, said that a thunder-clap or thunder-bolt would carry him off one of these days, or else he would burst: 'Moreover, my friends, his gut is already rotting, full of you know what.'"

† A translation quoted in L'Estoile.[14] Let us note that the Leaguers spoke out more boldly against the kings' miracle-working power than did the Protestants, who never frontally attacked this very popular belief; under Henry III the Leaguers never failed to deny the dishonored king all powers in this sphere. This did not prevent Henry IV, after his coronation at Chartres, from "touching" people, and crowds from coming to him; the belief easily survived the revolts.

king, after forty years of warfare, is unable to have this recognition of the Protestants accepted as a simple legal definition: the right to build churches (outside the towns), to convene synods, to be seated in tribunals equally divided for debates in which Protestants and Catholics come to grips. Henry IV has to grant to his subjects weapons against himself, against his successor; he supplies them with fortresses, weapons, and troops; and each year he gives them some money to maintain this army within the kingdom, this army whose job is to defend the small Protestant minority against renewed Catholic outbursts. The price is a high one, for this king who has also bought the peace of the Leaguers, the backing-down of Mayenne, and so many more things. But the compromise, a revival of the attempts made during the course of the past years, at Saint-Germain and elsewhere, has the very great merit of ending the war, and restoring peace to a ravaged France—a France which, although she probably has not yet learned tolerance, has seen the extermination of her most fanatical children.

IX

"Catholic France" and Modern Man

COMPARISON is not reason, said that perceptive man Montaigne; yet, without overworking the process, and considering the sum of the years 1600 through 1660, when modern France was "made," we might designate this lively and awkward period as her adolescence: pugnacious, gloriously powerful and self-confident, spreading out in all directions, with a success at least equal to that of the preceding century, this period is actually richer than the second part of the seventeenth century, from 1660 to 1690, when diversity withdrew before choices which, if not necessary, were at least imposed upon it. This adolescence is extremely triumphant amid the social and religious dramas it experienced, the dramas which are its growing pains. From all points of view, the seventeenth century is the richest, the most alive: in the shade of the Sun King, of Versailles and the great classics, we tend to forget the achievements, the exuberant richness of the years when France, less exhausted than Sully and Barthélemy Laffemas said, momentarily catches its breath and rediscovers, in new tonalities and a more confident style, the creative drive of the sixteenth century, as well as its religious intensity, its scientific curiosity, its love of beautiful pictures and buildings. This France is simultaneously rich in holy people who return to the Catholic Church that prestige which wars and polemic had greatly blunted, and in Cornelian heroes, in love with glory or scientific truth; an affable France in which, without the Caisse des Pensions, without Colbert or Chapelain, scholars from the whole world arrange to meet in Paris, at the Place-Royale or at the homes of Father Mersenne or Étienne Pascal. There is an astonishing richness whose epitome could almost be pinpointed to 1636-1637 when, at the moment when the Spanish re-invade France and De Corbie is threatening Paris, Corneille puts on *Le Cid*, and Descartes publishes his *Discours de la Méthode pour bien conduire sa raison et chercher la vérité dans les sciences*, when Saint-Cyran, the confessor at Port-Royal, clashes with Cardinal Richelieu, who soon afterwards will have him imprisoned—the dark beginnings of that Jansenist adventure which stirred up Paris for more than twenty years. All this intense and diversified life is built on an uneasy foundation: there are almost constant public disturbances; despite the firm grip of Richelieu and the sharp practices of Mazarin, there are revolts of *parlementaires* and nobility, Protestant assemblies and wars. And beyond all this, much less noticeably, there is the widespread agitation of the popular movements, both urban and rural; the endemic revolts of the *nu-pieds* and the *"croquans,"* revolts that are unceasing despite the commissioners distributed throughout the provinces—those *intendants* who are hated by the poor even more than the former magistrates were. During this early half-century, France is a land of great contrasts and wonderful triumphs in the two spheres which, as they did in the preceding centuries, still regulate civilized life: art and religion.

► **CONTRASTS IN THE EARLY
SEVENTEENTH CENTURY**

A period both disturbed and disturbing: even on the political level, where the pendulum-like oscillation of order and disorder, following the succession of regencies and kings, gives the impression of a badly regulated ballet, of unevenly applied power. These political crises nimbly and precisely reflect the movements that disturb the social order from below, movements which are not yet as assiduously studied as is the Day of the Dupes.* They bear, in a word, the mark of an intellectual brawl, something other than a continuation of the sixteenth century; the quarrel involved in *Le Cid*, for example, is an expression of this.

---

* The *Journée des Dupes* refers to 12 November 1630 when Marie de' Medici, in co-ordination with Gaston d'Orléans, hoped to persuade her son, Louis XIII, to dismiss Richelieu. Her lack of success, thus the dupe, in this venture led to her exile.— Trans.

Just as in those good, reliable treatises, inherited from an antiquity which was hungry for political theory, passed on by Bodin and several others, so in France: order follows disorder for sixty years. The first two Bourbons had the good fortune to have—belatedly—a male heir, and the bad fortune to die while still young. Out of this situation arose a Regency after 1610 and after 1643, when queens who were born outside the realm and who were carelessly kept uninformed of their new country and its affairs, had to rule a whole group of intractable aristocrats and *robins* who were delighted with the foreign women and ready to make sport of all the councils of the Regency. This unrest can be quelled rather quickly by the strong hand of a Richelieu, the skillful one of a Mazarin. But for years, all those whom royal authority gradually, and often severely, succeeded in silencing—like Henry IV and Biron, Richelieu and others like Cinq-Mars, De Thou, and Marillac—all those took things in stride: in the days of a Condé, nobles receive their signal and example from the royal entourage itself, but under Louis XIII, the queen mother herself works in rebellion against her son; nobles aspire simultaneously to profit from royal weakness, and to extort funds and pensions, even to the point of exhausting Sully's treasury or later the financial revenues; they compel recognition in government councils, to which the kings have long since ceased to summon them; provinces are aroused to revolt (purely aristocratic, that is); there are conspiracies in the Louvre itself; Paris is besieged. These aristocratic revolts are rather dangerous:* Mazarin flees before them, Condé no longer dares to return to France after his 1652 defeat and takes refuge in Spain until 1659.

Right beside the nobles, in the thick of the Fronde in conjunction with the nobility, are the *robins* and, especially, the *parlementaires* of Paris. The latter are legal officials of the highest rank, entrusted with preserving the laws of the kingdom and with interpreting law according to them; these men are no less dangerous than the nobles, especially when they are led by someone as ambitious as Gondi, from 1648 to 1652. The Parlement of Paris, like all the French *parlements*, registers the new laws and enactments before they go into effect, and has the right of *remontrance*, indeed the right to refuse the king their registration. In itself there is nothing presumptuous in this: laws cannot merely accumulate, but must be made consistent; this must be done before the law goes into effect. Consequently, the Parlement of Paris is a court of justice, yet it makes use of its privileges of *remontrance* and registration to assert its own control, and to limit royal authority. It argues from a merely nominal resemblance to the Parliament in London, which is a representative assembly of England (poorly representative, perhaps, but

---

* Not to mention the misdeeds these disturbances entail whenever their troops pass: "The companies of Canillac and Dienne did not commit any less pillaging in the mountains than those of the Baron de Saillans in the plains." [1]

that is not the point) and consequently a political assembly. The Parisian *parlementaires*, too, would like to play a political role, by wielding the judicial weapons at their disposal. Such claims were already being asserted during the disturbances in the sixteenth century; but Catherine de' Medici convoked the Estates-General, that truly representative body of the nation. Moreover, the *parlementaires*, as well as the nobles, were brought to heel by Henry IV, as for example when he forced, though not without some difficulty, the registration of the Edict of Nantes. The brazenness of the *parlementaires* increased in proportion to several causes: the Estates-General were not convoked after 1614, *parlement* offices were made hereditary and thus were stabilized, and, finally, there was the English example, in 1628 and especially after 1644, of the great disturbances occasioned by the conflict between Parliament and King. The Parisians are extremely heedful of this example. The goal of the *parlementaires*—the acquisition of a regular and uncontestable power of control—is never attained. Just as for the nobility—and perhaps even more rapidly, for these jurists carry the meaning of the State deep within them, steeped as they are in Roman law; illegality weighs upon them no less than does the lack of the little Gonesse rolls and bread—once the king raises his voice, each one returns to his row, to his seat, to his duties. The king, or the queen-regent, would have a good means of getting rid of the *parlementaires*: by replacing them. But they would have to be reimbursed. And the French monarchy, always needy and penniless and often even close to bankruptcy, hardly ever contemplates such an operation, which would be expensive. Except for a few rare periods like those of Sully, the first ten years of Colbert, or part of Fleury's ministry, there was a chronic deficit of public finances under the monarchy. This was the result of several major causes, which need only be enumerated: the absence of a comprehensive bookkeeping system, despite the Chambre des Comptes; the scope of expenses, always settled without any concern for receipts, especially expenditures for wars and, later, for buildings and the court; the incoherence of the financial system, bearing on only part of the population, and handed over very unequally to the tax-farmers across the realm (salt taxes and *tailles*); finally, the good will of the bourgeoisie, which subscribes to the loans, accepts the bankruptcies, and makes up the deficits.

The Protestants are still causing disturbances, at least during the early period of the disorders; they do so less out of a desire to resume the the struggle ended in 1598, than out of fear of Catholic plots, and desire to forestall them. It is true that at each clerical assembly—held, as a rule, every five years—the bishops persistently clamor for the abolition of the Edict of Nantes, the re-establishment of Catholic unity; and they will not cease to do so until 1685. Alarmed by a few noble intrigues, in the Rohan-Sully family among others, the fortified Protestant towns like

Montauban and La Rochelle take up arms, when Luynes repairs to the Midi in 1620, to re-establish Catholicism in the Béarn and when, particularly, Richelieu decides to fight to deprive the Protestants of their military privileges under the Edict. The relentlessness with which Jean Guiton and the people of La Rochelle hold out against the famous siege of 1628, expresses the fears the Protestants experience when they see all their rights, accorded them thirty years earlier, removed; and the bitter disappointment they experience when the word of Henry IV, given them at that time, is broken. However, with the granting of the Peace of Alais in 1629, the Protestants, deprived of strongholds, weapons, means of agitation, retreat; there is silence for forty years, until about 1670—a total political submission first and foremost, as Mazarin recognized, but one which perhaps also conceals an important social renewal in the ranks of the Protestants, the definitive setback of the nobles to the advantage of the urban bourgeoisie and doubtless the rural districts, along the routes that connect the large Protestant centers—Poitiers, La Rochelle, Montauban, Cahors, Agen. This period of composure almost certainly conceals some slackening of the fervor, after the grave ordeals of the years between 1620 and 1630, and awaits the terrible awakening between 1670 and 1685.

The Parisian insurrections of 1648 and 1649, however, exceed the bounds of a parliamentary revolt, even supported by the coadjutor's lackeys. The Parisian bourgeoisie gets mixed up in it, and countless lampoons of Cardinal Mazarin indicate that the cloth merchants and artisans are among the followers of the movement. Likewise, the long siege of La Rochelle is not merely the fanatic resistance of Huguenots whose exasperation reaches the point of appeal to the English; at that time, La Rochelle is also one of the richest French towns, and has its place among those Atlantic ports like Saint-Malo, Nantes, Bordeaux, and Bayonne, which get the greatest part of Spanish trade and money; a gaudy town, so much so that Richelieu's neighboring diocese might, to an ambitious eye, seem dingy. In the early part of the seventeenth century, French society experiences the full effect of the economic and social disruption provoked by the sixteenth century; the uninterrupted flow of gold, then of silver, begins to halt; not at all paradoxically, this is the time when Potosí and all the other large sources in the Americas begin to run dry, when American silver is more and more stretched out by base coinage, "black pennies," and credit; and, in these years between 1620 and 1640, the social consequences of the price rise, of inflation, begin to make themselves felt. The newly-rich bourgeois builds and furnishes his house, has himself "portraited" in powdered wigs and fine suits of black cloth with discreet white cuffs. He increases his donations and his pious organizations which, at his death, can help rid him of now and again having strained the interdictions forbidding usury. The bourgeoisie live in the grand manner the nobility can no longer maintain, during this period when the latter have already begun to come into the towns, dreaming of settling down there only to find under their eyes this unprecedented ostentation of the bourgeoisie. Nothing is more indicative of the nobility's feelings than the "lobby" of the Estates-General in 1614; there is the constant question of *roturiers* and *vilains*, of their loss of respect for their betters; frequent exchanges of blows with sticks or sword blades occur, and rude encounters. During the meetings, the nobility protests against the purchase of noble land by the urban bourgeoisie, against the letters patent of nobility that are generously sold by the king, and particularly against the activities of the forgers.*

Here is still another sign of the ascent of the merchant bourgeoisie, which is trampling down all the flowerbeds: having filled the ranks of the *noblesse de robe*, it crushes them; these new nobles protest—in their own way: not with sword in hand, but with fine, duly registered laws defending social precedences. Thus, the Parlement of Dijon says in 1625:

> Everyone is forbidden to assume the quality of nobility without express authorization . . . to bestow the quality of "lady" on wives of merchants, attorneys, notaries, and bailiffs, and these women are forbidden to allow it, under pain of one hundred *livre* fine, and three hundred for repetition of the offense . . . and lawyers and doctors and their wives are forbidden to wear clothing and headgear of silk or satin.

Likewise, the sumptuary laws of the time forbid or regulate, with a harshness indicative of their ineffectiveness, the wearing and use of fabrics woven with gold or silver thread. This law has a double purpose: like the law regulating the wearing of silk and satin, it defines the outward signs of the social hierarchy; also, it limits hoarding, that dreaded rival of monetary circulation.†

There is no doubt that we see merchants and *robins* who agree in their opposition to Mazarin in 1648; yet Mazarin's fiscal policy is there for a reason, and represents a temporary derivative of the conflicts occurring now and then in the background; the financial system is another contemporary evil, and the evil accrues to the rural districts. The bourgeois, who possess converted *rentes* and who see the increase of the *taille,* and the revival of the tax on the *Aisés,* are not happy. But what

---

* This guilty activity of kings, or of swindlers, never ceased for long. The entire sixteenth century was a fine era in this respect, and there are numerous echoes of it. Thus in the *Journal des guerres civiles* (1648): "The said Des Jardins, forger, having sold several letters patent of nobility, and for fifty thousand *écus,* so the story goes. . . ." [2]

† Similarly, they forbid the manufacture of silver dinner services, or recall them for monetary uses. . . .

can we say of the rural population, which endures both the weight of the *tailles* augmented by the king, and the ceaseless demands of the lords' agents who are entrusted by the nobility to render the greatest possible "return" on their fees? These tax collectors are themselves run down by their masters—who never find their revenues sufficient—to the point of selling their lands, unless they are so buried under debts that the "warrant" for seizure intervenes. Upon the ruins of the nobility, all during the seventeenth century, the bourgeoisie establishes itself as landed property-owners.[3] Thus the charges become heavier, partly because of the long-range policies of Concini, Richelieu, or Mazarin, partly because of the social changes; and they seem especially heavy, perhaps, compared with the previous ease. Throughout western France, previously inundated with Spanish money, rebellions, both rural and urban, are more frequent and violent than elsewhere. But there are signs of disturbance every-where: against the collectors of the salt tax, and against the collectors of all the detested fees like the "aids" and *tailles*. The popular outbreaks are an aggressive reaction which the bourgeois, and sometimes even the magistrates, do not always bother to quell—perhaps out of fear that they will be struck back, but also out of an unavowable solidarity with those lovers of justice, whose rage is all the more formidable since their leaders are often women, who are protecting the last *douzains* of the household.* An *intendant* complains thus (when upon other occasions he might be grateful for the help lent him by some bourgeois in controlling the popular furor):

> Now, although it was very likely within the power of the other lower-class magistrates of our above-mentioned city to stifle the nascent sedition which ordinarily begins weakly and feebly, be it out of cowardice or complicity, or both of them together, they stood with their arms crossed and watched, under their very eyes, all that violence, rage, and fury can inspire in a populace that lets itself be carried away by its first impulses.[5]

Sometimes the town produces and nurtures peasant revolts: in the poor provinces like the Limousin and the Rouergue, where rebellions go on year in, year out, between 1636 and 1643, the towns, which were af-

---

* The Russian historian Porchnev, quoted above, has followed these popular movements from 1623 to 1643, seeking indications of class struggle—not an easy task, since class consciousness at this time is almost mute. The quotations from the papers of Chancellor Séguier, preserved in Leningrad and gathered together at the end of Porchnev's book, are priceless. Thus, concerning the role of women, there is the following, occurring at Montpellier in 1645 (p. 702): "The tax levied on the artisans, because of the happy accession to the Crown, has given rise to popular disturbances begun by women and pursued very heatedly by their husbands." And in answer, from a rural parish: "There is a group from the Figeac election district which held several armed meetings. But it is a poor parish, accustomed to such disturbances. . . . And there were more armed women in this meeting than men. . . ."[4]

fected by commercial progress and which suffer more than the "flat-lands" from its decline, set the example, encouraging rebellion in the rural districts:

> And it would be necessary for the king's service to make a note-worthy example of Villefranche by punishing its chief inhabitants and officers, who are the cause of the sedition, and who kept it going for ten months. . . . And all the *croquants* from the country-side, poverty-stricken peasants, would not have defaulted had it not been for the example of those in Villefranche.[6]

However, Villefrance-de-Rouergue does seem to have been an exception; in those interior regions of western France as in Normandy, the crises reached an acuteness apparently not experienced by the east (ravaged, it is true, by the toughened soldiers of the Thirty Years' War) and the Parisian basin. Porchnev's texts and many others give excellent illustrations of the authorities' impotence in the face of those sporadic uprisings that are unconfinable despite all efforts, impossible to suppress except after havoc has been wrought: royal agents are mistreated, houses burned, roads cut off and travel on them forbidden. Doubtless this is not the same as an organized and continual guerrilla warfare: but they are at the mercy of panics, "fears," which are increasingly frequent; there are angry outbursts, village riots, all of which dissolve into the nearby forests*—then months, or at least weeks, of silence and calm. The worst years for these poverty-inspired insurrections, these murderous rebellions of *croquants* and *nu-pieds*, are apparently those late in the reign of Louis XIII, when the calamities of the war in the east and the north are added to agricultural disasters extant just about everywhere: already the years between 1630 and 1632 are marked by difficult famines—then again, throughout a good part of France, in 1637-38. From then on, until the Fronde, there is no rest for the *intendants* and the officials responsible for maintaining peace in the rural districts. In those difficult years, the long-range policy of the Cardinal, coming to grips with the Hapsburgs, is slowed down by the burdens of interior disorders.

Endemic peasant revolts, popular urban revolts, accomplished by the little people—people unable to make their voices heard, people of whom we know little. In spite of the (relative) solidarity of the towns and countryside, when faced with the cumbersome financial system, the

---

* "The *crocans* continue, and even increase their thefts, burnings, murders, and meetings; in the Verg forest, our governor Monsigneur de Bourdeille scours the countryside . . . They visited the forest . . . but found none of the enemy to fight. . . ." [7]

major contrast remains between the newly-rich town and the countryside excluded from the compass of enrichment; between the "flatland,"
in the toils of mediocrity, burdened by the demands of kings and lords,
and the towns, sustained for more than a century by the accelerated
trade with new worlds, launched into conquest and exploitation of new
markets, and become the meeting places of the *hommes sçavans* of the
day.

The eighteenth century is presaged by the early seventeenth, as regards the fertile and limitless activity of the bourgeoisie. In Paris they
build as much as the nobility, if not more—on the outskirts of the Place
Royale, and in the Marias district, which contains as many bourgeois as
aristocrats. The architectural style of this creativity is the private *hôtel*:
shaped like a horseshoe around an interior court, isolated from the street,
combining, with its double arrangement of rooms, one side facing the
court and the other the garden, all the period's resources for entertainment and for convenience. The façade of the *hôtel* is decorated with
pediments, and its stucco is set off by alternating red brick and white
or gray stone from the limestone quarries of Montmartre; this is to be
the model for all urban architecture until the nineteenth century. It is a
building intended to receive a large group of people, conceived more
for receptions at home than for the comfort of its inhabitants. The seventeenth-century *hôtel* is also important as an object of interior ornamentation. Merchants and *robins* are aware of the merit of well-fulfilled lives
and happily successful careers; they have more and more furnishings,
tables, and chairs, and their pride is lavished on those full-length and
half-length portraits, ordered in Paris from the greatest masters: Philippe
de Champaigne, Le Brun—beautiful pictures, replete with dignity, in
which the well-cared-for wig is arranged upon a large white collar which
sets the head apart from the large, black robe with many folds, wide
sleeves from which emerge carefully arranged cuffs, again white, with
fine lace tucks and fluting; the hand is either open in the broad gesture
of the pleading lawyer, or closed upon a little notebook, held at the tips
of well-manicured fingers. Everything exudes wealth and self-satisfac-
tion.

Merchants, financiers, *robins*—men whose professions leave them leisure time, and bestow upon them the taste for reading, learning, and
receiving friends who are equally fond of books and discussions: the
towns, overburdened with *tailles* and stirred up by the intense emotions
of the nobility and the *parlementaires*, are already centers of an intellectual and artistic life in which the upper classes participate enthusiastically. Thanks to Latin, which is the vehicle for ideas from one end of
Europe to the other, and thanks to the freedom of travel and exchange
across this same Europe (which nevertheless remains very diverse),
this intellectual and artistic life is astonishingly varied. At Father Mer-

senne's with the Minims on the Place Royale, or in Nevers, the little town along the Loire where he teaches several years, Italians and Flemings meet at the end of an arduous trip, but with the cheerful cordiality of scholars who respect one another, and who come to discuss mathematics as well as ethics, physics as well as theology. "Persons famous for their knowledge and love of belles-lettres," or the merely curious who are rather proud of being admitted into these learned gatherings, meet on specified days at the home of the Dupuy brothers, or at Théophraste Renaudot's on Mondays, or Étienne Pascal's in Rouen or in Paris. Between August 1633 and September 1642, three hundred fifty-five such conclaves occurred at Théophraste Renaudot's.* Open to "any soul come to confer in public about all sorts of matters concerning physics, ethics, and other disciplines," these learned gatherings do not bring together only the great names of the day—Mersenne, Peiresc, Gassendi, Descartes, the young Pascal†—and the discussions may just as easily turn to little discourses of scant interest. However, the assiduousness and urgency that marks them is sufficient indication of their interest for this learned society of the day, gathering together clerics and laity: Harlay, Archbishop of Rouen, Antoine Godeau, Bishop of Grasse, Gassendi, Jean Morin, Jacques Sirmond, Naudé, "who might be called, without flattery, a living library," Louis Mauduit, and Hugo Grotius from Sweden. These are groups of friends—who, naturally, do not always agree (Mersenne is friendly simultaneously with Descartes and Gassendi)—that constantly correspond to find out about things, to pursue the discussions brought up by their books and lectures.‡ Before Colbert, the scholarly world is organized and extended over all this very highly intellectualized bourgeoisie in the large and small towns; and the scholarly societies have a retinue of learned amateurs.

Men and women of good will also can be found—perhaps in greater numbers, since discussion there is less demanding—in the new *salons* that house the imitators of that Parisian woman born in Rome, Madame de Rambouillet. These lovers of beautiful language and refined manners, the followers of Vaugelas if not of Malherbe, gather in *ruelles* § hung

---

* Furthermore, these are put into print, under the title *Première, deuxième* . . . *Centurie des questions traitées des conférences du bureau d'adresses.*
† If we are to believe Fontenelle, the historian of the Académie Royale des Sciences founded in 1666, Mersenne's house is the best-known establishment of this sort: "It has been more than fifty years since people who were in Paris used to visit Father Mersenne who, being a friend of the most capable men in Europe, took pleasure in providing their place of contact. Gassendi, Descartes, Hobbes, Roberval, the Pascals, father and son, Blondel, and several others, gather at his home. He would propose mathematical questions to them, or ask them to make some experiments concerning certain views; and never did people cultivate with greater care those sciences born from the union of Geometry and Physics."
‡ The *Correspondance de Mersenne*, for example, is edited by J. Tannery, Cornelius de Waard, and René Pintard. Yet countless others await publication.
§ Women generally held their *salons* in their bedrooms and often sat on a bed on a raised platform in an alcove. The *ruelle* is the space between the bed and the

with blue or green, to have their clothing—rich with the ribbons and
feathers, the style of the day—admired, to speak gallantries and coquet-
teries in a language whose circumlocutions are rapidly becoming excessive (Molière's *Précieuses Ridicules* is written in 1659). A society game,
one which would set its refinement against the crudity of the court people, the life of the *précieuses* is an aspect, almost a style, of urban life,
dictating dress and speech with a success varying according to the meeting place; particularly, it is a Parisian* phenomenon which, in its way,
presages and prepares for the very civilized court of Louis XIV.

The literary and scientific life still shows traces of foreign models; in
this respect, the seventeenth century is a continuation of the sixteenth,
on no less general a scale; but the lines of force have changed. Whereas,
in the preceding century, Germany and especially Italy dominated the
exchange, the first part of the seventeenth century is characterized by
Spanish influence. Italy does not lose its position, and remains an artistic
exemplar: Poussin spends his life in Rome, and antique models have a
prestige Rembrandt lacks; but the Spain of Philip IV, the Siglo-de-Oro
Spain, with the weight of its economic prestige and of its extremely
fertile writers of romance and plays, invades everything. The works of
Calderón, Cervantes, Lope de Vega, arrive in Rouen and La Rochelle
in the holds of ships from Seville—those truculent storytellers who disclose to the astonished French this Spain, still magnificent, already poverty-stricken; a world of violent passions in which honor and love rule
the game, a world of picaros and hidalgos, of showmen with dogs, of jug-
glers, and dissolute shepherds†—the miraculous world of Velasquez and
Murillo. At that time Germany, torn by war, laid waste by the voracious
troops of Wallenstein and Tilly, lacking direct contact after the sack of
the Rhenish provinces, the Burgundian regions, and Franche-Comté,
fades into the background. There is a long silence in the east and north,
where the Netherlanders and the Dutch continue to fight one another
until 1621, despite their belated revival: Lorraine, a stronghold of the
Counter-Reformation, very Catholic in the days of Georges de la Tour;
Burgundy, which is rediscovering a popular theatrical life after 1650;
Dijon, town of mountebanks, whose straightforward art served as a model
for Molière and delighted generations of laughing Burgundians.[8] Yet
this primacy of exchange with southern countries, emphasized even more
by the activity of the most expanding contemporary religious orders—

---

wall, the alcove, where chairs were arranged. The Marquise de Rambouillet's *chambre
bleue* was known far and wide. In the seventeenth century, the word *ruelle* was the
most common word for what we now call a *salon.*—Trans.

* This is so despite an abundant literature: *L'Astrée,* the novels of the Scudérys—
Madeleine's *Le Grand Cyrus,* Voiture, and Scarron, and the numerous works on the
order of the "Defense of the Kingdom of Coquetry," "Laws of Gallantry," "Tender
Friendships," "Lotteries of Love," "News of the Precious Prudes," etc.
† Just a modest example would be Cervantes' *Diologue of the Dogs.*

the Jesuits and Capuchins—means that the most intensive cultural life shifts toward the interior and the west: Lyon no longer has the prestige of the previous century, but Paris, aided by royal policy, Richelieu's Academy, and scholars, increases her role; it is the same with Corneille's Rouen, Father Bredeau's Nevers, and all the towns where the Jesuits, reinstated after 1603, are actively rebuilding under the leadership of Father Martellange, who is the temporal coadjutor and architect of the order.

Is this picture entirely one of contrasts? Of these contrasts, some of which ushered in the Baroque, these few pages can give only a rapid evocation. Many elements of the picture are still missing, and some of the continuities, which we must limit ourselves to conjuring up in a word: the persistent taste for ancient literature, the relentless practice of witch-burnings, those hecatombs of the Franche-Comté and Lorraine; the customs of social games—anagrams, light verse, little songs—and, in the same houses at the same time, theological disputes. This period, like the sixteenth century, is one of saints and heroes, of people who are at once humanists and mystics. Yet they are clearly more distinguishable than they were a hundred years earlier.

► **THE SAINTS OF THE CATHOLIC REVIVAL**

Between 1590 and 1640—a significant chronological frame of reference—religious fervor in urban France seems several degrees higher, if we may compare fervor and fever. It is as if, since weapons were unsuccessful in settling a conflict painful for everyone, people's minds fall back on persuasion, and especially upon example, for demonstrating the superiority of Catholicism. Each person feels himself responsible for the common lot, and each carefully examines himself, projecting a gigantic reconquest, which shall be the work of all, not just of the Jesuits. The time for weapons is past, as is the time for reconciliation parleys: Henry IV once more tries his hand at the latter, with his former companions-at-arms, and experiences no success. The Catholic fervor busies itself with other tasks: preaching, teaching, reforming. This is the true era of the Counter-Reformation.

To this everyone gives the best of himself and of his goods. The fervor expresses itself, first of all, in many new institutions: establishment of convents, donations for the construction of churches and the decoration of chapels, not to mention the expenses entailed by the entries (which are legion) into the religious life, for at this time every candidate to an order must furnish a considerable amount of capital. At this time, too, all Paris is astonished to see religious establishments proliferate on every street of the town; there can be no doubt that bourgeois and nobles thus devoted millions of *livres* to the glory of God. Also, houses were tirelessly and easily changed into convents—at least until the difficult years of the 1660s.*

This fervor is further expressed, quite naturally, in a spiritual life rendered easily available to us by writings and testimony, a sort of revival better known than the preceding, since spiritual writings are easier reading than the minutes of notaries. This aspect has attracted the tender attention and admiration of many researchers,[9] who are skillful in describing all its nuances: from Francis de Sales to Condren and Bérulle. There are distant echoes of St. John of the Cross and St. Teresa of Avila, the great Spanish mystics of the preceding century, who guide the thought and the prayer of this new generation. Also, there are the commentaries inspired by St. Augustine who, particularly for Bérulle, is still popular.

This new religious life benefits, then, from the well-established economic support provided by the whole of the sixteenth century, and from an amazing crop of administrators, organizers, and mystical temperaments, endowed to a very great degree with an admirable finesse of thought and common sense. Whence the atmosphere of the time, overstrained with great meditations and noble undertakings, among the associates of Madame Acarie and the Abbé Olier; whence those lasting creations whose great religious career long survived the disappearance of their founders. The variety of efforts, if not intentions, also expresses the human richness of this movement.

In addition to the encroaching Jesuits, what great names, what active orders! Even before the new seventeenth-century institutions, religious life is animated by the exceptional presence of a few groups: Madame Acarie, Bérulle, and one order—the Capuchins. Cardinal de Bérulle is a great theologian and traveler: he goes to the Mediterranean regions, only slightly infected by Protestantism, in order to profit from their experiences; and to Spain where, over the course of several months, he negotiates with a few of Theresa of Avila's Carmelites, trying to persuade them to cross the Pyrenees and come into France—which is, to Spanish eyes, already the land of the Antichrist; he goes to Italy, and in Rome admires the Oratorians of Philip Neri, bringing them back to France in 1611. Bérulle is a great figure of this self-confident Catholicism which proves its vitality by its new foundations, by its forward strides.† All the same, he is good in argument, when confronted with St. Francis de Sales, the Bishop of Geneva, or with Condren; or when confronted with those enormously popular pioneers, the order of that other St. Francis,

---

* This movement of funds and property is known only through the exclamations of contemporaries: Eight convents, in a given year, on the Rue Saint-Antoine! But the archives control their temporary secret.
† He is the fortunate author of a great phrase, which rather nicely sums up the serene faith of the man and his period, of which the main thought is Redemption: "God has entrusted our selves to ourselves."

he of merchant Italy: the Capuchins. This order had long been accustomed to urban preaching; they swept away crowds of people—many more than did the Jesuits—with a skill which is sometimes a little strained.* The Capuchins imposed a new image of their patron saint, an image at once more dramatic and less benign, like the St. Francis painted by Zurbaran; they knew, too, how to hold people's attention by preaching on the most traditional subjects: the crusade, dear to Father Joseph, and many others.† Finally, they were able to inspire the same kind of painting from one end of Europe to the other, from the Italy of Caravaggio to the Lorraine of Georges de la Tour, a painting directed toward mystical contemplation: *The Adoration of the Shepherds* furnishes a beautiful encounter between these two friends of the Capuchins.

Thus, in the very early years of the century, while the Jesuits are barely beginning to settle down again (they return in 1603), day-to-day religious life is stimulated by the preaching enthusiasm of the Capuchins, of Francis de Sales, Bérulle, Canfeld, Coton, and Condren. This is the period when Francis de Sales publishes advice and pleasant exercises for arriving at that perfect love that is the goal of all Christian life; in 1608 there is the *Introduction à la vie dévote*, a flowery and easy-to-read breviary that gently leads the reader to the contemplation of God: the "little way," it is called by some, who, turning to more difficult paths, look toward Spain. Nevertheless, the "little way" is not a negligible one; it is attentive to the individual, whom it grants a dignity that is a reconciliation of the humanistic impulse with the Catholic faith. The preachers who voluntarily deal with "the knowledge we have of God through his creatures" do not make a mistake. Beyond this first spiritual itinerary, the period is still one of great mystics: after his *Introduction*, Francis de Sales writes his *Traité de l'amour de Dieu* (1616); beyond the devout life, there are the Carmelites and their formidable spirit of asceticism; the partisans of the "super-eminent" life in great debate with the supporters of Bérulle. These fiery souls, who reform Montmartre, who delight in the boldness of Port-Royal's Angélique Arnauld,‡ who

---

* Until the end of the century, the Capuchins maintained a high prestige, due primarily to their preaching art. For proof, this comment: "Father Honoré, a Capuchin monk, accompanied by Father Nicolas and other members of the same order, made a very beautiful preaching tour to Marmande, which began in the month of November, 1691. . . . At four in the afternoon, Father Honoré would preach a sermon; on certain occasions, he would put a rope to his neck, making honorable amends for the sinners, whom he caused to cry aloud for forgiveness and mercy. Almost everyone wept. . . . There was an unbelievable crowd of people, who flocked there from all over. . . ." [10]

† "Saturday, January 6, 1946, Twelfth-day; after dinner, to the sermon of Father Georges, the Capuchin who told us that the kings of France ought to conquer all the world . . . and he concluded that, in this year of 1646, the Turks ought to be dispossessed and driven from Constantinople. . . ." [11] (The Father Joseph referred to is François Leclerc du Tremblay, a close friend and adviser of Richelieu.—Trans.)

‡ This is long before the appearance of Saint-Cyran, consequently long before that

dream of charitable foundations, of orisons, of "life in God"—from Jeanne de Cantal to Vincent de Paul—form the most mystical generation France has ever known.

This religious atmosphere has yet another characteristic. Shortly after the civil wars, the higher clergy overrides its Gallican bias and, in 1615, accepts the decrees of the Tridentine Council, which the *parlements* refuse. For the Church in France, a visible revolution in the forms of worship dates from this reception, that is, from this willingness to reform. They become more rigorous, and there is no longer any place in them for the medieval imagination, which left the Church open to Protestant criticism; the freedom of movement within the office, during which, at the point of the sermon, the faithful chimed in whether or not asked by their *curé* to do so, is henceforth considered unseemly; the same is true of the harvest celebrations, during which, two or three times a year, the clergy consented to transform the Church into a place of laughter and games, which doubtless seemed to them completely innocent.* On the same level as this kind of purification of medieval liberties can also be placed the discreet revision of the lists and virtues of the saints, which once had flourished—the work of the Benedictine Maurists, and numerous diocesan chapters. In this manner, worship becomes more hieratic and the mass becomes less familial, more distant from the average parishioner—who gradually loses his right (which had been customary) to challenge his *curé*, to talk to him in public, and to discuss his statements. With the obvious exception of the hymns, the faithful are reduced to silence. Worship has become more solemn: a profound change, with far-reaching psychological implications.

On this path of reconquest through internal reform and good example, it is possible also to locate the famous Company of the Blessed Sacrament, a pious association of laity and priests, founded in 1627 by the Duke of Ventadour.† Directed simultaneously toward charity and toward the conversion of the ungodly or the Protestants, the Company rapidly made a major place in French society; not content with reform from within, it took on surveillance, teaching, and censure, and, even after its dissolution by Mazarin in 1660, had a few triumphs in this di-

---

of Jansenism, in this convent not more nor less worldly than the others. (Angélique Arnauld was the abbess of Port-Royal, and sister of the famous theologian and defender of Jansenism, Antoine Arnauld.—Trans.)

* At the end of the century the most famous of these medieval fetes in the Church is again condemned in the most horrified tones, by a theologian: "The ecclesiastics appeared, some in masks, others dressed like women, infamous people, or actors. . . . There they danced in the choir, and sang profligate songs, and ate fat meat even at the altar. . . ." [12]

† The Company is a secret society founded by Henri de Lévis, Duke of Ventadour. Mazarin is said to have referred to them as the Cabal des Dévots and, though officially dissolved, they are suspected of having been instrumental in getting Molière's *Tartuffe* banned after its 1664 performance.—Trans.

rection. The Company of the Blessed Sacrament, or the Cabal des Dévots, comprises the same state of mind,* the same men whose mental attitudes, in those days of *Tartuffe* and *Don Juan*, quickly alarmed all milieux. It is an Inquisition of the laity, lacking the former's powers or its safeguards: the Company of the Blessed Sacrament betrays a clerical temptation rejected by the seventeenth-century Frenchman—and not just by Mazarin, who gave in to numerous complaints with which people besieged him. For that matter, of all the foundations of the period, this was the only one to be thus discussed, and then rejected.

For these great souls, from the sweet and tender "very dear Philothea" to whom the *Introduction à la vie dévote* is offered, to Louis de Marillac, were capable not only of great outbursts and stirring, impassioned writings, but also of beautiful establishments augmenting the still-extant medieval orders. The latter, which people are content to reform within their own narrow framework, remain dedicated to the intention of their founders; at the same time the impetus for the education of priests, for charitable works, grows. The charitable orders of Vincent de Paul are well known: the Daughters of Charity in 1633, with Louise de Marillac; the Salpêtrière; the Foundling Home (*Enfants trouvés*) in 1638—all of which offer so many proofs, if indeed they are necessary, of the poverty of the times and the eroding away of the medieval relief institutions. There are female orders consecrated to contemplation, like the Carmelites† and the Order of the Visitation; and especially, the teaching orders, designed to assure the education of the lower clergy. Even Vincent de Paul, obsessed with the poverty he encountered everywhere flaunted in broad daylight, stepped outside his habitual concerns to attend to the matter, and founded the Lazarists (the Congregation of the Mission) in 1632; in 1650, Olier, a friend and disciple of Bérulle, and *curé* of Saint-Sulpice, established the Sulpician Fathers, a school for young priests in the parish he himself had reformed. But, within this sphere of teaching, the greatest creation of the times was Bérulle's Oratorians, "imported" from Italy in 1611. Meant at the outset to play the seminarian role called for by the Council of Trent, like the Lazarists and

---

* The "program" of the Company is contained in these few lines by its founder: "Receive the unfortunate, the plaguestricken, the convicts, peasants afflicted with gallstones or who lack seeds; rescue the innocent from the provost's archers, and the debtors from usurer's knavery; reform the dress of the Marseille women, who exhibit their breasts; run freethinking bookstores into the ground; purify the Saint-Germain fair and the Palace gallery; attack gambling and dueling; protect the young provincials, who arrive in Paris by coach; educate teachers for elementary schools; drive out the Jews, the Protestants, the Illuminati. . . ."

† After 1610, the Carmelites of Paris, founded in 1603, swarmed to Pontoise, Dijon, Tours, Rouen, Bordeaux, and Châlons. These titles are by no means a complete list, for the new orders are too numerous, especially the ones for women: the Recollect Augustinian Sisters, the Capuchin Sisters, the Ursuline Sisters, the Benedictine Sisters of Calvary, the Sisters of Our Lady of Charity and Refuge, the Benedictine Sisters of the Perpetual Adoration of the Blessed Sacrament, and so on.

Sulpicians, the Oratorian establishments were very quick to admit young men who had no intention of being priests. In the 1640s, and particularly in the region around Paris, where they already rival the Jesuits,* they experience great success as eager teachers, not only of the humanities,† but also history (including history of the periods succeeding antiquity) and the physical sciences—they are open to lessons from things. By this very orientation, the Oratorians abandoned the education of young priests; actually, despite a few attempts (and these were on a local scale) the intellectual reform of the lower clergy never came to much; the Council of Trent proposed the ambitious program of one seminary per diocese, but this was not within reach of a clergy where the commendam rule is prevalent, and where the multiple benefice, the play of royal favors, continue to encourage, alongside of the great outbursts of mysticism, comfortable careers in which piety has but a meager place;‡ to say nothing of the lack of a staff of teachers, despite the Theological Faculty, whose teaching is not appropriate for the demands proper to the apostolate in what today we would call a missionary field.

However, as the century progresses, the primacy of the Jesuits in the Catholic revival uncontestably asserts itself. As the outer flank of the reconquest, the Society establishes itself everywhere: in the towns, even the most mistrustful; near princes, the upper nobility, even the king. The activities of the other orders are sometimes rather overshadowed by the immense achievement of the Jesuits, who are constantly building, increasing their professed houses and *collèges*, and helping in the administration of the urban parishes. The support of the authorities—of Henry IV himself, after the beginning of the century—and the boldness with which the teaching fathers in the *collèges* Christianized the humanists' antique heritage, without fearing to heap disdain upon the Gothic Middle Ages,§ are the major elements of their success; there is also the skill with which they handle confession, that subtle interplay of nuances that enables them not to offend or shock the most scrupulous of souls

---

* The educational rivalry increases with theological divergencies: the Oratorians who, as loyal followers of Bérulle, are faithful Augustinians, are soon tempted after 1640 by the Port-Royal dialectic. Their respect for Descartes is equally strong. More reasons than necessary to dig a ditch which the Jesuits have no desire to fill in.

† The Oratorians are the first to teach the basic subjects in French, not Latin— before Port-Royal. This sensible reform explains their success.

‡ Among many reasons, let us recall the poverty of the lower clergy, who can scarcely support the ordinary vocations.

§ Charles Perrault, during the Quarrel of the Ancients and Moderns at the end of the century, emphasized this ostracism, which has great ramifications for art: "There were men paid and hired to make (antiquity) enter deeply into the minds of the young men put under their care; men who, dressed in long black robes, with square hats on their heads, offered them the works of the Ancients as not only the most beautiful things in the world, but as the very ideal of the beautiful, and had their laurels all ready should these young men arrive at imitating those divine models. . . ." [13]

with too much rigidity. The Gospels speak in such severe terms of the rich as to be disturbing to those good, newly-rich, merchant bourgeois —but for the Jesuits, the rich man has not committed a crime before God for his laden table, nor for the luxury of his clothing or house; he is criminal only insofar as he is callous toward the poor.

These are pleasant remarks to hear. But then Sunday mass, "touched up" by the Society, is also a pleasant fete to see; the Jesuits, who are great builders, have made by their architects, enormous churches with one wide nave, completed merely by juxtaposed side chapels. By virtue of one or two domes and wide bays these naves are full of light. The new church is made to receive the literate faithful, who come to mass with their Missals; the altar, placed in full light, is made to be looked at and admired. For a richness of decoration augments this "theatrical" arrangement: old-style façades, superimposed tall pediments supported by Doric or Corinthian colonnades; the interiors are fitted out with marble and gold decorations, and with paintings; there are communion tables, auxiliary chapels—the appeal to visual delight is everywhere, without fear of excess. Doubtless the introduction into the religious music of almost secular pieces is of similar importance: the evening prayers lean toward the operatic, and female singers hold a major place there; after their turn at singing, these women take up the collection. But this innovation is not unique with the Jesuits. Airy architecture and luxurious ornamentation have led us to speak of a "Jesuit style"; but both the term and the thing have recently been called into question by the historians of the Society. And the question remains open. In this we find the plastic expression of a new idea of religious life: the Society would have it as pleasant and attractive as possible to this world of noble ladies and newly-rich bourgeois to whom all the Society's care is directed. Is this the price to be paid for reconquest?

To do this, the Jesuits are active everywhere, present everywhere;* they mingle in worldly and scientific life, participate more than anyone else in the Academies and the discussion of "philosophy." However, the Jesuits seem especially concerned with working for the upper bourgeoisie and the nobility, at the risk of opening themselves to popular discontent, for the humbler classes are astonished and indignant at their buildings and their overweening activity.† But despite this, and despite

---

* Even in Canada; the Jesuits, along with a few other orders, particularly the Ursulines, set themselves up in Montreal and attempt to convert the Hurons.
† Here are two proofs, in different styles. At Puy in 1634, a bourgeois exclaims in his diary: "Ah, how people curse, and will go on cursing, those who have settled themselves here . . . because they are insatiable, and never content with the goods of this world." At Paris in 1643, in D'Ormesson's *Journal*: "Thursday, April 23, I went to hear the Jesuit Father Lingendes' sermon. Previously I was conversing with Father Lombard, who tells me how this popular hate continues against them, and that they almost dare not go out in the streets."

a few defeats of a temporal nature, by 1640, at the time of the centenary of their founding, the Society is enjoying a prosperity unequaled in
the kingdom: this is at the very moment when the quarrel with the
Jansenists—which, however, is really of another time*—is about to begin.

▶ **THE HEROES OF 1636**

In December, 1636, Pierre Corneille put on *Le Cid*, a tragicomedy;
several months later the *Discours de la méthode pour bien conduire sa
raison et chercher la vérité dans les sciences*, by René Descartes, appeared in the bookstores. Two works, two men—unquestionably exceptional ones, but still they are an expression of their time and serve to
complete its image. The Catholic France of Louis XIII, the France of
the royal vow of 1638,† extols other values too: the Cornelian hero, who
is the hero as well of the other contemporary writers of tragedy and
tragicomedy; and, on the other hand, the scientist, skilled in astronomy
and mathematics, astrology and music.

When Corneille dramatizes the thwarted loves of Rodrigue and Chimène, he is glorifying an old French ideal, that of chivalry. This hero is
an heir of the Middle Ages, a noble knight, who confronts extreme
dangers and is able to renounce everything, even love. He bears the
torch that Francis I, king of France, was the last to pass down, haloed
with a reputation all the more flattering because it is due to a sympathetic
legend ("Pavia, all is lost save honor," a memorable phrase). The Cid,
Rodrigue, that great-hearted hero who loves father, king, and Chimène,
is not accidentally from Spain, the land of honor. The French nobleman
recognizes and admires himself in the character of the Cid, persuaded
beyond a doubt that he practices the same virtues: blind courage, limitless devotion, sacrifice. Corneille knew his Spanish legends well, just as
did Cervantes when he had Don Quixote make it Sancho's duty to say
nothing about a withdrawal he deems dishonorable. And, with a spite-
fulness Richelieu little appreciated, he added the duel, for which the
nobility had been struggling against the Cardinal over a ten-year period:
the right to duel is, in 1636, the privilege of giving expression to those
lofty virtues, that sense of honor, which makes noble souls. D'Artagnan
—the real one or that of Dumas, it makes little difference—by dueling
on the Pré aux Clercs, defends the high opinion of self of this privileged
body, whose privileges are dwindling and whose good conscience re-

---

* By which time the great names of this period have disappeared: Francis de Sales
died in 1622, Bérulle in 1629, Madame Acarie after 1618, Jeanne de Cantal in 1641,
Condren in 1641; Olier, absorbed in his parish of Saint-Sulpice, and Vincent de Paul,
who dies in 1660, remain apart from the controversy.
† Louis XIII dedicated France to the Blessed Virgin Mary in 1638.—Trans.

mains his last refuge, nourished on his own account. A tongue of fire passing over all that ("to me, Count . . ." and later, the famous "Let him die," of Horace)—in this the prestige of the Cornelian hero is easily visible.

This noble heart, which does not trifle with honor and does not hesitate to defy authority (Camille in *Horace*) and all of society, like the martyr Polyeucte, is not the exclusive property of Corneille, nor even that of his four great tragedies; as quickly prone to lyrical effusions, where "honor" recurs in every line, as to unrestrained laughter during the happy endings—the noble heart can be found everywhere: on the stage and in novels, consumed by pride (already in Honoré d'Urfé's *Astrée* in 1627), greedy for glory at the cost of some violent acts, of the great battles of which no one tires. A considerable distance behind Elizabethan England, France set to work on the theater, and put in it those actions in which commingle laughter and tears, that brutality which only too well reflects the manners of court and châteaux; this is Corneille before *Le Cid*, mixed comedies (*Galerie du Palais, Place Royale*), and after 1643, *Don Sanche d'Aragon*; but it is also all the other contemporary tragedians: Benserade and Rotrou, who deal in Cleopatras, Augustuses, Rodogunes, in that tragicomic style that is the true style of the period. In the image of this tormented society, impassioned with grandeur and greedy for violent joys, their engravings ring with great sword fights; the evil and the great-hearted die, while "Harlequin, with his *gascade* leaps and his buffooneries, makes the unhappy see that he knows how to make them roar with laughter." [14] And, for Corneille and Racine, antiquity is a particularly valuable frame of reference, for it supplies distance, removal from the tragic surroundings, which attenuates the violence of these impassioned hearts, these hearts which, a dozen or so years later, will be reflected in the *Lettres de la Religieuse portugaise*.*

There are the same heroes, the same floods of nobility, in the novels: those about the *Précieuses*, by Scarron, Voltaire, even by Benserade and Rotrou, are becoming stylish; these little novels sell as well as the fat theological books and scientific publications of Gassendi, Peiresc, and Descartes—so much so that the bookstores on the Rue Saint-Jacques buy manuscripts from the authors for several hundred *livres*, a profitable practice for the less rich authors. Rotrou, in 1636, sells four tragedies for 750 *livres*; thirty years later, Molière sells his *Tartuffe* for 2,000; in the

---

* Intensely emotional outcries, which reflect a whole age. The Third Letter: "I have lost my reputation, I have exposed myself to the fury of my parents and to the severity of the laws of this country against nuns, and to your ingratitude, which seems to me the greatest of all misfortunes . . ." Fifth Letter: "Alas! I have suffered your scorn; I have borne your hate in all the jealousy I felt because of the attachment you were able to have for another; I should have had at least some passion to combat. . . ."

following century, an author who is clever in business can make a fortune—as did Voltaire. But then, Boileau was already lamenting: "Making a mercenary profession out of a divine art. . . ." There are comic novels, The Pedant Tricked, The Lottery of Love, Tender Friendship —so much good reading for this new and numerous public of *robins* and merchants, of nobles and *roturiers* for whom reading is simultaneously a relaxation and a lesson. The *homme généreux*, the well-born and at least good-hearted man who loves life, its joys and its dangers, triumphs in this new literature. The theater and the novel—relayed the lyric poetry of the preceding age, the game of the gallant court; the theater is the game of a whole society, and so on, in its own way, is the novel.

The other masters of the noble risk and of adventure are the scientists in search of steadfast truths: Galileo, who submits to Romish censure and does not succeed in detaching himself from his "discovery"; Descartes, obviously, enthusiast of all the sciences who, one fine day, decides to take up anatomy and devotes months to it in The Hague, where he dissects and rebuilds the mechanism of that still so mysterious human body. It is he, too, who gives himself the time to think about research, to share it with his friends—the other scientists with whom he corresponds, debates, and discusses for years, and offers them through his valuable attention the *Discours de la méthode*, that short introduction at the head of three little treatises on "geometry," "dioptrics," and "meteorology." For the whole learned world, this is an intellectual itinerary whose landmarks and rules are already known to a Mersenne. But Descartes then appears as the most noble of all: the man who dares doubt the external world, himself, and God: he is freed quickly from this doubt, but for a moment he is lost in the forest, without a compass, without any means of getting out of it, other than by always walking in the same direction without looking back. These are good rules, still examined today by the apprentice philosopher ("never accept anything as true . . ."); but we cannot forget the unheard-of daring involved in his departure.

Having lost everything up to his redeeming *cogito*, Descartes regains everything: the ethics of his country and his contemporaries (which he is careful not to disturb unnecessarily, preferring flight to Holland to insure the peace of mind he needs for scientific work—for Descartes knows well how much scientific research costs: "To provide for the expenses of the experiments he would need to make, and moreover to prevent anyone's importunacy from snatching away his free time . . ."); and finally, God: the God of traditional religion, consequently a Catholic God, whose truth is demonstrated by Scholastic arguments, without searching further: "Since I knew of some perfections that I did not have.

I was not the only being that existed (if I may, I shall make free use of the terms of the Schools here), but that there must by necessity be some other that was more perfect." [15] Also, the *Méditations métaphysiques* (the basis of a metaphysic which doubtless was necessary, and so distinctly separated from sciences) are not read very much any more.

Yet Descartes is at the center of the scientific movement of his day, with the *Méthode* and the *Regulae*; while he is not a precursor who, like Mersenne, Gassendi, and many others, had toiled at physics, mathematics, and anatomy. Thus he says in the *Traité des passions:* "The final and farthest cause of the passions of the soul is none other than the agitation with which the spirits move the little gland in the center of the brain." The same is true of his famous vortex theory. Descartes is the marvelous intellect of his period, among those who surround him: the man able to define that exemplary method—by virtue of which people should be able to understand, and ultimately to know, the world—that path which will show a way out of the indecisions, the doubts, the indefinite possibilities of the sixteenth century: the great Cartesian expression, "Those long chains of very simple and easy reasonings, which geometers customarily use to arrive at their most difficult proofs, had given me the opportunity to suppose that all the things which fall under man's knowledge follow upon one another in a similar way." [16] It is quite possible that Descartes is not so perspicacious as Mersenne or Gassendi, those masters of the Machine; but it is also important that Pierre Gassendi and Descartes had for years been having a fine scientific quarrel, because Gassendi's experiments—with their too quickly built system, at too great a remove from prudent experimentation—annoy Descartes the physicist and anatomist. It remains no less true that the philosopher, proclaiming the universal value of his mathematical method, gives his contemporaries the weapon which establishes the definitive retreat of sixteenth-century sentimental naturalism, and presages the new science: his precision and his concern with demonstrative clarity, what people then called the *esprit de plan.* As a matter of fact, the young Pascal, devoting himself to his mathematical investigations, experimenting at Puy-de-Dôme with atmospheric pressure, demonstrating the existence of a vacuum before an enthusiastic audience* at Rouen, is the living illustration of this scientific spirit, which has just found those rules without which no knowledge could be established.

That this systematic rigor was able to disturb scrupulous minds—as was the early daring of methodological doubt—is certain. But Des-

---

* This enthusiasm for science is one of beautiful, purely speculative minds; neither the technical applications, nor the idea that these might exist, is yet present. Denis Papin and his digester are of this century, this generation just after Descartes (during which, however, the *Journal des Savants* is already periodically publishing reports about machines). This is the passion to know for its own sake, not for the sake of action.

cartes, who remained a good Catholic until his death, was the special target for personal attacks; the Jesuits are content with keeping his works out of their *collèges* until his death. Afterwards, things go differently. But in the scientific world, between 1620 and 1640, others applied those long chains of reasoning, seasoned with good common sense, to matters of faith. They face the danger of confronting their faith with their science, without daring to say aloud that, in case the two prove contradictory, they will sacrifice the former to the latter. These men are the erudite free-thinkers, the "Paduan" disciples, whom Mersenne thought to be legion in Paris: horrified, he raises their number to fifty thousand. They are a curious breed who trouble the sleep of Pascal, who lives in hiding, quietly, fearing scandal and its dread consequences.* Some people have thought to find these men everywhere (because they were so well hidden), and have put into the same atheistic bag Naudé and Gassendi, Bouchard, Patin, Cyrano, and Descartes himself (dubbed "the philosopher in the mask"). These scholars fulfill their Christian duties *more majorum*,[17] and unburden themselves to no one; but among themselves, in little groups of safe friends, they meet in unfrequented cabarets or at one another's houses, to discuss the great problems which are simultaneously the prey of the philosopher and the theologian; they publish nothing unless it be of anonymous authorship, or of only discreet innovation like Naudé's *Apologie pour les grands hommes soupçonnés de magie* (1625). It is impossible to bring these men to light, despite so much contemporary suspicion and Pascal's wager†—until, at the end of the nineteenth century, the day a scholar discovers the revealing, but still extremely debatable, confessions of J. J. Bouchard. In all probability, they were very small groups, for to seek or train followers is to risk the stake, about which no one is keen; they are a kind of atheistic avant-garde, in a world where science and faith will soon be confronting one another openly.

Yet during those years around the middle of the century, the debate is not yet over; the more time passes, the more scientific enthusiasm spreads through the bourgeois and noble public. Women dabble in it;

---

* Except for a few exceptional cases whose careers ended at the stake, as for example Jules César Vanini, of whom Moréri speaks: "J. C. Vanini was burned at Toulouse on April 19, 1619 . . . he was a native of Naples, teaching atheism in France at the beginning of the seventeenth century, and having been convicted at Toulouse he was sentenced to death. They say that when he was ordered to make due apology and ask the pardon of God, the King, and Justice, he replied that he did not believe there was a God, that he had never been disrespectful of the King, and that as for Justice, he consigned it to the Devil. . . ." A profession of faith hurled in the face of the executioner, or a last bit of bravado?

† This refers to Pascal's proposition that we must lay odds on God's existence or His non-existence. If we wager against His existence, and it turns out that God indeed does exist, then we stand to lose everything. The three other possibilities, however, lead either to a gain for us, or at worst, a draw.—Trans.

attics, even bedrooms, are cluttered with glasses through which everyone scans the heavens, straining to read astronomy in them. The *Femmes Savantes* are an amused echo of this. But let us recognize at once that, in matters of faith, discretion is prevalent.* To be sure, the Protestants had said so much about saints and miracles that one would have good reason to consider this the cause of the general discretion. The great debate between faith and a science which is very slowly gaining strength, occurs only at the end of the century: Pascal, who was obsessed by this problem,† did not have the time to deal with it. Hence, that curious silence, perhaps attributable to Descartes himself, which for thirty or so years imposed itself on his metaphysics and his physics with the same authority.

► **THE JANSENISTS**

Another reason for this silence, a reason not Cartesian nor even philosophical, is the scope of the theological and moral debate stirred up by the Jansenists and the Jesuits for nearly three decades, 1643-1668, which leads us from *La Fréquente . . . Communion* by Arnauld to the Peace of the Church in 1668. It is a religious controversy having multiple political and social aspects, in which roles are played by the king and Rome, the Sorbonne and the Parisian Parlement, the parish *curés*, the Port-Royal nuns and the faithful, hermits of the Granges and mere bourgeois from Saint-Germain l'Auxerrois. The entire capital becomes aroused, then the provincial towns are won over; and the life of the Church of France is branded for more than a century. When at the beginning of the nineteenth century the last of the Jansenists disappear, their name is still synonymous with austerity and greatness of soul.‡

---

* Renaudot's *La Gazette* reports, in 1650, a miracle: blood sprang forth from a tree cut down on the Feast of the Annunciation, a punishment for the Godlessness of a woodsman who dared to work on that holy day. It comments: "Concerning which miracle, I thought I ought to inform the worthy public that it is equally wrong to give credence to the first rumors people scatter about concerning miracles and to pass them on without proof as articles of faith—as some superstitious people do—as it is to ignore them, when they are found to be accompanied by official proofs, given by the authorities of the Church."

† The eighteenth Provincial Letter: "Whenever Scripture presents us with some passage whose first literal meaning is contrary to what sense or reason recognizes with certitude, one need not try to repudiate these in order to submit them to the authority of the Scripture's apparent meaning; rather, Scripture must be interpreted, and one must seek another meaning, that agrees with this visible truth. Because the word of God is infallible in very fact, and the connection between the senses and reason within their own sphere is certain too, these two truths must agree."

‡ Thus, in *Le Rouge et le Noir*, the Jansenist Abbé Picard, head of the seminary of Besançon, is depicted to us as sympathetically as the face of the Congregationalist Vicaire Frilair is blackened. This long intramural struggle with the Jesuits has earned the Jansenists virulent condemnations, even in our own day: M. Préclin, in an introductory history text for Clio, settles the question once and for all. "Saint-Cyran

The point of departure for this great Jansenist debate is *La Fréquente Communion*, written by Antoine Arnauld in 1643. Not that Saint-Cyran and Jansen are not important to the matter: but Jansen died in 1638 and his book, *Augustinus*, which was published in 1640, did not cause a great immediate stir—a fat theological work in School Latin, crammed with quotations from commentators on Saints Augustine and Paul. The few other publications written before 1643 and inspired by the Jansenist spirit did not cause any great backwash, either; for example, Séguenot's treatise *La Virginité* (1638). Saint-Cyran (who died in that same year, 1643) made a name for himself in Paris as the confessor at Port-Royal; he attracted to the convent those Parisians who yearned for the austere life—recluses who, after 1637, meet close by the convent in the Chevreuse Valley. He was not afraid to offer sharp criticism of certain of Richelieu's political operations which offended Christian morality, and this earned him his long stay, from 1638 to 1643, in the Bastille. But despite the severity of Saint-Cyran, Parisian religious life was not affected until the appearance of *La Fréquente*, as people called it then. Within a few months the Jesuits—the direct targets of this little treatise which used all the Christian authorities to demonstrate subtly that communion, so important a religious act, should not be taken several times a week—and friends of the new theologian bring the debate before the public consciousness. This work that "charmed the flower of the schools and of youth," according to Bossuet's expression, is the manifesto, as moral as it is doctrinal, of a conception of Catholicism which very quickly encounters an extraordinary consent for which—if we believe the evidence, and we have little reason to suspect it—the Jesuits themselves were the first ones responsible. Olivier d'Ormesson notes: "Monsieur Talon says that everyone considers it bad that the Jesuits should take it upon themselves to refute this book through the mouth of Father Nouet, who ascribed to them a quantity of false opinions which he does not enumerate; that they are being done a great injustice. . . ." Further on he adds: "I bought and read this book [*La Fréquente Communion*] and have seen only very good things in it." [18] Thus go the sermons, discussions, and endeavors in the Sorbonne, where outbursts are frequent, and simple Protestant sermons which deal bitterly with contemporary practices and predestination.

For the debate is located on two levels, and both are in question as long as the quarrels last: dogma—or rather certain points of dogma, for the Jansenists, who call themselves Catholic and wish to be Catholics, do not venture to call everything into doubt—and morality, that is, Catholic practices. Obviously these two levels are closely interconnected, but the

---

was a saint *manqué*, with a confused and immoderate brain . . . Aberrant doctrine. . . ." In the best instances, it is "the Jansenist heresy." *See* R. Mousnier, in the Crouzet series.

Jesuits' position varies widely from one to the other: they are happy to speak of the Jansenist "heresy," but are more cautious about the question of morality; while, for the Jansenists, the most important thing is "feeling God in a special way." The doctrine of Port-Royal is formulated by the *Augustinus*: St. Augustine is reformulated by Jansen into a mystical idea of grace and predestination which undoubtedly borders on Protestantism, and the good Fathers on the Rue Saint-Antoine deny themselves no opportunity of crying out "warmed-over Calvinism." The heart of the matter—and the reason why the nuns of Port-Royal are Jansenist before Saint-Cyran's arrival at the convent—is the deep humility of the faithful soul, engulfed by God, the soul which is nothing and counts for nothing before divine grace, before the righteousness of Christ on the Cross: irresistible grace and predestination follow next. In consideration of this, the Jansenists reject nothing of the Tradition, challenging neither the sacraments nor the miracles; they show a special tenderness for Bernard of Clairvaux, the patron saint of Port-Royal who, in his day, sometimes found himself in trouble with the Papacy. They loudly proclaim their love for the Virgin, mother of Jesus, and their attachment to the Church of Rome; at the most, they sigh for the Church of the early centuries.* The Jesuits examined the *Augustinus* line by line, hypercritically, and very quickly extracted certain passages which they finally condensed into the famous five propositions by which the book was contested until the eighteenth century: the Jesuits claimed to have condemned the whole sect on the basis of five expressions "extracted" from the spirit, not the letter, of the *Augustinus*—expressions along the lines of "Christ did not die for all men." The Jansenists readily agreed with the condemnation of these expressions, but constantly claimed that they were not to be found as such in the *Augustinus*. An endless debate, and one without any possible agreement.

It is the Jansenist morality which is the most important as regards the social history of France. This morality is the bitter and vivifying fruit of this doctrine and, as has often been remarked since, the basis of all

---

* There is a great deal of orthodoxy in all this—but the standard in this matter is not a scale, where one puts the good on one side and the bad on the other. Let us note, too, that the Jansenist positions do not incline, either, toward any sort of nationalism. The Jansenists are people who are too troubled, too highly aware of the presence of God at every moment of our life—very far from Bérulle. So, without speaking of Pascal and the Miracle of the Holy Thorn, a low-born Jansenist comments thus upon a dry spell overcome by prayers at the end of the century: "Everyone correctly attributed such a change to the intercession of Saint Geneviève, whose statue we took down and carried through Paris in a procession . . . these reflections strengthened us all in the belief in this great truth, attested by Scripture, that it is the hand of God, angry at our sins, which sends all the different scourges that afflict us; just as it is the same hand of the Lord, moved to mercy by our tears, which subsequently spreads his divine generosity over us." [19] (The miracle of the Holy Thorn refers to a relic of the Holy Thorn preserved at Port-Royal which cured Pascal's niece, Marguerite Périer, of an abscessed eye.—Trans.)

morality. Predestination, which implies the freedom of God, also entails that of man, who chooses the good, not for the reward promised, but gratuitously, for its own sake. When the Jesuits accuse Port-Royal of encouraging *libertins*—what does our way of living matter, since, whatever our life may be, if we have grace we shall be saved?—the Jansenists, on the contrary, assert the value of the act itself, which is not a matter of bargaining and is not connected with any fear of the heavenly police. Port-Royal acknowledges good works, to be sure; but for themselves, not as an exchange of courtesies in which eternal life would respond to the rhythm of daily good deeds.* This moral exigency and the "revaluation" which results from religious acts when they are regarded through a sense of incontestable holiness, are what simultaneously cause the difficulty of Jansenism, whose audience could only have been taken from people sufficiently cultivated to enter into those arduous reasonings, and its unheard-of success with the Parisian bourgeoisie, who were educated, and accustomed to these theological cavils. And within this bourgeoisie, Port-Royal was completely successful in its recruiting: among the *parlementaires*, who have long been hostile to the Jesuits and who are eager to take offense at the laxity into which the Jesuit confessors have fallen—particularly those around the great men, around royalty itself, in those days of Anne of Austria and of the young Louis XIV. This is the time when easy victories pile up for the Jesuits: the Sorbonne, the King, and Rome are for them, the Pope condemns the five propositions as early as 1653, the *Lettres Provinciales* are condemned in 1660, and the Port-Royal nuns are broken up in 1664—these are completed by the relentlessness of the Jesuits, making the recluses and their friends seem sympathetic even to those who were neutrals in the struggle.

Thus, for the Jesuits, Port-Royal is the enemy who must be conquered, at least until the peace of 1668, at which time the Protestants undergo a new spell of persecutions. The Jansenist achievements became too widespread, too intolerable, for that Society which considered it its duty to rule the ruling classes; especially when the latter turn to the Chevreuse Valley or the Parisian convent, avidly reading *La Fréquente Communion* and then the *Lettres Provinciales*, when, finally, a number of little works are written in the shadow of Port-Royal to support its positions. These are agile refutations of all the Jesuit theses,† grounded in great

---

* This recalls Calvin, in some respects, and presages Kant who, in the *Critique of Practical Reason*, is a secular Jansenist, with the moral law deep in his heart.

† The Jesuits, teachers of Rome, extol papal infallibility; previously this thesis had been rejected, at the Council of Trent, but the Jesuits stick to it. Yet the Jansenists know of a pope who declared himself fallible (Seconde Chamillarde): "On the contrary, it is infallible that the popes can be mistaken, and fail in their judgments. We have too many proofs of it, and here is one that ought to convince you, one that you can still less reject as it comes from the same popes you believe infallible. Read the fourth chapter of the first book of *Dialogues* by Saint Gregory. 'Why are you surprised, Peter, that we who are merely men make mistakes? Have you forgotten

theological knowledge and a resolute faith in the value of their cause. But the weighty replies of the followers of Loyola and Molina gather dust on the bookstore shelves: to the Parisians, the wind seems to be blowing from only one direction, and the *Lettres écrites par Louis de Montale** appear to be the last word in theology. There are other Jansenist triumphs—the Recluses (*Solitaires*) and the Elementary Schools (*Petites Écoles*). The people who, at the summit of their career, abandon responsibilities and honors, family life and worldly life, to make a retreat in Port-Royal, present an astonishing example of disinterestedness; these same great minds undertake education and open Elementary Schools, furnishing excellent teaching, and in French too—reaccepting the responsibility, and on a wider scale,† for the great boldness of the Oratorians, a daring that bore great fruit in this entirely Latinized educational system, where even reading and writing are taught in Latin. These schools are completely detached from the pleasures and amenities of life. Jean Racine and a few other *honnêtes hommes* are educated there; and when dozens of young men desert the Collège de Clermont to attend them, the Society of Jesus finds one more reason—a minor one but nonetheless not negligible—for fighting the sect.

At the point where the young Pascal writes, at Arnauld's request, the *Provinciales*, all the Parisian *robins* are won over, as well as a good part of the merchant bourgeoisie and the lower clergy, and even a few nobles. So are former members of the Fronde, like the Duchess of Longueville; a fine opportunity to accuse Port-Royal of political conspiracy, the one vice that is still lacking. The movement goes beyond Paris and gains in the provinces, in the large towns like Rouen, Orléans, and Toulouse, and in other more modest ones, like Pamiers and Beauvais: bishops and *curés* get mixed up with it,‡ as well as old supporters of a Gallican Church, and young *abbés*, all of whom find, in their own way, spiritual nourishment in this great dispute.

Then the religious exaltation thus spread across France is increased by virtue of the Miracle of the Holy Thorn (March, 1656), when Pascal's niece brings the proof of divine assistance to the good cause; next,

---

how David, who had the spirit of Prophecy, passed an unjust sentence on Mephibosheth, the son of Jonathan, when he gave credence to the false witness of his servant Siba?' " (The allusion is to Gaston Chamillard and his *Seconde lettre de M. Chamillard . . . à un de ses amis touchant la possibilité des commandmens aux justes, pour monstrer que la première proposition condamnée par le Pape Innocent X est de Jansénisme* published in quarto at Paris in 1655.—Trans.)

* Pascal adopted the pseudonym of Louis de Montale when he first wrote the book whose full title is: *Les Provinciales, ou Lettres écrites par Louis de Montale à un provincial de ses amis et aux RR. PP. Jésuites sur le sujet de la morale et le politique de ses pères.*—Trans.

† Port-Royal, hostile to Scholastic rhetoric, teaches French, and gives preference to translation over composition; their pedagogical success is incontestable.

‡ "He was established as a *vicaire* in a Rouen parish called Saint Étienne des Cordeliers . . . there he made known the Gospels, which were then greatly ignored." [20]

through the enormous success of Pascalian eloquence, slicing Jesuit casuistry in two with frightening zest,* and, ultimately, persecution. The Formulary imposed in a highly administrative fashion upon all the clergy, directing them to condemn the five propositions, very quickly proved the best means of spreading the wicked doctrine throughout France. How could one not excite at least curiosity with this condemnation: "I, the undersigned, submit myself to the Apostolic Constitution of Innocent X, Supreme Pontiff, given the 31st day of May in the year 1653, and to that of Alexander VII, his successor, given the 16th of October 1656; I both sincerely regret and condemn the five propositions extracted from the book by Cornelius Jansenius, entitled *Augustinus*, in the proper meaning of the same author, as the Apostolic Seat has condemned them in the same Constitution. I swear it so. May God and the Holy Gospel help me." Several other Formulary texts were used, more verbose than this one: the sense and the sibylline tone of the whole remains. Especially effective is the maltreatment, and the men—like Monsieur de Saci, who advised not signing and was deprived of the sacraments like a common criminal—thrown into the Bastille. The twelve chief nuns of Port-Royal, led by Angélique de Saint-Jean, were dispersed into safe convents in Paris. They bear their exile with such simplicity of soul that they stagger those who must lead them back again to the straight path, and they have to be sent back home.

Port-Royal is at the height of its glory. Paris is grumbling against royal despotism, and, in the years between 1661 and 1668, when the young king appears in all his radiance to confront Europe, the capital is ready to declare itself for the martyrs who are victims of royal arbitrariness and of M. de Péréfixe. And once the peace is signed in 1668—by virtue of the diplomatic skill of Lionne, who plays upon the Jesuits in Rome to obtain that signature with reservations, who complies with the scruples of the Jansenist conscience—and once Arnauld is received by the king, the "Sect" is as alive as ever throughout the kingdom, at least in the towns; it is strengthened by the support of a good part of the lower clergy and about twenty bishops, and by the sympathies secured in some orders like the Oratorians and the Maurists. This great moment of French Catholic thought is exalted by the painful fighting: it has become next-of-kin, in its struggle with Jesuit Ultramontanism, with the Gallican movement; it fills up the urban French world with its examples and its statements, spills over even beyond the frontiers into the Netherlands and Italy. At the moment when scientific life abroad (with Huyghens and Newton) is triumphing over that of France, and when

---

* Pascal does not shrink from violence of expression: "The Jesuits are people without words, faith, honor, or truth; they are doublehearted and doubletongued. . . ." Nor does he fear to call upon God: "If my letters are condemned at Rome, what I am condemning is condemned in heaven too. . . ." [21]

literature is reduced to a courtier's exercise, the Jansenism of the 1660s—a superior moral exigency, a new form of the traditional rejection of Ultramontanism*—attracts to itself an élite which, speaking out, expresses a moment of the French conscience.

---

* The Pascal of the *Provinciales*: "The Inquisition and the Society (of Jesus), the two scourges of truth. . . ."

X

❊

The Era of Classicism

"The Age of Louis XIV"

❊ ❊

THERE are some who believe that France and French civilization after 1660 are concentrated into one person, Louis XIV, and one place, Versailles. The king, and the framework created in the image of the monarchy as represented by the son of Louis XIII: it is this sense of monarchial grandeur by virtue of which Voltaire sets himself to extolling, in the 1750s, "the age of Louis XIV." * The expression has remained, and has even become popular, being eagerly applied to Augustus, Pericles, Leo X, and other great builders, and lovers of monumental glory, concerned with leaving a monument of their power to posterity: great politicians, and certainly Louis XIV is descended from this line.

However, the *Grand Siècle* has been so highly praised, so glorified by generations of writers and historians with monarchial affections, that it has become difficult to gauge it precisely: it is true that the king himself, in the image of his predecessors, Louis XI or Henry IV, was careful of his reputation: his *Mémoires*, a history of his reign written at great expense (not to mention the newspapers, *La Gazette de France, Le Mercure, La Muse Historique*) to sing of the achievements of the reign, are proofs of it. This monarch, consequently, has been glorified even in

* All the more so in that he makes of the work the occasion to denigrate the next king. Louis XV. who does not appreciate true talent.

his stalemates, even in the military defeats and the frightening poverty at the end, when the king, weighted down with familial mourning and attacked by all Europe, confronts the storm and, when it passes, thinks about initiating a new policy—on the eve of his death. Yet 1709-1713 represents the acme of the crisis, although the beginning of his reign knew the distress of an accumulation of bad harvests and commercial stagnation, against which Colbert struggled until his death. The ostentation of the reign, then, coincides with economic crisis: from 1660 to 1680, Colbert distributes gifts and pensions to artists and scientists from all over Europe, Louis XIV triumphs over Spain and the Holy Roman Empire, if not over Holland. The king of France "was then like the sole king of Europe," simultaneously feared and admired, and soon imitated throughout Europe, from the German courts to that of England's Charles II. But then after 1680, when the commercial world comes to life again and the courtiers establish themselves at Versailles, there is a revival of those forces opposed to absolutism, and the great king is not successful in destroying them: the daring of condemned Cartesians, the cries from Protestant martyrs and the fearlessness of the Jansenists, only for a moment subsided—not to mention the violent reaction following the king's death and the retreat of Madame de Maintenon, that advisor in dark days and unhappy old age.

One might say without paradox that this age of Louis XIV is no longer than that of Leo X: it lasts about twenty years, and already his primacy is escaping him and his ascendancy is contested. This is the age of French classicism, the beautiful days of the fetes at Versailles, where Racine and Molière are held in high honor, and where the king imposes on his court, and on the town, a formal style of life, in which intense emotion is contained and repressed. The classic age is a time of putting things in order, if not into a state of obedience: out of the passionate fertility of the preceding period, the king suppresses and buries everything that does not serve the monarchy: the Jansenist scandals, the aristocrats' unrest. Even science and art are brought under control: Colbert reorganizes the Académie Française of Richelieu, his forerunner, and creates an Académie des Beaux-Arts, which is to define official art, and an Académie des Sciences. To this last Colbert is the most generous: aiding and supplying them with the means for their experiments and research is a fine program, even if the founder, in so doing, is thinking of his own glory. The king directs, organizes, and controls: he closes half the Parisian printing shops and puts the rest under the surveillance of his police lieutenant. Such rigorous control is amputation *manqué*; after 1685 and particularly after 1700, those who were condemned and reduced to silence for some dozen or so years are doing well again, and resume their place in French life.

► **THE DIFFICULT TIMES (1660-1680)**

During this twenty-year period French economic life, insofar as it is
linked to international trade, undergoes along with the latter a contraction due in large measure to the depletion of monetary specie. The
Americas slow down their production to the point of supplying only an
infinitesimal amount; the hoarding that follows the increase in the price
of precious metals does the rest. This economic contraction entails a
decline in prices and a slowing down of commercial, and then handi-
craft, activities: gradually urban stagnation is generalized, and ends up
by affecting even public finances. After 1680, there are rather vague
hints of a recovery of large-scale trade, which, after rises and declines
and brief fluctuations, fully asserts itself in the following century. But it
seems that French participation in this recovery is moderate, if not weak;
many facts indicate this: the unceasing pursuit of precious metals, the
prohibition upon the gilding of calashes, the inventories of the "silver
plate in Churches, beyond what is necessary for the decorum of the
divine service," and so forth and so on. Stimulated by the achievements
of the English after the founding of the Bank of England, and by the
first deliveries of the Brazilian gold-panners, this commercial revival
was, as it were, thwarted in France by the additional economic and fiscal
burden of the quasi-continual wars, by the very serious famines which
bore down with all their weight, particularly in 1693-95 and in 1709,
and finally by the exodus of the Protestant merchants and craftsmen,
bringing about a loss of manpower, ruptures in relations, and interruptions of trading currents. This is a new misfortune, augmenting these
others that are more classic and, probably, more serious in the second
half of Louis XIV's reign than in the preceding decades.

It is in the first economic context that Colbert's mercantilist policy—
sometimes called Colbertism—is located. As a matter of fact, the great
minister exercised a financial and economic influence whose facets were
multiple: without reforming an oppressive financial system, he attempted to regularize the receipts of taxes and to improve the state of
agriculture without attaining equity—in short, he tried to relieve the
peasants' burdens. Treasurers and tax farmers are watched, even condemned, after Fouquet—who had been no worse, nor more dishonest,
a superintendent of finances than had his predecessors. All of these efforts to improve receipts did not produce the expected results, for two
reasons: because the system for farming out taxes hardly permitted efficient control, and because the constantly increasing weight of expenses
always won out: for a few years, from 1664 to 1672, the diligent minister
was able to manage the royal coffers without having recourse to the traditional expediencies—loans from reliable towns, conversions of *rentes*,

sales of offices and positions, even monetary manipulations. But then, overcome by the spendthrift king and by the vices of the fiscal and financial system, he returned like his predecessors to the offering and creation of offices; after his administration, public finances felt the effects of all this, especially, as the sinister years passed by, during the slump created by the famines.

Yet for twenty years Colbert stimulated this faltering economic life in order to increase exports and, consequently, to increase the influx of precious metals. His program was an unwieldy one, involving the creation of factories, the reformation of guilds, encouragements and subsidies for trading companies, particularly those colonial companies receiving the exclusive monopoly on trade with the Antilles, Canada, and Guinea. Leffemas and Richelieu had already tried this before, and in the same spirit: this mercantilism is an old economic doctrine, daughter of sixteenth-century Spain: it puts prime emphasis on draining precious metals into France from abroad—something that was easy from 1550 to 1600. Undoubtedly Colbert put more enthusiasm into his plans than had his predecessors; he tried to profit from the unfortunate experiences of Richelieu, whose companies had not been too successful, and he was far-seeing, even to the point of looking askance at the wealth of the Church, and of contemplating a retirement of monastic vows in the hope of diminishing the recruitment of those not-too-productive communities. Especially, he thought about organizing foreign trade, of limiting the purchase of those commodities of little value, agricultural products and wood, and, on the contrary, selling fabrics, woven goods, glass, porcelains—luxury products manufactured in duly controlled, guild workshops, or in new factories sown across France according to local aptitudes: weapons at Tulle, tapestries at Aubusson, etc. Colbert exerts himself for these plans without thinking of the consequences, and with a tenacity which the public did not often echo: *Lettres, Instructions, Mémoires* from the minister, which are in the main published, prove his ardor. He had the misfortune of setting up his great machine a century too late; of seeking to drain the Spanish metals, which had always been assumed to flow like water from Seville to Lisbon,* into France—at a time when these metals are becoming rare, when Spain reveals her poverty and the galleons are returning almost empty. This mercantilist logic, which was born in the days of Philip II, could not succeed. Doubtless this failure in itself does not suffice to explain all of Colbert's lack of success: we can easily see that his appeals to the reliable towns, asking their co-operation in launching a new company, go unheeded; the fam-

---

* Other proofs of this very current monetary notion: the French diplomats impose upon Spain the enormous sum of 500,000 gold *écus* as a dowry for Maria Theresa; and Mazarin is thought of as a Machiavel preparing for the War of the Spanish Succession. This notion is not necessarily true.

ine of 1622, the epidemic, and the billeting of soldiers, are quite good reasons for refusing the ten or twenty thousand *livres* requested. At this time when the Dutch, powerfully aided of course by their bank in Amsterdam, take over maritime transport, impose themselves on all the colonies, and transform Amsterdam into a warehouse for all Europe, the French bourgeois and nobles, to whom Colbert had granted the unimpeded right to large-scale trade, do not plunge into the conquest of the maritime routes: Santo Domingo makes progress, and trade with the Antilles is consolidated; but not in any proportion to the hopes of the minister, who is in love with an overweening conception. At the end of the century, Vauban understands this and he writes in his *Dixme royale:* "It is not great amounts of gold and silver that create the large and real riches of the State . . . the real riches of a kingdom consist of the abundance of commodities whose use is necessary to sustain men's lives, commodities they would be unable to do without." [1]

Did these economic difficulties exert pressure upon social relations? It does not appear that a strict determinism links the two during this period. As at the beginning of the century, the contemporary chronicles supply an abundant share of evidence concerning the rivalry that sets the *noblesse de sang* against the rising classes, both the legal profession and the merchant bourgeoisie, a rivalry that makes *robins* turn on one another at the very entrance of the courtroom, makes them argue—or sometimes do even worse*—about protocol, with a brutality which leaves far behind the stage business of Molière on the same subject. In this area, the greatest impulse came about because of the revision and controls undertaken by Colbert's committee, to stabilize the nobility's titles and residential districts. This purification, which lasted a good ten or twelve years despite the promptness insisted upon by the king, is actually the result of protests as old as the century, against the conferment of nobility, and the ease with which the *roturiers* had long been swelling the ranks of the nobles. The *noblesse de robe*, the decorated orders—all are screened, to the satisfaction of those whose entry into these good societies was not illegitimate: "We spoke with M. de Sourdis of the ceremony that took place this morning at the Cordeliers, for several Knights of Saint Michael, which (order) has been restored to honor, receiving people of rank . . . the number of knights has been reduced to one hundred, and it has been rid of all the riffraff." [3] From now on, it is more difficult to become a noble—and Colbert's census, when there was such gnashing of teeth and so many *roturiers* put back in their places,

* The following is a limited example, perhaps, but one laden with meaning: "M. Antoine Ducup, judge magistrate to the Senechal of Lauragais, against M. Jean Faure, lawyer from the Parlement of Toulouse, who gave the latter a sword-thrust in the stomach, in payment of being reproached for not having bowed to him." [2]

serves as a prelude for the formation of that caste which, in the closing years of the Old Regime a century later, the nobility became.

There were, to be sure, some beneficiaries of this economic stagnation: hucksters and speculators in scarce wheat, whose profits are not negligible. Yet those who make the most out of these difficulties are still those who profited from the problems of the public finances: the chronic deficit will become more pronounced, to the point of bordering upon catastrophe when, at the end of the reign, the revenues are eaten up several years in advance—for the greatest good of the treasurers, bankers, and tax farmers, both the great, like Samuel Bernard, and the small, like petty savings-bank clerks.* Nevertheless, these are dangerous careers, and sumptuous fortunes. The financiers shamelessly acquire riches, through complex operations which are to the immediate profit of the king and their own long-range profit. Others who were favored, in addition to the four thousand financiers to whom Colbert wished to make restitution, were the purchasers of royal offices: multiplied by all possible means, divided semi-annually and quarterly, these offices are not always the ridiculous functions like that of the licensed master burial crier. In quite a few professions their role is important, and comfortable fortunes are consolidated there, with genuine discretion which does not allow large profits any more than it necessitates the financier's risks.

Let us look more closely at this solvent wealth: a sworn expert architect, who in addition owns a building concern, dies in 1706, leaving his widow two very attractive houses: one is an eight-room house in Paris, with a stable and courtyard—a small *hôtel*; the other is a smaller summer house in the country, at Épinay-sur-Seine.† In each house we discover all the signs of opulence: tapestries "going all around" the walls of each room, except the kitchen—Flemish or Bergamot tapestries, "old" ones at Épinay, newer ones at Paris; not to mention the curtains on the doors, thirty-nine ells in one place and thirty-one in the other; then the mirrors, more valuable than the furniture which is oak, walnut, or pear; each large room, be it an ordinary room or a bedroom, has these mirrors, which are designated as the primary decoration, and carefully described (sixteen inches, twenty-six inches of glass, frame, etc.); and finally, the silverplate, carefully distinguished from the fine pewter utensils and decorative crockery, and hallmarked on each article—candlesticks, forks, and spoons. Épinay, which has several mirrors but no silverplate, is a reserve of wood, bundles of firewood, and especially wine: "nine demi-hogsheads and two demi-squares of local red wine from the said

---

* All Paris periodically speaks of these extraordinary fortunes: a mere savings-bank clerk dies leaving his heirs five million *livres*, as well as some gems for distribution to avoid legal actions.

† This is taken from the inventory of Maître Nicolas Liévain, made after his death, and is one chosen among many.[4]

Épinay in the present year." The detail of the inventory gives us a picture
of a life as comfortable as the domestic arts of the day permit. A conversion of the sums that are supplied for each furnished room, even in
francs germinals, would not be very meaningful. Let us merely indicate
that the furniture of the Parisian house is valued at a total of 2,568
livres and of the Épinay house at 698; added to which the silverplate,
not counting the "table settings of fine pewter," is valued at 763 *livres*.
This impression of a comfortable life would be completed by adding
the contents of the libraries, the carriages and horses in the stables—all
of which are not "gray-haired and superannuated" like our licensed architect's own horse—and the trips from Paris to Épinay in the summer
months, a kind of vacation taken a stone's throw away from the town in
a rural setting. This bourgeois existence certainly seems to be one of domestic economy, in which the great concern is with furnishings and ap-
pointments—thus, it is quite different in its setting and particularly in
its way of life from that of Versailles and the court, where, in a setting
whose scale is entirely different, everyone spends without reckoning.
The opposition between the town and the court is not merely a theatrical one.

► THE KING: VERSAILLES

The great idea of the king's reign—we may well use this expression for
this king who was able to change his means, but who never, for one day
during the fifty-four years of his personal reign, lost his concern for
glory—was to make of the French monarchy a kind of model for all of
Europe, if not for the world: did he not receive at Versailles men even
from Siam? Such a task had been well prepared for by the Cardinal-
ministers: we need look no further than Richelieu, who ordered the
razing of the fortified castles, and organized the commissions of *intendants*, and Mazarin, whose diplomacy in Westphalia in 1648 secured the
recognition of French as the official diplomatic language. This absolute
monarchy will go on existing, with all its institutions and machinery intact, until the end of the eighteenth century, so well did Louis XIV know
how to persuade his contemporaries, and posterity, that it was impossible to surpass him, his court, and his councils—and, in particular, impossible to surpass his château, that great royal operation he had
worked on until his last years, that haughty example of power and order,
established by the king who well deserved the epitaph of Massillon's exordium opposite his mortal remains: the "most illustrious of the kings
of Christendom."

It was, first of all, the good fortune of Louis XIV that he, the king
who loves his profession, "never relaxing an iota of his diligence" until
his final days, and an administrator by preference and fact, should encounter the minister, a man of work and method, less clever governor

than taskmaster, a bourgeois completely devoted to the monarchic ideal. Both the king, jealously guarding his authority, and the minister, more overwhelmed with responsibilities than with titles, moulded the face of the monarchy for twenty years and, from 1664 to 1668, when all the reorganizations are under way, experienced the exaltation of founders. These reorganizations include the reform of the ministries and councils, the restoration of royal authority in the provinces, the supervision and control of the divided clergy, aroused by the Jansenists' polemic, and the delimitation of the nobility and bourgeoisie—with a daring and a rigor that stunned contemporaries in all three estates. The Parisian bourgeoisie which, at the beginning of the reign, still has Frondist tendencies, and is swept along by the religious dispute, scarcely appreciates the young king's first outbursts of authority. In 1666, this doggerel poem is circulated:

> Surrounded by the glory of his reign,
> With Cæsar's wisdom, Alexander's prowess:
> It's said that God did with this King endow us,
> Might He, alas! but take him back again!

Fouquet's trial turns public opinion in the minister's direction. The Jansenists are not slow to denounce the tyranny of a despotic king, but they do not advocate tyrannicide. And even among the nobility there are a few who do not have Saint-Simon's pen, who are, and will be for a long time, indignant: when the king claims he has the right to subject the nobility to taxes and when the required manifestations of servility become excessive. The Chevalier de Quincy thus relates the inauguration of the equestrian statue of the king, on the Place Louis-le-Grand on August 13, 1699, when the provosts and *échevins* bowed to the statue "so low, they touched the necks of their horses," and notes: "It seemed to me that this ceremony smacked of Nebuchadnezzarism." [5]

Louis XIV wants to be obeyed throughout his realm, an extremely natural desire, but an immense task, and one at which Colbert wore himself out, even to dying of overwork. It is difficult to declare that this aim is attained by 1715. If one compares the advances to the troubled days that came before, the bad memories of the Fronde (that obsession of the young king) and the weaknesses of Mazarin, forced to use trickery in Paris itself, they are undeniable, yet extremely limited. As for the government, it is clear that Louis XIV perfected a well-oiled machine: the councils meet on the appointed date and their functions are well determined; the ministers are granted an imposing staff; by the end of the century, there are more than nine hundred "secretaries to the king" at Versailles, each responsible for a narrowly limited task, each forever at the disposal of the king who makes himself "directly sensible" of them. This represents a system of government different from that of, for example, a Francis I—that other great king, who did not have a

Colbert by his side. And when the man in charge of this machine is Louis XIV, who lets no day go by without thinking of business, who is "informed of everything," "receiving and reading dispatches"— then the *bureaux*, ancestors of modern administrative systems, give their utmost, and the ministries work and govern. With the indolent Louis XV, the indifferent Louis XVI, things will be different.

In the same fashion, the king makes the provinces increasingly aware of his presence, through the *intendants*: those functionaries, not officers, who are established in an administrative [fiscal] division, the *généralité*, and who are always granted full powers of justice, police, and finance (according to their title). The *intendants* are, by law, the chiefs of all administration; they are able to set aside cases, to revise the tax rates and enact statutes. Usually the former Maîtres des Requêtes in the Grand Conseil, these new representatives of the king, assisted by subordinates whom they themselves recruit (sub-delegates), are remarkable agents of centralization. Now, as early as the beginning of the eighteenth century, these *intendants* restrict themselves to economic duties, such as recording the movements of prices and commodities. They are the king's statisticians who are going to try their hand at reform, but reform primarily in the economic sphere—which, not surprisingly, means that their reforms are for the most part a failure. Previously, in the days of Richelieu, the *intendants* and their then temporary envoys provoked a rather loud hue and cry, so that, at the beginning of his ministry, Mazarin agrees to discontinue them. Since they are responsible for control and rectification, the *intendants* get in the way of the magistrates and financiers whose actions they have come to supervise. All these officers, presidial judges, treasurers, and elected officials are local people, well settled into the functions from which they often derive more pride than profit—loyal servants of the king, they are nonetheless accustomed to total independence which allows them to protect, more or less consciously, the interests of their class as well as the general interest and they do not bear up well under the *intendants'* control and decisions. The failure of administrative centralization lay first in the struggle between the two sets of personnel, in which the older, and the more solidly rooted in the provinces, wins out more by erosion than by violent struggle.* But the failure of the *intendants* lies also in the unequal struggle conducted against administrative diversity in France: to which Colbert, as a good administrator, would perhaps have put everything in good order, he who organized the Cinq Grosses Fermes around Paris and who, one fine day, wished to unify the usages of the *régale*

---

* Though impatient words and gestures were not lacking; as far back as 1643 in Toulouse: "Someone named Landes, a treasurer of France, in the center of the town's public Square where there were a large number of people of quality, and also the populace . . . said that it was not at all necessary to pay the *tailles'* surcharges, nor to put up with the *intendans* in the province, more especially since they were the cause of all the surcharges, and were thieves as well." [6]

in all the dioceses of the realm.* But the king, faithful to a tradition going back to the Capetians, making France a mosaic of provinces more than a unified kingdom, does not go that far: charters, urban and provincial privileges, and local rights maintained in the provinces (in proportion to their annexation)—he revokes none of these, any more than he touches those of the regions annexed during his reign.† Thus, everything conspires to impede that centralization which the *intendants* symbolize in their *généralités*: the superimpositon of the administrative divisions, the practice of customary law in the north and written law in the south (with an enormous margin of uncertainty along the Massif Central, for the greatest benefit of provinces like the Auvergne), the very maintenance of the still powerful courts run by the lords—a lord who is a high judge under Louis XIV is still using his power of life and death—and finally, the variety of the forms of fiscal administration. The king superimposed one machine upon so many others, but he did not have the tranquil audacity of the members of the Constituent Assembly, a century later. Doubtless he makes himself better understood than his predecessors, doubtless he is more concerned about knowing what is happening, "listening to the least of my subjects," and many wrongs could be righted during the Grands Jours in Auvergne—but it does not go much further.

The sovereign's efforts to increase his ascendancy over the clergy move in the same direction: the Concordat of Bologna, granting the king the right to appoint bishops and *abbés*, is already a generous concession. Louis XIV, imbued with the divine character of his authority, wanted a good bit more. A man of great piety—even in the days of La Vallière and others like Madame de Montespan (D'Ormesson, in the *Mémoires*, mentions an extremely edifying fast day in 1665)—and very careful about his official duties, Louis XIV neglects none of his ecclesiastical obligations either, and touches at least as many scrofula victims as his predecessors.‡ He congratulates Bossuet, who makes his *Politique tirée*

---

* The Cinq Grosses Fermes refers to the main customs area, with a plethora of internal tolls and duties, which Colbert wanted to unify into one customs unit. *Régale* means royal prerogative, and here refers to Colbert's attempt to exercise the royal prerogative to pre-empt the revenues of vacant sees and abbacies for the king's coffers.— Trans.

† The principle is certainly understandable. The provinces newly integrated into royal France find their annexation more bearable because their traditions and rights are not appreciably changed. The Third Republic, after all, acted no differently when it decided, at the time Alsace and the Moselle were recovered after the First World War, to keep the laws which had been in force under the German regime, concerning the churches and the schools.

‡ M. Bloch, in his *Rois thaumaturges*, gives this text of a poster calling together the diseased people. It is obviously the current model:

"On the part of the King and M. the Marquis de Souches, Prévost de l'Hôtel of His Majesty, and the Grande Prévôté of France,
We wish to make it known to all those to whom it appertains that next Sun-

des propres paroles de l'Écriture sainte a divine-right theory of the monarchy. In open conflict with Rome concerning the southern bishoprics, whose spiritual and temporal *régale* eludes royal administration, Louis XIV demands of the clergy that beautiful expression that comes from the mouth of the same Bossuet: "We are so closely devoted to your Majesty that nothing could separate us from you," followed by the declaration of 1682, which for ten or so years was taught as the law of the land. The accord with Rome in 1694 brings this Gallican triumph to an end: Louis XIV, better advised by Jesuit confessors and Madame de Maintenon, is no longer the head of the Church of France, any more than were his predecessors—but the meaning of his attempt is clear.

These undertakings were so limited, and so well limited, that it is not overbold to advance this assertion: the glory of Louis XIV was essentially served by two follies of grandeur, both of which he is said to have repented upon his deathbed: his wars, and his buildings, to which he devoted himself ceaselessly for fifty years. At first the wars were fought in lace cuffs, surprise attacks that risked nothing—a region invaded, a government backed into a corner by the measures of the despair between 1708 and 1712. On several occasions, Louis XIV was not afraid to fight all Europe; his reign contributed much toward making the kingdom of France coincide with the limits of linguistic France, especially if one counts the 1659 acquisitions. Yet whatever glory might accrue to the king from these wars, he was not always victorious: as early as 1672 there is a defeat in Holland, and at the end of the War of the Spanish Succession in 1713, Louis XIV, that monarch by divine right, admits the right acquired in 1688 by the English to choose their own king, and to prefer William of Orange over James II, as well as the Spanish grandees' right to choose the successor to Charles II. These are the early adumbrations of a principle of international law destined for a fine and long life: the right of peoples to self-determination. But from triumphant meetings in interminable and ruinous wars, Louis XIV remains the king who is "not only contemplated, but admired, by the whole world," in spite of everything: because he plays the starring role for half a century, and also, perhaps, because no failure can dishearten him. After 1713, in his last two years, does he not prepare an entirely new policy which completely transforms his system of alliances and proclaims a striking revenge for the humiliations he has suffered at the hands of the English? After his death, Europe felt a vacuum, and gave itself twenty-five years of peace.

The memory of these wars is preserved and, if one thinks of Louvois'

---

day, Easter, His Majesty will touch those afflicted with Scrofula, in the galleries of the Louvre, at 10 A.M., for which no one can claim ignorance; and those who are afflicted with the said disease may go there if they see fit."

burning of the Palatinate, even maintained. The territorial gains are there —Franche-Comté, Strasbourg, and the pieces of Flanders that were gradually nibbled off. But the buildings, too, bear witness: it is true that Versailles (to restrict oneself to the essential building) is not merely the plastic and architectural expression of royal prestige, but is also the setting of a new life, in which the nobility, the ministerial bourgeoisie, and the humbler domestic staff meet one another every day. There are the social relations of other days, the ceremony, a life of presentations at court—and, beyond the iron gates, there is a new urban life in that town created around the château for him, out of nothing. Louis XIV gave to the French soul more than a décor, more than a new style, in this setting some distance from Paris—yet, in another sense, close to Paris, for Paris is present in its artists and artisans, its indispensable purveyors to Court life, who participate as silent and undaunted witnesses in the decay of the nobles, the insolence of the financiers—silent, for the time being.

The château has its long and rather well-known history, which in essence would be the following: at the beginning, the king conceived an envious admiration for Fouquet's little château of Vaux-le-Vicomte, Italianized like a Renaissance château, but opening its symmetrical façade onto a superb garden by Le Nôtre. With Fouquet imprisoned, Louis XIV salvages his foremen, Le Vau and Le Nôtre (Mansart comes later), and, as early as 1661, has them work on transforming his father's modest shooting lodge, a little building of red brick on white stone, set among the marshy forests oozing with water and rich game. The king, who has at his disposal Saint-Germain, the Louvre, Fontainebleau, among others, certainly seems at the beginning to have wanted to create a setting for fetes: his château is, in the early years, primarily the place where the court holds its merry-making: as early as 1664, all the court is installed at Versailles to participate in those fetes given under the title of *Plaisirs de l'île enchantée*. Then he thinks of a residence, then, gradually, of a resort—which makes of Versailles the new and definitive backdrop of the reign, where there are daily fetes, well ordered, following etiquette and the king's pleasure. There are a dozen or so years of preparations, of structures adapted to the earlier buildings that have been preserved, and, from 1682 on, the king and court come and set themselves up there, even though the work is far from completion. For that, Colbert, who has left us his accounts, had to survey, drain, transport stone and marble, employ up to thirty thousand men, and spend hundreds of millions.* Thus the château, by the processes of modifica-

---

* Hundreds of men were killed or wounded: in 1668, "a woman who had lost her son in a fall while he was working on the scaffolding at Versailles . . . presented an incomplete petition . . . reviled the king, calling him whoremonger, deceiver, tyrant, and a thousand other abuses." 7

tions and slight alterations in the plans, turns out to have the appearance of a gigantic Parisian *hôtel*, with its interior courts, its buildings at right angles, and its outbuildings set back off the square; while the long façade facing the gardens, the state room, fountains, and music directly conjure up Louis XIV's life of official entertainment. The receptions and the arrangement of the ceremonies, whether indoors or out, command perspectives of the gardens, the Grand Canal, or simply the Hall of Mirrors. This is the necessary* setting for an activity that daily moves several thousand people—not including the domestic staff.

From the days of the *divertissements* and *plaisirs*, Le Brun and his associates actively carry out the ornamentation: royal commissions wish to perpetuate, in marble and bronze, the memory of sweet moments—Cupidons and Amors, winged and triumphant. As the palace façade lengthens, the horizon emerges along the symmetrical avenues. Le Brun must supply everything, hordes of paintings, frescoes, and sculptures, as if to people the wide surfaces and cut the vast perspectives. The reign is narrated in Allegories, with the king as Apollo or Alexander, with so many Psyches, Mars, Hercules, and Venuses—in a mythology that is at once familial and symbolic. Did the ornamental profusion impress contemporaries? It was made, certainly, to dazzle.† In this respect, the large mirrors in the Hall of Mirrors are an even greater luxury; in the days when making a thirty-six-foot-square mirror means paying for twenty thousand hours of manpower—a fortune—the mirrors in Versailles may readily represent the greatest magnificence.[11] To posterity, the transient images of water and mirrors are less important than the antique glory with which the king desired to surround himself. Colbert, pensioning and heaping commissions upon artists from all over Europe, founding academies of painting, sculpture, and music, to which he attracts both Frenchmen and foreigners—Tubi, van der Meulen, and others—Colbert, Director of Letters and Arts, has left some important texts concerning this antique inspiration, which continues that of the Renaissance, but codifies it and makes of it the exclusive canon of French art. He writes to the director of the Académie de France at Rome, founded in 1666 and an ancestor of the French École de Rome: "Have

---

* Though some contemporaries, peevish spirits or cantankerous enemies, could claim not to believe this: "Expenses incurred on Buildings as little known to the public as they are useless to them, and on fountains that withdraw from nature by dint of being magnificent, are becoming ridiculous." [8]

† There are abundant numbers of admiring descriptions; it is still true that many especially appreciate the themes: "So vast a quantity of all sorts of work of all the diverse parts of painting, that is history, portraiture, landscape, seascape, floral, and fruit," said one man[9] while visiting a royal exhibition in 1667. Terseness remains, it is true, the rule of the day: "After dinner, I went to see the fresco paintings of Monsieur Mignard in the vault of the dome of the Val de Grâce; they are very beautiful." [10] (The Val de Grâce was a Parisian convent and the frescoes referred to are in the church. Today it is a military hospital.—Trans.)

them work diligently on the terminal statues, the vases, and, generally, on everything I ordered from you; but pay careful attention that the sculptors copy Antiquity purely, without adding a thing to it." * And in another letter, he does not hesitate to prescribe measurements to be taken with the greatest exactitude, so that the reproduction may be absolutely identical with the model. For Versailles, and through Versailles, academicism, that exclusive worship of the antique (so exclusive that the Gothic had never been so inveighed against as by Le Brun's associates and followers), is born and is to be maintained for more than a century —by virtue of the very reputation of all things Louis-Quatorze.

The décor is magnificent: a two-hundred-thirty-foot-long hall, ornamental lakes, fountains—a setting dreamed by a king who wants to impress Peter the Great, and the Turkish sultan as well. But Versailles is more than that. Far from Paris, its Fronde and its "populace," it is a well-ordered society where that lackey Colbert is responsible for revising and controlling noble titles, and for putting everyone in his place: *princes du sang* and well-titled nobles who are admitted to the daily ceremonies and presented to the king according to a set form; but also the *robins*, the secretaries for the Ailes des Ministres, and the innumerable household of the palace and the new town.

The wings of the château, which project toward the town, are occupied by a numerous population of pen-pushers, advisors, registrars, royal secretaries, bourgeois, and *robins*, all mixed together; these are the representatives of political power, of the State. In their realm, they are formidable, and fully aware that they control the machinery of government, insuring the administrative life of the kingdom. They are not arrogant or ambitious as are the nobles and great ecclesiastical personages—Louis XIV would not have borne that—but they are workers devoted to the king, and to him alone; feared by the courtiers (Madame de Sévigné and Colbert), they are relentless in their work for the progress of this monarchic autocracy of whom they are the best servants; simultaneously they are remote and discreet witnesses of court life proper. The king rewards their zeal with offices and noble titles, now parsimoniously distributed and regarded as the greatest possible honor.

There is still another world: the ten thousand or so servants employed in the château, and in addition the servants of those nobles who have gradually settled in the new town during the course of the reign— coachmen, footmen, kitchen servants, personal maids, gardeners, and

---

* Correspondence of the directors of the Académie de France at Rome, letter dated February 1, 1680. All this entails an appreciable impoverishment—for example, all Flemish art, from Rubens to Rembrandt, is discredited in the setting of Versailles, although not at Paris and still less at Lille or Amiens, areas frequently in touch with the Low Countries and which serve as fringes of trade and influences from the border regions.

wine-butlers. It is an entire small staff which, better even than the ministerial secretaries, insures the necessary connection with Paris. The capital supplies furniture, clothing, and fabrics because Versailles does not,
nor ever did, have the trades necessary for equipping and maintaining
the palace and its inhabitants; a whole one-way traffic is thus carried out
through this household, one which knows all about the life at court,
spreads doings and exploits far and wide, and broadcasts all sorts of news
to the dispossessed capital. This is something to which Louis XIV is not
blind—one day he upbraids the laziness of Philip V: "Don't imagine
that public opinion does not know about it; they are better informed
than anyone else; if you send out one of your letters, they know it before I do." By virtue of this, there is no obstacle between the king and
public opinion—anything Louis XIV might possibly wish to hide, Madame de Montespan or Samuel Bernard, the town is informed of; and
rapidly so, without recourse to the *Gazette d'Amsterdam,* that implacable puritanical and republican newssheet which welcomes all the gossip
from Versailles. But in the other direction, from the town to the king,
there is little communication. What is happening in the country, what
the common opinion of him is, of these the king knows very little—
only what the dispatches of those *intendants* who are zealous, but careful
about their careers, or the reports of La Reynie for Paris, are willing to
tell him. For the end of the reign, at least, Vauban and Saint-Simon
have recorded this opinion. But generally, a screen, to say nothing of
royal vanity, masks everything: the court is the tree hiding the forest.

The king certainly is not unaware of the lady's maids whom, as everyone knows, he greets with extreme politeness; or of his ministers and advisors whom he receives, listens to, and directs; but his usual entourage
consists of the *noblesse présentée,* as the contemporary expression calls it
(though it is a poor expression; the essential feature of this nobility is
not that it is presented, but that it is kept, which is much more significant). To a certain extent, Louis XIV admired Spanish etiquette, with
its extremely deferential tributes, and he wanted to have near him a few
thousand nobles who might serve as the down-stage actors, the supernumeraries of a perpetual ceremony, regulated like a ballet or an extremely glorious dramatic production. The king, at the center of the
court, stages a show of the greatest names of France, who are attentive
to his slightest gestures and desires. The nobility who, until the 1650s,
were unruly, boisterous, and dangerous to royal authority, are by 1680
domesticated and arranged in files or groups according to the ceremonies, are occupied day in, day out, with the monarch and his actions. A
century earlier, the hottest heads were taking up arms and conducting
war upon war against the king; at the end of the seventeenth century,
the most exalted of the great men takes up his pen—and exhales forty
volumes of his bitterness. A fine success for the man who was able to at-

tract around him those four or five thousand supernumeraries. He needs them, they need him; there are continual fetes, doubtless pleasant, for at least twenty years. There are daily ceremonies, from the king's arising to those ambassadorial receptions and presentations of foreign princes that are flattering to both hosts and guests. But the nobles drawn into all this found near the king something they had been lacking for decades: the wealth of pensions, offices filled by title only, ecclesiastical benefices received in commendam, dowries for daughters and officer's commissions for sons. When Henry IV wanted to get rid of Mayenne and his fellow plotters, he loaded them with gold and sent them back to their estates; and so, as early as 1610, if not before, the plots recommenced. Louis XIV, on the other hand, receives the rebel Condé, but he sets Condé up near him: the gain is obvious. Obvious, too, for the nobles; without the generosity of the king, how many would have been able to maintain the style of living necessitated by Versailles: an on-the-spot local *hôtel*, since Paris is too far away to allow a trip to the château, even once a day; a carriage and stables, and the household presupposed by mansion, carriage, and horses; a wardrobe according to the tastes of the day, to one's mistresses' fantasies, the costume balls, "all those little ribbons" and "canions," which are so expensive.* Apart from the princes of the blood—who live at the château besides—and the greatest families like the Condé, few nobles are able to maintain this style of living upon their own resources: consequently, the king fits them out, provided they be there and make themselves seen. Court offices multiply—chamberlains, butlers—and go to the most industrious, just as do the best military posts and other things of this sort. With a hint of scorn, no doubt, the king distributes generously: Madame de Sévigné perceived this when she said "what he flings about."

Such is the upper nobility, maintained by the king to do nothing, especially, to make no plots—slaves of the royal person, shut up in a golden cage, but nonetheless confined: several thousand courtiers, for whom Versailles is the end of the world, for whom all one's art goes into making oneself seen, obtaining a favor, having the chance to hand the king his shirt or a glass of wine; for whom all one's ambition is to be among his intimates, among the two or three hundred who are present at the *grand lever*, or the fifty at the *petit coucher*. This is a life of in-

---

* Despite all the king's generosity, the nobility, from which a large part of the Parisian luxury professions earn their living, pays poorly and is always in debt. The bourgeois businessmen bitterly complain: "The nobility often shows off its splendor, never by serving the king the way they might by military service, but by all kinds of expenditure . . . As far as I am concerned, a noble is a man who is able to contract huge debts by his bad behavior, and unable to pay one of them. They even think that man who pays loses face. . . ." [12] *Cf.* Don Juan and Monsieur Dimanche. (Characters in Molière's *Don Juan*—M. Dimanche is an example of a creditor easily intimidated and impressed by his debtor's fancy phrases and exaggerated politeness.—Trans.)

terminable presentations, of long and patient periods of idleness, of social games and long waits, of contemplation of the king eating, for
hours; a life of powerful intrigues, in which the smile, the amenity, are
the lessons of diplomacy. Beplumed, in full dress from morning on, their
bodies bathed in perfume (for palace etiquette restricts bathing time)
—the court nobles live for the royal presence alone. Look at the little
marquis in Molière, who depicted his age so cruelly and so well: "As
for me, just as long as I can be at the *petit coucher.* . . ." [13] This is, to
our eyes,* a humiliating life. Forgetting the honor and glory of combat,
and that medieval military ideal that won it privileged place at the head
of society, that nobility now places its ambition in the daily service of
the court, in the intrigues and the "worldly" distractions. At the very
best, we can say that, having long been hostile to work, manual or
otherwise, and being anxious not to lose face, the nobility accepts as its
goals the fetes and entertainments of a gilded prison.

Perhaps these superficial remarks explain the attraction of the court
in its first twenty years. In the days of Lully, Molière, and Racine, of this
young king drunk with his own glory, with his triumphs in love and
military victories, the life of the court has all the most brilliant attractions; the king succeeds in making the idle nobles feel carefree,
concerned with nothing but to please, to shine in those large fetes
mounted by the king to celebrate triumphant peace treaties, outstanding events of his family life. At the beginning of 1669, when the king
wishes to celebrate with his court the Treaty of Aix-la-Chapelle, he pays
100,000 *livres* (a fortune today) to offer his guests collations in the
gardens, theater on the green (a ballet by Lully and *Monsieur de Pour-
ceaugnac*); then dinner, fireworks, fountains, and dancing late into the
night.

In this sphere, as in that of the plastic arts, Louis XIV established
the style for a century—and with more originality than he did for painting and sculpture. He had Chapelain and his fund for Letters,† and
Lully, the Superintendent of Royal Music, helped him to acclimatize
theatrical performances (ballet, opera, and drama) to Versailles; these
performances form, along with the games and balls, the skeleton of the

---

* And to the eyes of some contemporaries: Madame de Sévigné put up with the
system but escaped from it as often as possible, and we will not even speak of Saint-
Simon and La Palatine (Charlotte-Elizabeth of Bavaria, second wife of Monsieur
—Philippe, Duc d'Orléans, Louis XIV's brother—Trans.), whose indignations are well
known. Some nobles, accustomed to camp life, remained faithful to the military ideal
of the nobility and refused the life of Versailles: "You do not yet know that a courtier is a real chameleon. . . . The courtier is in the habit of grovelling at the feet
of ministers and favorites; he prostrates himself servilely. His endearments are false,
he is ungrateful once he has succeeded, and he curries favor. . . ." [14]
† Though Chapelain was a mediocre poet, Colbert put him in charge of dispensing
royal prizes.—Trans.

fetes. In the days of Francis I, hunts, large excursions, tournaments, and mock combats were the basic entertainment of the royal entourage; later, under Henry III, ballets were performed at the Louvre for the king; and Henry IV had musicians and singers come from Italy for Marie de' Medici. But in giving so large a place to drama, Louis XIV is accepting as a standard for court life the taste of the town, that is of Paris, where from 1640 to 1660, under the influence of the cultivated Mazarin, Parisians adopted two forms of entertainment. On the one hand, there were dances and ballets, simple productions of old dances like *bourrées, pavanes,* and *voltes* led by a *vielle* and a violin, with the dancers "masked and dressed in ballet costume";[15] or else more elaborate compositions of varied pace: *Les Rues de Paris, Les Fées des forêts de Saint-Germain, Les Effets de la Nature.* On the other hand, there is Italian opera, whose triumph is enormous from 1647 or 1648 on: plays sung in front of large sets, enlivened by ballets, and *entrées en scène,** in 1647, Rossi's *Orfeo* surprises and enchants some, and disappoints others. But the opera comes into its own, alongside the spoken drama of Corneille and many others. During 1669 and 1670, the Parisian repertory is jammed: Mairet produces seven plays (*Silvie, Sidonie,* etc.), Rotrou twenty, Boisrobert six, Pierre Corneille twenty-four, Thomas Corneille sixteen.

Consequently, the town's taste becomes, by the king's will, that of the court: Corneille, Molière until his death in 1674, and Racine until *Phèdre* in 1677, work for Versailles, they are sponsored, pensioned, and coddled by Louis XIV—it is a generous time.† But more than tragedy or comedy it is the ballet and the *comédie-ballet* that were most successful at court: Molière and Corneille cater to this taste by inserting interludes and danced *entrées* into some plays, which cut the pace of the play. Lully is the master of the Versailles fetes: a prolific genius, he charms a generation of courtiers and most of all the king, who is delighted both to dance at costume balls dressed as Apollo and sunbedecked, and to initiate new dances like the minuet and gavotte. Annexed to the royal service after 1661, Lully writes ballets and operas staged with luxurious costumes and sets: they are as much spectacle as music, though Lully brings all his attention to bear on the orchestration of the music for his theater. There is no doubt that in these theatrical triumphs between the years 1660 and 1680, received with applause in Paris and at court, is expressed the classical ideal described at length by

---

* A term used for the acts in opera-ballet when each act has a separate subject.— Trans.

† Molière's boldness—*Tartuffe, Don Juan*—is well known; so great is his daring that the king's protection alone saves the artist from the worst censure. The two plays, with their *ex machina* conclusions, pose great problems: Don Juan, well before Figaro, tells the nobles some harsh truths (IV, 6): a freethinker says on stage, "I believe that two and two are four. . . ."

Boileau: an ideal of restrained feelings and mastered passions which, to a certain extent, the king imposes as the role of that still "unkempt world" of his nobility. The communion of the theater is, however, much more: the spectator's "holy thrill," united for an instant with the actor who plays for him, is a great school for taste and finesse that prepares for the eighteenth century's delicacy—men like Marivaux and Rameau owe the king a great deal.

For that matter, these fetes and theatrical entertainments very quickly won over contemporaries, who were dazzled by the marbles and mirrors of the palace, but also charmed by the ballets and the plays. There were foreign ambassadors, invited somewhat ostentatiously by the king; courtiers laughing and applauding, discreetly, after him; and, especially, foreign princes: Voltaire records this all in his 1750 *Siècle de Louis XIV*. Neither Fontainebleau nor the Louvre's colonnades count any more, and the most common ambition is to create a Versailles elsewhere in Europe. Charles II of England populates his court with Frenchmen, insists upon a music master coming from Paris, and requests plans from Le Nôtre for his gardens; likewise, the German princes, while waiting for Frederick II and Potsdam, found an Academy of Sciences and one of Fine Arts; they build, grant pensions, produce Molière plays, translate. The style of Versailles casts a spell.

Despite the Dragonnades, the Revocation of the Edict of Nantes, and the razing of Port-Royal; despite the burning of the Palatinate and the ravages in Holland; despite the constantly heavier taxes, with the *capitation** and the *dixième** added at the end of the reign; despite the gloom at the defeats and famines, despite "the old fright," as La Palatine calls her: the king remains Louis the Great, because he is king of Versailles.

► **THE REFUSALS**

The assembling of a nobility that hurls itself into servitude, the envious applause of foreign princes and their ambassadors, the crowds of artists and scholars singing the glory of this unequalled Maecenas—this concert of adulatory praise cannot let us overlook the limitations of this system. There are many Frenchmen, refugees in foreign countries or silent witnesses, who do not participate in this flattery competition. They think, as does an anonymous man in Utrecht, that this monarchy is inspired by Asiatic despotism: "An imitator of the Kings of Asia, slavery

---

* Direct taxes to supplement the income from the *taille*. The *capitation* was to be paid by everyone, of every class, in proportion to his income. Since assessment was lenient and collection irregular among the nobles, it can hardly be said that they paid their share. The *dixième* was ostensibly a ten per cent income tax, for which the same principles of assessment and collection obtained. In effect both taxes were additional *tailles* of which the peasant bore the brunt.—Trans.

alone pleases him." [16] At a time when bookstores are watched and printshops closed, the silence of the opposition, confronted by the zeal of the authorities, is understandable. But the religious policy in particular brings a whole segment of public opinion against the king. Jansenists and Protestants by turns are hunted down and mistreated; new martyrs are hurled upon the roads of Europe and tracked down like criminals. Yet on the other hand the philosophic and scientific investigations in which Descartes' contemporaries were so fearlessly engaged are carried on; there is an advance of Cartesianism, in both method and doctrine, and a more general advance, commonly called the Enlightenment.

It is the Protestant persecution that caused the greatest stir in Europe, earning the king a lasting hatred on the part of Frenchmen who were exiled in Holland and elsewhere, and were poorly suited to their adopted countries. It also earned him, despite their indignant protestations, the secret gratitude of German princes, happy hosts of French Huguenots.

The Revocation of the Edict of Nantes in 1685 was the final step of a dogged policy of persecutions and pursuits which began, or very nearly so, with the notion of personal rule. The restraint exercised over undesirable Protestants had several aspects of increasing severity: theological discussion, that is, persuasion, was in effect abandoned, except for lofty personages like Monsieur de Turenne, who was taken on by Bossuet; conversion through financial means, coined according to Pellisson's rate schedule and his fund, establishing unequal charges, depending upon the social quality of the converted individual, could not be a serious means of reducing heresy.* These two methods were replaced by more effective coercion: limitations brought to bear on the exercise of worship and the founding of Protestant schools and academies, Sedan and Saumur in particular, by a strict interpretation of the text of the Edict. Then there are vexatious civil measures, which in 1679 forbid the Protestants to practice certain professions—for example, bookselling. Thus the Protestants find themselves forbidden to hold their funerals after six in the morning and before six in the evening; the number and duration of the synods are regulated with constantly increasing severity. At the same time, daily life becomes more difficult from one year to the next, so numerous become the forbidden professions; the jurisdictional powers of the equally divided chambers, initiated in 1598, diminishes as well. In numerous towns in the Midi, where Protestants are in the majority, they do not wait until 1685 for their exodus, and there are small discreet leavetakings presaging the great one.

---

* Paul Pellisson, though more famous for his *Histoire de l'Académie française* as Louis XIV's historiographer, also administered a fund specifically instituted to convert Protestants.—Trans.

Even before the Revocation, the legal persecutions had taken a still more odious turn, with the conversion of the young and the Dragonnades:* attributing Catholic opinions to children met in the street, when they make the sign of the cross when a procession or banner passes, the police authorities have them seized and placed in convents where they are raised—at their parents' expense—as Catholics. At first only children over fourteen could be the object of this tender concern, but the age limit is lowered to twelve, then to seven. During the difficult years from 1680 to 1685, in towns like Nîmes or Montauban there are no more errand boys, no more children playing or wandering about; their parents raise them carefully secluded in the house's garden, let them go out only in their own company, and are careful to keep the doors tightly closed. But they are fortunate if these doors remain closed: this is the same time when the zealous *intendants,* acting without orders from Versailles, hit upon the best method of all: the billeting of the Dragoons. This sad obligation to billet soldiers, which the townspeople, fearing for their furniture, cellars, daughters, always try to avoid, becomes a means of extorting conversions. The yields obtained are extraordinary and arouse the admiration of Louvois upon receipts of brilliant reports in which the turncoats are figured by the tens of thousands. Moreover, in 1683, a Poitou *intendant* complains of no longer knowing where to place the troops at his disposal for this low task, since once billeting is announced, conversion comes about before it can be effected.

On October 18, 1685, at Fontainebleau, Louis XIV signs the Edict revoking the one his grandfather signed at Nantes after forty years of war—convinced, it has been asserted, that there are no more Protestants in France, something which perhaps the astonishing figures offered by the dragonnading *intendants* and the accounts of Pellisson might have made him believe. But too many articles of the Fontainebleau Edict deal with the fate of royal subjects who have remained Protestants, to make it possible to see this act as a mere official report of liquidation. On the contrary, Louis XIV, according to the terms of the preamble, certainly seems convinced of the necessity to re-establish the kingdom's religious unity, a task Henry IV and Louis XIII had also set themselves, and which only the foreign war and the lack of time prevented them from realizing. The Fontainebleau Edict is a combat measure, intended to coerce the last Protestants into embracing Catholicism: it is the culmination of the gradual and multiform diminution undertaken during the previous twenty years. With a severity leaving no room for any solution other than the heresy's disappearance for a century—Protestantism

---

* Name given to the repressions and persecutions of Protestants in the Cévennes and throughout the Midi in general, carried out by the royal Dragoons from about 1680 to 1685, under orders from several authorities, but especially the policy's prime mover, Michel de Tellier, the Marquis de Louvois.—Trans.

has no more legal existence until 1787—the Fontainebleau Edict forbids Protestant worship, throws its ministers outside the kingdom, closes its schools, and forbids its believers to leave the country, threatening the galleys for men and the seizure of body and wealth for women.* Thousands of Protestants, according to some estimates two to four hundred thousand, chose that risk and that solution, despite the troops watching the borders and the hardships of exile. Vauban, who, like so many others (particularly Arnauld and the Jansenists who are careful always to distinguish themselves from the Protestants), momentarily approves of the Revocation, quickly becomes aware of the scope of the movement. The Protestants use the way stations spontaneously set up by Alsatian Protestant towns like Mulhouse, Colmar, and Strasbourg; the Huguenots of Normandy and Paris benefit from the proximity of the Netherlands, and leave by sea from Nantes, La Rochelle, and Bordeaux. The bourgeois of the large Protestant localities abandon their native land, preferring exile to the betrayal of their faith. Weavers from Nîmes, ship outfitters from La Rochelle, laceworkers from Puy, wool merchants from Rouen, discreetly sell out a part of their assets and, if they can, transfer funds to their relatives living abroad; they line their clothing with gold pieces, load themselves up still further with things like plans for weaving machines, addresses of their connections; and, entire families strong, they leave their homes and towns, traveling by night, hiding by day, until they reach the border. On the other side, they are warmly welcomed, and called to Geneva, Berlin, The Hague, Kassel, and Hanover. They are a real élite. Aware that they have escaped a hell, they bring to these and other towns, along with a strict faith and their various skills— merchants, artisans, lawyers, teachers—French tastes and the French language with its demanding and logical ways of thought. Brandenburg and many other little German principalities are lucky.

Nevertheless, not everyone leaves. In many a rural town in the southwest and in Languedoc, those who are unable to leave France, for lack of material means, relations, or for many other dramatic reasons, submit to the law. Some, converts and tormented by their consciences, have brought about disturbance to the parishes, for these new Catholics have not for an instant lost their habits of free discussion and the independence of their former religion. Very soon the bishops will be complaining about these intractable members of their flock. Other have chosen a more difficult way: overtly practicing Catholicism, respecting its obligations and rites, but secretly lapsed, conspiring in small family circles, mixing two forms of worship, two faiths—at the cost of endless conscience pangs. Finally there are some, perhaps the least numerous, who have landed property in the mountains near Valence, Tournon, or Nîmes, and take refuge in the villages, rediscovering here and there

---

* Article Ten of the Edict.

some small rural groups who were led to Protestantism by the ministers in the course of their trips from Geneva to Pau, Poitiers, or Bordeaux: meager communities whose prior attractions are nil, but which assume importance after 1685. Fortified both by these displacements and by the tranquillity assured them by the mountains which have neither roads nor good means of access for royal agents, these interior refuges constitute a new stage in the formation of the Protestants—not a negligible stage, either, since even today it leaves its mark on the religious map of France, from Génolhac to Chambon-sur-Lignon. This is a new heroic period for the Protestants: the time of the Desert.* They gather in the high mountains, or at the foot of Mézenc and Aigoual, around ministers returned from Geneva. Discreet groups travel an entire night in order to participate in the meetings, where the faithful create an atmosphere heightened by danger. These assemblies constantly are threatened, which explains the armed uprisings at the end of the reign. When the king, on the basis of well-informed denunciations, decides to persecute the Protestants of the Desert and use his Dragoons there, the mountainous Cévennes region becomes the center of an interminable guerrilla warfare, in which the Camisard peasants, masters of this wild region without access or important towns, victoriously resist the royal troops and even the Maréchal de Villars. At the end of the reign, and even after the Treaty of Utrecht, the Camisards still hold the high country, and have saved, through their relentless struggle, the place of the Protestants in the national community.

There are other revolts, and other victims, of which the royal policy cannot completely dispose. These, the Jansenists, stand up at the end as at the beginning of the reign, against monarchial absolutism. Left in peace after 1668 when De Lionne obtained the agreement of Rome herself, the friends of Port-Royal nevertheless have continued their career as Catholic reformers. In the earlier battle the convent itself lost its right to educate novices; gradually, their forces dwindle. The convent of the Champs loses the brilliance of the little spiritual capital with which it shone in the 1650s; the recluses of the great generation—Nicole, Lancelot, Hamon—have disappeared and are not replaced. The Elementary Schools have fewer pupils, fewer teachers. The great Arnauld leaves Paris, despite his return to favor, and spends long years in the Netherlands—where Jansenism is active around Louvain, where Jansen and Saint-Cyran were students—and at Ypres, where Jansen had been bishop. What the "sect" loses in brilliance, through death or the curb put

---

* In French the word *Désert* implies not only the Biblical overtones of Wilderness, but also a specific period of French history: when Protestant ministers and organizations repair to the remote areas of the Cévennes and Languedoc to pursue their clandestine activity. There are two distinct periods: the Heroic Desert, from 1685-1762; the Second Desert, from 1762 to the Revolution.—Trans.

on polemics, it seems to have gained in extension: in many towns both small and large, the urban clergy is won over. The works published from 1643 to 1660 are still read, and the difficult theology of the Messieurs continues to furnish the spiritual bread for the bourgeois members of the *parlements*. But beneath this apparent calm which gives the impression, because the great vocal outbursts of Arnauld and Pascal have ceased, of a lusterless religious group, the enemies of 1650 are still face to face: the Jansenists are badly resigned to silence, and the Jesuits are in no way satisfied with their 1668 defeat. At the first possible opportunity—not the too-clever *Réflexions morales* by Quesnel but the *Cas de conscience* by the *curé* of Notre-Dame du Port at Clermont—both the polemics and the persecutions reappear. The *curé* from Auvergne simply asserted that the Jansenists sign the Formulary, with the private conviction that the five propositions are not contained in the *Augustinus* —something Arnauld had said over and over forty years earlier. But the *Cas de conscience* admits to the diplomatic deception of 1668, and the occasion is too fine a one not to be exploited immediately.

Without too much concern for his Gallican scruples, Louis XIV complains to Rome of the Jansenists' lack of discipline, and obtains (with no difficulty save the long delays for reflection, drafting, and transmission customary to the Roman Curia) the Bull *Vineam Domini* in 1708. This is the first condemnation of the nuns and of all those endorsing the *Cas*, placing them in the position of disobedience to both Church and King; the last twenty-two nuns are carried away to the ends of the realm—where they are, moreover, completely happy in this renewal of the 1664 persecutions which, to their eyes, proves the justice of their cause. But this deportation, of persons as aged as they are venerated, stirs up a surge of indignation in Paris: *curés* in their pulpits, parishioners meeting in the street, are as much excited as were the Parisians of 1660, and strongly disapprove. They soon meet at Port-Royal des Champs on Sundays, in the large, empty house which has become a pilgrim shrine in the middle of the woods—there are long walks in the garden where Nicole and the great recluses chatted, prayers in the convent chapel, and highly impassioned evocations of Mother Angélique and of Pascal. In the face of this confusion—the endless carriage processions across the countryside south of Versailles, the violent sermons of the *curés* in Paris and Rouen which are relayed to him—the exasperated king piles up, year in, year out, measures which turn out to be entirely apt to stir up the general indignation of the Parisians and to exalt the faith of the Jansenists: the buildings, then the chapel, are torn down stone by stone, and when the Jansenists meet in the little cemetery adjoining the convent where Racine and Pascal are buried, the graves, in their turn, are destroyed, and the remains gathered into a common ditch in the neighboring village of Saint-Lambert.

To put an end to the matter, Louis XIV obtains a new Bull in 1713, the famous *Unigenitus*, a detailed condemnation of Jansenist writings and doctrine, from Jansen to Quesnel. But, in the two subsequent years, the old king comes to know the strength of the religious movement whose disappearance he desires, which, like Protestantism, holds its own in turn and faces up to him. Fifteen bishops, led by Cardinal de Noailles, Archbishop of Paris, refuse to accept the Bull within their dioceses, arguing simultaneously from the pope's having, contrary to Gallican tradition—which the king thirty years before was relentlessly defending —interfered in French affairs, and from reservations inspired by the very basis of the debate, namely, the definition of "heresy." The Parisian Parlement, Jansenist to the core and the traditional defender of Gallicanism, falls into step, and, after momentarily contemplating refusing to register the Bull, submits to the royal will, contingent upon the approval of the French clergy. Faced with the steadfastness of the bishops and De Noailles, the king finally decides to convene a national council in compliance with those Gallican traditions invoked by the opponents of the Bull. The meeting arranged for September of 1715 never took place; with the death of the king, the several hundred imprisoned Jansenists leave prison, and the Jesuits replace them there. The regent abandons plans for the council; the struggle between Gallicans and Ultramontanists, Jansenists and Jesuits, is not over.

Less noisy, finally, and less gloriously persecuted—but undoubtedly no less dangerous—are the followers of Descartes: for under this name, this label, the rationalists are henceforth known. It is true that they have been more circumspect than the Jansenists, less of a nuisance than the Protestants, since Descartes did not hold any heretical positions, and *a fortiori*, any anti-religious ones. Moreover, until his death, nothing had been attempted against the great traveler who preferred, first the free climate of Holland, then the patronage of Queen Christina [of Sweden] to a stay in Paris. But after 1650, everything changes: the Jesuits, who in the preceding period were content to brush Descartes out of the way of their teaching, stir up accusations. In 1671, the Sorbonne officially issues a general censure on all his writings; shortly afterwards the Oratorians and a few other communities who teach Descartes must submit to this harsh decision. Yet it is at this very moment when his great followers, the Oratorian Malebranche and the Dutchman Spinoza, are taking up the Cartesian meditations and are extending them, each in his own way, in the direction of his own profound logic: Malebranche into psychology and mysticism; Spinoza into rationalism and pantheism.* During these

---

* Malebranche, *Recherche de la vérité* (1674), the author of an overly famous formula: "Better to renounce all else than to renounce reason." Spinoza, *Tractatus Theologico-politicus* (1670).

same years, however, Cartesian philosophy—officially forbidden or not —becomes a veritable mania, on the part, at least, of Parisian public opinion: like astronomy and physics, philosophy, when studied along with them, is exciting. People take "lessons in Cartesianism." Monsieur Rohault, in 1664, almost makes a profession of them, teaching "the philosophy of Descartes, experiments with the lodestone and its different effects" [17] in small groups—obviously outside the schools. Arnauld, when consulted concerning the judgment prohibiting everything not in Aristotle's *Physics*, asserts, on several occasions, Descartes' good faith. With the greatest clarity, he distinguishes between science and the mysteries of religion, "for the philosophic ways of reconciling our mysteries with the opinions of physics are not at all those of faith." The rigidity of the accusations was doubtless able to limit and stem this fervor for philosophizing; despite Colbert's lures and the generosities of the Academy of Sciences (founded in 1666), it also contributed to keeping the greatest names of the day outside of France: Spinoza stays in Amsterdam, Newton continues his mathematical investigations in Cambridge, and Leibniz continues his in Germany. Huyghens, who has come to France, flees in 1685. Science is encouraged, philosophy forbidden: the former languishes, despite the Observatory and the Academy; the latter lives, despite the condemnation.

The best proof of this Cartesian inheritance that can be put forward is the undeniable and imposing progress of the critical spirit in the towns —even in those most formidable and most delicate matters of faith* over which the Sorbonne, the Archbishop of Paris, the Society of Jesus, and the king in his council—that authority simultaneously civil and ecclesiastical—exercise a vigilant surveillance. It is clear that in the 1670s and 1680s the world of scholars, scientists, and philosophers—these are inseparable—hold sway over the majority of mankind. Some *abbé*, dealing with certain pseudo-miraculous practices, declares: "The monks of ——— girdled pregnant women with a belt of St. Margaret, whose story they would not be able to tell without laying themselves open to the derision of the learned world." Clearer still than these exclamations, escaped from some perverse spirit, is the disappearance of the witchcraft trials, that great legal and social phenomenon of the seventeenth century. These were still frequent, even thrilling, in the 1630s, when Mersenne, Gassendi, and Descartes were living and arguing—dozens of little makeshift, matter-of-fact trials in Franche-Comté or Lorraine, or else great provincial events like Gaufridy at Aix, Urbain Grandier at Loudun, or Barbe Buvée at Auxonne; between 1672 and 1682 the persecutions

---

* And, even more so, in others: a soldier telling about a siege says: "We began by shelling it and hurling red-hot broadsides. Most of the bombs burst in the air, which the burghers took to be a miracle, and we, for a sign that the bombs were worthless."

cease. The date 1672 marks the year when the Parlement of Rouen, beset with thirty-four sorcerers from Carentan doomed to the worst fate, finds itself dissolved by the king, who breaks up the proceedings and, in effect, halts the trials, despite the indignant protestations of the judges. The year 1682 is the year when the king, in the often-quoted enactment against soothsayers, poisoners, and other magicians, decides to allow trials only for real sorcerers. The suits that begin to come before the courts then are libel suits: "He called me a witch." Despite some resistance, magistrates and administrators certainly seem to have decided among themselves that witchcraft is not, after all, so very frequent. This is, not the fruit and extraordinary virtue of a royal act, but the result of a long intellectual development. Medical certifications become more common—for a long time, doctors were describing the neuroses of witchcraft suspects and their denouncers, and there is the recognition of that mentality of automatic suspiciousness whose ravages had been enormous. In 1641, Cyrano de Bergerac had already protested against the "inhumanity" of the trials; in 1660, a bookstore in Lyon publishes the French translation of a Rhenish Jesuit's work* devoted to the trials, in which the mental confusion through which the judges, lawyers, and criminals moved is analyzed and demonstrated with faultless logic, capable of getting through to even the most prejudiced and obstinate of judges and suspects.† Thus, although the idea of demonic possession is not denied, witchcraft goes out of daily life, out of the mentality of the judges and—at least in good part—those under their jurisdiction.

Something even more bold: in 1678, an Oratorian, Richard Simon, publishes an *Histoire critique du Vieux Testament*. Armed with a very extensive and erudite knowledge of the Bible, Simon applied to it those methods which had been clarifying texts from pagan antiquity for more than two centuries; he made a philological and historical analysis, and in his book—which caused a sensation—he gives his conclusions.‡ Thus he diminishes the part played by Moses in the writing of the Pentateuch, and several other—for that day—bits of daring along the same order. The

---

* Entitled *Advis aux criminalistes sur les abus qui se glissent dans les procès de sorcelerie. Dédiés aux magistrats d'Allemagne. Livre très nécessaire en ce temps icy, à tous Juges, Conseillers, Confesseurs (tant des Juges que des Criminels), inquisiteurs, prédicateurs, advocats et même aux Médecins.* By the P.N.S.J. Roman Theologian, printed in Latin for the second time at Frankfort in the year 1632, and rendered into French by J.-B. Villedor.

† "Either she evinces fear, or not. If she does (perhaps having learned of the torments she is to suffer, realizing, in a word, the deplorable position she is in) this is the greatest sign, they say, because her conscience is accusing her. If she evinces no fear at all (trusting in her innocence): that cannot be allowed to be a good sign; for they say that witches are more accustomed than good people to parading their innocence, and showing their assurance." [18] And the same goes for tortures, types of confessions, etc.

‡ Bossuet's *Discours sur l'Histoire Universelle* (1681) is almost entirely an eloquent refutation of Simon.

book is reduced to a pulp, and the author excluded from the Oratorians; this step forward, which establishes Biblical exegesis in France, is condemned. The shock, however, was great. Richard Simon continued his historical and philological work in long years of silence, but his first book is a great expression of the spirit of the time.

After 1680, while the royal hand grows heavier, critical thought continues its conquests. Philosophy and the sciences interest an ever greater number of people, and scientific discoveries encourage philosophic daring. There is a whole world of little groups of *sçavans*, both within and outside of the world of the official academies, recalling (with the excited inquiries into the meridian and its length, the earth, the place of the planets in the world) the atmosphere of the great period during the 1630s. Highly reputed circles are formed: the great Condé is surrounded until his death by a large group of scientists who speak more freely, knowing protection to be more certain. For too many, precautions are still necessary: Holland, the refuge for all those within enslaved France who sigh for freedom,* is at the heart of this European scientific life. Treatises in which Cartesians, supporters of vortices,† and Newtonians confront one another, are published at Amsterdam or The Hague. Likewise, there are the bold books for which Parisian bookstores would never take responsibility—commentaries on Richard Simon, polemics concerning the Protestant exodus as well as about the plurality of worlds. Despite seizures and the surveillance exercised over the mails,‡ all these books, all this philosophy, reach Lille, Amiens, and Paris—prefiguring the activity that was to unfold over the course of the eighteenth century. The most important, the most significant of the books coming out of Amsterdam at the end of the reign is undoubtedly Pierre Bayle's famous *Dictionnaire historique et critique* (1697). Bayle, a minister's son who sought refuge in 1685, was a true *philosophe* in the eighteenth-century sense of the word: by virtue of his patience in attacking the most venerated authorities by small, subtle blows; his patience in judiciously distilling a quasi-universal skepticism; his faith in *la raison raisonnante*.

Thus, a deep opposition: science is already triumphant, both inside and outside of France, and rationalist philosophy accompanies it; both penetrate into ever wider areas, conquering a larger public from one year to the next. All this, at the very hour when the divine right monarchy,

---

* The expression is that of Jurieu, in the title of a lampooning satire published at Amsterdam in 1689.
† Old Scholastic customs: for some Cartesians, Descartes has replaced Aristotle, and is as incontrovertible as the latter had been during the preceding centuries.
‡ "I have discovered many things touching upon the commerce of Dutch books, and if I did not know what I know with such certainty, I would have difficulty in believing the great quantity of books that are sent daily to Paris and its environs. This commerce is completely ruining the Parisian book trade." [19]

that political and religious ideal, receives its most beautiful illustration: that great king who wishes to be supreme master in that château unique in all the world. Louis XIV and Versailles: the flowering of the monarchic idea or its swan song?

XI

The Economic and Demographic Revolution of the Eighteenth Century

REVOLUTION? Perhaps the word is a little strong, in these areas where there are no sudden changes or violent convulsions. But it alone has the force to indicate the scope of a movement which is equaled only, and in another area, by the other Revolution, that of 1789, which, although its importance has not been overrated, cannot alone explain everything. Before La Fayette and Robespierre, before Hoche and Bonaparte, let us set into position this potent economic renewal that transformed all Europe. Without daring to claim—as have done some Brazilian economists who are delighted to claim that their country's gold has played an immense role in European life*—that the French Revolution is the

---

* A naïve interpretation, nothing more: many other attempts, and not naïve ones,

offspring of Brazilian gold exploitation, let us recognize that the period of the *philosophes* was one of great prosperity, flooding all of French life with riches; it was a period comparable to the long sixteenth century's revival, even to its appetites for luxury items. But to us the eighteenth century's achievement seems more complete, affecting all of society, not merely the towns. And the reverberation of the revived eagerness became multiplied and modified: a new humanism, directed toward action, anxious not merely to know but to do, responds to the former humanism enamored only of lessons from antiquity.

Thus the first peculiarity of the years preceding the Revolution is its economic aspect. In addition to a fuller population explosion than the one in the sixteenth century* the necessities of French life were entirely changed. The advances during the sixteenth century had swollen towns with wealth and inhabitants, accelerating the rhythms of large-scale international commerce† from the Mediterranean to the Atlantic, and from Italy to the Netherlands. The eighteenth century witnesses much more: rural life itself becomes easier and more bearable, protecting the mass of the population from those appalling attacks that punctuated earlier days: the famines. Thus a new phenomenon is added to the more classic one of Brazilian gold—which, after a long depression, replaces Spanish gold and silver, and gives a second wind to large-scale trade all over the world. Already the best-situated peasants—farmers holding seventy-five acres, large-scale husbandmen, small owners of an adequate estate—can participate in commercial life, can trade regularly, not intermittently, at fairs, can make purchases in exchange for their sales. The day laborer and hired help can at least earn their livings there. In this way the rural French market is opened to urban products; there is an enormous impetus to production, a long-unsatisfied need, which increases urban wealth and simultaneously creates a pressing need for new means of communication from the town to the villages. The eighteenth century is a great period of road construction—something indispensable to the new economic life.

Urban population increases without that of the rural districts proportionately decreasing (unlike the nineteenth century's population movement); the average length of life increases, gaining a few precious years, and approaches about thirty,‡ an advance all the more remarkable since

have been made to diminish the Revolution of 1789—to reduce it, for example, to a Freemason plot.

* The very approximate figures generally accepted indicate this: around 1500, thirteen million Frenchmen; sixteen million around 1600, not more than fourteen or fifteen million at the death of Louis XIV despite the impressive seventeenth-century territorial annexation, and, finally, twenty-three or twenty-four million shortly before 1789.

† A significant evaluation: French foreign trade goes from 215 million *livres* in 1716, to 900 million *livres* in 1750.

‡ Messance figures, according to observations made for a few generations in the middle of the century, that the length of life passed from twenty-two or -three years, to

not much is happening in medicine, whose means are still very limited. From the 1730s on, it is obvious that throughout France the country becomes richer, in both men and wealth—the great famine of 1709 is definitely the last slaughter in which several million Frenchmen disappeared in a few months: there are intermittent scarcities of food, particularly in 1726-27, which kill off old men and young children, but nothing comparable to the great slaughters during the real famines. French, and doubtless European, prosperity in the eighteenth century continues until about 1775, without returning to the former horrors which were gradually forgotten. A crisis opens up within the French economy, one that continues until the early years of the Revolution, at least until 1709: this is an important crisis, a contraction after more than a half-century of expansion, coinciding with the reign of Louis XVI: it sheds light upon the pre-revolutionary social and political atmosphere.[1]

▶ PROGRESS IN RURAL AREAS

England experienced, during this time, a much more powerful agricultural revival than that of France. People refer to it by using the legitimate expression "agricultural revolution." Its essential element is a long-term transfer of property, a multiple development of farming, in which enclosures play a role of prime importance. For France, however, using the expression "agricultural revolution" would be somewhat overstating the case, since, at any rate, agricultural progress could not be based on a similar transfer of property.[2]

French agricultural production increases, but without the waving of a magic wand; even without destroying small ownership to the advantage of large-scale farming. The rural landscape has been slowly and imperceptibly developing since the sixteenth century; the fruits of these gradual transformations, and of several other causes not as yet fully understood, became apparent around 1730. Now, with regard to enclosures: France went through some decrees for enclosure of the common land— along the lines of those in England, a country France greatly admired, in all matters during the century of the Enlightenment. These were the result of the *intendants'* initiatives: local decisions, taken in province after province around 1770, lasting until 1777. While this movement is being compounded in England, France is timidly trying it, not without recriminations, which we find even in the grievance-lists* in which the restoration of the common lands is often called for. In reality, it is the

---

twenty-seven or -eight; an acceptable estimate, despite the scornful criticisms of which the author is an object today.
* These are the *cahiers de doléance*, or *cahiers*: the listing of the complaints, by class or estate, in each electoral district during the elections for the 1789 Estates-General meeting. These lists also included recommendations for reform.—Trans.

whole problem of collective easements which is thus being posed: in some provinces, for local reasons—which usually revolve around the ravages of the flocks moved from the lowlands of the Midi to the Alps or, in Provence, the survival of the Roman law which is foreign to the notion of collective property and the action of the great landed bourgeoisie, anxious for fat returns and good income—the question was debated as early as the sixteenth century. What is called agrarian individualism is not born of a sudden change of ownership in the nineteenth century. In the plains of Northern France, even before the "pilot farms" like those in Liancourt, the requirements of a few large property owners, or their tenant farmers, were able to bring about a certain loosening of the traditional easements. These large landowners were anxious to set aside a large manure heap for their vast, continuous pieces of land, and eager to spare a meadow, rich in topsoil and well irrigated, from the havoc of collective pasture rights—and numerous old customs permit them to exercise this selective right over the common lands. Their requirements, at any rate, precede and presage the real movement in the eighteenth century. This is an age-old attack, of unequal scope depending upon the region; all the same it is not too well known, since in each rural community's internal economy, it becomes mixed up with individual efforts—the family regroupment of lands and the opposing interplay of inheritances and divisions. Agricultural individualism knew some fine days in the eighteenth century; but the Revolution did more for it than the enclosure decrees, more even than the 1789 Constituent Assembly and the rural exodus of the nineteenth century.

Many social forces act in the opposite direction, working to maintain the traditional rural community. These forces include the pride of the nobleman, be he fresh from the urban bourgeoisie or a longtime landowner, in wandering unimpeded over his terrain which, for him, is hunting grounds; and this hunting would be sharply curtailed, at least on horseback—forbidden—by hedgerow stake fences.* In the same fashion, there is the attachment to tradition and particularly to collective ownership, since the common lands are a great resource for the humbler classes, whose goats and few sheep have no grazing land other than the common heaths and the chaff remaining after grain harvests—to say nothing of the resources obtained from the forest. On occasion (the example comes from Lorraine), the small day laborers can look favorably upon the division of all the wealth from the communal lands, when it is made among all the inhabitants of a parish, not merely those who are already landowners; in these cases, the division enables them to have

---

* The collective easements withdraw only gradually. To forbid passage, there can be no question of being satisfied with a public notice or a heap of stones mixed with straw, erected in the middle of a field; for a long time only enclosures can be effective.

access to land in corners long since abandoned to thorns, although it is hard to clear; but such complete division is rather rare. Thus French agricultural prosperity in the eighteenth century was not the result of a social upheaval, as the disappearance of collective easements and the division of communal lands implies; wished for by some large-scale farmers, refused by others—and the same for the little country people— carried out in Lorraine and in Flanders but by no means contemplated in the Forez and Auvergne, these transformations do not constitute a conclusive explanation.

Meanwhile yields and worldwide production are improved: large landowners who have accumulated great blocks of land are interested in rural progress; nurtured on agricultural literature,* English models, and Physiocrat proclamations, they have made experiments, and try new methods of plowing and sowing. Others, farmers or husbandmen in the Beauce or Picardy, undertaking to clear the lands of the heath or the forsaken swamps, "had the generosity to sacrifice acres of land and years of harvests in efforts for the rural economy." The great step forward is the withdrawal of fallow lands—that disgrace of French agriculture which shocked the Englishman Arthur Young during his trip to France during the closing years of the Old Regime. This withdrawal is slow, since the great obstacle to the practice's disappearance is the whole of the collective rural life. Nevertheless, in some localities, the fallow land is "stripped," the land is sown instead of being left fallow after the grain is harvested—and it produces more: the empirical discovery of Western Europe in this realm is that of the virtue of fodder plants (clover, sainfoin, and alfalfa) which simultaneously furnish abundant feed for cattle and restore to the soil the nitrogen consumed by the wheat. The preceding centuries were not unaware of these plants, which grew in town gardens or in neighboring meadows to feed draft animals; introduced into the old rotation system, they thus make possible, at the same time, better wheat yields and better-fed livestock in greater numbers. This, in turn, permits better manuring of the fields and larger harvests; consequently, turnips, turnip-cabbages, alfalfa, and other fodder plants become a part of the plant rotation in the large estates of northern France. In the southwest, corn has gradually been gaining since its importation from America at the end of the sixteenth century; now it, too, overthrows the two-field system. It is cultivated alternately with wheat, and furnishes

---

* Throughout the century, and especially after 1750, agricultural books were extraordinarily popular. Anglomania, the Physiocrats, and Jean-Jacques Rousseau, in chronological order, had something to do with this. According to a bibliography appearing in Paris in 1810, twelve hundred books on agronomy were published in the eighteenth century, as opposed to one hundred thirty in the seventeenth, and one hundred in the sixteenth.[3] In the preface to his translation of the *Georgics*, Abbé Delille goes so far as to speak of the "agromania" of his day.

either fodder or grain; in either case it gives the peasant in Aquitaine, favored by his warm and damp climate, considerable comfort. Young was struck by this: "The border of corn marks the line separating the good husbandry of the Midi from the bad of the northern part of the kingdom. As long as no corn is in evidence, you see very rich soil lying fallow; but never after." Perhaps Young somewhat exaggerates this contrast, but his words are still striking; bad husbandry in the north, good in the south, in the eighteenth century; two hundred years later, we reverse the terms.[4] Also, after 1760, potatoes are gradually added; this contributes to the groping study of increasingly complex rotations—especially since it readily appears, in the regions around Caux in particular, that fodder plants are winning out in occupying the soil, not merely for the long season from August to the November of the following year, but for at least two or three seasons—thus destroying the one-field rhythm, in favor of more complicated alternations. Yet these enormous gains in cereal yields, and the consequent increase of livestock linked to them, are not universal. As a matter of fact, the success of fodder plants is assured only on enclosed land; moreover, some regions off the beaten track, having more solidly established traditions and a somnolent urban life—for it is true that the impetus comes mainly from the towns—saw nothing of it.*

However, with a few exceptions, it does seem that rural life everywhere is emerging from that chronic mediocrity prevalent in past centuries: the progress in large-scale farming, withdrawal of collective easements, and technical changes do not account for all the improvements. Other reasons were brought into play independently of the increased demand coming from the towns—reasons that were scarcely apparent and are still not readily seen. Archival documents give the impression that the wheat-marketers and hucksters, those large-scale traders between the towns and the rural areas, are less numerous with their suits, their clashes, and their violence than in the preceding periods; therefore, speculation —that great cause of brutal rises and sudden shortages of wheat—is less active. This is a mere impression, which would require confirmation and explanation. Another hypothesis is that of climatic variations. While in the preceding centuries the family record-books and memoirs never cease to complain of the winters (rains, winds, terrible frosts), a temperance seems to have settled in during the eighteenth century: the mild winters should have had a beneficial effect on the harvests, but this presupposes great climatic variations, and it is difficult to establish these with any degree of exactitude, and equally difficult to explain.†

---

* For example, at the end of his demographic inquiries M. Goubert asserts that Basse-Bretagne, Sologne, and Quercy are regions in which overmortality—that is, famines and epidemics—continued to rage throughout the entire century.[5]
† The problems have been posed with respect to the sixteenth-century rigors by Braudel in his *Méditerranée*.[6]

All of this means that, of all these rural transformations, the clearest aspect is this result: the increase of income and population, owing to the "population revolution of lower-class mortality," as Labrousse says. Even the poorest, the day laborers who have only their strong right arms, not the smallest patch of land, make the best of it and manage to live; their gain is the most obvious. Even in bad years the rural destitutes, reduced to begging in the dead season of winter, are not refused the piece of bread for which, in one way or another, they have begged; the price of the wheat they buy increases, but their wages as day laborers, indispensable to rural living, rise even more.[7] In this way the summer months help the winter ones, the good days bring work, and the poorest rural inhabitants keep themselves alive. From that time on, the birth rate surpasses the death rate; observers like Messance see in this fact a new necessity, before Malthus takes fright at it and raises his cry of alarm.* But the small farmer with some landed property, the farmer simultaneously cultivating his own lands and a few fields rented from a rich landowner, and (with greater reason) the *brave laboureur*, as Voltaire says, who has a plow, oxen, and horses, and cuts the figure of a large farmer —all these peasants, better off than the hired help, have gained something too: a more or less greater comfort, an ease of living even during the worst years; these make them forget, little by little, the great disasters of former times. The small peasant can feed himself all year long. Often he even finds himself with a surplus at the end of the agricultural year— a few sacks of grain in the depths of the granary, which he himself is able to sell. But this directly negotiable surplus earns him more than his subsistence; he sells his grain in the neighboring town or to some collectors, and he "lays in" money. A remarkable fact of this century is the multiplication of fairs and markets—a sign of the massive increase in buying and selling. The almanacs, whose use is increasingly widespread throughout the countryside, mention everything about rural life— current rumors, phases of the moon, practical advice on works and days —and they never fail to enumerate these fairs carefully. Shortly before the Revolution, more than five thousand fairs in five hundred communes are mentioned. The peasant draws about himself a new commercial apparatus, put at his disposal to insure the sale of his poultry and livestock, the improvement of which promotes its proliferation; consequently, his sales increase, as does his buying power, though perhaps in smaller proportion. Finally, there is a greater profit for the vineyardist whose crop had always been sold much more than that of the

---

* In 1756, Messance writes: "It is even necessary in the small town and rural parishes, that there be in a given year more births than deaths, as much to recruit men for the large towns as to repair the ravages of wars, plagues, epidemic diseases, and other scourges, which afflict humankind from time to time." [8]

grower of cereal plants—the latter needs forty to fifty acres to feed his family, while the vineyardist can supply them on two hundred and forty square yards. The demand for dinner and vintage wines increases, during this half-century of prosperity; the famous vineyards, those of ecclesiastical origins or those set up by princes during the Middle Ages, improve their wine-making techniques and their distribution networks: at this time Burgundy, Alsace, Champagne, and the region around Bordeaux acquire some of their present-day character.

Thus, cautiously and slowly, the French peasantry enters the lists of commerce. There is immense movement in the regions famous for wine, large business for the husbandman, tenants becoming accustomed to fairs, the first of the horse traders. The small peasant's appearance is timid. He is happy (after having clinked his glass of wine at the inn, in token of sealing a bargain in these areas where rounds of drinks and *vins d'honneur** are of the same traditions) with making several very modest purchases: incidental agricultural supplies, pruning hooks, hoes, sickles, and wooden shoes; more rarely, pieces of fabric; even less often, a dress or some boots. For long decades to come, peasant life remains fundamentally uncomfortable, and the peasant is not about to trust in his ease.† Still badly lodged in his airless and lightless house (for the expense of windowpanes is a needless luxury), with improvised furnishings—a large hutch, a cupboard, a table and benches, large wall-beds— the eighteenth-century peasant is concerned primarily with his tools; he buys sickles and axes and, little by little, scythes which win out over the land by means of the progress effected over artificial meadows. Thus, at the same time that his works and yields are improving, the peasant contributes to increasing urban activity, which is stimulated first of all by the landed proprietors. Both urban and rural prosperity are closely allied: from the country to the towns, there is the same continuing atmosphere of rising and healthy prices, of increasing comfort, along with the nuances imposed by the variety of economic and social conditions.‡

---

* The wines offered by municipal authorities to the important visitors of their towns. —Trans.

† Who does not know that passage in the *Confessions* where Rousseau tells how, as a young man, he was served black bread and poor soup by a cautious peasant, then, as he gained the latter's confidence, white bread, bacon, ham, and decent wine. Rousseau's peasant was thinking about the salt-tax collector; the salt tax disappeared, but the mentality has survived for a long time.

‡ This prosperity of 1730-1775 might seem to be contradicted by the poverty and squalor that Young reveals to us; but he is traveling at the height of the crisis, in a later period, and comes from a country whose agriculture is even more advanced. He always judges things by reference to an unparalleled English model; his observations, moreover, are not without a certain pessimism, despite the quality of most of his evidence. On the other hand, agricultural progress was not universal, nor was it ever invulnerable to local relapses. D'Argenson writes as follows, in August of 1748: "Our provinces in the interior of the realm and south of the Loire are plunged into deep poverty. The harvests are only half the size of the ones last year, and those were

► **URBAN PROSPERITY**

Between towns and countrysides the ties both strengthen and multiply:
the peasantry uses more and more money, and enters into the commercial circuits that are modified for its use. The necessary mental adaptation comes more slowly than the adaptation of techniques; around 1850,
how many villages there still are, where it seems the rule is to purchase
only the minimum from town, and where even the peddlers bringing
the small equipment—files and pliers, as well as thread, needles, and
little books—are not always well received.[9] Moreover, the towns are
more directly and more noticeably linked to the country, through the
landed proprietors, who are the greatest beneficiaries of the rural prosperity with no effort on their own part, and who, alone, give life to the
urban economy. The receipts of the fees in kind, a percentage of the
harvest, varies with the harvest and thus increases when the yields improve: hence, *banalités* and tithes cause added amounts of grain and
other products to enter the proprietors' granaries. When, because of a
better arrangement of their crops, the Lieusaint peasants harvest seven
hundred sacks instead of five hundred, the tithe-owner from Melun
gathers in seventy sacks instead of fifty. Thus, through landowners and
clergy, large amounts of wealth are transferred to the cities and harvests
ultimately are sold on urban markets. In the same towns, money is
spent. This is the principal ingredient of the urban progress and unquestionably is more important than the flow of Brazilian gold onto the
market place of world trade. (This gold, however, did render great service
in a country where credit is not yet figured in bank notes, contrary to
the Dutch and English practices, where national banks have an essential
place in the economy.) Thus both population and activity in the towns
are increased and expanded;* the urban prosperity is in perfect correspondence with the rural.

These landed proprietors are the bishops, nobles, and the bourgeois,

---

extremely poor. Wheat prices are rising, and beggars besiege us on all sides." Or
again in 1752: "One of my *curés* sends me word that, since he is the oldest man in
the province of Touraine, he has seen many things, and excessive periods of high
wheat prices, but that he does not recall such great poverty—not even in 1709—as in
this year."

* Messance attempted to calculate the population advance in the large French towns,
from the average birthyears on, multiplied by a variable coefficient. He gives interesting "orders of size" for the periods 1700-10 and 1750-70; there are slight increases
in regional centers: Clermont-Ferrand from 17,100 to 20,800; Roanne from 5,100 to
6,500; Aurillac from 5,800 to 7,200. A falling-off in the Mediterranean ports, in
these days when the Atlantic clearly prevails over the Mediterranean: Marseille, from
97,000 to 90,000. An advance in Paris, which goes from 509,000 to 570,000 (but
common opinion gives the capital 700,000 in the middle of the century). Messance
did not, unfortunately, subject Nantes and Bordeaux, those great beneficiaries of the
eighteenth century, to his calculations.

who acquired landed wealth from choices of safe investments. Among all these beneficiaries of rural progress, a minority lives at Versailles, far from its lands, entrusting to diligent superintendents the care of its interests. But most are in the nearby town—even the nobles for whom the old, uncomfortable châteaux, far from all pleasant society in this century where worldly life is so pleasant, seem to lack all the amenities —in small, bright provincial capitals like Dijon, Colmar, or Toulouse, or else in sleepy regional centers like Moulins on the Allier; the small towns of this period, those with ten or twenty thousand inhabitants, are the usual residences of the *hobereaux* who take such pride in their wealth and social situation. Favored simultaneously by the increase of crops and the price rise, these landowners who do not like living on their land and who are provided with abundant capital, use this capital in the towns. Contemporary economic life does not offer them a great variety of investments: money speculation and dealing in silver through banks are hardly possible except in the main trading places: from 1724 on, the Paris Bourse begins to acquire form and stability during the course of this century. Likewise, at Bordeaux and Nantes, there is a whole group of lenders, an international world in which Portuguese, French, and Italians rub elbows and trade with the Atlantic ship outfitters, who are always hard up; this is true even in Lyon, which no longer enjoys the great days of the sixteenth century when it competed with Antwerp on the world silver market. As a matter of fact the banks—even the ones in Paris like the Mallet bank, founded in 1723 by a Swiss who preceded Necker by a few years*—have rather limited initiatives. Such lack of daring is ascribable to the excessive caution of a possessor of landed capital, however effortlessly acquired, as well as to the unfortunate experience of Law between 1715 and 1720; Mississippi gold and illusory Louisianian expectations swamped the Rue Quincampoix with too much wealth not to produce a timorous reaction. In most of the towns, the bourgeois lend to needy peasants directly and at high rates; to safe friends and acquaintances they lend small amounts and, with due allowance made for frequent disappointments and proceedings, at little profit.

Another form of investment, without much attraction for the eighteenth century, is in durable goods which in the twentieth century is offered through multiple paths of borrowing, from the Bourse to holders of capital. Until shortly before the Revolution, the slowness of technical progress and the relative simplicity of craft equipment exclude appeals of

---

* The Mallet bank, founded immediately after Law's bankruptcy by descendants of sixteenth-century Protestant refugees who went to Geneva and returned to France, wants to be a safe bank, as do the other, subsequent Swiss institutions. The Mallet bank, which has had a very good clientele since its inception, still exists. For its second centenary in 1923, it published a modest brochure succinctly recalling the history of this house: a felicitous effort, which has not been imitated.

this order. The cabinetmaker or weaver replaces his plain implements in the same rhythm as the peasant renews his, even somewhat more rapidly. Only the factories need more, but they represent only a small portion of the period's industrial activity. Around this, and around such new enterprises as the Anzin mines, the earliest limited partnerships can be incorporated during the course of the century; the early ironmasters at Creusot and Saint-Étienne appeal for funds to friends and to the bourgeois in a neighboring town. In any case, this manner of employing capital has yet to find an important place in French economic life.

It is more noteworthy—because in this case demand is automatic—that the landed proprietors did not seek to return capital to the land, stimulating a rural progress of which they would have been the direct beneficiaries. Long-term loans to farmers and husbandmen to promote enclosure, for the purchase of seed and equipment, or for the improvement of livestock—at this time when even the most comfortable peasants are without funds sufficient for long and exacting restoration—is hardly a practical speculation, unless it be for a few devoted scientific agronomists who create "English-styled farms," as Young says of the Liancourt farm.* The capital which originates in the land does not return there, primarily because owners live in the towns, are not happy in the country, do not follow the working of the fields, and do not see the advantage of these burdensome changes which the peasant rarely solicits on his own.

The great means through which the landed proprietors flood the French economy is consumer goods. All these newly-rich people think especially of purchasing furnishing, rugs, and fabrics; they increase their household staffs, improve their daily menus, enrich their wine cellars, and, in particular, have things built. Few profitable investments, much expenditure for luxury items: the eighteenth century is characterized by urban luxury and comfort. The effect of this spending is quickly revealed in the towns' economic life: a new palace built for a bishop, the proliferation in the new residential districts of large towns of private *hôtels* whose models were established by the seventeenth century, furnishing executed with taste but without much regard for expense—and everything done decorously. All this means that the entire craft population is put to work, and, when there are not enough of them, towns like Nantes are forced to import carpenters, roofers, weavers, and cabinetmakers from the calmer regions. Furthermore, guild trips† around France are

---

* Young spent a great deal of time with Frédéric-Alexandre Plessis, Duke of Liancourt, at the latter's model, progressive farm at Liancourt, near Beauvais, in the Oise.—Trans.

† The translator has been informed that, as late as the 1920s, these same guild trips, *Tours de France*, were made by boys from the Auvergne who, in their fathers' company, "toured" France as chimney sweeps, much to the fright of the younger children who were not used to such sooty faces and odd accoutrements as were necessary to lower the boys into the chimney.

French Industries at the close of the Seventeenth and Eighteenth Centuries

ENGLAND

FLANDERS textile
LILLE ANICHE ANZIN
coal coal
AMIENS cotton
ARDENNES metallurgy
PICARDY textile
SEDAN wool
ROUEN cotton
REIMS wool
LORRAINE metal
NORMANDY VALOIS
textile LOUVIERS SENLIS silk
CHAMPAGNE textile, glass
EVREUX cotton
PARIS tapestry, etc.
CHÂLONS
CORBEIL paper
VOSGES
BEAUCE VITRY-Le-FRANCOIS cotton ALSACE
BRITTANY textiles textile textile
paper textile PONTPEAU textiles
GÂTINAIS textile LANGRES metal
metal MULHOUSE
MAINE textile ORLÉANAIS textile cotton
textile TOURS
ANGERS TOURAINE SOLOGNE FRANCHE
cotton silk woolen NIVERNAIS glass, pottery COMTÉ metal, metal
INDRET metal
BERRY Lé CREUSOT
POITOU textile NEVERS metal
textile, glass CHÂTEAUROUX
POITIERS AUBUSSON tapestry
ROANNE
LIMOGES porcelain
ANGOULÊME AUVERGNE THIERS LYON silk
paper paper, metals FOREZ
paper, glass, metal glass, metal SAINT-ETIENNE
Atlantic BRIVE cotton porcelain ANNONAY paper DAUPHINY paper
Ocean VELAY lace
le PUY AUBENAS silk
BORDEAUX
GUYENNE glass VIVARAIS
silk
NIMES glass
LANGUEDOC MONTPELLIER silk
TOULOUSE CASTRES silk, woolen
woolen
PYRENÉES metal

The Typefaces for

REGION Sixteenth Century
REGION Eighteenth Century
Regional Products Sixteenth Century
Regional Products Eighteenth Century
○ CITIES Sixteenth Century
◑ CITIES Eighteenth Century

accelerated, the large towns are swelled to the detriment of the small centers, and, especially, all the urban professions are enriched.

This urban prosperity is led by the two principal "industries" of the period, building and textiles. In the popular mentality, because the numerous guilds cover a good part of the craft activities, building constitutes the model guild—a good proof of the work being done in the towns: "When building goes, everything goes." Textiles are important, because the cotton towns like Rouen, Mulhouse, and Paris profit from the increase of the vogue that carries the worldly public toward calico, that light fabric which is still expensive but whose varied tones are easy to print.

Behind the artisans, overwhelmed with orders they cannot fill fast enough, behind the trader, whether on a grand scale or with a short range of activity, commercial capitalism is stimulated even more than "industrial" life—or rather, artisan life, for the state of techniques forbids any major renovation of the professions. France at this time experiences nothing like the English Industrial Revolution, those technical discoveries which, between 1740 and 1780, gradually restore the textile industries; these cross the Channel only at the end of the century, especially between 1815 and 1830. But these discoveries are of limited significance, and are in no way comparable to a new source of energy, steam, which was put to work after 1850. Thus, the demand for craft products increases quickly, at this time when production can develop only in terms of the labor force, that is, slowly. There is, consequently, the continual and gradual price rise, a sign of prosperity and an indication of the pressure exercised by demand; there are a great many attempts to multiply the sources of energy, on both large and small rivers, by diverting watercourses—quickly resulting in too many; there are mills, often abandoned today, whose ruins are even now a manifestation of this attempt at overequipment. There is too the development of a rural artisanry around towns like Amiens and Beauvais in Picardy, when urban manufacturers, following England's example, equip peasants to work in their rooms or cellars on raw materials, projects, and orders supplied by the manufacturers themselves. There are, again, many obscure, badly understood and badly known attempts to improve the yields and techniques of each profession: this is the underlying significance of the "industrial" part of the *Encyclopédie*, when Diderot's friends make plate after plate, design after design, explanation after explanation, elaborating the techniques employed by all the professions, in France and elsewhere.* And finally, there is the acceleration of trade, and the efforts

---

* A member of an academy in Marseille expresses this concern for techniques: "Even the mechanical arts are an occupation not unworthy of an Academy member"; and the plates of the *Encyclopédie* made as much of a name for this dictionary as did its backhanded slaps at the Church.

made to free it from urban and provincial impediments, the tolls and customs that limited both internal and foreign trade. On the one hand, this "industrial growth" encouraged the decline of the guilds, laboriously restored to health by Colbert, and the multiplication of free professions, the *chamberlains* working at home; on the other hand, it promotes the first concentrations, the factories that are small juxtaposed workshops* rather than large enterprises, as well as the limited partnerships, like the Anzin and other mining companies. All things considered, the level of industrial techniques makes a meager response to the appeal represented by the commercial advance.

And this commercial advance represents the century's greatest triumph. Owing to the Antilles, Santo Domingo, Martinique, and Guadeloupe—which, after a hundred or so years of the slave trade and progressive encroachment of the plantations, have been transformed by the planters into the richest colonial domains—the maritime trade experiences an unprecedented forward movement. The same movement provides a great deal of capital for Bordeaux and Nantes, the two large Atlantic ports and the two major way stations for this West Indian trade —despite the competition of Marseille which operates simultaneously in the Atlantic and in the Indian Ocean trade. The success of the Antilles trade, which increases the number of wharves and docks along the Garonne and Loire, is not one of spices or precious metals, as in the sixteenth century; it is one of new beverages, discovered during the days of Louis XIV, and quickly adopted by the good society of Paris and then by that of the small provincial towns: those new luxuries of the table —coffee, tea, and cocoa. The earliest "attempts" go back, to be sure, to the 1640s, when Arabian coffee came into the realm through Marseille, when the style very quickly merged into serving it, at the same time as the wines,† in the afternoon. As early as the reign of Louis XIV, coffee is as much appreciated at Versailles‡ as in the Parisian *salons*. But in the seventeenth century, coffee and tea are luxury items for the capital city alone; in the following century they become the reigning luxury of the towns. These new products from the islands, which do not yet reach the countryside and are not really going to permeate it until the end of the nineteenth century, pass into urban eating habits—never to leave them—within several decades. They do so with a hint of emotion, of

---

* At Amiens, Van Robais gathers together 1,800 workers in this way.

† "M. de la Devèze never lets us leave without offering us a cup of coffee, followed by some glasses of a nice wine." [10] Dinner wine would not be drinkable; hence the progress of wine-growing?

‡ A few minds, a few palaces, serve as detractors, in the midst of the court's general favor. In 1712, La Palatine writes: "I cannot stand either tea, or coffee, or chocolate. I cannot comprehend how people like those things. I find that tea has a taste of hay or straw, coffee of soot and lupine, and I find chocolate too sweet." The good German lady adds: "But what I would eat with pleasure would be a good *birambot*, a good beer soup."

style, strongly marked with snobbism; as early as 1696, the *Mercure galant* could write: "People have the same eagerness of it (coffee) as for wheat, and they fear being without it as they would fear lacking bread. Whenever it becomes scarce and expensive, news of this scarcity and expensiveness is distressing news for the public." Let us understand by this that the beverage that is so common today, coffee with milk and sugar, is an unprecedented luxury then; and in this sugared coffee with milk, two of the three ingredients are supplied by the Antilles. Tropical sugar cane is bringing to bourgeois and noble tables, in relative abundance, the sugar that once was so rare it was long considered a pharmaceutical product. To these three beverages, as well as sugar and molasses, must be added tobacco, whose use is particularly widespread during this period, to complete this panorama of products which cause Voltaire to regard these islands as so precious, compared to the areas of Canadian snow which produce, at most, wheat and fur. These new island products are the rapture of the frequenters of the *salons*, the academies, the reading rooms, and, particularly, the coffee houses.

Finally, in addition to the achievements of large-scale commerce, the legal world—busied with more frequent litigation, greater numbers of notarized deeds, affidavits, distraints, and cases, all of which the intensified commercial life involves—also profits from urban prosperity in its own way. Notaries, process-servers, lawyers, judges—all the *robins*, the "liberal professions," are swept along in the same movement. Contemporary justice—who did not denounce it?—is slow, because it is pettifogging, but also because it is overwhelmed by too many lawsuits; it is corrupt because it takes shameless advantage of the waves of wealth that break over urban life.

Even the common people of the towns can profit, in certain respects, from this new wealth. It is true that wages followed at a very great distance behind the price rise, a fact in which the abundance of free manpower played its part. But the journeyman carpenter or the silk weaver has work to do, for artisans do not lack orders; here, as for the rural day laborer, the gain can be seen in comparison with the preceding period, the difficult years during the seventeenth-century depression. In some localities, in the more favored towns like Paris or the Atlantic ports, there is a modest ease, with wine on the table every day—ordinary wine, certainly, but it is better than water. Throughout the urban areas, what is gained is, again, the security of life, sheltered from the wholesale mortality that punctuated former times.

The profit in craft and commerce succeeded in augmenting the profit from the land. It is this urban prosperity that we have to thank for the remarkable town planning of the period: precious, private *hôtels* that are responsible for the charm of the old residential districts like the Faubourg Saint-Germain, and that of small provincial towns like Riom or the more haughty Nancy. The efforts of the seventeenth century are continued and broadened: there are, as well, the freer and more airy prospects—the courtyards in Nantes and the Tourny *allées* in Bordeaux; streets paved and lighted at night, despite enormous costs and difficult installation. More and more the towns become places where it is pleasant to live; there is intimate comfort in the new *hôtels*, whose smaller rooms are easier to heat, and civic comfort too, because the town is gradually becoming better equipped. This is the setting sought after by the nobles themselves, a setting in which the blossoms of the regional civilization can bloom freely; this is the type of life so often described by nimble-penned provincials, enamored of their little regions, who discover in their capitals how sweet it is to live with this Janus-like aristocracy that is both noble and bourgeois. In this way, eighteenth-century prosperity makes a double fortune: in the provincial capitals, never before so active except during the period of the *philosophes*; and in Paris, the political capital (despite the royal sojourn in Versailles) as well as the administrative, economic, and intellectual one. For a long time the capital has been exceeding its traditional limitations, populating its outlying districts (Temple, Saint-Antoine, Saint-Marceau) and, crossing gardens and vineyards, grows until it meets the surrounding villages: Belleville, Auteuil, Passy, Saint-Denis. Empty spaces and gardens become rare within the town itself, especially on the right bank. The left bank is still quite open south of the Luxembourg Palace, and the banks of the Bièvre, a meeting place for curriers and tanners, are still swampy and only sparsely inhabited. Thus Paris grows outward from her interior, gaining on the periphery—particularly in the west, where the vast empty spaces that separate the Invalides from the Champ-de-Mars are being built upon— the lands which are being inhabited along the extensions of the Champs-Élysées and the Rue Saint-Honoré. Far from those great former axes, the Rue Saint-Jacques, the Rue Saint-Martin, and the Seine still glutted with ports, the town branches out and grows—an important prelude to the gigantic growth in the nineteenth century.

► ROADS AND WATERWAYS

Every town, then, lives by its connections with Paris, with Ferney and Vincennes, and with the Atlantic as well; compared with the preceding centuries, the eighteenth differs in yet another way on the level of trade, due to the new and more intense rhythm with which the services for post and travel are developed, and roads and canals built, in order better to link Paris and the provinces.

From the days of Francis I to those of Louis XIV, this type of concern was not entirely lacking; some traces of it, moreover, survive: a canal from the Loire to the Loing river, the Briare canal, brought into being at the end of the sixteenth century; roads around Paris, constructed by Sully and planted with trees; and even Riquet's too-famous Canal du Midi, joining the Garonne to the Mediterranean, traffic upon which never equalled that which passed along the Briare canal. Yet actually, for many reasons—lack of men and money, failure to discern the urgency of these needs—the efforts of the Valois and the early Bourbons were not urged very far forward. And, until the century of the coach, sea and land transportation remained risky, despite their advantage as much for efficient administration of the kingdom as for commercial traffic. Waterways are constantly used despite low water, sand, or rock shoals; roads too are constantly used despite cave-ins and the fact that they must be detoured, to avoid enormous mud holes, over fascines through open fields. These expeditions are always dangerous and are slowed to the rhythm of the way stations (one month from Paris to Bayonne): from the pine regions, coal and cheese from Auvergne go down the Allier and Loire to Orléans where they are retailed and sold on arrival—while the bargemen, with their gear on their backs, go back up to their point of departure. All this has certainly changed during the course of a half-century of prosperity.

Of these two means of transportation, the waterways undergo the fewest changes. New canal construction connects different river basins: the Canal de Centre links the Loire and Saône; the Canal de Bourgogne, the Seine and Saône. In particular, there are arrangements along the natural waterways which are used by light and numerous groups of boats: towpaths along rivers whose access is difficult, in order to ease the job of the bargemen. Thus in the long bends in the Loire between Roanne and Balbigny, the little well-graveled path survives today, though for a century it has been abandoned. Waterways, then, remain frequently traveled, especially by commercial transports, since travelers turn more and more, as the century progresses, to the roads.

Both the government and public opinion feel the need to develop roads, encouraged by the real advances in carriage-making technique—better and better suspension, more and more resistance to shocks and jolts. As early as 1715, a board from the Ponts et Chaussées of the Conseil de Finances is entrusted with building wide roads radiating out from Paris toward all the provinces. The rules of maintenance, the creation of a corps of engineers, the organization of road traffic, and, finally, in 1747, the foundation of an École des Ponts and Chaussées that survived all the revolutions: these are the major stages of work upon the roads, that great spiderweb around Paris, upon which the macadamed network of the nineteenth century is traced. In this manner the monarchy, fully conscious of what it is doing, reinforces the administrative, commercial, and intellectual primacy of Paris.

Even with due allowance made for the technical processes of surveying and paving, this gigantic work was effected less by an extraordinary financial effort than by the affliction of the French peasant. Between 1726 and 1738, there was gradually and cautiously instituted a *corvée royale*, which lasted some forty-odd years (until 1776), despite unanimous complaints and protests. Like the manorial *corvée* (which moreover has, here and there, fallen into desuetude), that of the king requires the peasant to supply ten to thirty days of labor annually, with beasts of burden, wagons, and digging tools for road construction. At times these *corvées* are rather far from the peasants' homes, which prevents them from returning there in the evenings; and often the *corvées* come just at the time of the autumn or spring work. Shortly before the Revolution, one of the worst memories of the rural population is of this *corvée*, which they cannot even avoid by monetary payment.* From *généralité* to *généralité*, the *intendants* compete with one another, seeing things on a grand scale, and executing, at the cost of the heavy sacrifices imposed upon the rural population, those straight, well-paved, and shaded roads which are beautiful enough to excite even the admiration of so hard-to-please an observer as Arthur Young.[11]

At the same time, and especially from 1770 on, the Ponts et Chaussées organizes, upon these major roads where traffic is not yet heavy, regular services between towns—and, given the layout of the network, chiefly between Paris and the large provincial centers. Great advances are made over the preceding century, with the coaches that "arrive and depart when they can"; the *diligences* and *turgotines*,† which are faster than the mail coaches, leave on a fixed day, have a set itinerary, and a definite schedule. The trip is not yet a pleasure outing: the weak springs and close air forbid this. Anyone who travels only in summer often prefers to go alone on horseback; for a long time the inns along the roads advertise, "We accommodate travelers on foot and horseback," a notice that in some places has been removed only recently.

Moreover the roads and postal services animate the towns, but have much less effect on the countrysides. Local communications between the flat regions and the towns do not experience the same improvement and remain chancy: muddy dirt paths, impractical during rain, dusty and still broken up during dry periods. Despite the greater frequency of peasant travel, despite the important role of peddlers on the highways and byways, the Ponts et Chaussées found neither the time nor the means to

---

* D'Argenson writes in 1748: "The large *corvée* roads are the most horrible *taille* that has ever had to be endured; the labor and sustenance of the day laborers is forced beyond their strength; they all decide to seek refuge in the small towns. There are numerous villages which have been deserted by everyone." After 1776, the Ponts et Chaussées arranges their construction and maintenance by contract with private concerns or with charitable workshops taking in the unemployed.

† Furetière defines *diligences* in his dictionary: "People call a *diligence* certain conveniences, either boats or carriages, that are well equipped, traveling several highly frequented places in less time than others take." (*Turgotines* are the coaches of the royal shipping and passenger service.—Trans.)

complete its network of large arteries with capillaries; lacking these latter, traffic is spasmodic and, on the whole, rather poor. Arthur Young noted simultaneously the technical success of these large roadways and the little traffic that they invited. The network of local roads, a necessary complement to the large ones, is instituted only in the following century.

However, as Ferdinand Brunot has pointed out nicely in his *Histoire de la langue française*, the monarchy accomplished more for the linguistic and intellectual unity of the nation by this road-building than by the centuries of centralization or by the famous Edict of Villers-Cotterets which imposed French as the official legal and administrative language. Before as after 1539, many townspeople, not to mention peasants, were content to understand French without speaking it, as do old people in Auvergne or those speaking Bas-Breton even today. But in the eighteenth century, the roads facilitated exchanges, and encouraged townspeople to take trips to the smaller towns or the country: business trips, nature walks imitating Rousseau, and, finally, the itineraries of the new social types whose profession is to cover France: peddlers and journeymen of the Tour de France.* Little people, commanding neither carriage nor coach—for even traveling together in a coach is a luxury: the trip from Paris to Lyon costs the large sum of two hundred *livres*—who value the level ground underfoot and the shade of the roads, travel through France simultaneously by preference and by necessity. Not for a moment do they hesitate to leave the roadway for a side village, and willingly they stop to chat with the mistrusting peasant alongside his field; they talk, they educate themselves, and, gradually, they entertain and teach too. There are two social types which the century of the Enlightenment certainly did not invent: journeymen traveling from town to town, forming little groups of workers into guilds—the Middle Ages knew these; and the peddlers, who sell the peasants small sewing materials, almanacs, and all sorts of books—already in the seventeenth century, their number is great and the profession well known.† But around 1750 these men are

---

* The spread of French in every province is measured by the number of large roads, where traffic becomes accelerated as time passes; thus, during the days of the great investigation of the language question, the Limoges Friends of the Constitution write in their *Lettre à Grégoire*: "The French language is used only in the principal towns, on the connecting roads, and in the châteaux." [12]

† Brunot quotes this nice text from 1660: "A peddler? A mercer who carries a basket hung from his neck; full of silk, ferret or wool ribbons, braid, aglet knots, combs, little mirrors, little baskets, needles, hooks, and other such low-priced little things. There are others here and there who carry Almanacs, ABC booklets, the ordinary and extraordinary news-sheets, saints' lives and little romances about Mélusine, Maugic, the four Aymond sons, Geoffrey à la Grand'Dent, Valentin, and Ourson; diverting items, earthy, dirty, nasty songs dictated by unspeakably filthy minds, satirical songs, pastoral poems, court airs, drinking songs—all composed by worshippers and prophets of Apollo, inspired by that Angel of the Abyss, and used by those who are devoted to his service." [13]

legion, and bring into the countryside their little collections of stories, their tales of the saints, their prescriptions and illustrated precepts; books undoubtedly more highly valued than the lives of the saints, the little prayer books, and all the other books for instructing beginners that the *curés* lent their catechists. There is no question that we are a long way from the time when the peasants' thatched cottages become reading rooms, or when the peasant peruses today's regional, daily paper. As a matter of fact, reading is still not widespread, due to a lack of time—especially in the summer—and a lack of curiosity and necessity as well. The almanacs and narratives about the four Aymond sons, which the peddlers can leave in the village, tour the parish in the evening by means of oral retransmission; but the small-wares peddlers spread a whole popular literature through France, from the main roads to the remote villages—the basis of today's folklore.

Similarly, the journeymen guild-members are never more talked about than during this period;* the heirs of the old trade guilds, speaking a language that is part-French, part professional jargon, they are quick to leave any place where work is poorly paid. In each town they are solidly organized to withstand any hard luck—bad season, sickness, unemployment. They are rather bold, aware of their strength which allows them to be free from any impositions on the part of their employers, even to the point of not being afraid to boycott them. The workers of the Tour de France are also great frequenters of the new roads, where their groups form, break up, meet, and also—rather often—fight.† They too, in a way different from that of the peddlers, are disseminators of the national language, and constitute an open, informed, and more active élite among the humbler townspeople who are about to play so great a political role in the years between 1792 and 1794.

In this way, French—the irreplaceable instrument of national unity—makes great strides throughout the entire realm during this half-century of commercial prosperity. As along the roads, so near the towns: the language makes the patient, slow, and uncompleted conquest of its own domain, while Europe, whose châteaux are copied from Versailles and whose princely courts are organized in the likeness of Louis XIV's etiquette and entertainments, speaks French too. To the (aristocratic) universality of the French language, extolled by Voltaire and by Rivarol

---

* In the seventeenth century they had some difficulty with the Company of the Blessed Sacrament, who were rather concerned about the morality and the Christian practices of these carefree travelers.
† An Example: "The King being informed that several young people from the various arts and crafts in the town of La Rochelle had for some time formed a society which they had given the title of *Société des Compagnons du Devoir*, that these individuals who, among themselves, have signs for recognizing one another, had given those who are not members the name of Gavaux, that they mistreat them whenever they meet, and prevent them from joining masters of different professions. . . ." [14]

in his famous speech before the Berlin Academy, replies the spread of the national idiom within French boundaries: the setbacks of patois and even of Latin. This is not the smallest achievement of this progress in the means of communication and exchange between 1730 and 1770 —the road of the Enlightenment, from town to town, academy to academy, with distant ramifications as far as the borders of Europe: Berlin and Weimar, Vienna, Cracow, St. Petersburg, and Odessa.

► **THE CRISIS OF THE YEARS 1775-1790**

After 1775, there are dark shadows in this picture of prosperity and wealth; the unfortunate Louis XVI, well before the terrible years, experiences this misfortune. There is a crisis in the French economy coincident with his reign, and one not in his power to reduce. At best, he could only have mitigated the sufferings of his subjects, which appeared all the more unbearable to them since the memory of the former frightening periods of poverty had grown indistinct in the popular mind after forty good years—almost two generations. Thus this crisis which is not so catastrophic as the famine years like 1694 or 1709, and which, also, is not a long deep recession like the seventeenth century's, and at the very least like the years from 1640 to 1680—the fifteen or so years when both town and country are affected by a slowing-down of business and profits—appeared unbearable to many; hence, its social and political implications, exacerbating class antagonisms, by its inroads into fiscal receipts and the weak royal finances. Through this, the crisis of 1775-1790 belongs to the history of the Great Revolution.

The origin of the crisis, like that of the previous prosperity, lies in the rural situation: an economic crisis of the Old Regime, one might say, in comparing it with the crises of the twentieth century and the second half of the nineteenth, whose origins are in the iron industry, and whose stoppages and depressions reverberate throughout the whole economy of a region, or a group of regions. Thus the crisis of Louis XVI's reign is a rural one. Consistently poor harvests due to bad weather heap up from 1773 to 1789; yields are smaller; there are occasional lost harvests and widespread incompetency, which suffice to create financial difficulties among small farmers and farmers on whose land the leases regularly increased in the preceding period, and even greater difficulty among the day laborers, the first to be affected. Until the good wheat crop of 1790, the grain harvests do not fill the granaries.* To this must be added the

---

* The years 1788 and 1789 are among the worst; that winter is often proclaimed the worst man's memory has ever known: "That year there was a severe winter, which began on Saint Andrew's Day [November 30] and continued until January fourteen or fifteen; there was a great deal of snow and ice, which caused a famine; many walnut trees, and others, were frozen; there was little grain, and no wine." [15]

terrible drought of 1785, not a negligible factor, when the meadows turned yellow with the sun and the fodder harvest was so meager that by autumn most of the livestock was destroyed for lack of reserves to feed them in the winter. In the regions where vineyards furnished more than the family's supply, there must also be added crises of abundance and of overproduction, resulting from a conjunction of good wine-producing years and reduced urban consumption. Against this accumulation of disasters the peasant is defenseless: neither funds established to compensate for agricultural calamities nor replaced cultivations make up for the severe winter or the drought of 1785. This persistence of bad harvests overwhelms the entire peasantry: the husbandmen's profits dwindle; the small farmers see their salable surplus disappear, and, peradventure, taste again—without any pleasure—bread mixed with bran and fern during this time when harvesting becomes difficult. The day laborers and the landless hired help too quickly spend what they earned during the summer; beggars and vagrants multiply, as does springtime terror in the countrysides, as storehouses use up their last reserves. No doubt this is a situation of food scarcity rather than famines, and so say the contemporaries, who are so badly frightened by these remediless misfortunes. Lacks of food are hard to bear: the rural population, overwhelmed with taxes and fees, all the heavier as their own resources dwindle away,* protect themselves as best they can, hiding sheaves of corn in the woods before the tithe-owner passes by, to lessen the share handed over to the Church; taking things to the lord's mill and oven only for form's sake, risking grinding and cooking the grain at home in order to pay less, for these services too, in *banalités*. With greater reason, the peasant who has no more of the necessities of life no longer buys tools and fabrics, either in towns or from the peddlers. The acquisition of such items as these is put off from year to year, until better times, and in this way the rural misfortunes, in their turn, redouble the urban crisis.

The landed proprietors, those "natural" intermediaries, in one way, lose even more: their revenues, at least those levied in kind, in proportion to the harvests, have diminished along with the latter, but in greater proportion since the peasants have not failed to emphasize, by virtue of a vital piece of deception on their part, the losses, for which nothing can compensate. Seizure and the expulsion of a few indebted farmers at the height of the crisis are not remedies. These annual revenues, consequently, are badly mishandled, and expenses follow their movement: building, purchases of fabrics and furniture, expenses of the table, wine cellar and servant staff, as well as the scale of living, are all reduced. Doubtless only Versailles courtiers, whose debts the king pays at the

---

* Obviously it is easier to hand over to the lord ten sacks out of a harvest of one hundred than five from a harvest of fifty: the percentage is the same, but the important thing is what remains—ninety in the first instance, forty-five in the second.

right moment, can maintain themselves, but they are a minority among the landed proprietors.

In this respect, both trade and artisanry are directly, and doubly, affected: rich people, who spend all the more willingly as their revenues do not ask much work of them, are forced to count their money and spend less; the rural masses, who in the preceding period began to go into town regularly to fit themselves out with essential products like fabrics and tools, fall back upon themselves and cease to nourish a different, but not negligible, commercial flow. By a concatenation of events identical with those of prosperity, all urban activities are rapidly slowed down—all luxury trade; some are paralyzed, as is the case with building. Here again several secondary causes are able to help the slump, as wine did the rural crisis. There is a dearth of cotton during the American Revolution, and difficulties due in part to the Franco-English commercial treaty of 1786; these add to the financial problems and to the general slump of printed cloth, be it Oberkampf's calicoes or the beautiful silks from Lyon. Even the Antilles trade feels these effects just before the Revolution, despite the tyranny of fashions in food. Even the best-placed artisans and manufacturers, as well as both small and large merchants, complain in their turn and blame taxes or the English competition. Then, at the point when wheat is scarce and—because of speculation—quite expensive, they disband their employees, workers, apprentices, and sellers, who join the ranks of the unemployed; similarly manufacturers, like the silk-mill owners in Lyon, no longer have work for the weavers who, in ten or twenty villages around Lyon, Amiens, and Rouen, work at home for them: this is the final blow to the rural, family economy in these urban backwashes. At any rate, unemployment frees a large working force of journeymen and artisans; if they want more work, they must work for rapidly declining wages. Guild leaders, large-scale merchants, manufacturers and tradesmen, in their own turn, experience a complete slump in their businesses, lower their scale of living, and consequently contribute to maintaining the urban crisis. In the same way the liberal professions are indirectly, but no less seriously, affected.

Lack of food, higher wheat prices, lower industrial prices, vagrants on the roads and in the forests, unemployed workers, small *rentiers* reduced to nothing:* across all France, poverty and dissatisfaction constantly increase, setting countless victims of the crisis against the royal government and, particularly, one class against another. There are catastrophic events in the towns: shortly before the Revolution, a wallpaper factory

---

* Paris, which was affected no more than other towns, and which has a population of six or seven hundred thousand people, will shelter some hundred thousand paupers, unemployed and small *rentiers* without any funds, in the years just before the Estates-General.

in Paris burns; mounted guardsmen charge workers begging for bread; there are battles between employers and workers, bakeries looted, convoys bringing flour attacked at the gates; these significant urban demonstrations on the part of the Fourth Estate, at this point, do not cause serious disorders. It is a question of manpower, for the journeymen workers in the guilds or the factories, or else the independents, are not yet numerous and represent only a small part of the population.

The struggle in the villages—known as the *réaction nobiliaire*—was more important: the aristocracy, seeing its revenues melt within a few years, did not accept this unexplained ruin. It turned first of all toward the manorial agents and the *intendants* who zealously hunt down the peasants to recoup the losses their masters suffered; a ferocious struggle, in which these little people, for their part, relentlessly and immoderately use and abuse manorial authority. The 1780s are a period of intense emotions, renewed panics and fears in which flails and pitchforks are quickly ready to join in self-protection against the overwhelmed peasants' many enemies, be they imaginary or real.

Next, the revision of the registers pertaining to landed property (*terriers*)—of which the rural population retained such bad memories at the time of the Revolution—is of the same inspiration, but with wider implications also. The simple proceeding consists in having some notary clerk come from town, someone accustomed to deciphering old, unintelligible scribbles of law office or château, and having him nimbly transcribe and make a fair copy of all the manorial archives which, stored in various locations, are half-eaten by rats, decayed by mildew, and forgotten by the peasants. Babeuf plied this trade, and from it retained a holy horror of the manorial regime. The noble, or the new chatelain— the bourgeois settled on his land—discovers these, without lifting a finger, privileges fallen into desuetude; whether prescribed or not— for about this there is room for discussion regarding both the privilege and the length of its prescription—and what a fine windfall, this privilege uncollected for twenty years, or prescribed for thirty years of neglect, and claimed of the peasant just before their prescription: how will he pay the capital accumulated during twenty-five or twenty-eight years of neglect? The chatelain revives all the recoverable privileges, and consequently overwhelms the peasants with what are in fact "new," arbitrary demands that add to the already heavy obligations which had continued.*

At the end of the eighteenth century, the gilded nobility of Versailles

---

* It is in the same spirit that the aristocracy obtains from the king the famous military ruling of 1781 making it impossible for the *roturiers* to gain access to the ranks of the army: this is a cruel dispossession of the sons of the good bourgeois at a time when—with the pedagogical prestige of the military schools abetting these new vocations—the bourgeois are invading every career open, or partly open, to them.

and the dull provincial nobility, driven back onto their manors ever since the damage wrought by the economic crisis dwindled away their revenues and kept them from holding their position in the towns, live turned toward the past, that lost paradise, and restore the medieval manor in their thoughts as if a return to the past were possible: the *réaction nobiliaire*, therefore, collides with the peasantry, as much worn out by their common impoverishment as the nobility is exasperated by it.

The peasants and bourgeois also are victims of another master provoked by the economic crisis: royal authority. Obviously the additional burden accrues to the peasants, since royal taxes are added to the tithes and lords' fees. But peasants and bourgeois alike are without tenderness for the direct taxes: *taille, capitation,* and *vingtième,** and indirect taxes: customs dues on beverages, the tax on salt, and so on, which the tax-farmers, greedy for heavy collections, gathered. The crisis in this area also caused lively reactions: the fiscal receipts did not increase† when royal expenditures swelled the expenses occasioned by the American Revolution. The important fact, however, does not lie there: everybody, everywhere, feels that these taxes (which, moreover, are badly collected), are an unbearable burden, and even that they are the cause of the poverty and economic difficulties felt in the towns and the country. Rather than impute the crisis to atmospheric calamities and to the mechanisms set into motion by the country being thrown back onto the towns, Frenchmen see the origin of it in the fiscal system, which has many faults, known and recognized by all, and begun by the iniquitous actions of the privileged. The incomplete and badly conducted attempts at reform multiplied, to end the increasing deficit—that immediate cause of the Revolution—by Louis XVI, and from Turgot to Necker seem, to the eyes of bourgeois public opinion, to constitute the very confession of the responsibility that falls upon the fiscal system. From taxes, public opinion effortlessly passes to those who establish them, and those who insure their collection: frequently, in these tumultuous years, one sees collectors of the salt tax and royal agents greeted with pitchforks in the villages and in the noisy suburbs of the large towns. The small, local agents, the ministers, and the king's entourage—these are to be blamed for the public poverty; the king escapes it, at least in the popular milieux, because the old, monarchic faith remains alive—there are many expressions of the faith in the grievance lists. But, with this

---

* The *vingtième* was an income tax of about five per cent, often levied more than once per reign.
† They tended to be lower, since there was an economic recession. But the indirect taxes, especially the "aids," by virtue of their mass—in terms of the population increase—maintained the receipts at an almost stable level.

exception, the economic crisis contributed more than a little to questioning, through the fiscal policy, the entire political and social system. Hence its prime place in both the underlying and immediate origins of the Revolution.

XII

Fêtes Galantes
and the Enlightenment

The Century
of French Europe

THE brilliant eighteenth century! On the very day the old king dies, it bursts into joyful fireworks. Voltaire saw these on the Rue Saint-Denis, in front of the taverns, on the road leading to the royal basilica. And from this month of September, 1715, until the performance of *Le Mariage de Figaro* at the Trianon in the presence of Marie Antoinette —that merry and bewitching queen—French society life seems to be a perpetual fete, set to the rhythm of the light and tender music orchestrated by Rameau and Mozart, in a setting of well-tended gardens and little Trianons nestled in greenery. A few discordant cries create, amid these fetes, an at least momentary disturbance: then the ball begins again, the ladies laugh in the glimmer of candlelight. There are the *parlementaires*, continually discontented, always chasing after the political offices refused them by the monarchy, happy to adapt themselves to claiming they are "Fathers of the Country." This is a popularity easily acquired, by using an expression becoming increasingly employed; a dangerous popularity. There is the fully dignified retreat of the Jesuits, vanquished in their century-long struggle with the Jansenists, and forced to leave the kingdom for a half-century, as their society vegetates

and then disappears—dissolved by Rome. There are lamentations
and protestations by the man of nature, that *philosophe* who is unlike
the others, who values neither the theater and its fictions nor the *salons*
and their venomous talk—that misanthrope who, as Voltaire piteously
protests, wants to make man walk on four feet: the terrible Jean-
Jacques, announcing the end of an age.

The too brilliant eighteenth century! Whoever glances through the
books of its exploits—sumptuous evenings at Versailles, large receptions
at Madame du Deffand's, solemn meetings of the academies at Berlin,
Dijon, and Montpellier—receives the impression of a world in a hurry.
The friends of Monsieur de Talleyrand Périgord, Bishop of Autun and
large financier of the clergy, taste along with him these sweetnesses of
life, which are so dear to them and which they will find never again;
these survivors of the storm return to the gilded, paneled *salons*, with
well-schooled servants, after 1815; they recognize the ornament of their
young and carefree days, but only the ornament. For what is essential
has departed with Rivarol—that inexhaustible master of fine wit—with
Voltaire, with D'Alembert and his *encyclopédiste* cohorts, and with the
noble hearts of the Marquis de Condorcet and of so many others like
Fréron, who would not really have killed that snake.* The essence of
these days is that spirit, always lying in wait for the witty remark; but
it is also a subtle bond, a stamp of fineness, by which is revealed the
attentive intelligence, rational and intuitive at one and the same time,
the charm of this fine society that does not have a good conscience.
Time passes too quickly in those witticisms, those games, while at stake
is a whole world. *Après moi, le déluge* should have been said by the
well-loved Louis XV, who nevertheless became angry in his old age, and
who succeeded in carrying out the strongest reform of the monarchical
government ever undertaken. The truest part of this expression is precisely that everyone feels the *déluge*, as portended by those Parisians who
believe to be perfectly possible the escapade of a French queen with a
frivolous Cardinal de Rohan in the Versailles shrubbery. That much
too famous puzzle of the Diamond Necklace, certainly a strange affair,
boils down to a play given by moonlight. Do not all the *salons* of the
period give themselves over to plays several times a week—even that of
the bluestocking Mademoiselle de Lespinasse—where there is serious discussion of the influence of climate on morals and politics, that subject
Montesquieu took up from Montaigne and Pascal, out of which he made
a trite theme of daily conversation.† Great ideas and little tidbits of

---

* Allusion is made here to the epigram of his enemy Voltaire, who wrote:
    L'autre jour, au fond d'un vallon,
    Un serpent mordit Jean Fréron.
    Que pensez-vous qu'il arriva? . . .
    Ce fut le serpent qui creva!—Trans.
† A new perspective from which to define the fact of civilization: "Everything has
been said and we come too late, for there have been men and ideas for more than

gossip, in the multiple rhythm of the mind: the years pass too quickly, in the glory of those conversations excelled in by Voltaire, as talented as anyone in words, conceits, as well as possessor of a wit which easily raises itself to the level of the greatest problems. Rousseau is not a good representative—he who is always serious, too serious, and who legislates for eternity—the father of Robespierre and of republican virtue.

In point of fact this eighteenth century, which the Revolution made into its own prelude, a eulogistic but subordinate role (intellectual origins, political origins: a litany with convincing claims) was actually a blossoming much more than a preparation for revolutionary events. The eighteenth century sees the flowering of a society finally brought under an organized government, where sword thrusts give way to witty words which blanch their victims to pallor under make-up but do not kill; it sees the flowering of an urban life, which finds its equilibrium in the antagonism of bourgeois and noble, and apes Paris, the town whose superior repute does not detract from the originality of the provincial capitals. The charms of these little towns equal those of Parisian life: rich in their traditions, in their vogues (mock-heroic plays in Dijon, instrumental music in Besançon and Strasbourg), in their *salons* and academies, in their *philosophes* and their writers, great and small (Bordeaux has Montesquieu, but each town has several local glories, important in contemporary life, although the mainstream of literature has not deigned to retain their names). So many towns, so many diverse riches, the sum of which, if it be possible to add them up, constitutes the refined and smiling civilization of the century of the Enlightenment— again under the banner of Voltaire, that devil of a man whose name, after his death, comes to mean a turn of mind; that prince of the *philosophes* who fills up the century, from his emprisonment in the Bastille in 1717 to his transfer, thirteen years after his death in 1791, to the Panthéon—the man of Ferney and of Paris, with the disquieting and unbenevolent smile presaging his long legacy.

► THE REGENCY ATMOSPHERE

During the long reign (from 1715 to 1774) of Louis XV, that king who ruled hardly at all except during the last four years of his life, the regency of the Duc d'Orléans, with its public disturbances, its atmosphere of complete relaxation in all spheres, its freedom, and its ostentation, constitutes both a preface to the century and a summary of it.

---

five thousand years," claims La Bruyère. But such an idea which, buried in Chapter 23 of Montaigne's first book of *Essais*, encountered no echoes at the close of the sixteenth century, is the subject of all eighteenth-century conversations. It enters into the heritage of public opinion, that amorphous entity that takes shape because it frequents *collèges*, and then—by virtue of the life of communication, reading, and newspapers—acquires life and constitutes a power in the state.

The Regent, and Regency Paris, set the tone until Louis XVI; the air of the years between 1715 and 1724 is that of the *salons* and academies, where the greatest battles are brought into the open. All those who could not or would not show themselves during the terrible years of the Spanish Succession are now in the limelight, and will remain in the foreground without Cardinal Fleury, Madame de Pompadour, or Louis XV obtaining any more than a truce amid these long battles, whose starting positions were arranged when the game began, soon after the death of Louis XIV. Already, Montesquieu and Voltaire were acquainted, amid disorders and cries of the *parlementaires* and Jansenists: the young Voltaire of the Bastille days, and the stern Bordeaux magistrate of the *Lettres persanes*. All this at a time when the Duc d'Orléans—that boy beloved of Charlotte-Elizabeth of Bavaria, and rather proud of his role as Regent—keeps his habits, and launches his fine suppers, Opera balls, and fashions for years to come, until, in fact, the virtuous protests of Jean-Jacques.

Following 1715 are the years of reaction (even though this somewhat heavy term conjures up the Thermidorian period, or the reign of Louis XVIII): the attitude of the *parlementaires*, hurling themselves with undisguised pleasure into those vigorous objections, into those refusals to register laws, as that right had been withdrawn for fifty years by the stern hand of a great king—an attitude that flatly negates the preceding order. The death of Louis XIV liberated all those political and social forces reduced to silence by the Sun King, if not subjected to his law: the Jansenists leave prison; the nobles, deprived of any voice in the royal counsels, convinced by Saint-Simon that their vocation is to govern and not to serve as symbols, the *parlementaires* who are often Jansenists to boot—all lift up their heads and cast blame on the dead king's entourage, on Madame de Maintenon and the Jesuit confessors to whom too many evils are imputed. At least until 1718, the Regency was a period of foolish experiments and of unchecked reaction.

For the upper nobility—the dukes and peers, the marquis and counts of Versailles, who invade the councils and create the short-lived regime called the Polysynodie—the revenge is total, though brief: Saint-Simon, who had been waiting a long time for this day, swept along with him the aristocracy for whom the honors of governing were more attractive than its responsibilities; while conciliatory to the Fronde, the Polysynoodie is a new attempt on the part of the aristocracy to recover that participation in political power which had so long been lost. But this undertaking, tolerated, if not patronized, by the Regent, was no more successful than the taking-up of arms in the preceding century. Saint-Simon's companions* were lost in multiple intrigues, overwhelmed with

---

* From the very beginning, impatient ambitions and divergent interests created endless imbroglios, through which Saint-Simon moves comfortably; but he alone, perhaps,

concerns for precedence, greedy for power but incapable of applying themselves to the duties of their new trusts, and thrown off by daily administrative difficulties; they knew neither how to organize their government nor how to make it accepted by public opinion. In 1718, the Regent re-establishes the ministers and councils instituted by Louis XIV, and, without disturbances or revolt, this new attempt on the part of the nobility to restore its political functions darkens hopelessly—until the Assemblée des Notables which, on the eve of the Revolution, reawakens the final ambitions of that class the monarchy itself had ruined.

The "restoration" of the Parlement is more concerted, and also more persevering. The Parisian Parlement, which in the middle of the seventeenth century claimed to advise the king, and which consequently plays a double political and judiciary role, found its ambitions intact after a half-century of coercion. These ambitions were nourished on the honorable conviction that Parlement is the true guardian of monarchic traditions, but also on the less admissible desire to gain the political prestige that would complete its own exalted idea of its function. After the great meeting in which Parlement decides to set aside the king's will in favor of the Regent, the latter must pay for this good turn. With great pleasure, the *parlementaires* recover their *remontrance* and registration privileges and do not deny themselves use of them, thus exercising a truly permanent control over the Regent's acts. True, these councils, populated with nobles and entrusted with replacing the ministers, give proof of both their spirit of initiative and their incompetence; whence, in part, the interventions. But in its excess, this fervor found the check French kings traditionally applied to them: as early as 1718, the Regent again takes up the old remedies—the jussive letters and *lits de justice*.* The Jansenist quarrels and the *philosophes'* daring, however, revived the pugnacity of the men at law, beyond that brief period when revenge was complete. Defenders of the Jansenists, attackers of the Society of Jesus, protectors of privileges and the privileged against the monarchy, the *parlementaires* stir up trouble, give justice a vacation in order to obtain recognition of their political right, exile themselves

---

sees clearly enough into the situation of both the Regent and his friends: "We were unable to blame him for not wanting to take risks for us, to unify Parlement with its bastard sons against him at the critical point of deciding on the power of the Regent, or of risking an outburst and a suspension of such major and urgent affairs, when he could only lose by such a risk, and we even more, whom the public, disposed as it is with respect to us, would blame for everything, for having wanted to mix our private quarrels with the regulation of government." The point at issue here concerns the famous meeting of Parlement when, indemnified by the will of Louis XIV, it must set it aside to return all the power into the hands of the Regent, at the expense of the bastard sons, and in particular, of the Duc de Maine who entered "bursting with joy," and left "totally shorn."

* A *lit de justice* is the formal procedure by which the king could force Parlement to register one of his decrees. It usually involved his making a personal appearance at the Palais de Justice and formally ordering the registration.—Trans.

and then return—checkmated. In 1732, 1756, and 1771, Paris lights up and sings the praise of the "Fathers of the Country," who soon become resigned and submissive. The reform undertaken between 1771 and 1774 by Louis XV—putting an end to the sale of offices, reducing the Parisian Parlement's sphere of action, and preparing an exact definition of judicial authority—is a radical one. It could have marked the end of the political agitation, had it not been abandoned by Louis XVI, by way of a joyous accession: the *parlementaires* regain their prerogatives and daring, and, until 1789, remain the most passionate troublemongers and (no matter what they say) the most active demolishers of the monarchy.

Finally, there are the Jansenists who, in the autumn of 1715, leave prison, demanding revenge. They quickly obtain substantial satisfactions: the exile of the king's confessor, Father Le Tellier, the imprisonment of a few other members of the Society of Jesus, and particularly the setting aside of the Bull *Unigenitus*, whose publication and indeed final registration is still dubious in some dioceses. This encounter of the Jansenists, those austere and morally exacting men, with the Regent is a peculiar one. The century is rich in these unexpected alliances—in 1771 Voltaire thoroughly supports the *dévot* party, the forbidden friends of the Jesuits, against the *parlementaires* at the time of Maupeou's reform; but this reform is unquestionably one of the more stimulating. In this case as in those preceding, the Duc d'Orléans grants only a short revenge to these curious friends: he is still Regent when the *Unigenitus* Bull is finally registered; besides, the Bull regulates nothing, since the Jansenists dispute this condemnation as they did the others, and especially since they continue to form within the Catholic Church a group prompted by a faith and an equally lofty ethic—hence their fervor and ardor for the good fight, not to mention certain popular victories such as the miracles of Saint-Médard in 1727. In the eighteenth century the Jansenists won over the lower, urban clergy and experienced an impassioned popular success. Barbier, that worthy memoirist of the beginnings of the century, records it in 1727: "The entire second order of the ecclesiastics, the largest part of the Parisian bourgeoisie, of the *robins*, of the third estate, and, which is more pleasing, even women and the people—everything is let loose against the Jesuits." [1] There lies the principal objective, until the great proceedings instituted against the Constitutions of the Society in 1761. But for a whole century, the Jansenists waged a war on two fronts: against the Jesuits, out of habit and conviction and, in their ideas, to purify and reform the Catholic Church; and then against the *philosophes* whose boldness is hairsplittingly surveyed: they are the first, for example, to denounce the blasphemousness of the *Esprit des Lois*, as soon as it is published. Their newspaper, *Les Nouvelles Ecclésiastiques*, exercises its spirit in lengthy columns and thrusts its bitter attacks against various people.

In a word, the years of revenge following 1715 are those of all sorts of daring and freedoms, after the cheerless and silent years of virtue under the monarchy: in an atmosphere of fetes, of laughter and pleasure, the forces contained, repressed, and condemned under Louis XIV are liberated. Like many reactions, this one is violent, and—since the Regent has long refused to be its instrument—it exceeds its goal. But the wrinkle it made furrows the subsequent period, despite the sobered Duc d'Orléans, and, later, despite Fleury. Without a doubt, the best indication of these new freedoms is the publication in 1721, by a nimble-penned Bordeaux *parlementaire*, of that light, flippant book which paints the portrait of France in an ironic and merciless indictment. Does not this "Persian"—born sly—venture the greatest crime by denigrating the religious protection of which French monarchy has been insured for centuries? At the turn of a page, in five words, he reduces the sanctity of the scrofula-curing king to the level of that prestidigitation in which his region is so rich: the royal miracle is very simple: "*Ce roi est un magicien!*" The tone has been set. This century of verbal liberties respects nothing.

The social upheavals brought about by Law's bankruptcy had their part, too, in the century. This Scotch banker, who so well understood the advantages of paper money and who saw things with a long view in proportion as success and public favor accompany his initiatives, was unquestionably not understood by his contemporaries,* not to mention the jealousies and the enemies his success stirred up against him. His failure, the July, 1720, bankruptcy, also marks these troubled times: for a long time to come, it turns the average Frenchman away from paper money and perhaps from the taste for speculation and banks. But more immediately, his failure ruins *rentiers*, possessors of assets small or large, and bourgeois who have borrowed money or sold land and houses in order to participate in the promised Mississippi fortune. Law's failure enriches not only the Duc de Bourbon, but also the nimblest to catch the gossip on the Rue Quincampoix—tavern waiters and lackeys who were well placed to know the news and to indulge in the speculation that ran rampant for more than ten years. Once the disturbance is quelled and the concerns of the banker, who takes refuge in Italy, are liquidated, Paris finds itself—to the astonishment of some and the indignation of many—"enriched" with some several hundred newly-rich, who promptly install themselves in fine *hôtels* and live on a grand scale in their turn; lovers, as only the newly arrived know how to be, of all the novelties of the day. This financial and social crisis—whose precise extent is very hard to gauge—contributed in no small way, among the

---

* Saint-Simon says of him: "Law was a man of system, and so deep that no one understood anything about him."

contemporaries of the Duc d'Orléans, to belief in the idea of a new world where all sorts of daring could have its place. Opinion, the "public," which is astonished by nothing since the king's death, accepts the Regent's fickleness in affairs of state, and the daring of the Jansenists and the *parlementaires*; it applauds Montesquieu and leaves Voltaire in prison. Such is the "good society," that of the *salons* and the fetes in the Regency style, the society which will rule over Paris until the end of the century.

► **SALONS AND FÊTES GALANTES**

Perhaps never in the history of modern France has the joy of living asserted itself with such frankness, a frankness that has, nonetheless, no trace of cynicism, as might be suggested by a comparison with the *manants*, whose life is so difficult even during the fat years from 1730 to 1770. Until Rousseau, until the great Romantic and socialist nineteenth century, those favored by chance and by the social order feel no shame in living in fully attractive luxury and leisure; only a century later does discretion or bravado become the rule. But the eighteenth century experiences neither these scruples nor these hates, at least at its beginnings, and worldly life attains its greatest glamor.

Worldly life or urban life—they are synonymous: it would be unthinkable, then, to live in one's château, lost amid one's peasants. What was still acceptable behavior in the sixteenth century is no longer so in the days of Diderot, and the only ones who remain in their old residences are the lesser nobility—those who gradually sold their inheritances in the preceding centuries and have nothing left but their dovecote and their name (as was true of Chateaubriand's father at Combourg).* They are peasants among their peasants, and no longer have enough wealth to take advantage of the century's great prosperity; the crisis of the reign of Louis XVI overwhelms them even further. Meanwhile, nobles of average and high degree, merchants with quickly made fortunes, men of law, and officeholders live a more than pleasant life in town: houses which are already comfortable, well-kept squares and streets, many meetings, *salons* where women hold first place, and charming fetes in parks or on lawns where the guests dance the gavotte, play comedies, and sing opera. The towns are also feverish with great conflicts; dances are interrupted to evoke the *Encyclopédie* and *Candide*, Calas and *Émile*, and the American Revolutionaries. Witticisms, the sweetness of friendly encounters, word-plays by Voltaire and by Rivarol, the play of ideas; never, even in the days of the Hôtel de Rambouillet and the *Précieuses*, never, even in those days of courtly knights, was

---

* As Young saw him, in a famous passage in the *Voyages*.

France so rich in fine minds, in wits like Usbek or Zadig, or in enthusiasts like Rameau's nephew or the *vicaire* from Savoy. No one in Europe is able to resist so many enticements, so many charms.

There is, first of all, the comfort of town life. People build with a double aim: being comfortable at home, and being able to entertain—or such seems the goal of this enterprising century. The increasingly numerous private *hôtels* consist of small, intimate rooms, where the *salons* combine one into the other for great festivities and where everything is provided for unostentatious and uncrowded receptions: it is an established fact that family life, constrained within the parent-child framework, is—if we can risk this linguistic anachronism—lower-middle-class. But, if it is true that everyone, nobles and shopkeepers, financiers and merchants—those masters of the century—lawyers and notaries, keep *salons* and receive their friends and their music teachers and perhaps some philosophizing *abbé*, they do so with less ceremony and more simplicity than in the preceding century. Apart from the follies of the greatest financiers, the biggest receptions are held more and more often by new public institutions like reading-rooms and academies. And the *salon* of the *philosophes* no longer aims at being a Hall of Mirrors in miniature; it gathers several intimates in a window alcove, in front of the gaming table, that passion of the day; the fashion is that of little secrets, the whisper into the ear, the great news spread about with understanding smiles: all these *philosophes* are more or less conspirators, and Rameau's nephew shocks everyone by saying aloud, in a public hall, what everyone has agreed to murmur in the nook of a *salon*. Finally, because they love their comfort and the warmth of an apartment whose small rooms can be easily furnished and better heated,[2] these good companies give themselves a new setting, one adapted to this new definition of life in society. Even Versailles and court life follow this movement toward comfort and intimacy: the Petit Trianon is constructed from plans having nothing in common with those of Louis XIV; the interior arrangements at Versailles are redone in the same direction. As a matter of fact, neither Louis XV nor Louis XVI sets any value on their predecessor's great ostentation; Marie Antoinette plays the shepherdess. But there is this slight difference: Paris imposes its tone upon the close of the century, including Jean-Jacques' rantings against worldly life, against the large receptions with their lies and vanities—the magnificent language of a frightened man's anathemas.

Thus is life transformed in these small, secret *hôtels*. They are set back from the street, opening onto large gardens with straight and symmetrical lines, as at Champs and Vaux; while the streets, whose maintenance has been improved and which are wider, safer, better paved, and cleansed of their filth, cease to be a nocturnal thieves' alley, by virtue of their lighting, and particularly, of the watch and improvements in the urban police force. The courtyards and the widest boulevards become places for promenading and meeting; city planning, an art rediscovered from antiquity, creates a new urbanity.

The eighteenth-century notion of luxury is no longer fond of overly large buildings: its special leaning is toward interior arrangement and suites of furniture. Instead of the spacious Louis XIV *fauteuils*, the style of Louis XV prefers small furniture: consoles, pedestal tables, dressing-tables, writing desks, with many secret drawers, chairs, and small *fauteuils*. Following the new style, Parisian craftsmen create filiform, twisted feet, and chair backs covered with bright-hued calicoes in various designs; the heavy, sculptured, *bombé* cabinets and mighty tables with antique columns are temporarily abandoned for delicate, graceful furniture attuned to the contemporary mode of dress, which is more restrained, less beribboned and befeathered, than in the days of Louis the Great.

Finally, urban life still presents the attraction of another luxury whose importance keeps growing throughout the century: the table. The profession of [the chef] Vatel becomes one of the most sought-after skills in all the large towns, and gastronomy becomes something of a passion of the century, as much as games of chance and discussion. There are fine suppers in the style of the Regent, not that of Louis XIV who used to wolf his food like some Pantagruel, and there are delicacies for financiers, whose names survive for certain choice dishes; it is the honor of a great house, noble or bourgeois, to have a talented cook with well-known specialties, as it is today to have a professional who boasts of his duck with oranges. Finally, on every table of good society, big-town or small-town, the beverages from the islands are given the place of honor. Michelet, in a famous passage on the qualities and the spirit of the Regency, made coffee the great prime mover of Parisian life: first the timid beginnings under Louis XIV, during the days of Arabian coffee and mocha; then the strong coffee of the *Lettres persanes* and from Réunion; and at last, in the days of the *Encyclopédistes*, the stimulating, light, and nervous coffee from Santo Domingo. Whether this be one of the brilliant intuitions with which the work is crammed, or merely a concurring opinion, fifty years after the visionary Michelet, Rambaud states that no one has measured the scope that "the changes which the almost simultaneous use of these articles, coffee and tobacco, . . . equally unknown to both Antiquity and the Middle Ages, were able to exercise on the French . . ." (let us add, in the towns).[3] And this occurs in a country in which heavy wine consumption already constitutes an important stimulant—to the point of justifying the expression "wine civilization" sometimes used to contrast France, Spain, and Italy with the Scandinavian and Anglo-Saxon countries. Research on this point remains to be done, but there is no question that contemporaries felt

the "arousing"* effects, admitting that it loosens the tongue and facilitates repartee, in days when it is not good to be socially backward, and
they honored those new enterprises destined for so beautiful a future:
the "coffee houses."

What opportunities the eighteenth century offered for meetings, witticisms, and scholarly or political discussions! Well might coffee be in
honor: there are the *salons*, opened by all those having some ambition
(even if only to be seen). Tax-farmers-general, bankers, merchants, and
manufacturers, exactly like the *noblesse d'épée* and the *noblesse de
robe*, have *salons* where women mill about, taking their revenge upon
the Chrysales† of the seventeenth century. And alongside these luxurious *salons*, there are the academies, the reading rooms, and the Masonic
lodges—new centers of the intellectual life, as well as the worldly.

Brilliant receptions or discreet, private conversations: anyone who has
some leisure and enough income has his day. In the age of the *philosophes*, this has become as normal as it was in the preceding century to
put money aside and acquire a plot of land several leagues from Orléans or Dijon. Numerous families offer a striking contrast from one century to the other: the thrifty grandparents are extremely economical in
their scale of living for dozens of years, in order either to round off a
landed inheritance outside of town, or to enlarge a business constantly
being threatened in these difficult times; and their grandchildren in the
1750s, who devour all their income in parties and dinners where fine
palaces and scintillating conversationalists do honor to their hosts. More
often than not, the mistress of the house, with a shade of bluestocking-
ism, leads the show in these *salons:* a marriage of science and literature, based on the *hôtel* of the Marquise de Lambert opened toward the
end of the seventeenth century and much frequented as early as 1710.
Madame de Tencin and Madame Geoffrin imitated this with brilliance,
as well as with a great knowledge of the world. After 1750, the game
becomes political: there are Mademoiselle de Lespinasse, and especially
Madame Necker, who caters to her husband's political ambitions. The
Parisian *salons* gather together famous men, like the old Fontenelle in
all his glory as *premier philosophe*, who loves its houses "where people
go to speak with one another, even, on occasion, with wit"; in Paris,
they are still the meeting places of academicians, present or future.‡

---

* Many virtues, even unexpected ones, are imputed to coffee: some memoir writers
recommend it to Catholic priests because it "is conducive to chastity." The *Encyclopédie* seriously asserts that the Turks attributed the falling population of their state
to their enormous coffee consumption.
† A character in Molière's *Femmes Savantes* who stands for common sense and
straightforwardness.—Trans.
‡ In his *Mémoires*, Hénault, the president of the Parisian Parlement, unequivocally
states this concerning the *salon* of Madame de Lambert: "One had to pass through
her in order to get into the Académie Française." [4]

In the provincial *salons,* where the illustrious men are not so brilliant, the regular visitors trade in literary news, new books, and light verse. But everywhere there breathes this "spirit of liberty" which, to Diderot's eyes, is the spirit of the century: freedom of subject matter, on which there are no taboos and (as Hénault again says) freedom of *la belle galanterie.* These gallant entertainments—or at least the philosophy behind them—we see reflected (precisely?) in the plays of Marivaux, with their games of love and of singularly refined coquetry, those games so cruel and futile, those disguises and subtle feints also typical of Marivaux,* which were never able to please the great-hearted Jean-Jacques and his Thérèse, who is so simple, so meagerly gifted at these witty thrusts and wounding conceits.

The academies and reading rooms are more serious gathering places than the *salons,* and almost exclusively masculine; their success is perhaps even greater, and certainly more characteristic. Before 1715, many of these academies were founded in the provinces; but in the 1750s, each average-sized town, of perhaps twenty thousand inhabitants, has its own. Some, the one in Montpellier, for example, are actually branches of Colbert's Académie des Sciences, and furnish learned, Parisian society with reports and studies; other, less ambitious, aim simply at improving the use of French within their region and at developing the arts and sciences—the Amiens society states that it "works jointly with everything that can improve the language, develop taste, and cultivate the mind." However, the most widespread concern, and the one essential to academic work, is the study of the sciences and of their application; the sciences are not separated from each other, and are considered as "the means for making people happy." † Dissertations and discussions on questions of physiology, physics, and mineralogy occupy the meetings; agronomy is very popular, and certain meetings, like the Académie des Sciences, Arts, et Belles Lettres in Orléans, concern themselves with nothing else. Endowed with large sums of money by generous patrons, who make it a point of honor to finance competitions, literary tournaments, and studies (a new form of patronage), the academies, the pride of their towns, stimulate local writers and scholars; sometimes their range exceeds the regional framework, by virtue of an exchange of publications and of the quality of the work. Let us merely call to mind the role of the Dijon Academy in the career of Rousseau, who presents his treatises there in 1750 and 1754.

Public libraries and reading rooms are neighbors of these academies, and often are full of the same men, so eager for knowledge; sometimes

---

* Another, more corrosive echo, is Choderlos de Laclos' *Les Liaisons dangereuses.*
† The Marquis d'Argenson, with respect to the Entresol Club, uses this expression which presages Saint-Just: happiness is a new idea in Europe. It also marks the passing of science into the realm of the technical, the great step which the seventeenth century did not take.

they are established by private wealth (as by Bouhier, the president of the Dijon Parlement) and sometimes by public subscription thanks to the initiative of a *philosophe* like Henri Gagnon at Grenoble. They spring up everywhere. At the end of the century, Toulouse boasts of having "four beautiful and rich public libraries," where theological works inherited from the previous century and erudite Benedictine works stand beside one another on the shelves. Rich in research equipment as well, the libraries collect published scientific works, fat dictionaries, by Bayle or Trévoux, and they give a great deal of space to the newssheets which, quite naturally, have proliferated: the *Journal des Savants*, historical and political journals (Panckouke's being the most famous), short-lived news-sheets, especially literary ones, keeping the provinces up to date on new things in Paris. These libraries lend out their books; they have a reading room and, alongside the actual library most of the time, a room for conversation—where the garrulous exchange their impressions, discuss, and comment, exactly as in an academy, a café (also often a meeting place), or an English-type club, like the famous Entresol Club in Paris.

Finally, the intellectual life has other frameworks, born with the century: Masonic lodges varying in role and importance. Introduced from England after 1721, coming through Dunkirk, Amiens, and Paris, these lodges—with their emblems, their secrets, their initiation rites, and the egalitarian diversity of their membership—fit effortlessly into the scene at a time when the academies admit only nobles and upper bourgeois; they are societies for thought, and achieve great success. The freedom of their discussion and the diversity of the paths they cross, from Rosicrucian mysticism to the most arid rationalism, explain this favor; they are in no way anticlerical, as are those of the nineteenth century (bishops and *curés* come gladly, in great numbers), and rather resemble the academies in their general concerns, discussing the great, stylish questions and commenting also upon the newssheets, the *Observateur littéraire* or the *Journal de Trévoux*. Thus, without their being among those chiefly responsible for the Revolution,* they have their share in the spread of philosophical ideas.

Thus this highly intellectualized and worldly life becomes a varied one: with gay *salons* and pedants in the Masonic lodges, each provincial town lives according to the rhythm of these meetings, be they solemn or intimate, and each town is an active intellectual center, enlivened with competitions and games participated in by bourgeois, nobles, and clergy. From this time forward, the nobility is not the only group setting the pace for urban life; it shares the initiative, and the leadership of taste and public opinion, with the liberal and commercial

---

* Despite its excessive character, this idea, which flatters some short-sighted Freemasons, was launched by some who are obsessed with revolutionary conspiracy; it has had a long life.

bourgeoisie, while the clergy, dwindled down during the century of the Enlightenment, weakened in number if not in talent and reduced to the defensive (it is good form not to be devout), is led on by the upper and the lower in this life and in this great change of ideas accompanying it.*

The gayest expressions of this society, devoted to pleasures of the mind, are the *fêtes galantes*. Watteau, Lancret, and Boucher offer us the finest images of these dances and games of love; of these Watteau, for whom the title of "painter of *Fêtes Galantes*" was created, is the first. The young Louis XIV at Versailles in the 1660s, in the days of his wild passions, had dreamed of islands where affairs of state could never reach him: one of the first Versailles fetes, in 1664, was entitled *Plaisirs de l'île enchantée*. Watteau, in his *Embarquement pour Cythère* (1717), reveals to us what success the royal enterprise experienced at the beginning of the following century: the *Amour paisible*, the *Assemblée dans un parc*, and the *Menuet* are so many faithful images, in a delicately sunny setting, of that invitation to the dance, those pilgrimages marked by amorous piety. The pastorals and fetes painted by Watteau,† paintings admired throughout many generations (from Nerval to Renoir), and Boucher's pastoral paintings, in which the same deeply moved tenderness and the same grace are found—these are the best plastic evocations of those promenades in the park, those light dances, minuets and gavottes, accompanied by the thin harpsichord music of François Couperin "le Grand," or some *air à danser* by Rameau.

Jean-Philippe, Rameau, France's greatest musician of that century which, in the German-speaking countries, is that of Johann Sebastian Bach and Wolfgang Amadeus Mozart, gave an unprecedented brilliance to choral and concert music, which the seventeenth century had discovered and had begun to appreciate in the days of Lully.‡ Rameau, for many years an organist at Dijon and Clermont, spent twenty years

---

* The crisis of the French clergy shortly before the Revolution is well known; Latreille has painted a good picture of it.[5] The contemporaries were especially struck by the numerical weakening, which accounts for a great decrease of vocations, particularly monastic ones. For example, Messance quotes Rouen, the town with a hundred steeples: in 1759, the twenty-one male orders have 418 members, the eighteen female ones, 528.

† After Watteau, the century is still rich with varied talents: the licentious Fragonard, the emphatic and moralistic Greuze. And then there is Chardin, a painter attentive to the lower-middle class, who does not live in this rhythm, but preserves the traditional virtues in his moderate comfort. Nonetheless, he seeks the refinements of costume of which high society sets the example: the *Benedicite* and the *Mère laborieuse*.

‡ Lully's popularity was enormous in his day. Nonetheless, music was then considered a minor art, alongside literature: La Fontaine tells us so. Rameau, Diderot, and Rousseau contributed in no small way to giving a more honorable place to this "diversion of the senses." In 1706, the *Mercure* writes: "Madame, do not expect that I am about to apply myself to very exalted matters: it is only a question of music"—fifty years later, this notion is unthinkable.

as the conductor of the orchestra of La Pouplinière, that great financier who wanted his Passy receptions to equal those at court; next he becomes Louis XV's Compositeur de Cabinet. His musical tragedies, heroic pastorals, lyric comedies, ballets (not to omit mention of his large body of harpsichord works), and above all the six opera-ballets that do the most for his reputation, constitute an abundant body of work in which the recitative, chorus, and symphonic accompaniment already occupy the place which will be theirs in the nineteenth century. Using gay love plots, such as *Fêtes de l'Hymen et de l'Amour*, *Castor et Pollux*, and *Surprises de l'Amour*, Rameau writes well-ordered music in which the orchestration attains a mastery long admired by his successors, an orchestration equally subtle and ethereal.* Sung drama, in which emotion is even greater than in spoken, classic drama, takes the lead then and becomes different. Toward the end of the century, Grétry's comic opera, in its turn, conquers the public. Lyric drama, gradually freed from ancient forms, like ballets and court entertainments, brings the definition of its genre to a close, at the same time that it wins over a large audience. In the second half of the century, how many of Voltaire's friends, who cannot bear Jean-Jacques, at least grant him the unequaled merit of having composed the *Devin du Village*.†

The *rapprochement* of Watteau and Rameau is classic, and it expresses a precious moment in both Parisian and French life. But this achievement in the refined expression of delicate feeling surpasses the limits of France, from Dijon to Aix-en-Provence: as early as 1720, Berlin owns an *Embarquement pour Cythère*, and the *Amour paisible* is at Potsdam. Every court in Europe discusses the *trumeaux* by Boucher and the *Fêtes Vénitiennes* by Lancret. In the musical domain, where foreign countries have their masters, an undeniable affinity unites the Bach of the *Brandenburg Concertos* with the Mozart of the *Paris* Symphony [No. 31 in D, K. 297] and the *Marriage of Figaro*. Throughout all Europe, society life follows the lead from France and, quite often, despite what people may say, equals the French manner. At a time when Frenchmen have their attention turned toward foreign countries, unreservedly admiring England with her *habeas corpus*, not ceasing to praise it from 1734 on (Voltaire's *Lettres anglaises*), to the point of justifying the expression of "Anglomania"; when Frederick II and Catherine II are applauded as they announce the great reforms in their states; when even

---

* Somewhat overlooked in our day, so brilliant and triumphant are the nineteenth-century music in the lyric sphere and twentieth-century music in the symphonic, Rameau was recently rediscovered in the *Indes Galantes*; the orchestral richness of this occasionally dramatic opera was sometimes astonishing. It remains true that Rameau dominated music in his day (he died in 1764), exercising a strong influence on Mozart; and he was a theoretician, whose studies—*Traité de l'harmonie*, 1722, and *Démonstration du principe de l'harmonie*, 1750—have been very highly valued.
† An esteemed composer, Rousseau also advised Gluck.

China plays a successful role among the *encyclopédistes*—then, Europe erects no barriers against the publications and great men which come from France. In the days of Louis XIV, both large and small princes had begun to build well-copied miniatures of Versailles, where a court set up along French lines completed the imitation. In the following century, it is the books, paintings, costumes, and furniture of France that it is good form to import; French is spoken in all the courts, at Frederick II's as at Catherine's, because it alone has the desired subtlety. The young Goethe, after a visit to Strasbourg, wonders for a moment whether he will write in French or German. Hundreds of Frenchmen, who sometimes have no talent other than that of speaking French, are employed in Vienna, Prague, and Berlin as children's tutors, and even in the great noble families of Russia: from St. Petersburg to Lisbon, people crave French architects, music masters, and writers. So great is the prestige of Parisian life that the richer people come to establish themselves in that capital where everyone feels at home. Already, at the end of the century, Casanova says: "Only in Paris does one live, elsewhere one vegetates."

In the century of the Enlightenment, Europe is charmed by Parisian cosmopolitanism and by the universality of French thought; she becomes a French Europe. This statement is—provided the limits are well understood—an exact one; but from *salon* to academies, at Berlin or St. Petersburg, let us always understand that we mean the Europe of high society: bourgeois or noble, this exists everywhere just as it does in France, be it northern Italy, Beccaria's homeland, the banks of the Rhine at Mainz or Cologne, or the Austrian Netherlands, which are in large part French-speaking.* This is true more so in the east, if not in Berlin itself, where Frenchmen are numerous and where the French *collège* maintains cultural ties which are valuable for the descendants of the 1685 exiles: in Saxony, Austria, Russia—it is only the nobility who speak, read, and sing French; in central and eastern Europe, the bourgeoisie is very small and too poorly established economically and socially to participate in this craze which, besides, requires leisure, income, and contacts—even commercial ones. For the bourgeois of St. Petersburg or Vienna, the English or German intermediaries make a screen. All the more reason why, throughout Europe, Francomania does not affect the peasant classes—or the common people in the towns. They lack everything: leisure and income. Eighteenth-century French Europe, whose monumental inheritance is so impressive, is the construction of a small, aristocratic minority.

---

* England, where the nobility is not a caste, and where high society is both bourgeois and noble, more than elsewhere, did not participate in this enthusiasm for France—for many reasons.

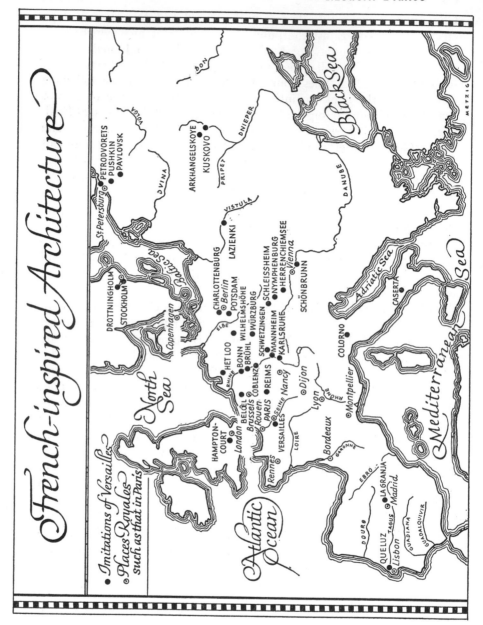

French-inspired Architecture

● Imitations of Versailles
⊙ Places Royales such as that in Paris

► **THE ENLIGHTENMENT: THE
SPIRIT OF THE PHILOSOPHES**

On the purely intellectual level, France by herself does not enlighten
the whole world: there exist the prestige of Leibniz, but especially the
renown of Newton, to remind us of this fact. The progress of the sciences yields in no way to the literary successes: one has merely to
understand the diffusion of Voltaire and Montesquieu, those political
thinkers, in the larger setting revealed to us by the *Encyclopédie* in
which each of the nine muses has her place. Also there is public opinion,
which the pronounced century-long advances in education render increasingly important: toward this opinion, even in his most intimate
correspondence, the greatest of the *philosophes* is constantly turned.

The collective work of the age, that monumental *Encyclopédie,*
planned, prepared, and realized by Diderot from 1748 to 1765, is unquestionably the greatest expression of the art and spirit of philosophy.
Diderot is the guiding spirit for ten or so years aided in the sciences by
D'Alembert. The former gathered around him "to demonstrate as much
as it is possible, the order and sequential connection of human knowledge," all those who with their particular talent and knowledge (Rousseau for music) feel "bound by the general interest of humanity and
by a feeling of reciprocal benevolence"—great expressions of the century's optimistic humanism. But the *Encyclopédie* is not a scientific synthesis: the *encyclopédistes* themselves confess, and not without some
regret, that the one system which will account for all knowledge is not
within their grasp; ever since the failure of Descartes' vortices, about
which Newton was right, the hope of attaining this system is not very
persistent. Diderot's friends simply are convinced that each science
must have its methods, its "general principles which are its basis"; that
between one science and another there exist aids and connections to be
carefully established: this care does not exclude the enthusiasm or
faith in mankind* which enabled the editor of the *Encyclopédie* to
bear up under both the rebuffs of the less pleasant collaborators—to
be begun by D'Alembert himself—and the publication troubles when,
as early as 1752, the condemnations rain down upon them and force
endless delays. This faith is also a faith in scientific progress, which to
them seems particularly admirable in the area of natural sciences, owing
to the work of Réaumur, Trembley, and, above all, Buffon—whose *Histoire naturelle* was published from 1749 on and whose *Théorie de la
Terre* was published in 1744.†

---

* Diderot: "Mankind is the unique term, from which we must depart and to which
everything must be returned."
† In the natural sciences the advances in observation are decisive: the earliest micro-

The *Encyclopédie,* which described the professions, arts, and sciences, is a discreet apology of human progress, detached—despite its blind spots—from all authority and dogma; just as Buffon, condemned for having contradicted Genesis in his *Théorie de la Terre,* yields, so Diderot does not hesitate to repeat purely orthodox articles about Christianity, Theology, Adam, and Hell throughout his dictionary. Despite many moments of daring, the *encyclopédistes* are more than once condemned to inconsistency: orthodox with respect to Providence and impertinent, even impious, in the article about Juno. But beyond its voluntary contradictions; beyond, too, the divergencies and uncertainties brought about by the unevenness of the collaborators and the wide dissimilarity of their convictions (D'Alembert is close to believing in universal mathematics, but is hardly seconded), the *Encyclopédie* presents the world with an attempt to co-cordinate all the acquired knowledge of the period. It is a balance sheet, or rather a *summa,* granted to be necessary in a time when it is admittedly impossible to unite all the sciences into one system of thought; it makes its point by offering a tableau of material civilization, of the state of the professions and techniques, of fashions and styles; it offers still another picture of its curiosities, and its tastes for history, for travel (an echo of the countless stories the Jesuits told in preaching to the noble savages) into space and time (ancient and modern science; philosophy).* But the encyclopedic spirit is one also of desire to open perspectives, to dominate discoveries, and to seek out the order men can put into the world: an opening onto a future† which they wish and believe to be better. That is the basis of the philosophic spirit animating Diderot's co-workers.

Diderot, a good worker in this great venture, likeable in his contentions with his lively-penned *philosophe* colleagues with their petty literary ambitions, touching in his reverence for his old dressing gown and his sympathy for the whimsical nephew of Rameau—Diderot, reasoning and arguing for thirty years, his pen always alert and festive,‡ is the

---

scopes do not appear before the end of the seventeenth century, with a single lens trained on the source of light. These are simple instruments which permit many discoveries; the ordinary microscope of today, however, was not effected before 1880.[6]
* Spinoza and Leibniz articles.
† Sometimes with unexpected ramifications: in his own field, each *encyclopédiste* sees beyond the present—as H. de Guibert in his *Essai général de tactique* (1772) presages the soldier-citizen of the Revolution.
‡ His verve, sometimes naughty (for so he was disposed) is nevertheless quick to conjure up the great problems in a few words. *Le Neveu de Rameau* is crammed with his well-matured views, as is *Jacques le Fataliste.* If one wants a description of the crisis beginning in the years 1770-1774, Jacques has written: "The year is a bad one; we can scarcely supply our needs and those of our children. Grain is expensive! No wine. And if only there were work; but the rich are entrenching themselves and the poor do nothing—for every one day that there is work, you lose four. No one pays what he owes; creditors are so harsh they drive you to despair. . . ." Turning the page, ideas on population: ". . . People never have so many children as in times of poverty.—Nobody reproduces as much as beggars do.—One child more is nothing to them, they will be fed by charity. . . ." (And I pass over the rest.)

good type of these *philosophes* who swarm around him to encourage and help, and also to exploit him: men like Holbach, Helvétius, Raynal, and so many others of lesser talent.

The *Encyclopédie* does not adduce a philosophic doctrine; concerning the great questions of the day, those like religion and government, which raise their heads daily, the *philosophes* do not have a common position either. The approach of these impassioned temperaments is undoubtedly the same: motivated by a similar spirit of free criticism, they have the despotic absolutism of the French Monarchy and the Catholic Church as a common target. But points in common stop there. Doubtless it is not a negligible thing to have the same enemies and to stand face to face with the same Bastille and the same Jesuits; but the century's weighty legacy would not be understandable without the divergencies which assert themselves, particularly after 1750. These are the days when Voltaire's sarcastic pen annotates Rousseau's writings, seeing in them more of the foolish than the lofty. Thus the divine right of the monarchy and the most esteemed practices of the Catholic Church are constantly and tirelessly discredited, attacked, and disputed. The Archbishop of Paris condemns and royal edicts forbid; books are no less successful for that, and make money for bookstores and for their authors, hidden or not behind borrowed names. But dissension in the camp of the *philosophes* is great: an abyss separates Voltaire from Rousseau and tomorrow, Brissot from Robespierre.

Voltaire put his stamp upon philosophic impiety: his fiery polemics and his virulence which go so far as to be a sweet mania (at one point signing himself *Ecrlinf*, that is, *Écrasons l'infâme*) fill the air of the times. Looking at matters more closely, however, it does seem that well before the *Lettres anglaises* and the *Essai sur les mœurs*, a part of the bourgeoisie and the aristocracy was gradually making its way toward impiety, or at least toward deism. Very quickly it became good form no longer to mention religion except to smile at it, to limit oneself to obligatory practices and even to exhibit a strong mind, free from "all those fables." Moreover, there is nothing surprising in what Necker states in his *Importance des opinions religieuses*, of 1788: "For some time now, you hear nothing mentioned but the necessity of composing a moral catechism in which no use of religious principles and outmoded incentives would be made, and that it is time to make a separation." The breadth of the theological and moral debates, sustained for almost a century within the Church, helped encourage indifference; there were the violent polemics of the *Journal de Trévoux* and the *Nouvelles ecclésiastiques*, the decisions of the *parlements*, ordering the burning of the Ultramontane bishops' orders; there were the English influences, and in particular the works of Locke preaching tolerance among all the Christian sects. All this, the long public disputes, encouraged doubts and introduced certain forms of unbelief. The hostility to Rome and the Jesuits, which flourishes in Paris during the century, carries in its wake a rash distrust of all theology. Voltaire certainly added a great deal to this through his talent for emphasizing in two striking words what others explain in fifteen pages (thus the famous sally: "God made man in his own image"), and then through his tireless hostility to all aspects of government, administration, or justice which reveal the influence, avowed or not, of the Church: persecutions of Protestants, abuses of power committed by bishops like Mirepoix. The problems are not those that will be posed under the July Monarchy or at the beginning of the Third Republic; but the "Voltairian" spirit takes shape around 1750 and gradually destroys all respect for the men and the things of the Church. How else can we explain Louis XVI's gesture of having a Cardinal arrested like a common criminal, in the open street?

Voltaire, that champion of tolerance,* and the upper bourgeois and nobles who read him fondly, are not exactly atheists. Voltaire grants more readily the existence of a God than of His priests and His Church—a God who would create the world without intervening in it any more, once the levers were flicked. He especially thinks that this God and this religion, which he can do without, are indispensable to the common people, who are no more capable of guiding themselves morally than politically. From the social point of view, religion is a good thing, and Voltaire never wearies of repeating this, for some might mistake it: "We are dealing with a number of rascals, a whole slew of little, brutal, drunken, thieving people: preach to them if you want that there is no Hell and that the soul is mortal. As for me, I shall scream in their ears that they will be damned if they rob me." [7] These are the words of a policeman, or of a large landowner jealous of his wealth: the honest piety of the poor, on which the literature of the *philosophes* did

---

* This does not mean that Voltaire and his *philosophe* friends were free from all prejudices: up to the Revolution, while the Protestants end up in 1787 by obtaining the granting of a civil state, and while actors, another category condemned by the Church, are coddled, feted, and overwhelmed with honors, Jews remain on the fringes of this society. In eastern France, at Metz, for example, they have their own separate district, away from the rest of the town, as in central Europe. Without exception they are everywhere foreigners whose curse is not forgotten; witness this statement concerning Jews who came from the Bordeaux region at the end of the seventeenth century: "And as several of them have become very rich, this unfortunate nation knew how to arrange such strong protections that it is more dangerous, in the regions they inhabit, to have anything to do with a Jew than with a Christian: the few resources people found among them at the close of the last reign, ended up by persuading them they were absolutely necessary to the state, by making them believe that they were naturalized, and by making them want to forget that accursed people, who must be and will always be wanderers and vagabonds, cannot settle down. . . ." And Voltaire himself declares in his *Dictionnaire philosophique:* "An ignorant and barbaric people, who have for a long time combined the vilest avarice with the most detestable superstitions and the most invincible hatred for all people who tolerate and enrich them. Nevertheless, we ought not to burn them."

not touch, is thus a blind spot for the owner of the château at Ferney, who attacks priests and dogma, sparing neither the Holy Books nor the Church Fathers—and scarcely sparing his Jesuit masters.

A wave of *raison raisonnante,* until the day when the citizen from Geneva lifts his passionate voice and states his position on religious feeling: "Conscience. Conscience. Divine instinct . . . ," cries this *vicaire* from Savoy, who is very quickly condemned by both Rome and Geneva, and who rediscovers, between good and evil, mankind and his freedom. But this Jean-Jacques, who is no less prideful toward the great (as in the very famous letter to the Comte de Lastic), does not nourish in his heart this disdain for the common people, for the masses, that dwells in Voltaire and a few others. In the years between 1750 and 1780 Rousseau, whose sentiment attains the level of a passionate logic, gives sentiment its place; he is applauded by an entire generation, that of Madame Roland,* not to speak of Romantic posterity.

On the political level, the separation is no less great. Before 1750, the *philosophes* are cautious reformers whose daring is calculated and limited: their daring is that of royal advisors, justifying enlightened despotism. After 1750, after the *Discours sur l'Origine et les Fondements de l'Inégalité parmi les Hommes,* and particularly the *Contrat social,* it is no longer a question of improving the monarchy, of passing from absolutism to limited monarchy: it is Revolution at its most complete, the Revolution which those living between 1789 and 1794 were to be unable to achieve.

Voltaire in his *Lettres anglaises* (1734), and Montesquieu in his *Esprit des Lois* (1748) are neither republicans nor democrats. Voltaire saw England, in haste, without asking himself too many troublesome questions; in particular, he read Locke, the theorist of the 1688 Revolution which praises the monarchy whose king shares power with the nation. Trusting in his foreign institutions, as much as he distrusts everything French, Voltaire is easily persuaded that the reality and the principle of that equilibrium of which Locke spoke so highly are one—rotten boroughs, corrupt elections, and the confusion of powers in local administration are of small concern to him. He never tires of praising that monarchy in which the House of Commons makes the laws implemented by the king, and in which neither a Bastille nor a Châtelet exists. Montesquieu is more systematic: he has sought and found his examples in antiquity as well as in modern times; he has read and re-read his compatriot Montaigne,† for whom he feels some affinity. He does not scorn general considerations—of which the twentieth century is very fond,

---

* She cries warm tears while reading the man she calls "the divine Rousseau." Though he is less impassioned, Kant owes him just as much.
† "Compatriot" in the sense of coming from the same region of France, near Bordeaux.—Trans.

calling it the philosophy of history—and, putting himself in the shoes of Plato, Bodin, and several others, he shows how tyranny, monarchy, and republic, regimes so different in their principles, generate one another through the processes of internal decay. Finally, he fully appreciates Locke and the *Essay on Civil Government,* and extracts its theory of the separation of the executive, legislative, and judicial powers—by which that huge book, the *Esprit des Lois,* less read than admired from a distance, constantly guides political thought even today.

England, therefore, is the model: the best-governed kingdom in Europe; for there the citizen is protected by law against everything arbitrary,* the king respects the law he has not himself formulated and he leaves the legislative branch in the hands of representatives of the nation. In addition to the separation of powers, which has the magnificent quality of preventing the monarchy from degenerating into a republic, Montesquieu approves of the division of the legislature into two branches: the Commons, the lower House, and the Lords, the nobility— the function of the latter being to serve the king, no longer by arms and military service as in the Middle Ages, but by controlling the acts of the lower House representing the totality of the nation. To Montesquieu's eyes, the noble lords and the Anglican bishops who sit in the upper House are the staunch mainstay of the monarchy—privileged and royalty are closely linked.†

These critics of absolute monarchy and of the order it supports had far-reaching effects—doubtless farther-reaching than the *philosophes* thought. The nobility, which, particularly for its life at Versailles, had long been discredited, has not regained its prestige by being compared with the nobility on the other side of the Channel. On the eve of the Revolution, Beaumarchais flings the most powerful darts (enumerating the qualities demanded of a manservant); likewise the monarchy is attacked in a thousand and one ways and is boldly reformed. Nevertheless, these liberals, Voltaire as Montesquieu, would accept a monarchy that would follow their advice; Voltaire exclaiming one fine day, "Ah, Louis XIV, had you but been a philosopher!" really meant, really

---

* The *habeas corpus* was all the more appreciated by the *philosophes* since the deviations in their language often placed them under the threat of *lettres de cachet*: both Voltaire and Diderot experienced these. Montesquieu writes: "At present, England is the freest country in the world, and I make the exception of no Republic. I call it free because the ruler does not have the power to do any imaginable wrong to anyone, for the reason that his power is controlled and limited by law."

† In this way Montesquieu gives the nobility a role which the kings of France have contested for centuries, and then taken away: in 1789, Louis XVI will also deem the monarchy and the privileged inseparable. On the other hand, Montesquieu has no tenderness for the court nobility, and boldly writes: "Ambition in idleness, baseness in pride, the desire to become rich without working, aversion for the truth, flattery, treason, treachery, breaking of all his promises, scorn for his obligations as a citizen, fear of a prince's quality, desire for his weakness, and, more than all that, perpetual ridicule thrown upon virtue: these, I believe, form the character of the greatest number of courtiers." [8]

thought, "Ah Louis XV, could you but listen to your *philosophes!*" Monarchy is like religion, there is some good in it. It must be retained, provided it lets itself be advised, provided it repudiates its arbitrary practices. Voltaire would be even less demanding than Montesquieu, attached to his theory and to its qualities of balance: he offered his services to two kings who refused them, Frederick II and Louis XV. With the latter, at least, he had one satisfaction: Madame de Pompadour listened to him.

Rousseau writes with a different-colored ink: he is neither the king's chamberlain nor even the president of a Chambre in a *parlement;* this musician who promises himself not to write, so much does the literary tribe displease him, becomes excited by academic competitions. In 1750 he carries off first prize in Dijon for having maintained that civilization and artistic progress corrupt mankind, which is good in a state of nature; he looks at a refined society with a distorting mirror. Missionaries and travelers speak convincingly about the noble savage; Jean-Jacques believes them, and his prose gives countenance to this idea which, between 1775 and 1780, did much for the popularity of the good-natured Franklin and the prestige of the American War of Independence. In 1754, Rousseau repeats his performance and competes on the basis of inequality among men: he does not obtain a prize. The good academicians in Dijon were frightened by his theories, which could not pass, as they had in 1750, for an amiable paradox. But the idea no longer leaves him; in 1762, he publishes the *Contrat social,* or *Principes du droit politique,* which bases the state upon a new law: a rapid work, clear in its overall lesson about sovereignty and equality—a moment of capital importance in French political thought.

All human society rests on a contract between the participants; it matters little whether the contract be tacit or well accepted during a given age. Consequently, all sovereignty lies in the people who accept this contract, who prepare and draft the terms and conditions of its implementation. Rousseau read Montesquieu, but wants to go further, for, basing authority on this agreement among all citizens, he also bases civil equality upon it. And the *Contrat social,* a study of the principles upon which the state rests, upsets that order of all things that eighteenth-century French society had secured: there can be no question of divine right or of an authority coming from above, for the king is king only through the sovereign will of the people, that is, through the totality of the contracting parties, the nation. The latter can, to be sure, give itself a king, but it also establishes the rules according to which he reigns; in particular, it can give itself another political regime:

> The people is a people, therefore, before it gives itself over to a king. This very act is a civil act, presupposing public debate. Consequently, before examining the act by which a people elects a king,

it would be good to examine the act by which a people is a people; because this act, being necessarily anterior to the other, is the true basis of society.[9]

Voltaire and Montesquieu give the monarchy different functions, to make it acceptable to *philosophes* and to enlightened public opinion. They lend support to a threatened institution, and plan reforms which would enable a consolidation without, in principle, changing anything: the English monarchy, too, certainly has its Church, and even its miracle-working kings. With Rousseau, everything is different: the throne is already overturned, and the fundaments of society are not there but in that equality of small landowners who are free men—who, because they are landowners, are attached to their native land, and who participate in the state's administration.* By that very point, Rousseau shows himself to be more attached to equality than to citizens' freedom: he has a feeling for social solidarity, so constituted by the consent of every participant; consequently, he goes much further than Montesquieu, since he condemns privileges and the privileged orders. In Montesquieu's eyes, the courtier is a man encumbered with numerous vices, attributable in part to his duties. Rousseau is briefer in his condemnation: "Rich or poor, powerful or weak, every idle citizen is a knave."

The *Contrat social* is thus the charter of the democratic principle. This citizen of Geneva, living in a small republic which he loves and occasionally defends against its detractors (*Lettre à d'Alembert sur les spectacles*, in connection with the article about Geneva in the *Encyclopédie*), gives a definition of popular sovereignty—which, thirty years later, triumphs in the Tuileries, on that terrible day, August 10, when two rights and two political principles confront one another in an exchange of grapeshot and blood: divine right against the right of people to self-determination, proclaimed by the Convention at the end of 1792. Voltaire and the others delivered the vanguard attacks; Rousseau drove out the heavy artillery. The Old Regime, both inside and outside France, never gets over it. Deep within himself, Rousseau is an enthusiast of justice, with an intransigence not practiced by Voltaire. One day he writes to a gainsaying academician from Dijon—a man who enjoys life, and, now and again, a philosopher:

Luxury feeds one hundred poor people in our towns and causes one hundred thousand to perish in our rural areas. The money pouring

---

* Rousseau is attached to the idea inherited from antiquity according to which only the owners of a plot of land are real citizens—his political equality lays the foundation for social equality. People have given an improper fate to the famous curse in his *Discours sur l'Inégalité*: "The first one who, having fenced in a garden took it into his head to say, 'this is mine,' and found people simple enough to believe him. . . ."

from the hands of the rich to those of the artists, in order to supply
their unnecessary things, is lost to the subsistence of the husbandman; and the latter has no coat precisely because others must have
braid; our kitchens need gravy, that's why so many sick people lack
bouillon; our tables need vegetables, that's why the countryside
drinks only water; our wigs need powder: that's why so many
poor people have no bread.

Rousseau is one of those sympathetic and impulsively generous Al-
cestes* who, noting with horror that civilization cannot flourish without social wastefulness, prefers, in a beautiful impulse, to abolish civilization rather than to perpetuate injustice.

What has been the diffusion of these great themes of French political thought, both critical and constructive, these themes discussed and
reproduced by a world of small literary men, *philosophes*, and disciples
of the greatest? Postal advances and communications progress in general
have facilitated transmission of books, little lampooning satires, and letters read in *salons*. But the essential lies in the progress of reading, that
is, in elementary schools and *collèges*: the public of the *philosophes*
is going to grow with the century. It does not extend yet to the rural
areas which, except for those just outside cities, still have no contact
with the new ideas.

Nevertheless, educational changes are important, especially on the
level of secondary education.† The universities remain very similar to
one another, very hostile to all changes in their methods and teaching,
which are looked down upon by the *philosophes* and by decent people,
at a time when scientific progress is accomplished outside of them, and
when a farmer-general is the greatest chemist of his period. But the *collèges* are the period's greatest triumph: they spring up everywhere, even
in the smallest towns of some thousand inhabitants, gathering together
twenty or a hundred and fifty pupils, augmented by allowances for private lessons and for the lodging of boarder-students (as they had several
centuries earlier, the *collèges* played this role near the universities).
These establishments, desired by the bourgeoisie for the instruction
of their children beyond the elementary level, still teach Latin, but they
give some place within the humanities, which are their base, for French

---

* Alceste is the main character in Molière's *Le Misanthrope* whose name is synonymous with that of a blunt, plain-spoken critic of society.—Trans.
† Brunot, studying the progress of the French language, once gathered together a
dossier concerning this problem (see his Volume VII). But an examination remains
to be made, one with immense possibilities: P. de Dainville has recently proved the
richness of such research for the area northeast of the Parisian basin (*see "Effectifs
des collèges et scolarité aux XVII⁰ et XVIII⁰ siècles dans le N.-E. de la France,"*
Population, X (1955), No. 3, pp. 455-488).

and, more particularly, for spelling, which is valued but not always respected, even by the *philosophes*. Outside the humanities, natural sciences, history, and geography are increasingly respected among the Oratorians who, after 1762, take over a good many of the Jesuit *collèges*. The great noble families and the financiers of high degree continue to entrust their children to tutors and, after *Émile*, these young people are brought up like so many little disciples of the *philosophes*. But as a whole, the bourgeoisie—the men of law, the merchants, the *rentiers*— supply the largest percentage of this large academic population; some children of artisans, some of the lesser nobility, and, very rarely, some peasants' sons complete these forces; they constitute the future clientele of the *philosophes*, of the academies, and Masonic lodges. This intellectual promotion is brought about by the teaching orders: the Jesuits, until their expulsion, Oratorians, Dominicans, and Benedictines.

For the lower classes, so far as concerns reading, writing, and arithmetic, the advances are less marked; the Physiocrats vainly proclaim that education is necessary to the peasantry for the improvement of their techniques and learning of new farming methods. Quite frequently the *philosophes* are not in agreement. Voltaire rails when he finds no labor for Ferney and regrets that the peasants send their children to school, which, he feels, is unnecessary for them. It is common to think, with some pity, that the humbler classes can do without all instruction, and can live among their antiquated notions.* Nevertheless, the lower clergy, the peasants, in mountainous regions like the Jura, and the artisans and journeymen in the towns, beg for elementary schools: reading and writing are already indispensable to the domestic personnel, who are so numerous, who daily rub elbows with their witty masters and who, legitimately or not, use their libraries, and participate in their intrigues. In the mechanical professions, the need is also great. Most of the time, private initiative underwrites these foundations: a rich landowner or an academician who is well inspired and well esteemed in his district, donates some money to recruit a schoolmaster for the winter; often coming from Dauphiny, Savoy, or even Italy, participating in the educational labor market with those three feathers—reading, writing, and arithmetic—in his cap, the schoolmaster is a new social type. Often a rather rough diamond, he teaches how to read printed books, how to write one's name, and how to add up simple lists; this is undoubtedly meager fare in a time when manuscripts differ greatly from printed books and when computation assumes the precise knowledge of re-

---

* A curious piece of medical advice in 1721, from the king's physician: "The preparation of toad powder [against the plague], such as it is described in this statement, is nothing special, and the high repute of this remedy does not seem to me to be based on precise observations. However, since the Public values it so highly, I agree that this statement be printed." [10]

gional weights, measures, and money.* Once the schooling is finished, the stock of knowledge seems slim: barely enough to read the almanac, whose material consists of traditional data, harvest dates, prices, and hearsay.

If Voltaire and Rousseau have a reader in the village, it is the *curé*; and in some localities, perhaps there is some notary or court clerk, living in seclusion in a hamlet. This is a very sparse public, except in the nearby suburbs of the large towns: Hurepoix and Ile-de-France, in the south and north of Paris, in frequently traveled areas, the vineyards of the Côte-d'Or hills from the Jura to the Alps; the broader traffic and the travels of rural people themselves create bonds and furnish opportunities for talk and inquiry. The peasant who, once a month, delivers fowl and cheeses to a great house, chats at church with a whole world of servants—a world that has a veneer of Diderot or Rousseau. This is another aspect of the spread of the Enlightenment, one that Madame du Deffand or Madame Roland, reading the *Essai sur les mœurs*, understood very well. But this personnel surrounding them, these menservants who occasionally read to while away idle hours, and who chat on doorsteps with neighboring coachmen or cooks—what image do they develop of *Candide* or the *Contrat social?* These humble townspeople play an important political role between 1789 and 1794—in the Jacobin clubs, for example. In Paris, from 14 July to 9 Thermidor, the role of these lower classes is preponderant; and even an approximate knowledge of the mentality of these intellectual frameworks that incite the revolutionary crowds would be of prime interest.

What is certain, at least, is that the immense majority of the rural population was not affected by the progress of the Enlightenment: the old, more or less superstitious beliefs, faith, and particularly the Catholic practices remain intact.† Sunday attendance at mass and Paschal

---

* School regulations are established in many places, such as the Jura, Burgundy, the east and north, which are more advanced in this sphere than is the Midi. For example, in Yonne: "There will be paid monthly to the Teachers 6 *sous* for beginners, 10 *sous* for those who can write, and 15 *sous* for those learning plainsong and arithmetic; they will not strike the pupils with their hands or feet, nor with sticks or rods, but only with switches, and in a spirit of charity, under penalty of the teacher's suspension for this fact alone; those not having the means to pay monthly, will be provided for by Charity in compliance with the foundation." 11

† One illustration among many of this stability of popular beliefs in rural areas is this encounter between learned men and the rural population in the Tarn in 1774: "Criminal procedure begun by the judge of the Viscounty of Lautrec against the authors of the murder committed in the parish of Saint Martin de Cornac upon the person of Pierre de Lalande, surveyor to the King, employed in Languedoc. This surveyor entrusted with drawing up a map of the province [one of the Cassini maps], climbed the towers of churches and châteaux for his work in triangulating a region. The peasants were convinced he was working magic which was occasioning the ruination of their fields, and, when they saw him on the roof of Saint Martin's church, they gathered into a mob shouting: '*Aro y son, courran ye anem esparaqua es tua aquellis mauditos personnas qui benoun porta la mort aysi.*' ('There they are just now,

communion are still solidly entrenched in rural customs; confidence in royal authority, in the benevolence of the king similarly are maintained, and are attested to by the grievance lists drafted for the Estates-General. If the peasants have a place in the Revolution, if they prepare themselves for burning châteaux, after having begged in the grievance lists for the abolition of tithes, dovecotes, and *corvées*, it is by virtue of the social antagonisms exacerbated by the crisis of the years between 1775 and 1789—not the fruit of the *philosophes'* propaganda, which scarcely extends beyond the urban setting. But this setting, it is true, plays the greatest role in the growth of the Revolution.

---

let's go kill and quarter those accursed men who come bringing death here.') They assailed him on the church roof, forcing him to come down; when he was on the ground, they knocked him senseless with stones and pickaxes, threw him in a ditch, and covered him with several cartloads of pebbles." [12] (The Cassini were a family concerned over the course of two centuries with mapping and surveying all of France. —Trans.)

CONTEMPORARY FRANCE

Nineteenth and

Twentieth Centuries

XIII

The Bourgeoisie Triumphant

1789-1845

THE eighteenth century of scientists and *philosophes*, of Lavoisier and
Condillac, had only one word on its lips: Liberty. (A word of which the
age of Louis XIV was already fond, not, at times, unparadoxically.) To
hear and believe all the enemies of despotism, to see members of the
Constituent Assembly and of the National Convention in their meetings, to see the Jacobins, ceaselessly invoking the Freedoms: the Revolution of 1789 had to wait a long time—with the help of Lamartine's
talent—for the coming of Freedom. Does not the Declaration of the
Rights of Man on August 26, 1789, consecrate to Liberty the majority of
its seventeen articles? But after Michelet, Jaurès, Mathiez, and Georges
Lefebvre, no one today can doubt the fact that the Great Revolution
was, even more, a social revolution—that of the advent of the bourgeoisie; and despite the convulsive changes during the Old Regime, despite the attempt at restoration after the defeats of 1814-1815, this
bourgeoisie has kept the primary place it made for itself as early as 1789,
and has not lost it in France even today. As early as 1792, bourgeois
France addresses a liberating message to the world: from Paris, the new

regime propounds its virtues and good offices to all Europe, and Europe hears this call, spread by the soldiers of the Year II and soon by the armies of Napoleon Bonaparte, more or less clearly. The whole nineteenth century is illuminated by this unprecedented social upheaval, when Europe, momentarily "French" around 1810—but in a fashion far different from the artistic and worldly diffusion of the Enlightenment—ultimately frees itself from those helmeted missionaries of a new world. Everything, however, does not return to order in 1815—this is attested to by the nineteenth-century revolutions, and, in particular, the great holocaust of 1848—and in France herself, the bourgeoisie resists the assault of those who learned nothing in twenty years of exile; it faces them and finally, in 1830, prevails for more than a century. "Bourgeois France" has succeeded "Old France."

Within the perspective of this history, the story of those twenty years, so portentous with important events, so glutted with struggles having multiple social repercussions, cannot be traced in detail; but the rhythm of revolutionary life, and especially the arc of its success and pauses, must be conjured up to illuminate the balance of the whole, and the bourgeoisie's progress in the following century. From 1789 to 1794, the Revolution is a continuous forward movement: the earliest solutions are rapidly outstripped and compromise is again called into question. The year 1789 was undoubtedly decisive, but with the Old Regime vanquished and the new one built by the Constituent Assembly, it remains true that from the flight to Varennes until January, 1793, through royal will and the pressure of foreign war, the constitutional monarchy constructed by the moderates in 1789 is first challenged, and then beaten; beyond the spring of 1793, in the short space of a year (July, 1793, to July, 1794) the Mountain Convention, fortified with the popular support necessary for the salvation of a threatened nation and republic, drafts what is actually a short-lived social democracy. Thermidor is the major pause. From that time until 1815, the bourgeois champions of the new regime, renouncing popular support without rallying themselves around the former state of affairs, attempt to stabilize the Revolution and give it a form as acceptable as was the 1791 compromise. Napoleon became involved, imposed his own solution, and went after the conquest of Europe—that liberation dreamed of by the soldiers of the Year II and the legislators of 1792. A personal regime, but one as remote from Tradition as from the Revolution in France, the Napoleonic empire has other repercussions throughout Europe, where it means political and social upheavals, and sometimes economic difficulties: always a "Frenchification" replacing European traditions no less ancestral than the French Old Regime; hence, from 1813 to 1815, that great revolt of "nations."

Whatever the importance of these compromises—the Republic of the Directory, Consulate, Empire—and whatever the legacy of certain effects of the period 1794-1815 (the Legion of Honor and the Imperial University, for example), it is the beginnings of the Revolution which, in France, weighed most heavily upon contemporary destiny. The year 1789, when the social and political frameworks of the French monarchy collapse, holds a place of honor there. A good part of the future of France is determined between May 5 and October 20,* when royal hesitations, the scruples of the six hundred "lawyers" who composed the representation of the Third Estate, and the enthusiasm of the Parisian lower classes took their place before the footlights—actors in the foreground of that year and years to come. Bold in laying down the law and in formulating new texts, the deputies of the Third Estate, who dared resist the king, and who, after June 20 and the famous Tennis Court Oath, obtained a roll-call vote and the recognition of the Constituent Assembly, are seized by paralysis when the king assembles his troops around Versailles and dismisses Necker in July. Legally—at least as long as a new legality is not instituted—Louis XVI is the head of the army and is in no way bound to choose his ministers from the bourgeois majority in control of the Constituent Assembly. These men of law and their jurists' revolution were saved on July 14 by the insurrection in the Faubourg Saint-Antoine and by the rabble that besieged and captured the most infamous of State prisons. Faced with a king who wants to sacrifice neither his privileges nor his power, who, as successor to Louis XI, Louis XIII, and Louis XIV, finds himself protecting his nobility (and defending his authority of divine right)—and faced with the royal "plot," the little people from the shops, the unemployed journeymen, and the impermanent French Guards, gathered and procured weapons (which they will keep until 1795), ready to shoot against the Swiss mercenaries of Monsieur de Launay, and to fight for the Constituent Assembly.

The second fortnight of July and the early days of August are no less important: this is the period of the Great Fear, that uprising of an entire peasant population who, alerted for months by the flurry of the lords' reaction, the drafting of the grievance lists, and by lack of food, rise up on hearing reports from Paris and the frightening rumors traveling across France. This revolt turns against the châteaux and the custodians of those charters in which the lords' rights are deposited and preserved; doubtless originating in panic,† the Great Fear is a vast social uprising.

---

* In 1789 (English translation by R. R. Palmer, *The Coming of the French Revolution*, Princeton, 1947), a short, admirable book which appeared shortly before the Second World War, Georges Lefebvre has nicely extracted the essential characteristics of this year which has no equal in the history of France, perhaps of the world. It is a book which, owing to circumstances, has not had all the success it deserves, and which ought to be in everyone's hands.

† In an article already cited, Baehrel shows how frequent panics were in the days gone by, in times of famine; nonetheless, the fact remains that the Great Fear is of another ilk than these, as are the sporadic revolts of the *croquants* and *nu-pieds*. (See below in Notes, VI, 17.)

The spontaneous revolt of peasant France against the manorial regime and this rural participation in the Revolution certainly seems to be unprecedented in world history. The Great Fear is the joyous fire into which the peasants throw their "feudal" burden. In the decrees from August fifth to eleventh, the Constituent Assembly will vainly declare all, or almost all, of these rights redeemable and not abolished; but the peasants will want to hear no further mention of them: they refuse to redeem them, or to pay them annually, pleading in court, for years offering resistance, either by passive inertia or with arms. The Convention's decree of July 17, 1793, which finally abolishes all the feudal rights maintained as title to property by the Constituent Assembly, serves only in effect to sanction this peasant revolution—the only one participated in by the entire French countryside.

Finally, once the Declaration of the Rights of Man is voted (August 26, 1789) but not ratified by the king—the same as the decrees proclaiming the abolition of the principle of the manorial regime, even as its maintenance is partially legalized—October fifth and sixth seem to renew the pattern of July 14. The king refuses to "pluck" his clergy and nobility, and the ideas of an aristocratic plot solidify more and more while, as early as July, the first emigration toward the German Empire is carried out. In the closing days of September, there are new troop movements around Versailles, and the impotent Assembly is once more saved by the Parisians who bring back the king and deputies to Paris. But on the morning of October 5, the Parisian women play a major role: after a moderate harvest, the Parisian food supply is in a sorry state, and the march on Versailles is something of a hunger march (on the return trip, the procession brings back ". . . the baker, the baker's wife, and the baker's errand-boy."* But the Assembly particularly, invaded on the night of October 5 by a crowd of Parisians mingled with undisciplined National Guards, had little appreciation either of the service rendered or of this crowd, bent upon causing dread. These men had already been frightened by the assault made upon the Bastille and then upon the châteaux throughout France; now they see many deputies of the three estates rallying about them, all disquieted by this "populace." On October 20, the Constituent Assembly intends to take precautions against all subsequent popular commotion and proclaims martial law: this is the first step in a separation which is later to be expressed both in the system of electors who are qualified by virtue of their property (*régime censitaire*) † and in the repressions under the Directory.

---

* The allusion here is to the marching song the victorious throng sang as they returned to Paris with their demands met, as well as their insistence that Louis XVI and his entourage settle inside Paris and not elsewhere outside the city—Versailles, Rambouillet.—Trans.

† At this point the word *cens* no longer refers to quitrents (see note p. 162), but rather to a tax payment establishing the property qualification for enfranchisement.

. . .

After 1789, Frenchmen lived the Revolution at a very irregular pace. The Parisians are linked to political life in a daily manner by clubs and sections; they are sensitive to the slightest nuance of the political contingency, and are enthusiastic and active, even in the discouraging and tedious years between 1794 and 1799. "Stocking-knitters," propagandists, the orators of expectant and anguished evenings—these are the great actors, in the best times, of the liberal revolutions, those acts of faith throughout the land on July 14, 1790 and July 11, 1792; and in the worst—the feverish period of September, 1792. The towns outside Paris are kept well informed by the Parisian press which, at least until 1792, is numerous and varied, and by the clubs, which pass on reports, studies, and watchwords from Paris, especially the Jacobin Club and its hundred and fifty provincial affiliates. The towns have followed the Parisian events more calmly, with a different awareness of the political choices, as the crisis in the spring of 1793 shows. But already in the provincial towns, revolutionary personnel is becoming scarce and the gradual substitution of middle bourgeoisie for upper bourgeoisie in political leadership, which is the great fact in Paris between 1792 and 1793, cannot be brought about, because the supporters of the Old Regime are still there. These groups need not lie low as they do in Paris because the lower classes are less numerous and less informed than in the capital; they do not exercise that strong pressure which Paris has so long witnessed. Thus the provincial towns follow, sometimes against their will; but yet they too live the Revolution, with the temporal lag and calm that result from their non-participation in these great events. Ultimately the rural population, affected so far as the roads permit, where a "rural bourgeoisie" of notaries and large-scale husbandmen become interested, followed the progress of the Revolution—much further behind. With the burning of the land registers and the establishment of local chapters of the Constituent Assembly (municipalities in the main), the attention of the countryside, which had been captured by the final struggles enacted higher up against the defenders and beneficiaries of the decrees of August 5-11, 1789, did not, after the peaceful year of 1790, follow the progress of political life. The exception is the religious question, long less dramatic than is generally thought, if it is true that each local investigation reveals a high proportion (fifty to sixty per cent) of *curé* "swearers," and a constitutional episcopacy firmly established as early as 1791; only the western *départements*, Brittany and the Vendée, the Nord, Basse-Alsace and several cantons in the southeast, experienced uprisings which, moreover, were not serious, until the conscription of 300,000 men in the spring of 1793. Actually,

---

If one was campaigning to become a direct elector, the *cens* was rather high; he would be called an *électeur censitaire*, someone qualified to vote in an assembly because he has sufficient property and could afford the tax thereon.—Trans.

only the echoes of royal policy seem important: Varennes is a major
event in the sense that, spread abroad throughout all of France, it exposed the attitude of Louis XVI toward the new regime to the naked light
of day. In this connection, the interpretations and veerings of a frightened Constituent Assembly are of little importance; the king's attempt
at flight remains treason, and a logical and sentimental continuity manifests itself from June, 1791, to August 10, 1792 and January 21, 1793: the
king refused the compromise of a constitutional monarchy, constructed
along English lines, which the Constituent Assembly set forth in 1791.
Going so far as to rest his hopes of restoration on the success of the foreign armies threatening Paris in 1792, the king pushes the revolutionaries toward the Republic, something no one would have considered
three years earlier. The iron chest discovered in the Tuileries put an
end to the matter; but in the rural areas, where the muffled echoes of the
Parisian *journées* and of the court proceedings scarcely arrived, the royal
treason followed as a matter of course from the abolition of royalty. A
heavy blow to a thousand-year-old tradition, the coming of the Republic mortgages the future even for those who, in the rural areas, are concerned only mildly about the political regime under which they live.
The subsequent attempts at restoration, moderate under Louis XVIII,
demanding under Charles X, will never again arouse that enthusiasm,
will never again revive that popular faith, simultaneously religious and
political, which the grievance lists indicated a few years earlier.*

The work of the great Committee of Public Safety and the Mountain Convention might have marked anew, as in 1789, a decisive step in
French social development: the plan to redistribute land to poor citizens was of another ilk than changes due to the sales of national
property (*biens nationaux*),† which profited a minority of bourgeois and
peasants. But this great project, like so many other anticipations of
the Convention in those days when it was following Robespierre and
Saint-Just, had an ephemeral life, and its career ended with that of its
leading spirits on 9 Thermidor. The First Republic came close to being a
real democracy, based on the economic and social independence of the
citizens. The followers of Rousseau, pondering the *Discours sur l'Inégalité* and the bases of the *Institutions républicaines*, were not heeded
by the Convention along this terrain of a second revolution which
would reshape the civic face of France, already greatly revamped between 1789 and 1791. Such is the deep meaning of Thermidor.‡ Be-

---

* It is a gradual, but lasting disaffection, one that varies according to the region and
the social frame of reference. In the towns, especially Paris, the effect of the treason
is more striking: on June 23, 1791, Danton cries out to the Jacobins: "The person
declared to be king of the French. . . ."

† The *biens nationaux* were primarily the land and buildings previously belonging to
the Church, the Crown, the king's personal domain, and the *émigré's* estates.—
Trans.

‡ Doubtless at the expense of some simplification: in a brilliant essay, *Bourgeois et*

yond the personal quarrels, beyond the blunders of the men overtaxed with the crushing task of insuring the salvation of the country—from within and from without—and beyond the little contingencies of these tragic days,* there remains the choice of the "Plain," of Sieyès, and many other real revolutionaries. The Republic looks into the past; no longer having a king, its ideal still remains the 1791 monarchy; the Republic can be liberal and bourgeois—it does not have to be democratic. And the whole political policy of Thermidor, from 1794 to 1799, consisted in stabilizing this precarious equilibrium of a regime that is in fact bourgeois, simultaneously refusing royal restoration on the one hand and the assistance and demands of the democrats on the other. It is a difficult policy, existing between the pressure of the lower, urban classes, especially the Parisian ones, who, moreover, are deprived of food because of the financial crisis and the royalist offensive, buttressed by religious disorder and intrigues on the part of the returned *émigrés*. This attempt to stabilize the Revolution in its bourgeois norms, from one *coup d'état* to another, alternately eliminating opposition from the Right and from the Left, is continued in 1799-1800 by Napoleon, whose compromise saved, in its turn, the basic revolutionary conquests —that is, those of 1789 to 1791. And, until the dark years of blockade and defeats, Napoleon's regime created no hostilities capable of unsettling it—despite the advance of despotism. These same conquests are maintained, in turn, in the Old French vocabulary of the Charter of 1814-1815 ("the grace of God," "the Charter bestowed"), despite the Ultra-Royalists: the object of a final debate between 1825 and 1830, they are certainly the basis of bourgeois primacy.

► EVALUATIONS OF THE REVOLUTIONARIES: EQUALITY

"Men are born and remain free and equal in rights." In this little sentence, in the first article of the Declaration of the Rights of Man (August 26, 1789), a sentence that suffices to deny all the values of Old Regime society, the French have placed special value on the second term: equality; and, more precisely, equality in law. Because, aware that they—unlike the American revolutionaries—are working for mankind and not just for French citizens, the 1789 Frenchmen are not so blinded that they forget to acknowledge the inequality of fact, or, as they said to the Assembly, not without ambiguity, "of nature." † There were during these two years—when the Constituent Assembly refined its principles

---

Bras nus, a sociologist, Daniel Guérin, has maintained an entirely different thesis, which has been as much discussed as it is enticing. It has not carried with it the support of all the specialists in the French Revolution.

* Without speaking, either, of the lack of personnel, which weighed heavily upon political life in 1793 and 1794.

† "Inequality is in nature itself."

and confronted them with the realities inherited from the Old Regime —a series of debates indicative of class concerns and innovating ambitions which continued to ignite, under the eyes of the most experienced men, both the necessity for total reconstruction from basement to attic and the complexity of interests lodged in the old house. The bourgeois had ended up by making itself fairly comfortable in this old house; they succeeded in the discreet acquisition of noble property (farming out of the tithe or many other fees), and commercial privileges of certain companies. The best-known and most typical debate is the one that came after the night of August 4: in the name of inviolable and sacred property rights, the deputies resumed in good faith what they had enthusiastically wanted to abandon the night before. (The result of the debate about property rights appears in Article 17 of the First Declaration.) From August 5 to 11, the abolished fees became redeemable; and even the tithe, renounced by the clergy as by everyone else, must continue to be levied until such time as new resources shall be bestowed upon the clergy.

Going into detail, it is true that the Constituent Assembly then proceeds to the most complete demolition work it has to accomplish: the ruin of feudalism. Beginning with this abolition of privileges, different forms of equality are distinguished step by step. First of all, fiscal equality: not only do the privileged classes lose their right to live at the peasants' expense, but they are also subjected to general taxation. To the double aspect of their fiscal privilege corresponds a double definition of beneficiaries: all members of the Third Estate, but especially the urban bourgeoisie overwhelmed by direct and indirect taxation, express satisfaction with knowing the tax is better assessed; for the peasants, the abolition (in fact, if not in law) of the manorial regime is actually an economic preferment: they recoup, at the lowest estimate, a quarter of their harvest, of which they themselves can now dispose. This is a valuable, negotiable surplus, and partially explains their passivity in the years after 1793. The *corvées* and the external signs of superiority of birth* disappear at the same stroke, and the noble thus appears as a rural bourgeois, nothing more—whatever may be the prestige he preserves among the peasants in some areas.

Moreover, the ruin of the manorial regime signifies civil equality: the posts reserved for nobles—ranks in the army, administrative offices —are open to everyone, according to the common usefulness; the bourgeoisie also exposes legal careers to reorganization and the inheritance of offices disappears (if not their venality, maintained for some offices even into our day), benefiting the century's new, educated, and rich bourgeois. The same is true for the law of primogeniture, which ob-

---

* Hunting privileges, jurisdictional powers; in 1790, the titles themselves.

viously affects noble properties, and which also will entail an equaliza-
tion. The reorganization of the judicial and administrative institutions,
following these decisions, eased the placement of a new personnel, all
the more numerous as the champions of the old order stood aloof or fled
the country. As First Consul, Napoleon implements in fact this establishment of civil equality by creating that new corps of civil offices which
the bourgeois hastened to fill: financial administrations, prefectures, and
so forth. However, the upheaval was most appreciable in the Army, not
in the administrative life, where the legal profession was still too conscious of its origins and the bourgeois had long been zealous servants of
the monarchy. The officer corps, however, whose ranks quickly were
depleted by emigration, rapidly became populated with these young
promotees, the military glory of the First Republic, and soon of the Empire: the military expression "a marshal's baton in his knapsack" soon
acquired a wider meaning—that of civil equality in general.

The Revolution also gave Frenchmen administrative equality and
equality before the law, no longer seen from the angle of estates and
social divisions, but from that of geography: as far back as the night of
August 4, certain towns, joining in the inimitable movement of freely
made sacrifices, had announced their renunciation of fiscal or commercial advantages; and so did provinces firmly connected with exemptions
and royal favors, maintained or granted for centuries. The Constituent
Assembly, in fact, accomplishes a complete reorganization of French
administrative life which, as perfected by the Convention and the Consulate, expresses this "geographic" equality: the *départements, arrondissements, cantons,* and *communes,* with their elected or nominated councils and tribunals, insure the application of the same laws and the same
penal or fiscal system to everyone, from one end of France to the other.
Certain local characteristics may have suffered by this, but good administration of the country gains by it—to the mixed satisfaction of
the citizens.

However, the Revolution maintained one exception in this territorial
unification. The deputies' generosity does not extend to the overseas
territories remaining French during this period—the three islands in the
Antilles (Guadeloupe, Martinique, and half of Santo Domingo), the
comptoirs in the Indies. In all these areas, political inequality and
deprivation of freedoms are maintained, to the detriment of the natives.
In this respect, the Constituent Assembly was under the influence of the
Antilles lobby directed by the Lameth brothers, who successfully argued
for continuing slavery. France lost Santo Domingo by it, but the institution is to be maintained until 1848 in the few territories recouped in 1815.

Still more important is the establishment of economic equality, a reflection of the rather summary views contemporaries nourish concerning the country's necessities of life. But this total equality of individuals,

employers and workers, merchants and shipowners, commands a large part of the early nineteenth-century capitalist advance, and it is a keystone of bourgeois domination. First of all the Constituent Assembly attacked the system of guilds and trade councils which varied greatly throughout France but was generally considered detrimental, since it interfered with the manufacturers' and merchants' spirit of initiative. In 1791,* societies and guilds with privileges are discontinued, as are such regulations as trademarks and inspections which control them: the employers and guild masters are no longer anything but individuals, and the work they supply is free from all obstacles and collusion. In the same year, on June 14, the Constituent Assembly also votes for the discontinuance of all workers' trade associations in the heart of the guilds or workers' unions.† This law, seen by some as a true-to-type manifestation of class, establishes a sort of equivalence, a mistaken equality, in which employers and journeymen are considered as equal entities. But this is an absurd guarantee, setting the employer, the man handing out work, face to face with the worker, who has only his work. The Le Chapelier Law,‡ complete with similar arrangements for rural labor, opens a new perspective upon the oppression of the working classes: that which existed during the years 1815-1850, that of Lyon in 1831, and others.

In the same direction, but with less social implication, go a few other abolitions of an economic nature: the trading companies—that is, the famous East India Company, which gets itself talked about until the Terror—and the mining companies lose their monopolies, to the benefit of shipowners' and landowners' equality. Similarly, but with an obvious social aim, such indirect taxes as *octrois, traites,*§ salt taxes, and beverage duties—loathed by the population for centuries—are discontinued. If there is any area at the close of the century in which Frenchmen felt their lives to be eased, it is certainly this one. And when Napoleon, running short of funds, boldly runs the risk and re-establishes some of these taxes in 1804 under the name of amalgamated taxes (*droits réunis*), he does so with a circumspection which is evidence of the scope of the rancor accumulated against these levies: charges which at best accentuate

---

* Not until then. The Constituent Assembly hesitated; at a time favorable to their discontinuance, on August 4, it changed its mind, deciding only two years later, perhaps due to the effect of the very clear economic recovery in 1791.

† The word in question is *compagnonnages;* it evokes an old tradition descended from the guilds. The *compagnonnages* served as insurance and mutual improvement societies. Their social solidarity and self-respect were quite high.—Trans.

‡ There is apparent progress toward equality since the monarchic legislation organizing the guilds authorized the employers' associations, when workers' unions were forbidden. But the *de facto* inequality is no less flagrant.

§ Octrois were duties levied by a town on foods and other goods to be used within it; *traites* were taxes levied on articles which came into or went out of the realm, or which passed from one province to another.—Trans.

the inequality of social conditions, insofar as they fall with a heavier hand on the lower classes.

Despite some caution or hesitation relating to the variety of the local situations and the ignorance of the deputies—notably in matters of agrarian law, where members of the Constituent Assembly and the Convention finally retained the collective rights over land and the communal lands—the establishment of equality is then the work of a class. When the Constituent Assembly proclaims equal access to offices and civil service positions, it is working for itself, not for the Fourth Estate. Unquestionably nothing demonstrates this point better (unless it be Le Chapelier's Law), than the establishment of political equality. After the Constituent Assembly has proclaimed the sovereignty of the nation, it rejects at least a third of the citizens from the body politic—those who have not the necessary "faculties" to take part in it. Thus the *censitaire* system distinguishes between the *actif* and *passif* citizens,* the latter, who enjoy the civil rights granted everyone, are unable, perhaps temporarily, to participate in political life. Despite the protests of newspapers and clubs,† wealth is the sole criterion for political qualification. And nothing intimates it more clearly than those early days of 1791: paying a contribution equal to three days' work is little; following the best calculation, there are, in 1791, four million *actif* citizens and two million *passif*. But, as elections are always held in two stages,‡ the *censitaire* system extends its eligibility to the functions of electors and those of the deputies. The basic organizational idea is that leisure and property are necessary prerequisites to a just evaluation of the general interest, an idea inherited from antiquity; it proved injurious to a good many of those who had played so important a role in 1789—servants, rural day laborers, and journeymen in Parisian guilds.

The 1791 Constitution, whose electoral arrangements are weighed down by an assembly frightened by the consequences of Varennes, therefore sanctifies citizens' political inequality, alienating from political life all those whose daily bread is not insured and whose independence is

---

* The distinction between *actif* and *passif* citizenship was first propounded by Sieyès: an *actif* citizen had full political rights and paid taxes; *passif* citizens, though possessing natural and civic rights, did not pay taxes and could not vote.—Trans.

† At the Constituent Assembly, Robespierre, virtually alone, protested against the establishment of the *cens* and the slight alterations produced after the Champ de Mars "massacre"—in the name of the Declaration of the Rights of Man. Article 6: "Law is the expression of the general will. All citizens have the right to assist, personally or through their representatives, in its formation." This protest went unseconded in the Assembly.

‡ Direct representation is not a current notion, doubtless because direct administration, known through experience, is applicable only in small areas: ancient cities, Swiss cantons, and Italian republics—especially because the representation of thousands of electors by one frightened man seems impossible. Despite the strides of trade and mathematical sciences, large numbers cause fear, particularly in this rather unfamiliar area, where the representatives and the represented ought to remain closely linked.

not guaranteed. Popular pressure in Paris shortly after August 10, 1792, brings the Legislative Assembly to renounce this dispossession (which the monarchy, when it convoked the Estates-General in 1788, had not practiced within the Third Estates). Consequently, the Convention was elected by universal suffrage, and the Republic inaugurated under this aegis.

But the men of Thermidor returned to the 1791 system; without restoring the basic distinction between *actif* and *passif* citizens, they restore the *censitaire* system of eligibility which, in effect, restrcts political action to a landed and inherited plutocracy. Napoleon, in a generous gesture, re-establishes a universal suffrage which is no longer useful and rests upon the six hundred citizens in each *département* who pay the most taxes. The same inspiration still exists from 1791 to 1815: the Restoration and the July Monarchy, however, are less generous than the Assembly. During these thirty or so years, *passif* citizens are legion, since (with a *cens* of 300 francs), the electoral body consists of 90,000 people until 1830, and 180,000 (with a *cens* of 200 francs) from 1830 to 1848— a little more than one per cent in the first instance, and a little less than three per cent in the latter.

Therefore, the new society built at the beginning of the nineteenth century is a classless society—egalitarian in its primary source more than in its everyday reality. Doubtless the bourgeoisie there shares with the former privileged people the dominant social influence, but its triumph is reinforced by the elimination, more or less complete according to the electoral systems, of the lower middle class—of the artisans and an early urban and rural proletariat. In this construction, the contemporaries were particularly sensitive to the hostile innovation of the Old Regime. Thus royalist theorists, like De Maistre and De Bonald, discuss not only the principle of sovereignty, but also the political qualifications of the bourgeoisie. To their eyes, the latter is the "economic" * class, while the nobility is the political leader: the bourgeois actuate the material life; the nobility have the role of leadership. These are theories which belatedly and weakly answer to the bourgeois ambitions that have been expressed for centuries and are satisfied after 1791.

► **EVALUATIONS OF THE REVOLUTIONARIES: FREEDOMS**

The Constitutional Monarchy of 1791 and the Republic of 1792 each take up their position under the standard of liberty, toward which the nation has been aspiring for as long a time as Voltaire and others have

---

* *Économique*, as used here and below, has a meaning somewhat different from its English equivalent. It indicates the bourgeois concern for economic matters, business, but also has the implication of a prudent thriftiness.—Trans.

been conjuring up the Anglo-Saxon example. And even if several strains have been put upon its exercise as early as 1793, it remains an important part of the ideal program which generations of citizens and of men gradually have learned to respect.

"Everything that is not injurious to others" is the most general definition established by the members of the Constituent Assembly, anxious to have the regulations, restrictions, and chicanery of the Old Regime forgotten. In concrete reality, giving an altruistic delimitation, in 1789, of the free man entails a formal condemnation of the guilds, of salt-tax collectors and their searches, and the honorific customs through which, for centuries, the nobility has been persecuting the *roturiers*; again, this is the implicit abolition of worldly customs, which basically spring from the same state of mind: domination by an estate or a class through social coercion. Freedom and equality obviously meet in these affirmations: "The exercise of the natural rights of each man has no limit other than those assuring other members of society the enjoyment of the same rights." The insistence with which the 1789 Declaration keeps returning to the constraints certain social groups could exercise* was sufficient to demonstrate that there lies the heart of the problem: the Frenchmen of 1789 want to feel themselves free in their daily life.

The Declaration of the Rights of Man also exhibits the greatest care in defining not only freedom, but also the freedoms indispensable to the citizen. In the first place, the revolutionary legislators insisted upon assuring for themselves an English-type *habeas corpus*, safeguarding their individual liberty; the Declaration does not have the strict precision of English law and does not set a time limitation upon imprisonments on suspicion, nor does it for standing trial. This is doubtless a defiant move on the part of those bourgeois fearing popular "excess" as much as aristocratic plots; it is also a result of the difficulty of throwing off, all at once, the slow habits of French legal procedures. The Act of August 26, however, defines the essential of these liberal guarantees, whose recall is sometimes necessary in the democracy of the Fourth Republic: limited detention on suspicion; the absence of *ex post facto* laws; invalidation and repression of arbitrary acts; respect for the legal forms of arrest, accusation, and detention (Articles 7, 8, and 9). The hatred for *lettres de cachet*, for incarcerations ended as unexpectedly as begun, and for the abuses springing from the procedures employed in seeking offenders as well as in the investigation of matters, are all, to a great extent, the bases of these texts. From the outset, the Assembly expressed similar fears by decreeing the inviolability of its members. In this kingdom in which, despite several attempts made to ameliorate the course of justice

---

* Article 4: "These limits can only be determined by law"; Article 5: "All that is not prohibited by law cannot be forbidden, and no one can be compelled to do anything that it does not ordain."

—particularly in the days of Chancellor Séguier—the king's subjects never felt certain of tomorrow, especially in the eighteenth century when incriminating writings circulate so rapidly, these guarantees seem at a minimum; during its career, the Constituent Assembly concerned itself with them on many occasions, specifying certain formulas and cleaning up the laws regulating and applying these general principles, and adding to the originally provided safeguards one securing the freedom of movement. This is one of the great conquests of the Revolution: despite all the strains suffered from 1792 to 1815, universally defined individual liberty is once more intact, in the Charter which governs France until 1848.

The Revolution also granted Frenchmen freedom of conscience: that ". . . no one can be challenged because of his opinions, even his religious ones" is written as early as 1789. This "even" is sufficient to demonstrate that this daring extends beyond the political level. The Catholic Church, the state religion, never admitted to the presence of heretics in France: the Protestants saw their civil status restored in 1787, to the protests of the clergy; similarly, the Jews continue to be considered people on the fringes of society, tolerated there where they become implanted; and actors, who have always been excommunicated, are adulated by high society but banished from the sacraments and from holy ground. As early as 1789, it certainly seems that the place of the Catholic Church in France no longer is as it was: Protestants regain, in fact, their right to exist in the kingdom; and it is particularly to them, more than to the Jews who are simultaneously feared and despised, that Article 10 of the Declaration is addressed. In 1801, Napoleon will legislate for the Protestants as he has done for the Catholics; in 1806, he recognizes a Jewish tabernacle. And 1815 does not go back on these innovations which sanctify French spiritual plurality and mark the beginning of the qualitative advance of these two minority communities, the Protestant and the Jewish, during the nineteenth and twentieth centuries.

Where did the members of the Constituent Assembly and later the Convention derive their daring in so attacking the Catholic monopoly? Most of it came from the simplicity of their Gallicanism, rather than from a Voltairian spirit, which is less widespread than under the July Monarchy. As representatives of the nation, they overthrow the organization and the internal police of the French Church with the same offhandedness as the kings of France had long employed: recalling its property to make its own financial situation sounder, doing away with the tithe, substituting a salary graded as are the ecclesiastical functions to furnish the Church with resources, reforming the modes of recruitment, and even entrusting the choice of bishops to election, as in the early Church. They do all this without too much concern for Rome, manifesting a conciliar Gallicanism quite opposed to Ultramontanism, and, in the long run, very close to that of 1682. This imprudence, joined with several others, quickly provoked division within the Catholic clergy; and until 1801, the revolutionary assemblies had to debate the opposition between the conforming and the rebellious bishops, without being able to resolve the conflict. The Counter-Revolution took advantage of this internal war much more than did the more or less secularized cults, embroidered onto the Republican calendar and the Supreme Being. The Catholic conscience of the majority of Frenchmen was not disturbed by these quarrels, and neither the Cult of the Supreme Being nor the Theophilanthropists outlived their founders. Perhaps religious freedom could have been more securely rooted in law if the separation of Church and State, decided upon by the Thermidor Convention in 1795, had been maintained; but this was a sterile anticipation, unable to mould a new awareness of the connections between the dominant religion and politics.

The men of the Revolution were readers of an *Encyclopédie* (itself censored before being condemned) and of many, many writings published unsigned due to a legitimate prudence; they proclaimed the right of expressing one's thought, and used this right on a large scale, as early as the first weeks of the Estates-General, when an entire active and virulent press undertook to express the most diverse opinions. The People's Friend or the King's Friend, the 1789 press is the first to express French public opinion, since previous publications (*Gazette, Mercure,* etc.), carefully supervised by royal power, never enjoyed total independence. "Thus every citizen can speak, write, and publish freely. . . ." The distinct memories of letters opened by the Cabinet Noir, that permanent postal censor, and of printing shops condemned by royal power to close, prompt the deputies in the Constituent Assembly to consider this freedom of expressing one's opinion to be one of the most precious guarantees of the independence necessary to citizens, even though they quickly sense the dangers of this total freedom granted by law to anyone who has the material means of having himself published. The aristocratic newspapers are the first to disappear, in 1792 and 1793. Later on, freedom of the press has not ceased to be an issue, so great are its prestige and its political effectiveness. Under the Restoration and the July Monarchy, the liberal opposition continues to call for a freedom which the bourgeois of the latter part of the eighteenth century appreciated at full value, since they had been totally deprived of it. Without going to such despotic measures as did Napoleon, who designated the number of newspapers (four in Paris, one per *département*), the government, fearing this uncontrolled force, used every means of limitation: financial pressure first, cautiously, then stamp taxes on each issue, making newspapers very expensive items, even for a segment of the bourgeoisie. After 1836, with Girardin's introduction of advertisements and the penny newspaper, this pressure relaxes; but throughout the Restoration, it is an effective, if not elegant, means of indirectly limiting the expression and spread of opinions.

Finally, the members of the Constituent Assembly, accustomed for centuries to "Catholic" thought, and during a century of cosmopolitan philosophy habituated to a universalist representation of great principles, legislated—as we know—for mankind. The noble inspiration that animates them exists once again when, in 1791 and especially in 1792, the new regime collides with the *Complot des Rois* faced with threats from Vienna or Berlin, the Revolution rises in protest, denounces the privileges and despotism that hold sway beyond its frontiers, and finally declares itself ready to aid and assist people who would like to regain their freedom and sovereignty. Undoubtedly these fine arrangements did not have all the accordance that someone like Brissot, announcing the necessary war, imagines. If Brabant rose up against Austria as early as 1789, the following years are calm, and the Declaration of Pillnitz did more for this war—which does not end until 1815—than the appeals of the oppressed peoples. Undoubtedly, too, the days of Trees of Liberty and of the joyous abolition of Old Regimes did not last for very long; faced with the slowness of nations to embrace self-determination in the same sense desired by the Convention, the latter decided, in December, 1792, to proceed itself to the expropriations and other measures necessary for abolishing the Old Regime: the Convention turns into a conqueror. But after the annexation of Avignon and of Savoy, in "revolutionizing" the Netherlands, after Dumouriez's 1792 victory over the Austrians at Jemappes, it nonetheless does bring to Europe the promotion of peoples to sovereignty, which establishes a new law and trails a deep social transformation in its wake.*

Neither the liberal 1791 Monarchy nor the Republic of the Girondists, 1792-1793, speaks the last word of the revolutionary message in the realm of freedoms. Through a tragic reversal of things the Convention, an assembly no less bourgeois than the Constituent Assembly, was led to alter its own principles and to safeguard them in a more distant future. Thus, in 1793-94, in the days when the members of the Convention follow the persuasive authority of Robespierre, was formed the Jacobin tradition whose political influence continues down to our own day.

Monarchists in 1789, the members of the Mountain have, in the image of Robespierre himself, become Republicans, through the force

---

* In the same state of mind, the Convention created the right of sanctuary in 1793. The Constitution of the Year I, Article 120: "[The French people] give sanctuary to foreigners banished from their native land for the cause of freedom. They refuse it to tyrants."

of events: hence, in 1791 and particularly in 1792, the royal treason. The founders of a State resolutely new from this instant on—that one and indivisible Republic whose grandeur is so often evoked by Barère's speeches*—they wanted to create a regime that would surpass the preceding one, one which, at the very least, would cause it to be forgotten. Amid these battles, the Convention, assailed on all sides and betrayed from within, was struggling, but was also preparing a new world: the new Declaration of Rights, that of 1793 (called the Year I), the preparation of a civil and criminal Code, and especially the establishment of schools and universities—these are the major expression of this great concern.† Aware that they are establishing a Republic unique in its day, one fundamentally democratic, contrary to the patrician republics of the United Provinces of the Netherlands and Venice, the members of the Mountain set themselves three basic objectives: defense against foreign aggressors, internal protection against the Counter-Revolution, and finally, the establishment of a real democracy—that is, a social one.

Robespierre and his friends take up the government at the point when all Europe is allied against that France already called by some the country of the rights of man; the territorial integrity of the country is threatened (in spring, the Antwerp Conferences prepared a split), as is the regime established by the regicides. For the great Committee of Public Safety, everything is subordinated to the suppression of these plans of the allies: farm and factory products are requisitioned, able-bodied men are mobilized for the famous armies of the Year II, and there is an appeal to scientists, to Gaspard Monge, Bertholet, and Chaptal, to insure the outfitting and armament of the million men mobilized by Carnot. The fortress of France is besieged on all sides, yet in less than a year it triumphs over its adversaries. Republican France may have renounced carrying freedom and equality to all the peoples of Europe; but it knew how to save itself.‡ The Jacobins are, first and foremost, patriots, for whom the peoples' right to self-determination means pre-eminently the safeguarding of the Republic which the French made for themselves. The independence of the French nation is enacted, to the sound of

---

* Barère was prosecutor at the trial of Louis XVI.—Trans.
† The plans and achievements of the Mountain Convention in matters of public education are well known; let us merely call to mind: the plan for a free and compulsory elementary education—abandoned by the Thermidorians; the plan for free secondary schools (*Écoles centrales payantes*) also revised after Thermidor; the creation of the principal Grandes Écoles, which educated the upper cadre of the nation for a century and a half: Polytechnique, Ponts et Chaussées, Mars (equal to the École de Guerre), and Normale; and the large institutions: the Bureau des Longitudes, the Conservatoire des Arts et Métiers, and Muséum d'Histoire Naturelle.
‡ The Decree of April 13, 1793: "The Convention declares, in the name of the people of France, that it will in no way meddle with the affairs of foreign powers, but it declares at the same time that it will wrap itself in its own ruin rather than suffer any power to meddle with the internal regime of the Republic."

cannons and the singing of *La Marseillaise*, at Toulon and at Landau, at Wissembourg and at Fleurus—and in 1795, Prussia, Spain, and the United Provinces recognize it. When Godefroy Cavaignac rebuilds the Republican party after 1830, and when Gambetta wants to continue the struggle against Prussia in 1870-71, each of them evokes the Jacobin tradition to glorify their demanding patriotism. And after 1870, down to the Second World War, this aspect of the Mountain's policy retained profound repercussions—in spite of divergent currents.

Nevertheless, in order to face this gigantic effort and to combat a violent, dangerous internal opposition, the Jacobins had to go against their principle, within the country itself or in the conquered territories. Robespierre, obsessed like many members of the Convention by the idea of a foreign conspiracy, did not hesitate to strike even among his closest associates when he had the factions of Hébert and Danton condemned. But in the preceding months, the press, "aristocratic" meetings, all the supporters of the first stage—those who were suspected of being luke-warm—were prohibited. Under the impetus of the Committee of Public Safety, but with the active collaboration of the revolutionary tribu-nals and the Jacobin clubs, the Mountain Convention established a dictatorship of the Mountain "party." The Republic belongs first of all to the Republicans, and it must protect them against its enemies. The revolutionary government suspends the exercise of freedoms until the restoration of peace, in order to save these very freedoms of which the citizens are temporarily deprived; thus the dictatorship is provisional. The Committee of Public Safety declares its devotion to the promul-gated freedoms but, recognizing the special weakness of such a regime which, by definition, allows the schemings of the enemies of freedom, of those same people who, were they in power, would refuse to let the Republicans speak,* the Committee proclaims that it is sometimes nec-essary to suspend the exercise of freedoms, the better to preserve them. It is a grave sacrifice, especially in the period immediately preceding the Great Terror, when "heads fell like apples." Forbidding liberty, in order to save it, is a difficult task: when can this liberty, then, be said to be in danger sufficient to justify its being forbidden? The Convention, and the subsequent Jacobin tradition, retain one sure criterion: foreign war†—and so did the terrible Clemenceau in 1917 and 1918.

That the Jacobins were devoted nonetheless to the freedoms they had to set aside for long months, to the detriment of their popularity and their lives, is clearly established by their social demands. Despite their appearance of political expediency in the depths of the crisis, the "Laws

---

* In his report on December 25, 1793, Robespierre declares: "If they [the enemies of the Republic] invoke the literal execution of the constitutional sayings, it is only to violate them with impunity; they are cowardly assassins who, to strangle the Re-public in its cradle and go unpunished, force her to protect herself. . . ."
† In Robespierre's same report of December 25, 1793: "The revolutionary govern-ment needs extraordinary powers, precisely because it is at war."

of Ventôse," that redistribution of land so daring as to be unheard of in those days, indicate the concern for establishing the Republic upon real democracy, upon the actual economic and social independence of the citizens. From Saint-Just's point of view in the *Institutions républicaines,* and doubtless from Robespierre's too, the citizen is truly free when he owns a plot of land which can assure him his own invulnerability against his employer, his creditor, and his chatelain. Saint-Just says this in a deservedly famous maxim: "Man must live independent." The Constituent Assembly knew this concern, having denied the vote to servants and those paying few, or no, taxes. The Jacobins reverse the terms, and give everyone the means to be citizens— in order not to have to deny citizenship even to the lowliest in France. Consequently, real democracy comes about in the heart of a society of small producers; each owning land or a workshop, the means to feed his family, and the means not to have this modest sufficiency threatened, by either his neighbors or his competitors.* Jacobin democracy is fundamentally democratic; it bases freedom on a minimization of economic and social differences, without going so far as the "chimera" of property equality. The extreme disproportion of wealth is an obstacle to democracy, and for that reason is condemned; this is already an important step in safeguarding the deep meaning of universal suffrage. This ideal of the small rural landowners is beyond a doubt the basis, and the limit, of the social aspirations motivating the Jacobin tradition. Even in the twentieth century, it preserves a high reputation, which partially explains the tenderness for the southern peasantry manifested by the Third Republic's assemblies; it is at the base of all legislation for assistance to the aged, the disabled, and the "economically weak," and also inspired laws concerning inheritance. As an anticipation of a daring never to be renewed, the redistribution of lands provided for in 1794 gave the Jacobin tradition its socializing orientation.

Thus did the Mountain Convention propose to France, and later to the world, a democratic ideal† whose great changes go far beyond those of the first Revolution: shortly after the July Days of 1830, a Republican tradition issues from this ideal, and is enriched and diversified in the opposition to the bourgeois monarchy, to *Napoléon le Petit,*‡ then in the

---

* The "Laws of Ventôse," which were never carried out, redistributed to poor patriots the property of the *émigrés* and "suspects," of all those who, as enemies of the Revolution, no longer have their place in the Republic. Saint-Just says in his *Institutions:* "He who is shown to be an enemy of his country cannot be a landowner in it."
† The 1793 Constitution, in its Declaration of Rights, enshrines its essentials: public assistance, as well as education, individual freedom as well as property; it even recognizes the duty of insurrection—Article 35: "When the government violates the right of the people, insurrection is, for the people and each party of the people, its most sacred and indispensable duty."
‡ This is the title of Victor Hugo's famous attack on Louis Napoleon. Hugo, at first a supporter of Napoleon III, turned Republican as a result of "Napoleon the Little's" *coup d'état,* December 2, 1851.—Trans.

exercise of power—without forgetting its original inspiration. But con- temporaries were particularly sensitive to suppression—even temporary suppression—of the freedoms established only recently by the Revolu- tion, and that with difficulty: the Thermidor conspirators, whatever their diverse and profound reasons for attacking Robespierre, are joined by hatred for the tyrant and their loudly proclaimed will to restore free- doms. An extremely precarious restoration: the Thermidorians, simul- taneously threatened by the Royalists and by the heirs of the Mountain, are maintained by dint of *coups d'état*. And Bonaparte—First Consul, then emperor—scarcely remembered having been counted at one time among the friends of the younger Robespierre. The exercise of the free- doms proved very difficult, all the more so as French citizens unflinch- ingly submitted to all sorts of privations, including Napoleonic despot- ism, the re-establishment of State prisons, the suppression of freedom of the press, the regulation of printing shops, and the hurling into prison or exile of the rare opponents.* Re-established by the 1814 Charter, but severely regulated in practice by the laws surrounding them, the funda- mental liberties formed the subject of a precarious apprenticeship until 1848, when the question of the press, of a press of very limited distribu- tion, plays the chief role. Never totally suppressed, but more easily under- mined than egalitarian principles,† the liberties are nonetheless an essential part of the revolutionary heritage bequeathed to twentieth- century France.

► **NAPOLEON**

Having refused the destiny and the stale honors of a Monck, the young General Bonaparte, through his fifteen-year tenure as the head of France, gave the bourgeoisie the time and the means to consolidate a victory that the Republic of the Directory, from Fructidor to Brumaire, re- vealed as rather precarious. The retention until 1815 of the social con- quests, and the economic prosperity of the first decade of the century, strengthened the bourgeoisie's position as the dominant class—a position which the new, *rallié*‡ clergy and the still-emigrated nobility cannot con- test: through its long duration, and through Napoleon's political sense, which set itself equidistant between the last Jacobins and the Chouans,

---

* In a well-known letter to Fouché, Napoleon expressed his opinion on freedom of the press, as early as 1804, in his inimitable and outspoken style: "Monsieur Fouché, the reform of the newspapers will soon take place, for it certainly is very stupid to have newspapers which have only the inconvenience of freedom of the press, with- out the advantages."
† Monarchic theorists, basing society upon the traditional authority of the Catholic religion, doubtless have a hand in it: thus the freedom of conscience granted Prot- estants and Jews is, to their eyes, shocking; and so, with greater reason, is the religious indifference making headway among the bourgeoisie.[1]
‡ Literally one who has rallied; here the word refers to those former Imperialists and Royalists who have rallied around the Republic.—Trans.

the Napoleonic stage is the most important moment in the consolidation that has been in progress since 1794.

But Napoleon was more than the conscious instrument of the French bourgeoisie in its triumph over the Old Regime: the success of his exceptionally bold policies enabled him to face the permanence of the personal compromise he had imposed on his opponents between 1792 and 1799. With an uncommon sense of French grandeur, his success also inspired him with the idea of putting his mark on his compatriots' everyday life—what is sometimes called Napoleonic civilization. Finally, and above all, at the same time as he was building his imperial monarchy at Paris, Napoleon was the soldier of the Revolution in Europe, carrying the abolition of the Old Regimes in the knapsack of his Great Army, indelibly marking the destiny of Germany, Poland, and Italy. In Goethe's words, the Revolution crowned.

From the conspiring general, asserting himself with difficulty in the councils of 19 Brumaire in the Year VIII at Saint-Cloud, to the emperor of the French, anointed by Pope Pius VII at Notre-Dame in Paris on December 2, 1804—this career which stupefied many contemporaries and finds admirers even today, admits of few failures: the First Consul succeeds within several months in putting Austria out of commission, and skillfully negotiates the Treaty of Amiens, concluding a war which has lasted for ten years; he asserts himself with equal authority, even then not devoid of brutality, on unrepentant Revolutionaries and on ambitious Royalists (the execution of the Duc d'Enghien): "Not wanting any more parties and seeing only Frenchmen in France," provided they rally to the Consulate—that is, to his person, since he is the sole guarantor of the new policy; Napoleon re-establishes, after the unremitting public disturbances during the Directory, civil peace. In this pacifying work, the creation of prefects,* those heirs of the monarchy's *intendants* and the Convention's national agents, and the establishment of a new financial corps (the tax collectors [*percepteurs*], the *trésoriers*, etc.) doubtless count less than the *franc germinal*, the Civil Code, and especially the Concordat.

Protected as early as 1799 by several Parisian bankers, who participated in the preparations for the *coup d'état*, the First Consul retains these precious props which enable him to put an end to the financial ruin of the First Republic. From promissory notes [*assignats*]* to *mandats territoriaux*† and bankruptcy, the entire financial policy of the ten preceding years is a failure, brought to a climax between 1797 and 1799 by war and foreign intrigues. Napoleon reorganizes the public finances,

---

* The institution's strength derives less from the powers allocated to the prefects than to the disappearance of the *parlements* and of the officers who, before 1789, did a fine job of thwarting the *intendants*.
† *Assignats* were paper money issued by the Constituent Assembly payable out of the *biens nationaux*. The Directory substituted the *mandats territoriaux*, which could be converted into a specific amount of land, for the *assignats* in 1796.—Trans.

creates the Caisse d'Amortissement, and then, with the aid of Perregaux and Mallet, creates the Bank of France, which as early as 1803 has a monopoly on issuing notes repayable on demand. Finally in the spring of 1803 (7 Germinal, Year XI) the *franc germinal* is created, that franc containing 322 milligrams of pure gold, which will remain the French currency and will be stable until the inflation shortly following the First World War. A bankruptcy adding up to seventy-five per cent has a large place among the totality of the Consulate's financial measures: the Caisse d'Amortissement liquidated the debts inherited from the preceding governments, with *rentes* of five per cent distributed to the government's creditors in a proportion of twenty-five per cent of their claim. However, after the uncertainties, after the inflation and the deflation during the Directory, the measure was not shocking; it enables the Republic's creditors, and all those who participated in the frantic speculation between 1794 and 1799, to save more money than they had put in. But above all, the creation of safe currency aided economic prosperity. For years, the fine, harvested crops had not been producing urban prosperity, so greatly had inflation thrown prices and trade into imbalance, producing crisis upon crisis; after 1801, and particularly after 1803, despite the recurring war, France again achieves a cloudless prosperity, until the transitory blockade crisis of 1811-1812—and until the great depression that starts in 1817. The financial reorganization was one of the best proofs of respect for the First Consul's credit, as far as the business community, the bankers and merchants, and the urban bourgeois living off its *rentes* are concerned.

The second proof: the Civil Code promulgated in 1804. Amid pressing concerns, the Convention had begun the indispensable confrontation of the monarchic legislation with the new principles: a long, exacting, and extremely careful work which had remained unfinished in 1795, and which the assemblies during the Directory did not carry very far forward. The Code, that collection of laws, was consequently the work of Napoleon's precedessors and of the Consulate. Brought to its conclusion with the least possible delay, it represents, to contemporary eyes, the definitive legislation of the revolutionary conquest: it combines individual freedom, civil equality, the abolition of all vestiges of the feudal regime, and the uniform application of the same law throughout all France. Similarly, articles concerning property, and Le Chapelier's Law dealing with workers' strike federations, aggravated by the formal prohibition of all strikes, an impediment to employers' freedom, are proofs of the spirit in which the members of the Council of State and of the Consulate's assemblies were inclined to this code of new Law.* The judicial administration, reorganized especially in the Courts

---

* There is no need for the property law, expressly emphasized in the 1789 Declaration, nor is there any for the prohibition of strikes and strike federations, appealing

of Appeal, consequently has, after 1804, a clear code in hand—one drafted precisely and carefully—an instrument of a more expeditious and equitable justice than that which existed prior to 1789.

Finally, internal peace owes even more to the signing of the Concordat, and the re-establishment of an untroubled religious life throughout every region. The 1801 text which (with a few touch-ups in 1817) continued in force for more than a century, until 1905, reserves the nomination of bishops for the head of the government; but whereas the king of France was a personage of the Church through the anointing and the symbolism attached to him, the First Consul is a "secular" authority. The Concordat recognizes the distribution of Church property transformed into national property, and allows the tithe to be discontinued. The clergy becomes what the Constituent Assembly had wanted it to be: a body of officials who are salaried and subjected to a civil oath (Article 6). Finally, at the price of a canonically delicate operation—the exhortation to resign addressed by the Pope to refractory bishops, in order to renew the episcopal personnel according to the norms of the agreement (one-third pre-1789 bishops, one-third conforming bishops, and one-third new prelates)—at the price of this sacrifice,* the ecclesiastical personnel could be renewed. And religious life quickly regains a fervor exalted rather than weakened by the difficulties of the preceding years; a fervor which, in literate "good society," was also just being stimulated by the publication of the *Génie du Christianisme* in 1802. By returning to the clergy its place in everyday life, and ending all the dissensions that had marked the revolutionary years, Napoleon obviously answers the wish of the masses, who have abandoned not an iota of their traditional faith; he also deprives the Royalist Counter-Revolution, which has not lain down its arms—those *émigrés* refusing the First Consul's offers of amnesty, and the Chouans connected with the Count of Artois—of their surest prop among the peasant population.†

In 1804, when the Pope comes to Paris and agrees, to the advantage of someone who is called "Usurper" in London or Warsaw, to proceed

---

to Napoleon's authoritarian spirit. The mentality of these collaborators in the Council of State is largely sufficient for it: rather, his hand would be found in the articles dealing with the family and granting the father the greatest powers over his wife and children.

* With which a certain number of bishops refused to comply: the schism of the *Petite Église*, which resulted in some regions, is gradually ended during the course of the nineteenth century, with the help of Rome at the beginning of the Restoration. It never really endangered the policy of the Concordat. (The *Petite Église* was a faction within the Roman Catholic Church which refused to accept the Concordat and favored a Royalist type of Church.—Trans.)

† Napoleon attended to it personally: the 1806 Imperial catechism insists on the duties of the emperor: "To honor and serve our Emperor is therefore to honor and serve God Himself. . . ."

with a ceremony discreetly based upon that of the royal anointment, the illusion is complete;* the hand of God rests on the new ruler of France. And despite foreign difficulties, despite the confinement of the Pope and the 1813 Concordat extorted from him through captivity and violence, the Napoleonic regime remained the great beneficiary of the Concordat of 1801. On Easter day in 1802, when the *Te Deum* celebrates the peace both of weapons and of minds, the journalists in the employ of the police minister can boast of a new Augustus. The French, governed by a firm hand, do not regret the liberty they have lost in order to pay for their retained equality, their economic prosperity, and their religious tranquillity.

In the subsequent years, the weakness of both Monarchic and Jacobin opposition, the benevolent apathy of the peasant masses, and the diligent police efforts of Fouché enabled Napoleon to take an important step toward the re-establishment of social inequality within imperial society: of this, the Legion of Honor was the first indication. Established in 1804, it created a body of élite Frenchmen, the first defenders of the state. The creation of entailed property [*majorat*] in 1808 is a more decisive step: it enables the Empire nobility, averaging out the allocation on the basis of large landed property varying according to the basis, to assure themselves of their inheritance. The new dukes, princes, and counts certainly are granted neither tax exemptions nor the right to collect taxes on their lands, but the Emperor Napoleon is obviously trying to furnish the new dynasty with as stable a personnel as that of the Capetian monarchy. But the weak complement of this *majorat* nobility (some two thousand members) and the limits imposed upon their privileges, made it possible for the new institution not to upset public opinion too much; the latter, moreover, was muzzled.

However, the Emperor of the great Empire, from 1808 to 1810, had eyes for nothing but melting away the memory of the monarchy in the ostentation and glories of the new regime. Hence this too ornately dressed court, suffering boredom and maneuvering like an army, laughs at the ruler's liberties, the slang of Madame Sans-Gêne, and the temper tantrums of Elisa; hence, above all, the efforts of the new owner of the Tuileries to put his stamp upon the age. Louis XIV and Louis XV each had his style of furniture; Napoleon, in his turn, created that heavy, Empire style which imitates the Roman without its suppleness or grace: massive colonnades, overabundant cornices and medallions, gilding. Napoleon, too, wants to build: opposite the Tuileries, the two triumphal arches, simultaneously imitating antiquity and evoking the emperor's

---

* As emperor, however, Napoleon did not go so far as to accept responsibility for miracle-working powers, curing scrofula. In the popular mentality, this royal miracle did not survive the faith in the monarchy—as Napoleon must have been fully able to sense.

exploits, the Madeleine, an immense and cold temple of glory. David and Gros are the saving grace of this imperial artistic leadership which, in addition, did not last long enough to create a completely new décor. Abandoned by the "great" literature—Chateaubriand and Madame de Staël—and shamelessly and disproportionately praised by a band of insignificant poets seeking work year in, year out, Napoleon experienced real success only in the area of science: his support of industrial research and technical progress recalls the great work of a pleiade of scientists working on the momentum of the eighteenth century: naturalists (Cuvier and Geoffroy Saint-Hilaire), mathematicians (Monge and Lagrange), and physicists (Arago, Gay-Lussac, and Bertholet)—scientific progress in which the imperial government participates only meagerly. Napoleon at least gave a fleeting popularity to two types of public distraction:* first, the balls, both bourgeois and common, which proliferate during the Directory. Napoleon prefers these to theatrical productions, which are dangerous—political allusions are forbidden in them and the number of theaters had been reduced since the Consulate from thirty to eight. Secondly, there are military reviews, increased by the victories brought back from all over Europe, which gradually create a chauvinistic emotion destined—at least among Parisians—for a fine career. All things considered, this leadership of arts and letters, exercised by a patron who is absorbed in his wars, scarcely deserves the great name of "Napoleonic civilization." It is an artificial interlude between the refinement and the daring of the eighteenth-century rationalists, and the Romantic revolution, which is then beginning to take shape both within France and without. The Napoleonic era is, above all, the expression of a will to grandeur; and its greatest claim to glory is, not having bestowed the Madeleine on Paris, but having tottered the Old Regimes in Europe.

The Europe of 1810 is a French Europe—more so, doubtless, than in the days of the Enlightenment. By means of alliances and dependent kingdoms, Napoleon, conqueror of Prussia and Austria, absorbs into the great Empire, or into the French sphere of influence, all of Western Europe and a good part of Central Europe as well.

Dependable allies like Bavaria, adversaries dreaming of revenge like Prussia—all make their reforms along the French pattern: a simple, clear, and efficient administration is the first objective. In the eyes of some who have not forgotten those unfortunate attempts, Joseph II in particular,

---

* The First Republic did not know how to give the country governmental fetes: the attempts made within the setting of the revolutionary calendar, fete of Nature and the Supreme Being, did not summon up much enthusiasm. Under the Directory, in reaction to the virtue of the Republic, a life of pleasures was largely developed at Paris, at least in the days of the *Incroyables:* balls were its main manifestations, especially in the Tivoli garden.

Napoleon is a despot illuminated with genius. But the brothers and brothers-in-law who rule over the new states, like Westphalia and Italy, copy French institutions; and the Civil Code thus radiates well beyond the *départements* of the Empire proper. Revised and corrected by the Consulate, then, the French Revolution is expanded to a new field of application: to that feudal Europe, which served as refuge for the Counter-Revolution, and which, in turn, undergoes, perforce, a revolution from above, but without the agitation or the bloody experiments. The administrative redistribution into *départements* or circles, and into their subdivisions in turn, is the ruin of local particularisms, urban or feudal, which are so alive throughout the Empire; applying the Civil Code is an automatic way of abolishing all feudal rule*—in favor of the citizens' equality and the destruction of classes and privileges, to the profit of the peasants and bourgeois. Creation of a civil service along French lines means, in those countries where the nobles have not yet become the parasites they were in France, the loss of all social and administrative prestige, to the advantage of the judges, tax collectors, and the governor-prefects of the new administration. Related to the application of the Civil Code (with slight differences according to the country, particularly in Italy where concordats have been established), the secularization of the clergy's property is also an important step: sold as national property, or distributed to French dignitaries, these assets change hands to the local clergy's disadvantage. For Napoleon, all of this is a question of good administration; for the population of Westphalia and the Papal States, the French system is revolution—even if the titles of the Old Regime are retained, even if the décor of the Milanese Court conjures up the old Lombard realm, and even if the Bavarian dynasty does not budge from Munich. In this manner, civil equality and religious and individual freedom, which had already crossed French borders as early as 1792, reach Calabria and the banks of the Vistula around 1810: Napoleon continues to be the Bonaparte of the Italian Army, and of the generals of the Year II, as if all Europe were enacting the Revolution according to his wishes.

A long and ardous task, primarily because it is being applied to unprepared peoples, this European revolution did not have the success augured by the French model: it did not have sufficient time since, apart from the left bank of the Rhine and northern Italy, the French rule lasted only a few years; also, this rule came out of the baggage wagons of a foreign army which is all too happy to pillage, is hard on the occupied peoples, and is a burden insofar as local frameworks are lacking; for the inauguration of the reforms is accompanied by military and economic measures which quickly seem to be the heart of the system, and which

---

* And first of all, the liberation of the serfs, more numerous than in France.

weigh heavy: war taxes and tributes, conscription, control of foreign commerce in terms of the Continental blockade, and even the simple Napoleonic desire to favor the French economy over every European market: finally, in Catholic countries like Italy and Spain, the fate of the Pope arouses misgivings which in no small way contributed to discrediting the entire French system.

However, if Napoleonic Europe had rejected "Frenchification," this is also and especially for a deeper reason—the social structure of the countries subjected to this revolution. Northern Italy, the two banks of the Rhine, and the United Provinces are receptive regions, by virtue of their extensive bourgeoisie, who are both commercial and liberal, and are open to the new ideas even before the arrival of the French troops; they are ready to forgive the soldiers' pillaging, and especially to fill the new administrative ranks and to take maximum advantage of the social innovations brought from France. In addition, these bourgeois are the ones who have participated longest in the Revolution: the right bank of the Rhine since 1794, northern Italy since 1796—twenty years, during which a whole generation grows up to live in a new social order. There is nothing comparable in peninsular Italy, Spain, the Germanic regions along the Elbe, or the Illyrian provinces in which France's stay is short, where nobles and peasants constitute the mass of the population, where there are no towns, at least not any longer, and where the nobility and clergy are still the leaders—even when Napoleon has cast them aside and supplanted them by civil servants, grafted onto hostile regions as in Stendhal's temporary stay at Brunswick. Thus, in the Kingdom of Naples, Joseph is the head of the town where the majority of the townspeople follow and accept the new rule; but all the mountain areas escape him. There the nobles are dominant, even though dispossessed of their titles and duties, and they encourage their peasants to be hostile to the foreigners. After 1815, these same nobles will be less fastidious, during the time of the Austrian interventions. It is here that the Napoleonic revolution shows its true colors: it is a social revolution, and sets itself against the framework of the Old Regime; it needs the support of an enlightened public opinion—something the peasants in Calabria or the Tyrol cannot supply.

Thus does the patriotic reflex prevail. There is only one European country in which national sentiment works in favor of French domination: Poland. Carved up by her neighbors during the first revolutionary wars, Poniatowski's Poland remains faithful to Napoleon until Leipzig. But elsewhere, from Spain to the German states, where the presence of France caused feelings of national solidarity,* a rise of xenophobia puts

---

* For which Napoleon worked by destroying the mosaic of the German Holy Roman Empire, as in Italy, where the Kingdom of Italy lays the groundwork for the movement of 1848-1870.

an end to this domination. The 1813 campaign is one of political liberation and social restoration, the former discreetly hiding the latter.

The fall of Napoleon in 1814 swept all of Europe into this reaction,
including the regions outside France best adapted to the new regime.
However, the restoration of the old regimes, a brutal process everywhere,
could not, in some localities, be carried on without caution: some German states like Bavaria, and Piedmont in Italy, maintain liberal constitutions which safeguard certain French innovations.

And this amazing two-time fall (1814 and 1815) is also shaded with
French compromise. The restoration of the Bourbons is not a total reaction, even less than in Piedmont or Bavaria, and for good reason.
Louis XVIII, returning to France in the nineteenth year of his reign,
had understood—and if he had had any doubt, the One Hundred Days
set him straight—that a total reaction, a complete Restoration, were not
possible. Hence, the Charter. Hence, too, the fits of impatience of the
returning *émigrés*, who constitute the main part of the Ultra-Royalist
troops. Returned from abroad in baggage wagons, the Bourbons make
enough concessions in 1814-1815 to be accepted by the bourgeoisie; they
continue the great conquests and even re-establish a few freedoms suppressed by the emperor. The clergy, which accepted the previous regime, is momentarily satisfied with the re-establishment of the state religion. Only the nobles of the Chambre Introuvable and of the "White
Terror" * are dissatisfied, and show it, without being able to impose their
will upon Louis XVIII until 1820.

After the assassination of the Duc de Berry, the 1814 compromise is
threatened: when the chief Minister, De Villèle, has a new Chambre Introuvable adopt the law concerning the *émigrés' milliard*,† he causes a
great deal of concern; the projected law re-establishing primogeniture
ultimately evinces a methodical plan for the gradual restoration of the
Old Regime. The struggle that the liberal minority put up against the
Ultras in the Chamber of Peers, with the Parisian aristocracy, hostile to
De Villèle, close at hand, as well as all the parliamentary battles, had no
national repercussions. They make less noise than, for example, the punitive expeditions during 1815-1817 in the Rhône valley; even the *émigrés'
milliard* law, financed through a conversion of *rentes*, caused only the
Parisian *rentiers* to cry out. And it is still only Paris, the capital, that
closely follows political life. Polignac, with his rashness and his cavalier

---

* The Chambre Introuvable was the nickname Louis XVIII gave to the Chamber
elected in 1815; he was amazed that such a pro-Royalist group could be found. The
"White Terror" refers to a wave of crime in southern France committed by Catholic
Royalists against former supporters of Napoleon and the Republic, as well as rich
Protestants.—Trans.
† The name given by its opponents to the indemnity for the estates the *émigrés* lost.
—Trans.

attitude toward the constitutional arrangements which had hitherto been respected, manages to alert Parisian public opinion and finally to awaken the Parisians who, being outside of the electorate [*pays légal*] due to the *censitaire* system, find in July of 1830, a good opportunity to resume—for several days—their place in political life. The Revolution of the Three Days, skillfully nipped in the bud by Périer, Laffitte, Thiers, and La Fayette, culminates in Louis-Philippe and the bourgeois monarchy, which is as close as possible to the Bourbons, all the while guaranteeing the rebels of the *National* the maintenance of a regime in which the basic conquests of 1789-1791 will not again be questioned: after July, 1830, bourgeois France finally has the king and political system* it desires.

► **BOURGEOIS FRANCE**

Be he a *rentier* (in the days when living off one's *rentes* is still as frequent as it is comfortable), manufacturer, merchant, or banker, the bourgeois who admires himself in the person of Louis-Philippe—that good king garbed in the Tricolor, that friend of the umbrella,† that man so unassuming as to entrust his children to the Collège Henri IV—henceforth has the dominant social position, a position secured not without some trouble, and one which he believes has been due him for a long time. Assuming the economic leadership of the country, he enjoys an unequalled material security: neither the peasants, who are constantly threatened by atmospheric calamities, nor the workers, who are not yet specialists, nor the towns' shopkeepers, who are subjected to the harsh laws of the economic market, have so much security. Only the landed property owners, assured of their rental payments, are in a position that is as favorable—or more so. Consequently, the bourgeois under Louis-Philippe has a good conscience: does he not exercise an economic leadership acquired by virtue of his relentless work, not to mention that of his ancestors? He has, too, the feeling of comprising the brains of his country: the new University‡ following upon the anarchic disorder of the Old Regime is organized for him, in his interest, from the elementary schools of Guizot to the schools in the administrative seats of the educational districts. True, the agitation of eighteenth-century intellectual life has not survived the Revolution, but who complains about it? Finally, in the reign of Louis-Philippe, and with the help of a more skillful king who is directly concerned but no less audacious than his predecessor,

---

* Article 14 of the Charter was amended; hereditary peerages were discontinued.

† Louis-Philippe is often so pictured, identifying himself with the bourgeoisie through his umbrella.—Trans.

‡ The reference here is to the University of France which is not one institution but rather the entire educational system consisting of teachers, professors, inspectors, etc. See below, pp. 439-441, for more details.—Trans.

political life seems to be stabilized, nestled as it is between the hands of this bourgeoisie: the little world of the electorate, narrow-minded, limited, selfish, and not without naïveté; at least this is so until the hard years of 1846-47, when a suddenly serious economic crisis, the power abuses by the July King, and the progress in labor ideas and action all knock simultaneously at the door, and reveal to those who hardly dare believe their eyes, serious discomfort and enormous risks. Guizot, the leading thinker of a generation, is then condemned, perhaps not without some degree of irresponsibility.

While France is extricating herself from the revolutionary wars and finding the tranquillity of peace again, the economic life experiences a falling-off period; thus, the bourgeoisie is not favored as it was in the pleasant days of Napoleon. From 1817 to 1850, the slowing-down of economic activity is striking, compared with the good period in the eighteenth century when foreign trade was increasing from one year to the next. It has increased only thirty per cent from 1815 to 1850. Economists* impute this stagnation to three simultaneous factors: the worldwide scarcity of precious metals heightened, in a country that has just experienced the *assignat,* by an unbounded distrust of paper money; the slowness of technical progress, especially in the sphere of energy—for France, the Industrial Revolution comes in the years between 1850 and 1880; and finally, the weak banking arrangements hindering large enterprises. The experience of the railroads between 1842 and 1848 is cogent in this respect, where speculation and an insufficiency of real means combine their malpractices. The Restoration and the July Monarchy, therefore, were periods of little profit and scanty economic activity; periods when the bourgeoisie were able to establish their economic power, but under the worst conditions: a lack of credit, a lowering of prices, and a continued inadequacy of *rente.* All this comes down to the fact that the national market is of slight importance, and that the bulk of the peasantry is not yet integrated into the trade economy. And, too, the English strides on the industrial and commercial level impose a narrow protectionism forbidding all conquest of foreign markets at a time when the United States and Latin America, lacking everything, turn toward grimy, industrial England.

The economic success of the period springs, then, from commercial capitalism, and not from massive industrialization, which has not yet occurred; banks with some degree of scope—the old ones, Mallet and Perregaux, who continue to direct the Bank of France, and the new, especially James Rothschild, that French branch of an international, family

---

* Today's economists, that is. Contemporary ones are immoderate praisers of the system which will make a great deal of money for England under Queen Victoria: economic liberalism, which today is still confused with political liberalism. The work of Jean-Baptiste Say and others is the apologia for free competition, *laissez faire.*

organization—plunge into a few large operations when the law of 1842 tries to organize French railroad equipment; but they are the exception. And the local or regional banks, which receive few deposits and lend with excessive parsimony and prudence, play a more important role than the reputedly boundless fortunes of the Rothschilds. The surest beneficiaries of these slow movements forward are the merchants and manufacturers: the first ironmasters, unable to supply the demand for the construction of railroad tracks,* since forest furnaces and the old puddling processes are the only ones used. The owners of the textile industry, especially, took advantage of those English inventions which gradually moved onto the Continent—even during the Napoleonic wars. These were adapted to the woolen industries in the north and Normandy, and especially in the cotton industry in Alsace, at Rouen, and at Paris; and finally, there are the silk-makers, who have dozens of skilled workmen and silk-weavers working for them in Croix-Rousse, in outlying suburbs, and in the mountains around Lyon and in the mountainous Vivarais region—price-fixers and paymasters, large-scale merchants, and entrepreneurs—in those silks which, more than ever, are in style among the bourgeoisie. Without any competition, even from England, the Lyon silk industries conduct large concerns, the most prosperous of the period. Finally—although they are more organizers than industrialists, in the modern sense of the term—there are those who direct transportation, such as the mail- and stagecoaches that comb the roads, improving the network set up in the eighteenth century; the thousands of carters who live off this land and river traffic, just before the advent of the railroad, propel that sector of the French economy which unquestionably has made the greatest progress since the Revolution. But the railroad itself, in a state of constant growth, does not as yet affect the economy. Railroads are established with difficulty in regions where the technical mentality has not won out; the opinions of Arago (as late as 1838), of Thiers, and of many others, are proof of this incomprehension. There is the coal-carrying line from Saint-Étienne to Andrézieux (1823) and from Saint-Étienne to Lyon (1827), as well as lines from town to town, which later are laboriously connected, and total 1,860 miles in 1848.

It is only the towns that are making progress, and particularly Paris, which already amasses the population overflow of the French countryside, doubling its population in ten years (from 500,000 to 1,000,000); but this small urban market is enough for those who lead an economic life sheltered from foreign competition. They are sheltered, as well, from governmental intervention in the conduct of their affairs: in 1831, the prefect of the Rhône *département* is repudiated by the government for having threatened the economic freedom of the silk industries by

---

* The production of coal in France reaches 5,000,000 tons in 1848; cast iron, 400,-000 tons.

daring to levy a tax on wages, in the terrible conflict setting Croix-Rousse against Bellecour and the silk-weavers against the employers. With a strict logic in the spirit of the Le Chapelier Law, the bloody Lyon affair illustrates, even better than Guizot's famous "get rich," the mental atmosphere in which the wealth of the bourgeois advances "by work and by thrift."

In only one sphere—land wealth—does this ambition meet an obstacle. But during the Revolution, the landed property of the bourgeois made great strides: those who acquired national property were as often townspeople as peasants, and land remains an investment sought after, often more than money speculation, by whoever has made a tidy little profit. But, face to face with the bourgeois who has some landed property, there is the nobleman, returned from abroad, who has during his ten or twenty years of exile lost his taste for court life; he settles down on his land, whatever remains to him, to develop it, to supervise his farmers, to look after his own good, and to restore a fortune which, in many cases, has been compromised.*

The noble *émigré*, returning in 1814, may find himself next to a new noble of the Empire, or a dignitary of the Revolution or the Empire put on half-pay or granted a premature retirement by 1815—in this way Colonel Bugeaud makes the most of his vast estates in Périgord. We hardly need say that this return to the land, which brings the noble back to the head of his country parish after at least a century and a half of absence, has great social implications: prestige and financial recovery are the fruits of his constant presence. But this restoration of the nobles does not, strictly speaking, threaten the economic supremacy of the bourgeoisie—it merely defines its limits.

During this first half of the nineteenth century, the bourgeoisie retained the intellectual concerns of previous generations: occasionally Voltairian, it is particularly anxious to set up, according to the views of Condorcet and Lakanal, an educational system to form the the foundation of its cultural superiority. Few remain of the Church's educational institutions existing just before the Revolution: some are at death's door, their former *facultés* supplanted by the *grandes écoles* created by the Convention, and by the Napoleonic establishments of higher education. Others are more active: the *collèges* were temporarily replaced by the Écoles Centrales of the Convention—the very active *écoles de département*, open to adults as well as children—then the *lycées* and *collèges*. The Oratorian *collèges* (such as Juilly), objects of the emperor's concern, have even survived the imperial attempt at reorganization. Still,

---

* Balzac is a mine of information about contemporary society, though he is sometimes to be referred to with caution: the spirit of thrift, which is not the capitalistic spirit, is Grandet, etc. In this context, Monsieur de Mortsauf in *Lys dans la Vallée* acts both as a name and as an attitude.

the essential aspect of this new educational system was established with the imperial University in 1808, which was subsequently touched up and polished during the Constitutional Monarchy.

Napoleon's creation of the imperial University in 1808 gave public education an administrative framework that has undergone few changes during a hundred and fifty years: Supervisor in Chief, Board of Directors, Inspectors General, Rectors, Councils, and local inspectors in the educational districts—these are the main cogs of a machine which has long given satisfactory service. Within this framework, the basic institution is secondary education. Undoubtedly the emperor took the former schools of Law, Theology, and Medicine under his wing; but these schools do not yet undergo any major reform. He also added the Facultés des Sciences et Lettres, but at the outset these are mere extensions of the *lycées,* having the same staff and, consequently, very limited objectives. Since, on the other hand, the elementary schools and elementary education are not the object of Napoleon's concern—he abandoned them to the Brothers of the Christian Doctrine—all the innovations of 1808 are directed toward the *lycées,* which are to insure the education of the young ruling class: civil servants and officers, thinks Napoleon; merchants and lawyers, add his contemporaries. The *lycées* are subjected to a military discipline and endowed with Oratorian programs: Latin, Greek, history, rhetoric, and the fundamental principles of the mathematical and physical sciences, that is, of all the natural sciences. The conferring of degrees at the end of these secondary studies is entrusted to higher education. Within this organization, in short, religious orders have no more place, for the State recruits the teachers from the laity. Actually, the diocesan seminaries for educating the clergy continue to exist essentially as secondary institutions in the hands of the Church. Despite local difficulties, the Napoleonic *lycées* were approved by those for whom they were destined: numbering about thirty in 1808 (not counting the *collèges* in the communes which towns can open, if they like and at their own expense, for the upper grades), the *lycées* number a hundred at the end of the Empire,* and their students continue to increase.

In 1815, it became not the imperial but the royal University, the royal *lycées* and *collèges.* And until 1848, an indication of the solidity of the new institution and its favor among the bourgeoisie, the Restoration does not attack its statutes,† at least not in its essential arrangements; although the title and the functions of the Supervisor in Chief of the Uni-

---

* This figure is achieved by a decree in November, 1811. Let it be understood that we are counting only the *lycées* for boys. Napoleon did not take steps for the education of girls, except for daughters of the members of the Legion of Honor.

† Only the Chambre Introuvable even thought of doing so: a law projected in 1817 proposes the pure and simple discontinuation of the University, and a return to the pre-1789 institutions and system. This was one of those propositions which led Louis XVIII to get rid of this Chamber full of Ultras.

versity were the object of modifications on several occasions. However, although the 1808 University had accepted "the precepts of the Catholic religion as the basis of its teaching," the clergy, no longer in possession of an educational monopoly, endeavors to gain control of the University: during the Restoration, the Supervisor in Chief, Regents, and Rectors are often ecclesiastics; during the July Monarchy, many fewer, probably only in reaction to and because of the influence of the Protestant Guizot. The control of the University is the subject of great debates until 1850: the Congregation requests authorization to teach outside of the University; seminaries actively recruit and teach all the young, whether they are future priests or not; Catholic propagandists raise a hue and cry against a University in which the spirit of Voltaire is too widespread. The Church's freedom to teach, an end to the monopoly: such are the great themes—until the Falloux Law.

Nevertheless, like any institution that fills a need, the royal University, closely supervised by ecclesiastical authorities and maintained despite so many attacks, gradually grows stronger. The Facultés des Sciences et Lettres barely survive; as early as 1816 the Restoration discontinued a good number of these, which were only pale continuations of the *lycée* in the administrative seats of educational districts. Only the Sorbonne, renowned for having Guizot and Cousin, and later the Collège de France, with Quinet and Michelet, attract students. The Law Schools meet with more success, but are strictly supervised, so much do public law and the history of governmental institutions appear to be material for sedition. The most prosperous establishments of higher education are the Schools of Medicine, in the days when this field is making a great deal of progress, and when concern for health gains adherents as prescriptions[2] become more and more effective. Yet it is still secondary education which remains the most active part of the University system: small towns set up, at great expense, *collèges* staffed with the necessary faculty, for which they appeal to Paris. The royal *collèges*, especially, are organized with more and more precision: the creation in 1821* of the *agrégés des collèges*, who constitute the professorial ranks; and, in the same year, an educational statute which defines the programs and the length of the philosophy courses, and which controls the passing from one class to the next by examinations. After many ups and downs, the École Normale Supérieure assumes the responsibility in 1830† for educating the professors of the royal *collèges*. These are the

---

* Michelet presented himself at the first session in September, 1821; he passed third in a competitive *lettres* examination (third class and above: a competitive examination in *grammaire* recruited the *agrégés* from the fourth class and below). Michelet was put through tests in philosophy, Greek and Latin literature, and the analysis of old texts.

† A general competition [*Concours général*], established in 1748, among all the *collèges* in France is re-established during the Restoration.

broad, general outlines of present-day secondary education in France; unquestionably the *lycées* of today scarcely resemble the *collèges* of the 1840s—with their black-robed teachers, their courses given mostly in Latin, their preponderance of Classical literature, their absence of modern languages, and their harsh discipline which Jules Vallès finds disgusting, as he does so many characteristics of the period. But the dominant features of the institution, whose solidity and effectiveness is gradually proved, are already adumbrated.

Finally, the July Monarchy completes this structure in 1833 by giving elementary education its first charter. The Guizot Law is simultaneously the fruit of its author's Protestant idealism, and the acknowledgment of necessities which each day become more pressing: the ignorance of the lower classes obstructs their work in factories and workshops, and, in time, this deficiency becomes more perceptible. After 1833, each commune is directed to have a budget for education, and several communes can join together to create a school: teachers, educated by the normal schools in the *départements* and chosen by the municipalities with the aid of the *curé*, must receive a minimum salary, assured them by the school fees and the commune. The teachers are subjected to the control of the clergy and a group of inspectors, who make sure the programs are carried out. The elementary school thus established is neither compulsory nor free, although the municipality can exempt the poor from tuition fees; nor is it secular. Ministers from the various religions can legally teach without having any certificate, and the schoolteachers are subjected to clerical supervision. The law is applied slowly and unenthusiastically in the rural areas, where it appears less necessary than in the cities; and it is applied irregularly, depending upon the prefects' zeal for verifying these items of the local budgets: yet it gradually becomes respected. In 1848, the elementary schools number 50,000 pupils throughout France.* They create a new teaching faculty, one that originates in the lower classes, or very close to them—a source of worry to the rulers of the Second Republic. Thus a new type of rural "bourgeois" comes into being, alongside the notary, the doctor, and the *curé*; one which, little by little, educates a small part of the younger generation. Today the Guizot Law appears as the point of departure for the effort to which Victor Duruy will devote himself during the Empire, as will, in particular, the men of the Third Republic. For the contemporaries of Louis-Philippe, it was nothing more than a generous complement to the more reliable and useful institution of the secondary *collèges*.

.   .   .

---

* Perhaps one per cent of the school-age population: but the children of the bourgeoisie and nobility do not attend the elementary schools—they receive their rudiments at home or in certain *collèges*, in elementary classes, auxiliaries of the secondary classes in the *collège*.

There remains finally the fact that the liberal bourgeoisie found the political instrument of its choice in the system of the constitutional monarchy. The electoral *cens* eliminates any hint of democracy, and if the history of the changes in the electoral law early in the Restoration indicates any one thing, it is certainly that the bourgeoisie's major concern is to remove civic authority from all those who do not have the necessary abilities. The nobility, close to the peasants, are basically more favorable to the little people—of the country at least—than are the urban bourgeoisie. But in its thirty years of practice, the latter has gained something more than the biggest chunk of political leadership of France; the French governmental system, which according to the Charter is constitutional with its ministers responsible to the king alone (Article 13), was actually a parliamentary regime, by virtue of the pressure exercised by its Chambers and the conception inherited from the revolutionary assemblies. Even Royalists like Chateaubriand are by their own admission supporters of ministerial answerability to the Chamber of Deputies; even Villèle, whose every ambition was to restore a socially and politically powerful noble class, behaves like a parliamentary minister: defeated in the elections of 1827, he retires without trying to continue with the support of the Constitution—though it is also true that Charles X is certainly careful not to retain him. In this way, parliamentary rule entered the domain of custom before being proclaimed by a legal text: without a doubt Louis-Philippe, with his party of functionary-deputies, that sacred battalion which assures the perpetuity of Guizot's government from 1840 to 1848, distorted the rules of the parliamentary game and embittered the future supporters of Reform. But its practice is established nonetheless, and the Second Empire (by virtue of official candidacy) and even the conservative 1871 Assembly will submit to it, without argument. Thus the line separating the division of political powers is not exclusively the one laid down by the Charter, to the advantage of those representing France on a *censitaire* basis.

The very sign of this bourgeois satisfaction, and bulwark of this political domination, is the National Guards, restored during the July Monarchy. The obligation to outfit itself and to set aside a certain number of half-days each month for exercises and parades makes the Guards an essentially bourgeois institution, one for which the nobility, the majority of whom are Legitimists, obviously have no use, preferring the "real" army and the navy for their military careers. This civic guard, therefore, is the guard mounted by the conquerors around their chosen regime: something not without its bravery, particularly in its earlier days when poverty and the Republican ideal incite frequent insurrections in Paris and the larger towns. The National Guards in the Saint-Merri cloister and on the Rue Transnonain assure, with merciless vigor, the regime's defense, and it took an economic crisis, the long, listless, haughty ministry of Guizot, and the final scandals to bring about its—partial—release, in February of 1848.

Thus the early-nineteenth-century French bourgeoisie manifests a clear awareness of its leading role in this new society emerged from the long Revolution. Proud of the economic success it has acquired outside of the humble manual work which is no longer its role, and conscious of a material security well above the precarious one of the lower classes, it has a sharpened sense of its intellectual superiority, its culture, and its devotion to its leadership, which is being assumed in France by the totality of the social group. Whatever be its subsequent achievements— the massive fortunes accumulated as early as the Second Empire, through the first Industrial Revolution and the worldly success through the decline of the Faubourg Saint-Germain at the end of the century—the bourgeoisie has perhaps never since had so clear, so naïvely expressed a vision of its collective prestige and its victory over Old France.

XIV

Romantic Rebellions

THE bourgeois France of the early nineteenth century, the France which disintegrates in February, 1848, is a world in the process of regrouping and reorganizing: the new order of things has not entirely dispossessed the old, and the latter remains present, critical and violently hostile; the new order did not, in fact, seek to oust the old one entirely, so great was the prestige of past glories, of the illuminated châteaux. But the long dispute goes on, between the last supporters of tradition—of that regime which cannot be restored—and the newcomers, installed in the best seats, having the generous liberality of those who have vanquished perils, have feared the worst, and who are now sure of their triumph. This long quarrel, still alive and active in 1848, cannot make us forget all those who, in the wings or stage front—still-neglected supernumeraries or forgotten witnesses of yesteryear—are the victims of this regrouping and are preparing new tomorrows: officers on half-pay, left by Waterloo in mid-air; former soldiers of Napoleon's Old Guard, who will not readapt themselves to civilian life; rural day laborers, landless and too often jobless; village and town workers, crushed by [Lassalle's] brazen law of wages which even so cannot keep them from dying of their poverty—so many victims, too numerous and too uncomplaining, faced with those new nobles, those newly-rich who constitute the rejuvenated aristocracy of bourgeois society.

As yet, of course, all these are not articulate: sometimes they are too modest, and also aware of the difficulty of making themselves heard in this country of rhetoricians—but their misfortunes speak for them. Guizot's and Thiers' good conscience is not that of their entire class, but only of a large majority; and one does not need too tender a heart to see and feel all the discord which, with a backhanded blow, dismisses the good-thinkers of this overly reasonable world. The sadness during the days of peace, when that peace was bought with so many repudiations and treacheries, is a taste the French are not fond of, as they have recently shown again. No more do they like a sordid economy, or the hypocritical utilization of Providence for the ends of social submissiveness: so many bourgeois virtues found only admirers, and the young students hurling themselves against the barricades in July, 1830, are in revolt against the prudence and the passivity of older generations—the unreasonable students at the École Polytechnique will get themselves killed in the Faubourg Saint-Antoine, at a time when a beautiful career awaits them.

In the years between 1815 and 1848, France is not stupid: it is stifling. Those great men, the "Doctrinaires" of the *Canapé,** or the scheming prince of the Palais-Royal, are too skillful logicians to be lacking the systematic spirit. But opposite them stand rebel sons, the heirs of the Revolutionary giants; without scruples, and soon without caution, they look at the world and their contemporaries out of different eyes: they see the oppression of freedom in Greece, in Poland, and doubtless in France, see the dispossessed of this land, those picked as victims by an implacable class, those who deserve assistance and brotherhood. Abandoning the fine rationalizations concerning individual progress and enrichment through domestic and professional virtues, some call for pity, others for rebellion: always, these are cries from the heart, from these men for whom the imagination creates a new and better world. Hardly established in the world the Revolution has created, they already dream of going farther, trying out ten or twenty different paths. Gentle dreamers (but not always gentle in those days when even literature is in battle dress, from *Hernani* to *Marion Delorme*), they are present in February, 1848, and nourish the Second Republic with their noble plans, and their anticipations, even bolder than those of 1794: time has passed, social structures become renewed, and already the words "socialist" and "communist" have entered daily speech. A fruit of circumstance, a permanent state of mind, Romanticism is a great period in contemporary France—one that still leaves its mark on the civilization of today.

---

* Under the Restoration, the "Doctrinaires" were a group headed by Guizot who wanted to elevate the happy mean, the *juste milieu*, as a political ideal between the extremes of divine right and the people as sovereign. Their group was so small that it was said they could meet on a sofa.—Trans.

► **THE OTHER SIDE OF THE PICTURE: THE DESTITUTION OF BOURGEOIS FRANCE**

It is possible to take two measures against this greater or lesser destitution: for many young people, and for the less young who are veterans of the Napoleonic period, the air of *censitaire* France is unbreathable. There is, on the one hand, the occupation, then the nostalgic evocation of the great years, clumsily revived by Louis-Philippe's government by the bringing home of Napoleon's ashes and that interminable French and European peace; beyond that, the "White Terror" and the great plans of De Villèle, the pressure of clerical domination: the Congregation, people say, inspires a "Catholic policy" and—according to one's viewpoint—suggests or orders. In the Congregation's terms, this is the advance of a clericalism which very quickly found its antidote, which is the other side of the picture. And to complete it, there is the claustrophobia of all those who refuse to believe that the history of France, from Clovis to 1789, was destined to fulfill itself in the monarchy of Louis-Philippe. But, more deeply, this discontentment feeds on an economic uneasiness, which covers the entire period, until the years just before 1848 and a crisis which takes the bankers' and industrialists' prudence into account, and, above all, explains the real and profound poverty from which so many Frenchmen die each year—of hunger, of cold, and of that dreaded consumption which causes so much havoc, even in the best-protected social classes: working-class poverty which disgusted so many observers, not just the sentimental, like Villermé, or the lyrical, like Victor Hugo. There is also poverty among the still unstable rural population, among the vile multitude of day laborers who flee to the more active and accessible towns. For all those who submit to and suffer from the terrible realities of the years between 1815 and 1848, bourgeois France cannot have a good conscience: so many revolts, so many refusals, haughty or pitiable, dominate those sad sights, like the cold and damp *courettes* in Lille, and the parodic picture of Charles X's coronation, as ridiculed by Béranger.*

The "defeats of 1815" weighed heavily upon a long generation: Waterloo, and the betrayal; the occupation of a good half of the nation by Cossacks, Austrians, and Prussians; and the return, for the second time, of a king in baggage wagons from abroad—so many realities could not help but strike the imagination. The *émigrés*, returned from their new escapade on the banks of the Rhine or else come out of their châteaux, also bear the responsibility for making the shame more ap-

---

* *Le Sacre de Charles le Simple* in which anticlericalism, hate for the *émigrés*, and scorn for the new king all have their place. The piece is well known, and justly so: it is one of the most typical works of the Republican poet, the "Man-Nation."

preciable. To the humiliation of a defeat which finally ends a series of sensational victories and which imposes, by the terms of the second Treaty of Paris, a loss of territory, is linked that sometimes bloody arrogance of the Royalists, who triumph in the distress.* Furthermore, the occupation left some bad memories which long reminded people of 1815-1818, when the Allies, the infantry, awaited the payment of their war indemnity: thus Russian troops in Alsace passed into the popular and juvenile folklore to convey the werewolf and other diabolical myths. Once the first excitement was over, the year of the Hundred Days continued to represent, for many Frenchmen, the end of a great period, less by the very conciliatory policy of the French rulers than by the evocation of the Napoleonic era, which was renewed and augmented in thousands of ways: first by the veterans of Napoleon's Old Guards, whose officers were placed on half-pay, to the advantage of the Royalists making up the cadres of the new army established after 1818 by Gouvion Saint-Cyr. Both soldiers and officers, unable to return to their battle-fields or to their trade, and in no way anxious to resume the civilian life which they so often scorned, were the eager minstrels of their past exploits. Wounds, citations, and imperial orders of the day, decorations which the monarchic government dared not strip off, were the points of reference, the way stations in the fireside tales told in the evenings in the most remote villages. "Long live the Emperor," a seditious cry in the early years of the Restoration, reverberated first in the rural assemblies, where the old trooper of the revolutionary armies, who has seen Milan, Vienna, Berlin, or Moscow, cannot restrain himself from recounting his own exploits. Who, then, would not have thought, with respect to the Little Corporal, of the comparison with pot-bellied Louis XVIII, or Louis-Philippe and his umbrella? And who would then have been able not to let a disdainful phrase escape concerning the silenced weapons, a silence continuing even beyond the opportunity provided by the 1840 eastern affair? But 1840 is a good sign: no one listens to Lamartine and his *Marseillaise de la Paix*, while Musset's *Rhin allemand* is greatly applauded.

Very close to the veterans who, forgotten in their distress, have returned from imperial wars, from Berezina and from Leipzig, from Montmirail and from Waterloo, the color and design of the cheap prints, known as *images d'Épinal*, spread far and wide the memory of the great moments that inspired the first twenty years of the century. The exile of St. Helena, tormented by his jailers (this was known very early),

---

* Certainly most Frenchmen, especially at the time, would not have experienced much pain from the bruise of Waterloo, nor even the loss of Landau, Sarrebruck, or Savoie. But the *émigrés'* songs of victory rang in the ears of many people as painfully as did the invocation of the "divine surprise" in 1940, after a similar disaster. The psychological context explains the reverberations of 1815.

expanded upon by Victor Hugo and Béranger, those resonant echoes of the popular fervor, which was shifting from the platitudes of the present to the extremely fresh grandeurs and purified glories of the past, contributed in no small measure to help the contemporaries of Louis XVIII, as of Louis-Philippe, to put their finger on the dull monotony of their existence. Stendhal, who had his share of the past glory and published a life of Napoleon, made his greatest heroes, Julien and Fabrice, admirers of Napoleon: the latter is overwhelmed with once having been able to approach the great man, the former, closer to the mentality that owes its dejection to the turning point of 1814-1815, cannot be consoled for having been born too late, and for not having been able to live during this wonderful time when a carpenter's sons were able, after a few campaigns, to become Maréchaux of France.

But precisely here lies the other aspect of this daily tragedy: great actions, and the opportunity to roam over Europe other than as a tourist, are missing. There are no brilliant destinies; rather, there are little second-rate careers for which one has to wait—and the young people trudge along behind a trained personnel overworked by Louis-Philippe's prudent policy. Even and especially, one must pay court to a power which, for twenty years, has no longer been important in political or administrative life—the clergy. During the Restoration, at least, since during the July Monarchy the ascendancy was less clear-cut, this Catholic clergy, strengthened by the backing of public powers and zealous in demonstrating its devotion to the traditional regime, controlled, stimulated, or held back careers, made and unmade reputations, boldly and often tactlessly ruled good society—so much so that contemporaries, Voltairians or not, attributed this almost visible influence to a specialized sect within the ecclesiastical organization: the Congregation which, in the minds of its critics, retained much of the former Company of the Blessed Sacrament,* and with still greater effectiveness. In its effort to regain the positions lost in the turmoil—convents to restock, dioceses to revive—the French clergy, as if established in a missionary country where only the support of the civil authorities is certain, doubtless multiplied the efforts with mixed feelings. Hence this impression, sometimes even to the eyes of the last of the Gallicans, of control, of heavy, omnipresent surveillance.

The events of 1825-1827 confirmed these fears: the vote on the Sacrilege Law† by the Chamber of Deputies, the coronation of Charles X,

---

* For the Company of the Blessed Sacrament, see above pp. 305-306. Bertier de Sauvigny, in a recent thesis, has shown that, if there never existed a "congregation" under that name and with those evil goals, a secret association formed as early as the Empire, under the name of "Chevaliers de la Foi," paved the way for the Restoration, setting itself the task of consolidating it, through effective control of the personnel necessary to the regime.

† A law invoking the death penalty for sacrilege.—Trans.

restoring past solemnities* in every detail, finally and particularly, the
expiatory ceremony for the death of Louis XVI, held on January 21,
1827 in the presence of four thousand priests who stretched for four
hours in an endless procession through Paris, simultaneously expressing
Charles X's willingness to bring about a more complete restoration than
had Louis XVIII, and the Church's support of this undertaking. This
explains at least partially why anticlerical deism is no longer confined to
the bourgeoisie, as in the eighteenth century, but has also won over the
lower, urban classes. The misdeeds whose spread the Sacrilege Law is to
repress, were but brigandage; the sack in 1831, at Saint-Germain l'Auxerrois, of the bishop's palace calls attention to this new lower-class anticlericalism, as violent as it is irrational. The Parisian demonstration, set
off by a Legitimist provocation—the mass celebrated in memory of the
Duc de Berry assassinated in February of 1820—is a simple explosion of
impatience, short-lived and not immediately significant; but it is indicative: the insults to which priests frequently were subjected in the streets
of Paris during the same period locates its meaning exactly. During the
July Monarchy, whose political personnel is recruited from bourgeois of
Voltairian outlook, the Church's influence certainly seems to be receding, or at least is less visible, more especially as, on the educational level,
the Church must struggle for "freedom of education" against the governments of Louis-Philippe. Moreover, from 1830 to 1848, it is material
poverty, more than anything else, whose force is being felt.

The slow capitalistic outfitting of France during the *censitaire* monarchy is accomplished at the expense of a long generation of little people
who can do nothing but bend their backs and submit passively to the
hardest times that rural day laborers and urban workers have known for
a good hundred years. The progress made by machines, banks, and textiles, plus the slight development of metallurgy, coming in a period of
economic listlessness, enables the bourgeoisie to reap some fine profits:
for example, the achievements at Le Creusot and Fourchambault, and
those of the Koechlin family in Mulhouse and the De Wendels in the
Lorraine. But they have a terrible counterpart: the unbridled human
waste of a France that believes herself to be overpopulated.

Manufacturers and landed property owners constitute the overwhelming majority of the deputies during this period and, when it comes to
questions of tariffs and protection, they suffer no ideological divergencies:

---

* The coronation of Charles X was a reconstruction of seventeenth-century ceremonies: the same gestures, the same words, the same flights of doves through the cathedral. Charles X also claims his right to touch those with scrofula: a few miserable
people appeared—nothing like the crowds of years gone by. The more discriminating
Louis XVIII had renounced this consecration, and Napoleon, in 1804, was wise
enough to revise the whole ceremony, eliminating what seemed antiquated. Charles X
was not sensitive to such things.

following and accentuating the policy of Napoleon I, they increase the number of laws, particularly between 1820 and 1822, which establish the French market behind the protection of a comfortable tariff wall; not shrinking from total protectionism, they "protect" iron, silk, beet sugar, and wheat against foreign competition. The greater availability of Jacquard looms and the increase of rural silk looms, extending as far as the Isère, unquestionably enable the silk factories in Lyon to increase their output and to produce cheaper silk; nor do the strides made by this industry remain confined to the small consumption of national buyers. In scarcely different terms, the example would be applicable to the cotton industry, which particularly advances under the July Monarchy.

Louis-Philippe's public works, especially canals and the railroads' progress after 1842, introduce the only dynamic elements into this economy which has accomplished a gradual and cautious transition in the direction of the Industrial Revolution whose example is offered by England. But here again, be they forge owners or bankers, men hardly see further than their own businesses, their towns or their districts: the former are unable to supply the demand for cast iron and steel, yet keep duties up on English steel and rejoice in the growth of their profits; the latter help, and let themselves be taken by, an unrestrained speculation which, because of the absence of large banking concerns, can be neither channeled nor organized until the 1846-47 catastrophe: the bankruptcies of the earliest railroad companies, when banks and moneylenders are unredeemably ruined.

Louis-Philippe's last two years are further proof of this economic maladjustment: agricultural life, whose progress is so slow* in most regions, commands the whole of the economy, as in the eighteenth century. The crisis of 1846-47 is the last of this type: an Old Regime, as it were, when as early as 1846 bad crops, common to all Europe—add to this the potato blight and the great floods of the Loire, Saône, and Rhône in 1847—have repercussions throughout all economic life. The shortage of food, the high price of wheat in starving towns and the riots against the grain transporters: this is the lot of 1846 and 1847, years that bring along with them an industrial and commercial crisis, unemployment, and an even graver urban poverty which had no small effect on the events of February, 1848.

The difficulties of the urban lower classes are the best-known, yet they should not be separated from the rural poverty, for the link between the two is very strong. Agricultural day laborers and landless *métayers*, who have a hard time making a living, leave rural areas, attracted by the fac-

---

* The continuation of burning the land in all the old *massifs* would bear this point out. Similarly the statement, in an 1830 agronomy course, that yields of wheat are seven for one; it might be a slight increase over the eighteenth century (five for one, six for one).

tories, by their salaries, which seem enormous to these peasants who are unaccustomed to handling more than a few dozen francs per year.* And the overpopulated land scarcely detains them, particularly the farmers and *métayers*, who undergo conditions that grow harsher with each lease renewal; the large landowner is no less "harsh" than the manufacturer, and for the same reason—manpower is plentiful. But the rural poverty is less visible and less striking than that of the towns, where the first generation of these *Déracinés* huddle together. In Croix-Rousse in Lyon, on the Rue des Fumiers in Nantes, and in the Saint-Sauveur district of Lille (in 1828, Lille has 20,000 indigents in a population of 80,000), the workers of the large newborn industries lead a life of suffering, which horrifies all those who have occasion to observe it. The abundance of manpower, the bitterness of a competition exasperated by the mediocrity of the consumers' market, and the "economic" mentality of the ruling class suffice to explain the dreadful working conditions rampant wherever industry is renewed and transformed: unhealthy workshops without maintenance of hygiene, and, especially, low wages—not even enough for the worker to feed his family. In the textile industry, women and children work, adding their earnings to those of the head of the family, without so much as achieving comfort: for women are always paid less, only half as much, as often as not; and children receive a few *sous* for their fifteen-hour day. Every eyewitness of this working-class poverty recognizes the lamentable condition; even those most favorable to the economic regime and most optimistic, like Adolphe Blanqui, who believe they see hygienic improvement in the factories at the end of this period, cannot conceal their feelings about "this horrible existence:" †️ one involving thirteen-to-fifteen-hour working days, according to the season, no weekly rest periods, no saints'-days off as in the old days, and often, in the textile industries, unhealthy work. Children participate as young as four or five, turning indigo mills, gathering up the empty bobbins under the machines, watching automatic looms; families huddle together in cellars having neither floorboards, furniture, nor heat; they sleep on straw, never change their clothes, and are sapped by the alcohol-

---

* The worst of the cotton mills offer its workers from six to seven hundred francs a year—just enough not to die of hunger. Yet these few francs per day seem the end of the world to someone who is not in the habit of reckoning the expense of food and lodging.

† Let us quote at least these few lines from Adolphe Blanqui, a liberal economist, who cannot be suspected of mawkishness concerning the children in the *courettes* of Lille: "As one goes into the precinct of the *courettes*, a strange populace of sickly, hunchbacked, deformed children, pale and dirty looking, beset visitors and ask them for money. Most of these unfortunates are almost naked and the best of the lot are covered with tatters. But these, at least, breathe fresh air; it is only in the depths of the cellars that one can judge the torment of those who are unable to go out because of their age or the severity of the weather. More often than not, they sleep on the bare ground, on fragments of colza chaff, on the haulm of dried potatoes, on sand, or even on the fragments they have painfully gathered from the day's work." [1]

ism of the tavern-sanctuaries, ruined physically by consumption, and overrun with children, three-fourths of whom will not reach adulthood. Thousands of workers in Lille, Rouen, Nantes, and Mulhouse live in this manner. Undoubtedly not all of the towns are so characterized: in the Norman woolen industry, wages are higher and the workers are spared hovels and undernourishment; it is the same in Sedan or Reims. But even there, where more sufficient wages permit a decent life, the worker is not protected from emergencies, unemployment, or disease —which everywhere causes atrocious misery, mendicancy, and such mortality crises as the cholera epidemic of 1832.

Under the July Monarchy, however, subsequent to Villermé's investigation, the government and the Chamber of Deputies become aroused over the problem of child labor; not without scruples, since state intervention in this realm runs counter to the principles that inspired the 1791 Le Chapelier Law, that is, the employer's freedom within his business: his total independence. After much debate, a law passed in 1841 forbids the employment of children under eight, limits to eight hours the work of children from eight to twelve, and to twelve hours those from twelve to sixteen. The law was not applied, for it is applicable only in concerns employing more than twenty workers, and its control is in the employer's hands: the inspectors are indulgent, former manufacturers. The value of the 1841 law lies especially in its being a precedent, causing the admission of state intervention in matters of labor legislation.*

For the manufacturing worker, "to live is not to die," according to Guépin's phrase. Abandoned to his lot—and at his employer's mercy because of the 1791 law forbidding all strikes (the strike federations which initiate the right-to-work principle) and by the institution of workbooks [*livrets*],† an Imperial creation no one dreams of discontinuing—the worker can be only patient and resigned. It is not at all amazing that the silk weavers in Lyon, who have long been poorly paid but are particularly affected by the crisis of 1830, should revolt in November of 1831 against the silk manufacturers who, refusing arbitration (which is officially illegal) and the wage scales of the Prefect of the Rhône, claim their right to continue paying their starvation wages: the rebellion in Lyon on November 22-23, 1831, launched to the cries of "Live free working or die fighting," is certainly a hunger rebellion, but also the first major demonstration of revolt, the first violent demand for its right to live on the part of a new class which, in this unnamable poverty, has gained awareness of itself.[2]

---

* Several other generous proposals met with even less success, in particular, the limitation of the length of the female working day and regulation of sanitary matters in workshops.

† These *livrets* were devised to maintain a strict control over the worker's movements and conduct. The worker had to give his *livret* to his employer as soon as he was hired; the latter maintained a record of the worker's behavior in them.—Trans.

► **THEMES AND STYLES OF FRENCH ROMANTICISM**

From this oppressive, sad, and unfeeling world, the victims—becoming, more than impotent victims, beings sensitive to injustice or depravity—seek escape. Against the saccharine and sometimes haughty satisfaction of the new masters, vehement protests are raised, as passionate as the bourgeois triumph is reasoned and reasonable; exceeding the framework of social revolt or of conflict between generations, the cry in early-nineteenth-century France is Romantic. And it goes beyond the superficial game of *épater le bourgeois* (although people are not above playing this game; Gautier wears a red vest to the theater, where black evening dress is *de rigueur*), as well as beyond a national manifestation of a European movement. Yet foreign influences, like the example of the German *Sturm und Drang* and the very literary appeal of Ossian, do not count more for us than the details of *la bataille d'Hernani*, or the great parallel of Racine and Shakespeare. Romanticism is certainly an international literary movement, almost without national boundaries; one rich in correspondences and counterparts.[3] Yet it is an attitude of mind, a reaction against rationalism in the name of sensibility and religious faith—its continuations, one might say, its rebounds, into the twentieth century are proof enough of that. From the early lyrics of Lamartine and Hugo in 1820, to shortly before the Revolution of 1848, everything in France that lives a burning existence seeks a new way and is stamped with the seal of Romanticism: battles in *salons* or theaters, but particularly principles and values, come out of this general revision of living styles, at the very moment the beginnings of the Industrial Revolution displace men, overpopulate towns, and lay the groundwork for a new human conditioning. As often happens, the artist-priest predicts and heralds, with no knowledge other than an instinct of human Becoming, particularly vigorous among the Romantics—those men of history, those founders of history as we understand it today.

Heirs of the Rousseau of the *Nouvelle Héloïse* and the *Confessions*, and of Chateaubriand's self-identification in *René*, these turbulent writers of prose and poetry owe their success less to the rhythmical and colorful evocations of savage nature, than to their discoveries: they are the prophets who tell of the evil—or rather of the evils—from which this century suffers, growing up in the shadow of the Revolution and of Napoleon, having put hope behind, not before it.* Perhaps physically sick, they are certainly affected to the point of dying of it, as did Nerval in 1855. They are affected at least to the point of not hiding their con-

---

* *Le Mémorial de Sainte-Hélène*, written by the Comte de Las Cases and published in 1823, is read passionately by young people twenty years later.

fusion and their miseries: a poet distraught in a world where he has no place, says Vigny of Chatterton, and Musset constantly repeats it, as does Baudelaire later on in *L'Art romantique.* Everything seeks flight and retreat, before thinking about changing the world, while some of them, at least, let themselves attempt this after the outburst in 1830: Lamartine and especially Victor Hugo, who carves out a career through the Third Republic; they cannot avoid feeling that the conquest of happiness, that dream dwelt upon constantly by Stendhal, becomes more difficult in a France where they are stifling, they who are the well-bred sons of good bourgeois families, educated as much as possible in that period. By chance some are prizewinners of the Concours Général;* they turn down the bleak, quotidian life and sad careers of honors at the price of baseness and villainy. Instead, they serenade their muses with plaintive tunes, they have women whom they love along the edge of a deserted lake; they admire and visit, at least in the imagination, foreign countries, and spiritedly conjure up bygone days—what sanctuaries, what substitutes for this misery, this sorrowful living in such a sad time. But the retreat into an ivory tower, into a shepherd's cottage lost on some high pasture, or simply into an old, inherited family house at Milly, Nohant, or Othis—what a challenge, what an impossible flight. Each spring brings so many friends to Nohant, and Othis is too close to the main road to Flanders and Paris.

Moreover, despair does not win out. Balzac, who wants to work for the Monarchy and Religion—those two beacons which, he thinks, light his work—never tires of evoking this provincial life, declared by everyone to be sadder than the Parisian life: the country doctors, peasants, nobles, *émigrés*, and merchants in Tours. Others fight: Romantic drama, Romantic poetry, Romantic art, so many horses spurred to announce and establish a new esthetic which is to destroy outdated classicism, worn out after a long century of use and an uncontested reign. In 1830, Hernani won the great "battle" of the Romantic era. But, beyond these formal debates, there are the disputes over the three unities, and the virtues of drama and tragedy—controversies which sometimes get bogged down in literary game-playing†—the Romantics again pay homage to sentiment and sensibility, whose rights they assert in the face of *la raison raisonnante.* This new quarrel between the old and the new, more shattering and pathetic than the earlier one by virtue of its audience and the emotions aroused at least in Paris, is a reaction against that movement which had been going on for three centuries, the advances of the rationalist Enlightenment: the Romantic heart, Jean-

---

* Notably Musset, Hugo, Michelet.

† To be sure, style and forms are important. But excesses are commingled with them, to the point of causing us to forget the fact that Musset writes his comedies and proverbs in a language as pellucid as Marivaux's or La Fontaine's.

Jacques' and the young Chateaubriand's in the days of the *Génie du christianisme*, is simultaneously the source of inspiration and of knowledge; it lies in the breast of a religiosity asserting itself, not without some degree of arrogance, against the semi-official Voltairianism of the 1830s. The invocation of the Muses, the appeal to an inner being (in Nerval and Baudelaire), and the participation in a supernatural life—again an evasion—placed under the sign of poetic magic or infernal invocations (Nerval at twenty translates Goethe's *Faust*) are some of the expressions, among many others, of the primacy of feeling over intellect.* Genius beats its breast, and the Romantic school has no teachers but the inspiration of places and moments, nor has it any need for philosophy† to teach the gifts of Nature and the magic of poetry. After all, the Romantic school is a school because it refuses rational thought; in the name of this refusal, it discovers its models and masters in the past (from Shakespeare to Calderon) and at a distance (from Scotland to Germany) as was so well understood by Madame de Staël. These models and masters have this in common: they have escaped, willingly or not, the intellectualistic ascendency that marks Modern Times. "Daughters of fire," hobgoblins, and genii; prophecies and celestial whispers: the inspiration of Romanticism, the vision of this world and of the beyond, the incantatory revelation—these are the children of the mad women in the house, the Imagination.

Sweeping along in their wake Géricault and Delacroix in pursuit of predestined lands, Greece and the Orient, and in search of great human adventures and tragic features (*Radeau de la Méduse, Liberté guidant le Peuple*), the Romantics find along their way the plastic arts which, with them, abandon Roman traditions, repudiating them, as the alexandrine, in the same movement. But they also encounter music which, speaking more to the senses than to the mind, would have been the prime Romantic art, had Musset or Vigny been gifted with the ability to create symphonic compositions.‡ Despite Berlioz—that life and work in which the *Damnation of Faust* and the *Roman Carnival Overture* attest the existence of a French Romantic music—it is in Germany that Romanticism, on this level, finds its fulfillment: there are Beethoven, Liszt, Schumann, Mendelssohn, and particularly Wagner; and there is,

---

* A good gauge of this triumph of emotions and the moral confusion it represents around 1830 would doubtless be an enumeration of the character-types glorified in the Romantic novel: adventurers, financiers, convicts, and prostitutes.

† At least it has not found the philosophy for its day: neither Victor Cousin nor, later, Auguste Comte are in agreement with Romanticism, in the same way we can note a profound agreement linking Corneille and Boileau to Descartes. Romantic philosophy came later, at least in France, with Bergson—as opposed to the way things were in Germany.

‡ The ear that seems to have been most attuned to music was that of Gérard de Nerval, who delightedly devoted months to gathering words and music from the folksongs of the Ile-de-France, in "his" region of Ermenonville-Chaalis in the Valois.

as well, the incomparable advance of musical studies throughout all the German towns. In all events, Chopin and Wagner come to Paris, and the lyric theater, opera, and comic opera make particular progress: Rossini and the *Barber of Seville*, and, a little later, Meyerbeer, who arouses the enthusiasm of the Parisians just as Lamartine and Victor Hugo are triumphing. Did not the triumphs of theater music, continued during the entire century by Gounod, Bizet, and Delibes, prepare the way for the advances of symphonic music? Yes, insofar as these triumphs maintained the taste for an art still considered minor, an "accomplishment," which keeps builders like Pleyel and Érard busy at turning out the practice pianos which, for a century, will remain an indispensable piece of furniture in bourgeois houses. Romanticism and music are as inseparable as Romanticism and sentiment: but in this area, it is the inheritance of French Romanticism which bears witness, rather than the period itself.

Romantic man—if this type ever became fully incarnated, from Stendhal to Baudelaire—is prompted by the need to see on a large scale, not to be bogged down in the banal quotidian surrounding him. This greatness of soul, which remained for some years a simple and sometimes naïve exaltation of the self, an individualism extended into the dark colors of the most violent emotions and fantastic visions,* feeding upon the evocation of heroes (whether authentic or magnified was of small import)—this greatness of soul has its foundation in generosity. Especially after 1830, after that brief blaze of hope when, in Paris, Brussels, Italy, and Poland, freedom seems to be revived, the Romantic no longer dreams of his own destiny, but of oppressed nations for whom the pursuit of happiness takes place through a revolution, a liberation. The Polish—like the Greeks a while before, for whom Delacroix and Victor Hugo were moved and for whom Byron gave his life—become their brothers and the objects of a new compassion. Monarchists yesterday by virtue of an unexpected conformism, and Republicans as the hour of the Second Republic approaches, the sudden change has nothing to do with the politicians' retractions of the 1790s: it is a discovery of their day, a new awareness full of understanding for aspirations which, to a certain extent, are their own. Becoming aware that the burden of the 1814-15 victories is no less heavy for the Germans, Poles, and Italians than that of the bitter defeats is for the French in their very acceptance, they confuse those causes which, indeed, are extremely diverse.

Moreover, with them, literature opens not only onto the Greek victims of the Turks, the Polish victims of the Russians and Prussians, and Silvio Pellico's compatriots, the victims of Metternich, but above all onto an

---

* Though, in this realm, French Romantics had not the fertile imagination of their colleagues across the Rhine, from Hölderlin to Novalis.

entity which eighteenth-century literature, as engaged in politics as it was, had ignored: the people. The people, who had recently been the Fourth Estate, whose virtues—revealed in July, 1830, and even more in the horrors of the Rue Transnonain—and whose place are gradually recognized, particularly by the novel, which lends itself better than any other literary genre to this rehabilitation which is actually a revelation. Humble Parisians occupy the main place in *Notre-Dame de Paris*, and 1848 had not yet arrived when Victor Hugo had written—if not published—his *Misères*, that sketch for the *Misérables*, in which a Paris full of humble people, full of the frustration of great hopes and Republican undertakings, finds a place. But Victor Hugo is not the only one. During the same period, George Sand admires the peasants of the Berry, collects legends and traditions, and brings them to life in her *Maîtres sonneurs* and in many talkative pastoral novels, in the days before she flounders in the socializing harangue of *Compagnon du tour de France*; and especially there is Michelet, who does not have to discover those things that surrounded him ever since his childhood, and who, in 1847, writes a long profession of faith in the margin of his historical work, *Le Peuple*: the lower classes, ignored and scorned, have been returned to national and literary life—at least as objects of study or sources of inspiration. Undoubtedly the Romantics arrive late, at the same time living conditions impose upon the proletariat the impression, which becomes increasingly strong as the years pass, that they constitute an alien and reviled world within the nation. The Romantics, at least, took the only step attempted in their period toward avoiding this alienation.*

Dressing the lower classes in the virtues which neither the bourgeois nor the old aristocracy practice any more—abnegation, charity, and so forth—the Romantics are the brothers, in their generosity, of the socialist thinkers. The latter, in the same years between 1830 and 1848, build the ideal City, which is to place the narrow and unjust world where they live—with a touch of propheticism in the later Hugo, in Michelet throughout his works—and to foreshadow the growing role of the rural masses which will upset the early Industrial Revolution now sketching itself out. A beautiful curve leads from the great lyrics of the 1820s— greedy for beautiful emotions and enamored of "egocentrism," crystallized in their own being—to the social involvement and vision of the 1840s, no longer prophesying the fate of Elvire† but about that of the

---

* In part, Victor Hugo owes his lasting popularity to this sympathy for the poverty-stricken of his day: his romanticized work is always successfully republished. But he also owes this favor to the *Châtiments*, and to his Republican period, when he is emphatically anticlerical and when for years he demands the amnesty of the Communards; perhaps even finally to the deifying funeral in 1885 which left such lasting memories with the Parisians.

† Lamartine used this pseudonym to stand for two of his beloveds—indeed in the nineteenth century "Elvire" and "beloved" were synonymous—a Neapolitan girl, Graziella, and Madame Julie Charles.—Trans.

Poor People, finding in this human understanding the consolation, cried out for by so many frustrations.

Thus, too, the entire generation's endless passion for history can be understood. Some might say it is evasion, but that is not enough; doubtless the Middle Ages intrigues them, as does the East (in which so many of them travel, from Chateaubriand to Nerval), creature of a literary tourist boom that is still going on. But in this mysterious, sunbathed East, they rediscover the Greece of the hetaerae and the gloomy revolutions, and not the antique fragments of the Parthenon or of the Age of Pericles: the reaction against classicism takes at least this direction. The only exception is Renan, later and not without reservations. Similarly, in the re-examincd Middle Ages or the seventeenth century, history itself is a new form of thought: in place of genealogies, kings classified according to lineage, and compilations of heroic memoirs, what a revision everyone works at! There is not a Romantic poet without a work to his credit in which history is more than a pretext,* being relentless toward the seventeenth century whose reputation is too beautiful, and especially toward Richelieu, that disgraceful enemy of all freedom (Cinq-Mars, Marion Delorme). They apply their loveliest colors to the Middle Ages of the Burgraves and Jeanne d'Arc, and finally devote themselves to the Revolution, from the Girondins to Napoleon. Nor can we ignore the prolific talent of Alexandre Dumas who romanticizes the sixteenth century with the same facility as he does the Revolutionary period, in his *feuilleton* style that even today keeps young girls up into the wee small hours.

From this orgy of historic literature emerge the works of the historians; never was a period in French life so rich with these patient, daring artisans of the past. This period established history—if it be true that previous work weighs lightly compared with the output of these years, and, if it be true as well that, after Guizot and Thiers, Thierry and Quinet and Michelet, the passion for history did not cease to dwell in a number of French breasts: histories of the Revolution, histories of France, histories of European civilization. Talented journalists like Thiers and professors like Guizot and Michelet, particularly devoted to the history of revolutions, publish texts at the same time they write and pay homage to national histories. What Madame de Staël had begun in Napoleon's day, with *De l'Allemagne*, is continued and expanded thirty years later. Giving the educated public a taste for history, and offering it as well continuous stories, sometimes grandiloquent, sometimes crammed with battles like Thiers' *Histoire du Consulat et de l'Empire*, the historians, in their own manner and with uneven success (but even Lamartine's long, flowing history in 1847 sold magnificently), forge the

---

* Except Musset: who is not void of an historical sense, and has to his credit the *Rhin allemand*.

historical nation: that entity, that "person," as even Michelet says, whose life is that of all those who compose it. Guizot also discovers the history of the English Revolution; but the French one has more enthusiasts.

But within this vast historical output, devoted to recounting in a sustained and sometimes turgid narrative the recent events of which many expect a renewal, Michelet dominates from on high, with all his visionary genius which senses and writes the history of France with the enthusiasm of a discoverer, opening the ways to a new science. Bold in his hypotheses, quick to compare disparate facts, always rich with admiration before human work—be it of Jeanne d'Arc or the Revolution— Michelet paints for his contemporaries the most suggestive history of France imaginable. For him, history is a resurrection of the past which he lives ardently, without omitting a thing, insistent upon a total restoration. Misled at the end, when he writes *Les Jésuites* and *La Femme*, when he retouches and cuts his work, in a direction soon to be illuminated by the forthcoming publication of his *Journal*, Michelet nonetheless furnishes his contemporaries with the idea that France is a work of art whose poorly known, poorly sensed riches must be learned and loved. He gives a sense of direction to historical work and research; he reveals to those surrounding it, amazed at recognizing themselves, French temperaments, milieux, and periods. Because he is a great traveler, he knows France: he inserted in his *Histoire de la France* a *Tableau de la France* which one cannot abstain from quoting, so evocative is its every line of provincial psychological landscapes. Thus this description of the people in Auvergne:

> Burdened, like those in the Limousin, with I know not how many dull and inelegant habits, one would say a southern breed shivering in a northern wind, as it confined and hardened under that foreign sky. In vain they emigrate from the mountains each year; they bring back some money, but few ideas. And yet there is a real strength in this breed of men, a bitter vigor; tart perhaps, but perennial as the grass in the Cantal. . . .

Or again, of Flemish churches:

> These churches, which are kept up, scrubbed and adorned like a Flemish house, glisten with cleanliness and wealth in the splendor of their brass ornaments and in their abundance of white and black marble. They are cleaner than Italian churches and no less winning. Flanders is a prosaic Lombardy, lacking vineyards and sun. Above its churches, on the tops of its steeples, rings the knowing and regu-

lar carillon—the honor and joy of the Flemish commune. The same tune has been playing from hour to hour for centuries, and satisfies the musical needs of I know not how many generations of artisans, who live and die affixed to their workbenches.

And what strides in French historical studies follow him, as early as the days of Victor Duruy and Taine!

► SOCIAL THOUGHT

During the reign of Louis-Philippe—while the Romantics extol the "people," and this word, accepted increasingly to mean the lower classes, is already beginning to assume a religious cast by virtue of Pierre Leroux, George Sand, and several others—the discovery of the proletarian realities is completed. In this respect, there is nothing more noteworthy than the compassion of a liberal economist like Sismondi for the deprived proletariat, the victims of competition and *laissez faire*—those great principles of the bourgeois political economy. Criticism—literary or philosophical—thus designates a whole sector of this period's thought under the name of Social Romanticism, an expressive rubric for gathering together all the essayists from Saint-Simon to Proudhon, as well as for the Revolution of 1848. The undeniable affinities among them are worth emphasizing.

Economists or merely self-educated people, Catholics or atheists—all these men, leaning toward the nascent proletariat and toward this beginning Industrial Revolution, whose ominous future Michelet foresees, are not protected against some sentimentality. Buchez, to take only one example, describes the proletariat in the following manner: "Almost since the first day, they have had to live (let us understand that they work to live, working when they are four): they are destined to exist for one thought alone: the avoidance of hunger; attached to the earth like polyps at the point where they come into the world, they work and die." [4] Whether from personal experience, like Fourier, or through a deep insight into the transformations taking place, like Saint-Simon, they extemporize on the poverty of which no one can be unaware; that is the great *raison d'être* of their projects, of their prophetic predictions, of their religious exaltation. Who among them does not have disciples, does not found a school—if not a church—to preach the new society with a faith that cares little for the modes and processes of change. Hence the epithet "utopians" applied to those socialists, the predecessors of Karl Marx, crushed by "scientific" socialism, who did not escape the curse of the "superseded" precursors and philosophies. Though forgotten today, these teachers of the 1848 generation, who were read avidly, have as wide a public as *L'Histoire des Girondins* or *Les Chansons des* *rues et des bois;* they have had faithful disciples, devoted to their memory. Doubtless they deserve better than the poor reputation of being gentle dreamers, as the subsequent "Scientism" * evaluated them.

Each one is rich in his own precise views on the world in which he has lived and has suffered, for none of them is really a recluse or a professor comfortably installed in his university chair. Each has his experiences: Saint-Simon's broad vision, measuring things against the world he has traveled, from America to Europe; Fourier, employed in trade, and burdened with the experiences of a life spent as a bookkeeper for the profits of a small business. And in the diversity of their writings, data, and culture, they are less valuable for their systems and projects than for the incisiveness of their analyses, which Marx did not disdain— he who read them all and who knew how to borrow their expressions ("man's exploitation of man," for example), their reflections upon the organization of work. For all these, too, the point of departure is that demonstrated development of the working classes, who produce but have nothing, "that phenomenon offered by the affluent nations, where public poverty continues to increase along with material wealth, and where the class producing everything is each day more and more nearly reduced to enjoying nothing."

Of these French Utopian Socialists, who shape a whole new sector of public opinion, the most famous is Henri de Saint-Simon, prophet of the modern industrial world and of government by the producers. This ruined noble, this traveler who fought for American independence, who saw, as early as 1780, onto what vistas commercial capitalism was opening, succeeds at the end of his troubled life in training some disciples, no less than Augustin Thierry and Auguste Comte, who establish the most firmly rooted school of socialist thought of the early nineteenth century. Before its disappearance, it left its contemporaries the annunciation of the industrial world: "The industrial class is the fundamental class, the nurturing class, of Society"—a century later, the expression is trite, but in 1825 it was rich and weighty. Saint-Simon gives notice that the government of societies must be entrusted to those who produce, must, therefore, be economic, and at the same time scientifically, organized. He predicts universal association, its triumph in a truly positive and industrial regime, and the end of the age of barbarism: a time when "the hardest-working and most peace-loving class will be entrusted with the control of public power."

Saint-Simon offers his followers not a program but a vision of the future, one attractive by virtue of its broad scope and its originality—if

---

* There is a very slight pejorative nuance to this word which expresses a belief in the omnipotence of positive science in all fields. Though related to Positivism, the term Scientism is much more inclusive; Positivism will be used below, especially in the next chapter, only in a philosophic context.—Trans.

one remembers that, for many, landed wealth had remained the principal economic resource. Saint-Simon appeals to the creative enthusiasm of those for whom *industry* is no longer skill, in the old sense of the word, but a new, recent mode of activity open to all daring and all progress. In the feverish atmosphere of Charles X's reign, when Villèle's friends and then those of the king himself are increasing the outbreaks of clericalism and Ultra-Royalism, the school of Saint-Simon is founded in Paris by Bazard and Enfantin. They organize the school, publish the Master's works, especially the *Nouveau Christianisme*, establish a working-class order, and conceive a widely read newspaper, *Le Globe;** finally, to its misfortune, it turns into a religious sect which goes down in ridicule—without dying completely—as early as 1833. But the range of Saint-Simon's movement is very great: the disciples of the school, who will propel the economic life of the Imperial period, denounce the malpractices of *laissez faire* and propose the organization of work, out of which Louis Blanc makes his entire program. They contribute to the discrediting of private property, in favor of different forms of co-operation in which the producers would join together for the largest enterprises, whose development they envisage and which they study in their publication, *Le Producteur* (launched in 1825). Thanks to the fertility and the prestige of their propaganda, a whole portion of the socialist vocabulary even enters into the everyday language: exploitation and organization, production and consumption, bourgeois and proletariat. The fantasies of "Le Père" Enfantin may have prevented Saint-Simon's movement from becoming *the* movement of the nineteenth-century French bourgeoisie; it does not eradicate the deep influence exercised by the doctrine in every milieu—from students at the École Polytechnique to workers in the Ligue des Droits de l'Homme.

Charles Fourier, a little shop clerk, a scrupulous cashier with little talent at the art of selling, is not, like Saint-Simon, open to the future. He devotes years and unintelligible works to denouncing the sins of commerce, the "crimes," as he says, and to demonstrating how competition engenders mercantile feudalism. Full of compassion for the victims of the system and, through having lived in Lyon and Rouen, not ignorant of the "assassination of the workers" in the factories, he protests against this war waged by the rich upon the poor which, to his eyes, lies at the heart of the new civilization. As a remedy, he proposes his social science, a mathematics of the "passions," and those little groups of sixteen hundred people living in complete and economically self-sufficient communities—the phalansteries. Several such experiments, which were disastrous, were carried out in the nineteenth century at Sedan and

---

* According to a custom of the day, which has gradually been lost, *Le Globe* had a masthead device that met with some success: "To each according to his abilities, to each ability according to its works."

Paris. But Fourier, that obstinate bull occasionally full of verve, an old bachelor, went astray into a construction of the "passions" that had nothing to do with socialism: the phalanstery should include a total strength precisely determined by that bookkeeper, and the most diverse temperaments, which Fourier classifies psychologically in a manner that has never been taken seriously. He thus claims to utilize the "passions," those of children for dirt and refuse, and the *papillonne*, which he believes to be universal*: "Real happiness consists only in satisfying all the passions," he says; the regimentation of the women phalansterians' "passions" under the authority of an *Haute Matrone*, directing "the full advance of gallantry," seems farcical to us; but it is to be seen in the same context as the impassioned fantasies of "Le Père" Enfantin and, fundamentally, the literary Romantics' glorification of the sentimental.

These quasi-delirious whimsies did not prevent Fourier from founding a school and having followers, like Victor Considérant who devoted his life to spreading the ideas of this loquacious man from the Jura and, following Fourier's example, in vehemently denouncing the social disorder. This is a major step in Fourier's movement, since Fourier does not concern himself with the passage from a capitalist society to a phalansterian society any more than did Saint-Simon with the advent of a government of producers. Fourier is ultimately credited with having inspired the modern co-operative system—though this attribution is somewhat generous, since there is a large gap from the picture of the phalanstery to that of the consumer co-operatives, and even to Boimondau's production co-operative.

The Saint-Simon school falls at Ménilmontant into Enfantin's religious propheticism around 1833 (Saint-Simon died in 1825). Fourier dies in 1837. But there is already a profusion of disciples or new theorists, forming a battalion crammed with imaginative reformers capable of suggesting a better world to their contemporaries, capable, too, of frightening—for if the rural classes are ignorant of all this revolutionary literature, the urban bourgeoisie is actually trembling before so much audacity in so many areas. Cabet remained, along with Considérant, Leroux, Pecqueur, Buchez, Barbès, and Blanqui because his *Voyage en Icarie*—that smiling reverie about an egalitarian world in which the goods, the means of production, and the land were common property—created fear as a future danger. And yet, neither did Cabet, who settled in Texas to establish Icarus and to test his dream, meet with much suc-

---

* Fourier, enamored of classifications, is not without some picturesqueness: haunted by cuckoldry, he distinguishes forty-nine "simple" orders of cuckolds and thirty-one "composite" orders; but were his contemporaries, who were scarcely shocked at these views so little in keeping with conventional morality, sensitive as we are to this jest? Probably not. To understand these "fantasies" thoroughly, we should have to make a social study of Romantic sensibility. (The *papillonne* is the "passion" that dominates mankind, causing it to flit from one thing to another.—Trans.)

An Outline of Romantic and Revolutionary Geography

ENGLAND

⊙ WATERLOO

● BOULOGNE

VILLEQUIER
⊙ ROUEN

JERSEY

ERMENONVILLE
⊙ CHÂLIS
PARIS ⊙
PORT-ROYAL

STRASBOURG ●

COLMAR ●

BELFORT ●

LA CHESNAIE ⊙ ⊙ COMBOURG

TOURS ⊙ BLOIS
SAUMUR ●

BESANÇON ●

SAINT-POINT ⊙

⊙ NOHANT

MILLY
⊙

COPPET ⊙

LA ROCHELLE ●

LYON ●

⊙ LAKE BOURGET

SAINT-ÉTIENNE ●

● GRENOBLE

Atlantic Ocean

TOULOUSE ⊙

PARIS

PORTE SAINT-MARTIN ●

PALAIS ROYAL
TUILERIES
RUE TRANSNONAIN ●
CLOÎTRE SAINT-MERRI ●
THÉÂTRE FRANÇAIS ⊙ PLACE DES VOSGES
HÔTEL DE VILLE ●
NOTRE-DAME
⊙ FAUBOURG-SAINT-ANTOINE
⊙ ARSENAL
RUE DES FEUILLANTINES
RUE NOTRE DAME DES CHAMPS

● *Revolutionary towns*

⊙ *Spots dear to the hearts of the Romantics*

cess. But Louis Blanc, the most realistic theorist—author of the *Organisation du travail*, who takes up Fourier's criticisms of competition and demands state aid for the oppressed workers, threatened with extermination—is also the object of unbridled hatred, that of Falloux for example, a hatred that forced him to end his life in exile. It is true that Cabet and Louis Blanc, trusting in authority to reform society, and obsessed simultaneously by Robespierre and Napoleon, finally conjure up bad memories: Louis Blanc pays a visit to Prince Bonaparte, interned in the fortress of Ham where the future emperor will write *L'Extinction de paupérisme*.

But the personality dominating these socialist milieux just before 1848 and the *Communist Manifesto* is a man from Franche-Comté, Pierre-Joseph Proudhon, a devil of a man who, from 1840—when he suddenly becomes famous, at thirty-one, by publishing *Qu'est-ce que la propriété?*—until his death in 1865, continues to disrupt, terrorize, and bully his most renowned contemporaries. A defender of freedom who yet did not want to cause trouble; a lover of social justice who differs from his socialist predecessors; an acrid critic of economic contradictions but one incapable of constructing a system—this print-shop worker, largely self-educated, continues to alert all those who endured, directly or not, his ceaseless verve, his intellectual vigor, and his violent language.* "Born and raised in the heart of the working class, but also belonging to it from his heart and, especially, through the community of sufferings and of wants," he once declared himself devoted to "being able henceforth to work without stopping, through science and philosophy, with all the energy of my will and all the powers of my spirit, for the moral and intellectual improvements of those whom I am pleased to call my brothers and comrades." A lucid, uncomplacent observer of social realities, the Proudhon of the *Propriété* and of the *Philosophie de la Misère* (subtitled the *Système des contradictions économiques*) in 1846, has no doctrine, but seeks justice in equality and freedom. A man who thinks irascibly—and fights to the end of his life against men and systems—he is already in this period a recluse, and will end up a libertarian preaching anarchy:

> A form of government, or constitution, in which both public and private conscience, educated by science and law, suffices alone to maintain order and to guarantee all liberties; where, accordingly, the principle of authority, the institutions of police, the means of prevention and repression, and the system of civil service are re-

---

* With a feeling for slogans which made him more enemies than supporters—who does not know that famous cry, so bitterly criticized: "Property is theft"?—he is sometimes relentless about some of his contemporaries. Thus he once calls Louis Blanc "the stunted shadow of Robespierre"; and another time: "He believed himself to be the bee of the Revolution, but was only its locust."

duced to their simplest expression; and, for even greater reason, monarchic forms and centralization at the top disappear, replaced by federative institutions and communal mores.

As do other socialists, he lashes out at mercantile society and encroaching capitalism. Proudhon, the son of an artisan, retained during his entire life an unblemished admiration for his father, who fixed his prices without taking any profit; he also is the *enfant terrible* of socialism, a man of the workers' party who fights all his fellow-travelers. After 1848, we shall see him in his long quarrel with Karl Marx, as Courbet's portrait has depicted him: pug-faced and full of character, with a gaze simultaneously troubled, penetrating, and steady.

Just before 1848, there comes the Revolution prepared for and dreamed of by the men of February; it is not merely a political revolution, but the hope of a truly liberal regime, of a Republic. The word is charged with an additional sense; the eponymic heroes of the secret societies are no longer the men of 1789—Bailly or Camille Desmoulins —but those of 1793: Robespierre and Marat, indeed the Babeuf of 1796 whose legacy Blanqui obtained through Buonarotti. The Revolution must be a social revolution: the very word "socialism" has passed into the ordinary language, flung out by Pierre Leroux in 1834 and subsequently taken up and incessantly popularized. De Tocqueville notes it in January 1848, faced with a jeering Chamber: not this government or that minister, but the bases of bourgeois society, are in question. French socialists—however utopian they were—shaped the ideological conscience of the new working classes, preparing for productive tomorrows.

The moral poverty of the proletariat struck the men of 1830 no less than did their material distress: Fourier links the two, and it may be that Marx is indebted to him for this governing idea. Moreover, the greatest of these socialist theorists are concerned with religion and its place in the new world they are preparing and heralding. There are few among them, however, who think that the Catholic Church can retain the spiritual leadership of the socialist world. Fourier makes no place for it in his phalanstery, nor does Cabet in his Icarus; Proudhon—after 1848, at least—reveals himself to be as strongly anticlerical as he is anticapitalist; and Enfantin's Saint-Simon church is a caricature. Among the socialists, only Buchez dissents from Saint-Simon—in both his *Introduction à la Science de l'histoire, ou Science du développement de l'humanité* (1833) and his *Histoire parlementaire de la Révolution française* (1834)—claiming to retain his religious faith as nourishment for his democratic and socialist hopes. Between the Gospel and a society organized democratically along Saint-Simon's lines, he sees no abyss but rather a profound agreement; the Gospel, rightly understood, is the

basis for equality, as it is for the sovereignty of the people. Pierre Leroux and George Sand will concur; but coming after the great undertaking of *L'Avenir*, this appeal addressed to traditional religion to participate in a social regeneration goes unanswered. Thus Buchez and his
friends cut isolated figures, remote and poorly understood, precursors of
that small *Sillon* group which, at the beginning of the twentieth century,
will give new impetus to Catholic social thought.

For the Catholic Church in the 1830s has recently condemned not
just a Catholic socialist but a democrat: Lamennais. Actually, Catholics
were not very numerous and were concerned about the mounting Voltairianism produced by the policy of the years between 1825 and 1830
(which notably reveal an extraordinary sale of eighteenth-century *philosophes*, the "best-sellers" of the day), and about the lower-class anticlericalism which breaks out in 1831. These factory workers, who have
neither more Sundays nor Saint's days off, and who see in the practices
of religion the pastime of the rich—these masses whose numbers increase
from one year to the next, are abandoned. Worse yet, the clergy seems to
be particularly concerned with consolidating its reconciliation with the
Monarchy, which was betrayed in 1801, etc. Lamennais, Montalembert,
and Lacordaire have sensed this rupture, which—because of the tradi-
tionalist routine and the absence of all non-theological education and
information—is not apparent to the clergy. Lamennais in particular, a
man of lively sensibility, follows the rhythm of his day; this writer with a
stirring style, who had made himself known in 1817 with his resounding
attack against bourgeois atheism (*Essai sur l'indifférence en matière de
religion*) was, until its condemnation by the Pope in 1832,* the moving
spirit behind the democratic and Catholic newspaper called *L'Avenir*.
Ultimately he leaves the Church, and publishes *Les Paroles d'un croyant*
in 1834. This was one of the real landmarks of the period, a fiery book
which, by virtue of its eloquent language, revealed, to a large section of
the bourgeois, the change in social ideas; it was this book by an ex-
priest which did more to bring the lower classes closer to the priest
than all the prose of Buchez and his followers.

Lamennais in his *Paroles d'un croyant* reunites socialist theorists and
advocates association, which is to bring about the disappearance of
monopolies and poverty; he proclaims his confidence in the people, who
are more human and even more moral than the bourgeoisie or the former nobility; a little later he goes on to announce his hopes for it: "This
real people, ignorant and ragged, living from one working day to the
next, is still the healthiest segment of society, the segment where the

---

* The Encyclical *Mirari Vos* condemns the program of *L'Avenir*, its acceptance of
freedom of conscience and tolerance, and the rupture of the close tie the Church
intends to preserve between monarchy and religion. Montalembert and Lacordaire
submitted to it, but not Lamennais.

best sense, the most justice, and the greatest humanity is found. Others fear it: I put my hope in it." The *Paroles d'un croyant* helped in no small way to effect a temporary reconciliation in the spring of 1848 between the lower classes and the Church. But the liberal attempt to unfetter Catholicism from the monarchy, to end this close political alliance —the work of *L'Avenir* during its two-year existence—did not have the same repercussions: until the *ralliement*** at the close of the century, until the Separation [of Church and State] in 1905, the daring effort of 1830 is as if forgotten. This contributed greatly, though not so much as did purely sociological conditions, to the subsequent alienation of the masses from traditional religion. For want of listening in time to that priest who feels, better than everyone else, the development that is in progress, the Catholic Church, a century later, will have to consider France a missionary country, will have to increase the institutions specializing in reconquest, which are necessary for rechristianizing the working masses.

Finally—a factor more important than the concern of Saint-Simon, Fourier, and all those other "thinkers," or than the anxiety of a handful of Catholics—the working classes, victims of the capitalist advance, gain a voice. A workers' body of thought, an idea of class, nourished simultaneously by experience and by doctrines spread by the Utopian Socialists, is gradually born, and takes its autonomous place; this is the prelude to an ideological movement which continues in other forms to the present day.

But before writing, before speaking out, the working classes struggle, regrouping themselves in institutions inherited from the Old Regime (whose survival is tolerated rather than authorized), and living several brilliant years, until a new outburst. Workers' unions as well as mutual associations come to life again: the journeymen of the *Tour de France*, grouped by professions, divided into hostile cliques, always quick to bully and to brawl, as in the preceding century—these perpetuate the habits of the profession, their songs, their tricks of the trade, and their deep solidarity against management.† But often those who are without work rebel against the workers, maltreated as they are, who do have jobs. And many, particularly in Paris, argue against the useless rivalries and the endless violences, calling for the union of all wage-earners against their employers. The word "unity," from this period on, has considerable

---

* The "rallying" now referred to is the policy of Catholic support for the Third Republic encouraged by Pope Leo XIII in the 1890s; again, those who carried out this policy are called the *ralliés*.—Trans.

† *Les Mémoires d'un compagnon*, by Agricol Perdiguier, called Avignonnais-la-Vertu, published in 1854, constitutes the best document about working-class traditions, though it is very favorable to those customs and those violences which Perdiguier defended at the same time as many workers openly deplored their abuses.

value and significance because union must permit struggle. Herein lies the explanation for the advance of the mutual societies, those associations of mutual aid against sickness and unemployment, maintained through spontaneous contributions from the workers and sometimes from the employers; provident and insurance companies are authorized by law (and well thought of by the bourgeoisie); moreover, they are subject to a close police supervision in most of the trade associations. Thus, despite the precautions taken by the Le Chapelier Law, the custom of labor organizations advances through the collection of contributions and the holding of regular meetings. However, very soon after the economic crisis of 1817, the joint accounts of these mutual societies serves to help not the old and destitute who are unable to work, but workers on strike; it is then a combat weapon which, despite all the prohibitions, the workers use more and more. The mutual society and health insurance become a basis of solidarity; after 1825, prefects authorize these associations less and less, for the employers and the authorities consider them effective and dangerous weapons in the hands of workers wishing to improve their living conditions.

Indeed, despite the legal prohibition and the suits which follow the uprisings, factory workers defend themselves against their employers by strikes; the uprisings in Lyon during 1831 and 1834 go so far as to be riots. But these were preceded and followed by numerous insurrections —less vast and bloody—against such legalization; from the difficult year of 1817 until the great crisis of 1846-47, not a year goes by that some important uprising does not raise its head in one town or another. Under the July Monarchy, some years saw as many as fifty lawsuits initiated, and in 1840 there were a hundred and thirty.* The workers in Paris, Nantes, and Rouen defy the legal provisions and all the suits to obtain better wages: often they are hopeless revolts of limited success, and sometimes of none. But the fever for joint action creates lasting solidarities.

And then, these workers write.† In addition to the memoirs and brief studies devoted to the improvement of the workers' lot and to the survival of the workers' unions, the noteworthy initiative of the period is the establishment in 1840 of a working-class newspaper called *L'Atelier*. Very different from *Le Globe*, *Le Producteur*, and *Le Phalanstère*, which were reserved for doctrinal exegesis, *L'Atelier* is a monthly newspaper destined to follow day-to-day events—without hiding its preference for Buchez's social Catholicism. It is the particular mouthpiece of the working class, edited exclusively by workers.‡ Convinced they are in

---

* The precise figures are: fifty-one in 1837; forty-four in 1838; sixty-four in 1839; a hundred and thirty in 1840.
† They also talk. The Parisians send delegations to the liberal deputies and to their friends—Arago, for example. Whenever a law regulating factory work is under discussion, the delegations are numerous.
‡ By way of example, let us note Martin Nadaud's admiration for the undertaking in

a better position than anyone else to say what their needs are, and to analyze the reasons why the struggles between employers and workers gain in intensity each day, they edit and correct their newspaper themselves. They accept no "bourgeois" collaboration, as we would say today; both before 1848 and after, their studies and demands evince a lucidity which explains why *L'Atelier* was held in such high esteem during and after its ten years of publication. Run by print-shop workers who, by the nineteenth century, along with carpenters and jewelers, long had been in the forefront of the militant workers, the staff of *L'Atelier*, whose head is Corbon, is Democratic. They advocate universal suffrage and, on the social level, they vigorously criticize "industrial privilege" and recommend organization of work. There is nothing original in this program. The essential is the composition of the editing committee and especially the paper's circulation among the workers, implying an awareness and response. The men of *L'Atelier* are imbued with a feeling of their own dignity, a sense of working-class pride which enables them to say everything and—in August, 1841—to denounce the class struggle:

> Struggle and antagonism between employer and worker never cease for a moment; it is this struggle, always muffled though sorrowful, which is sometimes revealed in the world under the names of prohibitions, strikes, union, and assembly; it makes itself continually felt in each workshop.

In 1844, Guizot brings suit against *L'Atelier* for "provocation to hatred among the various classes of society"—unsuccessfully, it should be added. Legal harassments follow, particularly concerning stamps. Nonetheless, the newspaper proceeds with its career: it was the conservative Republic, just after June, 1848, that got the better of those on *L'Atelier*, by means of surety bonds—that is, by money. This working-class thought, expressed by *L'Atelier* clearly and without useless phraseology*—reassuring in certain respects, since it advocates fidelity to the Catholic Church and love for a job well done—astonished both bourgeois milieux and the Conservative and Liberal press who welcomed this comrade with a new style. Through *L'Atelier*, working-class thought is asserted; it took its autonomous place in the French community and began a long

---

his *Mémoires:* "The year 1840 marks one of the most important dates in the history of the working classes. We may see then something never seen in any other period: a group of workers uniting to establish a newspaper, saying to one another that in order to collaborate in their work, they must work with their tools during the day and their pens at night. For ten years they defended, step by step, the freedoms of their class."

* Example: the affirmation of working-class dignity: "Money is only an instrument of work; man is the intelligent being who produces and transforms all things with the help of the instruments in his possession."

career. The great themes of socialist thought during the period can be found in this newspaper, whose masthead device was "Liberty, Equality, Fraternity, Unity." Those on *L'Atelier* have a special predilection for solidarity and its unifying manifestations: they often conjure up an international (*i.e.*, Franco-English, during September, 1841, the period of Chartism) solidarity: "There exists among the great working-class family a community of interests so vast and so complete that as soon as one of their parties suffers or merely experiences a passing discomfort, the others immediately feel its effects."

Thus the Fourth Estate, ignored yesterday, becomes both a subject of literature, by virtue of the most generous of the Romantics, and the object of study and discussion by economists and above all the socialists; it is present in every townsman's conversation and concerns, finally lifting up its voice with a dignity and an assurance that astonish, delight, and trouble mid-century France—it is, in fact, a new force in society. The period from February to June, 1848, is to complete the demonstration.

► **THE REVOLUTION OF 1848**

The Orléanist Monarchy collapses like the Bourbon Restoration, without glory and without serious resistance; during three cold February days, as during three fine July days eighteen years earlier, a worn-out, unpopular regime falls under the blows of the Parisians, aroused from the Faubourg Saint-Antoine to the Hôtel de Ville. But with this general characteristic, the resemblance ends. February of 1848 is more than a short-lived political revolution: the Parisian victory is not betrayed, and the brief history of the Second Republic—actually from February to June of 1848—is also the portentous history of a revolt that had many aspects (Romantic, Socialist, and Bourgeois) ending in the triumph of a skillful kinsman of Napoleon, the conqueror of a sad conspiracy of sorcerers' apprentices. But through its European repercussions and its political and social work, the Second Republic makes its mark upon the destiny of contemporary French civilization: from the springtime of the people to the conservative Republic of Falloux and Thiers, these burning pages still mold many contemporary realities.*

The July Monarchy was abandoned both by the bourgeoisie who established it and by the National Guards, the regime's solidest support from 1831 to 1839, which refused in February to answer the call of Guizot and Louis-Philippe. Thus the Parisian bourgeoisie—politicians like

---

* We are not concerned here with taking up the political narrative of this revolution *manqué*. The recent celebration of the 1848 centenary was the occasion of numerous publications and commemorative studies: continuous narratives like Jean Dautry's *Histoire de la Révolution de 1848 en France* (Paris: Editions Sociales, 1957), or else the more or less extensive scholarly works published by Presses Universitaires.

Thiers, bankers, merchants, and manufacturers—participate in the Revolution. The economic crisis of 1846-48, which rocked the entire country (famines and bread riots as early as 1846, with a financial and then an industrial crisis bringing about bankruptcies and unemployment) cast, in their minds, aspersions on the government which could not bring it to a halt. The bourgeoisie was struck by the financial miscalculations, but no less by the revolts in the towns, where bakeries are pillaged, and in the country, where peasants simultaneously suffer from poor wheat and potato crops and from shutting-down of the railroad construction camps, which disband more than a half-million workers throughout France. Moreover, the infamous scandals of the same years, exposing the misappropriations in public administration, contribute to discrediting the personnel in office. Finally in 1847, at the same time as a number of the 1830 participants are deliberately breaking off with Guizot and his king and calling for reform, there is a rash of publications reviving the memory of 1789 in the minds of the educated bourgeoisie, but presenting accounts which, though not always harmonious, nonetheless reawaken a revolutionary sympathy scarcely appreciated by the king of the barricades. Almost simultaneously, in the spring of 1848, Michelet, Louis Blanc, and Lamartine bring out their volumes. The campaign of banquets from July, 1847, to February, 1848—that provincial and gastronomic tour by the supporters of the parliamentary and electoral reform that Guizot rejected*—is located within this atmosphere of discontent and excitement.

In the closing months of 1847, propagandists and memorialists announce the February Revolution: no one has prepared for it, and no plan for reforms or for political reorganization is ready—not even in the pocket of a Louis Blanc, or a Ledru-Rollin. And yet, everyone senses it, predicts it behind the banquets and the riots—the presentiments of an era richer in intuition than in organization. The Second Republic, from March to May of 1848, is a generous improvisation, nourished on memories of the first one, on a quasi-mystical confidence in the sovereign people, and on a blind faith in human brotherhood: it is Lamartine, defender of the Tricolor, who "went around the world" more sure of the people more than of himself: "A nation is as incorruptible as the ocean." The February *journées* arouse the enthusiasm of the humbler urban classes, who catch a glimpse of the end of their miseries; the momentary good feeling between the moderate Republicans of the *National* and the socialist Republicans of the *Réforme* in the Provisional Government is a

---

* Thiers and Odilon Barrot proposed the lowering of the electoral *cens* in order to make the electorate pass from 250,000 to 450,000 electors, and the reform of the statute of the civil-servant deputies, which formed the greatest part of the majority favoring the king. Although the campaign of banquets is bourgeois and moderate, the Radicals, that is the Republicans, took an increasingly important part in it as early as autumn.

promise, and even more, a realization: the establishment of universal suffrage, the abolition of slavery in the colonies, the abolition of capital punishment for political crimes, and the creation of National Workshops to
cope directly with the unemployment in Paris are so many generous measures to renew and continue the work of 1789-1793. The clubs and newspapers, which multiply more than they did in the early months of the
great Revolution, maintain political pressure on the Provisional Government, in a good-natured way which will not last. But for several
weeks, the applause of popular orators, the clergy's benediction of Trees
of Liberty, and the conciliatory delegations at the Hôtel de Ville, maintain the impression of a sure triumph for the new regime. For the Socialists, undoubtedly, the new political form must be the means and the opportunity for a final emancipation of the working classes—while the
Moderates are less far-seeing, or rather, they look elsewhere: to the
provinces, following without protesting, but unable to participate in
the revolutionary excitement in Paris or in the ardent life of the clubs.
In March, the Parisians celebrate the European revolution: Milan, Berlin, Vienna, and Frankfort, all Europe, the Europe of the disunited
Germanic Confederation and of partitioned Italy, is shaken by these
urban rebellions which demand simultaneously a liberal regime and a
national unification—which, since 1815, Metternich has obstinately refused. Although the first revolts, in Italy, precede the Parisian insurrection by several weeks, the Parisians have the impression that Europe
awakens to their call to free all people from the political servitudes reinstated after the imperial wars. Even if Lamartine, the conciliatory minister of foreign affairs, declares the will of the Republic not to interfere in
its neighbors' internal affairs, the Parisians cry aloud their feeling for the
international solidarity of popular movements, and once more march to
the cries of "Long live Poland," when affairs are already going worse.*
The spring of 1848, an early spring, takes a turn for the worse as early as
May, and particularly in June. The political incapacity of the leaders and
the bitterness of the bourgeois struggle against the Democrats is explanation enough. Yet March-April of 1848 has remained in the collective memory of the Parisian workers as a great moment of fraternal hope:
one that counts in the psychological life of a people.

The Revolution is taken over by the moderate Republicans when, in
June (22-24), the workers' insurrection is beaten down by the National
Guards and the Garde Mobile, the new troops recruited by the Provi-

---

* This optimism, which is not devoid of naïveté, the grandiloquence of these democratic leaders, and their lack of political preparation (the ministers of the Provisional
Government retained the personnel of the July Monarchy; Blanqui, who had been
plotting the forceful seizure of power for twenty years, has no plan for the future
government following his victory, etc.) explain the often-used and pejorative expression, still used today—*quarante-huitard.*

sional Government, shortly after February, from among the young, Parisian unemployed. The retrogression of the Republic dates from those terrible *journées*, followed by heavy repression: the conservative Republic legislates against the lower classes, then lets itself be subjugated by the Prince-President at the end of 1851. Definitively deprived of all Parisian backing, the Second Republic was the plaything of Louis-Napoleon Bonaparte.

The June *journées* are the outcome of the conflict between the hundred thousand workers, assembled in the National Workshops, and the 1848 Constituent Assembly, composed mostly of Monarchists and moderate Republicans. Universal suffrage did no good service to the Republic: in April, it supplied an Assembly which could have adapted itself to Louis-Philippe, indeed to Louis XVIII; several months later, it elects the emperor's nephew to the presidency of the Republic—political inexperience on the part of nine million electors, it is said. Actually, the bulk of the population, which is still rural and could not be affected by the Republican propaganda (that of the secret societies, before 1848, or of the newspapers and clubs after February), votes for the "notables" or for Napoleon—that is, for those they know. Notaries, *hobereaux*, and doctors (not yet as important as they will become) all declare themselves Republicans and have nothing to combat save the Socialist or Communist Party candidates—the "sharers" or "reds," the partisans of the Provisional Government which just increased taxes forty-five per cent (forty-five centimes to the franc). Similarly, neither Cavaignac, a professional general of the army in Africa, nor Ledru-Rollin, can claim to be as well-known in the rural areas as Louis-Napoleon Bonaparte, who was served excellently by the entire Napoleonic legend built up by the Romantics, all the lithographs and the *images d'Épinal*. In April, the Monarchists and the moderate Republicans win as many votes, and the same ones, as did Louis-Napoleon in December.

Between this Assembly, hostile to the Provisional Government, and the sole social realization, namely the National Workshops, inspired by Louis Blanc but mishandled by Marie, there is no possible agreement: the social demands in general create fear, and the dominant mentality remains that of the Liberals—*i.e.*, economic liberal—of the preceding era. The caricature of help for the Parisian workers, brought into being on the Champ de Mars, again facilitates the task of a majority without unnecessary scruples; the Workshops are expensive and do not produce, since nothing has been done to make use of the workers according to their abilities. The employers who sat on the Luxembourg Commission are even able to make the shameless claim that they lack manpower. The dissolution of the National Workshops, however, coming after the failure of Blanqui and Barbès on May 15, provoked a general uprising in the eastern and southern districts, from the Panthéon to Père Lachaise: for four days, the National Guards and the Garde Mobile, reinforced by National Guards called up from the provinces, were obliged to reconquer, street by street, the insurgent districts. Led by Cavaignac and other generals from the army in Africa who were accustomed to the harsh raids of the Algerian conquest, the Republic's troops carried out a merciless repression even to the last bastion of the Faubourg Saint-Antoine, where the Archbishop of Paris, mediating a surrender one evening, died. Hundreds of executions immediately after June 26, twenty-five thousand arrests, and thousands of deportations all presage the repression of the Commune in 1871. Proudhon conjures up these *journées:*

> That insurrection alone is more terrible than all those that occurred for sixty years. The Assembly's ill will is its cause . . . Atrocious butchery on the part of the Garde Mobile, the Army, and the National Guards occurred. People are executed at the Conciergerie and at the Hôtel de Ville; forty-eight hours after the victory, they execute wounded and defenseless prisoners . . . they spread the most atrocious calumnies about the insurgents so as to excite vengeance against them. . . . Horror! Horror!

And Lamennais curses Cavaignac, Falloux, and the others in his July 11 article:

> The Constituent people began with the Republic, they end with the Republic. For what we see is certainly not the Republic . . . but around its bloody tomb, saturnalias of reaction. The men who became its ministers, its devoted servants, will not delay in collecting the reward which is destined for them . . . Pursued by scorn, bowed down with shame, cursed in the present and cursed in the future, they will depart to rejoin the traitors of all ages. . . .

Newspapers are suppressed, clubs closed, the people disarmed, except for the regiments of National Guards, proved to be safe during the struggle —the reign of terror has arrived. Cavaignac's plenary powers, the Constituent Assembly's and then the Legislature's adroitness, the domination of the party of order, of which Thiers, Marrast, and Falloux are the masters—this is the Great Fear of 1848. Begun in the victorious union of the bourgeoisie and the working classes, the Republic lost that first aspect in June; its grimacing mask is now that of class struggle. But the Republic had been the work of the workers who rushed into the streets in February; it has lost its defenders who stir no more—neither in December, 1851, nor in 1852.

Directed by a conservative majority and presided over by an ambitious man who, from the Élysée very quietly prepares a new Brumaire, the

Republic of 1849 to 1851 allows itself to be swept along by Thiers and Falloux (and occasionally Montalembert) on the path of a *censitaire* regime, protected by the clergy and free of all its cumbersome troublemongers. Thus Louis-Napoleon Bonaparte can amuse himself by reestablishing universal suffrage, and appear more Republican than his narrow-minded conservative deputies. Thiers legitimizes the electoral law eliminating the lower classes—three of nine million electors—by extending the residence requirement from six months to three years, a clever formula for ridding the polls of members of workers' union, rural day laborers, and victims of unemployment and the recent crisis: the great stratagem of the Legislative Assembly is to "thrust back the vile multitude." This is a short-lived electoral law, important especially for its intention. The Falloux Law of March 15, 1850, which aims a blow at the statute of the Imperial University (certain of whose provisions never have been abolished) is of another importance, for it organizes "freedom of education" for many years, all the while creating deep grounds for educational division in France. By establishing private education alongside public, it revives and dignifies the anticlericalism which breaks out in the following period. The work of Catholics, of Montalembert and Falloux, the Law satisfies those defenders of *écoles libres** who, for many years, had been struggling under Louis-Philippe against the University's monopoly. It grants to private individuals the right to open schools, and in an extremely liberal manner since the only obligation imposed upon opening a private secondary course is for the director alone to have taught or supervised for five years and to possess a certificate of ability or the *baccalauréat*;† in the primary system, ministers from the various religions are legally schoolteachers, without any other formality. Moreover, the law authorizes the municipalities and the *arrondissement* councils, or the *département*, to subsidize all these establishments—upon the recommendation of the Academic Council. Then again, the Falloux Law places public education under the control of the clergy: the schoolteacher is under the wing of the *curé* and the mayor; members of the Congregation can be public schoolteachers; the normal schools can be discontinued by the mere decision of the General Council, through which the members of the clergy enter the system. Despite the opposition of all the Liberals in the Legislative Assembly, with Victor Hugo and even Cavaignac in the forefront, the Falloux Law was adopted by a large majority, led along in particular by Thiers (who was convinced that all teachers are socialists), and restrained by Catholics themselves, such as the *abbé* Dupanloup and Roux-Lavergne. The

---

* In France, however, an *école libre* is *any* private school: one not connected to, or sponsored by, the State.—Trans.
† These provisions are still the law today; as are those concerning the subsidies for local communities.

oratorical struggle between the little Voltairian Thiers and Victor Hugo is extremely indicative of the two states of mind. Thiers:

> I am prepared to give all primary education to the clergy . . . I formally ask for something other than those secular schoolteachers, too many of whom are execrable . . . I ask that the *curé*'s action be strong, much stronger than it is now, for I count heavily on him to propagate that good philosophy which teaches man that he is here to suffer . . . I say and I maintain that elementary education must not inevitably and necessarily be within everyone's reach: I shall even go so far as to say that education, in my view, is the beginning of affluence, and affluence is not set aside for everyone.

Victor Hugo replies:

> Compulsory education is the child's right which, make no mistake about it, is even more sacred than the father's right . . . An immense Public Education System, donated and regulated by the State, beginning with the village schools and leading step by step to the Collège de France, and higher yet, to the Institut de France; the doorways of Knowledge are wide open to every mind. Everywhere there is a mind, everywhere there is a pasture, there must be a book! Not a commune without a school! Not a town without a *collège!* I reject your law. I reject it because it confiscates Elementary Education, because it degrades Secondary Education, because it lowers the level of knowledge, because it debases my country. . . .

The Prince-President approves this law, which gives total satisfaction to the clergy (though some bishops and the Ultramontane Veuillot had sought more, or protested against the hygiene supervision established in the private schools), and, when he becomes emperor, he will complete the Falloux Law with the oath. This is a purge (especially of Guizot, Michelet, and Quinet); there are new reforms which suppress the competitive examinations [*agrégations*] in philosophy, history, grammar, and letters (replaced by a single one in letters), mathematics, physics, chemistry, and natural history (a single one in sciences); there is the imposition that academic robes be worn at all times, and that professors shave their moustaches.

In December of 1851, Louis-Napoleon Bonaparte frees himself of his toughest opponents; a year later, he proclaims the Empire: the unwieldy dictatorship of the first years does not last. Napoleon III, unlike many other lovers of personal power, eased the regime after 1860, and was to finish almost as he began—as President of a parliamentary Republic. His hesitations and retreats are no longer important: under his reign, France finally sees the Industrial Revolution, experiences a hitherto unseen prosperity, opens itself to the world—at least to the colonial world —in an atmosphere of positivistic conquest, of technological and scientific progress which heralds a new era. The hour of the Romantics is past and so are the revolutions in the working-class districts.

XV

"Positivist France"

---

*1850-1900**

ESPECIALLY between 1850 and 1880, that great half-century experienced a transformation in ways of life, a renewal of economic activities, which left the past centuries' population movements and scientific and technological innovations far behind. As participants in a second, and soon a third, Industrial Revolution, we are tempted to forget how much French life was already transformed in the nineteenth century. If it is true that the man of 1870 is still closer to his seventeenth-century ancestor than to his eighteenth-century one—particularly if he lives in the country—the 1880s certainly seem decisive. The great turning point† is there, in this time when the steam engine, stationary or mobile, begins to supply men with an energy whose returns, disparaged in the mid-twentieth century, are nonetheless quite superior to the energy of run-

---

* The date 1900 corresponds to no political definition: the consolidated Third Republic has been proceeding upon its irregular career for more than twenty years. It is a mere landmark, and a debatable one, preferred to 1895 and the close of the difficult years since 1873; therefore, once more, we have an indicatory date.

† This expression "great turning point," already used on p. 259, is beyond any doubt more indispensable to the nineteenth century than to the sixteenth: the daily life of millions of men begins to be changed, and subsequently the change is but accelerated. Intellectual and material conditions, levels of culture as well as of nutrition, are modified profoundly. The turning point of the sixteenth century affects several hundreds of thousands of individuals; that of the nineteenth century affects the masses.

ning water, men, or horses; in this time, iron, cast iron, and steel make a
growing place for themselves in architecture as well as in domestic life—
from the Tour Eiffel, with its inexhaustible popularity, to the Godin* of
three generations ago. The first Industrial Revolution overwhelms rural
and urban areas, the financial life of the feverish Bourse and the age-
old economy of a village in Languedoc, with a force and power compelling immediate adaptation—all this despite protectionism, that aid of the
State which then seemed the only safeguard.

Few Frenchmen of that time had a clear picture of the ins and outs
of these transformations, which were undergone rather than desired; this
is undoubtedly because technological and scientific advances are not as
closely linked as today. From the invention of something to its technical
popularization, the course is long and the years numerous, but from scientific research to technical invention—how deep an abyss! Papin's
digester dates from the 1680s; the first locomotives are built a good century later; the railroads' conquest of France does not occur until after
1850, in that latter period. However, the best-informed contemporaries
of Napoleon III and MacMahon, those who have leafed through Saint-
Simon and who become enthusiastic while reading Auguste Comte
and Renan, do not hesitate for a moment: the industrial era is the corol-
lary of scientific progress, of a progress taking place in all sciences constantly strengthening man's grasp of nature and of himself; physics,
chemistry, medicine, and especially astronomy are evidence of the ap-
proaching triumph of mathematics. This generation, which repudiates
the mystical leaps of Romanticism, and which boasts about even the
most prosaic realism, is also mad for rationalist science, but with a reasoned madness, a madness about to be triumphant, inspiring the entire
student élite of the 1860s, all that convinced personnel of the Third
Republic, working from 1877 to 1890, and even beyond that date since
Clemenceau, for example, is a good representative of it.

The triumph of Scientism, in a country whose social and economic
structures have been renewed, is accompanied (a prudent term, but can
one assert more: a link of cause and effect?) by a new public life, one
in which democratic opinions hold the greatest place, supplanting, a century after the Revolution of 1789, monarchic faith, which survives
with great difficulty in several unevenly resistant bastions: the Latin
Quarter, naturally, a few provincial nooks, cantons in Brittany or in Mis-
tral's Maillanne. At the same time, the life of the working classes changes,
encouraged by industry's enormous call for manpower, by higher wages,
and by the progress of city planning; and working-class thought proceeds in its career, linked to, yet separate from, the contemporary change
of ideas, always inspired by the Parisian-trained personnel who have
long been supplying activists and writers, and stimulated by the Parisian

---

* A stove so common in nineteenth-century France that its brand-name came to
stand for the article itself.—Trans.

example of the 1870 Commune and its daring attempts. In some areas, new aspects of French life take shape, consolidating more or less fortunately according to the time and the place; after 1895, the days of strong organizations will bring about the necessary consolidations, and will consecrate the coming of the "proletariat" into national life.

▶ THE FIRST INDUSTRIAL REVOLUTION: A NEW ECONOMIC AND SOCIAL FRANCE

Without getting too far ahead of ourselves, is it not possible to assert that post-1850 France experienced the first great industrial transformation? After so many unfortunate attempts on the part of the State, so many factories vegetating despite the subsidies, orders, and privileges from Colbert's time, and after the days of the manufacturers who did not manufacture but who assembled or distributed raw materials and the artisans' output, France (which in 1850 is still richer in artisans than in workers, which almost unaware of tall coke furnaces still produces its iron in small forest furnaces, in wooded plateaux and mountains) is decisively regenerated, industrializing in a continuous movement, despite crises of speculation and overproduction—a new type of economic crisis destined, it seems, to have a long future. This is the birth of contemporary France, where towns expand and rural areas begin to become brutally depopulated, where Paris and the Seine Valley acquire a million people every twenty-five years, and build more than 150,000 houses at the same rate. What is the driving power behind the transformation in this France of Saint-Simon, where Protestant industrialists are doubtless as numerous and efficient as the followers of Enfantin? The steam engine certainly plays a large role, entailing as it does both the renewal of transportation and the re-equipping of heavy industry. Yet in this country still producing little coal and lacking investment capital, the great incipient industry, metallurgy, could not have evolved without a spread of banks, without the rapid growth of loan societies, and even without the extraordinary abundance of gold during the first twenty years. The progress of the French economy and its crises—from 1873 to 1895 —are clearly linked to the rhythm of the European and world economy, including the most obvious national consequences, like colonization and then the imperialism of the 1880s. From Péreire and Talabot to Jules Ferry, supporters of a long-range colonial policy, it is liberal French capitalism which continues to progress.

French industry is rapidly fitted out with steam engines: where there were 6,000 in 1848, there are 28,000 by 1870, outfitting close to 23,000 establishments, and representing a strength of 340,000 horsepower.* This movement, continuing beyond 1870 (84,000 in 1900 for 2,000,000 horse-

---

* French horsepower equals 32,549 foot-pounds per minute, as compared with our standard of 33,000 foot-pounds per minute.—Trans.

power) and until shortly before 1914, explains the stagnation of the labor force during this period, even taking into consideration a more precise definition of the worker, as the large factories move ahead to the detriment of the artisans and those who work in their own homes. But, despite the high smokestacks and forests of factory belts, the advances in themselves responsible for the forward leaps of production (in all the industries, textile as well as nutritive) have undoubtedly upset French life less than the mobile engine, the locomotive. In a few decades, the railroad becomes the most important means of long-distance transportation: capable, at the end of the century of ruining inland transportation along rivers or canals—the Garonne and Loire. Complemented by a network of roads totaling 250,000 miles, the railroad gives life to even the remotest small village, just as the automobile is about to take over some of its work: 1,900 miles in 1850, 10,500 in 1870, 28,000 at the end of the century—the railroad has at its disposal several hundred thousand cars, 12,000 locomotives; it provides a living for more than a half-million railway employees. The companies sharing the major lines radiating out from Paris, like the royal roads inherited from the eighteenth century and the bourgeois monarchy, are founded during the Second Empire.* In this way, a totally new activity has taken its place in the country, one which rapidly becomes indispensable through the changes it brings about in regions far distant from the large centers. But the construction and outfitting of this railroad system necessitated an extraordinary economic effort: the capital essential for these vast undertakings, the companies, can be amassed only by the Bourse. French metallurgical output is still too low to satisfy demand, and for many years England supplies steel and locomotives, despite all the progress of French industry in the central and northeastern regions. The construction of railroad beds (ballast, tunnels, bridges, stations) moves tens of thousands of construction workers across France; there is an unprecedented call for manpower in the rural areas and in still-somnolent towns, resulting in a migration about which we know little. To be sure, the railroad companies rehabilitated in one way or another, a part of the cartage personnel on the major roads: between Marseille and Lyon, 50,000 carters earned a living from the road in 1850; but the upheaval caused by the railroads, from the construction period on, is very great.†

Because of this railroad outfitting, coal and iron consumption exceeds production, despite the enormous progress achieved throughout

---

* The various lines, which survived until 1937, and are continued after nationalization under the name of "regions," were established at the beginning of the Empire: Nord, Paris-Orléans, Paris-Lyon, and Lyon-Méditerranée in 1852; Midi, and the short-lived Grand Central in 1853; the Est and Ouest in 1854. Paris-Lyon-Méditerranée is a later merger, in 1862.

† Thabault, in his monograph on Mazières-en-Gâtine, has pointed this out extremely well.

France, and particularly in the north which, during the course of the Second Empire, comes to rank ahead of the basin around Saint-Étienne. Coal production rises to four million tons in 1850, and consumption to seven and a half million; in 1870, the respective figures are thirteen and eighteen million. The movement continues: in 1899, because the production of the northern basin rises from four to twenty million, production reaches thirty-three million—but consumption is forty-five million. The strides in steel manufacturing and the use (due to the Thomas process after 1878) of iron from Lorraine, on the other hand, enables the metallurgical lag to be reduced: in 1870, France produces 110,000 tons of steel; in 1880, 380,000 tons; in 1903, 4,630,000.*

The employment of the Bessemer converter and the improvements made on puddling furnaces in the 1860s and 1870s by Siemens and Martin permit increased production of iron and steel, whose uses grow: as early as the Exhibition of 1867, bridges, ships, and lighthouses made completely of iron are shown, not to mention the metal frameworks which become an essential element of the new architecture. However, the metallurgical industries do not become concentrated, nor do they adopt the most improved techniques, within a few years; toward the close of the Second Empire, they are still scattered—except for the four major centers: in the north, in Lorraine, and in the towns of Saint-Étienne and Le Creusot—throughout all of France, from the Landes to the Basse-Indre basin, the Ardennes, and Seine-Inférieure, the Comité des Forges formed in 1864 organizes the iron manufacturers, who at the outset include the greatest names of the day: De Wendels and Schneiders (who as early as the end of the Second Empire have at their disposal at Le Creusot 15 blast furnaces, 30 power hammers, 130 puddling furnaces, 85 steam engines—and they employ 10,000 workers), the Cails from Paris, and the Marrels from Rive-de-Gier. Large and well-equipped establishments are created and flourish, by virtue of which the price per ton of steel decreases by half in twenty years; also, the small forges in the wooded regions of the Aveyron or the Langres plateau vegetate while waiting to be shut down. Hence the area around Saint-Étienne has the Aciéries de la Marine at Saint-Chamond and Horme, and the small workshops of gunsmiths who still work at home under rather poor conditions; the De Wendel establishments actuate the large metallurgy industry in the Lorraine at a time when the small workshops of the neighboring Haute-Marne are still producing iron in the forests. Thus metallurgy takes shape, slowly eliminating the old craft processes and establishing, in the coal-producing basins—and soon in the large iron veins—heavy iron smelting, tall furnaces, steel works, wire drawing mills, and rolling mills, maintaining, in numerous traditional centers, different types of metallurgy,

---

* The metric ton, the one referred to throughout this translation, equals 2,204.6 pounds.—Trans.

producing industrial tools, nails, knives, scythes, and sickles. Then, around 1890, this industry turns toward bicycles—while awaiting the automobile, and a new destiny.

And so we see the large railroad companies and heavy metallurgical enterprises, directed by those strong personalities of the day who are linked to one another by so many family alliances or business contracts, who sit simultaneously in administrative councils and in the legislative body—the real masters of the new France, Eugène Schneider or Paulin Talabot.* All those large establishments had to be created with the help of public funds, and the support of credit. In this area, the important work was carried out during the Second Empire. First, "to promote the development of Commerce and Industry in France," the principal French banks are created; these are destined to form the financial backbone of contemporary France. Like the Bank of France itself, from 1857 on, their provincial branches grow, supplying a very flexible network—one adapted to commerce and local industries. For a long time they are organizations that draw off money rather than lend it; they absorb the savings of the rich who seek five-hundred- or thousand-franc securities, and who want safe investments, recommended by directors or agencies in whom these clients have confidence.† They do some of the work of the former banks: the small regional ones (which, however, have taken their part in the economic revival), but also the Parisian banks (Mallet, Rothschild, Mirabaud), which are directed primarily toward government loans and international businesses. Having quite diverse specialties—the Crédit Foncier, for example, specializes in mortgage loans—and being mainly commercial banks, they assume an essential role in economic life, a role not played by the national or municipal savings banks, which attract the capital of small savers to the sole benefit of public finances.

Second, the establishment of large enterprises is accelerated after 1867 when a new law supplies all the facilities to be desired for the development of the joint-stock companies which increase during this period.‡ These companies are formed with the capital amassed through the sale of stock; they are run by boards of directors designated at general meet-

---

* In 1869 a polemicist of the day enumerates these owners of railroads, heavy metallurgy, steamers, gas, banks, and credit associations—he finds 183 of them. Sixty years later, journalists and *chansonniers* will speak of the "Two Hundred Families." Is this a distorted reality which lives and survives like a myth?

† The Crédit Foncier is founded in 1852; as is the Péreire family's Crédit Mobilier, the only large bank not to last, a victim simultaneously of the excessive ambition of its directors—following, say some, in the footsteps of Law—and of its competition. The Comptoir d'Escompte is founded in 1853, the Crédit Lyonnais in 1863, and the Société Générale in 1864. The Crédit Foncier, established with a capital of sixty million francs, has two hundred fifty million by the end of the century.

‡ Statements enable us to follow their rhythm: 191 in 1868, 200 in 1869, 223 in 1870.

ings of the stockholders in which each participant has as many votes as he has shares of stock—a system which, in point of fact, benefits only the large-scale participants. The more numerous holders of only a few shares are satisfied with cashing their dividend, and do not concern themselves with the meetings. Hence the flexibility of the new formula, which is far superior to that of the extant limited partnerships; at the same time it makes possible the accumulation of commanding amounts of capital, it allows this capital to be managed by small groups, often united by their joint participation in similar large-scale businesses and hence linked by common interests. And also, for that matter, the quoted values at the Bourse steadily increase from one year to the next, despite all crises up to the First World War. It is true that this process occurs concurrently with speculation in government stocks, both French and foreign; such speculation always interests a certain number of banks and their clientele. Yet as early as the Second Empire, money and the Bourse became trite literary themes, from Feydau to Zola: it is the world of high finance. And the extremely large army of banking employees become the indispensable pawns of these new activities.

The progress in transportation and industrial production has also brought about advances in the commercial professions even in rural areas, where the inn (doubling as a grocery and general store, selling a great variety of products) puts the peddlers out of business within a few years. But the change is even clearer in the towns, due to the founding of department stores: *galeries* with all sorts of names, and then, from a lack of imagination, new *galeries*. There are the large Parisian establishments, from the Bon Marché to the Samaritaine;* those large houses experienced a success we can no longer imagine, accustomed as we are to self-service. Zola saw it well: "For the happiness of ladies" who can look and look again, leave without buying, look again and return, pay without haggling, examine without trying on. There is a totally new rhythm and also a totally new technique of retail trade: just before advertising and its sensational success in the twentieth century, the late-nineteenth-century department store is the leading stimulant of the new commerce. Moreover, the concentration and especially the en-

---

* The Bon Marché was founded in 1852; the Louvre in 1855, the Printemps in 1865; the Samaritaine in 1869, and the Galeries Lafayette in 1889. The increased elegance of city-dwelling women is linked to this department-store progress, Michelet thought he saw this elegance in 1842, when the price of cotton fell—everyone knows the famous passage in *Le Peuple*—"Every woman used to wear a blue or black dress that she kept ten years without washing it, for fear it might fall to pieces. Today, her husband, a poor worker, covers her with a flowered dress at the cost of a day's labor. This whole female world, which presents a dazzling, rainbow-like play of thousands of colors on our promenades, was not very long ago in mourning." The year 1842 certainly was not enough to cause this feminine springtime; the department stores have their part in the "revolution." But the people in the country will remain "in mourning" for a long time.

largement of the interior market are again in play. The commercial function develops and, between 1860 and 1900, its forces double.

This economic and industrial progress finally finds an extraordinarily
effective aid in the increase of monetary circulation: the discovery and
working of new mines in California in 1850, and later in the Transvaal,
conveyed a flood of gold to Europe and France; this partially explains
the increase in wages and the acceleration of trade over a good twenty-
year period. This benefits, first of all, those iron manufacturers, large
industrialists, and members of boards of directors who, to a large extent, are the nineteenth century's newly-rich, and who sometimes
began with nothing,* for Paris, if not France, is a place of economic
growth *à l'américaine*, more often set up by the preceding era's achievements, which were above all financial. It is for these newly-rich that
Haussmann† rebuilds Paris: beautiful houses along the boulevards with
broad, open views, on which horses and carriages prance; the *folies* of
the Champs-Élysées, Auteuil, and Passy; theaters where the light, frivolous *vie parisienne* in the style of *La Belle Hélène* and of *opera-buffa*
unfurls displays of sometimes dubious taste—but the Tuileries set the
tone, and the Faubourg Saint-Germain sulks haughtily. And it is for
these newly-rich that the first summer resorts close to Paris come into being, where business concerns detain this world of worried speculators:
first Deauville, Dieppe, and Enghien, then the more distant spas,
Vichy, Royat, and Plombières. But it is again for this same world that,
between 1860 and 1880, is born the *haute couture* of Paris—which, like
ready-to-wear articles, benefits from the sewing machine. It clothes an
elegant and increasingly international clientele; large houses like Pa-
quin establish, and maintain into the following century, a reputation in
England and the United States, despite competition from Vienna and
Berlin. Thus has this progress of financial, commercial, and industrial
capitalism favored Paris, because of the advance acquired and because of
the administrative, railroad, and banking centralization. A new capital
becomes established, illuminated by gas.

Financiers associated in powerful and often rivaling groups, daring
speculators who make a profession of playing the Bourse on the outside
market, industrialists, businessmen who do not disdain useful political

---

* There is Cognac-Jay of the Samaritaine, well known by its customers who, touched
by the entire (sometimes blundering) system of family advertising, ensure a fine
future for it. And the same for Boucicaut. And the obscure people, like the Norman
spinning-mill owner, Fouquet Lemaître, a worker who became a cotton-mill owner
and dies leaving a fortune of thirty-two million francs.
† Granted that major strategical concerns undoubtedly played their role, as did extremely profitable financial transactions concerning the compulsory sale of real estate.
"The Fantastic Accounts [*Comptes*] of Haussmann," said Jules Ferry. (This is a
pun on the then very popular *Contes Fantastiques* by E. T. A. Hoffmann.—Trans.)

action—who is not familiar with Alphonse Daudet's terrible charge, *Numa Roumestan?*—this whole inflamed, cosmopolitan world mixed up with considerable foreign connections is, to a large extent, a "rail feudalism," offspring of the shortened distances and industrial progress brought about by the railroads. But these upset rural life too: undoubtedly in a manner less visible, for the brilliance of the town—the rumor of scandals spread far and wide by a cheaper press careless of the greats of this world the moment misfortune hits them, the lure of a capital that is more glittering, in its very frippery, than ever before—all this urban splendor has thrown back into the shadows the quiet beginnings of a still-incomplete agricultural revolution.

The easy and accelerated traffic of agricultural products—and also of fertilizers and machines—explains the regional specialization, the great agricultural advance at the end of the century. Irregular, varying from region to region, more or less rapid depending upon the structure of ownership and cultivation, this transformation brought about by the massive commercialization of products governed agricultural life for a century, until the present-day crisis. The most striking example—since each region reacts differently, as attested by the arguments of the French geographical school from Demangeon's *Picardie* to Juillard's *Basse-Alsace*—is the one in Languedoc. A Mediterranean region of general farming such as the Coustière wine district, grazing mobile flocks in the Cévennes during the summer, and tilling wheat on the plain, Languedoc (once the railroads are built), devotes itself to vineyards, abandoning previous crops almost totally within about ten years. At the same time, wine-growing has deserted the north; the general direction of specialization is clear: an adaptation to regional climatic conditions, abandonment of the concerns for adequate supply peculiar to the traditional general farming. In some localities, as in the Comtat, irrigation improvements enable the summer drought to be coped with: the beginnings of an undeniable achievement. Elsewhere, the siliceous soil of the Creuse and Combraille are improved by liming, so much so that the areas of wheat cultivation are not, on the whole, reduced. The facility of trade permits the growth of a national, and soon international, market, mainly of the most perishable products: flowers from the Côte d'Azur, spring vegetables from Brittany and the Mediterranean Midi, fruits, and so on.

However, this specialization does not entail basic changes in ownership and cultivation. In neighboring countries, Germany and England, where large-scale farming is more important, the second half of the nineteenth century sees a much clearer rural exodus and a considerable extension of this type of farming. The most distinct movement, that of rural depopulation, although in 1900 the majority (59 per cent) of the population remains in the rural districts, does not imply advances in large holdings, but essentially the day laborers' departure to the towns, and in-

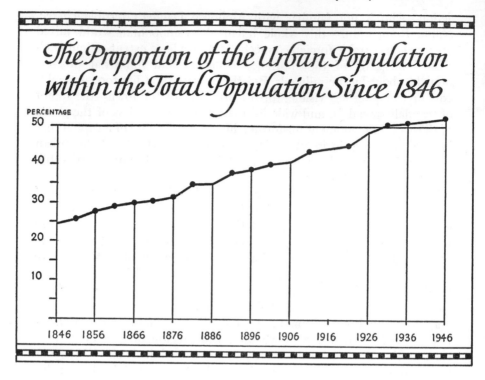

The Proportion of the Urban Population within the Total Population Since 1846

creased area for the small farming properties—but without much land consolidation. The solidity of traditions was unable to prevent crop change-overs—the reduction of wheat in Normandy and of vineyards in Aquitaine; it did maintain the cutting-up of land, and the redivision of plots in each part of communal terrain. Hence, despite the improvements of equipment—mechanical reapers, reapers and binders, sowers, and threshers*—even despite the extensive use of fertilizers, especially phosphates imported from North Africa, and despite the improvements in yields per acre, the economic situation is less favorable than one might believe. The drop in rural industries, particularly textiles, which were pushed aside by the concentration of factories and the 1880-1890 crises, contributed, it is true, to the situation. Nevertheless, the retirement of fallow land (twelve million acres in 1860, seven million in 1880, and their virtual disappearance after 1880), the increasing use of artificial meadows, often to the detriment of communal heaths, and improvements in the forest which, finding new uses and being kept

---

* This mechanical equipment came rather slowly: 100,000 threshers in 1862, 235,000 in 1892; 10,000 sowers in 1862, 50,000 in 1892. The hesitancy of the rural population toward these innovations is well known, despite the encouragements from agricultural schools and agricultural professors.[1]

up by the Eaux and Forêts, become increasingly productive—all these prove the scope of the agricultural revolution.

The village also changes: undoubtedly it still includes those peasant-artisans who held two professions in the traditional economy and supplied the peasant with basic, necessary manufactured goods—wheels, tools, and pieces of fabric. But their number diminishes in direct proportion to the proximity of the railroad: the villages become peopled with minor civil servants, schoolteachers, mailmen, pensioners, and particularly full-time artisans. The squares of small market towns have several shops, taverns—especially lively after Sunday Mass—grocery stores, selling a few newspapers a week, which call themselves general stores, as well as hardware stores and sugar merchants; in the *chefs-lieux* of the cantons, the doctors, pharmacists, notaries, tax collectors, cartwrights (who are agents for agricultural machinery) constitute an already considerable bourgeoisie whose settlement within market towns of more than two thousand helps to distort in our statistics the numerical reduction of people living directly off the land.[2]

Therefore rural France remains diverse: a farmer in the Beauce who, at the end of the nineteenth century, has ten to fifteen horses in his stables and all the current machines in his shed, who harvests wheat and sugar beets with better yields; the Bourbonnais *métayer* who takes orders from the "master" each Monday and divides his meager harvest in half; and the small farmer who cultivates his own land in Aquitaine, who has remained faithful, by virtue of an equally favorable soil and climate, to a general farming which is still profitable—all these are widely dissimilar types. They have made unequal use of the large opening onto the national market offered by railroad outfitting; but even the *métayer*, who is the least well-placed, nonetheless profits from it.

And yet this half-century was not a period of constant prosperity. The "launching" period itself, which practically coincides with the Second Empire, from 1850 to 1873, experienced some jolts which—since they affected with varying strength the nation's economic life—were hardly negligible. There are the 1857 speculation crisis, the textile difficulties after 1860, when the liberal treaty signed by Napoleon III opens the French market to English products and is protracted until 1866-67, for cotton, by the Civil War in the United States. Although French industry protested in 1860, before having suffered, it remains true that the bold attempt of the French agricultural and industrial economy to confront that of England—when the latter had had a comfortable technical advance for close to a century and had been devoted to free trade for ten years—disturbed an economic life traditionally limited within a national, protected framework. As early as 1871, the successors of Napoleon III are concerned with the return of protectionism.

Yet their triumph came with the great depression of 1873-1895: a world-wide, and not merely French, phenomenon, the crisis of 1873 can be traced to a depletion of the gold supply combined with the renunciation in many countries of bimetallism. Unquestionably France, which still remained strongly agricultural, felt this depression less than such nations as England. But French agriculture was affected simultaneously by the price drop, due to the progress of new regions, by the European influx of American wheat, as well as of Argentinian and Australian wool —this is the period of the great decline of French flocks—and by a crisis in the wine industry caused by the outbreak of phylloxera, which appeared around 1875 and continued until 1890, affecting all the vineyards in France. Though restored by American stocks, vineyards lost considerable ground in Aquitaine and the Charentes, and encountered new competition from Algeria. The textile, chemical, and metallurgical industries were affected from 1882 to 1885; and the textile industry had the particular handicap of the partial transferral of the industries around Mulhouse onto the western slope of the Vosges, after the German occupation of Alsace. The remedy found for this new economic crisis, after an attempt in 1882-83, was the adoption in 1892 of Méline's protective tariffs; this conservative from the Vosges was decisive in directing the French economy, since his protectionism has never been clearly revoked: the recovery following 1895 was carried out within the national framework—enlarged, it is true, by imperial conquests.

In this respect, the depression of 1873-1895 had consequences no different in France from those it had in the other, equally affected, countries of Western Europe; overseas expansion seems a necessity consciously presupposed first by governments, then by public opinion, which evolved rather quickly from 1885 to 1895. The work of the French colonial empire is primarily that of adventurers and missionaries who were isolated but supported by public authorities;* only from 1890-92 on does it become a work carried out on a national scale. The Ligue Maritime et Coloniale, a propaganda society among the youth, and the new Colonial Ministry, established in 1892, play a large part in it. However, there is a great deal of reluctance on the part of the Parisian petty-bourgeoisie, who remain quite set on *revanche*, and in the working classes, hostile to colonialism because of their humanitarianism. Finally, there is a great deal of ignorance, particularly in rural milieux. Conceived of by the business bourgeoisie as a safe market, both protected

---

* From this definition arises the augmentation of the first colonial domain's residue (Réunion, Saint-Pierre and Miquelon, Martinique and Guadeloupe, and the *comptoirs* of Senegal and India), through the "conquests" of 1830 to 1870: Algeria, Gabon, Cochin-China and Cambodia, Senegal and Djibouti. The great period certainly is between 1880 and 1900; this is the period when the empire takes shape with Tunisia, Tonkin, Annam, French West and Equatorial Africa, Madagascar, and finally Morocco.

and vast, for the industrial production, and also as a stable source of raw materials, both nutritive and industrial, the Empire has a well-defined economic role. Around 1895 there is no one who doubts that it is the "ambulance" which will enable them to overcome the crisis. Several factors—making use of four million square miles and administering sixty million men of different languages, cultures, and colors—immediately posed difficult problems whose existence the 1890 imperialists, except for the missionaries, hardly expected. Full awareness of them consolidates later.

Nevertheless, this stagnation, whose considerable effects cannot be minimized,* cannot distort the overall gain and the economic advance of the entire period. The gain and advance are attested to by several features: the rise of both agricultural and industrial wages, so marked until 1880; the development of foreign trade, in excess of ten billion francs at the end of the century,† through large companies like Messageries Maritimes and the Compagnie Transatlantique, and particularly Suez, which makes Marseille's new fortune; and finally, the general improvement in the standard of living. During the twenty imperial years, wheat consumption increased twenty per cent (in 1863, baking ceases to be a profession closely regulated by the government); sugar consumption increased fifty per cent, potatoes eighty per cent, wine doubled, coffee tripled—worldwide figures, which do not have a general significance; wine becomes more frequent on peasant tables, but coffee is not yet there, having become popular only in the towns. Alcohol also gains, doubtless, at that time, more in the towns than in the rural areas. But, all things considered, these figures are a good translation of the economic progress, and, if the population increases by four million (from thirty-five to thirty-nine million) between 1850 and 1900, it is already because of the increase in the average life span, indicating better living conditions and medical advances, and not because of an abundance of births which, on the contrary, diminish. This is a normal consequence, some say, of physiological improvement, evident although less noticeable to contemporaries than are the transformation of streets, new factories, and the large-scale works undertaken throughout urban and rural areas, unsettling familiar landscapes. In the towns, which already are becoming tentacle-like, and in the rural areas, where white bread and meat are be-

---

* In two spheres, at least: the first, where assertion ought to be prudent, is technical research which was stimulated, it seems, by the stagnation; but already, at the close of the nineteenth century, technical progress is closely dependent on scientific progress. The second is the revival of working-class and socialist action: in France as in England, the years between 1890 and 1895 are years of organization and establishment. But the French movement also has its own rhythm, about which we shall speak later.

† It rose to two and a half billion in 1851, and reached eight billion in 1869: the subsequent period obviously feels the effects of the depression.

ing consumed more frequently, Frenchmen at the close of the nineteenth century live better than their pre-1850 parents and grandparents, even when poverty, unemployment, or disease still lie in wait for them in a world which is still harsh.

► SCIENCE AND SCIENTISM

This economic progress is not born of a social transformation: the capitalistic and liberal society inherited from the July Monarchy remains fundamentally unchanged, but it handles things with an accrued power. The profit derived from this society by its masters is obviously greater than that of the manual laborer and of the wage earner. Yet the source of this profit is beyond any doubt the acquisition of a new mastery over nature, if not over men: a mastery arising from scientific progress, which increases during the half-century in a way never seen since. To use a happy turn of phrase, this is certainly the beginning of a second Creation: man creates a new world.

Throughout all of Europe, scientists are increasingly numerous in every area of knowledge; natural sciences diversify to such a point that universal knowledge, so long possible, becomes unattainable even in single disciplines like chemistry or physics. To explain how and why so many centuries of empirical or methodological research, from Descartes to Monge, from Mersenne to Kepler and Newton, from Ambroise Paré to Jenner and Laënnec, are becoming vastly fertile would carry us too far afield: we would have to follow the naturalists step by step from Paré to Buffon, from Cuvier to Lamarck; mathematicians, no less prudently, on more difficult paths, even to that non-Euclidian geometry of Riemann which, at mid-century, seems a quest of pure intellect, and which, a hundred years later, assumes such great importance. It is important to indicate here the spirit in which science triumphs—at the same time Renan becomes its herald in that great book, *L'Avenir de la Science*, a cry of confidence in reason, sure of its means and proud of the results obtained. The scientific method, a dialogue of hypothesis and experimentation, is set forth masterfully several years later by Claude Bernard,* and this lesson in method is chronologically sandwiched between the two most brilliant discoveries of the period: the strict application of mathematics to astronomy—Leverrier's deduction through calculation of the planet Neptune before it had been discovered—and Pasteur's revelation concerning the life of microbes. Then Auguste Comte's speculations about the three ages of humanity seem to be fully realized: humanity enters into the positive or scientific age, when all metaphysics loses its *raison d'être*, because it loses its reality. Spontaneous genera-

---

* *L'Introduction à la médecine expérimentale* is written in 1862. *L'Avenir le la Science* was written in 1848 and published later.

tion disappears from the postulates of the new medicine; Berthelot's chemistry brings about the earliest synthetics (methyl alcohol, acetylene), light and electricity are explained and mastered—more mastered, actually, than explained.

It would require many pages to compile a chronological catalogue of all those interrelated inventions which attracted universal interest, and are passed from country to country:* what boundless amazement for those contemporaries who follow these advances! Victor Hugo notes one day that the Académie des Sciences, recording the progress of chemistry during its Saturday meetings, is in the process of restoring and giving life to the old dreams of the alchemists; but he did not see what twentieth-century men saw: the transmutation of mercury into gold— the end of the great quest of all the Fausts of the Middle Ages. As early as 1848, Renan wrote that science is a religion which will furnish man with all the explanations his nature requires. Undoubtedly the strides made by medicine appeared the most extraordinary: not only because Pasteur's "revolution" (antiseptic processes, aseptic processes, and the discoveries of his followers in the Pasteur Institutes and in tropical countries) caused life expectancy to advance twenty years in one generation, but also because the application of a constantly improved chemotherapy to the human body demonstrated the unity of science, and the legitimacy of a total scientific unification—a unification of natural sciences to the social sciences.

For the scientific triumphs in the years between 1850 and 1880 are triumphs of the measurable, *i.e.*, of mathematics; to find instruments enabling observation of (or experimentation upon) the infinitely small, the cellular or microcellular, as well as the infinitely large (when astrophysics is born), is always to move forward along the same path. Biology links natural science to social sciences, demonstrating the facility of a transition which the theory of evolution, supported by the first great prehistoric explorations, masterfully upholds.† Thus the discoveries in the realm of the natural sciences increased and caused an enthusiasm which is the basis of Scientism: faith in a scientific progress‡ capable of gathering all the sciences into a single one based on mathematics, which would account for the universe and its galaxies, and of course for thinking man—indeed for God as well.

It is within this same movement that the social sciences become re-

---

* It is enough to recall, doubtless, that the basis of scientific work turns on chemistry and its atom theory, the wave theory of light, around electricity and electromagnetism, and finally, geology; chemistry, thermodynamics, electricity, and biology increase the bridges between science and technique.
† Darwin's *Origin of Species*, published in 1859, is almost immediately translated into all the spoken languages of the international scientific world.
‡ In this way the idea of progress, inherited from the eighteenth century, and the *encyclopédistes* in particular, acquired greater consistency and range.

newed and define their fields, repudiating all artistic ambition in order to seek the general laws of a human determinism more difficult to establish and analyze than physical laws. Experimentation being virtually impossible, the part played by conjecture (in statements like "the brain secretes thought as the liver stores sugar") explains the difficulties, but in no way contradicts the attempt. Taine explains, though not without some difficulty, the literature of England through physical milieu, race, and circumstances; the history by Fustel de Coulanges devotes itself to the patient, analytical search for causes and consequences, in which geographic determinism holds a major place. But before him, Renan published his *Vie de Jésus*, in 1863, from which he boldly concludes: "an incomparable man." Karl Marx—that founder of scientific socialism—in search of a precise evaluation of surplus value, exhibits in *Das Kapital* the same spirit. And at the close of the century, Durkheim, taking up a phrase—and an idea—from Auguste Comte, establishes sociology, the scientific study of human communities.[3] Social sciences will be the consummation of the scientific edifice dreamed of by Auguste Comte for the Positivist age: in 1863, Victor Duruy established the École Pratique des Hautes Études, in order to encourage scientific research and hasten this advent. This obviously does not mean that all France became Positivist: the new sciences, even the most useful to mankind, are still unknown and sometimes ignored. In many rural areas people prefer the "conjurer"—let us say bone-setter—to the doctor. In the Loire, there is a frequently heard old saw: "The tongue of a dog is worth the hand of a doctor." The scientific spirit, like the scientific movement, is the phenomenon of a minority.

Scientism's faith is aggressively rationalistic, its aggressiveness not hiding a certain scorn for religion and for Catholicism in particular. Obviously, *La Vie de Jésus* caused an uproar—Renan even lost his chair at the Collège de France; but Darwinism quickly, too quickly, appeared as a weapon against the teachings of Scripture. Perhaps, in fact, Pius IX helped set modern science against the Church by solemnly and globally condemning, with the *Syllabus* [*of Modern Errors*], all the errors of modernism, and other "isms": liberalism, naturalism, indifferentism, socialism. Like a besieged citadel, the Roman Catholic Church in 1870 promulgated the dogma of the Immaculate Conception or of Papal Infallibility, thus braving the storm majestically but with an unaccustomed rigidity, motivated perhaps by the scope of the assault.

The destinies of the Church of France, however, are closely bound neither to these great proclamations nor to the vicissitudes of the difficult relations between clergy and government. Protected at its beginnings by Napoleon III, treated less delicately from 1860 because of the backwash provoked by the Roman question, allied once more to powers under the

Moral Order* (which in 1875 authorizes Catholic higher education, the final stage of a reconquest begun in 1833 and 1850), abused in the 1880s when the Republicans adopt the divorce law and set up an elementary education system—all this could not conceal French Catholic vitality. It is a vitality of the masses, and particularly of the rural masses, whose clergy was still very much listened to. To take up the crosses, to recruit for the Papal Zouaves, to stock the seminaries, to supply the thousands of missionaries leaving to spread the Gospel in Africa and Asia, to parade in endless pilgrimages before the *curé* of Ars at Le Puy and soon at Lourdes,† to deliver the new devotions to the Sacred Heart of Jesus, Mary, and Joseph—to do all this, the clergy never appeals in vain to the rural districts, particularly in the west and in the mountainous regions. French Catholic life lacks neither saints nor teachers nor missionaries; but its action is primarily rural. The clergy no longer is numerous enough in the towns and the proletarian masses escape it; the bourgeoisie is divided, but Voltairianism remains good form, even among the Legitimists in the Faubourg. And finally, a tendency is taking shape in the villages, one that gains strength in the last quarter of the century and continues after 1900: the clergy is supported primarily by women—women who do not read, do not go out except for Sunday Mass, do not go to school. French Catholicism, in becoming a "thing for women," begins to lack profundity; the head of the family takes no further interest in it and becomes a seasonal observer, according to the quaint expression of G. Le Bras.‡ Withdrawal and vitality are not contradictory—but they presage the ghetto.

The young intellectuals who, educated during the Empire, bear the mark of Scientism—from Ferry to Clemenceau, from Vallès to Zola— are passionately anticlerical. Michelet, who re-edits his earlier works, and Hugo set the tone; Freemason lodges gain ample recruits and mold, in the still well guarded secrets of their initiation rites, the trained personnel of the Third Republic. The triumph of science must bring about the end of superstitions, and fanatic young people take "rationalist" oaths to hasten this end.§ Concerned with method, however, they prepare to work effectively for the new regime which is to succeed the Empire, elaborating a program of political reforms and plans for the spread of

---

* This is the label attached to the conservative policy, firmly rooted in the Church, announced in 1873 by the Duc de Broglie, then Prime Minister. The primary aim of the re-establishment of a "moral order" was the preparation for the restoration of a monarch. The subsequent reaction, until the 1876 elections, went against Republicanism: republican civil servants were dismissed, statues of La République were destroyed, etc.—Trans.

† The first "visions" of the Virgin occurred in 1857; at this time, Marianism experienced an incomparable and deeply significant period of thriving.

‡ A specialist in religious sociology.

§ The young Clemenceau swears in the Latin Quarter never to have recourse to a priest, no matter what the circumstances.

science—all at once. Future doctors, lawyers, and journalists, those enthusiastic readers of the eighteenth-century *philosophes*, also applaud
all the publications casting aspersions on those traditions; thanks to
Thérèse Raquin, Zola makes a name for himself in a few months in 1867.
Rationalist passion is found everywhere, not only in Vallès or Zola, but
in many a page of the *Littré* or the early *Larousse* as well. One example
is taken from the article on *Casuel* (perquisite fees) in the 1867 *Larousse*:
"The commercial spirit does not even halt before the coffin; everybody
knows that the length of prayers is in proportion to how much money has
been paid. . . ."

Reproaching the Church for taking a stand during the political debates of 1871-79, and disapproving of "political Catholicism," the anti-
clericals devoted themselves to stripping the clergy of their means of acting upon society—all the while carefully distinguishing between religion
and clericalism. It is toward this direction that the Ligue de l'Enseignement was founded in 1866 by Jean Macé, at Blebenheim* in Alsace; it
is with the same conviction of the necessity of taking the monopoly of
educating the young away from the clergy that the 1880-1886 education
laws were issued, after impassioned debates in the Chamber and in
the Senate. The granting of diplomas, which the Moral Order in 1875
had divided between public and *libre* professors, is restored only to
teachers in higher public education. Elementary education is set up for
those from six to thirteen: it is compulsory for every young Frenchman
—under the nominal responsibility of his parents; it is free—through
the abolition of the payments established by the 1833 law (without going
so far as the giving of free supplies, which is left to the municipalities'
good will); and, finally, it is secular—with Thursdays being left to the
parents' disposition for having their choice of religious education given
to their children outside of class. The clergy loses all rights of control
over the faculty, which is recruited from the elementary-teacher normal
schools in the *départements*—the "secular seminaries"; thousands of
schools were built throughout France from 1885 to 1900, and the education of millions of children was thus assured in a very brief space of
time. Furthermore, in 1880, the secondary education of women was established in *lycées* and *collèges* based on the model of the establishments
for men, not without noteworthy differences, which were subsequently
remedied. These establishments interfered considerably with the absolute monopoly the clergy enjoyed in this area by virtue of its convent
schools, where the daughters of the urban bourgeoisie were educated.
Yet these female students did not have a place in higher education until shortly after the First World War—an indication of how solidly an-

---

* The Ligue de l'Enseignement is not an offshoot of Freemasonry; if it is true that
Freemasons belong to it, many Protestants also come to it to fight against Catholic
clericalism.

chored the prejudices were. Until 1914, the only women students at the Sorbonne were foreigners—Russians particularly.

The 1884 law authorizing civil divorce, the discontinuation of prayers at the opening of parliamentary sessions, and the strict application of the never-abolished laws forbidding the Congregation in France are also translations of the same anticlerical spirit. Jules Ferry, Naquet, and Camille Sée lay the groundwork for an important development of public mentality; in this country in which unbaptized people are still a very small minority and Catholicism remains the religion of the great majority of Frenchmen, the 1880 laws herald the Separation, and educate public opinion to the idea—doubtless not new, but one not yet pushed as far as these consequences—of the total separation of spiritual and temporal power.[4] The years from 1880 to 1886 prepare for those from 1905 to 1907.

Within this world of steam and iron, are we to locate even artistic development inside the framework of Scientism? At a time when "wealth is a substitute for everything," when the engineer who is familiar with science appears to be the man of the future, intellectual life is swept along by this technical progress toward spiraling speculation. What Renan, in his *Prière sur l'Acropole*, calls "universal stupidity" [*panbéotie*] is the mark of the times, and it finds its merciless observer in the cruel Flaubert. A cultural depression marks the advent of the industrial bourgeoisie, which has no time to read, and unlike those of the previous century does not always have generations of soundly educated people behind it.* Bouvard, Pécuchet, and Homais are caricatured images stamped from the sickeningly base alloy of this new "good society" for whom all values, traditional or otherwise, have lost their meaning. The *Dictionnaire des idées reçues* by the same Flaubert rests on the same perspective; but the persistence of certain prejudices is significant, and nicely illuminates the implications of the "wisdom of the nation." Just a few examples: *Baccalauréat*: to inveigh against; "Erudition": scorn it as the mark of a narrow mind; "Agriculture": short of hands. Another good proof of this regression into stupidity is the political personnel of the Third Republic, who discontinue subsidies to the Théâtre Italien and Théâtre Lyrique, and who, in 1897, reject Caillebotte's gift, which is too rich in those innovators, Manet, Cézanne, and Renoir. The Second Empire was unquestionably better guided; in particular Napoleon III put an end, as early as 1863, to the control the Académie des Beaux-Arts exercised over artistic life: awarding the Prix de Rome, regulating State pur-

---

* There is moral depression, too, though generalizations in this area are more difficult; one can easily gauge, however, the gap on this level separating the triumphant bourgeoisie of the Jansenist seventeenth century from the world of concerns in Panama and with decorations.

chases, and establishing the activity of those who received the Prix de Rome. During the Third Republic, academicism raged ceaselessly: Clemenceau was virtually the only one interested in the new painting.

As a reaction against the Romantics' nobility and torments, but particularly an alignment on the side of scientific objectivity, literature wants to be a photographed report, an uninterpreted, untransfigured slice of life: the realistic novel is the best expression of the art which, to be truthful, claims to reject all choice. Zola writes a report of the Second Empire and Flaubert depicts the mores of provincial Normandy; poetry passes from this world and, at the end of the century, seeks refuge in the closed, inaccessible literary coteries of the Symbolists with their *recherché* difficulties. (Yet Baudelaire, refined and precious, is also in flight before this realism which he considers ephemeral.) Balzac is reputed to be the master of the new art because *La Cousine Bette*, *Le Père Goriot*, and *Eugénie Grandet* herald those who aspire to biographical criticism and learned reconstitution: from the *Comédie Humaine* to *Rougon-Macquart*, from *L'Assommoir* to the *Bête humaine*. Then Maupassant.

Actually painting preceded literature by at least a few years: Courbet, that stolid man from Franche-Comté who paints as a tree produces apples, who scorns Delacroix's East and is happy with the region where he was born, launches realism with the *Tableau historique d'un enterrement à Ornans* (1851), *Les Casseurs de pierres*, *Les Demoiselles de village*. Millet and Corot follow with their sowers and rural scenes. Scorning all mythology, all choice of learned subjects, as devoted to rocks as to the figure, Courbet frees painting from the slavery of the academic subject, painting of the type Puvis de Chavannes is then practicing as devotedly as Courbet is hurling his infantile passion into imposing "his" painting.

But, opposite Zola and Courbet, Baudelaire—of the *Correspondances*—Debussy, and somewhat later Mallarmé, are supported and discovered by the richest revolution that French painting has ever known: Impressionism, whose greatest displays date from the exhibitions of 1874-1876, inspires nonetheless the final forty years of the century, preparing and announcing the pursuits of the School of Paris. In the days of Cézanne, Degas, Manet, Monet, Renoir, and so many others, French poetic genius seems to be the gift solely of painting, so numerous are the canvases, rich with color, light, joy of life, and pent-up emotions: the painters surpass the poets, while the latter are losing themselves in the labyrinths of Mallarmé and Valéry. The new style is a rediscovery of color* for its own value, and of *plein air* painting. Who cannot imagine

---

* At the time when photography takes shape and becomes, at first, an art of the portrait, a record of features and hence a design, painting—which, after the 1870s, will be called Impressionism—turns toward color; the first impulse which will be followed, at the end of the century, by a new inquiry, that is, non-theoretical inquiry, into form.

Claude Monet's adventure of digging out a trench, climbing a scaffolding, and putting pulleys in his garden in order to create the famous
Femmes au jardin in 1867; who cannot envision the first amazement of
contemporaries at seeing the white light of the studios discarded and at
noticing, under the parasol, blue and green shadows on the face? Then
in the following years, the canvases multiply, canvases in which the
shimmers of light are rendered with a sort of passion: their predilection
for river banks, *La Seine à Argenteuil* or *L'Oise à Pontoise,* for the reflections on the water, derives from this love of color, placed by successive
contourless dabs, often on the surface of a design preserved despite this
search for color. This search is the great achievement of all the Impressionists, whatever their individual genius, from the tender Renoir, in love
with gay Parisian life and women, to Manet, painter of all the Parisian
landscapes, to Pissarro, constantly in search of new processes; yet to come
are the disturbances of the even newer forms of Cézanne, Van Gogh,
and Gauguin in the years between 1885 and 1890.

Rejected and banished from the official Salons, sometimes reduced to
poverty, the Impressionists were treated poorly by academic critics until
after the First World War. But it is because of them that painting, in the
modern period, became the dominant expression of modern art, relegat-
ing music* and literature to the background: *le boulevard des Capu-
cines* and *La gare Saint-Lazare, La fôret de Fontainebleau* and *Les
guinguettes de la Seine* entered into our artistic heritage in the same
movement, thanks to Monet, Sisley, and Renoir; similarly, a bit later,
La Maison du Docteur Gachet, Le pont de l'Anglais, and *La ferme au
Pouldu.*

▶ **PUBLIC LIFE AND DEMOCRATIC
   FEELINGS**

How did France become Republican? While in February, 1871, she sent
Bordeaux an Assembly in which the nobles, supporters of the Monarchy,
were more numerous than their ancestors had been in the Estates-
General of 1789, afterwards, France is to vote Republican, and to do so
continuously. And it is not only urban France which, for quite some time,
has been won over to "advanced" ideologies; it is also the France of the
villages and the remote rural areas, still imperfectly linked to the towns,
for the railroads in the *départements* have scarcely been built and the
bicycle has not taken its place in the daily lives of those in the country.

---

* French music is neither decadent nor even the province of a mere few, as is the
poetry of Mallarmé. The music from the operas of Gounod and Bizet is intended
for the people. Wagner remains, during this whole half-century, the idol of the "concerts" which are created then between 1860 and 1880—Pasdeloup, 1861; Colonne,
1873. But this musical public is more restricted than that of the Salons.

Actually, the problem is not merely one of the partial elections from 1871 to 1875 or of the propaganda of Gambetta, that devoted traveling salesman who visits the towns; the problem goes beyond this chronological framework, for it translates a development which is not a change of political sympathy but a transformation of the collective mentality.

In order to explain fully the progress of a democratic mentality, it goes without saying that the period between 1850 to 1900 alone is not enough: the assertion of parliamentarianism under the Constitutional Monarchy, the habits of French jurists, since the beginning of modern times, to vote according to the plurality of votes, as well as the collective life of French rural communities, in those days of still greater distance between people—all these important facts, traditions, and common working methods played their role.* But from shortly after December 2, 1851, to the Dreyfus Affair, there is an abruptly accelerated development which is not unrelated to the economic and social transformations.

In this area, the first ten years of the Second Empire are the ones that count; for the first time since 1815, when, under tranquil circumstances, elections with universal suffrage were held, the traditional guides of public opinion are in disagreement. The château, denied a restoration hoped for in 1848-49, has its candidates; or rather, it is not pleased with the clergy and does not support the candidates of the regime. The presbytery, which in most cases obediently follows the episcopacy allied to Napoleon III, has its own men as its official candidates, following the practice initiated by Morny—white posters, prefectoral circulars—and then, favor of the clergy. The universal suffrage mutilated by Thiers and his friends was re-established so well by Napoleon's nephew that the debate is carried to the public square, or rather to everyone's conscience. At the time of the 1848 elections, nothing similar had taken place, and the "notables" had been elected in great number. In 1852 and in 1857, the official candidates form a united front; these directed elections, with overly fine results, seem uneventful. Actually, beneath the dictatorial appearances, these elections conceal a gradual and certain awakening to political realities: the conflict between *monsieur* and *curé* —sometimes marked by little scandals which become quickly known in the rural areas where fairs and markets are increasingly frequent—has wide repercussions. As far back as this period, the ballot became the peasant's opportunity to test his political freedom: for a while, his habitual advisers do not speak the same language.† Only the Protestant

---

* And these are but the most important factors. Let us recall that Bloch poses this problem in the closing pages of his *Société Féodale*, wondering whether the taste for freedom, so much alive when he is writing his great work, published in 1942, is not a distant inheritance of the feudal customs of independence.

† After 1860, the terrible backwash of the Roman question created difficulties between Napoleon III's regime and the clergy. The Empire became liberal. Rural political conditions were much more confused. But full awareness has been won.

rural areas of the Midi and the Cévennes did not experience this momentary division; but their long practice of Calvinism conferred upon
them a considerable democratic "advance"; without any hesitation they
are Republican as early as 1848.

Unquestionably more important is the debate between the schoolteacher and the curé opened on the village square in the 1880s. Opened,
or rather enlarged: as early as 1848, in the days when the public elementary school and the normal schools were placed under the control of the
clergy, did the conservative bourgeoisie not reproach the schoolteachers
—in the voice of Thiers—for being horrible socialists? Now this control
is discontinued by Jules Ferry; religious education is no longer given in
class, and the schoolteacher teaches "natural" morality and good citizenship—nothing more. For the clergy in the 1880s and 1890s, the secular school is Godless, and it will remain so for a long time. If the lines of
battle were already drawn, the conditions under which the laws setting
up the public elementary school had been passed made the hardening
virtually inevitable. By contrast with the conviction, in ecclesiastical
milieux, that they were watching a diabolical project of dechristianiza-
tion, the reassuring words of Ferry during the course of the debates and
the care exercised to provide the clergy with the time necessary for
proper religious education do not weigh heavily. It is useless to look elsewhere for the origins of a conflict which, for a good quarter-century, had
been a struggle between two intellectual authorities within village communities. The young schoolteachers, educated in the normal schools in
order to receive a general education—more noteworthy for its humanism than for its adaptability to the local milieu—and also prepared to
withstand the oratorical assaults of the clergy who were often backed by
large property owners, generally took their task of dispensing cultural
education and civic information to heart. Coming from the lower
classes—sons and daughters of métayers, small farmers, mailmen, and
railway employees—and imbued with a sense of mission, they accepted
a challenge which could not be merely one of ideas and principles—if
indeed the combatants themselves, in accepting the challenge, are aware
of the change brought about on the spiritual level by the secular idea,
and by the ideal of equal toleration of all beliefs and of all differences of
opinion. The debate degenerated very quickly. Abusive generalizations
presented the schoolteacher as a materialist without any faith whose presence at church seemed a sacrilege, and the curé as a defender of all the
obscurantist superstitions, an enemy of science and the new world. But
on this side of the vocabulary and the too generously exchanged insults,
let us examine the controversy, sometimes even within four walls, which
was instituted: clashes of words, encounters of ideas arousing curiosity
and interest; gradually, readings and discussions; and, in the bargain, the

classing of Frenchmen into two permanently opposed groups, Right and Left—the Right synonymous with social conservatism, supported by the clergy, by traditional political and moral values, and by a long-nourished nostalgia for the monarchy, and the Left, synonymous with the expression of a desire for social and political progress, a democratic faith freed from religious or social constraints, and faith in a terrestrial future.

Stable in their posts to the point of spending their entire careers in the same village, holding an important social position by virtue of their learning—which enables them to converse with the doctor, justice of the peace, and road inspector—and also by virtue of the office of the town hall secretary, which falls to them so often, the schoolteachers were successful, and the elementary schools became the center of the French village during the Republic. The drop in illiteracy, as gauged by the examination boards, is a sign of their achievement; through rigorous training in "basic techniques" (reading, writing, and arithmetic) and also through the taste for general ideas patiently and more laboriously developed, the elementary school succeeds in causing illiteracy to decrease among military recruits—from 1900 on, the percentage becomes negligible. But it is important to see how much the schoolteachers' qualities of devotion and perseverance were aided by social development: the rural population has come to school because school answers an ever-increasing need for knowledge and culture; the small market town sends children with as much regularity as does the small city; the more remote areas, such as the regions in the Massif Central, come around more slowly. The compulsory nature of education, theoretically supervised by delegates from the cantons, friends of the school, designated by the Committee for Academic Inspection, was not enforced in cases of defaulting. This success of the schools is, in point of fact, explained by the moral and intellectual authority of the teachers, who were soundly trained in the normal schools, as well as by the social utility of the educational equipment acquired between the ages of six and thirteen, and finally, to a lesser degree, by a certain feeling of dignity attested to by the number of *certificats d'étude* that used to be framed and hung in a conspicuous place in the most beautiful room of the most modest dwellings.

At all times, school attendance dropped during the spring and summer months—from May to the end of July—when the children worked in the fields. Yet the school is necessary—not for the agricultural courses, which are not highly esteemed (whatever their real value), but for the training as human beings that is so necessary: to speak French, instead of a local dialect; to count in square meters and not in *journaux* or *boisselées*,* in cubic meters and not in cords; to write so that one can be understood when dealing with an inheritance or the purchase of a sowing machine in the neighboring town; to know the *départements* and their prefec-

---

* A *journal* was an old measure indicating how much land a man could plow in one day; a *boisselée* is an old dry measure, somewhat more than a peck.—Trans.

tures before leaving for military service. There are so many reasons for interest in the school—and these make the sarcasm and attacks of the curé, or, in the best instances, his reservations, easier to take. Thus does the public school, disputed in the towns where maximum attendance and enthusiasm are the rule, triumph in the French rural areas; and with it comes that simple faith in human progress and in the Republic which is the essential of its moral teaching. Quite obviously, the action is reciprocal: the development of a commercialized agriculture, railroad equipment, and technical progress contribute to spreading this basic confidence in Scientism. The Republican spirit is also a product of these economic changes, for the Republic is the offspring of the steam engine.

For many reasons, the mentality is more durable than the soon-superannuated technique contributing to its creation. Proof of this, in the closing years of the century, lies in the nationwide repercussions of one of the greatest collective debates known in the history of mankind—the Dreyfus Affair. This certainly does not mean that thirty-nine million Frenchmen—or even twenty million, discounting the children —knew about the Affair and classed themselves as Dreyfusards or Anti-Dreyfusards. But it can be said that there was not one small market town where these positions were not espoused by those new "notables" of the village—small tradesmen and civil servants—who kept themselves informed about the latest developments, receiving newspapers from Paris or from the regional center. And if the remoter areas, the hamlets in the wooded districts of France, were unaware of the development of a conflict difficult to follow and interpret, and unaware sometimes even of the name "Dreyfus," it nevertheless remains true that public opinion everywhere very quickly knew the broad outlines of the Affair: Justice and Truth on one side, the Nation and Military Honor on the other. It is in this sense that the "Affair" is the foremost crisis undergone by the Third Republic, well beyond Boulangism, that feverish Parisian outbreak, and Panama, that scandal among the financiers.

The significance of the Affair is measured in the discussions of 1898 and 1899: for months, uncertainty surrounds Dreyfus' innocence; hence the debates affecting every milieu, dividing families, classing the supporters of a new inquiry into the Ligue des Droits de l'Homme—which will survive and continue to serve a precious democratic cause—and classing the supporters of the authority of the judgment [la chose jugée] in the Ligue de la Patrie Française.* From the publication of Zola's letter, J'accuse, until the confession of Colonel Henry (January-August, 1898),

---

* It is during the Affair, more than during the days of Boulanger, that an important change is made in political tradition: the intellectuals of the Left are led into taking harsh positions against the General Staff and leaving the noisily asserted monopoly of militarist patriotism to the Right. After the interlude of 1914-1918, this cleavage will retain its importance until 1940.

the Affair stirs up Republicans and Nationalists, Anticlerics and Clerics; street demonstrations, trials by publicity, and parliamentary debates call attention to this excitement that involves so many great principles. After Colonel Henry's confessions, the Anti-Dreyfusard positions, however uncomfortable they may have become, are not deserted for a minute. The French Nation, convinced that the Army cannot reverse its decision without losing all its prestige,* even goes so far in February of 1899 to instigate an attack on the Élysée. But the important point of this crisis remains the combat in which Justice confronts Honor, Truth confronts Country, for long enough that many Frenchmen could become aware of the principles and rights upon which the political regime is founded —with which they are endowed through a fortunate concurrence of circumstances, almost inadvertently, in 1875. At that point an entire generation lives through an incomparable test of civic-mindedness, and an entire people becomes convinced, in these final twenty years of the century, that the Republican regime is the best of regimes, undoubtedly attributing to it many virtues which, in itself, it cannot have—to begin with, that of improving living conditions.

Let us put aside the liberal laws of the Republicans: freedom of the press, freedom of assembly and of association. For the French rural masses, those laws do not have much significance—at least not until the First World War. Only journalism enters, gradually, into daily habits in the towns and even more slowly in the country. The Press becomes the fourth estate, formidable and dreaded whenever scandals threaten. A stimulant of civic spirit, this organ of information is also a commercial affair; advertising helps it to survive, not without dangers, when, for example, it is a question of Russian loans.

But here we have one of the principal characteristics of this new political mentality: its civic-mindedness. Fostered by the schools, where the teacher misses no opportunity to extol France and the regime, and where the educational battalions inspire a love for military *panache* which remains alive even in the trenches, the Republican faith has its rites which are in no way artistic, since the Republic is Athenian only in Paris—and even there with modest prudence—but these rites, in their simplicity, are still important. The predilection for the Tricolor is shown on many occasions: on July 14, naturally, but also, in the large towns and in Paris, for such fetes as the opening of the universal exhibitions—in 1876, all of Paris is decked out, as witness Monet and Manet (*Rue Montorgueil, Rue Mosnier aux drapeaux*). In the smallest market towns, the celebration of July 14 is the object of a series of rejoicings which make out of

---

* And the Army, itself, is not far from sharing this opinion, since the War Council at Rennes, despite the evidence, still condemns Dreyfus with "extenuating circumstances." Dreyfus was cleared in 1906.

it both an official, serious fete (with its *Marseillaise*, its torchlight tattoos, and its speeches evoking the great ancestors of 1848, and especially 1789), and also a fete for the young and old: games, races, dancing, and feasting.

This civic-mindedness is still an everyday attitude in the sense that the management of municipal, if not national, affairs arouses great emotion: each time there is an open meeting of the Municipal Council, there is an attentive audience observing the words and deeds of their elected officials; the schoolyard meetings preceding legislative election are followed by the majority of citizens, who more often than not ask no questions and listen with a seriousness that would be surprising today. Finally, this civic sense is of a patriotic nature, devoted to national glories (extolled in the schools, where the history taught is resolutely moralistic and is devoted particularly to Alsace and Lorraine just after 1870, and again until just before the First World War).

We must also attribute to the patriotic civic-mindedness the very numerous music societies, brass bands (drums and bugles), and more rarely brass-and-reed bands—which everywhere serve simultaneously as preparation for regimental musicians and as a distraction appreciated in country and city alike. They have a standard repertory: military marches and chauvinistic music. Many things can be said on this point: the pride of the humbler classes, quite gifted in the main, forming a group made up of friends motivated by a common love for music, devoting their evenings to cornets and trombones. They are happy to participate in competitions in *départements* or on a national or international scale: brass bands from Bagnolet, from Fontenay-sous-Bois.

Despite so many shocks and jolts when the regime seems to be in danger—from Boulanger to the Separation; despite so many ministerial crises and stresses, from the assassination of Carnot to the Caillaux Affair; despite the lampoons and intrigues of the Faubourg Saint-Germain, the Duchesse d'Uzès, and the Jockey Club—France is the first decade of the 1900s became deeply Republican. And this is not an electoral choice, one that can be revoked from one election to another: it is a face of the collective psychology.

▶ **WORKING-CLASS LIFE AND IDEAS**

Yet the working classes remain a world apart; no one doubts this, neither the workers—even those who have become the most bourgeois—nor those who did not wear overalls and keep their distance. The class struggle is a social reality, which it is not yet good form to deny as a crackbrained, theoretical notion. At any rate, Thiers, at Versailles in May of 1871, chants victory in the name of "Order, Justice, and Civilization"; he makes no mistake about it. Neither does Gambetta, who established the Republic with the help of a new social stratum, not working class but petty-bourgeois, comprised of minor functionaries, retail merchants, and industrial or banking employees.

This separation of the classes is increasingly perceptible to the parties involved as the years pass. Undoubtedly, political incident is not there for nothing, since in June, 1848, and May, 1871, the best are killed in Paris, each carnage being followed by a long silence—from 1848 to 1860, from 1871 to 1890. But it was industrial life and economic development that weighed especially heavily in this sense. The Haussmannizing of Paris and of such large towns as Lyon and Lille, as well as the population pressure, results everywhere in the redistribution of land and people: in Paris, almost all of the eastern sector is working class, from the vicinity of the Bastille to Belleville and Ménilmontant, while the *boulevards* and especially the districts around the Arc de Triomphe are bourgeois. The former cohabitation of all classes in Parisian buildings tends to disappear and the establishment of new industries—chemical, in particular—in the peripheral areas act toward the same end: the "red belt" is formed in the nineteenth century. Proudhon cried out against Haussmann's Paris, with its public squares and gardens, its new barracks, its macadam, and its legions of street sweepers. Corbon says more simply: "The transformation of Paris having been forcibly made, the working population flows back from the center toward the outskirts; they made two towns of the capital: one rich, one poor. The latter surrounds the former." Moreover, capital and industrial concentration contributes to the separation of men: intra-company relations no longer have any reason to exist, and the confraternities died with the guilds; the owner, even when he is not president of an administrative council, or a salaried director, becomes an elusive individual, with whom the workers are rarely in touch. Thus, in the large industries at least, daily relations become relations within the same class. All the more so as, with the help of the crisis between 1873 and 1895, social elevation quickly becomes difficult: the workers who have become small employers are still legion under the Empire and these fine careers are possible in the provinces as well as in Paris. During the Republic, when the large companies are forming, this prospect closes. Hence the serious impression of a closed world, withdrawn into itself. When the defenders of labor's political abilities arrive, the pride born of this antagonism grows stronger, and class consciousness is no less active among the workers than on the other side.

The workers' conditions, however, improve during these fifty years, although there is no one set of conditions, far from it, ranging from the Parisian skilled workman living in the Marais, firmly established in the heart of a town he knows well, to the proletarian who has only his strong right arm, who is camped on the Rue de Lappe and is not sure about tomorrow.[5] Still, wages doubled, approximately; prices rose during the

Empire, then fell so much that nutrition—if not housing—made great strides. Thus, despite the tuberculosis and alcoholism which affect the entire society, but claim more victims there where the organism is less resistant, the end-of-the-century worker is more solid and is of better appearance than those who lived under the July Monarchy. Clothing also becomes more tidy, at least for fete days, since overalls remain the uniform for work, and often for every day but Sunday. But these changes do not make the workers into bourgeois, even those among them who are well-off, those in the Parisian luxury industries or in the new metallurgy— whose owners are willingly paternalistic, providing buildings for their personnel, and setting up canteens as early as this period. In order to merge into the bourgeois, they lack sufficient affluence and, especially, security; whether paid well or poorly, workers do not earn enough to assure a decent living for their families: women work, and often children do, too, for the 1841 law is overtly evaded by employers and personnel alike; apprenticeship is no longer protected, and a profession is learned haphazardly in a very tough combination of the tradition stemming from the workers' unions and sordid exploitation.[6] Finally, the working day is long, rarely shorter than ten hours; since women generally are paid at half the scale paid to men, even for equal work, and since the provinces are at a great disadvantage compared with Paris, working-class labor, often exhausting, consumes the workers. The average life expectancy increases much less here than elsewhere; the old worker grown gray in the harness actually does not exist—he dies before turning gray.

There is also the fact that the proletarian, like the specialized worker, has lived a sad and constantly threatened life: disease is a catastrophe which, for want of insurance, and even for want of sufficient help on the part of the workers' mutual societies, is irremediable; on this point everyone knows that France at the turn of the century is behind Germany and England. Another disaster is unemployment, due to the economic crisis and to the ill will of the employer who is always free to seek better workmen if the occasion arises; nothing guarantees work, and the worker knows he is at the mercy of this constant threat, which explains the success of the savings banks among these people—meager protection, at the cost of daily effort, against the dreaded bad days. This feeling of insecurity is sufficient explanation for the need felt by the workers to unite and consolidate themselves to defend not just one or two advantages but their right to live. Thus working-class life is voluntarily a collective life; even outside the factory, meetings are frequent, be they only in the taverns—the perfect meeting place (for private houses are often tiny), because the café offers drinks and, more important, newspapers to read, to discuss with others, following events at this time when the life of the labor movement is under discussion; let us recall a famous comparison: "In contemporary society, the tavern holds for the working classes the place the church held for past societies." Hence living conditions, traditions inherited from 1848 and even from the former workers' unions, and class consciousness all impel workers to form groups and associations which demand their place in the sun.

The importance of the labor movement strikes every observer as far back as the days of the Empire: *La Revue des Deux Mondes* published April 1, 1863, has an influential article by a liberal mind, Monsieur de Rémusat, who states, "One must take it for granted: what is on the move at this moment is the working classes . . . an intellectual and moral progress can be seen in their midst." This is obviously not to say that the workers are all models of virtue and intelligence: drunkenness and dissolute ways are rife among them as much as, if not more than, elsewhere. The *Sublimes*, the lewd habitués of the Bal Mabille or of the Banc de Terre-Neuve (the boulevards from the Porte Saint-Denis to the Madeleine) under the Empire are also types of workers—but they do not supply their class with a thing. Speaking and acting in the name of all, a few hundred men throughout France confer with theorists like Proudhon—who, moreover, wants to be a worker until his death—and Marx, and with the government too. They form an élite, in particular a Parisian élite. Through these men, who can be called by the fine name of "militants," the working classes assert their presence, demanding, and obtaining, as early as the days of the Empire, the freedoms necessary to enable everyone to fight the employers equally armed, and to reclaim their true place in national life.

Nothing is more noteworthy in this respect than the interest in educational questions shown by the workers.[7] Endowed with an elementary education, most of the time from public schools, but sometimes—as in Alsace and the region around Lyon—by the Ignorantine and Marist fathers, they find their intellectual equipment too light. Many of them, educated by the highly regarded mutual instruction of the public schools, have a passion for education, read a great deal, and retain the methods and tone of teaching even in their public life: the Ligue de l'Enseignement, founded by Jean Macé to encourage the development of education, indeed to combat those bourgeois prejudices which saw the schools as preparation for revolution, had many working-class adherents. Victor Duruy is popular among the Parisian workers when, as minister, he institutes in the *lycées* a special education, without Latin or Greek, lasting three or four years, for the purpose of preparation for commercial careers; this is true, too, when he favors the creation and extension of public elementary schools. Finally, men like Benoît, Corbon, and Proudhon are self-educated men who have thought about the general problem of education, and have organizational plans in which an important place is assured professional and adult education. These plans have confidence in Universalist education, a motivating force of social progress.

The educational problem, however, is thought of as existing within a greater struggle: the coming of a better world, of a brotherly world in which the worker ceases to be a proletarian, that is, ceases to be exploited; the labor movement is a movement for emancipation, of which education is a necessary condition.

The generation of Varlin, Tolain, Benoît Malon, inspiring the conscience of French labor until 1870, undergoes two influences and, torn as it is between two opposing ways of thought, exhibits even in those days the divergencies asserted into our own time. These two conflicting influences are those of Proudhon and Marx. The two men, who knew each other in Paris during the July Monarchy and who at that time got along rather well, broke brutally with one another just before 1848. And, until Proudhon's death in 1865, nothing brought them together; that hostility of temperament gradually became a hostility of doctrine and method. Neither in the study of capitalist society nor in the methods to be employed in destroying or reforming it, are they in agreement. Each of them has a nimble pen, and their influence is partially the result of this talent, which also helped tear them to pieces. Proudhon is lively, cantankerous, and often pig-headed; so is Marx, but who is not familiar with some of Marx's expressions whose formal impact caused all of their success: "Religion is the sigh of the creature overwhelmed by misfortune, the soul of a heartless world. . . ." Proudhon is a moralist, a worker who has more confidence in the people's instinct than in their reason; he wants Justice, and expects to attain it in the working-class world amid which he lives; when he studies the nature of private property, economic contradictions, or the ability of the working classes, he denounces the inhuman realities of economic relations, that is the injustices—with a virulent pen. As remedy, Proudhon has neither a system nor an overall plan, still less a *Weltanschauung;* he only knows that the working classes have but themselves, their professional action, their defense associations, and their production groups to count on; he has given hope to those who, for ten years, have lived under the blow of the June, 1848, repression: he incited them to regroup and to accept the facilities offered by the government of Napoleon III after 1860. Not that he is a Bonapartist; he is hostile to the State and the Army. And if he forsees a future society, it is an anarchic juxtaposition of small free communities working together joyfully. Proudhon taught the militant Parisian workers to mistrust all politics, all means of action, save the professional; this being done, he separates the workers from the Republicans, something which could not displease Napoleon III. Thus, during his lifetime, Proudhon drew the lines of force of working-class thought, simultaneously hostile to the State and to political life, devoted to the daily improvement of the workers' conditions, convinced that working-class emancipation will be the result only of wage-earners acting on the professional level. Renewed and made precise, these ideas form the basis of the "anarcho-syndicalist" labor tradition.

Marx speaks another language and his ideas, slower to take hold in France than in Germany or England, offer some different perspectives: Marx is the founder of Scientific Socialism; at one and the same time he is a believer in Scientism, and a fighter like Proudhon. He calls on the proletariat of every country to unite because, even after having shown the necessity of the advent of socialism, he knows well that the workers can and must help it along. Marx is a theorist, but also a man of action who devotes long days in London to preparing for the Congress of the International, listening to his fellow travelers, and drafting manifestoes. But obviously, the essential thing for Marx is the system—Proudhon's despised "theory"—which, explaining and demonstrating the mechanisms of capitalist society, predicts its downfall. From the *Communist Manifesto* in 1847 to the first volume of *Das Kapital* in 1867, he reveals himself as the greatest sociologist of his day: the study of the relations of production, the discovery of surplus value and of the class struggle are so many expressions of Marxist analysis which have become current.* Undoubtedly he owes to his predecessors, Saint-Simon and Cabet, many of the elements of his demonstrations. Before him, no one succeeded in making so clear a systematization; Marx, analyzing the means of production, can generalize his materialism into all of historical evolution in a vast panorama not without grandeur. Thus he wants to establish a history of human societies which is to be scientific; and his ultimate goal, unattainable in his lifetime, would doubtless be a social mathematics, figuring the surplus value and capitalist profit, establishing the algebraic laws and formulas of man's exploitation of man. But without achieving his aim, Marx, analyzing the class struggles in France, and later narrating the Commune to the eyewitnesses themselves, contributed in no small way to making his ideas and especially his hope for a better world, pass into the collective consciousness of the workers. Stimulated, in some manner, by the idea that the interplay of economic forces within the capitalist society works against this society and its masters, the workers will put more fervor into bringing about this liberation—the classless

---

* Let us recall an expression without going into the commentaries, which would necessarily be too long: "The relations of production in their entirety constitute the basis of society's economic structure, that is, they are the real foundation upon which the legal and political superstructure is erected, and to which correspond the definite social forms of consciousness. The mode of production of the material life generally determines the social, political, and intellectual process of life. It is not man's consciousness that determines his manner of being, but his social manner of being that determines his consciousness." Let us merely point out that, despite the abrupt character of this last phrase, it is not possible to reduce Marxism to a flat materialism as so many of his opponents and supporters have done.

society, the socialist society. Therefore, Marx supplies the labor movement with both an incomparable instrument of social analysis (which his followers did not always know how to use, respecting all the nuances of Marx's and Engel's thought), and a reason for hope, an impetus to accelerate this march of history in which the philosopher promises to the proletariat the greatest role.

The followers of Proudhon and Marx scarcely come face to face in the mutual, trade union, and workers' union associations which limp along at the beginning of the Empire. When, in 1864, Napoleon III recognizes the right to strike, and when, in the same year, Tolain and his English friends found the First International, which lasts from 1864 to 1872— "The International Association of Workers"—the militant life becomes more active. This surprises the government, and soon disturbs it—and disturbs the employers even more. The French section of the International, during the early years, supports Proudhon; shortly before 1870, during the ferment of the great strikes—La Ricamarie, Aubin, Le Creusot —the Marxist doctrine, which has been gaining the upper hand abroad from the outset, wins out in France. This is at the very same point when it becomes the official doctrine of the International at the Congresses of Brussels (1868) and Basel (1869). Hunted down and disbanded by the government, Tolain's Association becomes known to the workers; it numbers 240,000 adherents just before the War, and a few hundred thousand during the early years. The War, however, brings about its downfall,* although it furnishes the French labor movement with the opportunity for an exemplary era—the Commune.

From March 18 to May 28, 1871, Paris was governed by a handful of revolutionaries, only a minority of whom were Internationalists, who did not have a very precise program (except for a few expressions, the most famous being "land for the peasant, tools for the worker, and work for all"); moreover, they did not have enough time to make significant reforms. Simultaneously born of the "flinty fever" and the provocations of Thiers, who preferred an organized war (with the complicity of the Prussians again sitting in the capital) instead of negotiations, the Commune is a great period in the socialist tradition. Did not the Communards underwrite administrative life, exercise a scrupulous management of public funds, prevent all pillaging, in particular that of the Bank of France, simultaneously with an assertion of their faith in the future of a socialist society through their fragmentary work (regulation of work, organization of *chambres syndicales*)? † But the Commune, a govern-

---

* Essentially as a result of nationalist divergencies. Marx himself expresses his satisfaction with Bismarck's good work, which enables the axis of the Workers' International to shift toward Germany.
† Their function usually was that of a disciplinary tribunal set up to judge infractions of a union's rules and of the duties imposed upon its members.—Trans.

ment of the people by the people, is valuable as an example: Varlin, Courbet, Delescluze, and Rossel were as good as their word, and showed that workers are capable of self-government.

They still have their martyrdom: the bloody week of May 21-28 claimed many victims. And in return for a few acts of vandalism—setting fire to the Tuileries and to Thiers' *hôtel*, and for the execution of hostages—how many victims, from the Rue de Rivoli to Père Lachaise? Thiers and Galiffet triumph brazenly and immoderately in May of 1871, and the historians of the Commune estimate the number of Parisians affected by the repression to be around a hundred thousand. Yet to our own day, each year in May the "Wall of the Federals" [*Le Mur des Fédérés*] at Père Lachaise is decorated with flowers by labor organizations who have not forgotten "the heroic struggle of the proletariat."

After the Commune, the workers preserve the rights secured under the Empire: there is the right to strike, legally recognized since 1864, which enables the workers to combat their employers with equal weapons; the unwritten right, since 1868, to form professional associations. But the Parisian repression was so heavy that the labor movement could not rely upon them. For ten years there is almost total silence: a few small congresses after 1876, several appeals, and the virtually solitary work of Jules Guesde.

From 1880 to 1895, the labor movement seeks its means in the reorganization of the trade unions—officially authorized by the 1884 law; but also alongside the Fédérations Nationales de Métiers, which group workers by crafts,* alongside the Bourses du Travail,† which are local groups who make no distinction as to specialty, these years see the formation of the Socialist Workers' Parties, which are quite diversified according to the personalities of their instigators and their revolutionary ancestry: Blanquist, Marxist, and Proudhonian reformers form many agitated, loquacious little circles which gradually became rather influential among labor groups—influential enough that, in 1893, fifty Socialists sit in the Chamber of Deputies. Thus, in the everyday life of the working classes there is established the basic division between the narrowly professional associations, the unions, and the political parties, by no means indifferent to the workers' demands but resolved to use the political strength of the workers offered by universal suffrage.

At the same time, the first labor congress and, in particular, those

---

* In 1879 the Société Générale des Ouvriers Chapeliers de France is founded; in 1881, the Fédération Française des Travailleurs du Livre; in 1892, after several unsuccessful attempts, the Fédération des Ouvriers Mineurs.
† These were nationwide groups of workers who help provide one another with information about available jobs. Although often subsidized, and so controlled by municipalities, the Bourses functioned as social and educational centers. The motivating forces behind them hoped they ultimately would be the means of liberating labor entirely from both management's and government's control.—Trans.

preceding the establishment of the Confédération Générale du Travail [the C.G.T.], discuss the means for exerting the pressure that the workers have at their disposal to conduct their struggle: Aristide Briand is then the promoter of the general strike, which is to bring about a complete paralysis in the nation and allow a decisive victory over the employers; not without some illusions, the idea of a revolutionary action, independent of all politics and all parties, is glorified.

Education remains in the forefront of the workers' concerns: the Bourses du Travail have libraries and organize professional courses, especially courses in scientific and economic training. With the aid of technicians and men from the teaching profession—schoolteachers and professors—*collèges du travail* are created, especially at Paris.

Finally, the workers' actions and the daily struggle become more pronounced in the depression years, from 1885 to 1895: local strikes increase, and these, indicating the pugnacious ardor of the militants, arouse the enthusiasm of their leaders. On May Day in 1891, the Fusillade de Fourmies,* gives a new meaning to this festival of springtime; it becomes the workers' festival, the day when they gather together to celebrate their triumphs over the bourgeoisie, and to measure the progress still to be made. For many years May Day will remain a day consecrated to the memory of the dead workers.

Thus, working-class life gradually draws itself together; the broad vectors of its social action have already been established. In the subsequent period, under the impetus of first-rate personalities like Pelloutier and Griffuelhes for the C.G.T. and Jaurès for the group advocating political action, the world of the workers will settle organization and doctrine for years to come.

---

* The reference is to the execution of politically dangerous militants in the small mill town of Fourmies in the Nord. A similar "incident" also occurred at Béziers in 1907, during a major crisis affecting the vineyardists in Languedoc. Again, troops were called in to quell the revolt.—Trans.

XVI

The Dawn of a Scientific Civilization

1895-1914

AT the turn of the century—between the great economic crisis of 1873-1895, and the Great War of 1914-1918, now called, not without some cynicism, the First World War—France knows feverish days, piled one on top of another as if by some implacable Fate: interior crises like the Dreyfus Affair and the Separation [of Church and State] in 1905, imperialist shocks from Fashoda and the Boer War to the Moroccan affairs in Tangier, Agadir, the *"bec de canard,"** and finally, that excitement, that rising of hate and fear forming the basis of the war psychosis for which the summer of 1914 is preparing. Each day Paris vibrates with a new emotion; the *revanchard* spirit is not dead, and the Germanophilic pacifism of the Caillaux, the great socialist debates, and anticlericalism animate conversations and quarrels. More than ever, the capital sets itself apart, ahead of the peasant masses who form the body of the nation;

---

* The allusion is to a piece of the French Congo shaped like a "duck's bill" ceded to Germany in return for the latter's agreement that France could establish a protectorate in Morocco. This settlement is embodied in the Franco-German Convention, November, 1911.—Trans.

intensely it thrives on political incident and international crisis whose muffled echoes hardly reach the small market towns and the remote areas. Paris no longer finds time to breathe or to absorb the events as do the provinces: both the Exhibition of 1900 and the conciliatory visit of the King of England are occasions of nervous demonstrations, the fiery expression of anxiety.

Nothing but the daily hell, the vermin, and the cold wind of death, imposed for four straight years upon this generation born between 1890 and 1900, could have convinced them, when they arrived at the edge of old age, that the first decade of the twentieth century was a Belle Époque. Forgetting all the violences and destitution, forgetting Béziers and Fourmies, they convinced themselves, and forty or fifty years later, want to convince us that Paris and France were never more beautiful. And with what talent! Movies thrive on it, from the remote and charming *Mariage de Chiffon* by Autant-Lara, to Jean Renoir's *French Cancan*; there is a mythos about the Belle Époque, nourished by wonderful pictures, fond stereotypes—the director of the Moulin Rouge, the (Eastern) Prince Charming, the irresistible officer—refrains, and persistent catchwords, all of which are a bold betrayal, through "crystallization," of that so tormented period in the French past.

Yet the first decade of the twentieth century might have been a Golden Age, more than many other periods of the past: not because of the Moulin Rouge, or Robinson, or even that predilection for the rococo visible even today upon so many Parisian and provincial façades, on overelaborate balconies, in overwrought iron, or better yet, on the exterior structures of the Métro.

The exciting attraction of this stage of French history lies in its scientific movement: this is perceptible to everyone, at least in its exterior guises—that is, the technical strides which parallel it—in those years when the bicycle, the "little queen," takes its place in every home (the Tour de France is beginning its long career), when the automobile is already replacing the horse in the town streets, and when, finally, just before the war, man flies and crosses the Channel. There is also a dizzying progress of science for those who read and follow, gasping, the pace of the discoveries: the career of the Curies and Langevin, the daring of Albert Einstein, and the experiments of Planck. In this Europe that is living the final moments of its greatest glory, all the sciences seem destined for an overwhelming renewal: it is the end of Scientism, clearly discerned rather than proclaimed by all those affected by the general theory of relativity and Einstein's most brilliant pages on the new space-time continuum.

Natural and social sciences inform—they do not yet command—everyday life; and the new twentieth-century art of living is not yet born. But the new scientific spirit, animating first the physical sciences and then, gradually, the others, already finds a hesitant and uncertain echo, an unsubstantiated correspondence, as it were, in intellectual, artistic, and literary life: there are pictorial and musical inquiries whose innovations frighten conformists and others as well, and an anarchic disorder of literature bundled up in its traditions and its poetic arts. But the downfall of Scientism, whose fundaments crumble entirely, although this is much less evident than one would think, expresses itself first and foremost in the beginning of a religious, and more precisely Catholic, revival. This revival continued to expand and gain ever since the difficult years when Péguy, Sangnier, and several others entered into a daily struggle, and when Bergson, a new Romantic philosopher of the instinct, enthusiastically rehabilitated irrationalism in a marvelously rich language.

France is tormented, torn, overwhelmed by the immense tasks she takes over throughout the world. A colonial power and the homeland of revolutions, she is still, in the heart of a scientific and triumphing Europe, one of the primary centers of civilization; then, the War of 1914 imposes upon her the most arduous test a modern nation has undergone to this day.

► THE SCIENTIFIC REVOLUTION

Less than ever before, in learned Europe at the end of the nineteenth century, is scientific life narrowly French. For centuries—since the days when Père Mersenne was receiving his German and Dutch friends at the Minims and organizing real colloquies of mathematicians—scientific discoveries and their spread have known neither frontiers nor jealous nationalism. Scientists work for everyone, traveling all the more willingly, since the passport does not yet hold sway, at least in Western Europe; consequently, scientific progress is international. Pierre and Marie Curie at Paris, Einstein at Berne or Zurich, Rutherford at Cambridge, Planck at Berlin—and, later, Langevin and De Broglie at Paris, and Fermi at Rome: all form a scientific society scattered over the four corners of Europe, for in these days Americans and Russians are not very important. Suffice it to say that the revival of the early twentieth century is not French, any more than it is German or English; it belongs to each of the great names who marked a decisive stage, as well as to the laboratories and aides who participated in the sensational discoveries.

From the work carried out by the Curies in 1895, to the special [or restricted] theory of relativity of Einstein in 1905 and the general theory of relativity in 1915, there is a real Copernican Revolution, creating a new physics, discovering extraordinary perspectives in astrophysics and hypotheses concerning the structure of the universe. More rapidly, and more surely than in the days of Copernicus and Galileo, all of me-

chanics, the entire Newtonian explanation of the world with which generations of scientists had lived peacefully, collapses. Both Paul Langevin,
studying the atomic masses of simple bodies, and Max Planck, constructing his quantum theory to fill the recognized gaps in the wave theory of
light, play a major role in this transformation. Nourishing scientific
thought with a stimulant so powerful that he fed all postwar research, the
"father of relativity" brings to this thought, both by example (his use of
non-Euclidian geometry) and by the very definition of space-time, the
dowry of a new conception of science, so much so that the early years of
the twentieth century constitute a decisive stage, not only through the
discoveries brought about in this manner, but also through the defeat of
mathematical determinism, which had been the lifeblood of modern science for three hundred years.

Thus radioactivity and relativity, closely linked, constitute the scientific landmarks of the era. During the short period of ten or so years, all
scientists and all researchers are affected by the scope of the discoveries
and by their meaning. While almost everyone breathes the air of the
principles of mechanics, lives in an ordered universe from which he
would never imagine that he could be removed by experimentation, this
succession of experiments and theories leads each of them to a new
world: even an Henri Poincaré, whose mathematical corpus is so vast and
close to a restricted theory of relativity, finds himself upset and troubled.
One would be tempted to call this "Scientific Revolution" the revenge
of physics upon mathematics, if such simplification were not improper.
Better simply to note the enormous research field atomic theory and
relativity offer the scientific world: the twentieth century opens onto
this world of isotopes, neutrons, and electrons (which so soon are to become a part of ordinary language), and the research heralding Louis de
Broglie's wave mechanics (1925) and the fission of the uranium atom by
Frédéric Joliot-Curie (1938)—even the cyclotron and the atomic pile.

The first consequence of the physicists' revolution should, one would
think, have been the proclamation of their autonomy of the social sciences, the escape from the ambitions of Scientism and freedom from
mathematical mechanisms and all the grand axioms (only the measurable is scientific). But, in fact, the changes in physics occurred at the
very time the social sciences were setting their rules: in history, Seignobos
and Langlois publish their *Introduction aux études historiques* (1897),
a breviary of the "objective method." Simultaneously, the possessor of
a literary mind as subtle as Paul Valéry reveals himself, in his *Introduction à la Méthode de Léonard de Vinci*, to be the faithful and intrepid
follower of his teachers nurtured on Scientism. The universal determinism of men so educated gives way to a determinism of the social sciences, as if dallying on this side of the new physics. Let us quote this

fine passage from Rambaud's *Histoire de la civilisation française*, which
dates from the early years of this century:

> Even politics is not solely, as some seem to think, a matter of opin-
> ion. Well understood, it is a science, and even belongs to the so-
> called experimental sciences . . . it ought, if it is treated with the
> same scientific spirit, to lead to laws as certain as those of physics,
> chemistry, or physiology.

The social sciences had a ready explanation for the inauspicious backwardness in their development: at the moment when mathematics,
physics, and chemistry help one another and intermingle without any
one being the "servant," according to the Scholastic expression, of the
other; at the moment when biochemistry moves forward with giant
steps—the great concern, for the social sciences, is to make distinctions,
to define boundaries, and to stand guard over these boundaries with un-
failing vigilance. Psychology, sociology, political economy, history, and
geography are not without disagreement, and these smack of intramural, parochial squabbles (between historians and sociologists, for example), from which the syllabi and curricula of French *baccalauréats*
in philosophy still reverberate a half-century later.[1]

Thus the finest minds, the most gifted in intuition and knowledge,
those who, in the social sciences, knew how to show the way and go
beyond Scientism, took the form of precursors, debated, bantered, and
gibed at for a long time, even within the University. One example of
these "jeerers" (but from 1946!): Halphen, a partisan of "historizing"
objectivity, lets fly this arrow at Henri Berr, an "unflagging" precursor:
"None of his volumes under the general title of the *Évolution de l'Humanité*, which comprise the vast historic series of which [he] assumed the direction, bears—in addition to [his] prefaces . . . the slightest trace, either in his books or in his articles, of the ideas of which for
more than a half-century he has made himself the indefatigable apostle."[2]

In 1902, Berr founds the *Revue de synthèse historique* which pleads
not only for a history which while delighting in the trees of analysis
would not overlook the forest of synthesis, but which pleads also for a
history not cut off either from the auxiliary sciences or, especially, from
the related ones—ethnography and geography—which are indispensable
to a well-balanced understanding of the human past. At the same time,
Vidal de la Blache pleads with even greater talent for a human geography, broadly dependent on history and ethnography, and founds regional geography, a work of synthesis done on the scale of the "region,"
that triumph of the French Geographic School soon made famous by
men like Demangeon, Sion, and Brunhes. Finally, history tries discreetly to reform itself: Jean Jaurès carries out a socialist history which,
doubtless for ideological motives, sees things on a broad scale and does

not confine itself to political or diplomatic history; Lucien Febvre, for his part, publishes his thesis *Philippe II et la Franche-Comté* (1911), a study of political, religious, and social history, a vast panorama of a province and its social climate in the second half of the sixteenth century. There follows in 1922—but it was meditated upon and partially written as early as 1913—one of the first volumes of the series *Évolution de l'Humanité*, originated by Henri Berr: *La Terre et l'Évolution humaine*. By means of lucid demonstration, this book deals a blow at geographical determinism, a blow from which the latter has never recovered; but for one cause easily won, how many slownesses and resistances along the way! *Oportet haereses esse*, write the misunderstood precursors.

But Scientism met with a better end than this survival without glory and without works: it became diffused and popularized in the urban, even lower-class, milieux—and even into the country areas through the rural bourgeois who, after a century of full development, gradually constitute a new ruling, or sub-ruling, class. Science, or more precisely its mechanical application, dazzles and gives the authority of current opinion to a rather simple materialism nourished, first of all, by those material successes which alter the décor and the means of men's actions from one year to the next: to a large extent, the spread of Scientism becomes mingled with the progress of speed, in a world where man no longer moves about at a walking pace.

And yet we have only just reached the transition from steam to electricity and the internal combustion engine: the full effects of the inventions of Bergès, Deprez, Lenoir, and Forest are visible only after the First World War. But the contemporaries of Delcassé saw enough of it to gape in admiration, attributing these marvels to scientific progress and the ingenuity of scientists and technicians: electric lighting, electric motors, and electric transportation. There are the Parisian trolleys and the Métro, the movies of the Lumière brothers and Georges Méliès who projects the first filmed scenes from everyday life (*L'Arroseur arrosé*) and the first newsreels; bicycles are mounted on solid tires, then, thanks to Édouard Michelin,* inflated ones; and finally the automobile, which shortly before the war can go forty-five or fifty miles per hour, and which is already replacing the horse-drawn buses in the towns, obliging municipalities to pass decrees limiting speed at crowded crossings—indispensable security measures for both men and animals! Clouds of dust, cries of terror, motorists garbed like Eskimos—what amusing impressions progress offers when Armand Peugeot and Louis Renault are setting up their businesses! And in the closing years of this period, aviation is born:

---

* Bicycles quickly become widespread; they made a great deal of money for some Saint-Étienne industrialists who have much for which to thank this "steel charger."

Blériot crossed the Channel in 1909 and in 1913, Garros crossed the Mediterranean—and planes are already going a hundred and twenty-five miles per hour.

Electric motors gain ground from one year to the next, and find new uses in factories; the chemistry of dyes, fertilizers and also explosives makes great strides; but electrochemistry (electrolysis) in particular becomes a common process in the preparation of metals, among which duralumin appears just before the war. And the first plastics, galalith and bakelite, are contemporaneous with the first synthetic silks, appearing between 1900 and 1914. New industrial plants, new products—everything changing daily life comes out of the laboratories, out of the hands and the complicated instruments of the scientists.

Indeed, in this field of scientific wonder the most astonishing discovery, that of Branly, Lodge, and Marconi, is not known well enough to play its role in the flowering of a popular mentality rooted in Scientism: the crystal set is still too rare; similarly, in the simpler realm of telephone and telegraph, the invention does not yet have enough users. But the marvels of speed and light are more than sufficient. Not everything, naturally, is explained by these technical advances. Other elements—inherited from the preceding era and gradually spread abroad by the daily press with its satirical drawings and advertising—mingle with it. In these newspapers the photographic image is of great importance: convictions are won through reproduction of Forain's lithographs and those of many others. There are deeply resounding echoes of the recent and current quarrels and great debates: *curé* and schoolteacher confront one another on the square of the divided village, the Dreyfus Affair, and the Separation Law. Scientism diffuses itself as a faith in the future of humanity and of France; consequently, it is a repudiation of the "blind and obscurantist" forces of the past. Faith in progress also involves a virulent anticlericalism—sometimes coupled with pacifism in the areas where the Dreyfus Affair had the greatest repercussions. The conviction that today's world is finer than yesterday's is a vital force and a hope for everyone. This idea will go far: to the point of expecting the scientists to provide the indefinite prolongation of human life—a perfect example of the confidence in the limitless power of science.

And within this body of received ideas—which are acquired at the cost of simple personal experiential data and interpreted without research into the stream of events—the rejection of a theology and theogony is undoubtedly what is most essential. The Church is hostile toward the modern world and has been endlessly condemning all the changes which affect its realm, either closely or distantly, for fifty years. A few nuances of modernism do come into play, especially when the Pope speaks; but in this latter sphere, the everyday attitude of *curé* and bishop, the vengeful pastoral letters against the Godless schools and soulless world, count for more than Romish discretions. All this works for the advance of indifference if not anticlericalism. Science and its offspring Technology appear—doubtless too quickly—to be the substitutes for the banished Religion, even to the point of convincing the common run of mankind of their total incompatibility.* The fact is all the more important since at the same time Catholicism regains its audience in the intellectual milieux, if not those of the university, and begins an upward movement which is to grow stronger for a half-century.

► **THE CATHOLIC RECONSOLIDATION**

Unquestionably this Catholic renewal during the twenty years preceding the First World War is inseparable from the Parisian ideological battle being waged in the political assemblies, in the press, and on the Right Bank of the Seine. Between the Dreyfus Affair and the Separation of Church and State in 1905-1907, the link is obvious. And if it is true that, in its painful elaboration of the clear and partially new relations between spiritual and temporal powers, France presents the world with the spectacle of a bold construction, it is also certain that the Catholic Church, in this combat, cuts the figure of the accused now reduced to the defensive: so much so that the inventory of Church property made pursuant to the 1905 Law, the occasion of sometimes violent demonstrations throughout all France, brought about no modification of the positions taken while Combes was Prime Minister. In the same way it is still possible to point out in many of the positions in favor of religion, the will to defend a social order which the socialist advance seems gravely to threaten when the Workers' International asserts the active solidarity of the proletariat in every country. A Bazin or a Bordeaux, novelistic apologists for Family and Country as well as for Catholicism, take their stand—as, several years earlier, Zola took his. The fact remains, however, that the Catholic revival is still more the child of this scientific "earthquake" which occurred so suddenly. Its basis is an entire philosophic system of thought, furnished with magnificence by the literary, academic, and worldly success of Bergson; upon this thrive the Catholic literature, thought, and action of Claudel, Léon Bloy, Bourget, Estaunié, Sangnier, and Péguy.

Obviously neither the work of Bergson,[3] nor the early discussion concerning the value of science date from 1895: Brunetière, the holder of a key university post, did not hesitate to proclaim the bankruptcy of science in his ardor for attacking Berthelot and Renan. Many others, seeking support either in Descartes or in Kant, are satisfied with asserting

---

* What better illustration to indicate this state of mind than the title of a work (which all the same has little far-reaching effect—but that makes it all the more convincing) which appeared in 1912: *Peut-on croire sans être un imbécile?*

the limits of science which are incapable of knowing a moral world irreducible to physical phenomena. Actually, these controversies are minor, until the one that *L'Évolution créatrice* caused in 1907, utilizing physical indeterminacy and exploiting "the immediate data of consciousness": it supplies a new basis for irrational thought.[4]

Bergson's thought had such repercussions that almost overnight he became the undisputed master of the ideas of an entire intellectual élite. His pellucid prose, coming after that of so many unreadable nineteenth-century philosophers, the rightness of certain appropriate turns of phrase beginning with the too famous *élan vital,* and the very Parisian success of the Collège de France are sufficient explanation. Placing in the foreground the flux of life, the deep mystery of the self, and the reinstated intuition—as opposed to the reasoning excesses of Scientism—as the primary source of knowledge, Bergson blithely destroys the claims of rationalism as Berthelot conceives it. In the battle he joins, it is of small consequence if the demonstration is not always too convincing, or if sometimes it reverts to word-plays like *nature naturante* and *nature naturée;** many of his philosopher predecessors permitted themselves as much. But the critique of Scientism has been made: the Bergsonian consciousness is turned toward the metaphysical absolute and toward God who accounts for everything, first and foremost for the insufficiencies of scientific knowledge.

This philosopher, who is not a Catholic, did more for the Catholic revival than Blondel and Le Roy: he gave the impression that desiccating, rationalistic intellectualism was finally condemned, and that, *a fortiori,* materialism, at which a number of Positivists arrived by more or less circuitous paths, was identified with error—with the most monstrous error the nineteenth century was able to produce. This vital dynamism and irrationalism beneath the flashy finery of a precious intelligence echoes, intentionally or not, a whole body of foreign thought, from Schopenhauer to Nietzsche, and exalts the defeat of reason by the instinct and the forces of life. To be sure, there is no question of a superman with Bergson; in 1905 at the Collège de France the expression would have been much too daring, except for a Drumont, but the inspiration and the basic idea remain the same. Thus must be understood the multiple reverberations of a philosophy whose prestige did not survive its author, one whose weaknesses were very soon denounced, even by his followers—but a philosophy which came at the time when a great scientific revision facilitated an anti-rationalistic reaction—or, more simply, a scientifically inspired meta-rationalism which was the concrete attitude of many scientists and philosophers who were insensible to the

---

* *Nature naturante* renders *natura naturans*—the active principle in the universe; *nature naturée* renders *natura naturata*—the passive totality of things created. This distinction is present in Spinoza and goes back at least as far as Averroës.—Trans.

charms of Bergsonian prose. There is a Bergsonian style as well as philosophy; the following is an example from the *Essai sur les données immédiates de la conscience:* "But the moments when we collect our wits are rare, and that is why we are rarely free . . . We live for the external world rather than for ourselves; we do more talking than thinking; we are acted upon more than we act ourselves. To act freely is to recover self-possession, resituate oneself with pure duration."

All the same, the new philosophy would never have had so many adepts had literature not joined in at the same time. It seemed that Naturalism had had its day; a whole troop of writers enliven the literary scene; they make such a display of their religious feeling that their opponents often see it as a merely lucrative attitude. Occasionally even the terrible Léon Bloy attacks this little band of converts who please the clergy and public—and bullies Huysmans as well as Coppée and Brunetière.*

There are two directions to be distinguished in this literature—both of which, moreover, are equally successful. The first is the good prose, as pious as could be desired, which thrives on good sentiments in a time when the best seller is Georges Ohnet's *Le Maître de Forges.* Paul Bourget, who brings a profound psychology to bear upon a rather silly sentimentality, and, somewhat later, Henri Bordeaux, both furnish an ample supply of edifying novels on right-thinking themes: *Le Disciple, Un Divorce, Le Démon de Midi,* as many programs as there are titles which disclose the theme—no less than the *Roquevillard* or *Le Chêne et les roseaux.* Bordeaux and Bourget are, as it were, the leaders: behind them, or alongside in the best instances (like Estaunié's *L'Empreinte*), how many good, or not-so-good, novelists furnish magazines with serials, magazines like the *Veillées des Chaumières,* and *La Bonne Presse* which springs into life during this period—a whole world about which we lack statistics. Religion, work, nation, family: good reading for officers bored with barracks life, or for a bourgeoisie still hesitating between the Voltairian daring of an Anatole France and the still well-disposed traditional values.

Catholic poetry takes a higher tone, and the great names sing their faith outside the coteries and schools: Péguy in the *Mystère de Jeanne*

---

* This born pamphleteer, a minor author, is not, beneath his excesses, a poor judge of his day which rejected him and let him die in poverty. Thus he wrote of Huysmans, the deserter of Médan: "Converted at the lowest possible cost, without storming, without straining, and without twisting his back, he set himself to writing the literature of a convert—the kind that makes money . . ."; and of Brunetière: "that pedant with the style of a headmaster . . ." (Huysmans is called the "deserter of Médan" because he left the Médan Group, a literary clique under the aegis of Zola, which advocated Naturalistic subjects and documentary treatment. The miscellany *Les Soirées de Médan* contained work of both De Maupassant and Huysmans.—Trans.)

d'Arc and the *Tapisserie de Notre-Dame*, an inexhaustible singer of Chartres and his region; in 1912, Claudel publishes his *L'Annonce faite à Marie*, a medieval mystery play, and later, *L'Otage*, that Roman vision of the captivity of Pius VII. Both reveal their neophyte faith with a verbal richness and dramatic power which alone would suffice to explain their success. At the beginning of a long diplomatic, business, and poetic career, of the lyric songs of a man of action hastening to address himself to a task, the *Annonce* and the *Tapisserie* are the monuments of this revival of religious feeling.

Since the 1880s—when no writer dared say he was a Catholic and a kind of commiseration is reserved for whoever publicizes his faith—Christian spiritualism has gained an intellectual public which it has not had for two hundred years. To be convinced of this, we have only to see the circle of friends surrounding the most irascible and also demanding of these Catholic writers, Léon Bloy, in his last years (he died in 1914): scientists like the geologist Pierre Termier; writers like René Martineau and Jacques Maritain; musicians like Félix Raugel and Georges Auric, and painters like Georges Desvallières and Rouault whose *Sainte Face* nicely conjures up the tormented faith of the "adventurer of God." Bloy's daughters attend the *Schola Cantorum* of Vincent d'Indy, and the new religious music of Vierne and Franck is not unknown at the meetings at Bourg-la-Reine, where this "exalted Catholic" sweeps along enthusiastic souls in his wake.

A final characteristic: the place of men of the Church in this literary and artistic revival is more than moderate; Father Laberthonnière scarcely cuts a good figure near these philosophers. All those great converts at the beginning of the century came to Catholicism by addressing themselves first to lay people and only at the last moment to priests. It is to be thought that many of them do not live their faith with the same intensity: is it a question of education, a consequence of the "Republican" application of the 1801 Concordat, or more simply because the clergy engaged from 1880 to 1907 in this unceasing struggle devoted themselves to it entirely and were unable to be the leaders of this reconquest of an intellectual élite? Ultimately it is probable that the clergy was divided between moderates and integrationists, already linked in a typically French controversy.

Unquestionably the Moral Order, the beautiful years of 1874-75, and especially the restoration of a French Monarchy, with or without a white flag,* retain their adherents. The Catholic Royalists, just before the

---

* In 1871 and finally in 1873, the Comte de Chambord, known as "Henri V," the grandson of Charles X and Pretender to the French throne, negated all hopes of a Restoration. Though he would agree to a constitutional government, he maintained that France would have to give up the Tricolor, symbol of the Revolution, because "Henri V cannot abandon the white flag of Henri IV."—Trans.

War, are even endowed with a leader who will form, or rather mark, generations of intellectuals for several decades: Charles Maurras and the *Action française*, a daily forum for extreme-right Nationalism from 1908 on. There is an entire current of political thought served by great literary talent: Maurras, Daudet, Bainville. And Barrès, who is not of the group, but who contributed in no small way to the development of nationalistic themes, can be associated with them. *Action française*, however, exercised its influence especially in the period between the two wars; despite its condemnation by Rome, Maurrasian thought—primarily critical, and hostile to the Republican regime—maintained its spread until the end of the Third Republic. Eventually, after the "divine surprise," its role is of another nature. Extreme Nationalism, however, is not the ultimate originality of the Catholic revival: Royalist-Catholic thought seems rather to be a survival and soon a political myth with slogans ("the forty kings who, in a thousand years, made France"); the important characteristic of the first decade of the twentieth century is the rebirth of liberal and social Catholicism simultaneously under the impetus of Pope Leo XIII, whose social teaching did not have the same repercussions outside of France as it did within, and through the initiative of unusual Catholics: Marc Sangnier and Charles Péguy.

In 1891 and 1892, Leo XIII took two major steps: the first, political, by advising French Catholics to rally around the Republic which was consolidated through ten years of power. This was a wise position, beyond a doubt conforming with the preceding Roman political tradition which accepted negotiations with the First Consul in 1801, and recognized the Second Republic in 1848. Many conservative politicians, however, were hesitant about following Albert de Mun; years passed by in expectation, and the drama of the Dreyfus Affair ruined this policy of reconciliation with the regime. Actually the *Ralliement*, an affair restricted to France, is less important than the encyclical *Rerum Novarum*, in which Leo XIII shows his sympathies with the workers' conditions. Defining on behalf of the Church a real social doctrine, made urgent by the advances of industrialization and especially by the development of the class struggle, the encyclical is still considered today, in some milieux, the very basis of the Catholic Church's social policy; this is complemented, it is true, by the encyclical of Pius XI, *Quadragesimo anno* (1931), concerning the restoration of the social order. Refuting the socialist solutions of collective ownership and the removal of classes, the head of the Catholic Church established the two classes' duties of charity and justice,* gives them union as an aim, and, in particular, recommends the creation of

---

* "But the rich man and the employer should remember that to exploit poverty and destitution, and to profit from want, are condemned by divine and human laws alike. To defraud anyone of the fruits of his labor would be a crime that cries out to the vengeful anger of Heaven. *The wages you have stolen from your workers by fraud cry out to you, and their noise has risen to the ears of the God of the Armed.*"

Catholic unions which will work toward this aim.* In no country more than in France did the encyclical have greater repercussions—among both laity and priests—or arouse more varied efforts to give substance to this Catholic social program.

Efforts that are little known, even today, and which were misunderstood simultaneously by the conservative and the anticlerical milieux during the early years of the century, were the gradual formation of the first unions; scattered throughout Paris and the provinces these unions are composed more of employees than workers. Often badly led and confused with the "yellow" [or company] unions subsidized by employers to sow seeds of discontent among the workers, they have a hard time defending their independence against the employers and against the more powerful unions in the C.G.T. The trained personnel of the future Christian Confederation, people like Tessier and Poimboeuf, are formed in this dark struggle. In 1904, a group of intellectuals, prompted by Marius Gonin, set up the *Semaines Sociales,* an annual study meeting designed along university lines: lectures, discussions, and colloquies—dealing with such social topics as unions, work contracts, and the social obligation of public authority. Thus the *Semaines Sociales* gather together several hundred listeners—more numerous than the active participants; but workers are always in limited force in these meetings which are addressed to an intellectual élite and do not escape the dangers of a certain academicism. Finally, there are others who are in search of a new means for action upon the masses: experiments are carried out, and little groups prepare the postwar Catholic action.

Nevertheless two personalities dominate this great advance of social Christianity: Péguy, the man of the *Cahiers de la Quinzaine,* whose burning prose misled the myopic Sorbonne† as well as the bishops, who floundered in his politics. Péguy's heart thirsted for justice, and he was eager to give France the general appearance he imagines for her; Péguy is the fighter-poet who pleads all the good causes, attacking all privileges and all vices. A former socialist who repudiated the anticlericalism and pacifism of his youth, a Catholic perpetually dissatisfied with a Church

---

* "We have to praise loudly the zeal of many of our number, those who realize perfectly the needs of the present hour and who carefully explore the ground to discover there an honest path which might lead to the elevation of the working classes . . . We promise the happiest fruits from these unions, provided that they continue to develop themselves, and that prudence always presides in their organization . . . it should be taken as a universal and constant rule in organizing the unions in such a way that they furnish each of their members the proper means for him to attain, by the most convenient and shortest path, the goal he proposes for himself, which consists of the largest possible increase of bodily, spiritual, and material goods."

† Péguy and the Sorbonne historians, for example: "Historians usually write history without meditating upon its limits and conditions: undoubtedly they are right; it is better that each man works at his profession; generally it is better that an historian begins by writing history without looking into it so long. . . ."

which, according to him, betrays its missions,* Péguy assumes apparent contradictions, and heralds, through his "teaching"—which is through example—a new French type, one of the innovations of contemporary French civilization. Catholic Péguy has no sympathy with Royalism; he is Republican and Democrat, spontaneously close to his own, to the little people, who are suffering and hungry. Péguy is a Leftist (a usage made of his name thirty years later), which is certainly appropriate for a social Christian, who does not fear to quote Scripture to justify himself ("The horror of Jesus," he says, "is terrifying for the rich. He loves only poverty, and the poor."). Péguy accepts the heritage of the 1789 Revolution, and even of those of the nineteenth century. A fervent Catholic, he still does not deny his old teachers of the secular schools, whose greatness he is the first Catholic to recognize publicly, and in such an atmosphere: he foresees and says how much service this kind of school can render to a new religious life, accepting French spiritual pluralism and basing both his methods and goals on this frankly admitted reality.† An awakener of thought, a teacher of thought, avidly read by an entire generation of studious youth who are simultaneously charmed and rebuffed, Péguy shows a way; he is a stage in the contemporary French consciousness.

An idealist convinced of the necessity of destroying class and caste barriers, a man closer to political action than Péguy, Marc Sangnier, the founder of *Le Sillon*, represents the same movement, though perhaps more realistically. Sangnier saw, at the very moment when the Separation is prepared for and brought about, the immense advantage this rupture represents for the Church: it separates all organic ties with temporal power and can make of the clergy something other than an ally of the ruling classes. This rupture can also bring about a reconciliation with the lower classes, a total independence: a new Church can be born. Beyond the difficult moments, beyond the days when the first "furrow" is so difficult to plow, Marc Sangnier sees a France delivered from anticlericalism, peacefully effecting social justice in conformity with the Christian idea. A whole group forms around Sangnier whose thought, social rather than political, largely surpasses the daring of those in the *Ralliement* ten years earlier. *Le Sillon* is condemned by Rome in 1910 (in 1907, Pope Pius X had generally condemned all modernism as an abettor of heresies and had declared himself the intransigent defender

---

* "If God were fully served in His Church (He is served there with exactitude, but with such meager exactitude)."
† Still another fine passage from his *Cahiers*, which offer one of the most valuable panoramas of pre-World War One France: "We no longer believe a word of what our lay teachers taught us. We are fully nurtured on what was taught us by the *curés* . . . Now, our lay teachers have retained all our heart and they have our entire confidence. And unfortunately, we cannot say that our old *curés* have absolutely all of our heart, or that they have ever had our confidence. . . ."

of dogma and traditional positions); in 1912, Sangnier sets up La Jeune République, a league more comparable to the Ligue des Droits de l'Homme than to a political party. It is a small, numerically negligible group, yet its democratic and Christian ideal will exercise its influence on postwar political life.

Undoubtedly if we read all the condemnations of liberal Catholicism signed by Pius X, and even those of Leo XIII in his last years, if we see the sordid brawls at the gates of monasteries and churches during the inventory period, if we hear the whistles and catcalls in the early movies whenever a priest appears on the screen—then the voices of Péguy and Sangnier seem very soft during these ill-tempered years. Nevertheless, a whole new aspect of French Catholicism is in the process of taking shape—and affecting an age. The Catholic revival is not merely the reappearance of a traditional religion, a disturbed and out-distanced moment: rather, it is an emergent re-Christianization.

► ANARCHIST INDIVIDUALISM

In this country, the native land of Montaigne and Pascal, Proudhon and André Gide, in this French world where for centuries individual achievement has aroused more admiration than have collective efforts, the triumph of individualism cannot be presented as the fruit of circumstances, of fortuitous or prearranged encounters. In politics as in literature, in the theater as before easels, the early part of the twentieth century is marked by individual investigation and personal ambitions for discovery or success. For the most solidly organized parties, in an era when politics is more an affair of temperament than one of doctrine, to be themselves affected by militant anarchism—as with the schools of literature, insofar as the term still has any meaning in the days of Valéry and Apollinaire—all this did not develop and spread without relation to a past rich in examples and similar investigations, without relation to well-established traditions. Yet it is no less true that the 1900s and their atmosphere—at least in Paris, and particularly on the Right Bank—of putting Positivism to flight, of bankrupting Scientism (if not, in the eyes of the less experienced writers, of science itself), these years when the starry heavens above are called into question no less than the moral law within our hearts, were particularly favorable to this explosion of individualism, in the good or bad sense of the word. Finally, need we be amazed at the fact that artists, painters, musicians, and poets, more than any others, are the very sensitive witnesses of the great changes in this troubled world?

In political life, the most significant destiny is that of the forces devoted to defending the working classes; not that the Radicals, and the

Left or Right Republicans were indifferent. They are all inconsistent groups gathered around the few strong personalities who dominate the Assemblies. Through their lack of discipline and organization, within and outside the Chamber of Deputies, they would handily illustrate this individualism the Radical party will end up by exalting, if it is true that Alain, the "citizen against the powers," is the theorist of Radicalism, that "governmental anarchism."* But the fate of the labor organizations is an example. Indeed this is their period of reorganization: the socialists, scattered in little groups with precise ideologies, arrive at unity, thanks to Jules Guesde and Jean Jaurès. Marxists, Blanquists, Possibilists, and Alemanists meet again in the heart of the S.F.I.O. [Section Française de l'Internationale Ouvrière] which, in 1914, is not a negligible parliamentary force. Supported by the proletariat, petty civil servants, and peasants in *métayage* regions like the Bourbonnais, the Socialist Party, led by Juarès, presents the most well-established and well-organized appearance of any French party, as least from the 1905 Congress on. Supporting the Second International, they participate in its exchange of ideas and doctrinal confrontations; they set its parliamentary effectiveness against the intransigent, sterile theory of the German Socialist Party, led by Liebknecht and Kautsky. The Congresses of Paris in 1900 and Amsterdam in 1904 supply proof of its vitality.

At the same time, the trade-union movement achieves its unity. Thanks to Pelloutier, then Griffuelhes, the C.G.T. takes shape: Bourses du Travail, local organizations, *département*-wide unions† including all the guilds, and finally the Fédérations Nationales d'Industries all unite into one organization,‡ which continues to advance, despite serious difficulties after 1908, until just before the War. In 1912, it numbers 600,000 paying members.

Yet in their congresses and publications, the militants—workers, artisans, skilled Parisian workers, self-educated men, and "bourgeois" come to socialism through idealism—do not avoid the atmosphere of their times. Those following Proudhon prevail over the Marxists, and French socialism bears that mark, perceptible even today; as opposed to neighboring England, whose labor movement is more powerful and better organized, French socialism remains divided. While the English and Belgians established a sole organization including both unions and

---

* The expression is Proudhon's, and this patronage is not by chance. But Alain, in his *Propos*, abounds in characteristics as strikingly paradoxical.
† *Unions départementales* are Federations by *département* uniting the various trade and industrial unions.—Trans.
‡ Just before the War, this organization was improved: the Bourses du Travail—even if the name remained on the buildings where union representatives were present (*permanences syndicales*) and as part of the vocabulary—gave up their places to the compulsory unions in the *départements*. The Fédérations Nationales formed new and simpler groups: Slate-workers and Miners, Copper and Metal Workers.

parties working for the same emancipation of the proletariat, the French set up two organizations which, theoretically at least, are completely independent: certainly both the Party and the Confederation can aim for social revolution—the goal is identical, the means will be different. The party led by Jaurès—who is not himself a Marxist, practicing a parliamentary reform, insofar as the International allows him—may well attempt to "envelop" the C.G.T. The Syndicalists have no confidence in politics; bitterly they contemplate the ministerial careers of "deserters" like Millerand and Viviani, who act through corruption and threat, and Briand, who was the theorist of the general strike. These men believe in the inherent rightness of revolutionary action,* spontaneous on the professional level; they believe in the abolition of proletarian conditions by successive results, like the eight-hour day, within a factory. The ultimate recourse in this incessant struggle is the general strike, which would totally paralyze the nation's economic life. Finally, these revolutionary syndicalists can conceive syndicalism only as independent of political life; and they assert this typically French definition at the 1906 C.G.T. Congress at Amiens. Even today, a whole segment of the French labor movement continues to regard the Charter of Amiens as authoritative. The essence of the Charter lies in those two concluding formulas which were the most disputed after the War and whose exact understanding even now provokes ardent polemics in labor circles:

> 1. With respect to individuals, the Congress asserts the total freedom of the syndicalist to participate, outside of the union group, in whatever form of struggle corresponds to his political or philosophical conceptions; it confines itself to requesting him, in return, not to introduce his outside opinions into the union itself.
>
> 2. With respect to the organizations, the Congress declares that in order for syndicalism to attain its maximum effect, economic action must be directly exercised against employers; the confederated organizations considered as syndicated groups need not concern themselves with parties and sects which, outside and alongside, can, in all freedom, pursue social change.

Simultaneously fortified by theoretical discussions—like Georges Sorel's *Réflexions sur la violence,* and thinner, more readable studies by Pouget, Merrheim, and Griffuelhes, as well as the severe struggle waged against employers and the government from 1907 to 1911 during incessant strikes (the most important being that of the Railroad Workers in 1911, brutally crushed by Briand)—revolutionary syndicalism is then the most dynamic working force, as opposed to parliamentary socialism,

---

* Griffuelhes: "French Syndicalism is characterized by spontaneous and creative action . . . This action was not ordered by any formulas or theoretical assertions whatsoever."

which had been restricted to systematic opposition since 1905. Hence the lasting prestige of this syndicalist tradition, despite a certain slackening in the years immediately preceding the Great War.

This anarcho-syndicalism grew up under the aegis of Proudhon—also, through Georges Sorel, under the protection of Bergson. Primarily it is the work of first-rate personalities: Monatte, Griffuelhes, Merrheim. Because of this, because of the scorn of its trained personnel for the "ignorant people . . . who read filth . . . who play endless games of *manille*," the labor movement remains the achievement of a small minority which does not have a strong grasp on the world of the worker. But on the other hand, the militant worker, conscious of his duties, over-whelmed with responsibilities and harassed by the government (for whom, on the eve of May Day, detention on suspicion is a sanctioned method), is a pioneer, if not a hero; in this individualistic era, he is no aberration.

No more aberrant are the writers who breathed the anguished air of the prewar era—a war that for ten or so years has been foreboded in every milieu. Little does it matter that the masters of this great literature are read only by a small number of Frenchmen, that *La Revue Blanche* has but a small circulation, comparable to that of Péguy's *Cahiers*.* This literary world, at the time of the Exhibition of 1900 and before the War, is passionately individualistic: the cult of the Self is its first rule, from the young Léon Blum who is passionately fond of Stendhal—less the critic of Rome than the egoist, the father of Julien and Fabrice—to Barrès who advises young writers to seek the solitude that enables one to belong completely to oneself and to preserve one's interior life. Consequently this is the time when literature belongs to outcasts, re-viled by the common people but also by others—the heirs of Rimbaud; yet they themselves revile, refusing the world offered them by the end of the nineteenth century. Some escape toward another world in dreams: *Le Grand Meaulnes* by Alain-Fournier is a novel of rejection. Others choose their way, departing from the beaten paths: Nathanael is guided by a safe hand toward the fruits of the earth, offered him by the most amazing writer of his day who also created Lafcadio; Proust, at the same time, writes the novel about a world which feels itself disappearing, and which, especially, knows itself to be too rich in intelligence and sensibility. Yet undoubtedly the most typical, first of all because he was successful and had an audience the others did not receive until after the

---

* *La Revue Blanche* is taken as an example and many other "little" magazines would be worthy of our interest. There are the large undertakings, like *Le Mercure*, or the less important, like *La Nouvelle Revue française*, at its inception, about which André Gide noted in February, 1912: "We have 528 subscribers and dis-tribute 244 complimentary copies."

War, is Barrès: the exasperated patriot from Lorraine, the author of *Les Déracinés*, the teacher of an individualistic ethic no less demanding than that of the *Immoraliste* or of the author [Léon Blum] of *Le Mariage*.

The poets—successors and heirs of Mallarmé—like Valéry and Apollinaire, write for small coteries of initiates who alone can understand, and soon a commentary will be necessary in order to read the best-written works: thus *La Jeune Parque* or *Le Cimetière marin* are explained to the difficult exercise of the ear and the understanding by a friend of the poet. At a time when the popular or worldly novel continues to increase in circulation,* the highest literature becomes a realm reserved for a few who are able to appreciate the keen intelligence and, simultaneously, the sensualism hidden in this hermetic poetry; behind these the same concern expressed more simply by others, is still harbored: "One must try to live," cries the author of *Le Cimetière marin*.

Thus, the schools died with the century: no label, not even that of Symbolism (the last born of the schools), is appropriate for more than one author, or more than one coterie. The last of the Romantics died in 1885, with the pomp of national obsequies, justifiably imposing because of his popularity; in effect, Parnassians and Naturalists no longer matter. But the *mal d'écrire*, the fever of writing with originality, is no less widespread: perhaps the best indication of this literary anarchism is the growing preference for the journal, the memoir of minute individual facts narrated complacently day after day. Doubtless it is a remote inheritance from Romanticism, handed down by the Goncourts and others; though the daily chronicle has not yet become a genre or a source of revenue, it is a current practice: an immodest triumph of Self.

Actually, following the series of blustering manifestoes and the impassioned discussions which continue to rebound, one might place the entire artistic life of the period under the ensign of individualism—and not merely the literary set, overwhelmed by a heavy inheritance. And yet the musicians and painters, who hold so great a place—first place, many claim—at the head of European civilization around 1900, are more than individualists. Even though it is advisable not to linger upon the crop of theoretical and critical writings, even the table chat, concerning them, one is obliged to grant them a very wide significance, a more important credit than Symbolist conceits or Narcissistic meditations. And already the reports which sanctioned a French school in music and a School of Paris in painting, because of their international diffusion, were not mistaken.

With the end of the nineteenth century, Paris and then the large

---

* The creation of the first literary prizes, in the wake of the Prix Goncourt, helped a great deal.

provincial towns know the advance of symphonic music, which gradually creates a public for itself; it takes its place beside theater music, opera, and *opéra-comique* which continued to be well received from Rossini to Gounod. The latter sort of repertory becomes fixed, and no longer enriches itself at the same pace as in the days of Bizet and Massenet. The greatest achievement in this type of music is Charpentier's *Louise*, as tender an opera as could be wished for: opera and *opéra-comique* are henceforth considered "popular" in certain milieux; the operetta, a minor genre, carves out a career for itself. "Great" music or, as some say, pure music, continues to advance, aided by a whole series of institutions: not only the old Conservatoire where everyone, more or less, serves his apprenticeship, but also the Société Nationale de Musique (forged on the anvil of defeat by Saint-Saëns in 1871), which is freer and more daring than the old school; there is also d'Indy's *Schola Cantorum* founded in 1896, and finally the Sociétés de Concerts which each winter create new works, assuring them a public and an immediate success—or failure. Franck, Saint-Saëns, Fauré, and d'Indy were the first to nourish—and not without brilliance—this revival of French music at a time when German work, particularly that of Wagner, was dominating international musical life.

But whatever their merits and their works, these are less important in the French School than Debussy, Ravel, and Stravinsky—despite the ties that link some of them, such as Fauré, to contemporary poets; Debussy was also linked to the Symbolists, especially to Mallarmé. But Claude Debussy's greater importance unquestionably lies in the remote correspondence established between his investigations (and achievements) in musical technique, and the great movement of contemporary science; and the same is true of Ravel and Stravinsky who, with similar daring, also challenge an entire tradition of musical technique, established little by little from the sixteenth century on, and considered as immutable in its success—that of Bach but also of Rossini —as Euclidian geometry, the mother of Newtonian physics. Claude Debussy, with *Pelléas et Mélisande*, the great landmark of 1902, and *La Mer*, asserts an entirely new music, constructed of whole-tone scales, chords of sevenths, ninth, and elevenths, a music which accepts those dissonances usually rejected. Without abandoning classical techniques, Debussy utilizes new resources that bring cries from the critics, stir up long debates on his "verticalism," and prepare the way for the music of today.

Maurice Ravel—whose best-known work comes after the war—passes before 1914 as the very disciple of Debussy, utilizing the same innovations with the same audacity, and quickly acquiring a renown as great as his master's. As early as 1909, he is the famous composer of *Schéhérazade* and *Jeux d'eau*, and there will follow many other glorious titles like the *Rapsodie espagnole* and even *Ma Mère l'Oye*. But Ravel's music, still "classic" in its finish, causes less of an uproar than the major creations of Igor Stravinsky: *L'Oiseau de feu* in 1910, and particularly *Le Sacre du Printemps* in 1913. Rhythms and tonalities produced interminable discussion, when *Le Sacre* was presented in Paris before a public which had nevertheless been prepared for ten or more years. The Russian composer, who will become a naturalized French citizen after the war, appears from that time on as Debussy's equal and as one of the great founders of modern music.

Disrespectful of the hallowed rules, Debussy and Stravinsky are anarchists; yet for this very reason, they are much more than mere individualists: never in the history of music has so great an upheaval been effected, renewing traditional harmony, improving resources for expression and therefore for musical invention. Everyone knows what *Les Six*, that famous group between the wars,* and many others, owe to them.

The world of painting is still more prolific: the painters are talked about more than the musicians, and the wildest pictorial theories could be discussed in the days of the Nabis, Neo-Impressionists, Fauves, and Cubists. Art criticism, begun by Stendhal—much more than by Diderot, whose *Salons* are literary criticism—and made famous by Baudelaire, becomes a profession with recognized masters and apprentices, a press, rules, and paradoxes. Finally, on the occasion of the Exhibition of 1900, and in the years that followed, the discovery of exotic arts, African and Japanese, to say nothing of the Ballets Russes, contributed in no small way to facilitating learned elaborations in "isms" about the plastic arts; and in a less narrow framework, sculpture from Rodin to Maillot would obviously have its place here. In this way, the studio discussions, the blustering pages of critics, add more to the quasi-empirical, quasi-systematic investigations made by the painters of the period, extending the efforts of Manet, Renoir, Van Gogh, and Cézanne. Hence even at fifty years' distance, even with the famous historical perspective, it is difficult to characterize or explain the treasure-filled world of prewar French painting. Concerning this wonderful wealth, and its significance, there is, at any rate, no doubt. Gide says in *Les Faux monnayeurs:* "I have often asked myself through what marvel painting was ahead and how it happened that literature let itself be so outdistanced."

Yet how many artists are worthy of our mention! Take, for example, the strange Toulouse-Lautrec, lithographer and poster-maker, painter of brothels, circuses and animals, and the first to depict sporting scenes. Limiting ourselves to the most significant, we find two groups holding

---

* Under the aegis of Satie, "the six" included: Auric, Durey, Honegger, Milhaud, Poulenc, and Tailleferre.—Trans.

the greatest place: the Fauves who, coming out of Impressionism and also from Van Gogh, Gauguin, and Seurat, continue the quest for color. Matisse, Derain, and Vlaminck represent them well, particularly, perhaps, Vlaminck, the painter-runner-cyclist, more easily ranked behind this standard since he did not search for anything more, did not depart from this manner as did Matisse or Dufy. The brutally daring use of color remains the common fund into which, at least for a time, they all deposited: Fauvism had its finest hour around 1905.

Yet, on the whole, the Fauves are less important than the Cubists: the best of them rapidly let themselves become swept by the movement; and around 1910, the new school is so dominant as to cause the proliferation of doctrinal studies. Physical Cubism, Analytical Cubism, Decorative Cubism: Picasso (before 1914), Braque, Dufy, and Léger caused a revolution in painting. Reasoning their art, and especially analyzing their sensation and its reproduction, they imagined and rethought a new plastic space and recomposed it upon canvas: still lifes, human figures—but not landscapes—are thus the new objects of their studies, simultaneously theoretical and empirical. Cubism is an intellective art, seeking connections between the world of objects and the thinking self; simultaneously realistic and irrational, it is a discovery of the world, prompted by the deep feeling of the relativity of knowledge. According to a nice turn of phrase by Francastel, who has often emphasized it, a Picasso or a Dufy could understand and feel relativity better than many physicists. The following evidence comes from an artist, not an art historian:

> The problem of design is to represent a flat surface, masses, and objects situated in space. The solutions are countless. For our vision is above everything else empirical and conventional. Conventional is the design, conventional is the representation we make of this design, for we interpret this design according to our knowledge. It constitutes a suggestion.

Through its daring in a new vision of the world and through this deep correspondence with the scientific revolution, Cubism represents the most important stage in the pictorial life of Paris since around 1865, when Impressionism established a place for itself. Picasso and Braque, around 1910, were certainly able to make their contemporaries bristle and sometimes laugh, by the unexpectedness of some of their forms. Nevertheless they imposed their mark, and their art—the conventional, figurative, and geometric symbol—continues fifty years later to inspire those who came after them: Gischia, Fougeron, Pignon, and others.

Through its daring in deciphering space, Cubist painting once more expresses its confidence in man and especially in the conquering aspect of the scientific world, which, in effect, literature does not express—retarded as it is in the worship of sacrosanct techniques and immutable, stereotyped themes: the world which is made is but a setting for eternal man. The time has not yet come to speak of a new humanism. The word certainly lags behind plastic expression. The pursuits of Cubism also command aspects of contemporary, even everyday life: Cubist schematization, which we may call a sort of stylization, will reverberate thirty years later in furnishings and the manufacture of household objects; more quickly, through the poster, already transformed by Lautrec, the Cubists in large part asserted their new visions on the common man who, in the subways and on walls, learns to read in an unexpected line and a spot of color all the suggestive power of this unwritten language. Thus—after the War, certainly more than before it—Cubism dominates a vision of the world, that of the School of Paris, which the entire world, or at least its capitals, gradually discovers.

To be sure, writers, musicians, and painters affect only a Parisian public; and until after the War, with the popular spread of the radio and of posters, a minority even of this public: a small number of initiates, in groups which rarely mix with one another—despite a few exceptions like Gide, Blum, Maurice Denis, Fauré, and Debussy. Yet, despite these limits, despite academic reluctance (the Beaux-Arts will soon praise the Impressionists, the better to reject the Cubists, and Maurice Ravel fails in the Grand Prix de Rome in 1905), despite lack of understanding and catcalls, these great moments of French artistic life constitute the more fertile part of this civilization.

► THE FIRST WORLD WAR

From the one battle of the Marne to the other, for four years, France endured the heaviest weight of the First World War. With a fifth of her territory invaded, obliged to provide men for the eastern front and to help the Allies on the sea, she paid more dearly than any other power for the 1918 victory. In short, let us point out that twenty years later, in 1939, when the Second World War breaks out, France has not yet recovered; she still bears the mark—in her population, the slowness of her economic development, and especially in her collective psychology—of the losses and sufferings undergone during the four years of the first total war.

For more than a half-century, the French population has not been increasing rapidly: the birth rate keeps going down, yet due to medical advances, the average life expectancy is extended. This only made the human losses due to the war heavier: 1,400,000 dead—four per cent of the population. But still more precisely, this figure represents two young men in every ten sacrificed to the life of the nation; to which must be added 3,000,000 who are more or less invalid: some losing a limb or with disfigured faces,* ("*Les Gueules Cassées*"), others whose lungs are affected by gas: say again, out of ten men, four others have met with some difficulty in resuming their place in national life, with at least one out of four living off the relief of his fellow citizens because of total, or almost total, disability. Thus, of ten men who reached adulthood before 1918, four remain who have to help as many others of their fellow men live, and who must take charge of the families of the dead. Neither working women—although they are constantly on the increase—nor the constant immigration from abroad between the two wars were able to "compensate" for such losses.

To these human losses, which are heavier in rural areas than in the urban ones where special industrial allocations kept a part of the male population from the front, must be added, in a different sphere, the material destruction. Reconstruction lasted ten years: there were more than 300,000 buildings destroyed and 500,000 damaged; 31,000 miles of broken roads; close to 6,200 miles of unusable railroads; and 5,000 bridges down. Nor should we overlook the 11,600 square miles of arable land, meadows, and forests to be cleared of land mines and restored for agriculture;† the coal mines in the north flooded by the occupational forces before they left, and the plundered industrial installations.

Gradually Reims, Arras, Senlis, and Lunéville recover their look of old French towns—those products of past centuries' success, so quickly annihilated by artillery fire. Even Verdun, where the greatest battle of that long war was fought, recovers its urban appearance—alongside its charnel house.

While this immense rehabilitation work absorbs the economic strength of the entire nation, countries which did not undergo such disasters— the United States, Great Britain, and even Germany—are able to push ahead in industrial equipment and to emphasize their economic advance over a France that had been bled white.

But the spiritual sufferings—and the development of collective mentalities resulting from these—are no less important; the war veterans are marked for life by the existence they led for years in the trenches: mud, rats, vermin, gas, permanent alerts, hand-to-hand fighting, and the pounding of artillery, forced upon these men a physical attrition no one believed to be bearable, one that attacked nerves, lungs, and (since the stationary warfare contributed much to the spreading of alcoholism) digestive systems. The soldiers of the First World War, obscure heroes of a war of attrition who were marked in their flesh, made a civic *credo* of their solidarity in misery—"United as at the Front." Civilians were affected in other ways: in the worst way in occupied areas, since hostages

---

* Official statistics show 740,000 disabled out of these 3,000,000 wounded.
† These are minimum figures: thousands of roughly handled acres were not restored, but simply repaired by their owners.

and conflagrations were common measures; but even the areas away from the front suffered a war psychosis with far-reaching consequences: the streams of false reports the pious lies of the General Staff, all the "eyewash," the optimistic news unscrupulously promulgated on the public by the press and the government—all these left their traces. The great pessimistic crisis of 1917, which spared neither the front nor the rearguard, expresses the troubled spirits and the moral uncertainty felt by the entire nation in the thick of the fighting when Russia and the United States are changing the given factors of the war.

But these debates of conscience did not end in 1918—if only because of the meaning gradually given to the war: begun out of respect for alliances and to stand by "scraps of paper" whose importance was suspected by only a few Frenchmen, the First World War ends, thanks to Wilson, under the banner of the slogan "the war to end all wars," justifying all the sacrifices accepted by every French family. November 11, 1918 puts an end to an exhausting war, but also promises a future where "we shall never see that again"; the peace treaties and the League of Nations should have made of this hope a concrete form. Actually, as early as 1919, the Treaty of Versailles was denounced even in France as a *diktat*, imposing every possible humiliation on the Germans, including unilateral responsibility for the war (the famous Article 231). And it did not take long for the League of Nations, deprived of American cooperation, to prove its impotence in establishing that peace soon considered by some as the greatest of goods. Beyond the *détente*—the years from 1919 to 1924—following normally upon so long and so heavy an ordeal, the Great War long controlled attitudes of mind and indeed political options which France was still experiencing in 1939.

XVII

The Early Twentieth Century in France

Sciences, Arts, and Techniques 1919-1939

FRENCHMEN who lived through this period between the two wars remember it as bitterly as they praise—without stopping to think—the 1900 *Belle Époque*. And with some reason, for beyond the exhilaration of victory and the solace that came after such a long effort, there was no lack of dark years in this country which remained susceptible to the world's every quiver, to the world's every convulsive moment: the Russian Revolution, the American depression in 1929, the Moslem awakening, and European fascisms, all had their echoes in Paris, if not throughout France—while the nation remains in the grip of its own "interior" difficulties, both political and economic.

Thus, let us first evoke, within these twenty difficult years, the economic crisis which followed within two years of the world crisis: from 1931 on, France, in her turn, experienced a slump in business, a lowering of prices and wages, and the terrible deflation of 1934. The decline continues until 1938 and the artificial stimulus of the war effort, a decline signifying unemployment, poverty or at least financial embarrassment for millions of Frenchmen: workers, small-scale peasants, and petty civil servants lived through difficult years, despite the hope of 1936.

This is also a period of governmental collapse: the Third Republic no longer has the prestige it had before 1914. It is as if, in the political sphere, a spring had broken, after the great fruitions of the preceding forty years: parliamentary intrigues and wire-pulling lobbies often disgust informed citizens; neither the institutions nor the personnel are adapted to the new tasks of the state. Finally there is the sad day in July, 1940, when the parliamentarians themselves put an end to that Republic which had already just gotten through a February evening in 1934.*

In a word, these two decades are years of increasingly intense international crisis: despite some relief due to the efforts of Briand and Stresemann, what a long succession of distresses—from the French occupation of the Ruhr to the German conquest of Czechoslovakia! There is the failure of the peace, that slow erosion of the hopes and the achievements of Versailles, accelerated after 1933 and particularly after 1936: war in Spain, reoccupation of the left bank of the Rhine, war in Ethiopia, the occupation of Austria; then, Munich and Danzig: the war of nerves and propaganda besieged and misled the French well before September of 1939.

Nevertheless, amid these disturbances which, on the surface of events, disclose the anxieties and shocks of a world in profound transformation, French civilization is again renewed; despite all the extremely heavy handicaps—despite the systematic denigration of her neighbors, and sometimes some of her sons, despite the war in the Rif and the illusion of the Colonial Exhibition—she continues to stand for a particular form of collective life, a style of Parisian living, of French living which has no equal in the world when seen with some perspective and compared with that of other European nations or that of either young or old colonial societies. This form of life is still prized, as evidenced by the number of foreigners living in Paris, settled there permanently or for several months of the year, basking in this matchless human climate; another indication is the worldwide success of the Exhibition of 1937, in spite of so many traps in its brief career. During a time when the peoples of the planet are brought closer to each other by new means of transportation and cultural exchanges; when mechanical civilization makes extraordinary advances in the United States as well as in Western Europe and, little by little, in Russia; at this time, the originality of France is no less noticeable than a century or two earlier—and it acquires a new audience.

The fact is that France is in the front rank of the century's scientific and technical advances.† Unquestionably she is slower to adapt herself

---

* When, after the Stavisky scandal, troublemakers from the Right called for a demonstration that subsequently threatened to break into the Palais Bourbon and led to the fall of Daladier's second ministry.—Trans.

† In 1923, Thierry rightly notes: "Our entire civilization is one of physics."

particularly in the agricultural sphere and also in that of commerce, than Germany or England, and she is less fortunate than North America. Yet she provides herself with a powerful automotive industry and at the same time electrifies her rural areas, even the remote Alpine regions, and also builds dams and roads. Perhaps her engineers and scientists ought to be reckoning more and more with foreign "competition" in the international-patent and scientific-research markets: at least they still hold their good position.

France is present, too—perhaps even more noticeably—on the level of expression and transmission of ideas: an atmosphere of free, intellectual research, closely allied to the conditions created in the preceding era, suffuses all the activities of the mind. Despite the poverty of the press and radio, dominated by financial and economic interests which can in no way compare with the generous sixteenth-century patrons, the burning life of French intellectuals expresses this unequaled triumph which is the nation's liberalism.

Technical progress and liberalism surround the fundamental changes of social life as well: the industrial advance and the second revolution in transportation accentuated the rural exodus as well as the general rise of living standards. During the ten years of reconstruction, 1919 to 1929, the Frenchman's material life moves forward. If a peasant in the Haute-Loire continues to harvest his corn with scythes, to thrash with flails, and to feed himself on what he raises, he is rapidly becoming an anachronism. And the towns, from one decade to the next, are more comfortable and richer in diversions, and are all the more attractive for them: the ratio between town and country teeters in favor of the former, despite the constraint of the economic crisis after 1931.

But many innovations, even in the geography of the population, also upset social life: new élites are formed, insinuating their way into the bourgeoisie and aping it, recognizing it—despite all the revolutionary phraseology—as the dominant class. Thus, through a process of osmosis, French society restructures itself at a time when the crisis brings about the older structure's downfall. Yet masses and élites—who do not participate in the same forms of culture, do not have the same ideal of national life, and seem irreconcilable in the impotence of each to impose itself upon the other—continue to oppose one another. Beyond these electoral antitheses, this traditional cleavage between Right and Left, revolutionary "virtue" certainly seems to be lost: the year 1936, despite the momentarily aroused enthusiasm, is proof of this. Masses and élites move farther and farther apart, so moved by power of money unequally distributed by capitalist society: for the latter there are unequal theatrical achievements, as well as triumphs in *haute couture* and painting, which has become an object of snobbism; for the former, the wholesome joys of the Tour de France, cheap "Westerns," and the old refrains of Tino Rossi. France seen in profile and head-on—what different faces!

► NEW TECHNIQUES: ENERGY AND
TRANSPORTATION

What strikes the twentieth-century man reflecting upon his era, upon what surrounds him, is the rapidity of change in the world in which he lives: the speed of daily traveling is comparable only to the general acceleration of all movement, of history itself. Thus such a man perceives that his grandfather, who in 1880 saw the railroad and a few other innovations, was actually much closer to his seventeenth- or even his sixteenth-century ancestor than to himself. The 1930 Frenchman lives in a technical environment totally different from that of 1880 when steam engines, gas, railroads, and iron bridges represented the last word in material progress; but even more important than the revolution brought about by electricity, oil, and the movies, is the scope of this change. Each year brings an innovation that transforms an object of everyday use, a means of transportation or a machine. Technical research becomes a necessity* for industry and, lacking that, some knowledge of new achievements: annual shows and quarterly and monthly reviews increase, to establish the necessary communication between user and inventor; the exhibitions of the nineteenth century, held at intervals of seven to eleven years, are no longer adequate for this task, and the custom of holding them is quite naturally lost. Thus, all of daily living is made dependent upon technical progress: the machine becomes an everyday auxiliary, for the peasant who uses an electric centrifugal creamer as well as for the department-store accountants provided with calculating machines. This technological ubiquity, which continues to increase during the twenty-year period, articulates a scientific reality: the distance continues to dwindle between theory, laboratory discoveries, and calculations, and their applications; the laboratories for applied research, twentieth-century creations, bridge this gap. In the long run what remains slow is the spread of employment, for economic reasons certainly (the sometimes higher price of new working equipment), and for technical ones to a lesser degree, since the ordinarily used machine rarely demands any extensive professional education for its use; but particularly for psychological reasons: the vacuum cleaner in the city apartment and the tractor on the farm had no more insurmountable obstacle than the habit of using brooms or yokes. Thus, we can conceive how, though "invented" as early as 1890, there are no more than twenty thousand or so

---

* A necessity often misunderstood: technical innovation is slow to assert itself since the state of the scientific spirit (including the rational calculation of depreciation and even resale prices), is not widespread—not to mention the predilection for technical research. Even in 1940, Marc Bloch notes: "We have great scientists, and no techniques are less scientific than ours."

automobiles* throughout the nation on the eve of the First World War; they do not circulate abundantly until around 1930. The same is true of telephones, movies, or records. The sign marking these twenty years is the extension of electricity and the internal combustion engine.

At least it ought to be asserted that these are the technical applications which most changed French life; not that the advances in the domestic arts are negligible† (though they are slow to command attention outside a small, urban clientele), nor are the enormous attainments of the new biochemistry and pharmacy, which make a great deal of money for Rhône-Poulenc, nor even the strides made in plastics during the years immediately preceding 1939. The new industries born of chemical progress were scattered geographically and technically, owing to their narrow specialization: from the Parisian pharmaceutical laboratories to the Péage acetate factories in Roussillon (Rhodiaceta). From this scattering, too, comes their lesser relative importance, despite the exceptional progress they make.

The electric motor and the internal combustion engine furnished the mechanical civilization with a double strength: at a time when those coal mines operated for a century or more begin threatening to dry up, they put to work two new sources of industrial energy: hydroelectricity presents the greater advantage over coal and oil of being inexhaustible since it is fed by rain. Yet oil and electricity also offered many new means of transportation, complementing, and soon competing with that triumph of the preceding century, the railroad; the automobile, the motorcycle, and the airplane, so quickly adopted, constitute one more tightening of man's grasp upon nature.

As early as 1914, the output of France's coal-mining industry was insufficient to underwrite industrial life. Shortly before 1939, France produced forty-five million tons of coal; she imported, from Germany and England, the ten million tons she lacked. Hence, in particular, the disparity in her iron-making production (thirty to thirty-five million tons) and the weak steel production—six million tons. The perfecting of the new energy resources could only encourage strides in mechanization. But hydraulic equipment, consigned to regional electric companies whose financial means were frequently limited, was slow, especially after 1930; despite the good state of high-voltage, long-distance transportation, the steam-generating stations (easier to create, but returning lower profits since they are enormous consumers of coal) spring up at

---

* Gide goes to the burial of Charles-Louis Philippe: at Moulins, to get to Cerilly, the horse-cab drivers do not want to harness up their carriages. He has to look far and wide for an automobile. (Philippe died in 1900.—Trans.)
† Since 1945, Domestic Arts Shows have for the same reason become as national an event as the Auto Shows. Before the War, these shows retained the character of pioneer works ahead of their day, and sought to gather crowds—with dubious success: their present popularity indicates a new mentality.

ports and coal basins. Just before the War, the production in heat is virtually equal to that in water power.* The search for oil, pursued unenthusiastically and with only very slightly improved means, does not yield good results. Only one oilfield, Pechelbronn, located in Alsace as early as 1904 by the Germans, is operated shortly before 1939 and produces a hundredth of French consumption; the Middle East, the United States, and Mexico supply the rest—refined or not.

Despite these handicaps, both electric and fuel-oil engines assumed an important place in industrial life. First of all electric power has a flexibility of use the steam engine lacks—each machine can be equipped with its motor, particularly in the textile and metallurgical industries; and above all, electricity can give life to the fairly unimportant workshops, even in the rural areas, and restore to the mountain textile industries around Lyon and the craftsmen in the Jura an activity threatened by the previous period's industrial concentration in a few areas. Hence, the double and simultaneous success, in large-scale enterprises and in small workshops, of electrically powered equipment—particularly in cloth and spinning mills, though in fact these are less important than the revolution in transportation which followed upon the high installation expenses.

In the realm of interior and foreign relations, electricity and the gasoline engine bring still more momentous innovations: electric and Diesel motors equip railroads and urban transportation systems. The performance is superior,† economy over coal is considerable, and the rate of acceleration is more even—all these conditions suffice to explain why, at the very moment when some are discovering the charm of steam engines, they disappear: the Paris-Orléans-Midi (the present-day Sud-Ouest line) using the high lakes in the Pyrenees, outfits itself almost completely with electrically propelled engines; a part of the Ouest line does the same, and great plans are projected for all lines that must run up steep mountain grades. For shunting and short runs the companies also put on powerful Diesel machines. In a word, the major towns are serviced by an urban electric trolley car network which suffers almost immediate decline, after its heyday around 1930, because of the competition from automobiles. It is a slow retreat, since Paris keeps her last lines until 1935-1936, and even today, provincial centers like Lyon and Saint-Étienne have not totally given them up despite the flexibility of gasoline-powered buses and even the trolley buses.

Then the internal combustion engine changed transportation much more than did electricity: automobiles became the most important

---

* The figures for 1936 are: thermoelectricity, 7,600,000 kilowatt hours; hydroelectricity, 8,900,000 (half of which is for the Alps, and one-quarter of which is for the Massif Central).

† A locomotive has a very weak output of energy, on the order of five to ten per cent.

means of transport in the nation. Used to complement trains before 1914—at village stations and little towns where trains do not stop—then as a sports object and finally as an urban vehicle, the automobile gains new users and finds new uses each year:* there are trucks and delivery trucks, for light and short-haul transportation or for perishable commodities, and buses, taxis, and private cars for people. The industry which is created, especially around Paris, is concentrated in a few justly famous hands—Renault, Peugeot, Citroën—and the small prewar artisan undertakings, of the Dedion Bouton type, gradually disappear, absorbed by the large firms dominating the French market. Shortly before the War, all the factories together turn out 200,000 cars annually: more than 2,000,000 vehicles† circulate on the 186,400 miles of asphalt roads, equipped by an industry of tires and road-markers (Michelin), the latter quickly necessitated by the considerable traffic. The automobile is, at one and the same time, a more flexible working instrument than the train for the insurance salesman, the traveling salesman, and the businessman, as well as a toy and a means of distraction for the Sunday drivers who extend their range of action and avoid the fatigues of bicycles as well as the constraints of railroads.

From 1925-1930 on, bus lines were extended beyond the confines of the towns, and short-range connections around stations were abandoned to assure longer-range transportation: Paris-Côte d'Azur, Paris-Côte Basque; moving vans, fruit and market gardening transport practiced "door-to-door," town-to-town service from Roussillon to Paris. And thus highway transportation created serious competition for the railroads. Just before the War, there was the still unsolved problem of this rivalry, in which railroads, encumbered with public obligations (fares, reductions, legal obligations involving the maintenance of lines and the frequency of service), constantly lost ground, shutting down certain lines and stations, replacing light steam trains with even lighter railcars (*autorails*)—confronted with highway transportation which was free of their fares, itineraries, and schedules, and was subject to the formal safety controls. The Société Nationale des Chemins de Fer (S.N.C.F.), nationalized in 1937 by combining with regional companies, operates over almost 25,400 miles in 1939; most of the narrow-gauge railroads in the *départements* are abandoned and the secondary lines gradually closed, despite the protests of the Conseils Généraux Conservateurs and the tears of those lovers of the picturesque who are still charmed by the little trains in the *départements* rambling through the countryside. The few

---

* The automobile, like the bicycle around 1900, was the object of collective enthusiasm, which continues into today: in 1930 the *boulevards* used to ring with "At last I have a car, at last I have a car. . . ."
† That would be one car for twenty people, according to the statisticians; at that same time the United States was making many more—one car for six people.

lines in the *départements* which are not yet shut down in 1939 were to experience a glorious and short-lived survival from 1940 to 1945. The scarcity of gasoline gave them a clientele which had been lost for years, and an activity comparable to that before the First World War. For example: the Haute Loire-Ardèche network at the foot of Mézenc.

The internal combustion engine also equipped heavier-than-air flying craft. Aviation, which made great advances during the War and, in the closing years, participated in the operations, becomes a means of international, and then intercontinental, transportation. In 1927, Lindbergh succeeds in crossing the Atlantic: airports are built near every large town, as are layovers for pilots, and pilot training centers. Aviation lines soar in the glorious days of Mermoz, Doret, and Saint-Exupéry—the days of airmail and connections with South America. Then regular service departing from Le Bourget assures the fastest passenger service in Europe; by 1936, they transport 70,000 passengers and cover 6,200,-000 miles. Despite higher fares, the airplane takes its place among the normal means of transportation, especially for mail service.

Finally, electricity and oil also give a new life to sea and river navigation: liners and cargo ships run by fuel oil gradually come into use; self-propelling barges become more frequent on the rare canals and rivers and, in the north and the heart of the Parisian basin, do a large business.* In the realm of transoceanic navigation, French technique, always oriented toward performance, holds a good position—even first position, once the liner *Normandie* of the Compagnie Générale Transatlantique is launched. Yet, in the long run, this is less important than the commercial fleet.†

But the Le Havre-New York trip on the *Normandie*, the "Blue Ribbon" of the North Atlantic, or the Paris-Vienna trip by regular air service, are trips reserved for a small minority of Frenchmen: automobiles, motorcycles, and bicycles—along with railroads, certainly, which have not ended their career—are, among the new means of transportation, the only ones that transform daily life, activating exchanges through the new facilities they offer, aiding a human circulation such as the nation has never known from village to village, from farm to farm, from town to country or town to town. This incessant motion is multiplied tenfold by the Popular Front's institution in 1936 of paid vacations. A new mentality, too, gradually is created: even in the mountain villages where donkey carts and mules retain their backward supporters, the heavy and sturdy bicycle, and then the more complicated mechanism of the motor-

---

* One-fourth of the almost six thousand miles of waterways is navigable by boats of more than three hundred tons. And some hundred miles or so, like the Rhine, can bear canal boats of three thousand tons.

† The capacity of this fleet measures almost three million gross tons just before the War when France ranked seventh in the world. And she does not build very much—about forty thousand tons per year.

cycle, become part of local habits. This means that "going to dances" on Sundays preceded and prepared for the mechanization of small property, the advent of the tractor, which do not occur until after the Second World War. For townspeople, the car—be it the latest model or the quickly outmoded antique B2 Citroën—and the motorcycle were also means of more frequent contacts with the nearby or distant countryside; there are weekend fishing or hunting parties and vacation outings. France becomes still smaller, better known to many of her inhabitants— France herself, that is, and not the Empire; exploration and exploitation of the latter is reserved for a small, daring, and enterprising minority, cut off from the rest of the population by the large barrier of the long trip. The progress in communications contributed little to France's familiarity with the colonies; though often wished for, it was never carried out.

Linked to this progress of long- and short-range communication are the urban changes of the nation: the forward movement of medium-sized and large urban concentrations slows down in favor of the suburbs, villages, and small towns in the vicinity of large ones, where people find the space and the quiet they lack in the heart of industrial and commercial cities. Some large towns, like Lille and Saint-Étienne, even lose people; but the suburban increase alone does not explain this phenomenon. Thus people come in from Villefranche, Grigny, and Vaugneray to work in Lyon. Large firms, like Michelin at Clermont-Ferrand and Schneider at Le Creusot, build housing projects far from the factories with bus service to transport the workers; they even encourage workers to stay in rural areas, some fifteen to twenty miles distant from their plants —country workers are less restless than urban manpower. From 1931 to 1936, Paris loses 60,000 inhabitants; meanwhile the communes in the Seine and especially in the Seine-et-Oise, increase, disgorging their population each morning and regaining it at night. This considerably helped the whole area around Paris to absorb French strength; enriched by powerful new chemical, pharmaceutical, and automotive industries, the population of greater Paris numbers 5,000,000 in 1930—one-eighth of the population of France—who are served at this time by an enormous urban and suburban transportation network. Without counting either the usual railroads and their suburban network transporting a half-million people each day or private automobiles (about a hundred thousand), Paris has about a hundred trolley lines, covering a distance of more than six hundred miles, as many buses over nearly four hundred miles, and ninety-five miles of subways.

This second transportation revolution did not merely facilitate the exchange of men and merchandise, did not merely necessitate new developments in habitational patterns. It caused speed to become habitual; not simply that people became accustomed to ever-faster traveling, even over short distances, but much more that they acquired the sporting taste for record-breaking, and a rising average rate, the imitation of chases on roads and tracks, and the pleasure of going ever faster. Bicycle and automobile races express this new passion, limited at first to the cities, then spreading slowly into the rural areas. The nineteenth-century Frenchmen, with their railroads, had their means for rapid travel; their twentieth-century grandchildren acquired a second nature—a love for speed; it has become an habitual part of their makeup. Sporting competitions play a "model" role in this realm. Now, bicycling includes a whole range of tests on roads and tracks. The Tour de France on highways is typical; on tracks there are sprints and tests of pure speed, in addition to the chase and the middle-distance race. Automobiles also race, with duly recorded records.

► THE INTELLECTUAL CLIMATE

Intellectual life during these twenty years maintains its great prestige. Yet the nation's role at the apex of scientific research diminishes, at a time when new means of diffusion offer unprecedented cultural repercussions, and especially at a time when the atmosphere of freedom in which scientists and thinkers do their creative work remains an unparalleled achievement.

This is not to say that French science declines: it holds its position, and sometimes betters it within the century's worldwide scientific progress. The great results of the surgeons grouped around Leriche, the tuberculosis researchers from the Institut Pasteur, and the radiologists of Villejuif, are known throughout the world: hospitals in Hanoi or Brazzaville, and also in many European countries, copy French methods for training skilled medical personnel—researchers, teachers, and doctors. Facilities for hygiene thus serve science and medicine (both of which are becoming increasingly specialized) and become more effective from one year to the next; diseases like typhoid and tetanus disappear almost entirely, and tuberculosis gradually diminishes.

At the apex of physics research, French laboratories, directed by Irène and Frédéric Joliot-Curie, Jean Perrin, Paul Langevin, and Louis de Broglie (the latter "constructs" wave mechanics, relativity's final conquest, just after the War) remain in the forefront. Just before the Second World War, the Joliot-Curies at the Collège de France set off the first nuclear reaction at the same time that German, Italian, English, and American scientists are amassing significant discoveries along the same paths.

And yet output of the French physical scientists is more consistent than that of the social scientists: many of the latter, always concerned with defining their objectives and their methods (as in sociology), absorbed in academic polemics (political economists), have no far-reaching influence. Philosophers break away slowly from the meshes of Bergsonism which is at its height in the 1920s, and yet, because of Surrealism, irrationality retains all its charms; just before the War, the beginnings of existentialism, imported from Germany (Heidegger), take over. In history, a textbook fever seizes the academic world; there are extensive series for the use of students (not for the general public, who are left with second-rate history of wretched quality). These series are spread far and wide—a mixed blessing*—and absorb the intellectual strength of numerous scholars, who are teachers rather than researchers. On the other hand, geography, from the impetus given by Vidal de La Blache, achieves a place alongside that of history owing to Demangeon, Jules Sion, Roger Dion, André Allix, and Emmanuel de Martonne; similarly, the psychology of Georges Dumas and Henri Wallon, and the linguistics of Dauzat and Brunot.

All the same, from an overall perspective, it is obvious that as compared with scientific life abroad or that of the preceding era there is a slowing-down: one cause is lack of manpower, here as in many other fields, because of the burdens of the war—but there are many other reasons. All the research into difficult problems, conducted simultaneously in ten or twenty nations, becomes hard for one lone scholar to follow easily. Teamwork and exchanges of documentation are processes which become necessary and are less easy in France than in other countries. In France each scholar works on his thesis in his narrowly limited field, risking the loss of the broad perspectives which are rendered more imperative than ever by frequent discoveries in related areas. Historians, withdrawn into "historizing" history or "histories of events"—or even when they are open to syntheses and collaborations with other social scientists—are good examples of this, though not the only ones. Finally, research becomes expensive, whether that done in psychology laboratories or that done with the cyclotron; the days of researchers working in garrets or cellars, patching up their apparatus with string and old newspapers to conduct all the more sensational experiments, are over. Scientists, endowed with meager research funds from the universities where they teach, lack money, books, apparatus—and often even working space. Thus universities, as research and teaching centers, are simultaneously "prisoners of the worst bureaucratic red tape" and are deprived of money.†

---

* Some are unfinished today: Glotz, *Évolution de l'humanité*; others more "scholarly," such as *Peuples et Civilisations*, Clio. The life of historical science obviously lies, not there, but in the efforts of a few more daring historians: Georges Lefebvre, Albert Mathiez, Marc Bloch, Lucien Febvre, and Henri Pirenne.
† The expression, too harsh, is from Marc Bloch, whose great book, *L'Étrange Défaite*, which we often quote, was hidden under a bushel for a long time and recently republished by Albin Michel. (English edition: *Strange Defeat*, Oxford University Press, London, 1949, translated by Gerard Hopkins.—Trans.)

In 1936, the Popular Front government, aware of this double poverty, sought to remedy the situation and established the Centre National de la Recherche Scientifique. Several years earlier, a timid attempt at encouraging science had been made through the creation of a Caisse des Sciences; its means were weak and its effectiveness mediocre. Under the direction first of Madame Joliot-Curie and then of Jean Perrin, a new institution was accordingly organized, closely linked (through its recruiting) to, yet independent of, the universities. The institution, endowed with considerable funds and devoted to both theoretical and applied research, was still being "broken in" when the war broke out.

At the same time scientific life becomes harder, intellectual life is upset by the new means of communicating thought which gradually become part of people's habits. An entire daily popularization becomes possible, as does a greater number of informed people, at least for the more accessible aspects of intellectual life—not without the dangers of "pedagogical" simplification.

Printing moves forward: the press uses such new processes as telephotography, which allows for rapid reproduction of photographic negatives. But French newspapers, given over to often unavowable economic or political influences and very much disposed to big headlines, are not an important instrument of culture. Even in the weeklies, from *Marianne* to *Gringoire*, which are always concerned about political commitments—at a time when the large newspapers like *Petit Parisien* and *Paris-Soir* assert a factitious apoliticalism—articles are often notes hastily written by a reporter who is short on knowledge and more concerned with the elegant word or turn of phrase than the precise idea. Even the newspaper considered to be the most serious, *Le Temps*, contains very little information and scarcely bears comparison with its nominal counterpart in England.

Books, obviously, are more important than newspapers or even reviews, whatever may be the relative prestige of *La Nouvelle Revue Française* or *Europe*. However, outside the prolific textbook output, which made a great deal of money for Hachette and several others, book production is devoted mainly to literature, especially novels: the taste of the worldly public (*i.e.*, the very Parisian *salons*), the lure of ever-increasing autumnal prizes, and the awakening of foreign output, widely translated and spread all over France—all these crossfires of literary life favor the pre-eminence of the novel. Gallimard and Grasset vouch for the fortune of this "literature"; faced with this the older houses like Larousse and Colin, and younger ones like Les Presses Universitaires, strive to maintain on the market an output of indisputable intellectual quality—though without much circulation. Thus the publication of the *Géographie Universelle* and the *Histoire de l'Art* by Colin, of the

Encyclopédie française and the *Dictionnaires* by Larousse. But circulation figures cannot be compared with that of Gallimard's novel output.

But more and more the transmission and expression of ideas escape
this four-century-old medium in favor of the radio and the movies, and
even in favor of the telephone, which becomes an instrument of intellectual work as valuable as the magazine since it allows rapid and precise
exchanges of points of view between two individuals—even to the point
of partially replacing correspondence: Gide notes it, as an artist, in his
Journal, "How many beautiful letters have been lost in telephone conversations!" Radios have another implication: quickly ensconced in
each home, this sound-box conquers the largest possible public, for whom
it is the very sign of scientific progress; daily, the radio sends out all sorts
of news with the greatest possible efficiency, besieging the listener from
morning to night, outside of his work, and far from all critical contact
with his habitual social setting. Possessing both a presence and a persuasive power superior to all other means of information transmission,
radio-broadcasting, paradoxically, was left in private hands in France.
Poste Parisien and Radio Paris—fed financially by advertising which
abused this medium through the imposition of sung or spoken commer-
cials—competed with the State radio station and very soon propaganda
prevailed over information. This was true despite several attempts to
promote centers of educational radio: chats about popularized science,
professional, legal, and labor information, and regular news broadcasts.
Actually, except for theatrical, musical, or sports broadcasting, in the
realm of intellectual life, the radio has been satisfied with supplying information as fast as possible, preceding the newspaper without replacing it, and giving both propaganda and advertising the most intrusive
place; the Republic was not able to profit in its own behalf—so harshly
denigrated—in the same way as, beyond the Rhine, did Nazism.

Movies, which take a large place in French life after 1918, at the same
time as does the radio, offer different but no fewer resources from the
radio; these resources are superior to printing, especially from the 1930s
on, when words are added to pictures to annotate the visual action. Here
again, however, a meager profit was drawn from the movies, excluding
the scientific successes of Jean Painlevé and several strictly educational
films completed just before the War and intended for teachers. The
intellectual role of movies was limited to two areas: the weekly newsreel,
a newspaper filmed on the heels of the event and lacking any more explanatory significance than editorials in the dailies—despite the demonstrative means offered by pictures; and the documentary, a mere adjunct
of the program, one often restricted to folklore and the most picturesque
exoticism by not too demanding producers who are particularly concerned with serving up an inexpensive appetizer.

Thus the radio and the movies, more widespread in urban than in rural areas, enlarged the intellectual horizons of the nation, but did so, to a certain extent, by popularization of shoddy material. Hence, with the aid of the press, scientific charlatanism and false science are spread as widely as the more legitimate sort, and sometimes better: astrology, quack medicine, and occultism have more adherents as scientific conquests become more sensational. Thus the high prestige of medicine causes the success of Knock; it also serves quack doctors. Undoubtedly, scientists, caught up in their many tasks, were unaware of the advantages and dangers of these new means of spreading their ideas, and remained closeted in their laboratories and studies and, in the case of professors, before their already numerous students. Rhetoric and sensationalism thus presided over this enlargement of cultivated public opinion. Undoubtedly only planning or an educational effort disproportionate to the measures taken in the period could have avoided it. These measures included free secondary education in 1932; outlines for a general educational reform shortly before the War, and an extension—from age twelve to age fourteen—of compulsory education under Jean Zay's ministry.

Finally there remains, to the credit of French intellectual life between the wars, that climate of spiritual freedom conducive to all kinds of encounters and dialogues—better than in any other country in the world. This liberalism is unquestionably the heritage of age-old traditions deriving from the fact that, for want of being able to exterminate each other, groups antagonistic in spirit have had to put up with one another for a long time—Catholics and Protestants are the prime example. In looking more deeply into the period, let us grant that the Gallican tradition of the Church of France worked in the same direction, setting Gallicans against Ultramontanists, in arduous confrontations, since the Middle Ages; the same is true concerning the open debate, throughout the nineteenth century, between the supporters of the Old Regime and the admirers of the Revolution. The nineteenth-century liberal academic tradition, as developed little by little from Louis-Philippe to the early days of the Third Republic, expressed, on the level of higher education, that climate of free intellectual confrontation which remained its rule. The blows sustained by the University—particularly the quarrel between Michelet and the Jesuits, and the revocations occurring under Napoleon III—did a great deal to help demonstrate the necessity of a liberal life for teaching and research.

But between the two wars the whole of French intellectual life thrives in this atmosphere of free research—simultaneously because the recent, early-twentieth-century scientific movement appears to the eyes of cultivated men as the final condemnation of all dogmatism; and because the separation of the Catholic Church and the State, after the hue and cry over the brusqueness of the operation, bears fruit: there is the Church's complete independence, whose advantages the most far-seeing Catholics instantly perceive; and, reciprocally, the "lay" state is freed from the confusion of responsibilities which the political personnel were not competent to handle.

Finally and most important, the gradual diminution of struggles between the two schools was a basic element in the spiritual peace: not that there was a magical disappearance of the sectarian, anticlerical, and Freemason schoolteacher, any more than of the narrow-minded *curés* and the bigots railing against the Godless schools. But the public school is chosen more and more often by the large majority of Frenchmen, at least for the first degree; thereby it is the meeting-point at which all religious professions can live together under the single roof of educational "neutrality." And if rivalries still exist, especially in the postgraduate realm, they are loyal competitions between similarly organized structures: Catholic Action movements (Jeunesse Ouvrière Chrétienne, Jeunesse Agricole Chrétienne, Jeunesse Étudiante Chrétienne) and the various "UFOs" (Unions Françaises des Oeuvres Laïques d'Éducation sportive, artistique, etc.), grouped together under the aegis of the old Ligue de l'Enseignement, which in 1926 became the Confédération Générales des Oeuvres Laïques. Clubs, sports, musical education societies, and the first movie clubs thus underwrite the immense task of popular education; the secular works are financed by government aid, and the others by small groups of Catholics. What makes these problems hard to clarify is the variety of Catholic attitudes when confronted with the secular organizations, the post- and para-educational schools or works; for the most part, and especially as memories of the prewar struggles become blurred, these institutions are accepted and often preferred to the *collèges* or *écoles libres:* hence the success of the Éclaireurs de France over the Scouts de France, for example, is explained.* Yet for the most "integrist" of the Catholics, nothing is worth the *école libre*, where religious education orients all instruction, where the child is sheltered from contact with heretics of every shade and hue that could be encountered in a "lay" school; the former subsidize and give impetus to *collèges* and young people's movements—and do so with a mentality which cannot help but perpetuate the old quarrels.

Thus the French laity, in the closing years of this period, assumes a new appearance, one particularly perceptible in secondary and higher education—if not in primary. Abandoning the anticlericalism of Scientism and going beyond the facile slogan of neutrality, the lay spirit becomes synonymous with freedom, in research and in the expression of truth; synonomous, as well, with the capacity to embrace all the different

---

* The Scouts de France are sponsored by the Catholic Church.—Trans.

spiritual families which have become freely tolerated—from dialectical materialism to the many forms of idealism. It is in this atmosphere that we are to understand the impulse of interest stirred up between 1932 and 1939 by *Esprit*, the journal of Christian Personalism founded by Emmanuel Mounier; or again, the decades of Pontigny open to everyone,* or again the collective undertaking of the *Encyclopédie française* of Anatole de Monzie and Lucien Febvre. We must also regard the special position of the Gallican Church, within the Roman Church, in terms of this climate open to all intellectual and spiritual currents. Much more pioneering than all the other national churches, the Gallican is brushed by all the currents of ideas animating Roman Catholicism—including those unequivocally condemning this "laicity." Hence this "laicity" lays itself open to all sorts of attacks. As the democratic Republic refuses to silence its enemies, who advocate authority, tradition, dictatorship, etc., the "laicity" can justify itself only by letting all those speak who would not fear to impose their Truth by force—thereby destroying "laicity." From the Union Rationaliste to the Ligue Féminine d'Action Catholique et Sociale, passing by way of the young people in political parties (generally skeletal organizations), and the young people grouped together in lay, Catholic, Protestant, and Jewish groups—all these groups, although intellectual and spiritual life is unequally important in them, reflect, by their very existence, this typically French liberalism.

▶ **STANDARDS OF LIVING**

The scientific and technical progress did not benefit the entire population equally, any more than they advanced *pari passu* in this nation of old tradition which only in 1928 saw its urban population number more than its rural. Shortly before the War, the towns had a slight preponderance of population (fifty-three per cent); the statistics include among the "towns" large, lazy market towns, the *chefs-lieux* of the *département* or the *arrondissement* which fell far short of profiting from the necessary pace of modernization. As Marc Bloch writes:

> The endearing little town with its days at too slow a pace, the slowness of its buses, its drowsy administration services, the losses of time compounded at each step by a languid abandon, the idleness of its garrison cafés, its shortsighted political maneuvering, its small wage-earning craft professions, its book-bereft library shelves, its predilection for the habitual and its distrust of any surprise capable of disturbing its soft habits. . . .

The contrast between the regions north and south of the Loire, which is so distinct today, is already being adumbrated in the material life of

---

* Pontigny is a Cistercian monastery near Auxerre where international conferences were held for writers, artists, and intellectuals.—Trans.

France during these twenty years: in the north, agriculture and industry, swept along by the strides being made in metallurgy, become in a single movement outfitted, modernized, and adapted to the newest techniques, guaranteeing a rise in the overall standard of living; in the south, including all the Massif Central, the mountains, and the southern plains, industrialization affects a few scattered centers, and agriculture, which continues to dominate regional prosperity, is reactivated at a very slow pace and not without hesitations, reversals, and marked regressions. Thus the Basses-Alpes, the Hautes-Alpes, and the Lozère lose in population, and abandon the plowed fields to sandy moors or rubble; while the Nord and the Seine-et-Marne, the Seine-Inférieure and the Moselle, maintain their population and prosperity, despite significant developments in the ownership and farming of lands. On the geographical level as on the social level, the changes emphasizing this development, begun before 1914, have great importance and complex implications. A good example of the spread of mathematics into modern life, all of this is now audited and carefully measured by the Statistique Générale de la France, which has been constantly improving its measuring instruments since it was originated in the 1890s: figures, averages, and curves are the domain of applied statisticians and economists. On this question of living standards, wages, prices, and money are the principal barometers used; they alone furnish an extremely complex documentation—and often debatable interpretations. There is an entire field of new research which is just beginning to be exploited methodically since its initiation by François Simiand.

Of these implications, only the most important features can be outlined here. The first and most important fact is the improvement in the general standard of living: this finding results from averages—with everything that can be fallacious in an average dealing with forty million people of all ages and circumstances—but is still indicative. In twenty years French towns finally become equipped with what seems to us now to be minimum comfort—water, gas, electricity; rural areas receive electricity, and, depending upon local resources, begin the more difficult task of providing running water. Construction and housing move forward more sporadically: only devastated areas and the suburbs of the large towns divide areas into lots and start to build, owing to the facilities offered by the Loucheur Law. The brutal collapse of property income since the war partially explains this construction decline: being a property owner no longer provides enough to live on, when the Parisian wage earner devotes six to seven per cent of his wages to housing; before 1914, the percentage was between sixteen and twenty. Frenchmen travel more and more, especially in recent years, when city-dwellers see their right to leisure recognized by the 1936 law concerning vacations with pay; in twenty years, the number of registered bicycles more than dou-

bles, the number of automobiles is fifteen times higher.* The clearest
and also the least debatable strides are those in food supply (least debatable because the distribution of the 1,500,000 cars might admit of
many commentaries while it is quite clear that the stomach of a Rothschild has no greater capacity than that of an agricultural laborer in
Brie) : the annual per capita consumption of sugar moves from 40 to 51
pounds, of coffee from 6.5 pounds to 10, and wine from 105 quarts to
123. In this area, the changes already have variable meanings: the
average consumption of meat increases, but actually drops in towns
where dietetic advances involve a heavy demand for fruits and vegetables at the expense of the bread and meat which were more popular
before 1914. On the other hand, people in rural areas go to the butcher
and especially to the grocer more often than they used to: hence the increased consumption of "colonial" products—of coffee, chocolate, tea,
bananas, and oranges—passing into general consumption.†

Finally, if the consumption of wool and cotton remains stationary
during these twenty years, it is hard to conclude from this fact that there
is stagnation, since here a change in taste played a large role, as much in
simpler and lighter clothing, especially in the summertime, as in furnishings where triple curtains and slip covers become castoffs—"old-fash-
ioned" things. Despite the hard years of deflation and unemployment
after 1930, the improvement of the general standard of living is obvious,
compared with the prewar era—whatever the scope of the technological
falling-off proclaimed by economists comparing France to the rest of the
world, and to the United States in particular. On the other hand, if this
standard of living is compared with Mediterranean or Eastern Europe,
the eager immigration of Spanish, Italians, and Poles can be understood;
so that the most difficult work would get done, this immigration was
large in the mining regions in the north, the Lorraine, and the region
around Saint-Étienne—actually, there is a large immigration of construction workers throughout the nation. It is this standard of living,
described in their countries in the simplest fashion—in terms of current
wages and prices of consumer goods—which attracts them to France.
Consequently this immigration is different from that of the intellectuals
who come to Paris to seek an atmosphere in which to work; a third category of immigrants, also numerous during these twenty years, and even
more diversified, are those political refugees who also are very important
in national life.

·   ·   ·

---

* Bicycles: 1913—3,500,000; 1938—8,900,000.
  Automobiles: 1913—100,000; 1938—1,500,000.
† Jean Guéhenno in his *Journal d'un homme de quarante ans* wrote a moving pas-
sage on the annual orange that used to be bought before the First World War for
Christmas and which went rotten on top of the fireplace; it was contemplated each
day by the child to whom it had been promised as a priceless reward.

This enviable standard of living could be maintained by virtue of the inflation countenanced by the devaluation of 1925 and 1936—that is, the proliferation of paper money which, replacing the metal money of the nineteenth century, permitted monetary juggling having only remote connection with the reserves in the Bank of France. It could also be maintained by virtue of the protectionism inherited from the prewar era, which French policy continued to tighten up in order to protect its peasantry as much as its poorly equipped industries: the French national market—and to a lesser degree the market of the empire—thus tends toward national self-sufficiency. But this high standard of living policy, breached and battered by the world-wide crisis, nevertheless has its beneficiaries and its victims.

In the rural areas the victims are the small landowners, the direct development of whose land barely assures their existence: peasants in the Massif Central, the southwest, and the mountains, who are so sentimentally attached to their paternal inheritance that they paralyze any attempts at re-allocation; they lack the capital to mechanize their work —which would not make much sense anyway, since the plots are so scattered and small. These peasants, having no contact with the national market, cannot adapt their output to the urban demand; they vegetate and continue to farm a little bit of everything—rye or wheat, potatoes, some fodder—and maintain an all-purpose type of livestock which hauls, gives milk and meat, and hardly brings in a thing. This is the last evidence in the Haute-Loire, the Lozère, etc., of subsistence farming—a doomed system. There are intermittent exceptions and a few achievements, such as the very small landowners in the Vaucluse and Roussillon, grouped into co-operatives, who specialize in fruit growing and truck gardening; other exceptions are the peasant-craftsmen in the fruit-growing Jura region and the few sectors of large-scale cultivation in the Limagne, the Forez, and on the plains along the Saône, where the characteristics of the north's large-scale farming can be found.

The chatelains and *hobereaux* in the tenant-farming and *métayage* regions, like the Bourbonnais, the Vendée, and the southern part of Brittany, are victims who are perhaps more aware of, although more distant from, the mediocrity of the small peasants, if not their poverty. Revenues fall off because labor, lured into the towns, becomes rare; *métayage* disappears, gradually condemned by changing markets and changing mentalities. The peasants in the central part of France, freed from a constraining paternalism, maintain a respect for the château, and often even supply it with a few days' work each year. But these peasants do not give it their ballot. This is a less heavy loss than that of the tenant farms—and one of a different order.

On the other hand, north of the Loire, peasant life is more comfortable, even for the agricultural worker on a mechanized farm in the Beauce,

Brie, or in the Pas-de-Calais, because the proximity of towns and factories to the large-scale farmer—which enables him to adapt himself so well to the consumer's market—also compels him to pay wages higher than those in the Midi in order to retain the small amount of labor he needs. In the devastated regions of the north and east, the rehabilitation subsequent to 1918 encouraged re-allocation of land and enabled the small landowner to approach the national or regional market under better conditions. If, in short, it is true that, in both north and south, grazing is gaining over tilling, and animal husbandry—especially dairy farming —over grain, it is also true that the peasant in Normandy, even though he owns only a few acres, is assured a good revenue just "watching the grass come up." The greatest agricultural achievements, however, are located in the Parisian regions and in the north, where large-scale farming—rich with capital and machines, using the most complete crop rotations, knowing the chemistry of soils, adapting itself from one year to the next to the needs of the market—profits from the technical and commercial advance all the more, since it is in competition with the "backward" (at least technically backward) producers of the Midi and the central part of France.

The upper bourgeoisie (those peopling the upper administrative echelons through the intermediary of the École des Sciences Politiques and the École Polytechnique, and the boards of directors of the joint stock companies) and the middle bourgeoisie (*rentiers*, industrialists, and big businessmen) though continuing all the while to live on a grand scale, feel themselves growing frustrated, especially after 1936, and anxious; they become an embittered ruling class. Thus, they preserve a level of security and ease well above that of the common peasant or the working classes and quite comparable to that of the old, declining nobility. Yet the bourgeoisie senses the relative dwindling of their scale of living; this goes so far that they grow indignant, seeing laborers who have the leisure to go to movies.

Yet they continue to lead the life of a dominant class: their dress distinguishes them from the ordinary less than before, but it still bears the mark of first-rate craftsmanship; they are unquestionably reduced to a less numerous servant staff, but the overly dependent household crafts are less and less sought after and, on the other hand, the improvements in domestic arts allow this lack of manpower to be offset without too much effort; they are still rich in etiquette, *salons*, at-homes, and maintain themselves at Deauville, and at the Côte d'Azur in the winter. They inherit the fine residential districts of the large towns, the sixteenth *arrondissement* in Paris and Les Brotteaux in Lyon, and always do so with all the mere necessities for comfort—bathrooms, elevators, telephones —which at that time indicate a well-established fortune.

But, as a matter of fact, never has this fortune seemed so unstable: after more than a century of monetary stability (1801-1926), and an economic revolution—steam—which resulted in its favor, the time has come when the wealth of the bourgeoisie, shaken by the war as well, is partially exhausted and battered by the second Industrial Revolution. The industrial and commercial expansion of the United States, greatly accelerated from 1914 to 1918, and that of other new nations, is to the disadvantage of European capitalism; thus, annuities dissolve, without the annuitants realizing exactly why this quiet resource of coupons, the only income for many families even in 1914, evaporates so rapidly beginning prior to the crisis of the 1930s. Living off these annuities become increasingly difficult, and the sinecure regime of some officials excites envy among those very people who poked fun at it twenty years earlier.

The industrial bourgeoisie also experiences some disappointments, less serious, perhaps, but more irritating since they are exacerbated in the class struggle. The industrialists are imprisoned in mediocrity (except for a few large enterprises like Citroën, Renault, Peugeot, and Rhône-Poulenc) by a lack of capital (which is constantly attracted abroad and to government stocks despite the experience with Russia), backwardness of equipment, and the fallacious system of protectionism which avoids German, Anglo-Saxon, and Japanese competition but also shuts out foreign markets; working for a limited national market and a narrow colonial one, the industrialists flounder in piddling calculations, grumbling under a fiscal system whose bases established by Napoleon have never been systematically revised, and struggling against their manual and white-collar workers who have united to defend their wages. Thus each crisis brings about new difficulties, although certainly profits dwindle less than they claim (in order to soften the tax assessor), and never dwindle sufficiently to cause the technical and commercial renovations that would be necessary. The weak development of technical education, which in large part is in private hands and is neglected by small employers, who inherit their enterprise and educate their personnel on the job as did the journeymen of past times, is a partial explanation for this stagnation.

The liberal professions, for other reasons, are no more sheltered from a relative leveling-off of living conditions: civil servants joylessly see the hierarchical fan of salaries begin to close, benefiting the middle and lower categories; lawyers and doctors end up by having to work much more in order to maintain their positions. These latter are forced to bear the brunt, to the point of neglecting that culture which is the pride of a dominant class, to the point of feeling themselves chained like poor people to their tasks; they bitterly resent the harshness of the times.

Among the French between-the-war bourgeoisie, who are worried and all the more bent on enjoying their class privileges as they gradually

slip away, optimism is rare as is satisfaction with the way things are going: those who are contented include the heads of banks, large concerns,
and particularly the food business; the settlers in North Africa, the large-
scale vinegrowers in the administrative area around the *département* of
Oran, owners of olive plantations in Tunis and large estates in Morocco
who come each summer and spend their incomes and coddle their livers
at spas in France; doubtless too the newly filled strata of people who, by
the slow osmosis of scholarships,[1] workmen's promotions, and exceptional personal achievements, assure a very slow renewal of the bourgeoisie—but, all things considered, these are a small proportion of the
whole. This explains somewhat the panic of 1936 at the advent of
the Popular Front: industrialists and businessmen lead the panic. Even
the most liberal businessmen did not escape this impulse of fear for their
few pennies: the Protestant Alsatian textile industrialists, who perhaps
are paternalistic but benevolent, long concerned about working-class
achievements overnight became relentless opponents of their personnel.
Yet June of 1936 would never have led to this brutal rupture of French
society into two blocks had the worried, dominant class not been feeling frustrated for many long years; little does it matter that it could
quickly have reassured itself, faced with the timidity of those who
wanted "to let liberal capitalism have its last chance." It is the fright itself that is significant.

The lower urban classes present a no less complex picture: to all intents and purposes, a part of them remains outside the era's technical
transformations and watches the drop of its standard of living, both
relative and absolute. Craftsmen riveted to their workshops continuing
old professions, especially maintenance ones (shoemakers, blacksmiths,
and cartwrights),* or again, little residential district shopkeepers who
live thanks to an enfeebled annuity, and the poorly paid managers of the
large distribution companies like Potin and Casino are both threatened
by the rise of the "five-and-tens" [*Prisunic*]. An entire world vegetates,
becoming proletarian without daring to acknowledge it; they form the
bulk of the discontented tribe who await the aid and help of public
authorities or of a party of "social renovation" during the crisis years.

But this world is less noisy and less conspicuous than the working-
class proletariat. The development of mechanized industry and the concentration of enterprises which is so clear in the industrial branches
most affected by technical progress (like the metallurgical and chemical

---

* Let us understand that this group consists of the craftsmen in rural market towns,
where the electrician, mechanic, and gas-station owner gradually replace the cart-
wright and blacksmith. Similarly, the thousands of millers along the rivers whose
millstones turn a few weeks during the year—men who are ruined by the large
industrial milling—can be included.

industries), both entail the formation of a large labor mass—one that, at least in the large towns and the important businesses, acquires a sharp class consciousness and tackles its specific problems. Strictly speaking, it would be improper to postulate a working class: in terms of both class-consciousness and standard of living, there is a very large gap between the worker in a Renault factory and the journeyman in a small, provincial workshop where the worker is often still unknown to the Inspection du Travail. But there is at least a leveling and a more lively awareness of professional solidarity on a national scale. These twenty years signify considerable improvements in the proletarian standard of living: just after the war, in 1919, the eight-hour-working-day law assures the worker the satisfaction of an old union demand and, limiting the working day, grants to factory workers a part of the benefits brought about by the technical progress which has been around for long decades. In 1936, the forty-hour week and paid vacations constitute a new advance in the same direction—although the forty hours turned out to be difficult to maintain in the period immediately after the War. As for that other amelioration workers can expect from technical progress, wage increases, these were the object of struggles spread over twenty years, from strikes to collective agreements; these struggles were dominated by the "on-the-job" movement of June, 1938, which resulted in the Matignon Agreements on collective bargaining.

However, two problems dominate the workers' condition: first, insecurity, which certainly is not recent, but which the economic revolution does not mitigate. Undoubtedly compulsory insurance—slowly but gradually complied with—covering workmen's compensation and sickness, helps to make difficult times bearable. But the major insecurity is that of employment itself: the progress of machines increases the jobs for "specialized workers," who, on the automatic lathe for example, do not require special qualifications—and depletes the ranks of qualified workers educated by years of experience indispensable for running a business. Hence labor is pliable in the hands of employers who, especially after 1939, easily lay them off at the slightest indication of a slack in business. The weight of this insecurity about tomorrow upon the workers' mentality* is rather well gauged, on the one hand, by the prestige of the public post endowed with a pension—that of the post-office employee, for example—and better still, the professions halfway between civil servant and worker, such as that of the railroad employee. This is quite perceptible in the syndicalist literature of the Confederations. On the other hand, the insecurity can be measured by the great numbers of unemployed produced by the crisis, who maintain, until the war, "a

---

* This is one of the most powerful factors in their interdependence, until the strikes of pure solidarity so badly understood by the "bourgeoisie," and their class-consciousness.

labor mass" to the employers' advantage: 400,000 unemployed on relief each year between 1932 and 1938.

The second problem is that of working conditions; the man tied to
the machine, the man implanted on an assembly line of piecemeal work
over whose totality he has no control, the man no one asks to think, becomes an automaton. The machine dehumanizes work, even when it
puts an end to the difficult jobs of unloading and cleaning among others;
there are increasingly numerous jobs void of initiative and responsibility,
if it is true that alongside them, those affecting the making or maintenance of machines always require more qualification and attention. But
in enterprises taken as a whole, the jobs that have been automated always preponderate, jobs in which the fatigue and monotony of work
pose delicate problems of industrial psychology for engineers. "Ration-
alization," copied from American Taylorism, with its timekeepers and its
production accelerations, threatens the proletariat simultaneously with
physical and mental weakness. Friedmann quotes Merrheim's cry of
1913, during the time when the first attempts at Taylorism took place
in Parisian metallurgical industries; the entire reflection of the workers'
milieux for twenty years turns upon the theme Merrheim formulated
in its extreme state:

> How could anybody think that syndicalism would ever admit the
> Taylor system [of scientific management]? . . . Doesn't anyone
> see that it is capitalism's bitterest expression of scorn for the working
> class? Instead of increasing what little initiative there is among
> workers, they say 'become a machine.' Instead of utilizing individuals
> according to their qualifications and their aptitudes, they remove
> all average producers so as to use only brutes . . . intelligence is
> chased from workshops and factories. The only things which must
> stay there are strength without brains, robots of skin and bones
> adapted to robots of iron and steel . . . Workers not only have to
> be defended against the theft of their work: they have to be pre-
> served from physical debility, they have to save their right to be
> humans endowed with intelligence.[2]

An adaptation of men to machines, to the work rate, and to apprenticeship is studied simultaneously by the unions, doctors, sociologists, and
applied psychologists: a complete science of men at work is gradually
created in the *universités populaires** as well as in the realms of technical education; it is necessary for "humanizing" that new form of work,
the industrial mechanism, as caricatured by Charlie Chaplin in "Modern Times."

Can we say it thus: one must have worked in a factory, in the racket of

---

* As with the *collèges du travail* (see p. 513), these were part of the labor unions'
efforts at educating their members.—Trans.

gantries, of lathes studding steel, and in the rhythm of breaks and shopping errands, of repairs and output, in order to realize what eight hours daily of life represents; and how eight hours standing behind a counter, or ten hours in a business office, results in a different kind of fatigue! To be sure, the 1930 worker works fewer hours than his counterpart of 1860, and fewer hours than his engineer or his employer. But the subtleties of human fatigue forbid such oversimplified comparisons. Similarly there is the comparison of the engineer on the steam locomotive and the ticket collector in the station. The working-class mentality does not ignore these differences in the intensity of work and fatigue; it distinguishes a sometimes harsh hierarchy, if not an unjust one, in each trade association.[3] If labor in 1935 and 1936 displayed, with raised fists, a certain surliness—and much hope—in their demand, it is not by chance.

▶ MASSES AND ÉLITES

The encounter of words and facts, of theories and the technical and economic revolution: the class struggle, that keystone of Marxism, was ultimately admitted as a basic reality by the bourgeoisie itself, during this very time when the French economic crisis exacerbated the social conflicts. Thus a gap is hollowed out between the two worlds of bourgeois and labor, the two classes forming the most vital part of French society; it is somewhat as if the peasant world—slow to assimilate ideologies and new techniques, slow to embrace the radio and (even more) the movies, slow to look beyond its regional borders or even those of its *arrondissement*, still faithful to so many traditions lost in the towns, encumbered by so many social and religious taboos—were outside of the great controversy.

The dominant French class for more than a century, the bourgeoisie: will they, must they, stand aside? Strong with established positions and past achievements, strong with their culture whose supreme manifestations continue to dazzle the Old World and the New—to be sure, they will have nothing of this eclipse. Even though they repudiate liberal democracy whose egalitarian mechanism turns against them in the end when the emancipation of the workers moves forward: and there is a strong current within this class which looks nostalgically at neighboring authoritarian regimes. Even though convinced of the degeneration of the lower classes, indeed of the entire nation, even to the point of doubting the destiny of the Nation—these are the fruits of the critical thought of the brilliant and dangerous school of Maurras which has been holding so high a place for the past twenty years. But on the other side of the abyss which continued to deepen from 1934 to 1940, to the rhythm of shocks which each time were harder (February 6, 1934; June, 1936;

September, 1938; June, 1940), labor militants proclaim the imminent —and necessary, according to the best Marxist orthodoxy—advent of the Fourth Estate and the classless society. These are the hope of all those who each day are a little more enslaved by the new techniques which remove them from the French cultural tradition in favor of stupefying and commercialized distractions; as Marc Bloch has so nicely put it: "In the Popular Front—the real one of the masses, not that of the politicians —there was revived something of the atmosphere of the Champ de Mars, in the bright sunshine of July 14, 1790."

The bad conscience of a good part of the bourgeoisie is all too obvious:* most of the industrial leaders, the great administrators, and the officers on active duty—*i.e.*, a large proportion of the ruling classes—are convinced that the political system they obey is completely corrupt, that the country is incapable of effort or of resisting the slightest economic or military shock, and that everyone has been degenerated and perverted by unhealthy propaganda. These final censures harped on by a whole species of journalism and literature, overlook the fact that the regime and the people are also what the ruling classes have made them.

But this bad conscience is particularly revelatory of the fact that the ruling classes have run out of steam: they have lost their faith in their mission and are transferring the responsibility for this fall to others. The material reasons are obvious, and by a twisting of things, indicating to what extent simplified Marxist theses have passed into the common awareness, the economic decline seems, to them, to entail all the rest: the "sordid materialism" of the thirties is not there where people say it is. Thus living off high interest becomes a habit, if not ideal; poor fiscal citizenship, the avoidance of taxes, is not the deed of wage earners but of those who can dissemble, transferring income abroad and juggling sums in the accounting systems of their businesses. Better still, recourse to the government, to the public budget, becomes a current form of economic flight: the nationalization of the railroad companies, which had long been running at a deficit and replenished with public funds, was not a bad deal for them; likewise, when the network of bus lines becomes organized in the *départements*, it is characteristic that we see, in mountainous regions, private firms reserving the lowland lines—well traveled and promising easy profit—for themselves, while the *départements* must run the unprofitable lines. We know that rail and trucking competition also presents this same characteristic (see above, p. 545). It is the most conspicuous form of an economic "liberalism" rather different from that advocated by nineteenth-century theorists. As

---

* Does not the fact that free secondary education was agreed upon in 1932 also reveal the same state of mind? It is the sign of a liberalism inherited from a long tradition—actually from Condorcet and the revolutionaries of the Convention, consequently a Jacobin inheritance. But there also is the awareness of the necessary renewal of the ruling classes.

early as this period, liberal French capitalism lets itself be aided by the government—discreetly; yet it rejects the intervention of public power when the latter is in the way.

This running out of steam occurs not only on the material level; the dwindling of fortunes and income reveals singular deficiencies,* which include a totally "provincial" world view, not even on a colonial scale, and rarely on a European one, so much so that clairvoyants, scientists, scholars, and technicians foreseeing the future find themselves preaching in the wilderness. How to prepare for the future of the technical revolution, how to prepare the troops of engineers and teachers, at a time when this greedy bourgeoisie pays its children's professors less than it pays its servants? And this is but one example. After the Great War, the towns acclimatize themselves to mores undeniably freer than before, a reaction after four years of suffering, a widespread belief in a better world daily made more credible via electricity, movies, and radio. But the hard-pressed dominant class ceases to set the pace, unless one considers as "pace-setting" the bourgeois anti-feminism (slowness of the development of secondary female education, refusal to grant the right to vote, and changes in the Civil Code) clearly superannuated by the economic revolution and by women's increasing place in social life since 1914; to say nothing of their making of religious practice—often reduced to an unfervent Sunday conformism—the very sign of the right-thinker's belonging to the ruling classes. These are reactions of weakness. Basically, the best indication of this running out of steam is unquestionably the "cowardly appeasement" of Munich in 1938; but the bourgeoisie is not the only party to these difficult days.

Yet French culture, borne along by rich traditions and served by a constellation of artistic genius, reserved as it increasingly is for a public both cosmopolitan and narrow, again shines with an unsurpassed brilliance: even when the oil diminishes, the flame rises and shines stronger —just before the years of darkness. But—and this is a sign of the times— it shines more exclusively than ever in Paris: the provincial conservatories of music are losing strength, but Paris has never been so rich in composers who, continuing the pursuits of the preceding period and using the new resources offered them by the movies, produce an abundance of musical works which pass very quickly into the repertory of the grand concerts.† There is the same successful concentration in the realm of *haute couture*: the great French houses, like Chanel, dazzle a whole

---

* Literary evidence, to be taken with a grain of salt: Zola at the close of the nineteenth century "revealed" the moral and material misery of the poor; between 1919 and 1939, Mauriac "reveals" that of the bourgeoisie.
† It is not a question of drawing up a list, even of the choicest: in addition to the landmarks, like *Pacific 231* by Honegger in 1923 and the *Boléro* by Ravel in 1928, how many works by Milhaud, Auric, and Poulenc would have to be mentioned, beginning with those inspired by texts from Claudel, Valéry, Éluard, and Cocteau. Not to mention the success of jazz.

international public which, until the War, will continue to purchase on the Rue de la Paix, the Place Vendôme, and their environs, the graceful and tasteful results that become all the more matchless as *couture* completes the "chic" of its creations by the annexation of accessories. On industrial and commercial bases which, to be sure, are fragile, a real art of feminine elegance is perfected during these twenty years by Parisian *haute couture*. The same is again true of the School of Paris, with its diverse aspects, graced moreover with surrealistic fantasies; it invades galleries and exhibitions with its output simultaneously shocking and charming to critics and *amateurs*: the School is still dominated by the abundant and various works of Picasso, Matisse, and Braque.

But the most astonishing artistic development is the rebirth of legitimate theater which, in the nineteenth century, had sunk into the quicksand of the French Romantic declamatory style. Prepared for by the prewar work of Copeau and Dullin, this rebirth brings together several great names: the initiators, who remained masters until their death—Gaston Baty, Georges Pitoëff, and especially Louis Jouvet. The last, aided by his meeting with Jean Giraudoux and Jules Romains, and by the extraordinary decorative genius of Christian Bérard, inspired a moment in French art, rediscovering the real sense of theater in a respect for the text. From 1923 to 1934 at the Comédie des Champs-Élysées, from 1934 to 1939 at the Athénée-Louis Jouvet, and in his provincial tours, this actor-director dominates French theatrical life when, with *L'École des femmes* in 1936, he creates a new style of interpreting the classics.* With his friends Baty, Copeau, and Dullin, he then takes charge of the Comédie Française, under the direction of Édouard Bourdet; for three years it is imbued with the art of these craftsmen of the stage who secure for it a revival which it still is experiencing.† At the very moment when provincial music halls, ruined by the movies, are closing one by one, or else live only from intermittent tours, the Parisian stage again finds its greatness, and has a more numerous and informed public than in the fine days of Sarah Bernhardt and Mounet-Sully.

·   ·   ·

---

* The opening of *L'École des femmes* on May 9, 1936 was a French landmark—much more than the usual Parisian type. We have but to recall the ecstasies of the best critics—Seize in *Comœdia:* "Exquisite sets by Christian Bérard. No one has gone further in the art of suggesting a style without copying it . . . Where are we? There is nothing to recall a period exactly and yet the most untutored spectator could not have been mistaken: it is seventeenth-century France, it is Paris, it is the Place Royale, the Marias, the lighting of the old theater, the eternal décor of the *commedia dell'arte*. . . ." Louis Jouvet had been working at the sets for ten years.
† Jouvet's career, until his death in 1951, is unswerving: from *La Guerre de Troie* and *Électre*, to *La Folle de Chaillot*, *Don Juan* and *Tartuffe*, he is the model for a generation returning to the theater. Barrault, Bertheau, Vilar, and the dramatic centers are his successors.

The working class does not participate in this surge of French civilization in its most refined triumphs, or else it receives only vague reflections, faintly heard echoes—like the curious rubberneckers who, gathered around the entrance to the Bal des Petits Lits Blancs or at an opera premiere, see in the light of flashbulbs the last word in fashion; they know Jouvet, to be sure, not through his theater, but through movies—*Knock* again, *Entrée des Artistes*, *Hôtel du Nord*. For these people Picasso remains synonomous with madcap drawings, at a time when the most common advertising poster reflects the influence of Cubism—but again, it is too dim a reflection.

There are several rather clear explanations for this separation: one is that the workers' education, which is concerned more with political and social instruction than with cultural, affects only several hundred militants each year; the great movement of prewar *universités populaires* is listless, due to a lack of both teachers and students. Going to the people is no longer a form of civic-mindedness, and the people are attracted elsewhere: radio and spectator sports to say nothing of movies. Thus the best militant workers, those who lead the masses through their intellectual and verbal clarity and their character—a Monmousseau, for example— are educated primarily by their personal efforts at self-education, far from schools. These exceptions are better examples of the increasing diffusion of the cultural tradition than are the overly brilliant products of the École Normale, who are mostly hothouse flowers: but still they are exceptions.

By means of the gradual improvements in phonograph records, the radio broadcasts for the masses, transmitted on all frequencies all day long, the light, facile music with its fashionable old refrains: we know of course that at all times the Town, if not the Court, has hummed and jibed, at Mazarin as well as at Marie Antoinette. But with the radio, with all the force generated by millions of receivers, the little political ditty has been replaced by the sentimental ballad, whining or merry, but always a "love song"—next to which the old prewar successes seem to be masterpieces of taste and restraint.* To be sure, the radio also spread the taste for less facile music: the *opéra-comique*, operetta, and opera, rebroadcast each week, are also eagerly listened to—much more certainly than concerts of "classical music." But this has nothing in common with the triumphs of *Marinella*, *Valentine*, or *Fleur bleue*.

Both urban and rural families thus have, in their homes, daily vocal concerts; nevertheless, the urban masses still go out to assemble: but it is no longer at church, since the rupture between the Catholic Church and the working masses is total, the result of a long development begun in the nineteenth century and completed in this period between the wars; re-

---

* Maurice Chevalier, Charles Trenet, and Tino Rossi, its leaders, are national stars. Thirty years later, their Parisian counterparts are merely *boulevard* stars.

ligious life in the workers' world is weaker than today, when dechris-
tianization is not simply deplored but effectively combated. Spectator
sports have taken the place of the church, and are commercialized by
sporting associations seeking profits and the financing of their educational activities by Sunday exhibitions—for want of substantial government aid: this is the story for boxing, soccer, tennis, rugby, and cycling.
National championships with numerous play-offs, individual and group
competitions, sport demonstrations inflated by the press,* radio, and
movies, all attract enormous crowds, for whom the "stadium gods" are
truly national heroes: bicycle champions and the winner of soccer's
Coupe de France are foremost among them. The specialized sporting
press has the largest circulation of any daily or weekly: *L'Auto, Le Mirror
des Sports*. Spectators, however, preponderate over players, due to a lack
of equipment and training opportunities—despite the advances of
sports in the schools.

Beyond any doubt, the Republic has not felt much democratic concern for giving these urban masses the culture to which they have a right,
nor has it thought of reviving "the old paeans," in which a public can
live in mutual understanding: national holidays and unspectacular com-
memorations are limited most of the time to a beautifully rigged-out
military parade in Paris; they are even less elaborate in small towns without any garrisoned troops, where firemen and policemen supply the
bulk of the parade. And if July 14, again especially in Paris, is more than
that, if the dances on the public squares form an unparalleled tradition,
they are expressions nonetheless of a very old custom of games, and have
very little real link with the event in question.† In a word, delivered up
to these meager resources, the urban masses cannot look further, so
greatly are they overwhelmed by their working conditions.

Besides, their energies are directed primarily toward improving their
lot: the trained working-class personnel are the militants of the unions
and of the parties appealing to the workers. Revolutionary hope, so potent at the end of the last century, is still alive but diminished by the un-
forgettable experience of parliamentary deceptions, troubled by the
War (from the assassination of Jaurès to the crises of 1917), and unsettled by the Russian Revolution. Just after Versailles, the Socialist Party
and the C.G.T. went through a difficult period because the unexpected
success of Lenin led to a crisis of socialist consciousness; thus the dictatorship of the proletariat and Marxist teaching, which never enjoyed

---

* The President of the Republic attends the final match of the Coupe de France
at the Colombes Stadium which, despite its 60,000 seats, is too small on that day.
† From 1936 to 1939, however, an attempt was made by the governments of the
Popular Front to "organize leisure": initiations into theaters and movies, youth
hostels, cultural centers—this program, to which the name Léo Lagrange remained
attached, did not have the time necessary for any great results. Rather it underwent
underhanded disparagements, jeers, and boycotts from the bourgeoisie.

a very high reputation in working-class estimation, assumed an exemplary value. After the sad debates in the famous Congress of Tours in 1920, the socialist majority set up the Communist Party, belonging to the Third International (created by Lenin in the preceding year), while the minority set up a C.G.T.U. (Confédération Générale du Travail Unitaire)—allied to the Communist Party on the professional level.

This division among the working-class forces remains to our day; an attempt at union consolidation in 1936 on the basis of the Charter of Amiens did not last, ruined by Munich as early as 1938. The two political parties and the two nationwide unions—with their press, their militants' schools, and their youth—continue to fight over a group of adherents made sullen by the division itself. This very competition, without forgetting the great problems of the conquest of power and the socialization of a capitalistic nation, weighed heavily on the life of French socialism. Interminable doctrinal disputes, personal quarrels among staff brothers and enemies, and increases of posts for responsible people (even to a certain routine in the bureaucratized administrative machine)— all these realities explain the weakness of the labor movement during these twenty years. This weakness is particularly apparent on the union level: rivalries on a business-size scale separate workers from tradeunionism, and only a small minority subscribes. These rivalries also enable the Christian unions to make considerable strides. The C.F.T.C.—Confédération Française des Travailleurs Chrétiens—has been the great beneficiary of union pluralism.

It took the Fascist attempt on February 6, 1934—that surprise attack by discontented shopowners and non-commissioned officers which seriously threatened Republican institutions—to bring these two Leftist parties and the Radical Party together. From February 12, 1934, the "antifascist" general strike, to the Popular Front agreements of 1935 and 1936, the labor movement regains momentary vigor in unified action and hope —the reunified C.G.T. quintuples within several months. But until the success of May-June, 1936, in those elections when the new Chamber numbers a hundred fifty socialists and seventy Communists, mental reservations, constricting and stumbling calculations, continue to exist. The Popular Front turns sharply as early as 1937, less from enemy attacks than from division among its participants. Munich and the startled national conscience in autumn of 1938 does the rest. The Fourth Estate, as the contemporaries of Rémusat and Tocqueville used to say, is not ready to take up the standard from the bourgeoisie.

The immediate prewar years, from 1936 to 1939, are critical ones: between a dominant class whose concern over its own destiny impels it to condemn the entire nation, and labor refusing the revolution for which it had long been preparing, there is an abyss of incomprehension, fear, and sometimes hate. The most lucid Frenchmen are alarmed at it, all the more since the early months of the war, in the confusion of an improvised troop mobilization, did not silence the intense emotions—any more than did Munich in the preceding year. There is an ominous malaise reflecting two classes in the same nation which are gradually becoming convinced they are strangers; although this is not without some degree of exaggeration, since the cultural climate of this country whose civilization is so ancient does admit of exchanges, even barely perceptible ones, between groups. These include language and style of the press, of information in general, of posters; the more or less assimilated knowledge of stone treasures and evidence from centuries past; personal exchanges increased by the interaction of men, professional life, widespread leisure, and the slow rise of the proletarian élite (not without the risk of its becoming bourgeois); and finally by the interaction of those large groups on the border between the two classes: the petty functionaries, the retailers, and the lower skilled industrial personnel.

But above all there is one common denominator which revives the cultural sensibility of the urban population and decisively marks French urban life: the movies. In the large towns, and especially in Paris, the publics vary according to the movie theaters and residential districts; yet it is not possible to distinguish, as it is for music, between the public attending music halls and that attending the large concerts; movies attract every social class—the most refined and the most untutored. The some two thousand commercial-movie houses which contain about two million seats among them, in large and small towns alike, have in these twenty years become the most frequented places of entertainment. This new art, by its commercial flexibility as well as by its strictly artistic results, has become over several years the most valued form of entertainment. Just as in many other countries, urban civilization becomes a civilization of the moving picture.*

The French movies of the period have a long and complex history. Shortly before the War, Pathé had exercised a kind of worldwide monopoly over the production and distribution of films. After 1918, the strides of American movies, and then of other national film industries, terminated the French monopoly. On the contrary, the postwar market has been invaded by Hollywood productions. Gradually, until 1929 and the end of the silent films, there are formed simultaneously a distribution network (*i.e.*, theaters whose owners rent films, arrange their programs, and do their own local advertising), and, on the production set, a whole

---

* Let us be explicit about the word "urban." In rural areas, despite both the existence of itinerant enterprises and the attempts made by the various cultural societies, the success is less great, doubtless because the pace of the movies is too rapid for the peasant and also because the programs consist of worn-out and rejected films.

chemical industry producing and processing film, and the movie industry itself in studios around Paris and along the Côte d'Azur—although these in no way are comparable to those in California. These are extensive enterprises requiring enormous capital, so much so that movie production, itself artistic, is bound up with industrial conditions that have taken a heavy toll of quality: the producer, the man who supplies the capital, claims his right to recover his investment, and recommends tried and true formulas, filming plays, light comedies, musicals, and so on. The choice of programs by the theater owners, anxious to fill up their continuous showings (lasting fourteen to twenty-four hours), has a not negligible importance; this choice tends in the same direction: ease, good-natured vulgarity, and melodrama.

The importance of movies derives from the qualities proper to this new art. Silent or spoken, they command the attention of the viewer, who is isolated in a dark theater with the power of a sympathetic magic —which psychologists have yet to finish analyzing—which causes both the magical charm of the entertainment and its often advanced dangers: a real entrancement of children and the unsophisticated. At the very least, movies obtain an affective participation not demanded by the theater, where the plot is obvious to the viewer, and the esthetic emotion is distributed throughout the entire room and in an audience communality the movies do not incite. The seventh art is the one obtaining, more than any other, the most complete identification of spectator and entertainment. This is true even though the actor does not have to embody his character, as in the theater, and, in the hands of the director, can allow himself a good deal of perspective: what Louis Jouvet calls "a double entry art." Without paradox, it is possible to assert that the magic of the projected image itself creates this affective participation which only the greatest actors obtain in the theater by their "presence."

Despite surrealistic fantasies and the mediocrity of the output in the final years of the silent films, the glory of the French movies in these twenty years is not due to the stars—those faces on posters luring the good public on Saturday nights and whose enormous fees ruin the cinematic output—but to the great directors who, brought up in the days of silent films, produced the world's most astonishing cinematic harvest in the years between 1935 and 1939: Jacques Feyder, Jean Renoir, Marcel Carné, Jean Duvivier, René Clair, Marc Allégret, *et al.* Movies then attain maturity when this very young art finishes perfecting its visual and verbal language, when each director asserts his own style as actors and performers on the legitimate stage do theirs; when publics are differentiated: the great movie-club experts, enlightened amateurs who choose according to critics or credit titles—and on the other hand a fat public returning every Saturday to the same seat, no matter what the program might be. The high repute of movies is measured by these millions of spectators and by the popularity of the greatest stars: Raimu, Jean Gabin, Michèle Morgan.

American cowboy films, films by Chaplin or Disney, French films realistic even to a marked predilection for "tough guys" but always revealing well-drawn characteristics of society—all these entertainments inform and nurture the sensibility and the intelligence with an as yet unequaled effectiveness. In 1939, movie "consumption" is well on the way to becoming the major element of national culture.

XVIII

❀

French Civilization and World Civilization

❀ ❀

BETWEEN 1939 and 1956, the development is accelerated under our eyes: the pace of the history of civilizations is not that of political history, with its sudden fluctuations, maddening in their rapidity. There is no doubt, however, that cultures and educations, scientific life and artistic life, also experienced acceleration around the mid-twentieth century. In these heavily burdened years, from the abyss of 1940 to the resurrection of 1944 and the reconstruction of 1955, when French life is burdened with revolutionary factors—atomic energy, television, automation, social security, antibiotics—is not the greatest innovation the enormous progress in the full collective awareness of all these facts and its grasp of the new world being built? Long prepared for by the educational tools which caused the definitive drop of illiteracy, and by the progress of informative means like the press, radio, and movies, this full awareness makes of public opinion a sovereign power, and gives liberal democracy a hitherto unknown grandeur; it indicates the participation of the whole country in national and international life—most clearly so during the black years when the burden of disaster weighs on every conscience—whatever its reaction, and less clearly during the ten years of reconstruction, when many of the facilities, many of the intellectual and material comforts of prewar times, seem to have been regained.

Beyond any doubt, in this progress of the collective consciousness, the major event—whatever be the discussions or the reflections that the atomic bomb may call forth today, even in the humblest milieux—was the "strange defeat"of June, 1940. Coming unexpectedly after the long months of the "phoney war," when the rotting process of the waiting period carried on its work among the combatants as well as in the fields and factories, this even was brutally demonstrated by the anemia of the trained personnel (the army's general staff as well as union leaders), the enormous sclerosis concealed under the brilliant exterior of the intellectual tradition. For this "defeat of intelligence and character" not to be final,* it had to be a revelation, behind which many other reflections are to be aligned for years: the quietest little village, the most tranquil market town, had to experience realities long ignored, or left in a dark haze—the solidarity of France and the world, from Pearl Harbor to Stalingrad; the solidarity of France and her colonies. The Second World War, through its extensions beyond the battle of France until the final victory in 1945, until Berlin and Hiroshima, until the government in Algiers and the Brazzaville Conference, dominates this awakening of consciousness in a nation deeply transformed once again by the period after a conflict; nationalizations as well as the long open debate, still going on, with the colonies are proof of it. And the third Industrial Revolution, organizing and developing concurrently, seems, from that time onwards, not so much endured as understood and aided: a powerful contrast with the French society of yesteryear, so true is it that a desired economic change is not produced in the same way as stirred up by the mere interplay of forces spontaneously entering into competition.

However it is quite clear that this wider awareness about an increasingly smaller planet still remains irregularly accomplished, whatever progress is effected in fifteen years or so: urban and rural civilizations remain distinct—if not opposed, so much do towns seem to win out over, fight, and invade rural areas; the backward forms of rural life are now withdrawn into the high mountain ranges, taking refuge from the present as, centuries ago, they did from the invasions. But furthermore, despite Marseille, Lyon, Montpellier, Bordeaux, and Pau, Paris maintains its undeniable pre-eminence. Postwar Paris, which awakened from the sluggish sleep of the Occupation, remains a pole of attraction, and unquestionably it is the only French city living on an international scale—Paris,

---

* Must we remind the reader (but the history of the Second World War is not included in the secondary-education curriculum, and even its summary knowledge is already cruelly lacking among today's youth) that General de Gaulle announced a call to arms on June 18, 1940—the very day after the capitulation.

refuge of the cosmopolitan, seat of UNESCO, guide of the national consciousness; and, by contrast, the provinces still scarcely recovered from fratricidal struggles, again tempted by the deadly prewar calm. At a pace different from that of daily life, where propaganda, education, distractions, and leisure do not have the same meaning, the same tonality, where cultural continuities and discontinuities multiply in thousands of various ways, let us grant that—despite so many unifying institutions, administrative trained personnel, local and national practices of democracy, and national education—there are not one but many civilizations of unequal refinement and scope. Hence that impression of new richness for the traveler coming from the young nations, a richness all the nations of old Europe owe to their thousand years of long life—while France adds to this the scope of her universalized triumphs.

► **FRENCH VISION OF THE WORLD:
AN ENLARGEMENT**

For six years, France lived through the deadliest war known to history; the first great victim in 1940, and the first to rise up into the horrors of underground warfare, she came out of this test ravaged, but greater. Out of her long divisions she emerged united more solidly than she had been for a long time, and ready for the sacrifices of reconstruction.

In the Second World War, the meaning of combat made itself felt—whatever the choice made—upon everyone, at least from 1940 on (if it is true that, for some, doubt existed in 1939); and that those who did not want "to die for Danzig" were capable of seeking immediate peace. Actually, if public opinion was capable of hesitation in 1939, it was due simultaneously to both the pacifist propaganda in union circles and the Stalin-Hitler Pact. The fact remains that the most frequent reaction was that of good sense overtaxed by the preceding attacks and by the humiliation of Munich: "He (Hitler) will never have enough of it, each summer is a new attack. . . ." Enough. Once the phoney war ended in invasion, every Frenchman was caught up in the conflict. While the First World War had made the most of the quiet tranquillity of a rear area where business and the trade cafés pursued their glorious careers, after 1940 every Frenchman had to know the ends and the means of this conflict with an adversary whose continental victories multiplied unceasingly until 1942. There are a million and a half prisoners locked up in Germany, brooding over their powerlessness in morose ill-temper; the nation is cut in two by a line of demarcation difficult to cross; there is famine in urban areas; soon a million workers and youths are deported to furnish the industrial labor for an enormous war machine, not to mention for punitive reasons—the real deportation of those resisting the Occupational government and of Jews: the struggle is present in the life of every hour. The smallest hamlet in the unoccupied zone has its prisoner, or prisoners; later, its *maquis*, sometimes springing from a work camp for youth, sometimes created alongside the fostering village by exploiting the geographic advantages of mountainous southern France. All the greater reason why Alsace, Lorraine, and the Nord felt the even heavier weight of the Occupation and took the large part they did in the common resistance to foreign oppression.

But the war from 1940 to 1945 was not merely a national war of extraordinary immediacy: everything would have been simple had the French, undergoing every day an abhorred tyranny in their flesh and spirits, had only to unite to fight against the foreigner. Undoubtedly the Resistance was also this union, gathering together men of all political persuasions, of all social milieux. But the struggle took on another significance, for there was present at Vichy an old soldier covered with glory concealing the policy baptized National Revolution: a policy that included Maurrasian theorists of France first, "realistic"* politicians, believers in German victory, shock troops of Déat and Doriot, militiamen and Légion des Volontaires Français on the eastern front, as many promoters of an experiment copied from the Nazi revolution and long supported by people's confidence in the Maréchal of the Légion veterans. Yet on this side of these glorified manifestations, this abuse of confidence, the collaborationist regime was backed by a considerable part of the bourgeoisie: merchants benefiting from the illicit trade instituted by the Occupational forces, and from the black market; industrialists favored by the social peace of the Charte du Travail and by the professional regrouping established on the model of Fascist and Nazi corporate systems —great masters of the new economy, participating in the German war effort, like Renault and the contractors of the Atlantic Wall. Because of all this, that surge of a whole people which became the Resistance, roused by appeals from London, also has a social coloration: collaborationists and resisters are too neatly recruited from two opposed classes, at least until the end of 1943.

Thus the war was at first a struggle in everyone's conscience: the *de facto* government, provided with a formal legality acquired without debate in July of 1940, pushed all those who were unable to accept either a wait-and-see policy or collaboration, toward an illegality dictated by a higher law. Obedience to the law, the value of order and discipline, military or civil—these are among the many questions called into doubt during those ominous years when, from Vichy, Paris, and London, with the help of the radio and also the press, clandestine or not, duty was constantly invoked and was supported by policies which contended for their claim on the national conscience. This debate became more settled as time slipped by even to the point of disappearing without an object, after the

---

* Politicians form the right actually, rediscovering an old tradition—from 1815 to 1870—that had been confused since the Dreyfus Affair.

landing of June 6, 1944. But for four years of irregular fighting, the war thus carried out a selective destruction—less global loss than in 1914-1918, but those who disappeared were the best, carried by their valor to the front ranks of this national combat: *maquisards*, resisters deported in the violent haste of the summer of 1944, and victims of the final moments of the Liberation. This national and revolutionary shock has numerous martyrs, for whom many monuments have been constructed —monuments to the dead that differ from those of the preceding war. But excluding these funeral services and several episodic assemblies, the Fourth Republic has been no more generous toward its founders than was the Third which was born of less tragic combats. The new regime did not even concern itself with suitable commemoration of the famous parade in liberated Paris on August 26, 1944, proceeding from the Étoile to Notre-Dame—the greatest popular French demonstration in a hundred fifty years.

However, the War taught even the most cautious of those who held to a wait-and-see policy the solidarity of the entire world—much better than had the preceding war, which, in effect, was more European than global. How many walls, even in the lowliest dwellings, were covered with large, multicolored maps on which everyone painfully followed the hopes and fears: Kraków, Kiev, Rostov, Tobruk, El Alamein, Pearl Harbor, Singapore, Bir Hacheim, Warsaw, Rome, and that breathtaking liberation of France through the northwest and southeast!

Either from battle orders or from being hard-pressed by immediate forces in an unceasingly protracted conflict, what geography lessons, long shamelessly ignored—including that of the French overseas world where Free France rallied at Brazzaville and in the Chad around Eboué and General de Gaulle. Thus Africa, Europe, and the Pacific entered into the mental universe of the French through communiqués and the monitoring services of jammed radios; an intense emotional geography, but an important one.

Finally, these four years that lead France from the abyss to heights served to elevate the United Nations in the opinion of the entire nation: they helped England, constantly abused by Vichy propaganda, less than the Americans (of whose hostility to the government of Free France most Frenchmen were unaware), the 1944 liberators and the principal actors in the western front until the German surrender; but especially the long combat helped Russia, momentarily discredited in 1939 at the time of her alliance with Hitler—and, consequently, the Communist Party, which played a leading role in the Resistance. Even in 1939, the far Left, militated against by the tightrope policy* and by interior

---

* Over which the followers of Thorez did not have a monopoly. At the other extreme of the spectrum of political opinions, people were able to pass from Germanophobia to collaboration, to praise the "firm" policy lasting from 1920 to 1926, and treat opponents of Munich as warmongers.

Soviet developments—particularly the famous Moscow purges in 1937-1938—had a large following only in the days of the Popular Front. After the Liberation, the Communist Party acquired the electoral sympathy of a quarter of the adult population; a proportion that has held its ground for ten years, despite propaganda and parliamentary ostracism. The secure introduction of communism has been as much commented upon and discussed since all the political parties, including the socialists who, since 1948, have broken all ties with "the Party"—except those of parliamentary fellowship. This introduction derives simultaneously from the weakness of the anti-communist propaganda—simplistic, maladroit, and often in bad faith—and from the heritage of respect for authority and confidence in the indisputable promise, bequeathed to present-day France by fifteen centuries of Catholicism.

Thus, 1944 was a national victory, a victory for the Republic; yet it is a new Republic: despite significant innovations like women's suffrage, political works are less important than economic or social ones. Applying the revolutionary program of the Resistance, the first French government after the Liberation profoundly changes the French economy in a few months. They nationalize the major banks—Crédit Lyonnais, Crédit Foncier, B.N.C.I. [Banque Nationale pour le Commerce et l'Industrie], Société Générale—so completing the reform of the Bank of France initiated in 1937, and placing the basis of credit in the hands of the government. They also nationalize the sources of energy whose equipment, ravaged by the Occupational forces, is decrepit; this was a less immediately beneficial operation, since the coal mines, transmitting stations for electricity, and coking plants were in a piteous state. But government control of the production of energy enabled re-equipment plans to be carried out on a national scale once the reconstruction period passed: modernization of the coal mines, hydroelectric dams, and now atomic-powered generating stations. Finally, as retribution for a particularly cynical collaboration: the Renault automobile factories were put into the hands of the government, and the primary French producer of automobiles, kept going in competition with private concerns, preserved his position in the massive strides of this industry which today has become the foremost in the country.* Since the personnel of private companies, particularly in the banks, have been closely bound by family and professional ties to the ruling milieux in the government's administrations and have thus been able to maintain a modicum of control, there is perhaps something more important than the energy and credit "put at the nation's disposal": Social Security. This has been a gigantic work in preserving labor from the fear of tomorrow. Regrouping in one

---

* After a few difficult years of reconstruction and dearth of raw materials, the automobile industry has doubled its prewar output and gained foreign markets throughout the world: 1939—200,000 cars; 1954—500,000.

single body all the protections insured by the Caisse d'Assurance instituted twenty or thirty years earlier—sickness, accident, pension—Social Security, fed by employers' payments in the name of their employees, has been able simultaneously to encourage the use of medicine by the unfortunate, contribute to the sanitary renovation of the nation (made all the more urgent by the constant scientific progress), and even to collaborate with the Assistance Publique in medical research. Ten years after the difficult setting up of this enormous organization, the raised level of sanitation attests to the success of this manifestation of the old spirit of mutualism.

The Second World War has consequently brought about a sudden advance in the direction of socialism, creating institutions and businesses that place the French economy under the control of the government, all the while respecting quite a large sector left in the hands of private enterprise. Actually, though, the field left to free enterprise is still defined by the demands of planning: by the interplay of subsidies, by the encouragements and directives concerning territory development. Economic groups, presenting a united front against the administrations, save their freedom of action insofar as they know how to use their power, considerably increased by the Vichy government's corporatist regime: the sugar, oil, and transportation industries.

In a word, the War, for all intents and purposes, revived nationalism —in opposition to so many internationalistic malformations discredited during the collaboration. In every social class, this long participation in an excessive conflict gave rise to new and sharper—and lasting—awareness of the nation's place in the world. In 1953-1954, as the world's pace of transformation quickens, the crisis of the European Defense Community ample proves this to be so.

It is possible to assert without paradox that overseas France has never been as close to European France as during these years when "colonialism," banned from the new civilization being formed, is receding on all sides. The ease of the earliest colonial conquests, the penury of Frenchmen settling in these overseas territories, and the slowness of their economic and social development all rather easily explain an ignorance well expressed by the reception given the 1930 Colonial Exhibition, stamped with curiosity for the exotic. These factors also explain a profound indifference, despite Fashoda and the War in the Rif, the best indication of which was the failure of the Jeunes de l'Empire Français movement, created shortly before 1939—a difficult hour, it is true, to stir up vocational interest. The War accelerated the breakdown of colonial clichés: economies complementary to France proper, following the old inspiration of the colonial agreement, sovereign political guardianship in the more than patient wait for indigenous political and cultural progress—

rather close, basically, to assimilation. The Brazzaville Conference at the height of the war announced to France's overseas world a will for renewal, made all the more legitimate by the heavy participation of all overseas France in the war effort.

The Brazzaville promises are changed into an incongruous structure:* the French Union, in which both the Assembly of the Union and the High Council,† in a purely advisory capacity, very rapidly became the blinds of persistent relics of the past: the practice of a close, administrative guardianship, the maintenance of an economic treatment preferential to France proper, and the subjection of all indigenous peoples under forms which, in the long run, were very much like those that had been officially condemned. However, the new native élites—some of whom had not waited until 1945 to emerge—educated in France, strong both with their double culture and their hopes for the Liberation, grew indignant and then impatient: as early as 1945 in Algeria, and 1947 in Madagascar and Indochina, former comrades of the Liberation, volunteers in the Army of Free France, some of whom fought against the Japanese occupation and others who participated in the Tunisian and Italian campaigns, drew themselves up, amazed, saddened, and revolted by those cautions and those hesitations—rapidly come to be considered betrayals—on the part of France proper.

For ten years, France herself thus discovers the overseas communities through forgotten promises, violence, *coups de force,* diplomatic intrigues at the United Nations, and wars absorbing an enormous segment of French strength: Indochina, North Africa, Madagascar, and Africa south of the Sahara. The work of sanitary, educational, and economic equipment is by turns denigrated or exalted, according as it is evaluated in absolute terms (miles of railroads, roads, and hospital facilities) or by comparison with the equipment of France proper, and with population figures. African industrialization and agrarian reforms—sketched out here and there by daring civil servants (Secteurs de Modernisation among the peasantry)—define the enormous tasks necessitated by the deficient economy of all the territories that are "underdeveloped" and, to boot, are drained by their participation in the global war. Finally, the originality of the native Moslem, African, and Asian civilizations ceases to be the exclusive property of esthetic cliques or the object of scholarly compilations by sociologists and ethnographers who are un-

---

* Overseas *départements* assimilated into *départements* of France proper, like Guadeloupe; complex differences for Algerian *départements*; associated governments—Laos for example; protectorates who refuse an independent status in the French Union—Morocco and Tunisia; overseas territories under close administrative guardianship, like French West Africa, French Equitorial Africa, and Madagascar.

† Actually, these institutions never had any real existence: they had so little meaning for the overseas population that some territories refused to send their representatives to them; they did not have much more meaning for France herself. The Assembly of the Union (as far as its delegation from France proper is concerned) very soon appeared to be the refuge for deputies who had been scorned by universal suffrage.

known outside of universities. The native élite begin to find their voice, supported by linguistic, religious, and ethnic solidarities which are often very strong—Moslem for North Africa and Negro farther south. (This postwar period sees the birth of a North African literature in French. In September of 1956, the first "global" Conference of Negro-African Writers and Artists was held in Paris at the Sorbonne—an event of great significance, gathering together Negroes from Africa and both North and South America, under the chairmanship of a Haitian as President.) These élite are nourished simultaneously by French and European culture, in whose name they invoke the rights of the human individual, of the self-determination of peoples, in this country which remains, in the world's eyes, the homeland of the rights of man. Hence the discomfort of the government's daily life: that of a government which founded its colonial domain on the short-sighted alliance of conqueror and feudally organized tribe (kaid, etc.), while the colonial peoples' new representatives invoke the most celebrated French traditions in defense of their rights.

Thus for want of methodical scientific research (as is admitted even by ethnographers like Lévi-Strauss and tropical doctors), for want of a large, colonial population, with the exception of Algeria, France is unaware of her overseas areas and their problems, except when forced to grapple with them across the distortions of propagandists, amid the not disinterested interventions on the part of the Anglo-Saxon allies, in a tense climate where patriotism is the object of constantly higher bids. And yet the scheme of the work in progress becomes, step by step, more precise, at least at the political level. For at the cultural level, in the inadequate knowledge of non-European cultures, the hesitations accumulate on all sides. Finally, at the economic level, everything remains to be accomplished so that the young governments may rapidly raise their standard of living, industrialize on a massive scale, and take a place on the world market without risking another short-term economic "colonization." But in this all-important realm, if one refers to the bitter experiences of certain underdeveloped countries who arrived at political independence without regard for the economic future, the failing is a double one: the native personnel lacks applied economists capable of planning on an expanded scale, in step with scientific processes and present-day techniques—power systems, education, yields for investments and consumption. France herself does not have the wherewithal for lavish, long-term investments throughout the entire French Union: men and machines, which other powers assiduously step forward to supply, are cruelly lacking. The example of North and South Vietnam is clear.

The French economy, thrown into confusion by the War, lacks the enormous means necessary for the development of the overseas regions, for it has also to confront a new Industrial Revolution—scientific, actually, more than industrial; all this while the preceding one has not yet run its course.

War and Occupation simultaneously burdened economic life and carries structural changes in their wake. Destructions were extremely heavy during the ten years following 1945; however, public finances took the heaviest load, either through credits to disaster areas or through nationalizations. On the other hand, famine momentarily halted the rural exodus and for a few years gave vigor and prosperity to the directly developed small-scale farms in central and southern France: the post-1950 revival was painful, and adaptation to the new farming methods was made all the more difficult as the governments multiplied subsidies, protective tariffs, and taxation for wheat, enabling this archaic form of rural cultivation to survive. In the same manner, famine and the black market brought about a significant increase in retail trade: a half million concerns of all kinds—fabrics, grocery stores, and dairy products*—were created to profit from the scarcity of products on the markets. Ten years after the War, this method of distribution was omnipresent: the local grocery store, whose meager income completes a working man's wages, had a hard life. On the other hand, the Vichy regime, like its German model, under the pretense of a corporate system, instituted national professional organizations which survived it and gave the merchant and industrial bourgeoisie (indeed the liberal professions since groups like doctors played the same role) a framework and also supplied it with the means for a far-reaching economic policy, next to which the "conspiracies" of the prewar "two hundred families" seem extremely harmless. The employers' unions, which moreover were gathered together in the Conseil National du Patronat Français, played at unilateral liberalism: they denied the government's right to intervene to fix prices and protect consumers, yet called upon it to help them obtain export subsidies and protective duties or to insure "freedom" of work during strikes. A solidarity on the part of employers, more openly displayed and also more effectively maintained than before the war, answered to the workers' solidarity. The interest groups thus formed intervened shamelessly in political life. In short, these professional organizations—with the exception of a few areas like metallurgy, chemistry, and pharmaceutical houses—acted much more in the direction of conserving their profits, gained easily and at the least expense, than in the

---

* After 1945, fortunes made under the label *"au bon beurre"*—butter, eggs, and cheese (Beurre, Oeufs, Fromages) had as bad a press in the liberated and still starving towns as the peasant *lessiveuses* [scandals]. For several years the term BOF remained synonymous with profit off the common poverty, a newly-rich person who arouses indignation. (The *scandales des lessiveuses* refers to a practice, common among the rural population during the War, of hiding wartime currency in laundry pails in the hope that it would be more valuable after the War. To combat such speculation, one of the first measures was to issue completely new currency.—Trans.)

direction of modernization and scientific equipment—both constantly necessary.

Continuing the progress that has been occurring steadily for a century, a progress now stimulated by war and by military research into such areas as radar and the atomic bomb, science and techniques leap forward in the period immediately after the war: there is not an area in which enormously significant innovations do not come about to cause the transformation of scientific perspectives. This is true even in the social sciences which traditionally lag behind and are still inarticulate, and in which a generalized dubiousness calls into doubt frontiers, methods, and aims: history, sociology, political economy.* Unquestionably the most sensational strides are those in biology, enabling results in medicine and surgery which were unhoped for twenty years ago: antibiotics decisively push back the most terrible scourges—notably syphilis and tuberculosis. The average life span in France exceeds sixty years, momentarily settles at sixty-two: by 1964 this figure has been surpassed. Nevertheless, greater changes are increasingly under way, justifying one's calling this postwar period the Third Industrial Revolution—or Scientific Revolution, owing to electronics and atomic energy. The direct application of this recent progress to overseas economies would perhaps enable the young governments to press on, at the cost of a well-directed planning.

There is an obvious link between the bomb at Hiroshima, destroying thousands of human beings in an instant, and the projected atomic power stations of the Électricité de France. Created in an atmosphere of merciless competition between American and German scientists, the atomic bomb is the destructive use of a source of energy discovered by French scientists (such as Frédéric Joliot-Curie) in 1939. As early as 1945, France turned toward the peaceful use of this energy: hence the search for uranium and production for scientific ends—such as nuclear physics and medical research—and then for industrial ones. Since the war plants have been built at Châtillon, Marcoules, and Saclay; the last, for implementing expenses much more than for security motives, is organized and controlled by the government, and is oriented toward scientific use. But American and English achievements open the way for this industrial production which the Électricité de France was undertaking, a production which, by 1970, can bring about unprecedented industrial progress, supplying France with all the sources of industry she will require, and which coal and hydroelectricity cannot assure today. While the oil in Aquitaine can furnish a temporary contribution and at the same time important chemical raw materials—especially sulphur—the

---

* "Where is sociology headed?" one man asks himself; "What is the present-day calling of sociology?" asks another. These are two titles, mere examples, taken from the enormous literature which is not just French but international.

whole basic area of French industrialization, deficient for more than a century, is assured: creation of new industries in the languishing southwest, in the Massif Central, and the southeast; a decongestion of the Parisian region; the atomic or electric re-equipment of transportation —all these are vistas of an abundance of energy.

Today, electronics brings upheavals no less important. Originating in the electromechanics carried out by telephone and radio broadcasting technicians on electronic selection, it now is applied as much to industry as to office work; it has brought a revolution of the same magnitude as that of steam in the nineteenth century, relieving animal or human energy. The Press which loves great sensations has been choosing electronics and cybernetics as subjects for a long time: tortoises, mice, and bees have been the objects of beautiful reporting jobs, as have the machines that translate or compose music. Cybernetics brought about progress in many fields, including psychology, owing to the studied analogies between electronic circuits and feedbacks, and the functioning of the brain. Cybernetics does not replace the human brain for even if someone were to build a six-story house containing as many electronic tubes as the brain contains neurons, there is no proof that the miracle would occur. Electronics also holds a major place in scientific research and is employed in measuring devices, computers, and electron microscopes which enable observations in infinitely small areas—on the order of the micromillimeter.

Electronics allows for the large-scale automation of industrial work: with cheap machines, sometimes fifty or a hundred times less expensive than the old ones and much less cumbersome, electronic dial telephones enable the reduction of labor in unheard-of proportions (one or two hundred to one) and a production output ten to fifteen times cheaper. Thus, industrial electronics must engulf enormous transfers or reclassifications of labor, a reduction of working hours, and a new wage-price stabilization. Much less widespread in France than in the United States or England, this automation particularly affects the large firms around Paris: Renault's transfer machines with "electronic heads" installed in a chain is the best-known example. But electronics also changes office work, in which there have been few advances since the invention of the typewriter: classifying, selecting, and adding at record speeds, machines with cards and perforated strips, with cells and electronic tubes, totally abolish an enormous segment of labor. Used today in public administrations, banks (where in hours, statements for sixty to one hundred thousand customers can be made up) and concerns of some consequence for all today's complex accounting, electronic machines reduce the number of necessary office personnel—who then must be reclassified. It has been determined that a rapid diffusion of these processes would free a million office workers. Employers and unions debate automation:

while inevitable competition leads the employers to use electronic machines, the workers' representatives at the same time understand that the proletariat, white or blue collar, are not to pay the price (unemployment, labor displacement, reclassifications) for this change. This employment problem is already posed on a nationwide scale.

But it is not the only problem: wages, leisure, production, and consumption are also involved. The scientific revolution must gradually give a new look to the entire nation, changing her place in the world, following paths which as yet are far from being laid out: information problems, problems again of awareness and planning—whether private, in the large capitalistic companies, or public—within the framework of a scientific humanism yet to be created.

► CULTURAL RHYTHMS: FRENCH CIVILIZATIONS

National and social renewal, the acquisition of national and global solidarity—beginning with the French overseas territories—and the Scientific Revolution: all this is perceived unevenly by the mass of forty-three million Frenchmen. This fact is all the more important as the democratic regime returns the destiny of these Frenchmen, and of these profound changes, to the people by putting the ballot into everyone's hands— without doing much, despite the strides in the aforementioned means of dispensing information, about enabling everyman to place these means within his own universe. This is simultaneously a problem of information and of education because, whatever popularization is effected, cybernetics cannot be understood without a minimum of mathematical training, any more than the place in the world of Madagascar can be understood without some well-grounded notions of geography. Let us emphasize "cannot be understood." For cybernetics, calling upon extensive knowledge of mathematics and physics, thermodynamics and game theory, necessitates thorough study for its comprehension. All present-day scientific fields are at the same point: thus the state of astrophysics, biology, and "Bourbaki's" mathematics.

For ten years, French National Education has been seeking educational reform, always kept from being carried out by a study commission, without achieving any results, for many reasons—the main one being a lack of funds. Several attempts at reform have been undertaken sporadically concerning the second diploma: a pedagogy of interest, inspired by Scout psychology, carried out a very much debated experiment. Pedagogy, which is highly credited, aims at lessening the child's effort: it is true that never in our civilization has childhood been the object of so much concern and so many precautions. "The child king," say some, seeing the proportion of the most modest budget devoted to toys: a reaction of the collective sensibility in this period which has seen so many massacres of innocents from 1940 to 1945 and which knows that childhood is more threatened now by the H-bomb. Reinforcing the scientific training of secondary education without lessening its humanistic molding; specializing and intensifying the scientific and technical instruction in higher education; extending compulsory education to the end of the reformed secondary education level—such a program presupposes resources, equipment, and a larger teaching staff than exist in the present-day system which, inherited from the nineteenth century, has hardly been modified in the period between the wars. While they are waiting, more than in any other period in their history (for never has another civilization been so outdistanced by its sciences and techniques), Frenchmen live at different intellectual and material levels. As far back as the seventeenth century, it is true, there was an enormous gap between the Parisian living in the Marais, frequenting a *salon* of a *précieuse*, and the peasant in the Velay, a crude-mannered bumpkin. But unquestionably this gap is less perceptible in the early years of the twentieth century in the days when the railroad, the elementary school, and compulsory military service produced their full effects. Now it is important once more. Between town and country, province and Paris—what varying levels of civilization!

This is certainly not to say that rural areas are merely places of immobility or slow change, while the triumphant towns stand for places of speed and fast-moving life; nor would the idea be any more exact that it is a closed world, withdrawn into itself, when exchanges between town and country have never been as great as in these twenty years when townspeople have acquired the habit of a necessary summer migration to the country and its natural landscapes. While the latter continue to lose population—the rural population today amounts to less than forty per cent of the total—the towns, which continue to grow, mark contemporary civilization with their types of life; they bring to bear against the country a kind of constantly invading urbanization which some curse as "suburbanization," so greatly do the large victorious towns with their multiple functions seem to be the characteristic human habitat of today's world; they live from their connections with distant regions, even possessing an international reach, and devour space in "megalo-urbanisms" —nearby suburbs, large suburbs. Thus, even while it is losing its last rustic features—small gardens, animals raised for domestic consumption, all the things preserved by nineteenth-century rural migrants with a nostalgia for lost space and activities—the large town makes itself felt in the rural world: for their weekends, the bourgeoisie build country-houses far from smoke and noise; co-operatives and business committees renovate châteaux and ghost towns in the Haute-Provence and the Haute-Loire, for summer camps and for people with paid vacations; the ease of transportation and the enormous increase of automobile traffic since 1945 multiply daily and seasonal exchanges. Finally the city preserves its reputation for public and private comfort (but especially public: monuments, stadiums, meeting and entertainment places) and its rather exaggerated reputation for easy living. Undoubtedly this urban pressure on rural life is a function of distances and locations: the Brie region just outside Paris comes under the influence of the capital from one month to another; the wages of agricultural workers as well as the seasonal shifting about of labor around Meaux and Coulommiers, are also rather good expressions of this; in the Creuse and Savoie, linked so closely to Paris during the last century, Limoges and Lyon are more important today than is the capital, and exercise an influence of a different order. On the other hand, the villages perched on the hills of the Basses- and Hautes-Alpes, and the Ardèche with old, medieval houses (in a conspicuously fifteenth-century style) are the object of growing Parisian appreciation in which art, snobbism, and the simple attraction of bright sunshine all have a part. Yet on the whole, the growing "urbanization" of landscapes and of men is certainly a prominent feature of the contemporary period.

French rural areas, however, resist urban conquest, that pressure of many shapes and many subtleties—subtleties that make rural life an amazing repository of traditions, sayings, and beliefs which form the stock in trade of folklore. Thus a farmer in the Beauce driving a Vedette is interested in chlorination of water, and is settled in a comfortable house with a television set, a refrigerator, and bathrooms: is he not more like an American farmer in Illinois than a peasant in central France? And the pedestrian peasant mentality is met, not in him, but in agricultural workers who, for all their handling of tractors, sowers, and threshers, nonetheless remain closer in their poverty to the traditional modes of life. In the same fashion, the Mediterranean peasant in Provence who each evening goes out onto the village square for a game of *pétanque*, his neighbors, and his friends, is the next of kin of the townsman through his commercial life and his discussion, in which most of the small French peasants are not practiced; the same can be said of the vinegrower in Alsace or Burgundy, a merchant often traveling on the roads, and the peasants in the border areas.

However, the rural French cultures consist, in the main, of rejections. From a life paced by seasonal work and through the slowness of natural ripening, even in hothouse farming, the small French peasants retain, as they would quasi-hereditary acquisitions, an empirical caution which, until now, neither schools nor population have been able to conquer. Neither the movies, with their rapid pace and complex language—especially the quality production in the style of Bresson, Autant-Lara, and Clément—nor consequently television, nor the household comforts of

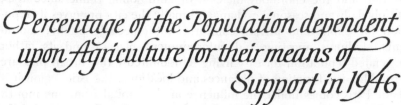

Percentage of the Population dependent upon Agriculture for their means of Support in 1946

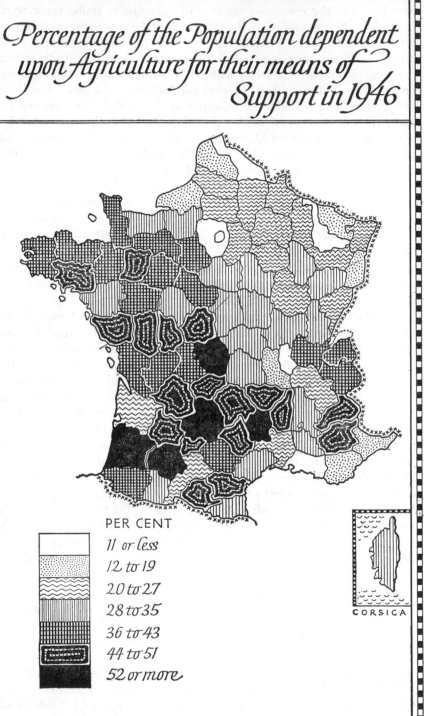

PER CENT

11 or less

12 to 19

20 to 27

28 to 35

36 to 43

44 to 51

52 or more

CORSICA

townspeople's apartments are really adopted in rural districts. In the heart of the Massif Central, the officials of the rural construction service [Génie Rural] responsible for the drinking-water equipment of rural communes, often have a hard time persuading the municipalities to accept their projects. And if it is true that radio has taken a place in peasant homes, it is through the convenience with which it informs, without effort, those who have grown unaccustomed to reading since elementary school: rural libraries or bookmobiles have not been especially successful; the headlines and local news in the daily (regional) newspapers are scanned, and so are the weeklies—preferably illustrated. But there are no treatises on agronomy, nor even novels: *Le Chasseur français* takes the place of both. Again, it is speed itself—on the road, in carrying out work, and in the exchange of ideas—which is refused by the peasant world: fine-speaking Parisians and speed-demons on the main highways are the objects of equal censure.

Thus peasant communities live a French life having its own tonality, as well as its regional variants, costumes, and fetes, piously maintained by praisers of the past—not devoid of commercial significance, as for example, in Brittany. French is spoken increasingly and replaces dialects; religious life, Catholic or Protestant, has lost the unanimous fervor of past centuries, but its practice among women remains high everywhere, and men are not totally separated from it as they are in some urban milieux: the church remains one of the poles of rural, public life, "one of the points where the peasant tests his freedom,"* along with the town hall and the school. But the human horizon of villages remains extremely limited: familiar roads, the market town, the neighboring town, and the Préfecture of the *département*, belong to the accepted universe; a few trips organized by the concern of the school or the "patronage of the *curé*" make several natural wonders known: the Ocean, the Alps—or even Paris, dimly glimpsed in a short week. But it is much more difficult to establish contact with the vast world, in perpetual flux—so different from what the schoolteachers recently let them glimpse—despite war memories, especially for the prisoners, and the information in newspapers or on radios. The same is true of intellectual and artistic horizons: not only Parisian life, but even the life of the capital of the *département* —the Autumn Exhibition of local landscape painters, or a lecture by Mauriac or Sartre, would not arouse interest. If a schoolteacher tactfully and patiently tries to set up a cultural or sports center, the success is almost certain: recently an artistic initiation has even been undertaken, with good results, in the Limousin. But it is a long and exacting work, for peasant life does not yet know what to do with leisure. Finally, in

---

* The phrase is borrowed from a memoir of the last war (*Déposition*, by Léon Werth), in which peasant life and mentalities in Bresse are analyzed with much subtlety and understanding.

those milieux where grandparents bring up children,* customs are preserved better than elsewhere—even those of entertainment; on Saturday nights, young people still prefer dances to the movies. Young people
from ten to twelve miles around meet at these dances among acquaintances, often next of kin. And, as regards entertainment, traveling circuses, as meager as they are, make up for everything else.

This is not to assert that rural areas are not developing: but they do
so slowly. And the most important factor in this change is, even today,
the economic crisis which has been crushing the peasantry for some
years; painfully it is endured, but owing to that very slowness, it is difficult to surmount. The fine peasant caution and common sense, so well
esteemed by specialists in electoral geography, constantly act against the
necessary agricultural revolution,† at least south of the Loire.

Towns against the cities: the towns inspire the rural population—
daily, owing to the special fares on trains and "workers'" buses and to
cycles, with or without motors, and definitively, as the housing problem
diminishes. Living in a town is often a sign of superiority, whatever one's
trade. Brought closer together by the War—during those long years when
towns were drained of strength, and when country people saw themselves become the object of unaccustomed attentions—rural and urban
people now find themselves alienated from each other by modes of life
which, except during the period of paid vacations or on occasions of such
family ceremonies as marriages and especially burials (not as well attended as before), are scarcely congruent.

To be sure, the transitions are multiple as is characteristic of any European nation with an old civilization. Mende or Charolles are large villages, even if Mende is a Préfecture, in which the population regards the
"stranger" who saunters through its streets with just as much curiosity
and defiance as in the smallest hamlet in the Haute-Loire: minus the
dogs at the heels of travelers. But similarly there are numerous small
towns which nevertheless have a factory of some sort, large weekly markets, and hotel facilities, not to be discounted, which occupy the position
of a necessary layover on a given road and which are a point of contact
between extremely different rural regions—none of them much like
towns. Sleepy towns like Moulins on the Allier, Lons-le-Saunier at the
foot of the Jura plateaus, and Sézanne-en-Brie are much less citified, for
example, than the tourist centers which slumber for six months and

---

* This is also a partial explanation for the peasant's attachment to the lands inherited from his ancestors—that major obstacle standing in the way of the rural
re-allocation of land throughout all of France.
† Dimly seen, however, as the tractor's progress indicates, under the pressure of
mediocrity and thanks to the efforts of technicians like R. Dumont, whose *Voyages
en France d'un agronome* and *Leçons de l'agriculture américaine* are extremely
important.

then in season are swollen with people taking cures—towns like Vichy, Lourdes, and Le Touquet. If it is true that many of these small built-up areas, grouping ten to twenty thousand people, keep, thanks to their local accent, their sometimes well-exploited historic memories and the simplicity of their provincial life—a charm and a flavor peculiar to them —they remain nevertheless halfway between rural and urban life: feverish, complex, marked by the industrial and commercial advances of the contemporary world, advances belonging to the centers whose populations number fifty thousand or more, and which have an important regional role.

From the peasant—too often having to fall back, because of economic contingency, on the action of proliferating and greedy marketers, forwarding agents, retailers, and intermediaries who cause food prices to go up five or ten times—to the city dweller—who keeps up with the economic pace of the region and of the nation, indeed the world—what a difference of mentality on this level alone! A female laboratory assistant working on the condition of silk in Lyon, a metallurgist in Strasbourg or Nancy, and the urban worker, aided by the professional instruction of unions or *collèges du travail* and by his newspaper, sees ahead and is concerned about day-to-day, enormous problems. Job and wage fluctuations and the rise or decline of a town or economic region are important to him. Le Mans, a new French automotive center, grows larger in proportion to Renault's success; but the old regions around Saint-Étienne, knocked about by the decline of the silk, ribbon, and cycle industries, seek to revitalize themselves: businesses are shut down, weaving mills are converted to the manufacture of stretch fabrics, iron manufacturers are absorbed by the Aciéries de la Marine. When unemployment extends over an economic region, the entire population is affected: men on pensions work part-time and "replace the young," small merchants see their customers' credit immoderately extended, and workers who do have jobs are threatened by the availability of labor which tempts the employers. Urban solidarity is multiform—but no less engaging than the ancestral village solidarity so lauded by those contemners of modern civilization. Whenever a labor dispute affects an important establishment, the entire town participates; at the first sign of a false step on the part of the employer, or the "forces of order," the solidarity strike breaks out, carrying the professional ranks in its wake, and sometimes all the workers in the town: for example the Michelin strike in 1947, the shipyard strikes at Saint-Nazaire and Nantes in 1954. And in the most peaceful instances, collections or union treasuries come to the aid of the strikers and enable them to hold out. Despite protectionism, industries and big business are bound to global economic life: the wool-producing region in the north lives off Australian and Argentinian wool, just as the cotton textile industry in the Vosges and around Alsace depends on

Egypt and India. Within the production committees, industrial life, the flow of regional capital, and investment projects are the object of discussion and instruction—with a candor that varies according to the good will of the employer. Regional capitals, today's large towns, specialized, open onto the national market, and more or less linked to European and global markets, experience a large-scale economic life, subject to fluctuations coming either from the government or from abroad, necessitating adaptations and conversions. An entire life, diverse and moving, is constantly being threatened in the present-day world: the ominous slump in French textile industries over the past five years, the constant progress of heavy metallurgy, and the devouring extension of all the chemical industries, from oil refineries to pharmacies, are thus expressed in urban life, as in the post-1953 revival of stock-market speculation and savings.

Social relations are also more complex: the village, in which large landowners, small farmers, day laborers, and the "notables" of the town—notary, schoolteacher, merchant—rub elbows according to a rigorous and respected etiquette, experiences a peaceful social life as the days go by; only vacation or election periods and trips to town bring them some transitory disturbance. Urban life is both more diverse and less calm: as it did before it offers, in its merchant districts and its promenade areas, many opportunities for encounters between classes clearly distinguishable by their dress, their modes of transportation, and their residential districts. But city dwellers, and the semi-city dwellers who work in town and travel each evening to reach their suburban houses or the nearby countryside, have multiple social relations through the various groups in which they move: sporting or artistic associations, learned groups, mutual societies, regional groupings (all the livelier as the receiving town is more insular), veterans' associations, and finally and most important, professional unions. For these groups are not all equally lively. Let us ignore theatrical and musical conservatories, groups of antiquarians, and archaeologists, who vegetate because the new means of cultural diffusion work in favor of Paris. Mutual societies, reduced by Social Security to a complementary role, no longer have the place they did before the war, despite great achievements, especially in the area of surgery. On the other hand, sports have more numerous and more enthusiastic supporters: even participation has grown, but particularly the groups of supporters who follow the soccer and rugby teams around, partially finance their recruiting efforts, organize receptions and *vins d'honneur* for the glory of the champions, and assure the maintenance of stadiums and bicycle-racing tracks. For these difficult tasks, directors of companies and supporters fondly spend no less than treasures. However, French sporting equipment is deficient, even in the most popular areas. For example, outside Paris there is only one bicycle-racing track in France that is open in wintertime—the one at Saint-Étienne. It is true that bicycle-racing used to seem condemned to death by motor-cycles.

All these associations, however, whose activities comprise a large part of the gastronomical banquets and meetings (in particular, the region-alist associations), on the whole, are prompted, financed, and directed not by the upper bourgeoisie who live in closed circles, but by the urban bourgeoisie: the merchants, the middle range of officials, and the trained industrial personnel who are greedy for easy Sunday entertainments. Even in that respect, angler groups or Amicales des Anciens du Train des Équipages are less important in urban life, despite all their good nature, than the corporate groups.

Even more than political associations (which hardly affect any but the capitals of *départements*), union life, extended since the War to all workers including civil servants, but balanced by an equal development of employers' associations, animates the large town. Rival unions*—fol-lowing a short period of reunification shortly after the Liberation—have split up the labor movement and weakened its action, but, through their very "competition," they have stirred up an intellectual fermentation and a sharper awareness of proletarian traditions. Beyond the region and the town, the civil servant-teacher, withdrawn into an autonomy that safeguards a semblance of unity; the worker linked with this or that inter-national movement through his federation or his union press; the mili-tant who spends long hours each week in discussing and collecting stamps; or the simple dues-paying member happily reading posters, perusing his professional newspaper—all these men are participating in a wide social life in which, today as yesterday, great economic and political prob-lems are posed. Election to Social Security, to joint production commit-tees, shop or craft gatherings, simple meetings of different militants, with familiar names and nicknames—CGTists, (the former) worker priests, "Christians"—it is around the firms, the Bourses du Travail, and the Maisons du Peuple, that the most ardent urban life revolves, a life

---

* The reunification brought about during the Resistance, and continued until 1948, had not affected the Christian movement which—of Catholic origin and recruited from the *jocistes* [members of the J.O.C.]—always remained apart from the C.G.T. For ten years, three union organizations divided the workers' support: the C.G.T., always present and the most powerful, whose leaders are linked with those of the Communist Party; the C.G.T.-F.O. [Force Ouvrière] inspired by socialists and fol-lowers of Proudhon, which attracts civil servants, especially post-office employees, and the labor milieux in the north; and the C.F.T.C. [Confédération Française des Travailleurs Chrétiens], Christian unions, on the upswing as compared with the pre-war period, with active militant workers, but particularly rich in employees. The C.F.T.C. prevails over the C.G.T.-F.O. because of both its pugnaciousness and its large number of members. Finally, the majority of teachers constitute an autonomous federation with two hundred thousand members who did not accept the 1948 secession, but did nothing toward reunification. There also exists a large autonomous confederation of trained personnel. (The "suffix" F.O. is taken from the weekly *Force Ouvrière*, representing a reformist wing within the larger C.G.T.—Trans.)

linked to daily economic vicissitudes and the most firmly established traditions of the labor movement: the proletariat's destiny, its persistent poverty, its tenacious hope, dominate the social life of the large town.

Last but not least, urban civilization has a more elevated intellectual tone than does the rural, and in a sense one more elevated than between the wars, owing to several provincial creations characterizing the present-day period: *lycées, collèges* (indeed *facultés* in the administrative seats of educational districts), consequently count for little, at least insofar as they are institutions. Alumni groups, inspired by nostalgia for a mad youth, become, in the main, opportunities for joyous gatherings of forty-year-old men who have escaped the monotony of family Sundays; parents associations, until now, have especially served the forces of administrative maneuvers in the obscure intrigues concerning reforms. The ties have yet to be created which might make secondary education establishments the urban cultural centers they ought to be, as the rural elementary school, with its projectors, agricultural library, and the devotion of its schoolteachers, has often succeeded in being in the villages. Attacked and slandered by the Vichy government from 1940 to 1944, neglected and asphyxiated from 1951 to 1955 by the second legislature of the Fourth Republic—which, like the Vichy government, has taken great pains over private education—it is true that the personnel in both elementary and secondary public education, overwhelmed by continually worsening working conditions, cannot secure this cultural diffusion by themselves alone.

Therefore, there is a greater role for these associations, which, in the buoyant years after the War, have taken up the old ideal of popular education and which, despite subsidy reductions and political in-fights, paralleling those of the unions, continue their work: People and Culture, Travel and Work, Youth Hostels with various labels, cultural circles of the Ligue de l'Enseignement—all organize touring trips, studies, lectures, and discussions, and help educational theater and movies survive. These activities are scattered, competitive,* and developed unequally according to the town and especially the range of a few leaders, who carry along in their wake both the young who are curious about the contemporary world, and the old, who preserve the nostalgic notion of a Caliban better armed for the class struggle.

It is harder to measure the role of television which, though rapidly expanding, is still in its infancy and makes a new cultural means available to city dwellers who, accustomed to the movies, are immediately won over. Despite the obstacle of its high cost, the television set has its ardent

---

* Here again, as in the public school, there is the image of the nation: unity in diversity seems ideal to some. Attempts have been made to unite denominational and areligious movements into one common work; they have never been able to obtain more than a federation of independent groups—which continue to compete.

supporters in every region reached by the transmitter. In the same way, the book and record clubs, production co-operatives which supply first-rate quality at fair prices, participate in the urban intellectual life on the family level, if not that of the individual. Their role has been constantly growing for the past decade or so: in the case of books, this is because of the selections, which distribution conditions often make it impossible for bookstores alone to accomplish; for records, because of the long-playing "revolution" enabling long scores to be recorded on a single record with a musical fidelity far superior to prewar impressions. Unquestionably these clubs do not have the same "customers" as do the Travel and Work associations; however, through the frequent exchanges among the youthful members and through the moderate cost of the subscription purchases, the scope of these associations is considerable.

It is particularly in the area of entertainment that the modern town is regaining vitality. Provincial theatrical circuits just manage to survive and the municipalities unfervently maintain the municipal theaters that receive them. In this area, a great work was undertaken after 1945— one that is now losing steam: the four dramatic Centers at Rennes, Tours, Saint-Étienne, and Colmar, which come once a year to Paris to refuel themselves, each season present several successful shows in all the urban centers of the thus created theatrical region: their success is effected by the devotion of their leaders, as well as their fidelity to the lessons and techniques of Copeau, Dullin, and Jouvet. Until his death in 1951, Jouvet encouraged the decentralization of drama (the future, he said), lending his theater, lavishing advice, and accepting official responsibilities with these young troupes, despite his burdensome tasks with the Athénée (*La Folle de Chaillot, Don Juan, Tartuffe*) and with the movies. The National Popular Theater (T.N.P.) plays a comparable role through its provincial circuits and its annual Festival at Avignon.

Helping the amateur troupes in the cultural centers around them to survive, the centers develop a taste for the theater which is transformed by the widespread use of movies, since the latter are now the urban entertainment par excellence.* The cinemas' shorter programs and their policy of continuous afternoon and evening shows assure the greatest flexibility in recruiting a public; movie clubs which present and comment upon works, and improve the audio-visual culture of 150,000 members, cinematic reviews and critical works, are gradually molding a more demanding public, one that is learning how to choose films and theaters

---

* The Centre National du Cinéma, which regulates this industrial art, subsidizes producers, and encourages quality and censorship, numbers 5,300 movies which have 2,600,000 seats, and 380,000,000 spectators each year. Production runs around a hundred full-length films each year, more shorts and newsreels. These are sold in about fifty foreign countries—leading which, obviously, are French-speaking countries like Belgium, Canada, and Switzerland—and have a place on the international market alongside American and Italian productions.

according to the director and the stars. Finally and most important, along with the enormous current production of melodramas, westerns, or light comedies, French movies are maintaining, as they maintained even during the Occupation, their high quality, turning out five to ten masterpieces each year—the "classics" of an art that profoundly informs sensibility and intelligence: alongside men like Renoir, René Clair, Carné, and Becker, a new generation of great directors is taking its place, one that in its turn brings its own vision of the world to the screen: Bresson, Autant-Lara, Clément, Clouzot, and Tati. More than the radio, often heard without being listened to, movies have become the principal mode of French urban culture: public authorities and the University recognize this primacy, contributing in no small way to the present-day differentiation of city and country.

In a word, each large French town has its own stamp, its own life, which ought to be called to mind at greater length: regional capitals, rich with monuments maintained by the press and regionalistic literature, like Dijon and Rennes; center of intense religious life, like Lyon and Strasbourg; gates of France open to the world, like Marseille and Le Havre; industrial cities, like Roubaix and Metz. Today as yesterday, each town is a miracle of men; the large French town is in the forefront, where so many French types, members of Free Thought and pious devotees of the Sacred Heart of Jesus, working-class missionary-priests, and Marxist followers of the *Nouvelle Critique*, planners and supporters of free enterprise, proletarians in white collars, laborers in overalls and caps, and young vaguely liberal employers who cannot move a hundred yards without their Cadillacs—all these live together, rub elbows, fight, and sometimes fraternize. However, the final and perhaps most significant characteristic: all these towns—even the oldest, even momentary capitals like Lugdunum, or capitals of a divided France (Bourges)—receive the best part of their vitality from the capital. Relations with Paris enliven the economic and the intellectual life, and, in the long run, do so to the benefit of Paris: people from Lyon who hoped for a decentralization to their advantage from the Lyon-Paris electrification recently have experienced bitterly this Parisian concentration. French life in all its plenitude is to be found only in Paris. Paris is a great urban mass containing one-sixth of the population of France. It is unlike any other city, in France or the world: the generous and swollen heart of French civilization.

Despite the Versailles of Louis XIV and of Thiers, Paris has been the capital for centuries, and has remained the heart and the mind of France.[1] From her "historic" center, where tourists from the world over saunter about in summer, tourists sensitive to the harmony of the old stones and to the light air of summer evenings, to the distant little town in the Seine-et-Oise or the Seine-et-Marne where, after an hour's subway ride and an hour's train ride, the suburbanite greedy for silence and air reaches his "pigeon-hole"—in this enormous urban area around Paris almost seven million Frenchmen are gathered, living a single ardent, proud life. Workers and employees live in the twentieth and twenty-fifth *arrondissement*, upper bourgeois in the beautiful sixteenth and seventeenth, residential districts; working classes in "red" suburbs from Bezons to Saint-Ouen, from Ivry to Montrouge; trained and technical personnel from the west, Versailles and Saint-Germain; large, more "mixed" suburbs from Draveil to Brunoy, and from Aulnay to Campigny-sur-Marne. Seven million Frenchmen, full-time Parisians in the heart of the town, daytime Parisians, nighttime Parisians, depending upon their work and their pleasures—all have an inimitable sense of French life even when they have no control over it. Posters of all descriptions, shop windows on the Rue de la Paix and the Rue de Rivoli arcades, newspapers, chosen carefully and precisely—since *Libération* is not *L'Humanité*, and *Paris-Presse* is not *France-Soir*—entertainments of unequaled variety, retrospective showings at the Cinémathèque and always avant-garde theater; finally—but this is not all—the free speaker, the banterer on the Rue Mouffetard as in Montreuil, in Levallois, and on the Boulevard Saint-Michel, who gives everyone the keen feeling that a greater freedom exists here than anywhere else. The French and the world took the measure of Paris, during those four black years from which the capital emerged with pride, strong in its martyrdom. In describing the Liberation, General de Gaulle sensed this well: "For more than four years, Paris was the remorse of the whole world. Suddenly the world became her lover. While the giant seemed to sleep, incarcerated and stupefied, people became used to her tremendous absence. . . ." Imagine France, imagine the world, without Paris!

That all France lives under the stimulus of the capital is more than obvious: the political and administrative centralization, the political regime, the network of railroads, highways, and air routes, the concentration of banks—all these are so many good reasons for it. It is possible to deplore it, and recommend one of several remedies. Decentralization was one of the great projects of the Fourth Republic; the results do not as yet lessen the capital's domination.[2] The only influential financial seat since the Second Empire, the Parisian region is now also the foremost commercial and industrial center of the country. All the large firms have Paris offices, for there they find only too clear advantages: the ease of office staff and of financial, fiscal, and customs operations, and the relations with competing or complementary establishments. Concerning commercial operations, to these same factors can be added the study and use of the nation's most concentrated consumers' market, which serves as a pilot area for all provincial markets through the press, through the

Roman Catholic Religious Practice

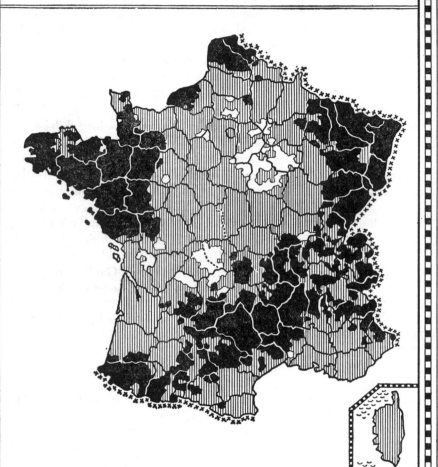

 Practicing regions

 Regions indifferent to Roman Catholic traditions

Uncommitted regions

CORSICA

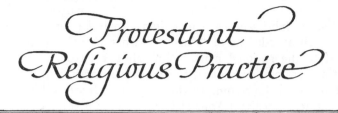

Protestant Religious Practice

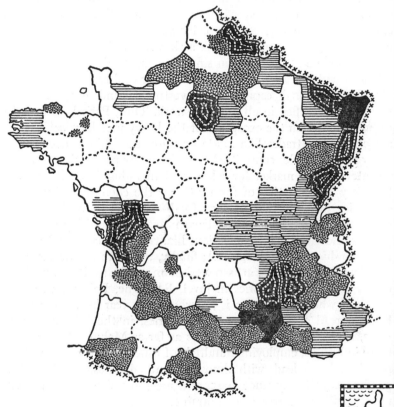

 From 1-9 churches or subsidiary buildings

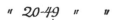 " 10-19 " " " " "

" 20-49 " " " " "

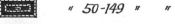 " 50-149 " " " " "

" 150-300 " " " " "

CORSICA

department stores' network of branches, and through highly centralized firms; in certain areas, this market also guides a part of the European one: Boussac fabrics or farm machinery, material for lighthouses and buoys, or cheap editions of "classics"—what French products are not sent out to the national market through Paris, from a single district (sometimes from a few shops), from a single department store, or from a single seasonal showroom? In this respect, it is astonishing to see the Manufacture Française d'Arms et Cycles, in Saint-Étienne—an old firm with a commercial circuit secured by a half-century of proven experience, a firm whose catalogue and whose monthly magazine (*Le Chasseur Français*) have the highest commercial circulation in France—prove no exception to this rule, and establish a showroom of samples. As an industrial center the Parisian region simultaneously enjoys effortless shipping relations with the English Channel and the coal region in the north, an abundant national capital for investment, and great resources of manpower qualified in all kinds of work. Thus, Paris lives on all kinds of industries, with the exception of the heavy metallurgical ones. There are old artisan trades like *haute couture*, furnishings, decoration, and fancy goods—trades committed to high-quality production, which retain an international market for sales; modern industries that come out of that very specialization of former times, the chemistry of perfume and cosmetics, of confection, of dyes; food industries born of the enormous consumer market; highly specialized industries, requiring numerous employees and elaborate organization, like the pharmaceutical or the electronics industries (Bull, I.B.M.); finally, there are the different sorts of metal-working, from the artisan workrooms of the twelfth *arrondissement* to the automobile factories in Javel, Boulogne, Poissy, and Colombes, a fifth of whose production is absorbed each year by the region around Paris. Spread out to the town boundaries, in the suburbs—more and more, in the greater suburban areas as far as Melun, Mantes, Meaux—these industries, employing hundreds of thousands of workers (the automobile industry leads with almost a hundred thousand), have been expanding continually since 1945, and are more dynamic than even the metal-working industry in the Lorraine.

On the administrative and political level, there is the same trend toward Paris. Who can be unaware of this, when the administrative staff in a *département*, completely overcome, badly aided by an as yet undefined regional staff, cannot help referring even the simplest questions to Paris—while the Council of State, that guardian of the law, bows under the weight of gracious appeals, advice, and requests. The same is true on the intellectual level. Education, scientific and technological research, publishing, the press (including the radio and the young television industry)—all of French intellectual life comes out of Paris and is concentrated back upon it; the *grandes écoles* and their most "profitable" preparation; the departments richest in teachers and students (there are as many French students in Paris as in the sixteen other universities combined), assure the pre-eminence of Parisian higher education over all others; for the same reasons, public secondary education in Paris is also better than that of the provincial towns—unless the super-abundance of Parisian students destroys that advantage. Even the National Center for Scientific Research has most of its laboratories and research centers at Paris; moreover, it is complemented by establishments along the same order that live off private or nationalized industry: iron works at Saint-Germain, petroleum at Rueil, S.N.C.F., coal mining. All the large publishing houses, even when they use provincial printers often far from Paris (as far as Abbeville, Bourges, and Mâcon), are set up on the Left Bank in the fifth and sixth *arrondissements*; the Parisian press, though it is now being set back by regional journalism, served as a press for the entire nation for a few years after the Liberation—and it remains highly superior to the regional efforts by virtue of the quality of its commentaries, and it indirectly nourishes the latter efforts. Poorly protected against bribery, despite the creation of the S.N.E.P. [Société Nationale des Entreprises de Presse], this press of political information, which is more vital and serious than it was before the War, owes its hold on both the Parisian and provincial public to its verve and technical progress, despite the importance of other information media. Even more striking than the contrast between Parisian and provincial newspapers is the contrast between Parisian broadcasting stations and regional ones —more and more the latter are mere relay stations.

A monstrous urban organism in its immensity, in the difficulties of supply and of traffic that it always creates, the Parisian region is still a unique testing ground for culture. For more than a century it has been the center of attraction for the scholars and artists of every country in the world; in the shadow of its libraries and museums, it maintains and nurtures a cosmopolitan population which, blending into French life, cultivates at the same time a thousand and one original characteristics. There are so many hothouse cultures whose hardiest cuttings enrich Parisian civilization, well beyond active particularisms, whether scientific, artistic, or indeed gastronomic: Chinese acupuncture, Japanese No, Negro music, Balkan cuisine thus have their adherents, and also, in the best sense of the word, their specialists. *Associations amicales** establish sympathetic ties with the most remote countries, and through their press, movies, and exhibitions, make known these manifestations of kindred or exotic civilizations. Sheltered by the Sorbonne, the Collège de France, and the École des Langues Orientales, research institutes offer to students intellectual means for these exchanges in the form of study groups,

---

* As, in America, the organizations styled "Friends of the. . . ."—Trans.

inspired by the most disinterested research. It is a real melting pot, with French preponderant, for these foreign colonies where political refugees, scholars, students, and artists play the most important role—whatever the quality of the assimilation undergone by less active groups of craftsmen, merchants, and unskilled laborers.

Simultaneously, Paris remains the center of France, a center in which all the orientations of French thought and culture are maintained, in the main through the effect of the centralization of the institutions, but also because of the exceptional equipment of its libraries and museums, and the atmosphere of freedom peculiar to the whole town. One has but to see, on the level of spiritual life, the role of the Jesuits installed in all the chairs of dogma in the Catholic Institute, the range of their *Action populaire* at Vanves, and their skillful leadership of the Catholic Youth in the A.C.J.F. [Action Catholique de la Jeunesse Française], the influence of Saulchoir, the large house of the Dominicans, their *Cerf* publications, their efforts to renew sacred art, alongside Sulpician traditions which, inherited from the nineteenth century, are still very much alive in their district.* In Paris too, with greater reason, small political groups on the fringes of the large parties enliven thought; they supply topics for reflection and propaganda, slogans and solutions, which pass discreetly into the common heritage after having been launched by these heretics. Thus on the Left there are Trotskyites of the Fourth International, the New Left, the Movement for the Liberation of the People, Independent Socialists, Young Republicans—to mention only a few.

Simultaneously an avant-garde and a living museum: this Catholic revival—due less to the achievements of a clerical party, the Popular Republican Movement [M.R.P.], than to the profound modernization of its faith by a minority, bearing lofty testimony in a de-Christianized world—this Catholic life, remote from all habitual religion, is primarily a Parisian phenomenon. The theatrical achievements of Vilar, Barrault, and Meyer—the heirs and successors of Cartel—are borne by a public whose theatrical sensibility is in proportion to the demands of its creators. Similarly, whatever be the reputation of the movie festival and the literary juries, the fate of a great film or book depends upon the reception granted these creations by the thousands of Parisians who attentively read the criticism of the weeklies and the monthly journals,† forming an

---

* An example of "Sulpician" survival is this publication announced in the *Bibliographie de la France* in October, 1953: "*Le Bon:* prayers and invocations to help cure the sicknesses of domestic animals, taken from the best authors. This book will render invaluable services to people with domestic animals." Similarly, a hundred quotations indicating survival of anticlericalism and Scientism could be cited.

† The intellectual range of these journals, not all of them widely read, is an indication of this astonishing wealth: existentialist, *Temps Modernes;* very literary, *Mercure;* "Christian personalist," *Esprit;* Jesuit, *Études;* Marxist, *Pensée;* Dominican, *Vie Intellectuelle;* "Progressist," *Cahiers Internationaux;* surrealist, *Lettres Nouvelles.*

independent and thoughtful judgment, which is the seal of success for all France.

To be sure, all Paris does not attend the exclusive movie houses on the Boulevards, nor the productions of the T.N.P. or of the Théâtre Hébertot. The Parisian urban region, an area of strong contrasts, also juxtaposes relics and experiments, novelties and traditions. Faced with this virulent Catholic intellectualism, sociologists, in love with religious practices and vitalities, note how much the sidewalks of the Boulevard Montparnasse "devitalize" Catholic men and women from Britanny who come to Paris from Quimper. Just as with the subway readers of the *Figaro* and the "Homeric" *Équipe*, so too Paris has its districts and its villages—each dominated by a principal function, each endowed with its own flavor, depending upon its age, its monuments, and its people. It would require many pages to evoke this discovery of the inexhaustible Paris lying beyond Haussmann's boulevards, to evoke the rendezvous of bums—the favorite subject of an entire literature. But if it is true that the Parisian working girl, who could never buy herself a dress with a Christian Dior label, reflects this Parisian chic—the town's most conspicuous attraction—by her dress and in the choice of her scarf and in her bag from the Prisunic, it is also true that in the intellectual and artistic fermentation that breathes life into the high places of the capital—painting exhibitions, the current stylish cafés, "La Nationale," and "Les Écoles,"—something else passes: a presence of mind, an unexpected curiosity even for the ball-playing child or the strongman in Les Halles— a presence, a curiosity, which applauded *Le Cid* "by Gérard Philipe and Jean Vilar," in the open-air theater of Suresnes, and which has every day the vista of the Louvre or the Pont Notre-Dame before its eyes. Here, more than anywhere else, an entire culture is incorporated into the sentient body of an entire people.

The leader of national civilization, the leader for thousands of faces as diverse as the needs of all the spiritual families and the artistic traditions of France; a discreet leader, in no way anxious for uniformity but rather for the divergencies which better unite France, Paris is simultaneously the most astonishing and the most fertile crucible of a global civilization which—at a time when everyone's attention is being forced, sometimes not without awkwardness, upon the original creations of Africa and Asia, at a time when, not without dangerous ambiguities, supranational creations are honored—is not yet, as much as it should be, a reality.

Bibliographical Notes

PART I: THE MIDDLE AGES

CHAPTER I.   *The Year 1000*

1. Richer, *Histoire de France*, tr. [into modern French] and ed. by Robert Latouche, Paris: Champion, 1937, II, 49.
2. Raoul Glaber, *Histoire*, ed. Maurice Prou, Paris: Picard, 1886, Bk. III, Ch. IX, ¶40. (Collection de textes pour servir à l'étude et à l'enseignement de l'histoire, vol. I.)

CHAPTER II.   *Feudalism: The Eleventh Century*

1. Doon de Saint-Quentin, *De Moribus et actis primorum Normanniae ducum*, Bk. III, ¶44, in *Memoires de la Société des Antiquitaires de Normandie*, vol. XXIII, (1865).

CHAPTER III.   *The Century of Great Progress*

1. *Ordonnances des rois de France de la Troisième race*, Paris: L'Imprimerie Royale, 1777, XII, 563-564.
2. Guibert de Nogent, *De vita sua*, tr. [into modern French] and ed. by Georges Bourgin, Paris: Picard, 1907, Bk. III. (Collection de textes pour servir à l'étude et à l'enseignement de l'histoire, vol. XL.)
3. *Liber miraculorum sancte Fidis*, ed. Auguste Bouillet, Paris: Picard, 1897, Bk. I, ¶13. (Collection de textes pour servir à l'étude et à l'enseignement de l'histoire, vol. XXI.)
4. *Ibid.*
5. *Exordium parvum*, in *Les monuments primitifs de la regle cistercienne*, ed. Philippe Guignard, Dijon, 1878.
6. Statutes of 1134, ¶VIII.

CHAPTER IV.   *The Capetian Synthesis*

1. Jean de Joinville, *Vie de Saint-Louis*, ed. Nathalis de Wailly, Paris: Hachette, 1914. (Eng. tr. by Joan Evans, *The History of Saint Louis*, New York: Oxford University Press, 1938—Trans.)
2. Guillaume de Saint-Pathus, *Vie Monseigneur saint Loys*, ed. Henri-François Delaborde, Paris: Picard, 1899, Ch. VII. (Collection de textes pour servir à l'étude et à l'enseignement de l'histoire, vol. XXVII.)

CHAPTER V.   *The End of the Middle Ages*

1. Georges Espinas, *Les origines du droit d'association dans les villes de l'Artois et de la Flandre française jusqu'au début du XVIe siècle*, Lille: Raoust, 1941, II, 100-101, #46.
2. Jean Froissart, *Chroniques*, ed. Siméon Luce, Paris: Renouard, 1869, I, #149. (An interesting English translation is a sixteenth-century one done by John Bourchier, *The Chronicles of Froissart*, London: Nutt, 1901-1903, The Tudor Translation series (this particular reference is in I, #149); an abridgement of the Johnes translation exists in paperback: *The Chronicles of England, France, and Spain*, ed. Dunster, New York: Dutton, 1961—Trans.)
3. *Choix de pièces inédites relatives au règne de Charles VI*, ed. Louis-Claude D'Arcq, Paris: Renouard, 1863. I, 59 (Société de l'Histoire de France, vol. CXII.)
4. *Journal d'un bourgeois de Paris 1405-1449*, ed. Alexandre Tuetey, Paris: Champion, 1881, entry for the year 1420.
5. Froissart, *op. cit.*, Prologue.
6. Christine de Pisan, *Le Livre des faits et bonnes moeurs du sage roi Charles V*, Bruges: Desclée de Brouwer, 1892, Ch. XVI.
7. *Journal d'un bourgeois . . .* , entry for the year 1429.
8. *Ibid.*, entry for the year 1420.

PART II: MODERN AND CONTEMPORARY FRANCE
MODERN FRANCE

CHAPTER VI.   *The Rural Milieu and Mentality*

1. Georges Lefebvre, *Études sur la Revolution française*, Paris: Presses Universitaires, 1954.
2. For modern Europe *see*, among others, Camille Ernest Labrousse, *La Crise de l'économie française à la fin de l'ancien régime et au début de la révolution*, Paris: Presses Universitaires, 1944, p. xxiv.
3. Roger Thabault, *Mon Village, 1848-1914*, Paris: Delagrave, 1944, p. 99 and *passim*.

4. For information on farming methods, *see* Marc Bloch, *Caractères originaux de l'histoire rurale française*, Paris: Colin, 1951, chs. VI and VII.

5. Labrousse, *op. cit.*, General Introduction.

6. Sébastien Le Prestre de Vauban, *Projet d'une dixme royale*, ed. Émile Coornaert, Paris: Alcan, 1933, p. 28.

7. *Ibid.*, p. 280.

8. *Ibid.*, p. 279. There are countless documents in archives, a few examples of which are: AD, Saône-et-Loire, B. 1297; BN, Mss, Anc. fonds, n° 21802, f° 234; complaints in family record books and memoirs (for example, Jean Burel, *Mémoires*, 1601-1629, ed. Augustin Chassaing, Le Puy-en-Velay, Marchessou, 1874, p. 451).

9. Olivier Lefèvre d'Ormesson, *Journal*, 1640-1672, ed. Chéruel, Paris, Imprimerie Royale, 1861, II, ix.

10. Gaston Roupnel, *La ville et la campagne au XVIIe siècle: Étude sur les populations du pays dijonnais*, Paris: Leroux, 1955. Striking examples are given from his Burgundy of the dread famines and epidemics, and of their demographic consequences; in particular, Part I, Chapter 1.

11. AD, Nièvre, B. 60.

12. Roland Mousnier, *Histoire Générale des Civilisations*, IV (Sixteenth and Seventeenth Centuries), Paris: Presses Universitaires, 1956, p. 162.

13. Boris Porchnev, *Nardonie Vosstania vo Francüpered Frondoï* (The Popular Revolts in France before the Fronde), Moscow: 1948, appendix, p. 654. *See* the French edition, Paris: S.E.V.P.E.N., 1963, p. 595.

14. AD, Nièvre, B. 44 and 81.

15. Fernand Braudel, *La Méditerranée et le monde Méditerranéen à l'époque de Philippe II*, Paris: Colin, 1949, Part II, Ch. 6. *See also* Braudel, "Misère et banditisme," in *Annales Économies, Sociétés, Civilisations*, vol. II (1947), No. 2, pp. 129-42.

16. Antoine Jacmon, *Journal*, 1627-1651, ed. Augustin Chassaing, Le Puy-en-Velay: Marchessou, 1885, p. 47.

17. *See* the first part of an excellent article by René Baehrel, *Annales Historiques de la Révolution française*, April-June, 1951, p. 113ff.

18. Vauban, *op. cit.*, p. 38.

19. Lucien Febvre, *Le Problème de l'incroyance au XVIe siècle: La religion de Rabelais*, Paris: A. Michel, 1942. *See also*, numerous articles in the *Annales Économies, Sociétés, Civilisations*, especially: "Sorcellerie, sottise ou révolution mentale," vol. III, No. 1, pp. 9-15; "De l'à-peu près à la précision," vol. V (1950), No. 1, pp. 25-31.

20. Jean-Baptiste Thiers, *Traité des superstitions selon l'Écriture sainte, les décrets des conciles, et les sentimens des saints Pères et des théologiens*, Paris: Dezallier, 1679, I, 97.

21.   Friedrich von Spée, *Cautio Criminalis*, tr. into French by F. B. Velledor, Lyon: Prost, 1660, Preface. (Spée, a Rhenish Jesuit, specifies the same situation in Germany more than elsewhere. [For full French title, see above p. 347—Trans.])

22.   *Ibid.*

23.   Henri Dontenville, *Mythologie française*, Paris: Payot, 1949, and its bibliographies. *See especially*, André Varagnac and his studies of prehistoric civilization such as *De la préhistoire au monde moderne, essai d'une anthropodynamique*, Paris: Plon, 1954.

24.   Marc Bloch, *Les Rois thaumaturges*, Strasbourg: Colin, 1951, reprint.

25.   Burel, *op. cit.* p. 480. Bloch has, obviously, collected many other examples, but few are as artlessly moving as this one.

26.   André Siegfried, *Géographie électorale de l'Ardèche sous la IIIe République*, Paris: Colin, 1949.

CHAPTER VII.   *Urban Progress During the Sixteenth Century*

1.   Lucien Febvre, "La première renaissance française," *Revue des cours et conférences*, XXVI (1924-1925), #11, May 15, 1925, pp. 193-210; #12, May 30, pp. 326-340; #13, June 15, pp. 398-417; #15, July 15, pp. 577-593.

2.   AD, Saône-et-Loire, B. 43.

3.   D'Ormesson, *Journal*, I, 208.

4.   AD, Haute-Savoie, B. 28.

5.   Charles Morazé, "Nouvel essai sur le feu," in *Hommage à Lucien Febvre, Éventail de l'Histoire vivante*, Paris: Colin, 1953, I, 85.

6.   AD, Haute-Savoie, *loc. cit.*

7.   Pierre Thomas du Fossé, *Mémoires pour servir à l'histoire de Port Royal*, Utrecht: aux dépens de la Compagnie, 1739, p. 443.

8.   AD, Saône-et-Loire, B. 1207.

9.   Burel, *Mémoires*, p. 374.

10.   AD, Nièvre, B. 42.

11.   Richard Ehrenberg, *Das Zeitalter der Fugger*, Jena: Fischer, 1896, especially Part II, Chs. 1 & 2. (Partial English translation by H. M. Lucas, *Capital and Finance in the Age of the Renaissance*, New York: Harcourt, Brace, 1928.—Trans.)

12.   *Ibid.*, pp. 36-37.

13.   B. N. Mss, Anc. f: 17262, 28.

14.   D'Ormesson, *op. cit.*, I, 122.

15.   Charles Sorel, *La Bibliothèque Française*, Paris: Compagnie des libraires du Palais, 1664, p. 158.

16.   M. de Monconys is thus quoted by Lucien Febvre in his "Sorcellerie, sottise ou révolution," *loc. cit.*

17.   Pierre de L'Estoile, *Journal, 1589-1611*, eds. Louis-Raymond Lefèvre and André Martin, 3 vols. Paris: Gallimard, 1948-1960. (Selec-

tions have been edited and translated by Nancy L. Roelker, *The Paris of Henry Navarre as seen by Pierre de L'Estoile*, Cambridge, Mass.: Harvard University Press, 1958.—Trans.)

18. D'Ormesson, *op. cit.*, II, 302.
19. AD, Mayenne, B. 2985.
20. AD, Loiret, B. 1383.
21. René Pintard, *Le Libertinage érudit dans la première moitié du XVIIe siècle*, Paris: Boivin, 1943, *passim*.
22. Ferdinand Brunot, *Histoire de la langue française des origines à 1900*, Paris: Colin, 1926, VII, 68.
23. Spée, *Cautio criminalis*, translator's foreword.
24. Esprit-Valentin Fléchier, *Mémoires sur les Grands Jours d'Auvergne*, Paris: Hachette, 1856, p. 113. (English translation by W. W. Comfort, *The Clermont Assizes of 1665*, Philadelphia: University of Pennsylvania Press, 1937, p. 121.—Trans.)
25. D'Ormesson, *op. cit.*, I, 129.
26. Published in Vienne by J. Poyet, 1616, 8 pages.
27. Published in Chambéry by Brossart, 1620, in 8ᵛᵒ, 8 pages.
28. Braudel, *La Méditerranée . . .* , pp. 374-420; the entire second part is relevant to this paragraph.
29. Henri Hauser, *La Response de Jean Bodin à M. de Malestroit*, Paris: Colin, 1932, p. 13. (English translation by George A. Moore, *The Response of Jean Bodin to the Paradoxes of Malestroit and the Paradoxes*, Chevy Chase, Maryland: The Country Dollar Press, 1946, p. 29.—Trans.)
30. Concerning the great international crises and particularly the bankruptcy of France in 1557, *see* Ehrenberg, *op. cit.*, Part III, and Braudel, *op. cit.*, Part II. (The English translation of the Ehrenberg does not include the third part.—Trans.)
31. Braudel, *op. cit.*, p. 408.
32. Frank C. Spooner, *L'Économie mondiale et les frappes monétaires en France, 1493-1680*, Paris: Colin, 1956, *passim*.
33. Braudel, *op. cit.*, p. 407.
34. Franz Borkenau, *Der übergang vom feudalen zum bürgerlichen Weltbild*, Paris: Alcan, 1934.

CHAPTER VIII.   *From Innovators to Fanatics*

1. Will E. Peuckert, *Die Grosse Wende*, Hamburg, Classen & Goverts, 1948.
2. Lucien Febvre, *L'Incroyance . . .* , *see especially*, Part I, pp. 11-226.
3. These are extracts from the description of the Boggio Reale in a chronicle of the trip of Charles VIII by André de la Vigne, *Vergier d'Honneur* collected in Louis Lafaist, *Archives curieuses de l'histoire*

de France depuis Louis XI jusqu'au Louis XVIII, Paris: Beauvais, 1834, I, pp. 334ff.

4. Giorgio Vasari, *La Vie des plus excellents peintres, sculpteurs, et architectes*, tr. Charles Weiss, Paris: Dorbon-Aîné, 1913, I, 45-46, Ch. 7, "Of Architecture." (This selection is not included in the Gaston de Vere translation, *Lives of the Most Eminent Painters*, 10 vols. London: Macmillan, 1912-1914. However, it is included in the paperback reprint *Vasari on Technique*, tr. Louise Maclehouse, ed. G. Baldwin Brown, New York: Dover, 1960, pp. 96-97.—Trans.)

5. Madame de Maintenon, *Mémoires*, Laurent A. de La Beaumelle, Amsterdam: aux dépens de l'auteur (et de l'éditeur), 1755-1756, I, 98.

6. Michel de Montaigne, *Oeuvres Complètes*, ed. Maurice Rat, Book I, #51: "On the Vanity of Words," p. 294. (English translation by Donald Frame, *The Complete Works of Montaigne*, Stanford: Stanford University Press, 1958, p. 223.—Trans.)

7. G. Vasari, "Preliminary Discourse to the Lives of the Artists," Weiss, I, p. 105; de Vere, I, xliii.

8. G. Vasari, "Preliminary Discourse to the Whole Work," Weiss, I, 10; de Vere, I, xxix.

9. Pierre Ronsard, *Odes*.

10. Lucien Febvre, *op. cit. See also* the noteworthy restatement which deals with the only "achristian" work of the period: *Origène et Des Périers ou l'Énigme du Cymbalum Mundi*, Geneva: Droz, 1944. As an indication of the deep faith of the period, Jean Dagens has patiently listed the publications and re-publications of spiritual works during the first half of the century: *Bibliographie chronologique de la littérature de spiritualité et de ses sources—1501-1610*, Paris: Desclée de Brouwer, 1952.

11. Jean Bodin, *Les Six livres de la République*, Paris: Du Puys, 1579, 4th ed. (*See* Kenneth McRae, ed., *The Six Bookes of a Commonweale*, Cambridge, Mass.: Harvard University Press, 1962; a facsimile reprint of the 1606 translation by Richard Knolles.—Trans.)

12. Dom Henri Leclercq, *Histoire des Conciles*, Paris: Letouzey et Ané, 1913, X. (This is a translation of Carl Joseph Hefele, *Concilengeschichte*, Freiburg im Breisgau: Herder, 9 vols., 1873-1876—Trans.)

13. Catherine de' Medici, *Lettres*, ed. La Ferrière, Paris: Imprimerie Nationale, 1880-1905, letter dated January 31, 1561, I, pp. 577-78.

14. L'Estoile, *op. cit.*, I, 660.

CHAPTER IX. *"Catholic France" and Modern Man*

1. Aurillac, 1643, quoted in Porchnev, *Nardonie Vosstania* . . . , p. 681.

2. François-Nicolas Baudot de Dubuisson-Aubenay, *Journal des guerres civiles*, ed. Gustave Saige, Paris: Champion, 1883, I, 94.

3. Bloch, *Caractères originaux* . . . , Chs. V & VI; Roupnel, *Ville et campagne* . . . , Part III.

4. B.N., Mss, Nv. fds fs, 18 432, fº 231.

5. B.N., Mss, fds, fs, 18938, fº 10, Normandy, 1640. *See also* Porchnev, *op. cit.*, pp. 644, 672.

6. B.N., Mss, Nv. fds, fs 18432, fº 247.

7. Pierre de Bessot, *Livre de raison* (1609-1652), ed. Philippe Tamizey de Larroque, *et al.*, Paris: Picard, 1893, p. 23.

8. Roupnel, *op. cit.*, Introduction to 1955 edition.

9. Henri Brémond, *L'Histoire littéraire du sentiment religieux en France depuis la fin des guerres de religion jusqu'à nos jours*, 11 vols., Paris: Bloud & Gay, 1916-1933 (this is the most famous); more recently, Louis Cognet, *Les origines de la spiritualité française au XVIIᵉ siècle*, Paris: La Colombe, 1949.

10. Philippe Tamizey de Larroque, ed., *Livre de raison de la famille de Fontainemarie* (1640-1774), Agen: Lamy, 1889, p. 39.

11. D'Ormesson, *Journal*, I, 341.

12. Jean-Baptiste Thiers, *Traité des jeux et des divertissemens qui peuvent être permis ou qui doivent être défendus aux chrétiens selon les règles de l'Église et le sentiment des Pères*, Paris: Dezailler, 1686, p. 440.

13. Charles Perrault, *Parallèle des Anciens et des Modernes*, Paris: Coignard, 1690, II, preface.

14. AD, Loire, B. 231.

15. René Descartes, *Discours de la méthode*, IV, section 34 in *Oeuvres Complètes*, ed. Charles Adam & Paul Tannery, Paris: Cerf, 1902, VI, p. 34. (Translated by Norman Kemp Smith, *Descartes: Philosophical Writings*, London: Macmillan, 1952—Trans.)

16. *Ibid.*, II, section 19, p. 19.

17. Pintard, *Libertinage érudit* . . . , p. 125.

18. D'Ormesson, *op. cit.*, I, 112.

19. Du Fossé, *Mémoires*, p. 437.

20. *Ibid.*, p. 331.

21. Blaise Pascal, *Oeuvres Complètes*, ed. Jacques Chevalier, Paris: Gallimard, 1960 (Bibliothèque de la Pléiade), pp. 791, 810.

CHAPTER X. *The Age of Classicism*

1. Vauban, *Dixme Royale*, p. 25.

2. AD, Aude, B. 2566.

3. D'Ormesson, *Journal*, II, 345.

4. AN, Y, 17 620.

5. Joseph Sevin de Quincy, *Mémoires*, ed. Léon Lecestre, Paris: H. Laurens, 1898, I, 118.

6. B.N. Mss, 17 296, 65 V°.
7. D'Ormesson, *op. cit.*, II, 552.
8. L.M.D.L.F. (Charles-Auguste de La Fare), *Mémoires et réflexions sur les principaux événements du règne de Louis XIV*, Rotterdam: Fritsch, 1716, p. 192.
9. Jean Rou, *Mémoires* (1638-1711), Paris: Agence Centrale de la Société, 1857, II, 18.
10. D'Ormesson, *op. cit.*, II, 403.
11. Jean Fourastié, *Machinisme et Bien-être*, Paris: Éditions de Minuit, 1951, pp. 127-128. (English Translation by Theodore Caplow, *The Causes of Wealth*, Free Press of Glencoe, Illinois, 1960.—Trans.)
12. B.N., Mss, 21 730, 156.
13. Molière, *Le Misanthrope*, II, 5.
14. Quincy, *op. cit.*, p. 178.
15. Dubuisson-Aubenay, *Journal*, I, 234, March 12, 1650.
16. L.M.D.L.F., *Mémoires*, p. 193.
17. D'Ormesson, *op. cit.*, II, 146.
18. Spée, *Cautio Criminalis*, p. 321.
19. B.N., Mss, 21 743, 132.

CHAPTER XI. *The Economic and Demographic Revolution of the Eighteenth Century*

1. For everything in this chapter, see the two great works of Camille Ernest Labrousse, *Esquisse du mouvement des prix et des revenus en France au XVIIIᵉ siècle*, Paris: Dalloz, 1932; *see also La Crise* . . . , vol. I (the general introduction to this work is an admirable concentration of the most basic writings since Mathiez, along with the works of Georges Lefebvre, about France just before the Revolution.)
2. Bloch, *Caractères originaux* . . . , 1956 edition, contains a close study of the changes in French rural areas at the close of the Old Regime, especially chapter VI.
3. Daniel Faucher, *Le Paysan et la machine*, Paris: Éditions de Minuit, 1955, p. 56.
4. Arthur Young, *Voyages en France*, Paris: Colin, 1931, II, 620. (English edition C. Maxwell, ed., *Travels in France*, Cambridge, England: Cambridge University Press, 1950.—Trans.)
5. Pierre Goubert, "Une richesse historique en cours d'exploitation: Les registres paroissiaux," *Annales: Économies, Sociétés, Civilisations*, vol. IX (1954), No. 1, pp. 83-93.
6. Braudel, *La Méditerranée* . . . , p. 230ff.
7. Labrousse, *Esquisse* . . . , I, 497ff.
8. Messance, *Recherches sur la population des généralités d'Auvergne, de Lyon, de Rouen, et de quelques provinces et villes du royaume, avec des réflexions sur la valeur du bled tant en France qu'en Angleterre, depuis 1674 jusqu'en 1764*, Paris: Durand, 1766, p. 2.

9.   Thabault, *Mon Village, passim.*

10.   Rou, *Mémoires* . . . , p. 259.

11.   Young, *op. cit.*, I, 91.

12.   Brunot, *Histoire* . . . , VII, Book III, p. 229.

13.   Daniel Martin, *Parlement nouveau, ou Centurie interlinaire de devis facétieusement sérieux et sérieusement facétieux* . . . *servant de dictionnaire et nomenclature aux amateurs de deux langues françoise et allemande*, Strasbourg: Letner, 1660, pp. 387-389, quoted by Brunot, *aux depens des heretiers [sic] de Feu Everand*, VII, Book I, p. 49.

14.   A.D., Charente-Maritime, B 1 722 (for the year 1742).

15.   A.D., Yonne.

CHAPTER XII.   *Fêtes Galantes and the Enlightenment*

1.   Edmond-Jean-François Barbier, *Journal historique et anecdotique du règne de Louis XV*, ed. La Villegille, Paris: Renouard, 1847, I, 263.

2.   Morazé, "Nouvel essai, sur le feu," I, 85; this article is rich, as always, with bold suggestions.

3.   Alfred Rambaud, *Histoire de la civilisation française*, Paris: Colin, 1938, II, 559.

4.   Charles-Jean-François Hénault, *Mémoires*, ed. François Rousseau, Paris: Hachette, 1855, p. 103.

5.   André Latreille, *L'Église et la Révolution française*, Paris: Hachette, 1946.

6.   See Émile Guyénot, *Les sciences de la vie aux XVIIe et XVIIIe siècle: l'Idée d'évolution*, Paris: A. Michel, 1941.

7.   François-Marie Arouet de Voltaire, *Dictionnaire philsophique* in *Oeuvres Complètes*, ed. Louis Moland, Paris: Garnier, vols. 17-20, 1878-1879, the article on God. (English translation by Peter Gay, *Philosophical Dictionary*, New York: Basic Books, 1962.—Trans.)

8.   Charles-Montesquieu, *Esprit des Lois*, III, 5, in *Oeuvres Complètes*, ed. Édouard Laboulaye, Paris: Garnier, vols. III-VI, 1876-1878. (There is an eighteenth-century English translation by Thomas Nugent, *The Spirit of the Laws*, New York: Hafner, 1949.)

9.   Jean-Jacques Rousseau, *Contrat social*, ed. Edmond Dreyfus-Brisac, Paris: Alcan, 1896, I, 5. (English translation, G.D.H. Cole, *The Social Contract* [Everyman's Library], London: Dent, 1913; New York: Dutton, 1935.—Trans.)

10.   B.N., Mss 21 630, 247 V°.

11.   Vermenton, AD, Yonne, BB.

12.   A.D., Tarn, B, 7 314.

CHAPTER XIII.   *The Bourgeoisie Triumphant*

1.   Félicité Robert de Lamennais, *Essai sur l'indifférence en matière de religion*, Paris: Tournachon-Molin & Seguin, 1817. For information

concerning the freedom of the Press, *see La Loi de Justice et d'Amour* proposed by Villèle in April, 1827.

2. Honoré de Balzac, *Le Médecin de campagne,* in *Oeuvres Complètes,* ed. Marcel Bouteron, Paris: Gallimard (Bibliothèque de la Pléiade), Vol. VIII, 1936.

CHAPTER XIV. *Romantic Rebellions*

1. Adolphe-Jérôme Blanqui, *Les classes ouvrières en France pendant l'année 1848,* Paris: Pagnerre, 1849. *See also,* the principal slighted evidence all of which contain moving pages: Eugène Buret, *De la misère des classes laborieuses an Angleterre et en France: de la nature de la misère, de son existence, de ses effets, de ses causes, et de l'insuffisance des remèdes qu'on lui a opposés jusqu'ici, avec les moyens propres à en affranchir les sociétés,* Paris: Paulin, 1840, 2 vols.; Ange Guépin, *Nantes au XIXe siècle: statistique, topographique industrielle et morale, faisant suite à l'Histoire des progrès de Nantes,* Nantes: Sebire, 1835; Alban de Villeneuve-Bargemont, *Économie politique chrétienne ou recherches sur la nature et les causes du paupérisme en France et en Europe,* Brussels: Meline, Cans & Cie., 1837; Louis René Villermé, *Tableau de l'état physique et moral des ouvriers employés dans les manufactures de coton, de laine, et de soie,* Paris: Renouard, 1840, 2 vols.

2. Fernand Rude, *C'est nous les canuts* (*La révolte des ouvriers lyonnais en 1831*), Paris, Domat-Montchrestien, 1953. (This is the most recent and most excellently done study of the frequently emphasized political and social importance of the insurrection in Lyon in 1831.)

3. *See* the studies devoted to the Romantic period in the collection, "L'Évolution de l'Humanité," particularly Paul van Tieghem, *L'Ère Romantique: Le Romanticisme dans la littérature européenne,* Paris: A. Michel, 1948.

4. Philippe-Joseph-Buchez, *Introduction à la science de l'histoire, ou science du développement de l'humanité,* Paris: Paulin, 1833.

CHAPTER XV. *"Positivist France"*

1. *See* Thabault, *Mon Village,* which analyzes carefully all these basic psychological realities.

2. Joseph Garavel, *Les Paysans de Morette: un siècle de vie rurale dans une commune de Dauphiné,* Paris: Colin, 1948. *See also* Thabault, *op. cit.*

3. Émile Durkheim, *Les règles de la méthode sociologique,* Paris: Alcan, 1895.

4. *See* "Conclusions," pp. 587ff. in Henri-Xavier Arquillière, *Saint-Grégoire VII,* Paris: Vrin, 1934; *see also* pp. 168-169 in the present text.

5. Georges Duveau, *La vie ouvrière en France sous le second empire,*

Paris: Gallimard, 1946—a masterful, if occasionally finicky study, of working-class life under the Second Empire.

6. Pierre Hamp, *Mes Métiers*, Paris: Gallimard, 1943. (This is the most noteworthy among many works concerned with the painful atmosphere of adolescent work; Hamp is more prolix an author than those of other inquiries and first-hand accounts.)

7. Georges Duveau, *La Pensée ouvrière sur l'éducation sous la Seconde République et le Second Empire*, Paris: Domat-Montchrestien, 1947. (An exciting book on this question.)

CHAPTER XVI. *The Dawn of a Scientific Civilization*

1. Sociology and history; *see* Armand Cuvillier, *Sociologie et problèmes actuels*, Paris: Vrin, 1958: history, science of the particular, sociology, science of the general, et cetera, ad infinitum.

2. Louis Halphen, *Introduction à l'histoire*, second edition, Paris: Presses Universitaires, 1948, p. 94.

3. Henri Bergson, *L'Essai sur les données immédiates de la conscience*, Paris: Alcan, 1889.

4. Bergson, *Ibid.*, tr. by F. L. Pogson, *Time and Free Will*, New York: Harper Torchbooks, 1960 (authorized); *see also* the translation by Arthur Mitchell, *Creative Evolution*, New York: The Modern Library, 1944 (authorized).—Trans.

CHAPTER XVII. *The Early Twentieth Century in France*

1. Jules Marouzeau, *Une Enfance*, Paris: Bourrelier, 1946.

2. Georges Friedmann, *Problèmes humains du machinisme industriel*, Paris: Gallimard, 1946.

3. *See* Hamp, *Mes Métiers*, which is amazingly descriptive.

CHAPTER XVIII. *French Civilization and World Civilization*

1. There have been some recent methodical studies of Paris by geographers, sociologists, and economists, several of which are published: René Clozier, *La Gare du Nord*, Paris: Ballière, 1940; Paul Henry Chombart de Lauwe, *L'Espace social d'une grande cité*, Paris: Presses Universitaires, 1952.

2. See Jean-François Gravier, *Paris et le désert français*, Paris: Le Portulan, 1947.

Index

About the Authors

GEORGES DUBY, Professor of Medieval History at the Faculté des Lettres, University of Aix-Marseille, was born in 1919; he holds the title *agrégé*, and the degree of *docteur ès Lettres*. Professor Duby edits the journal *Études Rurales* and is director of the Centre d'Études des Sociétés Méditerranénnes. His published works include: *La société aux XIᵉ et XIIᵉ siècles dans la région Mâconnaise*, *L'économie rurale et la vie des campagnes de l'Occident médiéval* (for both of which he received the Prix Gobert); and, with Professor Perroy, *Le Moyen Age* (Volume Three in the series "Histoire Générale des Civilisations"). He has taught Medieval History at the universities of Lyon and Besançon, and has lectured at universities throughout Europe, Canada, and North Africa.

ROBERT LOUIS RÉNÉ MANDROU is Director of Studies of the Sixth Section of the École Pratique des Hautes Études at the Sorbonne. Born in 1921, Professor Mandrou attended the universities of Lyon and of Paris, and holds the title *agrégé d'histoire*. His books include *Introduction à la France Moderne* (1500-1640); *Essai de Psychologie historique*, *La culture populaire en France aux XVIIᵉ et XVIIIᵉ siècles*, and *Classes et luttes de classes dans la société française au début du XVIIᵉ siècle* (the latter two forthcoming). From 1954 to 1962 he was Secretary for the journal *Annales: Économies–Sociétés–Civilisations*, and he holds the chair of Histoire Sociale des Mentalités at the Sorbonne.

JAMES BLAKELY ATKINSON was born in 1934. He has studied at Swarthmore College and the Sorbonne, and is currently working for a doctorate in comparative literature at Columbia University.